INTRODUCTION
TO
LAW ENFORCEMENT
AND
CRIMINAL JUSTICE

EIGHTH EDITION

HENRY M. WROBLESKI, LL.B.
Former Law Enforcement Coordinator
Normandale Community College

KÄREN M. HESS, Ph.D.
Normandale Community College

THOMSON

WADSWORTH

Australia • Canada • Mexico • Singapore
Spain • United Kingdom • United States

THOMSON
WADSWORTH

Introduction to Law Enforcement and Criminal Justice, Eighth Edition
Henry M. Wrobleski and Kären M. Hess

Acquisitions Editor: Jay Whitney
Assistant Editor: Jana Davis
Editorial Assistant: Jennifer Walsh
Technology Project Manager: Susan DeVanna
Marketing Manager: Terra Schultz
Marketing Assistant: Annabelle Yang
Marketing Communications Manager: Stacey Purviance
Project Manager, Editorial Production: Matt Ballantyne
Art Director: Vernon Boes
Print Buyer: Karen Hunt
Permissions Editor: Kiely Sisk
Production Service: Shepherd, Inc.

Photo Researcher: Suzie Wright
Copy Editor: Kirsten Balayti
Illustrator: Jim Daggett
Cover Designer: Yvo
Cover Images: Judge reviewing notes, police officer in helicopter, and speeding police car copyright © Corbis. View from inside police car copyright © Thinkstock/Getty Images
Cover Printer:
Compositor: Shepherd, Inc.
Printer: West Group

For more information about our products, contact us at:
Thomson Learning Academic Resource Center
1-800-423-0563
For permission to use material from this text or product, submit a request online at HYPERLINK
http://www.thomsonrights.com.

Any additional questions about permissions can be submitted by email to thomsonrights@thomson.com.

Library of Congress Control Number: 2005921828

Student Edition: ISBN 0-534-64668-9
Instructor's Edition: ISBN 0-495-00586-X
International Student Edition: ISBN 0-495-00809-5

Thomson Higher Education
10 Davis Drive
Belmont, CA 94002-3098
USA

Asia (including India)
Thomson Learning
5 Shenton Way
#01-01 UIC Building
Singapore 068808

Australia/New Zealand
Thomson Learning Australia
102 Dodds Street
Southbank, Victoria 3006
Australia

Canada
Thomson Nelson
1120 Birchmount Road
Toronto, Ontario M1K 5G4
Canada

UK/Europe/Middle East/Africa
Thomson Learning
High Holborn House
50-51 Bedford Row
London WC1R 4LR
United Kingdom

Latin America
Thomson Learning
Seneca, 53
Colonia Polanco
11560 Mexico
D.F. Mexico

Spain (including Portugal)
Thomson Paraninfo
Calle Magallanes, 25
28015 Madrid, Spain

Brief Contents

Contents

SECTION II:

 CONTEMPORARY LAW ENFORCEMENT   113

Chapter 4: Contemporary Policing: An Overview   115

SECTION III:

 CHALLENGES TO THE PROFESSION   243

Chapter 10: Terrorism: The Newest Threat to Our National Security   336

SECTION IV:

 LAW ENFORCEMENT AND THE CRIMINAL
JUSTICE SYSTEM   441

Chapter 13: Courts and Corrections: Law Enforcement's Partners
in the Criminal Justice System   443

Preface

Introduction to Law Enforcement and Criminal Justice was written to present an overview of the field and the numerous complexities within it. It also seeks to instill an appreciation for those who "serve and protect" our society and an understanding of this exciting, challenging profession.

The future of our lawful, democratic society depends in large part on those currently in the field of criminal justice and those preparing to enter it. Law enforcement officers have awesome power and tremendous responsibilities that must be met under constantly changing circumstances and in a way that protects individual rights and society's rights simultaneously—a tremendous challenge.

When we wrote the first edition of this text over 25 years ago, law enforcement seemed more predictable and faced different challenges than now. In the 1970s law enforcement was focused on restoring its image after the disturbances and civil unrest of the 1960s. It saw organized crime as a major national threat. Crime fighting was its most obvious mission. Victims were seen primarily as sources of information. AIDS, crack cocaine, drive-by shootings and children shooting children, domestic violence and terrorism were not perceived as problems. The first edition contained no chapters on community policing, problem-solving, juveniles or victims because these were not priorities. The beginnings of community policing could be seen, however, in the discussions of team policing and community service—helping citizens help themselves. The first edition also had no chapters on courts or corrections, focusing solely on the law enforcement component of the criminal justice system.

The current edition recognizes the interrelationships of the components of the criminal justice system and the need for coordination among them. As you learn about law enforcement, you will find three recurring themes in this text. The first theme is that of community or service orientation to law enforcement and the critical importance of partnerships, viewing citizens as co-producers of justice. A second theme is that of police officers as peace officers as well as crime fighters and a concern for not only criminal justice but social justice as well. The third theme is that of police officers' discretion in their role as gatekeepers to the criminal justice system. Each chapter in the text serves as an overview of an area that could be expanded into an entire course.

Major Features—Context Themes

Not unexpectedly, the text begins with chapters that provide needed background (Section I). Our present system of law enforcement did not just magically appear. It has evolved slowly, shaped by numerous factors, including social and political influences. Chapter 1 describes the evolution of law enforcement and the criminal justice system from its ancient roots to the present system. Chapter 2 describes the laws all U.S. citizens are expected to obey and how they came to be. Chapter 3 explores crime in the United States: what types of crimes are occurring and theories about why, who commits crime and the effect it has on victims. This section provides the context within which to understand contemporary U.S. policing: its history and traditions, the laws under which it operates and which it enforces as well as the individuals who choose to disobey the laws and their victims. Policing is, at its heart, about people.

Section II helps you understand the traditional organization and functions of law enforcement, most of which can still be found within our law enforcement agencies. First, an overview of the organization, goals, characteristics and culture is presented (Chapter 4). Next, two approaches to policing gaining popularity throughout the county are introduced—community policing and problem-oriented policing (Chapter 5). This is followed by a discussion of the general functions of most agencies, patrol and traffic (Chapter 6), and the specialized assignments frequently found in larger agencies, such as investigators, SWAT teams, school resource officers and reserve officers (Chapter 7).

Section III explores important challenges to the profession in the twenty-first century. It begins with a discussion of the challenge of policing within the law, apprehending criminals without violating their constitutional rights (Chapter 8). Next, the challenges posed by gangs and drugs, problems which have overshadowed the previous concern with organized crime, are discussed (Chapter 9). This is followed by an examination of the latest threat to our country—terrorism (Chapter 10). Then significant issues involved in policing are described, including discretion, discrimination, racial profiling, use of force, pursuit, liability, corruption and ethics (Chapter 11). The section concludes with a discussion of departmental issues, including recruiting and retaining officers, civilian review boards, sexual harassment, unions, moonlighting, privatization of law enforcement, accreditation and professionalism (Chapter 12). The final section (IV) places law enforcement into the context of the criminal justice system, examining its role with the other two components of the criminal justice system, the courts and corrections. The need for collaboration and cooperation among the three components has become an important focus during the past decade. Chapter 13 discusses the evolution of community justice and presents a brief look to the future.

This eighth edition has been completely updated, with all except classic sources cited being published between 2001 and 2005. Included are 36 new terms and 426 new cites.

New to This Edition

Specific changes within each chapter include the following:

- Chapter 1—History: the Department of Homeland Security and the reorganization of the Department of Justice; 2 new terms, 4 new cites.
- Chapter 2—Our laws: new Supreme Court precedents; the needs of society and the rights of the individual; conflict and consensus theory; crime control versus due process expanded; 2 new terms, 5 new cites.
- Chapter 3—Crime: the 8% problem; debate on amending the U.S. Constitution to include victims' rights; a parallel justice system for victims; 3 new terms, 41 new cites.

- Chapter 4—Contemporary policing: contemporary goals resulting from community policing; the importance of image; interoperability; E911, reverse 911 and phantom wireless 911 calls; 4 new terms, 20 new cites.
- Chapter 5—Community policing: the importance of community and social capital; analyzing the community; common mistakes in problem solving; involving and educating citizens—civilian review boards, citizen patrols, citizen police academies and ride-along programs; community policing, partnerships and the decrease in crime; 4 new terms, 20 new cites.
- Chapter 6—Patrol: management of patrol operations; global positioning systems (GPS); facial recognition in patrol cars; segways; personal vertical take-off and landing aircraft; 6 new terms, 58 new cites.
- Chapter 7—Specialized roles: crime scene investigation (CSI) units; psychics; gambling; K-9 case law; 1 new term, 51 new cites.
- Chapter 8—Policing within the law: 11 recent Supreme Court cases related to criminal procedure including informational roadblocks, *Illinois v. Lidster*; the requirement to identify oneself, *Hiibel v. Sixth Judicial District Court of Nevada*; legality of roadblocks and checkpoints; de facto arrests; protecting the rights of foreign nationals; 2 new terms, 29 new cites.
- Chapter 9—Gangs and drugs: prison gangs; hybrid gangs; gangs and community policing; the enterprise theory of investigation; statistics on current drug use; 1 new term, 44 new cites.
- Chapter 10—Terrorism: a new chapter, includes motivations for terrorism; methods used; the critical role of local law enforcement in homeland security; investigating terrorist acts; community policing and homeland security; intelligence gathering and sharing; asymmetric warfare; the role of the media in terrorism; 5 new terms, 62 new cites.
- Chapter 11—Police conduct: expanded discussion of discretion, the discrimination-disparity continuum; deadly force decision model; anatomy of a lethal force event; a model of circumstantial corruptibility; the hierarchy of wickedness; excerpt from *Walking with the Devil: The Code of Silence*; balancing and ghosting in data on traffic stops; 5 new terms, 33 new cites.
- Chapter 12—Departmental issues: the law enforcement candidate ride-along; human resource roundtables; retention techniques; types of civilian review; credentialing, 2003 Supreme Court rulings on affirmative action; 35 new cites.
- Chapter 13—Courts and corrections: gun courts; domestic violence (DV) courts; mental health courts; community justice; a look to the future; 1 new term, 28 new cites.

How to Use This Text

Introduction to Law Enforcement and Criminal Justice is more than a text. It is a learning experience requiring *your* active participation to obtain the best results.

You will get the most out of the book if you first familiarize yourself with the total scope of law enforcement: read and think about the subjects listed in the Contents. Then follow five steps for each chapter to achieve triple-strength learning.

1. Read the objectives at the beginning of each chapter, stated in the form of "Do You Know?" questions. This is your *first* exposure to the key concepts of the text. The following is an example of this format:

Do You Know?

- What the basic instrument of government is?

Review the key terms and think about their meaning in the context of law enforcement.

2. Read the chapter, underlining or taking notes if that is your preferred study style. Pay special attention to all information within the highlighted area and the magnifying glass icon. This is your *second* exposure to the chapter's key concepts. The following is an example of this format:

 The U.S. Constitution is the basic instrument of government and the supreme law of the United States.

The key concepts of each chapter are emphasized in this manner. Also pay attention to all words in bold print. All key terms will be in bold print when they are first used and defined.

3. Read the summary carefully. This will be your *third* exposure to the key concepts. By now you should have internalized the information.

4. To make sure you have learned the information, when you have finished reading a chapter reread the list of objectives given at the beginning of that chapter to make certain you can answer each question. If you find yourself stumped, find the appropriate material in the chapter and review it. Often these questions will be used as essay questions during testing.

5. Review the key terms to be certain you can define each. These also are frequently used as test items.

Note: The material we've selected to highlight using the triple-strength learning instructional design includes only the chapter's key concepts. While this information is certainly important in that it provides a structural foundation for understanding the topic(s) discussed, you may not simply glance over the "Do You Know?" highlighted boxes and summaries and expect to have mastered the chapter. You are also responsible for reading and understanding the material that surrounds these basics—the "meat" around the bones, so to speak.

The text also provides an opportunity for you to apply what you have learned or to go into specific areas in greater depth through discussion questions, InfoTrac College Edition assignments and Internet assignments. Complete each of these areas as directed by the text or by your instructor. Be prepared to share your findings with the class. Good reading and learning!

Ancillaries

To further enhance your study of law enforcement and criminal justice, several supplements are available:

- Study Guide—A workbook that includes key concepts and terms, chapter summaries with fill-in-the-blank questions, and practice test questions in multiple-choice format.
- The Criminal Justice Resource Center http://cj.wadsworth.com—An exceptional resource Web site containing links to over 3,000 popular criminal justice sites, jobs, news, and other interesting and relevant links.

- Careers in Criminal Justice 2.0 Interactive CD-ROM—With this CD-ROM, students can view video profiles of actual testimonials from people in the field and link to the various career options in the criminal justice system while also learning about job requirements and salaries.

  Also included is FREE access to the Holland personalized self-assessment test, designed to help students determine which careers best suit their interests, as well as tips on cover letters, resumes and interviews.

- CNN Today Video Series—Exclusively from Thomson/Wadsworth, the *CNN Today* Video Series offers compelling videos that feature current news footage from the Cable News Network's comprehensive archives. With offerings for Introduction to Criminal Justice, Criminology, Juvenile Delinquency and Corrections, each of these videotapes provides a varied collection of 2- to 10-minute clips on such hot topics as police brutality, terrorism, high-tech crime fighting tools, registering sex offenders, juveniles behind bars, elderly inmates and much more. Available to qualified adopters, these videotapes are great lecture launchers as well as classroom discussion pieces.

- Crime Scenes CD-ROM—An interactive CD-ROM featuring six vignettes allowing you to play various roles as you explore all aspects of the criminal justice system.

- Internet Investigator, Third Edition—A colorful trifold brochure listing the most popular Internet addresses for criminal justice-related Web sites.

- *Seeking Employment in Criminal Justice and Related Fields,* Fourth Edition—This book provides specific information on many criminal justice professions, helpful tips on resumes and cover letters, practical advice on interview techniques and includes a free copy of the *Careers in Criminal Justice CD-ROM,* Release 2.0.

Acknowledgments

We would like to thank the reviewers for the Eighth Edition: Lawrence Trostle, University of Anchorage; Robert C. Wadman, Weber State University; and William R. King, Bowling Green State University. For their valuable suggestions for the previous editions of *Introduction to Law Enforcement and Criminal Justice*, thank you to: William Castleberry, University of Tennessee–Martin; Lisa Kay Decker, Indiana State University; Darek Niklas, Rhode Island College; Charles Ousley, Seminole State College; James W. Robinson, Louisiana State University–Eunice. Constance M. Bennett, Seminole Community College; Kenneth Bowser, Westfield State College; Roger Brown, Golden Valley Lutheran College; Steven Brown, East Tennessee State University; William Castleberry, University of Tennessee–Martin; Lisa Kay Decker, Indiana State University; Vincent Del Castillo, John Jay College of Criminal Justice; Rita Dorsey, Shelby Community College; David G. Epstein, Brunswick Junior College; Chris W. Eskridge, University of Nebraska; Larry Gaines, Eastern Kentucky University; James N. Gilbert, University of Nebraska; Larry A. Gould, Northern Arizona University; George Green, Mankato State University; Martin A. Greenberg, Ulster County Community College; Edmund Grosskopf, Indiana State University; Daniel Gunderson, Chippewa Valley Technical College; Burt C. Hagerman, Oakland Community College; Hill Harper, Valdosta State University; Larry W. Hensel, Tallahassee Community College; Thomas Hinze, Riverland Community College; Robert G. Huckabee, Indiana State University; Robert Ingram, Florida International University; Robert R. Ives, Rock Valley College; Paul H. Johnson, Murray State University; William Kelly, Auburn University; Leonard Luzky, Ocean City College; Sidney A. Lyle, Odessa College; Michael Moberly, Southern Illinois University at Carbondale; Glen Morgan, Lincolnland Community College; M. G. Neithercutt, California State University—Hayward; James E. Newman, Police Academy, Rio Hondo Community College; Darek Niklas, Rhode Island College; E. W. Oglesby, Fullerton College; Charles Ousley, Seminole State College; Joseph Polanski, Sinclair Community College; Frank Post, Fullerton College; James W. Robinson, Louisiana State University–Eunice; Jack Spurlin, Missouri Southern College; James Stinchcomb, Miami Dade Community College; Jack Taylor, Oscar Rose Junior College; Gary W. Tucker, Sinclair Community College; Larry Tuttle, Palm Beach Junior College; Myron Utech, University of Wisconsin at Eau Claire; Tim Vieders, Niagara County Community College; James Walsh, Mount San Jacinto College; Douglas Watson, Northern Essex Community College; David A. Wilson, Turnbull Police Department; Dawn B. Young, Bossier Parish Community College; and Gay A. Young, Johnson County Community College.

We would also like to thank the survey respondents for the Eight Edition: Rob Deu Pre, Clatsop Community College; Egan Green, University of Tennessee at Martin; Pam Hart, Iowa Western Community College; Shihlung Huang, Fayetteville State University; Robert Hunt, Delta State University; David Jenks, California state University, Los Angeles; Wayne Longo, North Idaho College; Thomas

Luzinski, Concordia University of Wisconsin; Ihekwoaba Onwudiwe, University of Maryland, Eastern Shore; Jim Sandow, Triton College; Lynne Snowden, University of North Carolina at Wilmington; Roger Stielow, Troy State University.

Any errors in the text are, however, the sole responsibility of the co-authors.

A special thank you to Christine Hess Orthmann, content researcher and writer, and for her careful proofreading of page proofs. Thank you also to Jay Whitney, our editor; Jennifer Walsh, editorial assistant; Matt Ballantyne, production editor at Wadsworth; Peggy Francomb, our production editor at Shepherd, Inc.; and our families and colleagues for their support and assistance throughout the evolution of this text.

About the Authors

Henry M. Wrobleski, LL.B., is the former coordinator of the Law Enforcement Program at Normandale Community College. He is a respected author, lecturer, consultant and expert witness with 30 years' experience in law enforcement. He is also the dean of instruction for the Institute for Professional Development and is a graduate of the FBI Academy. Other Wadsworth texts Mr. Wrobleski has co-authored are *Introduction to Private Security*, 4th ed. and *Police Operations*, 3rd ed.

Kären M. Hess, Ph.D., has written extensively in the field of law enforcement and criminal justice. She has been a member of the English department at Normandale Community College as well as the president of the Institute for Professional Development. She is also a member of the Academy of Criminal Justice Sciences (ACJS), the American Correctional Association (ACA), the American Society for Law Enforcement Trainers (ASLET), the International Association of Chiefs of Police (IACP), the National Institute of Justice (NIJ), and the Police Executive Research Forum. In addition she is a fellow in the Textbook and Academic Authors' Association (TAA).

Other Wadsworth texts Dr. Hess has co-authored are *Constitutional Law*, 3rd ed.; *Corrections in the 21st Century: A Practical Approach*; *Criminal Investigation*, 7th ed.; *Criminal Procedure*; *Introduction to Private Security*, 4th ed.; *Juvenile Justice*, 4th ed.; *Management and Supervision in Law Enforcement*, 4th ed.; *Community Policing: Partnerships for Problem Solving*, 4th ed.; *Police Operations*, 3rd ed.; and *Careers in Criminal Justice: From Internship to Promotion*, 5th ed.

THE EVOLUTION OF LAW ENFORCEMENT AND CRIMINAL JUSTICE

This section provides the background necessary to understand contemporary law enforcement and its role within the criminal justice system and American society. Chapter 1 describes how law enforcement has evolved from ancient times to the present. It traces the development of important federal agencies that provide assistance to law enforcement and that also rely upon local law enforcement to fulfill their missions. Of special importance in the twenty-first century is the establishment of the Department of Homeland Security.

Chapter 2 explains how our system of laws evolved and the important role of the U.S. Constitution and the Bill of Rights in this evolution. Several amendments in the Bill of Rights guide how law enforcement functions and what it can and cannot do. The inherent conflict between individual rights and the needs of the country symbolized in the scales of justice and the resulting need for balancing crime control and due process are one focus of this chapter.

Chapter 3 details what has historically been the focus of law enforcement: crime. Controlling crime has been a challenge since our country was founded. Although our forefathers sought freedom, they also had a firm belief in law and order. This chapter looks at the types of crime found in our country today and at various theories of crime causation. The chapter also describes those who break the law as well as the effect crime has on its victims. The change in focus from punishing offenders to involving victims and the community to bring about community justice is explained and sets the stage for the remaining chapters of the text.

CHAPTER 1

A Brief History:
The Evolution of Law
and Our Criminal Justice System

The farther backward you can look, the farther forward you are likely to see.

—Winston Churchill

Do You Know . . .

- When and why law enforcement began?
- The significance of the tithing system, the Frankpledge system, Leges Henrici, the Magna Carta, the parish constable system and the Watch and Ward system?
- The origins of features of our criminal justice system, such as general alarms and citizen's arrests? The offices of constable, sheriff and justice of the peace?
- The origins of local responsibility for law enforcement? Division of offenses into felonies and misdemeanors? Jury by peers and due process? Paid law enforcement officers? Women in law enforcement?
- What significant contributions Sir Robert Peel made to law enforcement?
- Where and when the first police department was established in England and what it was called?
- What systems of law enforcement were brought from England to colonial New England and the South?
- When and where the first modern American police force began and what it was modeled after?
- What the vigilante movement was and why it occurred?
- When and how federal and state law enforcement agencies originated in the United States?
- Who the chief law enforcement officer at the federal level is?
- What the first modern state police agency was and when it was established?
- What the five levels of law enforcement are?
- What three eras of policing have been identified? The main characteristics of each?
- What effect the spoils system had in the 1900s?
- What the Pendleton Act accomplished?
- What effect the Equal Employment Opportunity Act had?
- What four phases of development the juvenile justice system has gone through?
- What was established by the Juvenile Court Act of 1899?

Introduction

The heritage of law enforcement is a source of pride, as well as a guide to avoiding mistakes in the future. Specific dates and events are not as important as acquiring a sense of the sequence or chronology of how present-day laws and our system of law enforcement came into existence. **Law** is a body of rules for human conduct enforced by imposing penalties for their violation. Technically, laws are made and passed by the legislative branches of our federal, state, county and city governments. They are based on customs, traditions, mores and current need.

Law implies both prescription (rule) and enforcement by authority. In the United States, those who enforce the laws are *not* the same as those who make them. Historically, in other countries, this was not the case. Often rulers both made and enforced the laws.

This chapter discusses primitive and ancient law and its influence on the development of English law and law enforcement. This is followed by an overview of the evolution of law enforcement in England from the Anglo-Saxon tithing system, through the Norman Frankpledge system and on through the centuries up to the establishment of the London Metropolitan Police in 1829, the development of city and borough police forces and the entrance of women into law enforcement in England.

Next the continued evolution of the criminal justice system in the United States is described, beginning with a discussion of early law enforcement, including the first police forces and slave patrols, the city police and the vigilante movement. This is followed by a description of the various federal, state, county and local agencies established over the years. Next the overlap in these agencies is discussed, followed by a description of the three eras of policing: the political era, the reform era and the community era. The chapter concludes with a brief historical overview of the evolution of our juvenile justice system and a recap of important dates in police history.

Primitive and Ancient Law

Law enforcement can be traced back to the cave dwellers, who were expected to follow certain rules or face banishment or death. The customs depicted in early cave-dwelling drawings may represent the beginning of law and law enforcement.

If a builder builds a house for a man and does not make its construction firm and the house collapses and causes the death of the owner of the house—that builder shall be put to death. If it causes the death of a son of the owner—they shall put to death a son of that builder. If it causes the death of a slave of the owner—he shall give the owner a slave of equal value. If it destroys property he shall restore whatever it destroyed and because he did not make the house firm he shall rebuild the house which collapsed at his own expense. If a builder builds a house and does not make its construction meet the requirements and a wall falls in—that builder shall strengthen the wall at his own expense.

Figure 1.1   From the Code of Hammurabi (2200 B.C.)

SOURCE: Masonry Institute, 55 New Montgomery Street, San Francisco, CA 94105. Reprinted with permission.

The prehistoric social order consisted of small family groups living together as tribes or clans. Group living gave rise to customs everyone was expected to observe. The tribe's chief had executive, legislative and judicial powers and often appointed tribe members to perform special tasks, such as serving as a bodyguard or enforcing edicts. Crimes committed against individuals were handled by the victim or the victim's family. The philosophy of justice was retaliatory: punish the offender. A person who stole the game from a neighbor's traps could expect to pay for the crime by being thrown into a pot of boiling oil or a cage of wild beasts. Other common punishments for serious offenses were flaying, impalement, burning at the stake, stoning, branding, mutilation and crucifixion.

 A system of law and law enforcement began earlier than 2000 B.C. as a means to control human conduct and enforce society's rules. Keeping the peace was the responsibility of the group.

The earliest record of ancient people's need to standardize rules and methods of enforcement to control human behavior dates back to approximately 2300 B.C., when the Sumerian rulers Lipitshtar and Eshumma set standards on what constituted an offense against society. A hundred years later, the Babylonian King Hammurabi established rules for his kingdom designating not only offenses but punishments as well. Although the penalties prescribed were often barbaric by today's standards, the relationship between the crime and the punishment is of interest (see Figure 1.1). The main principle of the code was that "the strong shall not injure the weak." Hammurabi originated the legal principle of *lex talionis*—an eye for an eye.

Egypt

The first accounts of a developing court system came from Egypt in approximately 1500 B.C. The court system was presided over by judges appointed by the pharaoh. About 1000 B.C. in Egypt, public officers performed police functions. Their weapon and symbol of authority was a staff topped by a metal knob engraved with the king's name. The baton carried by the modern police officer may have its origin in that staff.

Greece

The Greeks had an impressive form of law enforcement called the *ephori*. Each year at Sparta a body of five *ephors* was elected and given almost unlimited powers as investigator, judge, jury and executioner. These five men also presided over the Senate and Assembly, assuring that their rules and decrees were followed. From the Greek philosopher Plato, who lived from 427 to 347 B.C., came the idea that punishment should serve a purpose other than simple retaliation.

Rome

Like the Greeks, the Romans had a highly developed system to administer justice. The Twelve Tables, the first written laws of the Roman Empire, were drawn up by 10 of the wisest men in Rome in 451 and 450 B.C. and were fastened to the speakers' stand in the Roman Forum. The tables dealt with legal procedures, property ownership, building codes, marriage customs and punishment for crimes.

At about the time of Christ, the Roman emperor Augustus chose members from his military to form the Praetorian Guard to protect the palace and the Urban Cohort to patrol the city. Augustus also established the Vigiles of Rome. Initially assigned as firefighters, they were eventually given law enforcement responsibilities. As the first civilian police force, the Vigiles sometimes kept the peace very ruthlessly. The word *vigilante* derives from these Vigiles.

Another important contribution from the Roman Empire was the Justinian Code. Justinian I, ruler of the eastern Roman Empire from A.D. 527 to 565, collected all existing Roman laws. They became known as the *Corpus Juris Civilis*, meaning "body of law."

English Law and Law Enforcement

The beginnings of just laws and social control were destroyed during the Dark Ages as the Roman Empire disintegrated. Germanic invaders swept into the old Roman territory of Britain, bringing their own laws and customs. These invaders intermarried with those they conquered, the result being the hardy Anglo-Saxon.

The Anglo-Saxons and the Tithing System

The Anglo-Saxons grouped their farms around small, self-governing, self-policed villages. When criminals were caught, the punishment was often severe. Sometimes, however, the tribe would let offenders prove innocence through battle or through testimony by other tribespeople willing to swear that the accused was innocent. Additionally, the tribe sometimes allowed criminals to pay a fine for committing a crime or to work off the debt.

Over time, the informal family groupings became more structured. Alfred the Great (A.D. 849 to 899) established that all freemen belonged to an association binding them with a certain group of people. If one person in the group committed a crime and was convicted, all group members were responsible for the person's fine. Consequently all group members were careful to see that no one in the group broke the law. Every male, unless excused by the king, was enrolled in a group of 10 families known as a **tithing.** To maintain order they had a chief tithingman who was the mayor, council and judge in one. Society was so basic that it enforced only two laws: laws against murder and theft.

The **tithing system** established the principle of collective responsibility for maintaining local law and order.

Any victim or person who discovered a crime would put out the **Hue and Cry,** for example, "Stop, thief!" Those hearing the cry would stop what they were doing and help capture the suspect.

The Hue and Cry may be the origin of the general alarm and the citizen's arrest.

When capture was made, the suspect was brought before the chief tithingman, who determined innocence or guilt plus punishment. Theft was often punished by working off the loss through bondage or servitude—the basis for civil law, restitution for financial loss (Lunt, 1938).

If a criminal sought refuge in a neighboring village, that village was expected to return the criminal for punishment. This cooperation among villagers eventually resulted in the formation of **hundreds,** groups of 10 tithings. The top official of the hundred was called a **reeve.**

The hundreds also elected a **constable** to lead them in pursuit of any lawbreakers. The constable was the first English police officer and had charge of the community's weapons and horses. Finally, the hundreds were consolidated into **shires** or counties. The head of the shire was called the **shire-reeve,** the forerunner of our county sheriff.

The shire-reeve acted as both police officer and judge, traveling from hundred to hundred. The shire-reeve had the power of *posse comitatus,* meaning he could gather all the men of a shire together to pursue a lawbreaker, a practice that was the forerunner of our posse.

The Norman Frankpledge System

In 1066 William the Conqueror, a Norman, invaded and conquered England. As king of the conquered nation, William was too concerned about national security to allow the tithings to keep their system of home rule. He established 55 military districts, each headed by a Norman shire-reeve who answered directly to the crown. The Normans modified the tithing system into the **Frankpledge system.**

The Frankpledge system required loyalty to the king's law and mutual local responsibility of all free Englishmen to maintain the peace.

William also decided that shire-reeves should serve only as police officers. He selected his own judges, who traveled around and tried cases, forerunners of our circuit judges, in effect separating the law enforcement and judicial roles.

The Twelfth Century

William's son, Henry I, ruled England from 1100 to 1135 and issued the **Leges Henrici,** establishing arson, robbery, murder and crimes of violence as being against the king's peace. This set the precedent that for certain crimes a person is punished by the state rather than by the victim.

The Leges Henrici made law enforcement a public matter and separated offenses into felonies and misdemeanors.

Henry I's reign was followed by many years of turmoil, which lasted until Henry II became king in 1154.

 Henry II established the jury system.

Henry II's jury system, called an inquisition, required people to give information to a panel of judges who determined guilt or innocence.

For the next 100 years, kings appointed enforcement officers to meet their needs. When John became king in 1199, he abused his power by demanding more military service from the feudal class, selling royal positions to the highest bidder and increasing taxes without obtaining consent from the barons—actions all contrary to feudal custom. In addition, John's courts decided cases according to his wishes, not according to law.

In 1213 a group of barons and church leaders met to call for a halt to the king's injustices. They drew up a list of rights they wanted King John to grant them. After the king refused on two separate occasions, the barons raised an army and forced him to meet their demands. On June 15, 1215, King John signed the Magna Carta.

The Magna Carta

Our modern system of justice owes much to the Magna Carta, a decisive document in the development of England's constitutional government.

 The **Magna Carta,** a precedent for democratic government and individual rights, laid the foundation for requiring rulers to uphold the law; forbade taxation without representation; required due process of law, including trial by jury; and provided safeguards against unfair imprisonment.

The Magna Carta contained 63 articles, most requiring the king to uphold feudal law. Article 13 restored local control to cities and villages, a fundamental principle of American law enforcement. Another article declared that no freeman should be imprisoned, deprived of property, sent out of the country or destroyed except by the lawful judgment of peers or the law of the land. The concept of due process of law, including trial by jury, developed from this article.

The Next 500 Years

Several interesting developments in law enforcement occurred in the following centuries. In 1285 King Edward I established a curfew and night watch program that allowed for the gates of Westminster, then capital of England, to be locked, keeping the city's occupants in and unwanted persons out. Bailiffs were hired as night watchmen to enforce the curfew and guard the gates. Edward I also mandated that groups of 100 merchants be responsible for keeping peace in their districts, again making law enforcement a local responsibility. This system of law enforcement, called the **Watch and Ward,** provided citizens protection 24 hours a day, with the day shift called *ward* and the night shift *watch.*

An ever-increasing population and a trend toward urbanization led law enforcement to become truly a collective responsibility. If a man's next-door neighbor broke the law, the man was responsible for bringing the lawbreaker before the shire-reeve. The hundred decided yearly who would be responsible for maintaining law and order, with responsibility rotated among community members. Inevitably some people paid other members to serve in their place, beginning a system of deputies paid to be responsible for law and order. The paid deputy system was then formalized so that those whose turn it was to pay met and appointed the law enforcers. The abuse of citizen duty to serve as watchmen was pervasive, however, and led to petty thieves and town drunks serving as watchmen.

 During the fourteenth century, the shire-reeve was replaced by the justice of the peace.

The justice of the peace was assisted by the constables and three or four men knowledgeable of the country's laws. At first the justice of the peace was involved in both judicial matters and law enforcement, but later his powers became strictly judicial. The justice of the peace eventually became the real power of local government (Lunt).

With the passing of feudal times and the rise in the power of the church, the unit of local government in rural areas progressed from the hundred to the **parish,** the area in which people lived who worshiped in a particular church. Each year the parish appointed a parish constable to act as their law officer. This system of maintaining law and order in rural Britain lasted from the Middle Ages until the eighteenth century.

 During the Middle Ages, the **parish constable system** was used for rural law enforcement; the Watch and Ward system was used for urban law enforcement.

Developments in urban England required a different system of law enforcement. With urbanization came commerce, industry and a variety of buildings usually made of wood, since England was primarily forest land. For fire prevention purposes the town guild appointed men who patrolled at night on fire watch. They assumed the coincidental responsibility of preventing people from breaking into houses and shops.

Although the Watch and Ward system was primitive and not very effective, it was adequate until the Industrial Revolution (1750) began. About the same time, famine struck the rural areas, and large numbers of people moved from the country into the towns seeking work in weaving and knitting mills and in factories. Many, however, failed to find work, and England experienced much unemployment, poverty and crime.

In addition, political extremists often incited mobs to march on Parliament. The government had no civil police force to deal with mob violence, so it ordered a magistrate to read the **riot act,** permitting the magistrate to call the military to quell the riot. This is the forerunner of today's gubernatorial authority to call out state's National Guard in times of rioting or violent strikes.

The use of a military force to repress civil disobedience did not work very well. Soldiers hesitated to fire on their own townspeople, and the townspeople, who actually paid the soldiers' wages, resented being fired on by soldiers they had hired to protect them.

In addition to unemployment, poverty and resentment against the use of military force, the invention of gin and whiskey in the seventeenth century and the subsequent increase in the liquor trade also caused a rise in violent crimes and theft. Because many constables were employed in the liquor trade, they often did not enforce regulations governing taverns and inns. Furthermore the London watchmen were highly susceptible to bribes and payoffs.

Henry Fielding and the Bow Street Runners

In 1748 Henry Fielding, lawyer, playwright and novelist, was appointed chief magistrate of Bow Street in policeless London. Fielding fought for social and criminal reform. He defied the law by discharging prisoners convicted of petty theft, giving reprimands in place of the death penalty and exercising general leniency.

Fielding wrote and published pamphlets and books about London's poverty-stricken inhabitants and the causes of crime, calling for an understanding and lessening of their suffering. He also urged that magistrates be paid a salary rather than depending on fees and fines for their income.

During this time thieves and robbers moved freely in London's streets, looting and rioting. Although such riots inevitably brought soldiers, they sometimes did not arrive for two or three days. Fielding suggested that citizens join together, go into the streets and trace the perpetrators of crime and instigators of mob violence *before* they committed crimes or caused destruction. Such views made Fielding one of the earliest advocates of crime prevention.

Fielding was also instrumental in establishing the **Bow Street Runners,** the first detective unit in London. This amateur volunteer force, under Fielding's direction, swept clean the Bow Street neighborhood. When these runners proved successful, other units were organized. Foot patrols of armed men guarded the city's streets, and a horse patrol combated highway robbery on the main roads up to 25 miles from Bow Street.

Although the Bow Street Runners and patrols greatly improved control in the Bow Street area, other parts of London were overwhelmed by the impact of the Industrial Revolution. Machines were taking the place of many jobs, causing unemployment and poverty. The cities were developing into huge slums, and the crime rate soared. Children were often trained to be thieves, and for the first time in England's history, juvenile delinquency became a problem. Developments in England had a great influence on the juvenile justice system that would later develop in the United States. Citizens began carrying weapons, and the courts used long-term prison sentences, resulting in overcrowded jails and prisons. Punishments were also severe, with more than 160 crimes punishable by death.

Despite the rampant crime, however, most Londoners resisted an organized police force, seeing it as restricting their liberty. They had fought hard to overcome the historical abuse of military power by English kings and resisted any return to centralized military power. Then, in 1819 and 1820, two contrasting incidents helped people change their minds. The first was the Peterloo Massacre, an attack by armed soldiers on a meeting of unemployed workers that left 11 people dead and hundreds injured. This incident vividly illustrated the danger of using soldiers to maintain peace. In contrast, in the second incident, the Bow Street Runners broke up a conspiracy to murder a number of government officials. When the conspirators were executed, people saw that actions by professional peacekeepers could prevent a major insurrection.

In addition to rampant crime, Parliament was also concerned about poverty, unemployment and general conditions. Five parliamentary commissions of inquiry met in London between 1780 and 1820 to determine what should be done about the public order. It was not until Sir Robert (Bobbie) Peel was appointed Home Secretary that the first constructive proposal was brought before Parliament.

During the first few years of reform, Peel encountered strong opposition. In addition to this opposition, Peel faced the problem of finding a building for the newly created London Police. He chose an abandoned building built many years before for visiting Scottish nobility. This building became known the world over as Scotland Yard, as immortalized by A. Conan Doyle in his Sherlock Holmes mysteries.

Peelian Reform

Sir Robert Peel, often referred to as the "father of modern policing," proposed a return to the Anglo-Saxon principle of individual community responsibility for preserving law and order.

 Peel's principles for reform called for local responsibility for law and order; appointed, paid civilians to assume this responsibility; and standards for these individuals' conduct and organization. His proposals led to the organization of the Metropolitan Police of London in 1829.

The name *police*, introduced into England from France, is derived from the Greek word *polis* meaning "city." The principles of Peelian reform stated:

- Police must be stable, efficient and organized militarily.
- Police must be under governmental control.
- The deployment of police strength by both time and area is essential.
- The securing and training of proper persons is at the root of efficiency.
- Public security demands that every police officer be given a number.
- Police headquarters should be centrally located and easily accessible.
- Policemen should be hired on a probationary basis.
- The duty of police is to prevent crime and disorder.
- The test of police efficiency is the absence of crime and disorder, not the visible evidence of police action in dealing with these problems.
- The power of the police to fulfill their duties is dependent on public approval and on their ability to secure and maintain public respect.
- The police should strive to maintain a relationship with the public that gives reality to the tradition that *the police are the public and the public are the police.*

Peel's principles became the basis of police reform in many large cities in America. In addition, one of Peel's first steps was to introduce reform that abolished the death penalty for more than 100 offenses.

London Metropolitan Police (1829)

British police historian Critchley (1967, p.52) states: "From the start, the police was to be a homogeneous and democratic body in tune with the people, and drawing itself from the people." The London Metropolitan Police, called "bobbies" after Sir "Bobbie" Peel, were uniformed for easy identification—top hats, three-quarter-length royal blue coats and white trousers—and were armed only with truncheons. Their primary function was crime prevention through patrol.

Unfortunately the London Metropolitan Police were not popular. Soon after the force went on street duty in 1829, a London mob assembled to march on Parliament. A police sergeant and two constables asked the mob leaders to send their people home. Rather than dispersing, the mob attacked the sergeant and constables, killing the sergeant and critically injuring the constables. A jury of London citizens, after hearing evidence clearly indicative of murder, returned a verdict of justifiable homicide. In time, however, police officers discharging their duties with professional integrity created a respect for the law.

City and Borough Police Forces (1835)

Broad public use of the steam engine and railways and better roads helped move many criminals from London to provincial cities, such as Birmingham, Liverpool and Manchester. Soon the citizens of these cities demanded some police organization similar to London's. In 1835 Parliament enacted legislation allowing (but not requiring) every city or borough (unincorporated township) of more than 20,000 people to form a police force.

Women Enter Law Enforcement

 In 1883 the London Metropolitan Police appointed two women to supervise women convicts. Their numbers and functions later expanded.

In 1905 a woman was attached to the London Metropolitan Police force to conduct inquiries in cases involving women and children. Each year several more police matrons were hired.

Early Law Enforcement in the United States

When the English colonists came to America, they brought with them many traditions, including traditions in law enforcement. From the beginning they were concerned with avoiding anarchy:

> As the *Mayflower* rode at anchor off Cape Cod, some of the passengers threatened to go out on their own, without any framework of government. To avoid this threat of anarchy, the *Mayflower Compact* [1620] agreed that: "We . . . doe . . . solemnly and mutually . . . covenant and combine our selves together into a civil body politike for our better ordering and preservation . . . and by vertue hereof to enact . . . such just and equall lawes . . . unto which we promise all due submission and obedience" (Gardner, 1985, p.26).

The early colonial American settlements relied heavily on self-policing to assure the peace. Communal pressure was the backbone of law enforcement. The colonists were of similar background, most held similar religious beliefs, and there was actually little worth stealing. The seeds of vice and crime were present, however, as noted by Perry (1973, p.24):

> These colonists were far from the cream of European society; in many cases they represented the legal and religious castoffs. (Persons found guilty of criminal or religious offenses who were banished from Europe and exported to the New World.) Their migration served the dual purpose of removing socially undesirable persons from the Mother country and providing manpower for the outposts of imperial expansion.

Many features of British law enforcement were present in early American colonial settlements. In New England, where people depended on commerce and industry, the night watchman or constable served as protector of public order. In the South, where agriculture played a dominant role, the office of **sheriff** was established as the means of area law enforcement. Most watchmen and sheriffs were volunteers, but many were paid to serve in the place of others who were to patrol as a civic duty.

 New England adopted the night watchman or constable as the chief means of law enforcement; the South adopted the office of sheriff.

Many different types of law enforcement were tried in different parts of the country. Almost all used some kind of night watch system, with little or no protection during the day. The fastest-growing municipalities were the first to organize legal forces.

The First U.S. Police Forces

The first police forces in the United States were developed in Boston, New York and Los Angeles.

Boston   In 1631 the Boston court established a six-man force to guard the city from sunset to sunup, the first night watch in America. In 1636 a town watch was created and stayed in effect for more than 200 years. At first the primary function was to ring a bell in case of fire. In 1702 the police were to patrol the streets in silence. In 1735 they were required to call out the time of day and the weather.

New York   The first colonists in New York, then called New Amsterdam, were the Dutch who settled on Manhattan Island's south end. In 1643 a "burgher guard" was formed to protect the colony. Then, in 1653, New Amsterdam became a city (population 800), and the burgher guard was changed to a **rattle watch,** a group of night-patrolling citizens armed with rattles to call for help (Bailey, 1989, p.346).

In 1664 the British took over New Amsterdam and renamed it New York. Thirty years later the first uniformed police officers replaced the nighttime rattle watch, and four years after that New York's streets were lighted.

The system of watchmen was very ineffective. Often the watchman was sentenced to patrol as a form of punishment for a misdemeanor. In addition citizens could avoid watch duty by hiring someone to take their places. Wealthy citizens came to rely on hiring others, and the men they hired then hesitated to invoke their authority against the well-to-do. By the mid-1700s New York City's night watch was "a parcel of idle, drinking, vigilant snorers, who never quell'd any nocturnal tumult in their lives; . . . but would, perhaps, be as ready to join in a burglary as any thief in Christendom" (Richardson, 1970, p.10).

Due to a continuing increase in crime during the day, New York City hired an assortment of watchmen, fire marshals and bell ringers to patrol both day and night. In 1844 a paid day watch was established, consisting of 16 officers appointed by the mayor.

 In 1844 New York City established the first modern round-the-clock, paid American city police force, modeled after London's Metropolitan Police.

Soon other cities followed suit, including Chicago, Cincinnati, New Orleans, Philadelphia, Boston, Baltimore and San Francisco.

Although patterned after the London Metropolitan Police, New York police officers protested wearing uniforms. Not until 12 years later did the New York police adopt a full police uniform and become the first uniformed law enforcement agency in the country. Likewise, although Fielding established the Bow Street Runners (the first detective unit) in 1750, more than 100 years passed before American police agencies recognized a need for detective units. In 1866 Detroit established the first detective bureau, followed by New York in 1882 and Cincinnati in 1886. Other important differences from the London police were that police in the United States were armed and they were under local, not national, control.

Los Angeles   In 1850 California became a state, and Los Angeles incorporated as a city with a population of 1,610. During its first year, the city elected a mayor, a city marshal and a sheriff:

> The duties assumed by the sheriff and marshal included the collection of local taxes. The sheriff 's obligations required him to traverse a vast area on horseback, fighting bands of Indians and marauding desperadoes. Lacking paid assistants, the marshal was permitted to deputize citizens whenever necessary to maintain order (Bailey, pp.310–316).

In 1853 the city council established a police force of 100 volunteers, called the Los Angeles Rangers. Four years later they were replaced by the Los Angeles City Guards, who were charged with maintaining the peace. Finally, in 1869, the police force changed from a voluntary organization to a paid department.

Slave Patrols

Law enforcement in the South evolved differently. By 1700 most Southern colonies, concerned about the dangers posed by oppressed slaves, established a code of laws to regulate slaves, for example prohibiting slaves from possessing weapons, congregating in groups, resisting punishment or leaving the plantation without permission.

Not surprisingly, many slaves resisted their bondage, attempting to escape or lashing out through criminal acts or revolts. The threat of harm by slaves was compounded by their growing number; in some Southern states, blacks outnumbered whites by more than 2 to 1. The white colonists' fear of this large and potentially dangerous slave population led to the creation of special enforcement officers—**slave patrols** (Reichel, 1999, p.82). By the mid-1700s, every Southern colony had a slave patrol, most of whom were allowed to enter any plantation and break into slaves' dwellings, search slaves' persons and possessions at will and beat and even kill any slaves found violating the slave code. Asirvatham (2000, p.2) states:

> Twentieth-century Southern law enforcement was essentially a direct out-growth of the 19th-century slave patrols employed to enforce curfews, catch runaways and suppress rebellion. Even later on, in Northern and Southern cities alike, "free men of color" were hired as cops only to keep other African Americans in line [enforcing Jim Crow laws supporting segregation]. Until the 1960s black cops, by law or by custom, weren't given powers of arrest over white citizens, no matter how criminal.

Evolution of the City Police

When city police were first established, their only contact with their departments was face-to-face meetings or messengers. One early means of communication was a telephone pole light system to notify police of a call awaiting response. During the 1850s, however, telegraph networks linked police headquarters directly with their districts. Several decades later a modified telegraph system linked the patrol officers directly to the station. A fire alarm system, first introduced in Boston, was adopted for police use. Call boxes placed on city street corners were equipped with a simple lever that signaled the station that the officers were at their posts. A bell system was added that allowed the patrol officers to use a few simple signals to call an ambulance, a "slow wagon" for routine duties or a "fast wagon" for emergencies. The introduction of a special "Gamewell" telephone into the call box in 1880 made this a two-way communication system, greatly improving contact between patrol officers and their station houses.

The Civil War brought new social control problems. As centers of population became increasingly urbanized, fringe areas became incorporated suburbs of the hub city. These newly developed fringe cities had their own police forces, which fostered complex, uncoordinated relationships, compartmentalization and inefficiency.

Although cities developed police departments and maintained a certain level of law and order, this was not the case in many areas, especially the frontiers. In such areas Americans came to rely upon vigilante groups for law and order.

The Vigilante Movement

In response to the absence of effective law and order in frontier regions, as many as 500 vigilante movements were organized between 1767 and 1900 (Klockars, 1985, p.30).

 The **vigilante** movement refers to settlers taking the law into their own hands in the absence of effective policing.

The first American vigilante movement occurred from 1767 to 1769 in South Carolina:

> The disorder in the South Carolina back country of the 1760s was typical of later American frontier areas. . . . Outlaws, runaway slaves, and mulattoes formed their own communities where they enjoyed their booty. . . . By 1766 and 1767 the back country was in the grip of a "crime wave," and the outlaws were almost supreme (Brown, 1991, p.61).

Because there was no sheriff or court, "respectable settlers of average or affluent means" organized as **regulators** in 1767 to attack and break up the outlaw gangs and restore order. As noted by Brown (p.60): "An American tradition had begun, for, as the pioneers moved across the Appalachian Mountains, the regulator-vigilanted impulse followed the sweep of settlement toward the Pacific."

A characteristic of the vigilante movement was that the leader was usually one of the most powerful men in the community, thus making the movement highly respectable: "Two presidents (Andrew Jackson and Theodore Roosevelt), eight state governors (including Leland Stanford, Sr., founder of Stanford University), and four U.S. Senators had either been vigilantes or expressed strong support for vigilante movements" (Klockars, 1985, p.31).

An uneven judicial system and a lack of jails added to the strength of the vigilante tradition. The movement was evidence of the value Americans placed on law and order and the desire to be rid of those who broke the law. It was also evidence of a basic paradox in the illegal means used to the desired end: "Perhaps the most important result of vigilantism has not been its social-stabilizing effect but the subtle way in which it persistently undermined our respect for law by its repeated insistence that there are times when we may choose to obey the law or not" (Brown, p.72).

As the country grew and its society became more complex, federal and state agencies were established to meet needs that could not be met at the local level.

Establishment of Federal Agencies

Congress created several federal law enforcement agencies to meet demands created by the nation's changing conditions. The oldest federal agency is the U.S. Marshals Office, created in 1789. Figure 1.2 illustrates the most common federal agencies before the reorganization that followed the September 11, 2001 (9/11), attack on the United States.

 Among the earliest federal law enforcement agencies were the U.S. Marshals Office, the Immigration and Naturalization Service, the Secret Service and the Internal Revenue Service.

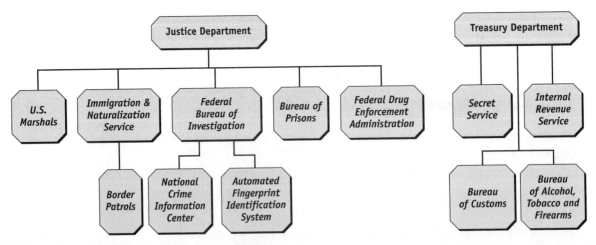

Figure 1.2 Federal Agencies, Original Organization

Judge Roy Bean dispensed frontier justice and cold beer in the Texas territory west of the Pecos River.

The Department of Justice

The Department of Justice is the largest law firm in the country, representing U.S. citizens in enforcing the law.

 The attorney general is head of the Department of Justice and the chief law officer of the federal government.

The Department of Justice's law enforcement agencies include the Federal Bureau of Investigation, the Federal Drug Enforcement Administration, the U.S. Marshals, the Immigration and Naturalization Service (pre-9/11) and the Bureau of Prisons.

The Federal Bureau of Investigation (FBI)   Created as the Bureau of Investigation and renamed the Federal Bureau of Investigation in 1935, this is the primary investigative agency of the federal government. Its special agents have jurisdiction over more than 200 federal crimes. Their responsibilities include investigating espionage, interstate transportation of stolen property and kidnapping; unlawful flight to avoid prosecution, confinement or giving testimony; sabotage, piracy of aircraft and other crimes aboard aircraft; bank robbery and embezzlement; and enforcement of the Civil Rights Acts. The FBI also provides valuable services to law enforcement agencies throughout the country:

- The *Identification Division* is a central repository for fingerprint information, including its automated fingerprint identification system (AFIS), which greatly streamlines the matching of fingerprints with suspects.
- The *National Crime Information Center (NCIC)* is a computerized database network containing records of wanted persons, stolen vehicles, vehicles used in the commission of felonies, stolen or missing license plates, stolen guns and other stolen items serially identifiable, such as television sets and boat motors.
- The *FBI Laboratory*, the largest criminal laboratory in the world, is available without cost to any city, county, state or federal law enforcement agency in the country.

- *Uniform Crime Reports (UCR)* are periodical publications provided by the FBI, which, since 1930, has served as a national clearinghouse for U.S. crime statistics. States report their monthly crime statistics to the FBI, which in turn releases information semiannually and annually regarding all crimes reported to it.

The Federal Drug Enforcement Administration (FDEA)   FDEA agents seek to stop the flow of drugs at their source, both domestic and foreign, and to assist state and local police in preventing illegal drugs from reaching local communities. They become involved in surveillance, raids, interviewing witnesses and suspects, searching for evidence and seizure of contraband.

The FDEA is charged with the full responsibility for prosecuting suspected violators of federal drug laws. It has liaison with law enforcement officials of foreign governments and highly trained agents stationed in all major U.S. cities and in 30 countries.

The U.S. Marshals   Marshals are appointed by the president and are responsible for (1) seizing property in both criminal and civil matters to satisfy judgments issued by a federal court, (2) providing physical security for U.S. courtrooms, (3) transporting federal prisoners and (4) protecting government witnesses whose testimony might jeopardize their safety.

The Immigration and Naturalization Service (INS)   The Immigration and Naturalization Service originally had border patrol agents who served throughout the United States, Canada, Mexico, Bermuda, Nassau, Puerto Rico, the Philippines and Europe. They investigated violations of immigration and nationality laws and determined whether aliens could enter or remain in the United States.

When the Department of Homeland Security (DHS) was organized in 2002, the INS was moved from the Justice Department to the Department of Homeland Security as two separate agencies: Citizenship and Immigration Service Ombudsman and the Bureau of Citizenship and Immigration Services, effective March 1, 2003. The DHS is discussed in Chapter 10.

The Bureau of Prisons (BOP)   The Bureau of Prisons is responsible for the care and custody of persons convicted of federal crimes and sentenced to federal penal institutions. The bureau operates a nationwide system of maximum-, medium- and minimum-security prisons, halfway houses and community program offices.

The Department of the Treasury

The Department of the Treasury also had several agencies directly involved in law enforcement activities, including the Bureau of Customs, the Internal Revenue Service, the Secret Service and the Bureau of Alcohol, Tobacco and Firearms. They too have been affected by the reorganization following the 9/11 attacks. In addition a new bureau may be added to the department to track monies flowing to terrorist groups.

The Bureau of Customs   The Bureau of Customs originally had agents stationed primarily at ports of entry to the United States, where people and/or goods enter and leave. Customs agents investigated frauds on customs revenue and the smuggling of merchandise and contraband into or out of the United

States. Since the reorganization of federal agencies, the Bureau of Customs is now within the DHS under the Border and Transportation Security directorate and has shifted its priority to fighting terrorism.

The Internal Revenue Service (IRS) The Internal Revenue Service, established in 1862, is the largest bureau of the Department of the Treasury. Its mission is to encourage the highest degree of voluntary compliance with the tax laws and regulations. IRS agents investigate willful tax evasion, tax fraud and the activities of gamblers and drug peddlers.

The Secret Service The Secret Service was established in 1865 to fight currency counterfeiters. In 1901 it was given the responsibility of protecting the president of the United States, the president's family, the president-elect and the vice president. The Secret Service has also been transferred to the DHS.

The Bureau of Alcohol, Tobacco and Firearms (BATF) The Bureau of Alcohol, Tobacco and Firearms is primarily a licensing and investigative agency involved in federal tax violations. The Firearms Division enforces the Gun Control Act of 1968. Under the post-9/11 reorganization, this Bureau has been transferred to the Justice Department and renamed the Bureau of Alcohol, Tobacco, Firearms and Explosives.

Other Federal Law Enforcement Agencies

Although most federal law enforcement agencies are within either the Department of Justice or the Department of the Treasury, other federal agencies are also directly involved in law enforcement activities, such as U.S. Postal Inspectors, the Coast Guard and the armed forces military police, as well as investigators, intelligence agents and security officers for other federal agencies.

Current Organization

The major changes occurring as a result of the attack on America on September 11, 2001 were the creation of the Department of Homeland Security and the transfer of several agencies from the Department of Justice and the Department of the Treasury to this new agency.

The Department of Homeland Security The recently created Department of Homeland Security (DHS) now oversees the U.S. Secret Service, the Bureau of Customs and Border Protection, the Bureau of Citizenship and Immigration Services (formerly the Immigration and Naturalization Service, or INS) and the U.S. Coast Guard. Other DHS agencies with investigative and law enforcement roles include the Transportation Security Administration (TSA), the Office of Inspector General and the Federal Computer Incident Response Center. Figure 1.3 shows the law enforcement agencies included within DHS.

The creation of the DHS is the most significant transformation of the U.S. government since 1947, when Harry S. Truman merged the various branches of the U.S. Armed Forces into the Department of Defense to better coordinate the nation's defense against military threats. DHS represents a similar consolidation, both in style and substance. In the aftermath of the 9/11 terrorist attacks against the United States, President George W. Bush decided 22 previously disparate domestic agencies needed to be coordinated into one department to protect the

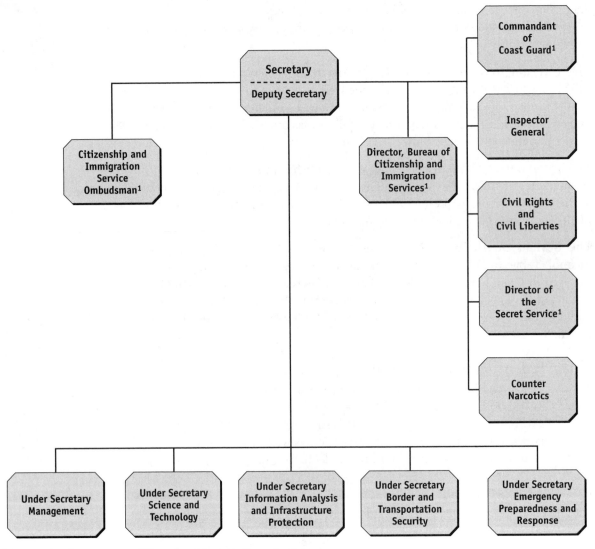

Figure 1.3 Department of Homeland Security Organization

[1]Effective March 1, 2003.

SOURCE: Adapted from DHS Web site, http://www.dhs.gov.

nation against threats to the homeland (DHS Web site, *http://www.dhs.gov*). The current organization of the Department of Justice is shown in Figure 1.4.

Establishment of State Agencies

Many federal agencies have state counterparts, including state bureaus of investigation and apprehension and state fire marshal divisions, as well as departments of natural resources, driver and vehicle services divisions and departments of human rights.

In 1835 the republic of Texas's provisional government established the Texas Rangers, a military unit responsible for border patrol. The apprehension of Mexican cattle rustlers was a primary task (Folley, 1980, p.88). In 1874 the Texas Rangers were commissioned as Texas police officers, with duties that included tracking down murderers, robbers, smugglers and mine bandits.

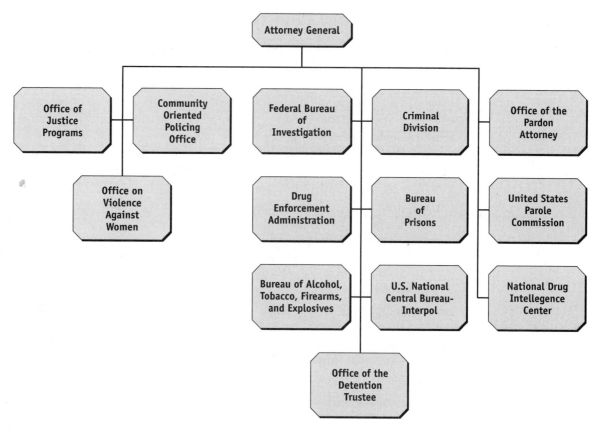

Figure 1.4 Current Organization of the Department of Justice

 The Texas Rangers were the first agency similar to our present state police.

Massachusetts was next to establish a state law enforcement agency by appointing a small force of state officers in 1865 to control vice. The state also granted them general police powers; therefore, Massachusetts is usually credited with establishing the first law enforcement agency with general police authority throughout the state.

Most state police agencies established before the twentieth century were created in response to a limited need. This was not the case in Pennsylvania, which established the Pennsylvania Constabulary in 1905 to meet several needs: to (1) provide the governor an executive arm for help in fulfilling his responsibilities, (2) provide a means to quell riots occurring during labor disputes in the coal regions and (3) improve law enforcement services in the rural portions of the state (Folley, p.66). The Pennsylvania state police served as a model for other states and heralded the advent of modern state policing.

Today the most visible forms of state law enforcement are the *state police*, who often have general police powers and enforce all state laws, but do not usually work within municipalities that have their own forces unless requested; and *state highway patrols*, who focus their attention on the operation of motor vehicles on public highways and freeways, enforcing state traffic laws and all laws governing the operation of vehicles on public highways in the state. The highway patrols usually operate in uniform and drive distinctively marked patrol cars and motorcycles.

Development of County Agencies

The two main county agencies are the county sheriff and the county police.

The County Sheriff

Many state constitutions have designated the sheriff as the chief county law enforcement officer. The sheriff is usually elected locally for a two- or four-year term, an obvious mixing of police and politics.

State law establishes the sheriff's powers and duties. Each sheriff is authorized to appoint deputies to assume responsibility for providing police protection, as well as a variety of other functions, including (1) keeping the public peace, (2) executing civil and criminal process (such as serving civil legal papers and criminal warrants), (3) keeping the county jail, (4) preserving the court's dignity and (5) enforcing court orders.

The hundreds of sheriff's departments vary greatly in organization and function. In some states the sheriff is primarily a court officer; criminal investigation and traffic enforcement are delegated to state or local agencies. In other states, notably in the South and West, the sheriff and deputies perform both traffic and criminal duties.

The sheriff's staff ranges from one (the sheriff only) to several hundred, including sworn deputies as well as civilian personnel. One major difference between sheriffs' offices and municipal police departments is that sheriffs often place greater emphasis on civil functions and operating corrections facilities.

The County Police

County police departments are often found in areas where city and county governments have merged and are led by a chief of police, usually appointed from within the department.

The Coroner or Medical Examiner

The office of coroner has a history similar to that of the sheriff and comes to modern law enforcement from ancient times (Adams, 1980, p.150). The coroner's principal task is to determine the cause of death and to take care of the remains and personal effects of deceased persons. The coroner need not be a medical doctor or have any legal background to be elected. In some jurisdictions, however, the coroner has been replaced by the medical examiner, a physician, usually a pathologist, who has studied forensic science.

Development of Local Agencies

In addition to federal and state agencies, much power was vested in local agencies.

District and Special Township Police

The United States has approximately 19,000 townships, which vary widely in scope of governmental powers and operations. Most townships provide a limited range of services for predominantly rural areas. Some townships, often those in well-developed fringe areas surrounding a metropolitan complex, perform functions similar to municipal police.

The Constable

Several states have established the office of constable, usually an elected official who serves a township, preserving the peace and serving processes for the local justice court. The constable may also be the tax collector, in charge of the pound, or authorized to execute arrest warrants or transport prisoners.

The Marshal

In some parts of the United States, a marshal serves as a court officer, serving writs, subpoenas and other papers issued by the court and escorting prisoners from jail or holding cells in the courthouse to and from trials and hearings. The marshal also serves as the bailiff and protects the municipal judge and people in the court. In some jurisdictions the marshal is elected; in others the marshal is appointed.

Municipal Police

The United States has more than 40,000 police jurisdictions and approximately 450,000 police officers, all with similar responsibilities but with limited geographical jurisdictions. The least uniformity and greatest organizational complexity are found at the municipal level due to local autonomy. The majority of these police forces consist of fewer than 10 officers. This level of law enforcement is the primary focus of this text.

Overlap

American police forces may be classified according to the level of government each serves. However, no uniform pattern of police administration exists at any level of government, and no mechanism exists to coordinate the agencies' activities and goals.

 The five levels of government authorized to have law enforcement agencies are (1) township and special district police, (2) municipal police, (3) county police, (4) state police and (5) federal police.

The preceding discussion makes evident how law enforcement in the United States did not evolve in a consistent, regulated or sequential manner, resulting in considerable duplication and overlap in providing services. Overlapping jurisdictions and potential competition when two (and often many more) forces find themselves investigating the same offense pose serious problems for law enforcement and highlight the need for education and professionalism.

The evolution of policing is much more than a history of agencies that have emerged to meet society's needs. Policing itself has evolved in how it views itself, its responsibilities and the most effective means to meet those responsibilities.

The Three Eras of Policing

Kelling and Moore (1991, pp.3–25) describe three eras of policing: the political era, the reform era and the community era.

The Political Era (1840–1930)

One basic difference between England's first police and those in the United States was that in England, bobbies could be fired. In the United States, this was not the case:

> In New York, for example, the first chief of police could not dismiss officers under his command. The tenure of the chief was limited to one year. Consequently, any early New York cop who was solidly supported by his alderman and assistant alderman could disobey a police superior with virtual impunity. So while the British were firing bobbies left and right for things like showing up late to work, wearing disorderly uniforms and behaving discourteously to citizens, American police were assaulting superior officers, refusing to go on patrol, extorting money from prisoners and releasing prisoners from the custody of other officers. . . .
>
> Perhaps the only good thing about the corrupt, inefficient, ineffective and disobedient early American police is that as an institution it could not be well controlled by anyone—not even the local politicians (Klockars, 1985, p.42).

 In the **political era,** police forces were characterized by a broad social service function, a decentralized organization, an intimate relationship with the community and extensive use of foot patrol.

During the political era, police got their authority from politicians and the law. This close tie to politics often caused problems.

Police Corruption   As in other countries, corruption became a problem in U.S. law enforcement. One primary factor underlying this corruption was the prevalent **spoils system,** whose motto, "To the victor go the spoils," resulted in gross political interference with policing. The winning party felt its members should be immune from arrest, given special privileges in naming favorites for promotion and assisted in carrying out vendettas against their political opponents. This system led politicians to staff many of the nation's police forces with incompetent people as rewards for support, "fixing" arrests or assuring that arrests were not made, and securing immunity from supervision for certain establishments or people.

 The spoils system encouraged politicians to reward their friends by giving them key positions in police departments.

Organizational Modifications   Reform movements began early but moved slowly against the solidly entrenched political "untouchables." Cities sought to break political control through a variety of organizational modifications, including electing police officers and chiefs, administering forces through bipartisan lay boards, asking states to assume local policing and instituting mayor–council or council–city manager municipal government.

Electing the municipal chief of police was common with the establishment of local departments. Remembering the corrupt officials who served as long as they pleased the king, the people elected police officials to serve short terms so they would not have time to become too powerful or corrupt. However, this system had several drawbacks. Not only were the officials not in office long enough to become corrupt, they were not in office long enough to become proficient in their jobs. In fact officials would just get to know their own officers and have enough experience to run the police department when their terms would expire. The position of police chief had also become a popularity contest. Furthermore, since terms were so short, officials often kept their civilian jobs and generally devoted most of their time to them, giving only spare time to running the police force. Therefore most municipalities decided that having a permanent police chief, with experience and ability, was the best way to achieve effective law enforcement. Today the elected police chief system remains in only a few cities.

In the mid-1800s administrative police boards or commissions were established. Comprised of judges, mayors and private citizens, the board served as the head of the police department, with the police chief following its orders. The rationale was that though the chief of police should be a professional and hold the job continuously, civilian control was necessary to maintain responsibility to community needs. This system lasted many years but had serious weaknesses; board members often proved more of a hindrance than a help, and the system fostered political corruption.

In an attempt to control corrupt police agencies and the incompetent local boards behind them, some areas adopted state control of local agencies, believing such a system would assure citizens adequate and uniform law enforcement. However, most cities and states found this was not the answer because laws were not equally enforced and the system lacked responsiveness to local needs. Therefore control was returned to local government in most instances.

The next system to be tried was the commission government charter. Commissioners were elected and charged with various branches of city government. This system, also on the decline, was as inadequate as the administrative police board.

The most prevalent current local system is the mayor–council or council–city manager government. The former is very efficient when the mayor is a full-time, capable administrator. The latter assures more continuity in the business administration and executive control of the overall operations because a professional, nonpolitical administrator manages the community's affairs. In either system the police chief is selected on merit.

The Pendleton Act   In 1883 a major step toward reducing police corruption occurred when Congress passed the Pendleton Act. Prior to this act, most government positions were filled by political appointment, with those appointed commonly incapable of performing their tasks well. One government worker who was going to be replaced by President Garfield shot and killed the president. This incident caused a public outcry and resulted in passage of the Pendleton Act.

The Pendleton Act created the civil service system for government employees and made it illegal to fire or demote a worker for political reasons.

The act established a Civil Service Commission to enforce its provisions. The new laws called for a test open to all citizens and for new workers to be hired on the basis of who had the highest grades. The act also relieved government workers from any obligation to give political service or payments.

The Social Service Function   During the political era, police served a broad social service function:

> Police ran soup lines; district or precinct stations were designed to provide brief lodging for immigrant workers when they arrived in cities; police assisted ward leaders in finding work for immigrants, both in police and other forms of work; and police provided a wide variety of other services (Kelling and Moore, 1991, p.7).

The department organization during the political era was decentralized, primarily because of lack of effective communication. Toward the end of this era, the call box made communication easier and helped to centralize the police organization.

During this era, police were usually close to their community. Foot patrol was the most common strategy used, bringing the beat officer into contact with the people. Most police officers lived in the area they policed and were of the same ethnic background.

Minorities   Little has been published about minority police officers in the early history of the United States. According to Sullivan (1989, p.331), African Americans first served as police officers as early as 1861 in Washington, DC. Most were hired in large cities, and by around 1900 they made up 2.7 percent of all watchmen, police officers and firefighters. That number declined until about 1910 when less than 1 percent of police officers were African American.

During this era many African American police officers rode in cars marked "Colored Police," were often hired exclusively to patrol black areas and were allowed to arrest only other black citizens (Sullivan, p.331). In addition, few were promoted or given special assignments.

 During the political era, African American officers were often segregated and discriminated against.

Women   Initially women were restricted to processing female prisoners and to positions as police matrons. Many misconceptions about a woman's ability to perform certain "masculine" tasks were dispelled as a result of changing social attitudes; yet room for improvement remained.

At the end of the 1800s, a movement to employ women as regular police officers gained support. In 1883 Marie Owen became the first woman police officer in the United States, appointed by the Detroit Bureau of Police. In 1910 the first regular policewoman under civil service was appointed in Los Angeles. Shortly thereafter, in 1912, the first woman chief of police was appointed by the mayor of Milford, Ohio. By the end of World War I, more than 220 cities employed policewomen.

A major reason for this relatively rapid acceptance of female peace officers was a change in the public's view of the police function and the newly accepted emphasis on citizen protection and crime prevention rather than exclusive concentration on enforcing laws and detecting crimes. Women were welcomed into police departments, where they were assigned to handle cases involving children and women:

> There is little doubt that early policewomen were assigned to handle children and their problems because of the female nurturing role. This role coincided with societal values that made mothers responsible for insuring that children grew up to be good citizens. Furthermore, the early policewomen's movement (1910–1930) received support from both national women's groups and prestigious civic and social hygiene associations (Hale, 1992, pp.126–127).

In 1925 August Vollmer opened the Crime Prevention Division in the Berkeley, California, Police Department. This unit was headed by policewoman Elizabeth Lossing, a psychiatric social worker. According to Hale (p.127): "The separate roles of policemen and policewomen were emphasized by the International Association of Chiefs of Police (IACP) at its meeting in 1922 where it was recommended that policewomen meet higher education and training standards than policemen. . . . The IACP stated that policewomen were essential to police work and recommended that police departments establish separate units."

 During the political era, the roles of policewomen were clearly separated from those of policemen, with women serving a protective and nurturing role.

Prohibition   The Prohibition movement (1920–1933) resulted from passage of the Eighteenth Amendment in 1919, which outlawed the manufacture, sale or transportation, including importing and exporting, of intoxicating liquor beverages within the United States and its territories. Manning (1997, p.91) suggests that Prohibition resulted in one of the most important transformations in policing in the United States:

> It placed what had been a relatively corrupt and symbiotic form of police organization in large cities in opposition to large segments of the respectable classes in the communities in which they functioned. The enforcement of Prohibition laws not only created hostility and hatred of the police and made contacts between police and public increasingly adversarial, it increased the opportunities for legally created and defined corruption.

Prohibition ended in 1933 with passage of the Twenty-First Amendment repealing the Eighteenth Amendment. The inability of the police to control consumption of alcoholic beverages might be likened to the contemporary challenge of controlling use of illegal drugs.

The Wickersham Commission and Police Professionalism   In 1929 President Herbert Hoover appointed the national Commission on Law Observance and Enforcement to study the American criminal justice system. Named after its chairman, George Wickersham, the commission devoted 2 of its 14 reports to the police. Report 11, *Lawlessness in Law Enforcement*, delineated the problem of police brutality, concluding that "the third degree—the inflicting of pain, physical or mental, to extract confessions or statements—is extensively practiced." Report 14, *The Police*, concentrated on police administration and called for expert leadership, centralized administrative control and higher personnel standards—in short, police professionalism.

The Reform or Professional Era (1930–1980)

In reaction to the shortcomings of the political era, the reform strategy developed, taking hold in the 1930s and thriving during the 1950s and 1960s, before beginning to erode during the late 1970s (Kelling and Moore, p.6).

 In the **reform era** or the professional era, police forces were characterized by authority coming from the law and professionalism; crime control as their primary function; a centralized, efficient organization; a professional remoteness from the community; and emphasis on preventive motorized patrol and rapid response to crime.

As early as the 1920s, August Vollmer was calling for reforms in policing. Vollmer was first town marshal and then police chief in Berkeley, California, from 1905 until 1932:

> Vollmer is often called the "Father or Dean of Modern Police Administration." Some of his important contributions include the early use of motorized patrol and the latest advancements in criminalistics. He suggested the development of a centralized fingerprint system that was established by the FBI; he established the first juvenile unit, was the first to use psychological screening for police applicants, and was the first to emphasize the importance of college-educated police officers (Roberg and Kuykendall, 1993, p.71).

Vollmer developed the first degree-granting program in law enforcement at San Jose State College. He also advocated that police officers serve as social service workers and that police act to prevent crime by intervening in the lives of potential criminals, especially juveniles. In addition:

> Vollmer's emphasis on the quality of police personnel was tied closely to the idea of the professional officer. . . . Another concern of Vollmer's dealt with the efficient delivery of police services. His department became the first in the nation to use automobiles and the first to hire a full-time forensic scientist to help solve crimes (Dunham and Alpert, 1989, p.27).

Manning (p.92) describes three changes made in the 1930s that were fundamental to altering the police role:
1. Crime statistics were linked to police professionalism through the establishment of the Uniform Crime Reports.
2. Police began to tie their fate to changes in crime rates as measured by these published figures.
3. Police began to symbolize their mission in terms of the technological means by which they were said to accomplish it.

Manning (p.92) suggests: "By the mid-1930s the use of the radio, of the automobile for mobile patrol, and the collection and systematization of crime statistics began to characterize large urban departments. . . . The police eagerly espoused, displayed, and continued to seek a technologically based, rationalized crime control mandate."

One of Vollmer's protégés, O. W. Wilson, became the primary architect of the reform era and the style of policing known as the **professional model.** Wilson accepted a professorship at the University of California, Berkeley, and in 1947 he founded the first professional school of criminology.

Like his mentor, Wilson advocated efficiency within the police bureaucracy through scientific techniques. He became police chief in Wichita, Kansas, and conducted the first systematic study of the effectiveness of using one-officer squad cars. Wilson's classic text, *Police Administration*, set forth specific ways to use one-officer patrol cars, to deploy personnel and to discipline officers.

Wilson (1950, pp.17–18) decried political influence on the police: "When the police department is controlled by the machine, political influence begins with the appointment of the recruit, rallies to save him from discipline, helps him to secure unearned wages or disability benefits, grants him unusual leaves of absence, secures an unwarranted promotion for him, or gives him a soft job. In countless ways the creeping paralysis of political favoritism spreads and fastens itself upon the force to sap its vitality and destroy its morale for the benefit of the party, at the expense of both the public and of the police force itself."

Wilson (p.388) also called for cooperation with the public: "Public cooperation is essential to the successful accomplishment of the police purpose. Public support assists in many ways; it is necessary in the enforcement of major laws as well as of minor regulations, and with it arrests are made and convictions obtained that otherwise would not be possible." The reformers sought to disassociate policing from politics. They were to become professionals whose charge was to enforce the law, fairly and impartially. The social service function became of lesser importance or even nonexistent in some departments as police mounted an all-out war on crime. Two keys to this war were preventive patrol in automobiles and rapid response to calls. This is the style of policing with which most Americans are familiar and have come to expect.

Unfortunately, the war on crime was being lost. Crime escalated, and other problems arose as well. In the 1960s violent ghetto riots caused millions of dollars in damages, thousands of injuries and many deaths:

> Most of these riots were triggered by incidents in which white officers were policing in black ghetto areas. The National Advisory Commission on Civil Disorder was formed to study the situation. The resulting Kerner Report (1968) was comprehensive and scathing, and placed a large part of the blame for the riots on racism in society and the severe under-representation of blacks in police departments (Sullivan, p.333).

As a result of this report and other studies, many cities began to actively recruit minorities for their police departments. The civil rights and anti–Vietnam War demonstrations and riots had other ramifications:

> They expanded civil protest beyond the inner city to middle-class colleges, main-street America, and television. They brought large numbers of middle-class and minority protestors into open conflict with the police. When the police employed tactics that included the use of force and mass arrests against protestors, they were portrayed as agents of repression who maintained order at the expense of justice. As a result, the rational-legal bureaucratic model of policing began to be questioned by a broader spectrum of the American people (Fyfe et al., 1997, p.17).

Blue-Ribbon Commissions   Kelling (2003, p.14) describes five national commissions that resulted from the turmoil in U.S. cities and controversy surrounding police practices in the 1960s and early 1970s:

- The President's Commission on Law Enforcement and Administration of Justice, which published its reports in 1967 and 1968, was influenced by urban racial turmoil. Among the outgrowths of its work were the Safe Streets Act of 1968 and the Law Enforcement Assistance Administration, which provided significant funding for police-related programs.
- The National Advisory Commission on Civil Disorders (popularly known as the Kerner Commission) was similarly inspired by riots and other disorders in many U.S. cities in the summer of 1967. Its report examined patterns of disorder and prescribed responses by the federal government, the criminal justice system and local governments.

- The National Commission on the Causes and Prevention of Violence was established after the assassinations of Martin Luther King, Jr. and Robert Kennedy in 1968. Its report, *To Establish Justice, To Insure Domestic Tranquility*, was published in 1969.
- The President's Commission on Campus Unrest was established following student deaths related to protests at Kent State and Jackson State Universities in 1970.
- The National Advisory Commission on Criminal Justice Standards and Goals issued six reports in 1973 in an attempt to develop standards and recommendations for police crime-control efforts.

The Law Enforcement Education Program (LEEP)   Following publication of the Presidential Crime Commission's recommendation that by 1984 all police officers be required to have at least a bachelor's degree, Congress created and funded the Law Enforcement Education Program (LEEP). This program poured thousands of dollars into police education, and by the mid-1970s, more than 1,000 academic institutions had police-related courses being offered to thousands of students nationwide. Eventually, however, LEEP was phased out of the federal budget.

Another relatively short-lived federal boost to the professionalization of law enforcement was the Law Enforcement Assistance Administration.

The Law Enforcement Assistance Administration (LEAA)   In 1968 Congress enacted the Omnibus Crime Control and Safe Streets Act; Title 1 of this act established the Law Enforcement Assistance Administration, which existed through September 1979.

LEAA worked in partnership with state and local governments, historically responsible for crime reduction and law enforcement. Congress affirmed this historical responsibility in the Act: "Crime is essentially a local problem that must be dealt with by state and local governments if it is to be controlled effectively." Of even greater significance is the statement of Richard W. Velde, LEAA administrator, foreshadowing the community policing movement: "Crime control is everyone's business. It is not just the business of the criminal justice system—of police, courts and corrections—but of all citizens who want to live in harmony and peace." LEAA awarded more than $9 billion to state and local governments to support tens of thousands of programs and projects.

The National Institute of Justice (NIJ)   The Omnibus Crime Control and Safe Streets Act also established the National Institute of Justice as a research and development agency to prevent and reduce crime and to improve the criminal justice system. Among the institute's mandates were that it sponsor special projects and research and development programs to improve and strengthen the criminal justice system, conduct national demonstration projects that employed innovative or promising approaches for improving criminal justice, develop new technologies to fight crime and improve criminal justice, evaluate the effectiveness of criminal justice programs and identify those that promised to be successful if continued or repeated and carry out research on criminal behavior.

Advances for Women and Minorities   A boost was given to women and minorities when the Supreme Court ruled in *Griggs v. Duke Power Company* (1971) that any tests used for employment must be job-related. Another boost was the passage of the Equal Employment Opportunity Act (EEOA) in 1972.

The Equal Employment Opportunity Act prohibits discrimination on the basis of sex, race, color, religion or national origin in employment of any kind, public or private, local, state or federal.

That same year, women began to seek positions as patrol officers. Tension and conflict resulted. Accepted as assistants to policemen, they were seldom accepted as partners on patrol:

> Clearly, policewomen on patrol have faced many obstacles from both their peers and management, who believed that they cannot perform patrol duties because they have neither the physical strength to do the job; the authoritarian presence to handle violent confrontations; nor the ability to serve as backup to their partners in high-pressure situations. Attempts by supervisors to either overprotect policewomen, or keep them from areas with high violence further reinforce the view that women are not capable of performing patrol (Hale, p.128).

During the reform or professional era, minorities and women obtained legal equality with white male officers but still often encountered discrimination.

The Kansas City Preventive Patrol Experiment   Another event during 1972 had a great impact on eroding the reform strategy; the classic Kansas City Preventive Patrol Experiment called into serious question the effectiveness of preventive patrol or rapidity of response, the basic strategies of the reform era. The Kansas City Experiment showed that "it makes about as much sense to have police patrol routinely in cars to fight crime as it does to have firemen patrol routinely in fire trucks to fight fire" (Klockars, 1983, p.130).

Increasing Challenges to the Professional Model   The professional model faced many challenges including the inability of "traditional" police approaches to decrease crime; the rapidly escalating drug problem; the pressing problems associated with the deinstitutionalization of thousands of mentally ill people, many of whom became homeless; dealing with thousands of immigrants, some legal, some illegal, many speaking no English; and the breakdown of the family unit.

Many began asserting that the police and the criminal justice system could not control crime and violence alone:

> All of the major factors influencing how much crime there is or is not are factors over which police have no control whatsoever. Police can do nothing about the age, sex, racial or ethnic distribution of the population. They cannot control economic conditions; poverty; inequality; occupational opportunity; moral, religious, family or secular education; or dramatic social, cultural or political change. These are the "big ticket" items in determining the amount and distribution of crime. Compared to them what police do or do not do matters very little (Klockars, 1991, p.250).

Kerlikowske (2004, p.7) points out:

> The [professional] model was neat and orderly, especially internally, and completely unprepared to deal with the social change, upheaval and the overwhelming demographic challenge of the 1960s. The thin blue line that had won wars abroad could not win peace or even calm in the neighborhoods

wracked by exploding crime rates and deep social unrest. Forgotten in the professional model was the familiarity that existed between officers and the community in the earlier era, when residents saw officers as neighborhood problem solvers and when their efforts attracted some level of community support. Instead, professional officers were viewed as an occupying army.

This unfortunate situation made the time ripe for the current era, the community era.

The Community Era (1980–Present)

Paralleling changes being made in the business world, many police departments became "customer-oriented," viewing people within the community as consumers of police services. Just as in business it is important to know what the customer really wants and needs, so in policing it became important to know what the citizens of a community want and need.

 Police forces in the **community era** are characterized by authority coming from community support, law and professionalism; provision of a broad range of services, including crime control; decentralized organization with more authority given to patrol officers; partnerships with the community; and use of foot patrol and a problem-solving approach.

In contrast to policing during the reform era, which was **reactive,** responding to crime after it was committed, policing during the community era is more **proactive,** seeking the causes of crime and trying to rectify those problems, thereby deterring or even preventing crime. The community-oriented approach to policing is the focus of Chapter 5. Largely because of civil service and a grassroots-inspired groundswell of general reform, most police forces have shaken the influence of corrupt politics. In contrast to conditions at the turn of the century, appointment to the forces and police administration generally are vastly improved. Police recruitment, discipline and promotion have been removed from politics in most cities.

Communications involving police service have also greatly improved. The radio and patrol car transformed the relationship between the police and the public and offered increased protection for everyone. The continuous expansion of the telephone in the 1960s and 1970s made it easier for people to call the police. Police dispatchers were added to tie radio systems directly into telephone networks and computers greatly increased the efficiency and effectiveness of operations. The use of fingerprint systems and the increased employment of women as police officers as well as many other advances occurred at an accelerated pace.

Despite advanced technology, which greatly improved police officers' abilities to respond to requests for aid and increased their mobility, the basic strategy of police has not altered. Crime waves in metropolitan areas prompt cities to improve their street lighting, to increase the number of police officers on the streets and to demand more severe punishment for the convicted criminals.

The human factor has assumed greater importance as police agencies cope with the tensions and dislocations of population growth, increasing urbanization, developing technology, the civil rights movement, changing social norms and a breakdown of traditional values. These factors have enormously compli-

Table 1.1 The Three Eras of Policing

	Political Era 1840 to 1930	Reform or Professional Era 1930 to 1980	Community Era 1980 to present
Authorization	Politicians and law	Law and professionalism	Community support (political), law and professionalism
Function	Broad social services	Crime control	Broad provision of services
Organizational Design	Decentralized	Centralized, classical	Decentralized, task forces, matrices
Relationship to Community	Intimate	Professional, remote	Intimate
Tactics and Technology	Foot patrol	Preventive patrol and rapid response to calls	Foot patrol, problem solving, public relations
Outcome	Citizen, political satisfaction	Crime control	Quality of life and citizen satisfaction

SOURCE: Linda S. Miller and Kären M. Hess. *Community Policing: Partnerships for Problem Solving,* 4th ed. Belmont, CA: Wadsworth Publishing, 2005, p.17. Reprinted by permission. (Summarized from George L. Kelling and Mark H. Moore, "From Political to Reform to Community: The Evolving Strategy of Police." In *Community Policing: Rhetoric or Reality,* edited by Jack R. Greene and Stephen D. Mastrofski. New York: Praeger Publishers, 1991, pp.6, 14–15, 22–23.)

cated law enforcement, making more critical the need for truly professional police officers.

Today's local police officers must be law enforcement generalists with a working knowledge of federal, state, county and municipal law, traffic law, criminal law, juvenile law, narcotics, liquor control and countless other areas. However, this accounts for only approximately 10 percent of what a modern police officer does. Today's officers spend 90 percent of their time providing a variety of services while protecting life, property and personal liberty. They must be aware of human factors and understand the psychological and sociological implications of their work. They must deal with all citizens, rich and poor, young and old, in ways that maintain the community's support and confidence. Policing and partnering with this greatly diverse citizenship is no small challenge or responsibility.

The distinguishing characteristics of the three eras of policing are summarized in Table 1.1.

The Evolution of Our Juvenile Justice System

Our juvenile justice system has its roots in England's feudal period when the crown assumed the protection of the property of minors. When the feudal period ended, duties previously assumed by the overlord were transferred to the king's chancery court, which followed the doctrine of **parens patriae.** Under this doctrine the king, through the chancellor, was responsible for the general protection of all people in the realm who could not protect themselves, including children.

Another English common law principle that influenced our juvenile justice system was that children younger than age 7 were incapable of criminal intent. Children between the ages of 7 and 14 were presumed to still be incapable of criminal intent unless it could be shown differently. After age 14, children, like adults, were held responsible for their acts and treated according to a strict interpretation of the law. In effect age had a direct bearing on how someone who broke the law was treated.

These English common law principles were brought to the United States by the colonists and formed the foundation of the juvenile justice system they established. The system evolved through four major phases.

 The four major phases in the development of the juvenile justice system were:
1. A Puritan emphasis
2. An emphasis on providing a refuge for youths
3. Development of a separate juvenile court
4. Emphasis on juvenile rights

The Puritan Emphasis

The concept of *parens patriae* and the notion that there was an age below which there can be no criminal intent were brought by the colonists to America. From the time the colonists first arrived until the nineteenth century, however, the emphasis was on Puritan values, which held that children were basically evil. Parents were responsible for controlling their children who were, in effect, their property. Children who broke the law were dealt with severely. Parents literally tried to "beat the devil" out of misbehaving children. This Puritan emphasis lasted until the 1820s.

Providing a Refuge

By the 1820s several states had passed laws to protect children from the punishments associated with criminal laws. Many states recognized the brutality of confining children in the same institutions with adult criminals. The first American institution to isolate children convicted of crimes from adult criminals was New York City's House of Refuge, established in 1825. This was the first juvenile reformatory in the United States.

In 1884 New York passed legislation allowing a trial judge to place children under age 16 who were convicted of a crime under the supervision of any suitable persons or institutions willing to accept them. During this period the state took over the parents' responsibility for their children, but not to the degree that occurred in the next phase of the system's development.

The Juvenile Court

In 1899 Illinois passed the Juvenile Court Act, creating the first juvenile court in Cook County and beginning an era of social jurisprudence. The court's primary purpose was to help wayward children become productive community members. The Juvenile Court Act not only created the first juvenile court, it also regulated the treatment and control of dependent, neglected and delinquent children.

 The Juvenile Court Act equated poor and abused children with delinquent and criminal children and provided that they be treated in essentially the same way, establishing a **one-pot approach.**

Most juvenile courts today have this same dual charge.

During this period, the philosophy of *parens patriae* was in full effect. The Chicago legislation grew out of the efforts of civic-minded citizens who saw the inhumane treatment of children confined in police stations and jails. The legislation, whose full title was "An Act to Regulate the Treatment and Control of Dependent, Neglected and Delinquent Children," included many characteristics of our current juvenile courts, including a separate court for juveniles, separate and confidential records, informal proceedings and the possibility of probation.

The Chicago legislation also required that children be given the same care, custody and discipline that parents should give them. The major goal was to save the child. This was also the first basic principle of the juvenile court—that of *parens patriae.* The state not only acts as a substitute parent to abandoned, neglected and dependent children, but also as a "superparent" for delinquent children.

In this role of superparent, the state could commit a youth found to be delinquent to a training school or some other correctional facility. The purpose was not to punish but to help reform the youth. Because this purpose was so dissimilar to the adult criminal court, a new vocabulary emerged for the juvenile justice system. Youths were not *arrested,* they were *taken into custody.* Their innocence or guilt was decided not at a *trial* but at a *hearing.*

It should be noted that many historians view the child-saving movement as a means to control the lower classes, not as a means to "save the children." As Hess and Drowns (2004, p.12) state: "The child savers were not entirely humanitarian, however; they viewed poor children as a threat to society. These children needed to be reformed to conform, to value hard work and to become contributing members of society."

Although establishment of juvenile courts was a tremendous advancement in the juvenile justice system, it presented some major problems. Because children were no longer considered "criminals," they lost many constitutional protections

Judge Benjamin Lindsey presided in juvenile court in Denver, Colorado, from 1900 to 1927. His court stressed a caring approach "in the best interests of the child."

Colorado Historical Society

1600

April 1631—Boston establishes the first system of law enforcement in America called the "night watch." Officers serve part-time without pay.

1700

1712—The first full-time law enforcement officers are hired in the United States by the City of Boston.

1767—The first organized vigilante movement occurs.

September 24, 1789—Congress creates the first federal law enforcement officer, the U.S. Marshal.

1800

1825—New York City's House of Refuge is established.

1829—The first police force in England is established, known as the Metropolitan Police of London.

1835—Texas creates what is later to become the Texas Rangers, the oldest statewide law enforcement agency in America.

1844—New York City establishes the first 24-hour police service.

1858—Boston and Chicago police departments are the first to issue uniforms to their officers.

1862—The Internal Revenue Service (IRS) is established as a part of the Treasury Department.

1863—Boston becomes the first police department to issue pistols to its officers.

April 14, 1865—Abraham Lincoln, on the day he was assassinated, approves formation of what is now known as the U.S. Secret Service.

1866—Detroit establishes the first detective bureau.

1883—Congress passes the Pendleton Act to reduce police corruption.

1899—The Juvenile Court Act establishes a separate system of justice for juveniles.

1902—Fingerprinting is first used in the United States to identify criminal suspects.

1900

1910—Alice Stebbins Wells of the Los Angeles Police Department becomes the first female officer with arrest powers.

1914—The Berkeley (California) Police Department becomes the first agency in the country to have all patrol officers using automobiles.

1912—The first female Chief of Police is appointed in Milford, Ohio.

1919—The Eighteenth Amendment is passed, commencing Prohibition.

May 10, 1924—J. Edgar Hoover begins nearly 50 years of service as director of what would later become the FBI.

May 11, 1924—Mary T. Davis becomes the first female officer to be killed in the line of duty.

1929—The Wickersham Commission addresses police brutality and the need for police professionalism.

1933—Prohibition ends with the passage of the Twenty-First Amendment.

1968—The Omnibus Crime Control and Safe Streets Act establishes the Law Enforcement Assistance Administration (LEAA–funded through September 1979) and the National Institute of Justice.

1968—The Kerner Report on racism and the underrepresentation of African American officers in police departments is issued.

1972—The Equal Employment Opportunity Act.

1972—Kansas City Preventive Patrol Experiment

1982—Wilson and Kelling's "Broken Windows" published.

1993—World Trade Center Bombing, February 26.

1990—Goldstein's *Problem-Oriented Policing* published.

1995—Alfred P. Murrah Federal Building, Oklahoma City bombing, April 19.

2000

2001—September 11, attack on United States.

2002—Establishment of Department of Homeland Security.

Figure 1.5   Important Dates in Police History

of due process in criminal proceedings. For example, often delinquents were not given notice of the charge, were not provided with a lawyer and were not given the chance to cross-examine witnesses.

Justification for the informal procedures used in the juvenile justice system before 1960 was set forth a century ago in *Commonwealth v. Fisher* (1905): "To save a child from becoming a criminal or from continuing in a career in crimes . . . the Legislature may surely provide for the salvation of such a child . . . by bringing it into one of the courts of the state without any process at all, for the purpose of subjecting it to the state's guardianship and protection."

By the 1960s, however, the U.S. Supreme Court began to seriously question the use of *parens patriae* as the sole reason for denying children many constitutional rights extended to adults charged with a crime, leading into the fourth phase of the juvenile justice system's development. These rights are described in the next chapter.

A Brief Recap of U.S. Policing

A fitting conclusion for this chapter is a brief recap of the sequence of events from the beginning of law enforcement in the United States to 2002, presented in Figure 1.5.

 SUMMARY

Our current laws and the means by which they are enforced have their origins in the distant past, perhaps as far back as the cave dwellers. A system of law and law enforcement began earlier than 2000 B.C. as a means of controlling human conduct and enforcing society's rules. Keeping the peace was the responsibility of the group. Many features of our present system of law enforcement are borrowed from the Greeks, Romans and particularly the English.

The English tithing system (groups of 10 families) established the principle of collective responsibility for maintaining local law and order. If a law was broken, the Hue and Cry sounded, the origin of the general alarm and the citizen's arrest.

The constable was the first English police officer, and he had charge of the weapons and horses of the community. In response to a need for more regional law enforcement, the office of shire-reeve was established. The shire-reeve was the law enforcement agent for an entire county.

In 1066 William the Conqueror invaded England and changed the tithing system to the Frankpledge system, requiring loyalty to the king's law and mutual local responsibility for maintaining the peace. Under his rule the shire-reeves were limited to law enforcement, and separate judges were appointed to try cases, in effect separating the law enforcement and judicial roles. William's son, Henry I, became known as Henry the Lawmaker. His Leges Henrici made law enforcement a public matter and separated offenses into felonies and misdemeanors. Henry II established the jury system.

The next significant development was the Magna Carta, a precedent for democratic government and individual rights. The Magna Carta laid the foundation for:

- Requiring rulers to uphold the law.
- Forbidding taxation without representation.
- Requiring due process of law, including trial by jury.
- Providing safeguards against unfair imprisonment.

During the fourteenth century, the shire-reeve was replaced by the justice of the peace. Later, during the Middle Ages, the parish constable system was used for rural law enforcement; the Watch and Ward system was used for urban law enforcement.

Of importance to English law enforcement were the contributions of Sir Robert (Bobbie) Peel. Peel's principles for reform called for local responsibility for law and order, appointed, paid civilians to assume this responsibility and standards for these individuals' conduct and organization. His proposals resulted in the organization of the first police force in England, the Metropolitan Police of London, established in 1829. In 1883 the London Metropolitan Police appointed two women to supervise female convicts. Their numbers and functions later expanded.

The early American settlers brought with them several features of English law and law enforcement, including those found in Leges Henrici, which made law enforcement a public matter, and in the Magna Carta, which provided for due process of law. Law enforcement in colonial America was frequently patterned after England's Watch and Ward system and later after the London Metropolitan Police and the principles for reform set forth by Sir Robert Peel. The first modern American police force, modeled after London's Metropolitan Police, was the New York City Police Department, established in 1844. The vigilante movement refers to taking the law into one's own hands in the absence of effective policing.

Although law enforcement was generally considered a local responsibility, Congress created several federal law enforcement agencies, under the jurisdiction of the Departments of Justice and the Treasury, to meet demands created by the nation's changing conditions. Among the earliest federal law enforcement agencies were the U.S. Marshals Office, the Immigration and Naturalization Service, the Secret Service and the Internal Revenue Service. The U.S. Attorney General, as head of the Department of Justice, is the chief federal law enforcement officer. The beginning of state law enforcement agencies occurred with the establishment of the Texas Rangers. Law enforcement in the United States is a cooperative effort among local, county, state, federal and specialized law enforcement officers.

The three eras of policing are the political era, the reform or professional era and the community era. In the political era, police forces were characterized by authority derived from politicians and the law, a broad social service function, a decentralized organization, an intimate relationship with the community and extensive use of foot patrol.

The spoils system encouraged politicians to reward their friends by giving them key positions in police departments. Cities sought to break political control by a variety of organizational modifications, including electing police officers and chiefs, administering forces through bipartisan lay boards, asking states to assume local policing and instituting mayor–council or council–city manager municipal government. In addition, in 1883 the Pendleton Act created the civil service system for government employees and made it unlawful to fire or demote a worker for political reasons. During the political era, African American officers were often segregated and discriminated against. The roles of policewomen during this era were clearly separated from those of policemen, with women serving a protective, nurturing role.

Police forces in the reform or professional era were characterized by authority derived from law and professionalism; crime control as their primary function; a centralized, efficient organization; a professional remoteness from the community; emphasis on preventive motorized patrol and rapid response to crime. During this era, in 1972, the Equal Employment Opportunity Act was passed. This act prohibits discrimination on the basis of sex, race, color, religion or national origin in employment of any kind, public or private, local, state or federal. This gave minorities and women legal equality with white male officers and prompted many women to seek patrol assignments. Despite the passage of the Equal Employment Opportunity Act, many minorities and women still often encountered discrimination.

Community era police forces are characterized by authority derived from community support, law and professionalism; the provision of a broad range of services; a decentralized organization with more authority given to patrol officers; an intimate relationship with the community; and the increased use of foot patrol and a problem-solving approach.

The juvenile justice system has developed through four phases in the United States: (1) a Puritan emphasis with severe penalties for juvenile crime (1776–1824), (2) an emphasis on providing a refuge for youths (1824–1899), (3) development of a separate juvenile court (1899–1960) and (4) emphasis on juvenile rights (1960 to present). The Juvenile Court Act equated poor and abused children with delinquent and criminal children and provided that they be treated in essentially the same way, establishing a one-pot approach.

DISCUSSION QUESTIONS

1. What common problems have existed throughout the centuries for people in law enforcement?
2. Why was there no law enforcement during the daytime for many centuries?
3. Why did it take so long to develop a police force in England? In the United States?
4. In today's society, how has the power of the *posse comitatus* assisted and how has it worked against law enforcement?
5. At present, how does the government respond to increased crime in the United States in comparison with the responses in the seventeenth century?
6. Should police chiefs be appointed or elected?
7. What demands are made on the modern police officer that were not present 20 or 30 years ago?
8. How well are women and minorities represented on your police force?
9. Where is your regional FBI office? What facilities and services does it offer?
10. Do you feel the process of justice should be the same for juveniles as it is for adults?

INFOTRAC COLLEGE EDITION ASSIGNMENTS

■ Use InfoTrac College Edition to help answer the Discussion Questions as appropriate.
■ Using InfoTrac College Edition, find the article "The Rise of Juvenile Delinquency in England 1780–1840: Changing Patterns of Perception and Prosecution." This article focuses on a neglected but historically

important transition, the rise to prominence of the problem of juvenile delinquency between the 1780s and the 1830s. Find 10 significant problems during this era that were studied by reformers and briefly state their effects on juveniles. Be prepared to share your analysis with the class.

■ Using InfoTrac College Edition find and outline the article "The End of Community Policing: Remembering the Lessons Learned" by R. Gil Kerlikowske.

INTERNET ASSIGNMENTS

Go to the Web site of the Pendleton Act and focus on *Background on the Pendleton Act*. Note the new special skills required with the introduction of typewriters. As you read the document, write down what strikes you as being the most important areas covered by the act. Be prepared to share your findings with the class.

BOOK-SPECIFIC WEB SITE

The book-specific Web site at http://info .wadsworth.com/0534552803 hosts a variety of resources for students and instructors. Included are extended activities from each chapter in which students write a policy, use critical thinking skills to make choices in response to a given scenario, use InfoTrac College Edition with direct links to articles for participation in topical discussion forums and analyze court cases using Web links for research.

Many activities can be printed or e-mailed to instructors. Plus, cited cases with Web links, interactive key term FlashCards, PowerPoint presentations, chapter objectives, and an extensive collection of chapter-based Web links provide additional information and activities to include in the curriculum.

REFERENCES

Adams, T. F. *Introduction to the Administration of Criminal Justice,* 2nd ed. Englewood Cliffs, NJ: Prentice-Hall, 1980.

Asirvatham, Sandy. "Good Cop, Bad Cop." *Baltimore City Paper,* May 2000, p.2.

Bailey, W. G. (ed.). *The Encyclopedia of Police Science.* New York: Garland Publishing, 1989.

Brown, R. "The American Vigilante Tradition." In *Thinking about Police: Contemporary Readings,* 2nd ed., edited by C. B. Klockars and S. D. Mastrofski. New York: McGraw-Hill, 1991.

Chapman, S. G. and Johnston, Colonel T. E., Sr. *The Police Heritage in England and America.* East Lansing: Michigan State University, 1962.

Critchley, T. A. *A History of Police in England and Wales.* Montclair, NJ: Patterson Smith, 1967.

Dunham, R. G. and Alpert, G. P. *Critical Issues in Policing: Contemporary Issues.* Prospect Heights, IL: Waveland Press, Inc., 1989.

Folley, V. L. *American Law Enforcement.* Boston: Allyn and Bacon, 1980.

Fyfe, James J.; Green, Jack R.; Walsh, William F.; Wilson, O. W.; and McLaren, Roy Clinton. *Police Administration,* 5th ed. New York: McGraw-Hill, 1997.

Gardner, T. J. *Basic Concepts of Criminal Law, Principles and Cases,* 3rd ed. St. Paul, MN: West Publishing Company, 1985.

Hale, Donna C. "Women in Policing." In *What Works in Policing,* edited by G. W. Gardner and D. C. Hale. Cincinnati, OH: Anderson Publishing Company, 1992.

Hess, Kären M. and Drowns, Robert W. *Juvenile Justice,* 4th ed. Belmont, CA: Wadsworth Publishing Company, 2004.

Kelling, George L. "The Evolution of Contemporary Policing." In *Local Government Police Management,* 4th ed., edited by William A. Geller and Darrell W. Stephens. Washington, DC: International City/County Management Association, 2003, pp.3–25.

Kelling, George L. and Moore, Mark H. "From Political to Reform to Community: The Evolving Strategy of Police." In *Community Policing: Rhetoric or Reality,* edited by J. R. Greene and S. D. Mastrofski. New York: Praeger Publishers, 1991.

Kerlikowske, R. Gil. "The End of Community Policing: Remembering the Lessons Learned." *FBI Law Enforcement Bulletin,* April 2004, pp.6–10.

Klockars, Carl B. *Thinking about Police: Contemporary Readings.* New York: McGraw-Hill, 1983.

Klockars, Carl B. *The Idea of Police.* Newbury Park, CA: Sage Publications, 1985.

Klockars, Carl B. "The Rhetoric of Community Policing." In *Community Policing: Rhetoric or Reality,* edited by J. R. Greene and S. D. Mastrofski. New York: Praeger Publishers, 1991.

Lunt, W. E. *History of England.* New York: Harper & Brothers, 1938.

Manning, Peter K. *Police Work: The Social Organization of Policing,* 2nd ed. Prospect Heights, IL: Waveland Press, Inc., 1997.

Perry, D. C. *Police in the Metropolis.* Columbus, OH: Charles E. Merrill, 1973.

Reichel, Philip L. "Southern Slave Patrols as a Transitional Police Type." In *Policing Perspectives: An Anthology,* edited by Larry K. Gaines and Gary W. Cordner. Los Angeles: Roxbury Publishing Company, 1999, pp.79–92.

Richardson, J. F. *The New York Police.* New York: Oxford University Press, 1970.

Roberg, R. R. and Kuykendall, J. *Police & Society.* Belmont, CA: Wadsworth Publishing Company, 1993.

Sullivan, P. S. "Minority Officers, Current Issues." In *Critical Issues in Policing: Contemporary Readings,* edited by R. D. Dunham and G. P. Alpert. Prospect Heights, IL: Waveland Press, 1989.

Walker, Samuel. *The Police in America: An Introduction.* New York: McGraw-Hill, 1983.

Wilson, O. W. *Police Administration.* New York: McGraw-Hill, 1950.

CASES CITED

Commonwealth v. Fisher, 213 Pa. 48 (1905)
Griggs v. Duke Power Company (1971)

CHAPTER 2

The American Quest for Freedom and Justice: Our Laws

We hold these truths to be self-evident: that all men are endowed by their creator with certain unalienable rights; that among these are life, liberty, and the pursuit of happiness.

—Thomas Jefferson

 DO YOU KNOW . . .

- What civil rights and civil liberties are?
- What the Declaration of Independence says about civil rights and civil liberties?
- What document is the basic instrument of government and the supreme law of the land?
- What law takes precedence if two laws conflict?
- What the Bill of Rights is?
- What specific rights are guaranteed by the First, Second, Fourth, Fifth, Sixth, Eighth and Fourteenth Amendments?
- What is established by the Exclusionary Rule?
- What criminal law does?
- What the difference between a felony and a misdemeanor is?
- What is usually necessary to prove that a crime has been committed?
- What civil law refers to?
- What the basic differences between a crime and a tort are?
- What Section 1983 of the U.S. Code, Title 42, stipulates?
- Where police get their power and authority from and what restrictions are placed on this power and authority?
- What the scales of justice symbolize?
- What two conflicting models of criminal justice need to be balanced?

CAN YOU DEFINE?

actus reus	case law	conflict theory	crime control
American creed	civil law	consensus theory	criminal intent
asset forfeiture	civil liberties	constitution	criminal law
authority	civil rights	constitutional law	custodial
bail	code of silence	*corpus delicti*	interrogation
Bill of Rights	common law	crime	double jeopardy

CAN YOU DEFINE? (CONTINUED)

due process of law	indigent	police power	statutory law
ecclesiastical law	infamous crime	power	strict liability
elements of the crime	intent	precedent	subpoena
equal protection	litigaphobia	procedural criminal law	substantive criminal law
equity	*mala in se*	procedural due process	substantive due process
Exclusionary Rule	*mala prohibita*		
federalism	*mens rea*	pure speech	symbolic speech
felony	misdemeanor	*scienter*	tort
fighting words	moral law	selective incorporation	warrant
grand jury	motive		zones of privacy
hearsay evidence	negligence	self-incrimination	
incorporation doctrine	ordinances	social law	
indicted	ordinary law	speech plus	
	petition		

Introduction

To assure each U.S. citizen the right to "life, liberty, and the pursuit of happiness," those who settled here established laws that all are expected to obey. The supreme law of the land is embodied in the U.S. Constitution and its Bill of Rights. Beyond that, however, each city, state and the federal government has continued to pass laws governing citizen behavior. Our system of laws is extremely complex and may be classified as follows:

- *Form*—written or unwritten common law
- *Source*—constitutional, statutory, case
- *Parties involved*—public, private
- *Offense*—criminal, civil

Each of these overlapping classifications are explored in this chapter.

The criminal/civil distinction is of interest to law enforcement officers because they must deal with those who break criminal laws and at the same time not violate the "criminal's" civil rights. Officers who do not deal legally with criminal matters may find themselves the target of a civil lawsuit. In addition law enforcement officers must be able to tell the difference between a criminal and a civil offense because they are responsible for investigating only criminal matters. Civil offenses are not within their jurisdiction.

This chapter begins with a discussion of the Declaration of Independence and the law that operated in the newly created nation. This is followed by a description of the constitutional law found in the U.S. Constitution and the Bill of Rights—the first 10 amendments, which guarantee all American citizens' civil rights and civil liberties—as well as the Fourteenth Amendment, which made the Constitution and portions of the Bill of Rights applicable to the states. Following the discussion of constitutional law is an explanation of criminal and civil law. The chapter concludes with a description of police power in the United States—

where it comes from and how it is restricted—and the needs of society balanced with individual rights and how this conflict has influenced development of the criminal justice system.

The Declaration of Independence

The Europeans' original immigration to the New World was heavily motivated by a desire to escape the religious, economic, political and social repressions of traditional European society. North America was seen as a land where people could get a new start, free to make of themselves what they chose.

Sometimes, however, reality did not fully coincide with the **American creed** of individual freedom, as seen in the treatment of Native Americans, the importation of slaves, the establishment of state churches and the repressiveness involved in such episodes as the Salem witchcraft trials. Nevertheless the spirit of liberty and justice remained strong. As noted by Myrdal (1944): "The American creed is the national conscience; a body of beliefs about equality, liberty and justice which most Americans believe in, in spite of the fact that America has, and always has had, multiple wrongs."

In the 1760s the British began taking away rights Americans felt were naturally theirs, and the American Revolution resulted. In effect, the United States was born out of a desire—indeed, a demand—for civil rights and civil liberties.

 Civil rights are those claims that the citizen has to the affirmative assistance of government. **Civil liberties** are an individual's immunity from governmental oppression.

Civil rights and civil liberties are recurring themes in America's development and reflect values that were forcefully stated in our most basic document: the Declaration of Independence. The Declaration of Independence is not only a statement of grievances against England but also a statement of alternative basic premises underlying human freedom. As Thomas Jefferson phrased it in the Declaration, the United States was demanding "the separate and equal station to which the laws of nature and of nature's God entitle them."

 The Declaration of Independence asserts that all individuals are created equal and are entitled to the unalienable rights of life, liberty and the pursuit of happiness. It further asserts that governments are instituted by and derive their power from the governed, that is, the people.

The Declaration of Independence was an idealistic statement of philosophy. It broke our ties with England but did not establish how the United States should be structured or governed. Each colony developed its own means of policing and protecting itself. The colonists relied heavily on laws they had brought with them from their homelands, England in particular.

Types of Law

In addition to the classification of law introduced earlier, several types of law must be understood to appreciate their complexities and effect on criminal justice. Recall that law is a body of rules for human conduct enforced by imposing penalties for their violation. Laws define social obligations and determine the relations of individuals to society and to each other. The purpose of law is to regulate individuals' actions to conform to the way of life the community or the people's elected representatives consider essential.

Social or Moral Law

Often, obedience to law is obtained through social pressure—ridicule, contempt, scorn or ostracism. **Moral** or **social law** refers to laws made by society and enforced solely by social pressure. Moral or social laws include laws of etiquette, "honor" and morality. When moral laws break down and social sanctions fail to obtain conformity, other laws may be enacted and enforced.

Precedents: Common Law and Case Law

The beginnings of law are found in social custom. Custom is simply **precedent**— doing what has been done before. In early times custom, religion, morals and the law were intermingled. Some early customs have, over the centuries, become law. Precedent explains why many good ideas in criminal justice are so slow to materialize.

Some customs were enforced physically rather than morally, and the violator was expelled from the community, sacrificed to the gods or hanged. Other violations of custom not felt to be harmful to the whole community were punished by the injured group or the injured individual with the aid of the family (self-help, vengeance, feud). As long as such vengeance might lead to retaliation, the sanctions behind the rules of custom were still purely moral. When the community began to protect those who had taken *rightful* vengeance, however, these persons became agents of the community. This kind of self-help met early society's needs when the right to take vengeance or redress was clear. It did not provide a way to settle controversies. Therefore courts were established to interpret customs and settle controversies. Custom was replaced by judicial precedent.

In England **common law** referred to the precedents set by the judges in the royal courts as disputes rose. This was in contrast to local custom or **ecclesiastical** (church) **law.** When Parliament supplemented and modified the existing legal principles, the term *common law* described the law in force before, and independent of, any acts of the legislature.

The common law brought to the United States by the early settlers forms the basis of modern American law in all states except Louisiana, which established and kept the system of French civil law. In essence common law describes the precedent generally followed in the absence of a specific law, known in the United States as **case law.** Case law refers to judicial precedents; no specific law exists, but a similar case serves as a model. When cases not covered by the law come before the courts, the judges' rulings on previous similar cases will, for all practical purposes, be treated as law.

Statutory Law

The United States has largely replaced common law (unwritten law) with **statutory law,** that is, legislated and written law. Statutory law may be passed at the federal or state level, and at either level it includes **constitutional** and **ordinary law.**

Federal constitutional law is based on the U.S. Constitution, its amendments and interpretations by the federal courts. Ordinary federal law consists of acts of Congress, treaties with foreign states, executive orders and regulations and interpretation of the preceding by federal courts. State constitutional law is based on the state's constitution, its amendments and interpretations of them by the state's courts. State ordinary law consists of acts of the state legislatures, decisions of the federal courts in interpreting or developing the common law, executive orders and regulations and municipal ordinances.

In addition, in most states, each county and city is given the right to pass laws for its local jurisdiction, providing the law does not conflict with the state's laws. Local **ordinances** (laws) are primarily enacted to protect the community.

Equity

The need for laws to change as society changes has long been recognized, as illustrated in a letter written by Thomas Jefferson in the nineteenth century:

> . . . laws and institutions must go hand in hand with the progress of the human mind, as that becomes more developed, as more discoveries are made, new truths disclosed, and manners and opinions change with the changing circumstances, institutions must advance also, and keep pace with the times. We might as well require a man to wear still the coat which fitted him as a boy as civilized society to remain ever under the regiment of their barbarous ancestors.

Indeed, laws that once made good sense now appear ridiculous. For example, an old law in Truro, Massachusetts, stated that a young man may not marry until he has killed either six blackbirds or three crows; and in Gary, Indiana, it was illegal to go into a theater within four hours of eating garlic.

Equity demands that laws change as society changes, resorting to general principles of fairness and justice whenever existing law is inadequate. It requires that the "spirit of the law" take precedence over the "letter of the law."

Equity describes a system of rules and doctrines supplementing common and statutory law and superseding laws that are inadequate to fairly settle a case. However if every locality and state were left alone, our legal system would be chaos. Fortunately our Founding Fathers foresaw this danger and wrote the Constitution of the United States, a carefully drafted document that established the workings of our democracy.

Constitutional Law

A **constitution** is a system of fundamental laws and principles that prescribe the nature, functions and limits of a government or other body. The U.S. Constitution was drafted by the Constitutional Convention of 1787 and became effective in 1789.

 The U.S. Constitution, ratified in 1789, is the basic instrument of government and the supreme law of the land.

The Constitution states that the legislative, executive and judicial departments of government should be separated as far as is practical and that their respective powers should be exercised by different individuals or groups of individuals. The

The opening paragraph of the U.S. Consitution clearly states its purpose: We the People of the United States, in Order to form a more perfect Union, establish Justice, insure domestic Tranquility, provide for the common defence, promote the general Welfare, and secure the Blessings of Liberty to ourselves and our Prosterity, do ordain and establish this Constitution for the United States of America.

legislature makes the laws, the executive branch, of which law enforcement is a part, enforces the laws and the judicial branch determines when laws have been violated.

Order of Authority of Law

If two laws conflict, a set order of authority has been established.

 The order of authority of law is the federal Constitution, treaties with foreign powers, acts of Congress, the state constitutions, state statutes and, finally, common law or case law.

The Bill of Rights

The Constitution organized the government of the new nation but contained few personal guarantees. Consequently some states refused to ratify it without a specific bill of rights. Ten amendments, with personal guarantees, came into effect in 1791. They became known as the **Bill of Rights,** a fundamental document protecting a person's right to "life, liberty, and the pursuit of happiness."

 The Bill of Rights refers to the first 10 amendments to the Constitution, which protect the peoples' liberties and forbid the government to violate these rights.

Individual constitutional rights are clearly specified in each amendment. Of special importance to criminal justice professionals are the First, Second, Fourth, Fifth, Sixth, Eighth and Fourteenth Amendments.

The First Amendment

 The First Amendment guarantees freedom of religion, freedom of speech, freedom of the press, freedom of peaceable assembly and freedom of petition.

Freedom of Religion   Citizens are free to worship as they see fit through two guarantees: (1) no law can establish an official church that all Americans must accept and support or that favors one church over another, and (2) no law is constitutional that prohibits the free exercise of religion. The First Amendment clearly separates church and state and requires that the government be neutral on religious matters, favoring no religion above another.

Freedom of Speech   The Supreme Court has ruled that the First Amendment does not protect all forms of expression. Highly inflammatory remarks that advocate violence and clearly threaten the peace and safety of the community spoken to a crowd are not protected.

Schenck v. United States (1919) established the "clear and present danger" doctrine and serves as a guide to the constitutionality of government restrictions on free speech (and free press). The Court held: "The most stringent protection of free speech would not protect a man in falsely shouting fire in a theatre causing a panic. . . . The question in every case is whether the words are used in such circumstances and are of such a nature as to create a clear and present danger that they will bring about the substantive evils that Congress has a right to prevent." *Chaplinsky v. New Hampshire* (1942) also established that use of **fighting words** likely to cause violence will not be tolerated.

The ban on words presenting a "clear and present danger" and "fighting words" is counterbalanced by the concept of **pure speech,** speech without any accompanying action. An example is the Americanism "Kill the umpire," commonly heard during baseball season.

Unlike pure speech, **speech plus** is not protected by the First Amendment. An example of speech plus is the action taken by striking employees in a picket line. If they physically prevent others from entering or leaving a commercial building, the police may be called to assure that those who wish to enter or exit the building are allowed to do so.

Courts have recognized that **symbolic speech,** involving tangible forms of expression, such as wearing buttons or clothing with political slogans or displaying a sign or a flag, is protected by the First Amendment. The Supreme Court has also held that burning the American flag is protected by the First Amendment, as is cross burning: "Cross burning can be a symbolic act that seeks to communicate a message and therefore can also have First Amendment protection" (Gardner and Anderson, 2003, p.219).

Freedom of the Press   The First Amendment guarantees the right to express oneself by writing or publishing one's views. The Founding Fathers recognized the importance of a free interplay of ideas in a democratic society and sought to guarantee the right of all citizens to speak or publish their views, even if contrary to those of the government or society as a whole. Accordingly the First Amendment generally forbids censorship or other restraint upon speech or the printed word. As with speech, freedom to write or publish is not an absolute right of expression. The sale of obscene or libelous printed materials is not protected.

The police and the press often come into conflict because of the Sixth Amendment guarantee of the right to a fair trial and protection of the defendant's rights. The guarantees of the First and the Sixth Amendments must be carefully balanced. The public's right to know cannot impinge upon others' rights to privacy or to a fair trial.

Freedom of Peaceable Assembly   Americans have the right to assemble peaceably for any political, religious or social activity. Public authorities cannot impose unreasonable restrictions on such assemblies, but they can impose limitations reasonably designed to prevent fire, health hazards or traffic obstructions.

Freedom of Petition   The right of **petition** is designed to allow citizens to communicate with their government without obstruction. When citizens exercise their First Amendment freedom to write or speak to their senators or representatives, they participate in the democratic process.

The Second Amendment

 The Second Amendment guarantees the right to keep and bear arms as necessary for a well-regulated militia.

The Supreme Court has ruled that state and federal governments may pass laws that prohibit carrying concealed weapons, require the registration of firearms and limit the sale of firearms for other than military use. Thus it is illegal to possess certain types of "people-killing" weapons, such as operable machine guns and sawed-off shotguns of a certain length.

The right of the states to pass laws regulating firearms rests in the Supreme Court's interpretation of the Second Amendment. In *United States v. Cruickshank* (1876), the Court stated that the amendment protected only the right of the states to maintain and equip a militia and that unless a defendant could show that the possession of a firearm in violation of federal statutes had "some reasonable relationship to the preservation or efficiency of a well-regulated militia," the individual could not challenge a gun control statute on Second Amendment grounds. All federal court decisions involving the amendment have used a collective, militia interpretation and/or held that firearms control laws are constitutional.

Dozens of federal and state court decisions have held that the Second Amendment limits only the federal government, not the states, and that the right to keep and bear arms is a collective rather than an individual right.

In November 1993, the Brady Bill was passed, mandating a national five-business-day waiting period for handgun purchases and that local law enforcement officials conduct background checks of prospective handgun buyers. The law took effect in February 1994. However in June 1997, the U.S. Supreme Court ruled 5–4 in *Printz v. United States* and *Mack v. United States* that the federal government is not empowered to require state or local law enforcement agencies to run background checks on prospective gun buyers. According to the Court, the background check provision violates the principle of separate state sovereignty. Justice Scalia, writing for the narrow majority, stated: "The Federal Government may neither issue directives requiring the states to address particular problems, nor command the states' officers, or those of their political subdivisions, to administer or enforce a Federal regulatory program. Such commands are fundamentally incompatible with our constitutional system of dual sovereignty" *(Printz v. United States)*.

As of November 1, 1998, the Brady Law was modified so an applicant can receive immediate clearance to purchase a gun. The issuing police agency can contact the FBI by computer and either receive clearance or be denied a permit for the applicant. However, because many police agencies do not have the computer capability to communicate with the FBI, the new system is somewhat imperfect.

The Fourth Amendment

 The Fourth Amendment requires probable cause and forbids unreasonable searches and seizures.

The Fourth Amendment has the most impact on law enforcement of any of the amendments, dictating how officers carry out their responsibilities without violating anyone's civil rights or civil liberties. The restrictions placed on law enforcement by this amendment are discussed in detail in Chapter 8. Only highlights are included here.

Searches   In most instances a police officer is not allowed to search the homes of private citizens, seize any of their property or arrest them without first obtaining a court order—a **warrant.**

The courts have ruled that in some instances it is permissible to arrest a person or conduct a search without a warrant. For example if a felony is committed in the presence of a police officer, the officer has the right to arrest the criminal immediately, without an arrest warrant. If police officers make such an arrest, they may search the suspect and a limited area surrounding the suspect to prevent the suspect from seizing a weapon or destroying evidence (*Chimel v. California*, 1969). Any evidence in plain view may also be seized.

The Supreme Court has ruled that the Fourth Amendment does not prohibit police officers from stopping and frisking a "suspicious person" if it was reasonable on the basis of the police officer's experience and the demeanor of the individual frisked (*Terry v. Ohio*, 1968).

Listening in on a telephone conversation by mechanical or electronic means is considered a search and seizure under the Fourth Amendment; therefore, such actions require probable cause, reasonableness and a warrant for their use. Congress has passed legislation that limits the use of wiretapping and bugging to the investigation of specific crimes and restricts those officials permitted to authorize them. *Katz v. United States* (1967) established that evidence of conversations overheard through electronic surveillance of a telephone booth was inadmissible because the proper authorization had not been obtained. *Berger v. New York* (1967) established that although electronic eavesdropping was prohibited by the Fourth Amendment, under specific conditions and circumstances it could be permitted.

Numerous Supreme Court cases have interpreted restrictions imposed by the Fourth Amendment. For example, in *Boyd v. United States* (1886), the Court held that the Fourth Amendment applied "to all invasions on the part of the government and its employees of the sanctity of a man's home and the privacies of life. It is not the breaking of his doors, and the rummaging of his drawers, that constitutes the essence of the offense; but it is the invasion of his indefensible right of personal security, personal liberty and private property." The findings in *Boyd* clearly suggest that evidence gathered in violation of the Fourth Amendment should be excluded from federal criminal trials and, consequently, contributed to the development of the Exclusionary Rule some 30 years later.

Exclusionary Rule   Without procedures for enforcing the provisions of the Fourth Amendment, the impressive constitutional language would be meaningless. Consequently the procedures and the power for their enforcement were vested in the courts. They must refuse to consider evidence obtained by unreasonable search and seizure methods, regardless of how relevant the evidence is to the case. Thus the phrase "innocent until proven guilty" in practice means "innocent until proven guilty by evidence obtained in accordance with constitutional guarantees."

The **Exclusionary Rule** is the direct result of the Supreme Court decision in the case of *Weeks v. United States* (1914), when the Court considered evidence seized unconstitutionally:

> If letters and private documents can thus be seized and held and used in evidence against a citizen accused of an offense, the protection of the Fourth Amendment declaring his right to be secure against such searches and seizures is of no value, and, so far as those thus placed are concerned, might as well be stricken from the Constitution. The efforts of the courts and their officials to bring the guilty to punishment, praiseworthy as they are, are not to be aided by the sacrifice of those great principles established by years of endeavor and suffering which have resulted in their embodiment in the fundamental law of the land.

In 1961 the Exclusionary Rule reached maturity when the Supreme Court, in the case of *Mapp v. Ohio*, extended the rule to every court and law enforcement officer in the nation.

 Courts uphold the Fourth Amendment by use of the Exclusionary Rule, which demands that no evidence may be admitted in a trial unless it is obtained within the constitutional standards set forth in the Fourth Amendment. *Weeks v. United States* (1914) made the Exclusionary Rule applicable in federal courts. *Mapp v. Ohio* (1961) made it applicable to every court in the country.

Since 1961 the Exclusionary Rule has applied to both the federal and state courts, and evidence secured illegally by federal, state or local officers has been inadmissible in any court. The Exclusionary Rule has important implications for the procedures followed by police officers, because neither the most skillful prosecutor nor the most experienced police officer can convince a jury of a defendant's guilt without adequate and lawfully obtained evidence.

The Fifth Amendment

 The Fifth Amendment *guarantees* due process—notice of a hearing, full information regarding the charges, the opportunity to present evidence in one's own behalf before an impartial judge or jury and to be presumed innocent until proven guilty by legally obtained evidence.

The Fifth Amendment *prohibits* double jeopardy and self-incrimination.

Grand Jury   The Fifth Amendment requires that before individuals are tried in federal court for an "infamous" crime, they must first be **indicted,** that is, formally accused of a crime by a grand jury. The grand jury's duty is to prevent people from being subjected to a trial when insufficient proof exists that they have committed a crime. An **infamous crime** is a felony (a crime for which a sentence of more than one year's imprisonment can be given) or a lesser offense that can be punished by confinement in a penitentiary or at hard labor.

Due Process   The words **due process of law** express the fundamental ideas of American justice. A due process clause occurs in the Fifth and Fourteenth Amendments as a restraint on the federal and state governments, respectively, and protects against arbitrary, unfair procedures in judicial or administrative proceedings that could affect a citizen's personal and property rights. Thus constitutional limitations are imposed on governmental interference with important individual liberties, such as the freedom to enter into contracts, to engage in a lawful occupation, to marry and to move without unnecessary restraints.

Due process requires timely notice of a hearing or trial that adequately informs those accused of the charges against them. It also requires the opportunity to present evidence in one's own behalf before an impartial judge or jury, to be presumed innocent until proven guilty by legally obtained evidence and to have the verdict supported by the evidence presented.

Due process requires that during judicial proceedings, fundamental principles of fairness and justice must prevail, including both substantive and procedural due process. **Substantive due process** protects individuals against unreasonable, arbitrary or capricious laws and limits arbitrary government actions. No court or governmental agency may exercise powers beyond what the Constitution authorizes. In contrast, **procedural due process** deals with notices, hearings and gathering of evidence. The vast majority of due process cases are in the area of procedural due process.

Because the Fifth Amendment is so vague, hundreds of cases have been heard. Important Supreme Court cases involving due process include *Brady v. Maryland* (1963), which held that the suppression of evidence favorable to an accused by the prosecution violates due process. *United States v. Russell* (1973) found that it was not entrapment for an undercover agent to have supplied the defendant with a scarce ingredient required to manufacture an illicit drug. In *Hampton v. United States* (1976), the Court held that it was not entrapment for undercover agents to be both providers and purchasers of drugs involved in the case.

Double Jeopardy   The Fifth Amendment also guarantees that citizens will not be placed in **double jeopardy;** that is, they will not be tried before a federal or state court more than once for the same crime. A second trial can occur, however, when the first trial results in a mistrial, when the jury cannot agree on a verdict or when a second trial is ordered by an appellate court.

Double jeopardy does not arise when a single act violates both federal and state laws and the defendant is prosecuted in both federal and state courts. Nor does a criminal prosecution in either a state or federal court exempt the defendant from being sued for damages in civil court by anyone harmed by the criminal act. This occurred in the O. J. Simpson case in which Simpson was found not guilty in criminal court, but later was found responsible for wrongful death in civil court and ordered to pay restitution.

Further, a defendant may be prosecuted more than once for the same conduct if it involves the commission of more than one crime. For instance if a person kills three victims at the same time and place, he or she can be tried separately for each slaying.

Double jeopardy is also an issue in asset forfeiture. **Asset forfeiture** allows the seizure of assets and property used in connection with a crime. Many police departments hesitate to use asset forfeiture for fear it would constitute double jeopardy if they also want to try the suspects in criminal court. However, as the result of two cases, *United States v. Ursery* (1996) and *Bennis v. Michigan* (1996), law enforcement can constitutionally use asset forfeiture without double jeopardy concerns.

To guide law enforcement in the appropriate use of asset forfeiture, Congress has approved legislation adding due process protections to assure that property is not unjustly seized from innocent owners. Provisions of the legislation include a *"burden of proof"* clause stating that the government must establish that the property was subject to forfeiture by a "preponderance of the evidence."

Self-Incrimination   In any criminal case, every person has the right not to be a witness against him- or herself; that is, individuals are not required to provide answers to questions that might convict them of a crime. This is called **self-incrimination.** Such questions may be asked at the very earliest stages of an investigation; therefore, the Supreme Court has ruled that when an individual is interrogated in the custody of the police, the guarantees of the Fifth Amendment apply. **Custodial interrogation** can extend to questioning outside the police station.

To ensure against self-incrimination, the Court ruled, in the landmark case *Miranda v. Arizona* (1966) that citizens must be warned prior to custodial interrogation of their right to remain silent, that what they say may be used against them in court and that they have a right to counsel, which will be furnished to them. If these warnings are not given, any statements obtained by the questioning are inadmissible in later criminal proceedings.

Although accused persons may waive their rights under the Fifth Amendment, they must know what they are doing and must not be forced to confess. Any confession obtained by force or threat is excluded from the evidence presented at the trial. Courts have ruled that the guarantee against self-incrimination applies only to testimonial actions. Thus handwriting samples, blood tests and physical appearance and voice tests, including repeating words in a police lineup, do *not* violate the Fifth Amendment. In addition *New York v. Quarles* (1984) established an exception to the Exclusionary Rule in that if the public safety would be threatened by delaying questioning, police may question a subject in custody without first advising of the right not to self-incriminate.

The Sixth Amendment

 The Sixth Amendment establishes requirements for criminal trials. It guarantees the individual's right to have a speedy public trial by an impartial jury, be informed of the nature and cause of the accusation, be confronted with witnesses against him or her, subpoena witnesses for defense and have counsel for defense.

The Supreme Court has ruled that state juries need not have 12 members and has approved state statutes that require only 6 members. Moreover the Court has ruled that jury verdicts in state courts need not be unanimous. In all jury trials the jury members must be impartially selected. The right to jury trial does not apply to trials for petty offenses, that is, those punishable by six months' confinement or fewer, such as shoplifting or minor traffic violations. Nor is a jury trial a right of juveniles.

The Sixth Amendment requires that accused persons be told how it is claimed they have broken the law so they can prepare their defense. The crime must be clearly established by statute beforehand. In general accused persons are entitled to have all witnesses against them present their evidence orally in court. Accused persons are entitled to the court's aid in obtaining their witnesses, usually by **subpoena,** which orders into court as witnesses persons whose testimony is desired at the trial. Facts not in the personal knowledge of a witness are called *hearsay.* **Hearsay evidence,** that is, secondhand evidence, cannot be used in criminal trials except in certain instances.

Finally, the Sixth Amendment provides a right to be represented by counsel. For many years this was interpreted to mean that defendants had a right to be represented by a lawyer only if they could afford one. The Supreme Court's first modern ruling on the right to counsel was *Powell v. Alabama* (1932), a case involving nine young black males, ages 13 to 21, charged with raping two white girls. The trial was held in Scottsboro, Alabama, where community sentiment was extremely hostile toward the defendants. Although the trial judge appointed a member of the local bar to serve as defense counsel, no attorney appeared on the day of the trial, so the judge appointed a local lawyer who reluctantly took the case. The defendants challenged their conviction on the grounds that they did not have a chance to consult with their lawyer or prepare a defense, and the Supreme Court concurred. However, in *Betts v. Brady* (1942) the Court ruled that a defendant's federal right to an attorney did *not* apply in a state court.

Twenty years later *Gideon v. Wainwright* (1963) reexamined the holding in *Betts v. Brady.* Gideon was an indigent charged with a felony in Florida, where counsel for indigent defendants was permitted only in capital cases. The trial judge denied Gideon's request for counsel, so Gideon defended himself and was convicted and sent to prison. He appealed and, in a rare occurrence, the Court agreed to hear the case and overturned *Betts v. Brady.* Writing for the majority, Justice Hugo Lafayette Black stated:

> The fact is that in deciding as it did that "appointment of counsel is not a fundamental right, essential to a fair trial"—the court in *Betts v. Brady* made an abrupt break with its own well-considered precedents. . . . Not only these precedents but also reason and reflection require us to recognize that in our adversary system of criminal justice, any person hauled into court, who is too poor to hire a lawyer cannot be assured a fair trial unless counsel is provided for him.
>
> This seems to us to be an obvious truth. Governments, both state and federal, quite properly spend vast sums of money to establish machinery to try defendants accused of crime. Lawyers to prosecute are everywhere deemed essential to protect the public's interest in an orderly society. Similarly there are few defendants charged with crime, few indeed, who fail to hire the best lawyers they can get to prepare and present their defenses. That government hires lawyers to prosecute and defendants who have money to hire lawyers to defend are the strongest indications of the widespread belief that lawyers in

criminal courts are necessities, not luxuries. The right of one charged with a crime to counsel may not be deemed fundamental and essential to fair trials in some countries, but it is in ours. From the very beginning, our state and national constitutions and laws have laid great emphasis on procedural and substantive safeguards designed to assure fair trials before impartial tribunals in which every defendant stands equal before the law. This noble ideal cannot be realized if the poor man charged with a crime has to face his accusers without a lawyer to assist him. . . . Betts was an "anachronism when handed down," and it should be overruled.

The court ruled 9–0 that the due process clause of the Fourteenth Amendment requires states to provide free counsel to indigent defendants in all felony cases.

The **indigent,** that is, people who are destitute, poverty-stricken, with no visible means of support, have such a right at any "critical stage of the adjudicatory process," including the initial periods of questioning, police lineups and all stages of the trial process. In 1956 in *Shioutakon v. District of Columbia,* the courts established the role of legal counsel in juvenile court. If juveniles were to have their liberty taken away, such juveniles had the right to a lawyer in court. If their parents could not afford a lawyer, the court was to appoint one.

The Eighth Amendment

 The Eighth Amendment forbids excessive bail, excessive fines and cruel and unusual punishments.

Bail   **Bail** has traditionally meant payment by the accused of a sum of money, specified by the court based on the nature of the offense, to ensure the accused's presence at trial. A defendant released from custody who subsequently fails to appear for trial forfeits bail to the court. Because bail typically costs one-tenth of its amount, it is often informally considered a punishment in itself.

The Eighth Amendment does not specifically provide the right to bail, only that bail will not be excessive. In 1966 Congress enacted the Bail Reform Act to provide for pretrial release from imprisonment of indigent defendants who were confined, in effect, only because of their poverty. The act also discouraged the traditional use of money bail by requiring judges to seek other means to ensure that defendants would appear for their trial.

The leading Supreme Court decision on excessive bail is *Stack v. Boyle* (1951) in which 12 community leaders were indicted for conspiracy, and bail was set at $50,000 per defendant. The defendants moved to reduce this amount on the grounds that it was excessive, and the Supreme Court agreed:

This traditional right to freedom before conviction permits the unhampered preparation of a defense, and serves to prevent the infliction of punishment prior to conviction. . . . Unless this right to bail before trial is preserved, the presumption of innocence, secured only after centuries of struggle, would lose its meaning.

The right of release before trial is conditioned upon the accused's giving adequate assurance that he will stand trial and submit to sentence if found guilty. . . . Bail set at a figure higher than an amount reasonably calculated to fulfill this purpose is "excessive" under the Eighth Amendment.

Cruel and Unusual Punishment Whether fines or confinement are cruel and unusual must be determined by the facts of each particular case. Clearly such excessive practices as torture would be invalid. The Supreme Court has heard numerous cases concerning cruel and unusual punishment and has held the death penalty itself to be cruel and unusual in certain circumstances if it is not universally applied:

- *Furman v. Georgia* (1972) stated that the death penalty violates the Eighth Amendment if the sentencing authority has the freedom to decide between the death penalty and a lesser penalty.
- *Gregg v. Georgia* (1976) held that the death penalty for murderers is not per se cruel and unusual punishment.
- *Rummel v. Estelle* (1980) ruled that a mandatory life sentence required by a state habitual offender statute is not cruel and unusual punishment.

The Ninth Amendment

The Ninth Amendment emphasizes the Founding Fathers' view that government powers are limited by the rights of the people and that it was *not* intended, by expressly guaranteeing in the Constitution certain rights of the people, to recognize that government has unlimited power to invade other rights of the people.

Griswold v. Connecticut (1965), a case involving the Ninth Amendment, addressed the issue of whether the right to privacy is a constitutional right and, if so, whether the right is reserved to the people under the Ninth Amendment or is derived only from other rights specifically mentioned in the Constitution. The Court in *Griswold* ruled that the Third and Fifth Amendments, in addition to the First and Fourth, created **zones of privacy** safe from governmental intrusion and, without resting its decision upon any one amendment or on the Ninth Amendment itself, simply held that the right of privacy is guaranteed by the Constitution.

The Tenth Amendment

The Tenth Amendment embodies the principle of **federalism,** which reserves for the states the residue of powers not granted to the federal government or withheld from the states. However, through the Fourteenth Amendment, many civil rights and civil liberties assured by the Bill of Rights were made applicable to the states.

The Fourteenth Amendment

The Fourteenth Amendment requires each state to abide by the Constitution and the incorporation doctrine of the Bill of Rights. It guarantees due process and equal protection under the law.

The Incorporation Doctrine Harr and Hess (2005, p.111) explain: "Considering the Constitution was aimed primarily at limiting the power of *federal* government, it seemed unthinkable that the federal government would be kept in line only to have state authority left unbridled. The **incorporation doctrine,** also known as **selective incorporation,** prevents the unthinkable."

In *Palko v. Connecticut* (1937), the Supreme Court held that there were rights "so rooted in the traditions and conscience of our people as to be ranked as fundamental," meaning "essential to justice and the American system of political liberty." The selective incorporation doctrine holds that only those provisions of the Bill of Rights that are fundamental to the American legal process are made applicable to the states through the due process clause. For example, if a state law were to abridge freedom of religion, it would be violating the First Amendment as applied to it through the Fourteenth Amendment.

Due Process   The Fourteenth Amendment limits the *states'* infringement upon individual rights. The Bill of Rights does not specifically refer to actions by states but applies only to actions by the federal government. Thus state and local officers could proceed with an arrest without any concern for the rights of the accused. The Fourteenth Amendment duplicates the Fifth Amendment, except it specifically orders state and local officers to provide the legal protections of due process. An important Supreme Court case related to the Fourteenth Amendment is *Brown v. Mississippi* (1936), which stated that a criminal conviction based on a confession obtained by brutality is not admissible under the Fourteenth Amendment due process clause.

Equal Protection   The Fourteenth Amendment also prohibits denial of the **equal protection** of the laws. A state cannot make unreasonable, arbitrary distinctions between different people's rights and privileges. Because "all people are created equal," no law can deny red-haired men the right to drive an automobile, although it can deny minors the right to drive. The state can make reasonable classifications, but classifications based on race, religion and national origin have been held unreasonable.

In addition to the great body of constitutional law, criminal and civil law also are important to the criminal justice professional.

Criminal Law

Criminal law includes rules and procedures for investigating crimes and prosecuting criminals, regulations governing the constitution of courts and the conduct of trials and the administration of penal institutions. American criminal law has a number of unique features. In establishing criminal law, the federal government and each state government are sovereign within the limits of their authority as defined by the Constitution. Therefore criminal law varies from state to state. Despite the many differences, most states have a tradition derived from English common law.

 Criminal law defines crimes and fixes punishments for them.

The Bureau of Justice Statistics defines **crime** as "all behaviors and acts for which a society provides formally sanctioned punishment." Crimes are made so by law. State and federal statutes define each crime, the elements involved and the penalty attached to each. The statutes that define what acts constitute social harm are called **substantive criminal law,** for example a statute defining homicide. A substantive criminal law not only defines the offense but also states the punishment. The omission of the punishment invalidates the criminal law.

Prosecutor Shelia Calkins gestures with her fists describing the fight between Thomas Junta and Michael Costin. Junta was accused of beating to death fellow hockey dad Costin after their sons' hockey practice in July 2000.

In most countries crimes and punishments are expressed in statutes, with punishments including removal from public office, fines, exile, imprisonment and death. Unless the act for which a defendant is accused is expressly defined by statute as a crime, no indictment or conviction for committing the act is legal. This establishes the difference between government by law and arbitrary dictatorial government.

Criminal law in the United States generally defines seven classes of crime: offenses against (1) international law, (2) the dispensation of justice and the legitimate exercise of governmental authority, (3) the public peace, (4) property, (5) trade, (6) public decency and (7) persons. Like English law, American criminal law also classifies crimes with respect to their gravity as felonies and misdemeanors.

> A **felony** is a serious crime, generally punishable by death or by imprisonment for more than one year in a state prison or penitentiary. A **misdemeanor** is any minor offense, generally punishable by a fine or a short term, usually not to exceed one year, in a jail or workhouse.

State criminal codes vary in their classification of offenses considered misdemeanors. Crimes usually defined as misdemeanors include libel, assault and battery, malicious mischief and petty theft. In some states the distinction between felonies and misdemeanors is practically discarded, the punishment for each particular crime being prescribed by statute.

Crimes have also been classified as *mala in se* (bad in itself) and *mala prohibita* (bad because it is forbidden). A *mala in se* crime is one so offensive that it is obviously criminal, for example murder or rape. A *mala prohibita* crime is one that violates a specific regulatory statute, for example certain traffic violations. These would not usually be considered crimes if no law prohibited them.

Proving That a Crime Has Been Committed

In addition to establishing what specifically constitutes a crime and the punishment for it, **procedural criminal law** specifies what must be proven and how, that is, legally within the constraints of the Constitution and the Bill of Rights.

To prove that a crime has been committed, it is usually necessary to prove:
- The act itself *(actus reus)*—the material elements of the crime.
- The criminal mental state *(mens rea)*—intent to do wrong.

Material Elements—The Criminal Act   Basic to the commission of a crime is the concept of *actus reus*—literally the "guilty act." The *actus reus* must be a measurable act, including planning and conspiring. What constitutes this forbidden act is usually spelled out very specifically in state statutes and is called the *corpus delicti.*

Contrary to popular belief, the *corpus delicti* of a crime is not the body in a murder case. It is, quite literally, the body of the crime itself—the distinctive elements that must exist for a particular crime to be proven. These **elements of the crime** make up the *corpus delicti.* Law enforcement officers are most responsible for proving that the actual act occurred—establishing the elements of a specific crime. Much more difficult to establish is the defendant's mental state.

Criminal Intent   The second key requirement of a crime is **criminal intent** or *mens rea,* literally, the "guilty mind." To convict someone of a crime, it must be proven that the defendant intentionally, knowingly or willingly committed the criminal act:

> The term *mens rea* means evil intent, criminal purpose, and knowledge of the wrongfulness of conduct. It is also used to indicate the mental state required by the crime charged, whether that be specific intent to commit the crime, recklessness, guilty knowledge, malice, or criminal negligence (Gardner and Anderson, p.35).

In some crimes intent is not an element. These are known as **strict liability** crimes. These offenses generally involve traffic violations, liquor violations and hunting violations. In strict liability crimes, defendants are liable regardless of their state of mind when the act was committed. Individuals who break traffic, liquor and hunting laws are generally not considered "criminals" and receive lesser penalties.

A liquor store owner cannot use the excuse that a minor who bought beer from the store looked at least 30 years old. A man who has consensual sex with a minor female cannot use the excuse that she said she was 21. Nor can the speeder claim ignorance of the posted speed limit or claim a faulty speedometer. Intent is not at issue—only the speed.

Intent is *not* to be confused with **motive,** which is a *reason* for doing something. Motive is not an element of any crime, but it can help to establish intent. If police officers can show why a suspect would benefit from committing a certain act, this greatly strengthens the case. A classic example is Robin Hood, who allegedly stole from the rich to give to the poor. He intended to steal, and although his motives were "righteous," he was still committing a crime. A modern example would be the actions of Dr. Jack Kevorkian, who helped terminally ill people to commit suicide. Although motive is not relevant to the issue of guilt or innocence, it can affect sentencing.

Another element of a crime that must sometimes be proven is *scienter,* guilty knowledge making individuals legally responsible for their acts. In other words the person committing the act knew that it was a crime. For example, to be guilty of harboring a felon, the person harboring the felon has to know the person is a felon, or the person who buys stolen property has to know the property is indeed stolen. This is closely related to *mens rea.*

Crimes can be categorized in many ways. You have already seen one such classification: a criminal act can be either a misdemeanor or a felony. Another common classification differentiates between violent crimes, or crimes against persons, and property crimes. Violent crimes against persons include homicide, rape, assault and robbery—actions that involve the use of force or the threat of force against a person. In contrast property crimes do not involve such force and include larceny, burglary, motor vehicle theft and arson. These crimes are discussed in Chapter 3. Consider next the third major type of law—civil law.

Civil Law and Torts

Although laws vary from state to state, generally such actions as trespassing, desertion of family, slander, failure to make good on a contract or similar actions against an individual would be covered under civil law.

 Civil law refers to all noncriminal restrictions placed on individuals. It seeks not punishment, but restitution. The offense is called a **tort**.

A tort is not the same thing as a crime, although the two sometimes have many features in common. The distinction between them lies in the interests affected and the remedy afforded by the law. A crime is an offense against the public at large, for which the state, as the representative of the public, will bring proceedings in the form of criminal prosecution. . . . A criminal prosecution is not concerned in any way with compensation of the injured individual against whom the crime is committed. . . . The civil action for a tort, on the other hand, is commenced and maintained by the injured person himself, and its purpose is to compensate him for the damage he has suffered, at the expense of the wrongdoer (Prosser, 1955, p.7).

Law enforcement officers recognize when a matter is covered by criminal law and when it is covered by civil law (noncriminal matters). An act can be both a crime and a tort.

 The distinctions between crimes and torts are as follows:

Crime	Tort
Public wrong	Private wrong
State prosecutes	Individual prosecutes
Seeks to punish	Seeks redress for injury
Criminal intent is required	Intent not necessary

The Law Enforcement Officer and Civil Liability

Citizens can bring action against the police and have been doing so with increasing frequency. Griffith (2002, p.6) suggests: "In the American system of justice, you're innocent until proven guilty . . . unless you carry a badge." He also suggests: "A law enforcement officer tried by the media in a racially charged case has as much chance of a fair hearing as a Wiccan priestess in Old Salem." Although somewhat exaggerated, this situation may cause the threat of civil liability to affect police officer responses, including arrest decisions, by creating a "lawsuit paranoia" (or **litigaphobia**) that can permeate and undermine the effective operation of law enforcement agencies and can affect every law enforcement officer, both professionally and personally. Daniels and Spratley (2003, p.54) note the dilemma in police pursuits: "In today's litigious society, departments can easily fall victim to the Catch 22 of vehicle pursuits: sued if you do and sued if you don't."

Chudwin (2003, p.10) describes the devastating effects the fear of being sued might have: "In a case in the Northwest, an officer reported that he and his partner did not fire on an offender pointing two pistols at the officers because they were afraid of liability if the pistols were not real. The offender shot and murdered one of the officers. The officers were more fearful of a lawsuit than being murdered."

Rutledge (2003, p.94) explains the three basic categories of civil cases that can be brought against police officials: "(1) under a state or federal statutory scheme that creates specific causes of action to cover particular subjects (employment, sexual harassment, public records access, vehicle pursuit, etc.); (2) under general tort law (for such things as negligence, false imprisonment, assault and battery, infliction of emotional distress, etc.); (3) under Title 42, Section 1983, of the U.S. Code, for alleged violation of federal statutory or constitutional rights by state and local officials acting under the color of law." This third reason, violation of the Civil Rights Act, accounts for many of today's numerous lawsuits.

The Civil Rights Act (Section 1983)   The U.S. Code, Title 42, Section 1983, passed after the Civil War in 1871, states:

> Every person who, under color of any statute, ordinance, regulation, custom, or usage, of any State or Territory, subjects, or causes to be subjected any citizen of the United States or other person within the jurisdiction thereof to the deprivation of any rights, privileges, or immunities secured by the Constitution and laws, shall be liable to the party injured in an action at law, suit in equity, or other proper proceeding for redress.

 Section 1983 of the U.S. Code, Title 42, stipulates that anyone acting under the authority of local or state law who violates another person's constitutional rights—even though they are upholding a law—can be sued.

The two basic requirements for a Section 1983 action are that (1) the plaintiff must be deprived of a constitutional right and (2) the defendant must deprive the plaintiff of this right while acting under the "color of the law" (*Adickes v. Kress and Co.*, 1970). Like criminal law, civil law has levels of "intent":

- Strict liability—the wrongdoer is liable even if no harm was intended (for example, keeping wild animals).
- Intentional wrong—the person knows the act was unlawful but did it anyway.
- Negligence—the person did not set out to do harm but acted carelessly.

Intentional wrong and negligence are the two categories law enforcement officers are most frequently involved with.

Intentional wrongs that may affect law enforcement include assault, battery, excessive force, false imprisonment, false arrest, malicious prosecution, intentional infliction of emotional distress, trespass, illegal electronic surveillance, invasion of privacy, defamation and wrongful death. Later chapters introduce procedures to minimize the likelihood of a civil lawsuit for an intentional wrong.

The second category of civil charges frequently filed against law enforcement officers and their agencies is **negligence,** the failure to use due care to prevent foreseeable injury. Routine police duties that most often lead to negligence lawsuits are care of incapacitated persons, duty to render emergency aid, caring for arrestees, aiding private citizens, investigating unusual circumstances and operating emergency vehicles carelessly, for example during high-speed chases. Given the inherently dangerous nature of police work, such as the carrying of lethal weapons and the authority to drive at high speeds, officers are unquestionably vulnerable to lawsuits when mistakes or errors in judgment occur that lead to unnecessary injury of a private party. The results of such lawsuits, even when judgments are in favor of the police, can have far-reaching, long-lasting adverse effects on the officers involved and their agencies, as well as on the police profession and the community as a whole.

The leading case for police negligence is *Byrd v. Brishke* (1972), in which the plaintiff claimed to have been surrounded by about a dozen Chicago police officers who repeatedly struck him. The plaintiff could not identify the specific officers who had beaten him, but his claim was that all those present were liable because they did nothing to stop the beating. The court concurred: "We believe it is clear that one who is given the badge of authority of a police officer may not ignore the duty imposed by his office and fail to stop other officers who summarily punish a third person in his presence or otherwise within his knowledge."

Officers must also come forward with information regarding other officers' misconduct, for any evidence of a **code of silence** is enough to justify a civil rights claim against a municipality. In any department where such a code of silence exists, civil liability is greatly increased. This issue is discussed in Chapters 4 and 11.

Much of the civil action taken against police officers and their agencies results from the tremendous power officers have and, indeed, require.

Police Power

Without means of enforcement, the great body of federal, state, municipal and common law would be empty and meaningless. Recall that *law* implies not only the rule but also enforcement of that rule. All forms of society rely on authority and power. **Authority** is the right to direct and command. **Power** is the force by which others can be made to obey.

Police power describes the ability of federal, state or municipal governments to enforce the laws they pass by granting government agents at each level the authority to use force against those who fail to comply with the laws.

 Police power is derived from the U.S. Constitution, U.S. Supreme Court decisions, federal statutes, state constitutions, state statutes, state court decisions and various municipal charters and ordinances.

Police power was defined by the Supreme Court in 1887 as "embracing no more than the power to promote public health, morals, and safety" *(Mugler v. Kansas)*. For example traffic laws are passed to preserve the general safety and to make the highways safe for the motoring public. Likewise, juvenile laws are passed to protect juveniles from parents, guardians, relatives or others who would endanger the youths' physical and mental welfare.

States' police powers are delegated to them by the Bill of Rights in the Tenth Amendment, giving the states those powers not delegated to the federal government.

 Police power ultimately rests with the people because their elected representatives create the laws that the police enforce.

Figure 2.1 illustrates the sources of police authority.

Note in Figure 2.1 that the arrows between the citizens, governments and courts go two ways—citizens are not only governed by laws passed by the legislation, interpreted by the courts and enforced by the police, they also play a role in establishing laws by electing the representatives whose actions and decisions ultimately influence policing.

Because each state is responsible for its citizens' health, safety and general well-being, they usually assign these functions to municipal police departments in the cities and to sheriffs and constables in rural areas. State legislatures may define the powers and duties of police officers; however, police officers' authority and powers cannot conflict with the Constitution.

Although the state legislature passes laws, the courts, the judicial branch of government, decide the purpose and character of the statutes, as well as whether these statutes conflict with the Constitution or are contrary to proper public policy. Acceptable police power requires that the regulations are (1) reasonable, (2) within the power given to the states by the Constitution and (3) in accord with due process of law.

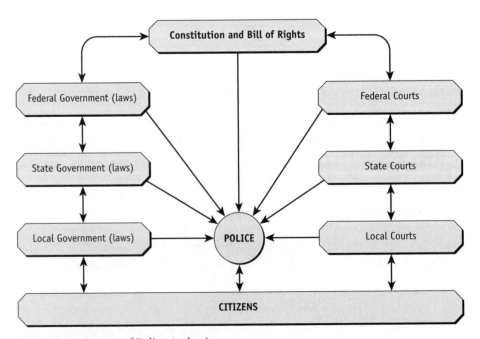

Figure 2.1 Sources of Police Authority

Police power is restricted by the Constitution, the Fourteenth Amendment and the courts.

Many have noted the irony and inherent conflict present in our system of law enforcement—the designation of a police entity authorized to use coercive force to eradicate violence and effect a peaceful society. This paradoxical scheme often places officers, whose defining characteristic is the right to use force, in an awkward relationship with the citizens they are sworn to serve and protect. In addition, law enforcement is faced with balancing the needs of society with the needs of the individuals within that society.

The Needs of Society and the Rights of the Individual

America was founded on the desire for liberty and freedom from England's tyranny. Although the Founding Fathers crafted our government to assure it would not impinge on individual liberties, the desire for law and order was also strong. They had brought with them the common law of England, and it was expected that these laws would be obeyed.

 The scales of justice symbolize the desire to balance the needs of society with individual rights.

This tension between society's needs and individual liberty has its roots in two conflicting views of social control: conflict theory and consensus theory.

Lady Justice defends the balance between individual rights and the needs of society represented by the scales of justice.

Conflict Theory

Conflict theory contends that certain behaviors are criminalized to keep the dominant class in power. The roots of this theory are found in Marx and Engels's *Manifesto of the Communist Party* (1848, p.419):

> The history of all hitherto existing society is the history of class struggles. Freeman and slave, patrician and plebeian, lord and serf, guild-master and journeyman, in a word, oppressor and oppressed stood in constant opposition to one another, carried on an interrupted, now hidden, now open fight, a fight that each time ended in either a revolutionary reconstruction of society at large, or in the common ruin of the contending classes.

Marx referred to the lower class as a "slum proletariat" made up of vagrants, prostitutes and criminals. The law was intended to maintain the power of the upper class and control this "slum proletariat."

Consensus Theory

Consensus theory holds that individuals within a society agree on basic values, on what is inherently right and wrong. Acts that are wrong are considered crimes. This theory goes back in history at least as far as Plato and Aristotle. Deviant acts are unlawful because society in general feels they are unacceptable behavior. French sociologist Emile Durkheim (1858–1917), in explaining the criminal law, suggests that crime is conduct "universally disapproved of by members of each society." An act is criminal when it offends strong and defined states of the collective conscience.

These two opposing views of social control parallel the two competing models within the criminal justice system: crime control and due process.

Crime Control versus Due Process

A major function of our criminal justice system is **crime control.** However, the Fifth Amendment of the Bill of Rights and the Fourteenth Amendment both guarantee citizens due process of law. *Due process of law,* as defined by Gardner and Anderson (2003, p.490), is "the constitutional guarantee that criminal arrests and trials must meet certain minimum standards of fairness (procedural due process), and that laws not violate constitutional rights (substantive due process)."

 Two conflicting models of the criminal justice system are crime control and due process of law.

It may appear that crime control is inconsistent with due process, but the two can operate together to benefit society. The emphasis on one model or the other may change from time to time, as illustrated in Figure 2.2. Seldom is a perfect balance struck.

The dual responsibility of seeking out and punishing the guilty while simultaneously protecting the innocent is one of law enforcement's greatest challenges.

 SUMMARY

If the fundamental values of our society are to be preserved and extended, citizens must understand and support those institutions and statutes that, in practice, reflect the principles set forth in the Declaration of Independence, the Constitution and the Bill of Rights.

The Declaration of Independence asserts that all individuals are created equal and are entitled to the unalienable rights of life, liberty and the pursuit of happiness. It fur-

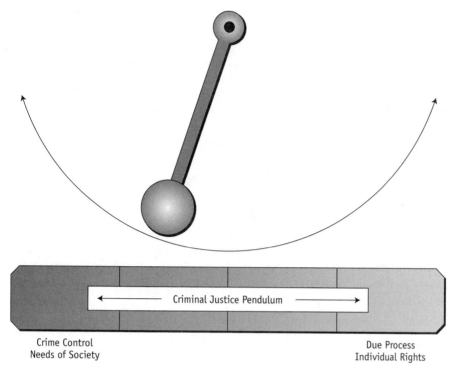

Crime Control
Needs of Society

Criminal Justice Pendulum

Due Process
Individual Rights

Figure 2.2   The Criminal Justice Pendulum

ther asserts that governments are instituted by and derive their power from the governed, that is, the people.

To achieve the goals set forth in the Declaration of Independence, the U.S. Constitution was drafted as the basic instrument of government and the supreme law of the United States. The order of authority of law is the federal Constitution, treaties with foreign powers, acts of Congress, the state constitutions, state statutes and, finally, common law or case law.

Some states, however, refused to ratify the Constitution if it did not contain personal guarantees. As a result the Bill of Rights was drafted, containing the first 10 amendments to the Constitution, which protect the peoples' liberties and forbid the government to violate these rights:

- The First Amendment guarantees freedom of religion, freedom of speech, freedom of the press, freedom of peaceable assembly and freedom of petition.
- The Second Amendment guarantees the right to keep and bear arms.
- The Fourth Amendment requires probable cause and forbids unreasonable searches and seizures. Courts uphold the Fourth Amendment by use of the Exclusionary Rule, which demands that no evidence may be admitted in a trial unless it is obtained within the constitutional standards set forth in the Fourth Amendment. *Weeks v. United States* made the Exclusionary Rule applicable in federal courts. *Mapp v. Ohio* made it applicable to every court in the country.
- The Fifth Amendment guarantees due process; it prohibits double jeopardy and self-incrimination.
- The Sixth Amendment establishes requirements for criminal trials. It guarantees the individual's right to have a speedy public trial by an impartial jury, be informed of the nature and cause of the accusation, be confronted with witnesses against him or her, subpoena witnesses for defense and have counsel for defense.

- The Eighth Amendment forbids excessive bail, excessive fines and cruel and unusual punishments.
- The Fourteenth Amendment requires each state to abide by the Constitution and the Bill of Rights. It guarantees due process and equal protection under the law.

In addition to constitutional law, the criminal justice professional must also be familiar with criminal and civil law. Criminal law defines crimes and fixes punishments for them. Crimes may be classified as felonies or misdemeanors. A felony refers to a serious crime, generally one punishable by death or by imprisonment for more than one year in a state prison or penitentiary. A misdemeanor refers to any minor offense, generally punishable by a fine or a short term, usually not to exceed one year, in a jail or workhouse. To prove a crime has been committed, it is usually necessary to prove the act itself *(actus reus)*—the elements of the crime—and prove the criminal mental state *(mens rea)*—intent to do wrong. In strict liability crimes, however, such as traffic violations, the defendant is liable regardless of intent.

Civil law refers to all noncriminal restrictions placed on individuals. It seeks not punishment, but restitution. The offense is called a tort. The distinctions between crimes and torts are as follows:

Crime	Tort
Public wrong	Private wrong
State prosecutes	Individual prosecutes
Seeks to punish	Seeks redress for injury
Criminal intent is required	Intent not necessary

Section 1983 of the U.S. Code, Title 42, stipulates that anyone acting under the authority of local or state law who violates another person's constitutional rights—even though they are upholding a law—can be sued.

Without means of enforcement, the great body of federal, state and municipal law would be meaningless. To ensure enforcement police have been given power and authority from local, state and federal sources. Police power is derived from the U.S. Constitution, U.S. Supreme Court decisions, federal statutes, state constitutions, state statutes, state court decisions and various municipal charters and ordinances. Police power ultimately rests with the people because their elected representatives create the laws that the police enforce. Police power is also restricted by the Constitution, the Fourteenth Amendment and the courts. Police have the power to enforce the laws so long as they do not violate the civil rights and liberties of any individual. The scales of justice symbolize the need to balance the needs of society with the needs of the individuals within that society. A similar balance is needed between the two models of criminal justice: crime control and due process of law.

DISCUSSION QUESTIONS

1. What specific restrictions are placed on police officers by the Bill of Rights?
2. Why has the Supreme Court said that state and federal governments can pass laws against carrying weapons when the Second Amendment specifically guarantees the right to bear arms?
3. Why were African Americans considered "unequal" until Lincoln was president? The Constitution existed; why did it not apply to African Americans?
4. What is the basic difference between civil rights and civil liberties?
5. In what well-known cases has the Fifth Amendment been repeatedly used?
6. What do police power and authority consist of?
7. The Declaration of Independence states that all people are created equal. Does this mean all people have the same opportunities?
8. If a person's reckless driving of a car injures another person who dies two weeks later as a result of the

injuries, could the reckless driver be charged with a crime, sued for a tort, or both? How would the type of charge affect the possible consequences faced by the reckless driver?

9. Should law enforcement officers be immune from tort action?

10. Should Fourth Amendment rights be extended to include general searches?

INFOTRAC COLLEGE EDITION ASSIGNMENTS

■ Use InfoTrac College Edition to help answer the Discussion Questions as appropriate.

■ Using InfoTrac College Edition, locate the review by Douglas Husak of "Philosophical Analysis and the Limits of the Substantive Criminal Law." This is particularly straightforward writing to students with no previous legal background. Pick one chapter and outline its contents. Be prepared to share your outline with the class.

■ Use InfoTrac College Edition to find *equality before the law* and to then locate *discrimination.* Outline how the various courts have viewed discrimination over the years.

INTERNET ASSIGNMENT

Use the key words *actus reus* to review what is called the "guilty mind" in criminal law. Write your own definition for *actus reus,* and be prepared to compare your definition with others in your class.

BOOK-SPECIFIC WEB SITE

The book-specific Web site at http://info .wadsworth.com/0534552803 hosts a variety of resources for students and instructors. Included are extended activities from each chapter in which students write a policy, use critical thinking skills to make choices in response to a given scenario, use InfoTrac College Edition with direct links to articles for participation in topical discussion forums, and analyze court cases using Web links for research. Many activities can be printed or emailed to instructors. Plus, cited cases with Web links, interactive key term FlashCards, PowerPoint presentations, chapter objectives, and an extensive collection of chapter-based Web links provide additional information and activities to include in the curriculum.

REFERENCES

Chudwin, Jeff. "Lawsuits, Training and Officer Safety." *Tactical Response,* Spring 2003, p.10.

Daniels, Wayne and Spratley, Lynette. "Lawsuit Defense: Protecting the Department from Litigation." *Law and Order,* June 2003, pp.54–59.

Gardner, T. J. and Anderson, T. M. *Criminal Law, Principles and Cases,* 8th ed. Belmont, CA: Wadsworth Publishing Company, 2003.

Griffith, David. "Swimming the Witch." *Police,* October 2002, p.6.

Harr, J. Scott and Hess, Kären M. *Constitutional Law and the Criminal Justice System,* 3rd ed. Belmont, CA: Wadsworth Thomson Learning, 2005.

Marx, Karl and Engles, Friedrich. *Manifesto of the Communist Party.* Chicago: Encyclopedia Britannica, Inc., 1984, p.419.

Myrdal, G. *The American Dilemma.* New York: Harper & Brothers, 1944.

Prosser, W. L. *Handbook of the Law of Torts,* 2nd ed. St. Paul, MN: West Publishing Company, 1955.

Rutledge, Devallis. "Chief Accountability." *Police,* October 2003, pp.94–96.

CASES CITED

Adickes v. Kress and Co., 398 U.S. 144, 151 (1970)

Bennis v. Michigan, 116 S.Ct. 994 (1996)

Berger v. New York, 388 U.S. 42 (1967)

Betts v. Brady, 316 U.S. 455 (1942)

Boyd v. United States, 116 U.S. 616 (1886)

Brady v. Maryland, 373 U.S. 83 (1963)

Brown v. Mississippi, 279 U.S. 278 (1936)

Byrd v. Brishke, 466 F.2d 6 (1972)

Chaplinsky v. New Hampshire, 315 U.S. 568 (1942)

Chimel v. California, 395 U.S. 752 (1969)

Furman v. Georgia, 408 U.S. 238 (1972)

Gideon v. Wainwright, 372 U.S. 355 (1963)

Gregg v. Georgia, 428 U.S. 153 (1976)

Griswold v. Connecticut, 381 U.S. 479 (1965)

Hampton v. United States, 425 U.S. 484 (1976)

Katz v. United States, 389 U.S. 347 (1967)

Mack v. United States (1997)—See *Printz v. United States*

Mapp v. Ohio, 367 U.S. 643 (1961)

Miranda v. Arizona, 384 U.S. 436 (1966)

Mugler v. Kansas, 123 U.S. 623 (1887)

New York v. Quarles, 104 S.Ct. 2626 (1984)

Palko v. Connecticut, 163 U.S. 537 (1937)

Powell v. Alabama, 287 U.S. 45 (1932)

Printz v. United States, 521 U.S. 898 (1997)

Rummel v. Estelle, 445 U.S. 263 (1980)

Schenck v. United States, 249 U.S. 47 (1919)

Shioutakon v. District of Columbia, 98 U.S.App.D.C. 371 (1956)

Stack v. Boyle, 342 U.S. 1 (1951)

Terry v. Ohio, 392 U.S. 1 (1968)

United States v. Cruickshank, 92 U.S. 542 (1876)

United States v. Russell, 411 U.S. 423 (1973)

United States v. Ursery, 59 Cr.L. 2191 (1996)

Weeks v. United States, 232 U.S. 383 (1914)

CHAPTER 3

Crime in the United States— Offenders and Victims

Something insidious has happened in America: crime has made victims of us all. Awareness of its danger affects the way we think, where we live, where we go, what we buy, how we raise our children, and the quality of our lives as we age. The specter of violent crime and the knowledge that, without warning, any person can be attacked or crippled, robbed, or killed, lurks at the fringes of consciousness.

—Statement of the Chairman, President's Task Force on Victims of Crime

DO YOU KNOW . . .

- What the three major sources of information about who commits crime are?
- What the eight Part I Index Crimes are?
- What other serious crimes present a challenge to law enforcement?
- What the most common types of white-collar crime are?
- What three key characteristics of computer-related crime are?
- What two characteristics of organized crime set it apart from other crimes committed by a group of individuals?
- What types of bias may be involved in hate crimes?
- What a ritualistic crime is and what must be investigated in it?
- What the classical and the positivist theories of crime causation state?
- What some causes of criminal behavior are?
- When violent offending is most likely to begin and with what group of offenders?
- What groups of people are most likely and least likely to become victims of crime?
- How crime affects its victims?
- What second victimization may occur?
- What victims' rights may involve them in the criminal justice system?

CAN YOU DEFINE?

aggravated assault	career criminal	delinquency	first-degree murder
aggravated rape	carjacking	delinquent	grand larceny
arson	chronic criminal	determinism	hate crime
assault	classical theory	direct victims	homicide
battery	cybercops	8% problem	identity theft
bias crime	cybercrime	embezzle	Index Crimes
burglary	dark figure of crime	fence	indirect victims

justifiable homicide	phishing	ritual	statutory rape
larceny/theft	pilfer	ritualistic crime	theft
malice	positivist theory	robbery	victim impact
manslaughter	premeditated	secondary victims	statement (VIS)
motor vehicle theft	primary victims	second-degree murder	victim statement of
murder	rape	simple assault	opinion (VSO)
negligent homicide	recidivist	simple rape	white-collar crime
organized crime	risk factors	status offenses	xenophobia
petty larceny			

Introduction

Crime is more than laws and cases. Crime involves hurtful acts committed by individuals against other individuals or their property. Until recently, however, crimes have been examined as acts against the state and prosecuted as such. This is changing. Whether it is called restorative justice, balanced justice or community justice, the system is beginning to view criminals, victims and society as all equally affected by criminal acts.

This chapter begins with a description of the major sources of information on crime and offers cautions on interpreting crime statistics. This is followed by an explanation of violent crimes including homicide, assault, rape and robbery; crimes against property, including burglary, larceny/theft, motor vehicle theft and arson; and crimes that are less serious in either their use of violence or the value of the property involved.

The chapter then discusses special challenges, including white-collar crime, computer-related crime, organized crime, bias crime and ritualistic crime. Next those who commit crimes are briefly described, including a discussion of why people commit crime, an examination of the biological and environmental causes of criminality, the problems of recidivism and the career criminal, as well as the juvenile offender.

The final major discussion is about those affected by crime—the victims— including an overview of victimization statistics and risk factors, followed by a discussion of a crime's effects on its victims and on indirect or secondary victims. Next the fear of victimization and how the criminal justice system may further victimize are examined. Then efforts to improve the treatment of victims, specific victims' rights during criminal justice system proceedings, the impact of victims' rights on offenders and the rest of the system and specific programs for victims are described. The chapter concludes with discussions of the role of the police in dealing with victims and police officers as victims themselves.

Sources of Information on Crime

Several sources of information about crime are available.

 The most frequently used sources of information about crime are the media, self-reporting surveys and official government statistics.

The Media

Much of what we know about crime comes from the media, which may over-dramatize and distort the true extent and seriousness of the problem. Study after study shows that the media focuses on crime and violence to the neglect of other aspects of law enforcement. In one study of over 1,000 articles, the "overwhelming majority dealt with crime" (*Marketing Community Policing in the News*, 2003, p.3.) As the adage states: "If it doesn't bleed, it doesn't lead."

In addition, researchers Chiricos and Eschholz (2002) found that the local television was more likely to portray blacks and Hispanics as criminal suspects rather than as victims or role models. In fact, they suggest: "Today's prevailing criminal predator has become a euphemism for young back male" (p.400). The media's focus on crime and violence and on minority offenders can produce a distorted picture of crime in the United States and should not be relied upon.

Further, researchers Weitzer and Kubrin (2004, p.497) found: "Many Americans report that they are fearful of crime. One frequently cited source of this fear is the mass media. The media, and local television news in particular, often report on incidents of crime, and do so in a selective and sometimes sensational manner."

Self-Report Surveys

Self-report surveys are typically conducted with school-age youths. For example, the *Sourcebook of Criminal Justice Statistics* includes such information as high school seniors reporting involvement in selected delinquent activities in the past 12 months, involvement with drugs and alcohol, and involvement in traffic violations.

Farrington et al. (2003, pp.933–934) studied the reliability of self-report surveys by comparing such reports with court data and conclude: "Criminal career research based on self-reports sometimes yields different conclusions compared with research based on official records." They found that self-reports produced a much higher incidence of criminal offending than did official (court) records, as shown in Table 3.1.

Official Sources

The two most frequently used official sources of crime data are the FBI's Uniform Crime Reports (UCR) and the Bureau of Justice Statistics National Crime Victimization Survey (NCVS).

The FBI's Uniform Crime Reports and NIBRS   Information about crime comes from statistics gathered from around the country. In 1930 Congress assigned the FBI to serve as a national clearinghouse for crime statistics. The FBI's National Crime Information Center (NCIC) instituted a program called the Uniform Crime Reports (UCR). The annual publication of this program, *Crime in the United States* (2003), reports that today, more than 17,000 law enforcement agencies, serving 93.4 percent of U.S. citizens, contribute data to the FBI either directly or through state UCR programs. The UCR divides offenses into two major categories: Part I and Part II **Index Crimes,** with Part I crimes being those that are most serious in either their use of violence or the value of the property involved.

 The eight Part I Index Crimes are murder, aggravated assault causing serious bodily harm, forcible rape, robbery, burglary, larceny/theft, motor vehicle theft and arson.

Table 3.1 Prevalence and Frequency of Offending: Court Records versus Self-Report

	Prevalence		Frequency	
	Court	*Self-Report*	*Court*	*Self-Report*
Age				
11	1.7	28.4	1.1	2.9
12	2.1	27.9	2.1	4.6
13	8.0	41.5	2.8	11.6
14	10.6	46.4	2.8	13.5
15	13.1	47.6	3.1	16.8
16	13.6	51.3	2.2	18.3
17	12.7	61.1	2.4	21.8
Total	34.0	85.9	4.6	49.2
Offense Type				
Burglary	4.7	22.3	1.6	3.2
Vehicle theft	23.8	33.1	1.8	5.9
Larceny	25.6	66.1	2.0	11.6
Robbery	3.3	8.6	1.2	5.6
Assault	12.7	61.3	2.4	11.4
Vandalism	8.4	47.9	1.9	8.2
Marijuana use	1.8	49.1	1.2	29.9
Drug selling	3.9	21.7	1.6	28.8
Property	27.5	71.8	3.6	14.3
Aggressive	17.4	70.4	2.9	16.1
Drug	4.5	50.8	1.8	41.1

Notes: Prevalence = % offending.

Frequency = Average offenses per offender.

SOURCE: David P. Farrington; Darrick Jolliffe; J. David Hawkins; Richard F. Catalano; Karl G. Hill; and Rick Kosterman. "Comparing Delinquency Careers in Court Records and Self-Reports." *Criminology,* August 2003, p. 941. Reprinted by permission.

A summary of the figures for the Part I crimes committed in 2003 is depicted in the Crime Clock (Figure 3.1). The Crime Clock should be viewed with care. Being the most aggregate representation of UCR data, it is designed to convey the annual reported crime experience by showing the relative frequency of occurrence of the Index Crimes. This graphic does not imply a regularity in the commission of the Part I offenses; rather it represents the annual ratio of crime to fixed time intervals. Figure 3.2 shows the distribution of the Part I offenses. The most recent UCR figures are available online at http://www.fbi .gov/ucr/ucr.htm.

The Uniform Crime Reports program is undergoing major revision, moving from its current system of summary counts to a more comprehensive, detailed reporting system, the National Incident-Based Reporting System (NIBRS). This

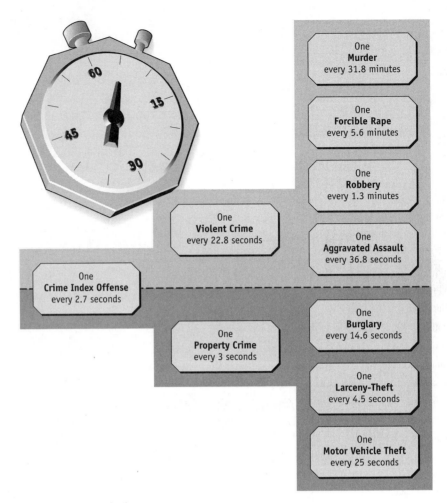

Figure 3.1   Crime Clock

SOURCE: *Crime in the United States, 2003.* Washington, DC: FBI, 2003, p.6.

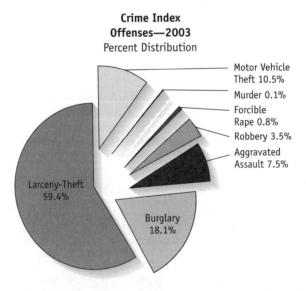

Figure 3.2   Crime Index Offenses, Percent Distribution[1] 2003

[1]Due to rounding, the percentages do not add to 100.0.

SOURCE: *Crime in the United States.* Washington, DC: FBI, 2003, p.11.

system is intended to replace the traditional eight offenses of the FBI Part I Crime Index with detailed incident information on 46 offenses representing 22 categories of crimes (see Table 3.2). According to McEwen (2003, p.402):

> Compared with the summary UCR statistics, NIBRS provides more detailed data. Crime analysis is enhanced by having details on individual crimes that can then be analyzed and summarized in a variety of different ways. NIBRS also expanded the number of reportable offenses in 22 categories, known as Group A offenses, to 46. The expansion to 46 crime classifications provides a means for police departments to analyze virtually every problem that might arise, including offenses related to domestic violence, use of guns, hate crimes and terrorism.

Table 3.2 The National Incident-Based Reporting System Group A Offenses

Arson	Negligent manslaughter
Assault offenses	Justifiable homicide
Aggravated assault	Kidnapping/abduction
Simple assault	Larceny/theft offenses
Intimidation	Pocket picking
Bribery	Purse snatching
Burglary/breaking and entering	Shoplifting
Counterfeiting/forgery	Theft from building
Destruction/damage/vandalism of property	Theft from coin-operated machines
Drug/narcotic offenses	Theft from motor vehicle
Drug/narcotic violations	Theft of motor vehicle parts/accessories
Drug equipment violations	All other larceny
Embezzlement	Motor vehicle theft
Extortion/blackmail	Pornography/obscene material
Fraud offenses	Prostitution offenses
False pretenses/swindle/confidence game	Prostitution
Credit card/ATM fraud	Assisting or promoting prostitution
Impersonation	Robbery
Welfare fraud	Sex offenses, forcible
Wire fraud	Forcible rape
Gambling offenses	Forcible sodomy
Betting/wagering	Sexual assault with an object
Operating/promoting/assisting gambling	Forcible fondling
Gambling equipment violations	Sex offenses, nonforcible
Sports tampering	Stolen property offenses
Homicide offenses	Weapon law violations
Murder/nonnegligent manslaughter	

SOURCE: Brian A. Reaves. *Using NIBRS Data to Analyze Violent Crime.* Washington, DC: Bureau of Justice Statistics Technical Report, October 1993, p.1.

Even though the NIBRS program offers expanded capabilities, it has been slow to be accepted at the state and local levels. Cost is a major consideration. . . . Other factors center on the differences between the two systems. The UCR has a hierarchy rule that allows for the recording of only the most serious offense in an incident, whereas NIBRS has provisions for recording all offenses in an incident. (For example, if an individual were beaten and robbed, the UCR would record one offense—assault—and NIBRS would record both offenses.) Adopting NIBRS can therefore have an impact on local crime statistics.

Departments who switch to NIBRS will doubtless see a significant increase in crime *statistics*, while actual crime may, in fact, be decreasing.

The Bureau of Justice Statistics National Crime Victimization Survey

The Bureau of Justice Statistics (BJS) National Crime Victimization Survey (NCVS) began in 1973 and, as previously described, gathers information on personal crime experience through interviews with approximately 160,000 people age 12 years and older in 86,000 households nationwide. The survey collects data on crimes against individuals and households, regardless of whether they were reported to law enforcement. The data from this representative sample is then extrapolated to estimate the proportion of each crime type reported to law enforcement and details reasons given for reporting or not reporting.

The NCVS collects detailed information on the frequency and nature of the crimes of rape, personal robbery, aggravated and simple assault, household burglary, personal and household theft, and motor vehicle theft. The survey provides information about victims' age, sex, race, ethnicity, marital status, income and educational level; their offenders' sex, race, approximate age and victim-offender relationship; and the crimes: time and place of occurrence, use of weapons, nature of injury and economic consequences. Questions also cover the victims' experiences with the criminal justice system, self-protective measures used and possible substance abuse by offenders.

BJS statisticians Rennison and Rand (2003, p.1) report that residents age 12 and older experienced 23 million violent and property victimizations in 2002, continuing a downward trend that began in 1994.

The UCR and NCVS Compared The UCR and NCVS differ significantly. As noted, the NCVS projects crime levels from a selected source of information and reports a substantially higher number of crimes than those reported in the UCR. Some analysts believe neither report is accurate and that crime is two to five times higher than either source reports.

The UCR captures crimes reported to law enforcement but excludes simple assaults. The NCVS includes crimes both reported and not reported to law enforcement but excludes homicide, arson, commercial crimes and crimes against children under age 12 (all included in the UCR program). Even when the same crimes are included in the UCR and NCVS, the definitions vary.

Another difference is how rate measures are presented. The UCR crime rates are largely per capita (number of crimes per 100,000 persons), whereas the NCVS rates are per household (number of crimes per 1,000 households). Because the number of households may not grow at the same rate as the total population,

Table 3.3   A Comparison of the UCR and the NCVS

	Uniform Crime Reports	*National Crime Victimization Survey*
Offenses measured:	Homicide Rape Robbery (personal and commercial) Assault (aggravated) Burglary (commercial and household) Larceny (commercial and household) Motor vehicle theft Arson	Rape Robbery (personal) Assault (aggravated and simple) Household burglary Larceny (personal and household) Motor vehicle theft
Scope:	Crimes reported to the police in most jurisdictions; considerable flexibility in developing small-area data	Crimes both reported and not reported to police; all data are available for a few large geographic areas
Collection method:	Police department reports to FBI or to centralized state agencies that then report to FBI	Survey interviews; periodically measures the total number of crimes committed by asking a national sample of 49,000 households encompassing 101,000 persons age 12 and over about their experiences as victims of crime during a specified period
Kinds of information:	In addition to offense counts, provides information on crime clearances, persons arrested, persons charged, law enforcement officers killed and assaulted and characteristics of homicide victims	Provides details about victims (such as age, race, sex, education, income and whether the victim and offender were related to each other) and about crimes (such as time and place of occurrence, whether or not reported to police, use of weapons, occurrence of injury and economic consequences)
Sponsor:	Department of Justice Federal Bureau of Investigation	Department of Justice Bureau of Justice Statistics

SOURCE: Bureau of Justice Statistics. *Report to the Nation on Crime and Justice,* 2nd ed. Washington, DC: U.S. Department of Justice, 1988, p.11.

trend data for rates measured by the two programs may not be compatible. Table 3.3 compares UCR and NCVS data gathering.

A Caution   Be mindful when interpreting official statistics that they reflect only reported crimes, and that these reports are voluntary and vary in accuracy and completeness. In addition not all police departments submit crime reports, and federal crimes are not included. Furthermore it is estimated that less than half the crimes committed are reported to the police. The true number of crimes, called the **dark figure of crime,** is unknown. Despite these difficulties, police departments make frequent use of the information from the UCR program.

Another caution: Any large-scale data collection program has many possible sources of error. For example in the UCR program, a police officer may classify a crime incorrectly; and in the NCVS, a Census Bureau interviewer may incorrectly record a victim's response. Crime data is also affected by how victims perceive and recall events. In addition clerical errors may occur at any stage. Both programs have extensive accuracy checks to minimize errors.

Regardless of the format used to compile information on crime, the need exists for crime to first be defined and classified.

Classification and Definitions of Major Crimes

The FBI classifies the Index Crimes as violent crimes, formerly crimes against persons, and property crimes.

Violent Crimes

The four Part I violent crimes are murder (homicide), assault, rape and robbery.

Murder (Homicide)   **Murder** or **homicide** is defined in the UCR program as the willful (nonnegligent) killing of one human by another. The generally recognized levels of homicide are (1) first-degree, (2) second-degree, (3) manslaughter (or nonnegligent manslaughter) and (4) negligent homicide. The first three categories are classified as felonies. Negligent homicide, however, is usually a misdemeanor.

First-degree murder is the willful, deliberate and **premeditated** (planned) taking of another person's life. A homicide that occurs during the commission or attempted commission of arson, robbery, rape or burglary is also usually classified as first-degree murder. **Second-degree murder** is murder that is *not* premeditated but the intent to kill is present. This charge often results from killings that do not involve weapons.

Manslaughter is differentiated from murder in that the element of **malice** is absent; the death was accidental with no original intent, hatred, ill will or disregard for the lives of others. In many states manslaughter is classified as either involuntary or voluntary. *Involuntary* manslaughter involves negligence, such as deaths resulting from automobile accidents. In contrast *voluntary* manslaughter, sometimes called second-degree manslaughter, is intentionally killing someone without previous malice but in the sudden heat of passion due to adequate provocation. For example a husband who kills another man he found in bed with his wife might be found guilty of voluntary manslaughter. Many instances of self-defense are also defined as voluntary manslaughter.

Negligent homicide refers to an accidental death that results from the reckless operation of a motor vehicle, boat, plane or firearm. **Justifiable homicide** includes killing in self-defense or in the defense of another person if the victim's actions and capability present imminent danger of serious injury or death. This classification includes killing an enemy during war, capital punishment, death caused by a public officer while carrying out a court order and deaths caused by police officers.

Assault   **Assault** is the unlawful attack by one person on another to inflict severe bodily injury. Assaults are frequently committed in conjunction with rape and robbery. Several states have two distinct crimes, assault and battery. Where two crimes exist, assault refers to the threats made, whereas **battery** refers to any physical contact that occurs. If only one crime exists, it is usually assault, and battery is included within that crime. Assault may be aggravated or simple.

Aggravated assault is an unlawful attack on a person to inflict severe bodily injury or death. Assault can safely be classified as *aggravated* if a gun, knife or other weapon is used and serious personal injury is inflicted. **Simple assault,** the most frequent type, has no intent of serious injury. It may or may not be accompanied by a threat. Hands, fists or feet are the most commonly used weapons. Most simple assaults result from emotional conflicts and are classified as misdemeanors.

Rape   **Rape** is having sexual intercourse through the use or threat of force. Rape may be aggravated, simple or statutory. **Aggravated rape** involves using force, threats of immediate use of force or taking advantage of an unconscious or help-less victim or a victim incapable of consent because of mental illness or a defect reasonably known to the attacker. **Simple rape** involves misleading a victim about the nature of the act being performed; for example having intercourse under the guise of a medical examination or treatment or knowingly destroying the victim's will to resist by use of a drug or intoxicant. **Statutory rape** involves sexual intercourse with a minor, with or without consent.

Robbery   **Robbery** is stealing or taking anything of value from the care, custody or control of a person by force or threat of force. Assault to commit robbery and attempts to commit robbery are included in the definition. Many states divide robbery into degrees.

This violent crime often results in injury to the victim. In half of the cases, rob-bery is accompanied by an assault upon the victim. Sometimes labeled as the most brutal and vicious of all crimes, robbery occurs in all parts of the country; its vic-tims are people of all ages, incomes and backgrounds. Robbers may shoot, assault or torture their victims to find where valuables are located. Many victims who have refused to cooperate, and even some who have, have been ruthlessly killed.

The preferred weapon of most robbers is the handgun. Other weapons used include knives, acids, baseball bats and explosives. Armed robbers frequently attack drugstores (often for narcotics), supermarkets, liquor stores, jewelry stores, gas stations, banks, residential homes, cab drivers and pedestrians.

A new form of robbery appeared late in 1990—**carjacking,** which is taking a motor vehicle by force or threat of force. Congress enacted the Carjacking Cor-rections Act of 1996 to establish strict penalties for persons convicted of carjack-ing, with sentences up to 25 years in prison for cases involving "serious bodily injury" to a victim.

Crimes against Property

The four Part I Index Crimes against property are burglary, larceny/theft, motor vehicle theft and arson. Although these crimes do not usually involve violence, they can leave their victims feeling violated.

Burglary   **Burglary** is unlawful entrance into a building to commit theft or another felony. Burglary has three subclassifications: forcible entry, unlawful entry where no force is used and attempted forcible entry.

Larceny/Theft   **Larceny/theft** is unlawfully taking and removing another's per-sonal property with the intent of permanently depriving the owner of the prop-erty. It includes shoplifting, pocket picking, purse snatching, thefts from motor vehicles, thefts of motor vehicle parts and accessories, and bicycle thefts. The cat-egory does not include embezzlement, "con" games, forgery, passing worthless checks or motor vehicle theft.

Larceny/theft may be classified as either a misdemeanor or a felony. It differs from robbery in that it does not involve force, threats of force or violence. The severity of punishment usually depends on the value and type of property taken, whether it was taken from a building or a person and the specific circumstances of the case.

Some states categorize larceny into degrees. **Grand** and **petty larceny** are common identifications for the value of property taken and punishment imposed. First-, second- and third-degree larceny also indicate a certain minimum value of the property taken and various degrees of punishment. The most common type of theft is the theft of items from motor vehicles and motor vehicle parts and accessories, such as cell phones, stereos and CD/tape players, pagers, CB radios, clothing and photography equipment.

Other forms of larceny are thefts from underground garages where maintenance equipment, such as lawnmowers, snow blowers, lawn hoses and fertilizers, is the target. Bicycles are also targets for thieves. Thefts from coin-operated vending machines, pocket picking, purse snatching and shoplifting are other forms of larceny/theft.

Theft can refer to several different crimes, depending upon state statutes. It can describe a type of larceny, a theft from the person, a theft by force or a burglary. The most commonly referred-to forms of theft are summarized in Table 3.4.

One of the country's fastest-growing crimes is **identity theft,** a crime involving misappropriation of names, Social Security numbers, credit card numbers or other pieces of personal information for fraudulent purposes (Fleck, 2004, p.3). Wexler (2002, p.29) calls identity theft a "national epidemic" affecting millions of consumers and costing billions of dollars. In December 2003, President Bush signed into law the Fair and Accurate Credit Transactions Act, increasing the penalties for identity theft and lengthening the statute of limitations for violations of the consumer credit law.

Motor Vehicle Theft   **Motor vehicle theft** is the unlawful taking or stealing of a motor vehicle without the owner's authority or permission. This definition excludes those who have lawful access to the vehicle and take it for temporary use. Motor vehicles include automobiles, trucks, buses, motorcycles, motorized boats and aircraft.

The economic impact of motor vehicle theft can be great, with drivers absorbing such losses through higher insurance premiums. It is difficult to obtain a conviction for auto theft unless witnesses see the person drive the vehicle away and make positive identification. It is also difficult to prove the suspect intended to permanently deprive the rightful owner of its use. Therefore the category of "Unlawful Use of a Motor Vehicle" was created to apply to suspects who merely have possession of a vehicle reported stolen.

One motive for auto theft is joyriding—the car is stolen, taken for a ride and then abandoned. Joyriding is often a separate charge where intent to permanently deprive is not in evidence. Autos are also stolen for revenge, for transportation, for commercial use and for use in committing other crimes, such as kidnapping, burglary and bank robbery. Autos are stolen and stripped for parts such as transmissions, engines and seats. Automobiles are also stolen, modified, given altered serial numbers and fraudulent titles and sold to an unsuspecting public.

Arson   **Arson** is intentionally damaging or destroying or attempting to damage or destroy by means of fire or explosion the property of another without the consent of the owner or one's own property, with or without the intent to defraud. It is a felony in all 50 states. Arson has increased more than 400 percent in the past 10 years. An estimated 1,000 people, including 45 firefighters, die each year in arson fires, and 10,000 people are injured annually. Annual damage estimates are

Table 3.4   Forms of Taking and Types of Theft

Shoplifting (retail theft) or price altering
- Shoplifting—the most common form of theft in retail stores—is the taking by concealment to avoid payment for goods.
- Price altering avoids payment of the full price of an object by lowering the amount on the price tag.

Taking by employee, bailee or trustee
- Employee theft of money and other objects causes large losses in business places.
- Embezzlement of funds or negotiable securities that are in the custody of employees, bailees or trustees.

Snatch and run
- The taking is observed, and the offender flees to avoid apprehension.

Till tap
- Thief opens cash register unobserved and takes cash and coins.
- While store employee has cash drawer open, money is grabbed and the thief flees (snatch and run).

Taking by trick, deception or fraud (stings, scams or swindles)
- Con games and operations.
- Deceptions and tricks to obtain property illegally.
- Obtaining property by false pretense.

Taking by force, or the threat of the use of force (robbery)

Taking during a burglary (trespass with intent to steal or commit a felony)

Taking by extortion (threats of future violence or threats to reveal embarrassing information—blackmail)

Taking from a person
- Purse snatching (a form of snatch and run).
- Pickpocketing.
- Rolling a drunk (taking from person incapacitated by alcohol, drugs or other means).
- Taking from a corpse.

Taking of lost or mislaid goods or money

Taking of objects or money delivered by mistake
- Example: a check for too much money is mailed to a person by mistake.

Looting
- Taking property from or near a building damaged, destroyed or left unoccupied by tornado, fire, physical disaster, riot, bombing, earthquake and so on.

Taking by failure to return a leased or rented object
- Example: failure to return a rented car or videotape within the time specified by state statutes or city ordinance.

Taking by illegal entry into locked coin box
- Vending machine, pay telephone, parking meter and so on.

Smash and run
- A store or other window is broken, and after snatching objects, the thief runs to avoid apprehension.
- Women drivers waiting at stoplights are sometimes subjected to this tactic. The thief breaks the car window, takes the woman's purse from the front seat and runs.[1]

Taking by illegally obtaining or using information
- Such as in the "insider trading" scandals. See the 1987 U.S. Supreme Court case of *Carpenter v. United States,* 108 S.Ct. 316. One of the defendants in the case was the coauthor of a *Wall Street Journal* column.

Taking by illegal use of a credit card or credit card number

Taking from a person with a superior right of possession
- People may acquire a superior right of possession over the owner of property because of a bailment, pledge or contract. State criminal codes may make taking from a person with a superior right of possession a crime.

Theft by possession of stolen property
- See 832 P.2d 337 (Idaho, 1992), 473 N.W.2d 84 (Nebraska, 1991) and 419 S.E.2d 759 (Georgia, 1992).

Ordinary theft
- Taking occurs observed or unobserved by owner or other people.

[1]The "bump" technique is also used. An expensive car with only a driver occupant is usually picked as the victim. While the victim is waiting at a stoplight, the victim's car is bumped intentionally. When the victim gets out of the car to view damages, one of the thieves distracts him or her while the other thief sneaks around to get into the victim's car. Because the victim generally leaves the keys in the ignition, the thief drives off in the victim's car. The other thief jumps in his or her car and also speeds away, leaving the victim stranded.

SOURCE: Thomas J. Gardner and Terry M. Anderson. *Criminal Law,* 8th ed. Belmont, CA: Wadsworth Publishing Company, 2003, p.359. Reprinted by permission. All rights reserved.

as high as $15 billion. One of the most serious problems often encountered in arson investigations is the joint jurisdiction of firefighters and law enforcement officers. All too frequently this results in duplication of effort and inefficiency.

Part II Index Crimes

The Part II offenses consist of several other crimes that can be either misdemeanors or felonies. They include counterfeiting, curfew violations (juveniles), disorderly conduct, driving under the influence (DUI), drug abuse violations, drunkenness, embezzlement, forgery, fraud (confidence games, etc.), gambling, liquor law violations (bootlegging, etc.), loitering (juveniles), offenses against the family and children (child abuse, neglect, nonsupport), other assaults (intimidation, coercion, hazing, etc.), prostitution and commercialized vice, runaways (juveniles), sex offenses (except forcible rape, prostitution and commercialized vice), stolen property (buying, receiving, possessing), vagrancy, vandalism, weapons violations (carrying, possessing, etc.) and many other offenses (bigamy, contempt of court; the list goes on and on).

Other Crimes

Many crimes do not fall neatly into the classifications just discussed.

Other serious crimes include white-collar crime, computer-related crime, organized crime, bias or hate crime and ritualistic crime.

White-Collar Crime   **White-collar crime** is occupational or business-related crime. The Part I offense of larceny/theft and several Part II offenses can also be classified as white-collar crimes. These crimes often involve billions of dollars and pose an extremely difficult challenge to law enforcement officers. In recent years, several agencies, including the FBI, U.S. Secret Service and American Society for Industrial Security (ASIS), have renamed this category of crime to reflect a change in scope, now referring to it as *economic crime*. To help fight white-collar crime the National White Collar Crime Center (NWCCC) bridges the gap between local and state criminal justice agencies and also links criminal justice agencies across international borders.

White-collar crime includes (1) credit card and check fraud including identity theft; (2) securities theft and fraud; (3) insurance fraud; (4) consumer fraud, illegal competition and deceptive practices; (5) bankruptcy fraud; (6) embezzlement and pilferage; (7) bribes, kickbacks and payoffs; and (8) receiving stolen property.

Unauthorized use of checks and credit cards (found, stolen or counterfeited) results in losses of millions of dollars annually. Securities theft and fraud may be perpetrated by clerks acting independently, by individuals who rob messengers and steal from the mails or by well-organized rings. Most securities thefts involve the cooperation of dishonest employees ("inside" people) and may involve counterfeit and bogus securities as well.

Insurance fraud losses lead to higher premiums for consumers. Because insurance is important to businesses and individuals, false claims for life, health and accident benefits affect almost everyone. Especially prevalent are fraudulent auto accident claims seeking compensation for treatments for personal injury, time lost from work and automobile repairs.

Consumer fraud, illegal competition and deceptive practices include thousands of different schemes to defraud the public, including offers for "free" articles, advice, vacations, mailing or unordered merchandise, phony contests, recommendations for unneeded repairs, "going-out-of-business" sales, unqualified correspondence schools and price fixing. Bankruptcy fraud, also called planned bankruptcy, scam or bust-out, involves purchasing merchandise on credit from many different suppliers, selling the merchandise for cash that is "hidden" and then filing for bankruptcy and not paying the creditors.

Embezzlement and pilferage, both forms of theft, are considered by many businesses to be their most serious problem. People **embezzle** when they steal or use for themselves money or property entrusted to them. To **pilfer** is basically the same, but on a much smaller scale. Cumulatively the losses from pilferage may be much greater than what some other dishonest employee might embezzle. Equally dishonest is unauthorized use of company equipment, personnel and time.

Bribes, kickbacks and payoffs are pervasive in the business world and are often used to obtain new clients, to keep old clients, to influence decisions or to obtain favors. They can involve anyone from the custodian to the company president, and they can occur in any aspect of a company's operation.

Receiving stolen property, although classified as a white-collar crime, often occurs in conjunction with such crimes as robbery and burglary. The person who buys and sells stolen property is of vital importance to most burglars, robbers and hijackers. Criminals depend on a **fence** (a professional receiver and seller of stolen property) to convert stolen goods into cash.

Computer-Related Crime Computer crime, also referred to as **cybercrime,** is a rapidly increasing threat to American businesses and consumers:

> Computer criminals are no longer masterminds, just crooks and creeps doing what crooks and creeps do. Today and every day thousands of people worldwide are being victimized by computer crime. . . . The computer crime hit parade includes distribution of child pornography, credit card fraud, industrial espionage, harassment, breaking and entering (hacking), solicitation of prostitution, child molestation ("traveler" cases), malicious mischief, and property destruction (viruses), and that barely scratches the surface (Griffith, 2003, p.18).

Martin (2003, p.52) also notes: "Criminals have embraced the convenience of computers, printers, faxes, personal digital assistants (PDAs), and cell phones right along with the rest of us." And Thomas (2003, p.14) cautions: "The use of computer networks and encryption technology by dangerous criminals, including terrorists, presents significant challenges for the FBI and the law enforcement community. Unless law enforcement enhances its technical ability to gather and process computer evidence, investigators and prosecutors will lack information needed to prevent terrorist acts and solve crimes."

Rantala (2004, p.1) reports: "Among 198 businesses responding to a 2001 pilot survey, 74% reported being a victim of cybercrime." According to Rogers (2003, pp.22–23): "As a result of 9/11, law enforcement has spent millions of dollars on conventional physical homeland defense. Computer security experts speculate the law enforcement community is still unprepared for a cyber-attack." Rantala (p.1) also notes that: "A cyber-attack may be just as dangerous as a physical attack."

Compounding the challenge is the fact that most computer crime is not reported. As Johnston (2002, p.52) notes, only 36 percent of the companies victimized reported the intrusions to law enforcement agencies. (In the survey, 85 percent detected computer security breaches within the last 12 months—from March 2001.) The FBI estimates that electronic crimes are running at least $10 billion a year.

Most big corporations have been victims of cybercrime, from employees' snooping through confidential files to criminals stealing trade secrets. The most common crimes are credit card fraud, telecommunications fraud, employee use of computers for personal reasons, unauthorized access to confidential files and unlawful copying of copyrighted or licensed software. While a large portion of cybercrime is committed internally by employees, companies and private users are finding themselves increasingly vulnerable to outside hackers. The estimated worldwide damage caused by the "I Love You" virus was $10 billion. The crime also challenged law enforcement with jurisdiction and prosecution issues, as the perpetrators were operating in one country while most of the actual victims resided in another country.

Computer fraud may involve the input data, the output data, computer time or the program itself. *Input data* may be altered; for example fictitious suppliers may be entered, figures may be changed or data may be removed. Some schools have experienced difficulties with student grades being illegally changed. *Output data* may be obtained by unauthorized persons through such means as wiretapping, electromagnetic pickup or theft of data sheets. *Computer time* may be taken for personal use, an example of pilferage. Some employees have even used their employer's hardware and company time to set up their own computer services for personal profit. The *computer program* itself might be tampered with to add costs to purchased items or to establish a double set of records.

One area of computer crime that is becoming more publicized is sex-related computer crimes, including child pornography. Albinsson (2002, p.40) notes: "New technology has proved both a blessing and a curse in the fight against child sexual abuse, making the production and distribution of pornography easier than ever before, but giving authorities important tools to hunt down offenders and trace victims."

A study by the National Center for Missing and Exploited Children (Wolak et al., 2003, p.vii) found that an estimated 2,577 arrests for Internet crimes against minors were made during the 12-month period starting July 1, 2000. They categorized the sex crimes against minors into three mutually exclusive types: (1) Internet crimes against identified victims (39 percent of arrests), (2) Internet solicitations to undercover law enforcement posing as minors (25 percent of arrests) and (3) possession, distribution or trading of Internet child pornography (36 percent of arrests). The study (p.7) found that almost all offenders were male (99 percent), non-Hispanic white (92 percent), older than 25 (86 percent) and acted alone in the crimes they committed (97 percent). Few (11 percent) were known to be violent.

No matter what type of computer crime is involved, some common characteristics are usually found.

 Characteristics of computer-related crime include:
- Computer crimes are relatively easy to commit and difficult to detect.
- Most computer crimes are committed by "insiders."
- Most computer crimes are not prosecuted.

Scott Peterson confers with his defense attorneys during his double murder trial in Redwood City, California, in July 2004. Peterson was found guilty of murdering his wife Laci and their unborn son on Christmas Eve of 2002 and was sentenced to death.

Unfortunately, few computer crime specialists patrol cyberspace. Those who do have been dubbed cybercops. **Cybercops** are highly trained police officers who investigate technological crime, and the demand for such training is growing exponentially.

Other sites and services allow computer-crime victims themselves to get more directly involved in the war on cybercrime. One example is the Internet Fraud Complaint Center (IFCC), created by the FBI and the National White Collar Crime Center (NWCCC). A dedicated Web site at http://www .ifccfbi.gov allows consumers and small businesses to file Internet fraud complaints online with the IFCC. Sometimes fraud is perpetrated by organized crime figures.

Organized Crime   Organized crime goes by many names—the mob, the syndicate, the rackets, the Mafia and La Cosa Nostra. A basic definition of **organized crime** is a continuing criminal conspiracy seeking high profits with an organized structure that uses fear and corruption.

 Organized crime is distinct from other forms of crime in that it is characterized by corruption and enforcement powers.

These features make organized crime especially threatening, not only to the police, but to our entire democratic process.

Organized crime is particularly challenging to law enforcement because of the numerous types of groups involved. The President's Commission on Organized Crime has identified 11 different groups: La Cosa Nostra (Italian), outlaw motorcycle gangs, prison gangs, Triads and Tongs (Chinese), Vietnamese gangs, Yakuza (Japanese), Marielitos (Cuban), Colombian cocaine rings, Irish, Russian and Canadian.

Despite the various and distinct origins of organized crime groups, many of them participate in the same activities, including heavy involvement in gambling, drugs, prostitution, pornography, loan sharking and infiltration of legitimate businesses, in fact, in anything that offers the potential for high profits. For example, La Cosa Nostra (LCN), the most well-known organized crime faction currently operating in the United States, is involved in drug trafficking, extortion, illegal gambling, money laundering, murder, obstruction of justice and a variety of financial fraud schemes.

Russian organized crime (ROC) is becoming a growing threat in the United States and may present law enforcement with its toughest challenge yet. ROC engages in money-laundering facilities and trafficking in humans (women and children sold as sex slaves and indentured household servants). According to Finckenauer and Voronin (2001, p.26):

> The threat and use of violence is a defining characteristic of Russian organized crime in the United States. . . . The common use of violence is not surprising, since extortion and protection rackets are such a staple of Russian criminal activity. Contract murders, kidnappings, and business arson have all been employed by Russian organized crime. Arson is used against businesses that refuse to pay extortion money. . . . [ROC is also] extensively engaged in a broad array of frauds and scams, including health care fraud, insurance scams, stick frauds, antiquities swindles, forgery and fuel tax evasion schemes. Recently, for example, Russians have become the main purveyors of credit-card fraud in the United States.

Zhang and Chin (2002, p.737) describe Chinese human-smuggling organizations: "Contrary to widely held conceptions about Chinese organized crime, most alien smugglers are otherwise ordinary citizens whose familial networks and fortuitous social contacts have enabled them to pool resources to transport human cargoes around the world. With the exception of a shared commitment to making money, little holds them together. These organizations have clear divisions of labor with limited hierarchical structures."

Most organized crime groups have their hands in the drug trade. For many such organizations, drug trafficking is their economic mainstay. Another challenge for law enforcement is found in the partnering of different organizations for profit in illegal narcotics. In addition, Hansell (2004, p.D1) reports that Internet fraud, called **phishing,** is rising and is linked to organized crime groups. He also reports that Eastern European crime gangs are likely to be behind the scams—most frequently some form of identity theft.

Many contend that the public and government play active roles in perpetuating organized crime and, in fact, are sometimes directly responsible for creating opportunities that allow such enterprises to thrive. Politicians and the citizens they serve must take an active stance against organized crime by discontinuing their associations with these entities. Research by Sung (2004, p.111) suggests that state and economic failures contribute to predatory organized crime: "Failure of the state to deliver key political goods such as security, justice and stability encourages criminal groups to perform state functions." Further, according to Sung: "Poor economic outcomes such as high unemployment, low standards of living and a reliance on an underground economy stimulates the growth of criminal syndicates as suppliers of demanded goods, materials and jobs." Yet another area of concern for law enforcement is the dramatic increase in bias or hate crimes.

Hate Crimes   The FBI defines a **bias** or **hate crime** as a criminal offense committed against a person, property or society that is motivated, in whole or in part, by the offender's bias against a race, religion, disability, sexual orientation or ethnic/national origin. According to Fantino (2003, p.36): "Hate-motivated crime has many faces and wide-reaching consequences. In most cases it represents the voice of intolerance and bigotry intended to harm and intimidate someone because of that person's race, ethnicity, national origin, religion, sexual orientation or disability." Bouman (2003, p.23) contends: "Hate/bias crimes destroy communities, as well as hoard resources from law enforcement agencies." Hate crimes may also be seen as a form of **xenophobia,** the fear and hatred of strangers or foreigners.

 Hate crimes may be motivated by bias against a person's race, religion, disability, sexual orientation or ethnicity.

FBI statistics indicate race is the most frequent motivation of hate crime, followed by religion, as shown in Table 3.5. In fact, racial prejudice motivated almost half of the 7,462 hate crime incidents reported to the FBI in 2002.

Schafer and Navarro (2003, p.1) suggest: "Hate, a complex subject, divides into two general categories: rational and irrational. Unjust acts inspire rational hate. Hatred of a person based on race, religion, sexual orientation, ethnicity or national origin constitutes irrational hate." They (p.4) also note: "Empirical observations show that hate groups go through seven stages in the hate process." These stages are illustrated in Figure 3.3.

Hate crimes differ from other attacks on people or property in some important ways, especially their viciousness, as shown in Table 3.6.

Offenses frequently involved in bias crimes include cross burning, swastika painting, bombing, hanging in effigy, disturbing a public meeting, graffiti, obscene letters or phone calls or face-to-face oral abuse. As with other types of crimes, the Internet is being used by hate groups to build a sense of community through encrypted messages, chat rooms, e-mail communication and Web sites.

One well-publicized crime of hate was the savage beating and death of Matthew Shepard, an openly gay student at the University of Wyoming. Just 21 years old, Shepard was brutally beaten, tied to a wooden fence miles out of town and left to die alone, allegedly by two men with strong antihomosexual convictions. Another widely publicized hate crime was the murder of James Byrd, Jr., an African American who was hitchhiking home. Three white men picked him up but instead of giving him a ride home, took him to a wooded area where they beat him unconscious. They then chained him to the back of their truck and dragged him several miles, his right arm and head being torn from his body in the process.

Table 3.5 Incidents, Offenses, Victims and Known Offenders by Bias Motivation, 2002

Bias Motivation	Incidents	Offenses	Victims[1]	Known offenders[2]
Total	7,462	8,832	9,222	7,314
Single-Bias Incidents	7,459	8,825	9,211	7,311
Race:	3,642	4,393	4,580	4,011
Anti-White	719	888	910	1,064
Anti-Black	2,486	2,967	3,076	2,510
Anti-American Indian/Alaskan Native	62	65	72	52
Anti-Asian/Pacific Islander	217	268	280	242
Anti-Multiple Races, Group	158	202	242	143
Religion:	1,426	1,576	1,659	568
Anti-Jewish	931	1,039	1,084	317
Anti-Catholic	53	58	71	21
Anti-Protestant	55	57	58	34
Anti-Islamic	155	170	174	103
Anti-Other Religion	198	217	237	73
Anti-Multiple Religions, Group	31	32	32	18
Anti-Atheism/Agnosticism/etc.	3	3	3	2
Sexual Orientation:	1,244	1,464	1,513	1,438
Anti-Male Homosexual	825	957	984	1,022
Anti-Female Homosexual	172	207	221	172
Anti-Homosexual	222	259	267	225
Anti-Heterosexual	10	26	26	6
Anti-Bisexual	15	15	15	13
Ethnicity/National Origin:	1,102	1,345	1,409	1,247
Anti-Hispanic	480	601	639	656
Anti-Other Ethnicity/National Origin	622	744	770	591
Disability:	45	47	50	47
Anti-Physical	20	20	20	21
Anti-Mental	25	27	30	26
Multiple-Bias Incidents[3]	3	7	11	3

[1]The term *victim* may refer to a person, business, institution, or society as a whole.

[2]The term *known offender* does not imply that the identity of the suspect is known, but only that an attribute of the suspect is identified, which distinguishes him/her from an unknown offender.

[3]A *multiple-bias incident* occurs only when two or more offense types are committed in a single incident. In a situation where there is more than one offense type, the agency can indicate a different bias for each offense. In the case of a single offense type, only one bias can be indicated.

SOURCE: *Hate Crime Statistics.* Washington, DC: Federal Bureau of Investigation, 2002, p.9.

The Hate Model

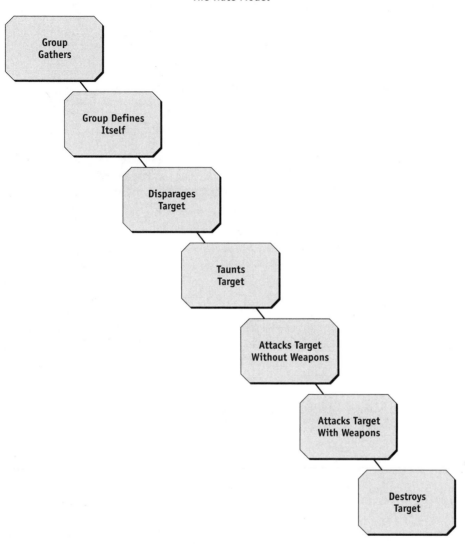

Figure 3.3 The Seven-Stage Hate Model

SOURCE: John R. Schafer and Joe Navarro. "The Seven-Stage Hate Model: The Psychopathology of Hate Groups." *FBI Law Enforcement Bulletin*, March 2003, p.1. Reprinted by permission.

One well-known hate group is the Neo-Nazi Skinheads, youths with shaved heads or closely cropped hair, usually between the ages of 13 and 25 and typically male. They sport Nazi insignia, tattoos and/or satanic symbols and preach violence against African Americans, Hispanics, Jews, Asians and homosexuals.

Passage of the Hate Crime Statistics Act of 1990 directed the U.S. Justice Department (DOJ) to collect bias-crime data nationwide. The program is voluntary, however, and no budgetary provisions were made. The U.S. DOJ has also created a hotline (1-800-347-HATE) that citizens can use to report bias crimes.

Many states have also passed legislation mandating the collection of bias-crime statistics. In addition, hate-crime laws have resulted in legislation providing

Table 3.6 Hate-Based Crimes and Non–Hate-Based Crimes Compared

Characteristic	Non–Hate-Based Incidents	Hate-Based Incidents
Relationship of victim to perpetrator	Most assaults involve two people who know each other	Assaults tend to be "stranger" crimes
Number of perpetrators	Most assaults have one perpetrator and one victim	Involve an average of four assailants for each victim
Nature of the conflict	Tends to be even	Tends to be uneven—hate crime perpetrators often attack younger or weaker victims, or arm themselves and attack unarmed victims
Amount of physical damage inflicted	Not typically "excessive"	Extremely violent, with victims being three times more likely to require hospitalization than "normal" assault victims
Treatment of property	In most property crimes, something of value is taken	More likely that valuable property will be damaged or destroyed
Perpetrator's personal gain	Attacker settles a score or profits from the crime	In most, no personal score is settled and no profit is made
Location of crime	No place with any symbolic significance	Frequently occur in churches, synagogues, mosques, cemeteries, monuments, schools, camps and in or around the victim's home

SOURCE: Adapted from Christina Bodinger-deUriarte. *Hate Crime: The Rise of Hate Crime on School Campuses.* Research Bulletin No. 10 of Phi Delta Kappa, Center for Evaluation, Development, and Research, December 1991, p.2.

additional sentencing options and penalty enhancements for convicted perpetrators. Currently all states have some form of hate-crime legislation. Table 3.7 summarizes the statutory provisions of hate-crime legislation state by state.

Many states allow victims to bring civil suits against perpetrators. In most of these states, victims can sue for actual and punitive damages and obtain an injunction. Suits can be brought regardless of criminal proceedings, with the burden of proof being a preponderance of evidence (a lesser standard than in criminal proceedings). In some states if the offense is committed by a juvenile, the parents are liable up to $5,000. The final area of criminal behavior to explore is ritualistic crime.

Ritualistic Crime   A **ritual** is a system of rites, a ceremonial act. Rituals are heavily linked to a belief system and may include symbols, artifacts, words, gestures, costumes and music. Whether this belief system is a formal religion or not, it is protected by the First Amendment right to worship as one wishes.

Rituals have a rich heritage. The Egyptians used amulets as good luck charms to ward off evil or to bring about good fortune. The Greeks practiced several forms of ritual, including hydromancy, similar to our wishing wells. They also put much faith in astrology and the signs of the zodiac. The Romans, too, practiced rituals, primarily fertility rites. Later in Europe and in the United States, witchcraft became a focus. In Europe more than 200,000 witches were killed for their beliefs.

Skinheads are a hate group that advocates white supremacy. They typically sport Nazi tattoos and have shaved heads.

All recognized religions have rituals meaningful to their members. Cults also use rituals to draw their members together. Satanic cults have one strong leader to whom all members give allegiance. Often the leader is worshipped as an anti-God—the embodiment of Satan and evil. Members are often youths who do not fit in with their peers and have no self-identity. In the cult they are accepted and given a feeling of belonging, worth and power. They are often influenced by heavy metal music and may dress in a punk style. Members of satanic cults frequently wear pentagrams and inverted crosses. Dark clothing is common, as is self-mutilation, such as sticking safety pins through nipples. *Satanic rituals* commonly include robes (red or black), daggers, candles, altars and pentagrams. They often involve chanting, occur at night and are conducted in strict secrecy. None of this ritualistic activity is illegal, and the majority of cults stay within the boundaries of the law. Some, however, do not.

When the rituals of a group involve crimes, such as desecration of cemeteries, grave robbing, cruelty to animals, child sexual abuse and even murder, they become a problem for law enforcement. As noted by Los Angeles Police Department

Table 3.7   State Hate Crimes/Statutory Provisions

Alabama–Idaho

	AL	AK	AZ	AR	CA	CO	CT	DC	DE	FL	GA	HI	ID
Bias-Motivated Violence and Intimidation	✓	✓	✓		✓	✓	✓	✓	✓	✓	✓		✓
Civil Action				✓	✓	✓	✓	✓		✓	✓		✓
Criminal Penalty	✓	✓	✓		✓	✓	✓	✓	✓	✓	✓		✓
Race, Religion, Ethnicity[1]	✓	✓	✓		✓	✓	✓	✓	✓	✓			✓
Sexual Orientation		✓			✓		✓	✓	✓	✓			
Gender		✓	✓		✓				✓				
Other[2]	✓	✓	✓		✓				✓	✓			
Institutional Vandalism	✓		✓	✓	✓	✓	✓	✓	✓	✓	✓	✓	
Data Collection[3]		✓			✓		✓	✓		✓			✓
Training for Law Enforcement Personnel[4]		✓			✓								

Illinois–Missouri

	IL	IN	IA	KS	KY	LA	ME	MD	MA	MI	MN	MS	MO
Bias-Motivated Violence and Intimidation	✓		✓		✓	✓	✓	✓	✓	✓	✓	✓	✓
Civil Action	✓		✓			✓			✓	✓	✓		✓
Criminal Penalty	✓		✓		✓	✓	✓	✓	✓	✓	✓	✓	✓
Race, Religion, Ethnicity[1]	✓		✓		✓	✓	✓	✓	✓	✓	✓	✓	✓
Sexual Orientation	✓		✓		✓	✓	✓		✓		✓		
Gender	✓		✓			✓	✓			✓	✓	✓	
Other[2]	✓		✓			✓	✓		✓		✓		
Institutional Vandalism	✓	✓		✓	✓	✓	✓	✓	✓	✓	✓	✓	✓
Data Collection[3]	✓		✓		✓	✓	✓	✓	✓	✓	✓		
Training for Law Enforcement Personnel[4]	✓		✓		✓	✓				✓	✓		

Montana–Pennsylvania

	MT	NE	NV	NH	NJ	NM	NY	NC	ND	OH	OK	OR	PA
Bias-Motivated Violence and Intimidation	✓	✓	✓	✓	✓		✓[5]	✓	✓	✓	✓	✓	✓
Civil Action		✓	✓		✓					✓	✓	✓	✓
Criminal Penalty	✓	✓	✓	✓	✓		✓	✓	✓	✓	✓	✓	✓
Race, Religion, Ethnicity[1]	✓	✓	✓	✓	✓		✓	✓	✓	✓	✓	✓	✓
Sexual Orientation		✓	✓	✓	✓		✓					✓	
Gender		✓		✓	✓		✓		✓				
Other[2]		✓	✓	✓	✓		✓				✓		
Institutional Vandalism	✓	✓			✓	✓			✓	✓	✓	✓	✓
Data Collection[3]		✓	✓		✓						✓	✓	✓
Training for Law Enforcement Personnel[4]												✓	

Rhode Island–Wyoming

	RI	SC	SD	TN	TX	UT	VT	VA	WA	WV	WI	WY
Bias-Motivated Violence and Intimidation	✓		✓	✓	✓[6]	✓[7]	✓	✓	✓	✓	✓	
Civil Action	✓		✓	✓			✓	✓	✓		✓	
Criminal Penalty	✓		✓	✓	✓	✓	✓	✓	✓	✓	✓	
Race, Religion, Ethnicity[1]	✓		✓	✓			✓	✓	✓	✓	✓	
Sexual Orientation	✓			✓			✓		✓		✓	
Gender	✓						✓	✓	✓			
Other[2]	✓						✓	✓	✓	✓	✓	
Institutional Vandalism	✓	✓		✓	✓			✓	✓		✓	
Data Collection[3]	✓				✓			✓	✓			
Training for Law Enforcement Personnel[4]	✓								✓			

[1]The following states also have statutes criminalizing interference with religious worship: CA, DC, FL, ID, MD, MA, MI, MN, MS, MO, NV, NM, NY, NC, OK, RI, SC, SD, TN, VA, WV.

[2]"Other" includes mental and physical disability or handicap (AL, AK, AZ, CA, DC, DE, IL, IA, LA, ME, MN, NE, NV, NH, NJ, NY, OK, RI, VT, WA, WI), political affiliation (DC, IA, LA, WV) and age (DC, IA, LA, VT).

[3]States with data collection statutes that include sexual orientation are AZ, CA, CT, DC, FL, IL, IA, MD, NV, OR, and WA; those that include gender are AZ, DC, IL, IA, MN, WA.

[4]Some other states have regulations mandating such training.

[5]New York State law provides penalty enhancement limited to the crime of aggravated harassment.

[6]The Texas Statute refers to victims selected "because of the defendant's bias or prejudice against a person or group."

[7]The Utah Statute ties penalties for hate crimes to violations of the victim's constitutional or civil rights.

SOURCE: Anti-Defamation League, 2001. Accessed from http://www.adl.org/99hatecrime/provisions.asp. Reprinted by permission.

Investigator Patrick Metoyer: "We don't investigate warlocks, satanists, vampires, Jews, Catholics, or Protestants. We investigate *crime.*"

 A **ritualistic crime** is an unlawful act committed during a ceremony related to a belief system. It is the crime, *not* the belief system, that must be investigated.

Indicators of satanic or ritualistic involvement in a crime include inverted crosses, candles, altars, animal parts, colored salt, incense, such symbolism as 666 (referring to an anti-Christ), swastikas or books on the occult. Normal investigative techniques are not effective with ritualistic crime. Usually multiple victims and multiple suspects are involved, and often logic will not work.

Juergensmeyer (2002) describes two notorious U.S. cults. A cult of the late 1900s was the People's Temple, lead by Jim Jones. Hundreds of his followers moved into a rural community called Jonestown in Guyana, South America. When the commune came under investigation, Jones ordered his followers to commit suicide resulting in 900 deaths. Another notorious cult was the Branch Davidians, led by David Koresh. In 1993 a 51-day confrontation between the cult and federal forces near Waco, Texas, ended with the apparent mass suicide of over 80 cult members, including Koresh.

Juergensmeyer also describes a current cult, the International Society for Krishna Consciousness, or the Hare Krishna, which originated in Asia. Members wear orange robes similar to those worn by Indian holy men. They shave their heads and meditate in strictly regulated communes.

Garrett (2004, p.62) notes: "Some law enforcers do not believe ritualistic crimes occur. Mark Rizzo, a noted law enforcement trainer on cults and the occult, warns this is a mistake. He says back in the '60s, '70s and '80s local law enforcement lived in the same state of denial about gangs. . . . Rizzo suspects these crimes are more prevalent than most people believe."

Having examined the various classifications and types of crime law enforcement must handle, consider next the types of people involved in such crimes and the factors contributing to their involvement.

Offenders—What Leads People to Commit Crime?

The reason people commit crime has been debated since crime was first defined. Some blame crime on the failings of the criminal justice system—understaffed police forces, lenient judges, overcrowded jails and prisons and overworked, burned-out probation and parole officers. Others blame society and the overwhelming absence of personal and community responsibility and accountability— abusive parents, permissive parents, inadequate schools and incompetent teachers, the decline of religion, media violence, drugs and high rates of unemployment. A detailed discussion of the causes of crime is beyond the scope of this text. Only the major theories are briefly discussed.

Theories of Criminality and Causes of Crime

The **classical theory,** developed by Italian criminologist Cesare Beccaria (1738–1794), holds that people are rational and responsible for their acts.

 The classical theory sees people as free agents with free will. People commit crimes because they want to.

A refinement of the classical theory is the *routine activity theory* developed by Lawrence Cohen and Marcus Felson, which states that the volume and distribution of predatory crime (where an offender tries to steal an object directly) correlates highly with three variables found in everyday American life:
1. The availability of suitable targets (homes/stores containing easily sold goods).
2. The absence of watchful guardians (homeowners, neighbors, friends, relatives, guards, security systems, etc.).
3. The presence of motivated offenders (unemployed individuals, drug abusers, etc.).

The intersection of these three variables increases the chances of a predatory crime occurring. This theory gives equal weight to the role of victim and offender. It also suggests that the opportunity for criminal action depends on the victim's lifestyle and behavior.

The classical theory of crime causation was called into question toward the end of the nineteenth century. Among the leading opponents was Cesare Lombroso (1835–1909), an Italian criminologist who developed the **positivist theory.** Lombroso's studies (1911) supported a biological causation for deviant behavior, suggesting that individuals who did not conform to society's laws and regulations were biologically inferior. *Biological theorists* hold that how a person acts is basically a result of heredity.

 The positivist theory sees criminals as "victims of society" and of their own biological, sociological, cultural and physical environments.

Lombroso maintained that criminals are born with a predisposition to crime and need exceptionally favorable conditions in life to avoid criminal behavior. Building on Lombroso's idea that environmental influences affect criminal behavior, some scholars developed the positivist view based on the concept of **determinism**. Determinism regards crime as a consequence of many factors, including population density, economic status and the legal definition of crime. This multiple-factor causation theory brought the positivist view into direct conflict with the notion of free will.

The Influence of Biology

A medieval law states: "If two persons fall under suspicion of crime, the uglier or more deformed is to be regarded as more probably guilty." Such a law is based on a belief that criminals are born, not made. While we've come a long way in our understanding of the causes of crime since the Middle Ages, a person's biological makeup continues to be among those factors many believe are correlated with criminality. Biological functions and conditions that have been related to criminal behavior include such variables as brain tumors, disorders of the limbic system, endocrine abnormalities, chromosomal abnormalities and neurological dysfunction produced by the prenatal and postnatal experience of infants.

Adoption studies have lent support to the biological theory of criminal behavior. A fairly powerful argument can be made for a biological basis of criminality when it can be shown that the adopted-away children of criminal biological parents grow up to display criminal behavior, especially when the adoptive (nonbiological) parents are not themselves criminal.

A counterposition to the biological theory is the *behavioral/environmental theory,* which suggests that criminals are made, not born.

The Influence of the Environment

Many environmental factors have been identified as contributing to criminality, including poverty, unemployment, the disintegrating family and drug and alcohol abuse.

Poverty is a pervasive, persistent, devastating threat to many of our nation's families, particularly to youths. Poverty encompasses a host of problems, including overcrowded and unhealthy living conditions in unsafe, crime-ridden neighborhoods; inadequate schools; limited access to health care; and single and/or teen parenthood. Poverty was identified by the Census Bureau as one of six parameters that indicate a risk to children's welfare, the other parameters being absent parents, single-parent families, unwed mothers, parents who have not completed high school and welfare dependence.

Unemployment is intimately linked to poverty. Numerous studies suggest that a booming economy leads to decreased levels of unemployment, alleviating poverty and translating into a drop in crime.

The *family* is another strong environmental influence on criminal activity. As mentioned, the Census Bureau has identified unwed mothers and single-parent families as two risks to children's welfare. Sadly, many families serve as the training ground for violent behavior, perpetuating what has been termed the "cycle of violence." Studies show: "Being abused or neglected as a child increased the likelihood of arrest as a juvenile by 59 percent, as an adult by 28 percent, and for a violent crime by 30 percent" (Widom and Maxfield, 2001, p.1). In many violent homes, drug and alcohol abuse is a continual presence.

Drug and alcohol abuse, although arguably linked to an organic (biological) chemical disorder or imbalance, is considered a significant environmental factor in crime causation. The role drugs and alcohol play in crime can be viewed two ways: (1) drug and alcohol use physically alters individuals, lowering inhibitions and increasing confidence, which can then lead them to commit criminal acts (domestic abuse, rape, assault, drunk driving, etc.) or (2) a dependence on drugs and/or alcohol may lead a person to commit crime to support the addiction (robbery, burglary, etc.). The relationship between drugs and crime is summarized by Menard et al. (2001, pp.269–270):

> Crime typically is initiated before substance use . . . [however,] once crime and substance use are initiated, each appears to increase the likelihood of continuity of the other. . . . The most plausible conclusion is that drugs and crime are related by mutual causation: crime affects drug use and drug use affects crime.

The Combination of Biology and Environment   Comparisons of groups of criminals with groups of noncriminals have failed to produce any single characteristic that absolutely distinguishes the two groups. However, a growing body of evidence suggests that the forces operating to stimulate criminal behavior may be a complex interaction between predisposing biological/genetic factors and certain environmental agents that trigger criminal tendencies.

 It is likely that criminal behavior is the result of both heredity and life experiences.

Put simply, biological abnormalities in some people heighten their sensitivity to adverse environmental circumstances, making them more prone to antisocial behavior. This relationship between genes and the environment is often viewed as synergistic; the genes alone won't cause the behavior, nor will the environment alone. When they function together in a specific combination, however, the individual will display criminal responses. Table 3.8 summarizes the major theories on the causes of crime.

Messner and Rosenfeld (2001, p.5) believe: "The American Dream itself and the normal social conditions engendered by it are deeply implicated in the problem of crime. [The American Dream is] a broad cultural ethos that entails a commitment to the goal of material success, to be pursued by everyone in society, under conditions of open, individual competition." They (p.10) suggest: "The American Dream has a dark side that must be considered in any serious effort to uncover the social sources of crime. It encourages an exaggerated emphasis on monetary achievements while devaluing alternative criteria of success, it promotes a preoccupation with the realization of goals while de-emphasizing the

Table 3.8 Review of the Major Theories of the Causes of Crime

Theory	Major Premise
Choice Theory	People commit crimes when they perceive that the benefits of law violation outweigh the threat and pain of punishment.
Biosocial Theories	
Biochemical	Crime, especially violence, is a function of diet, vitamin intake, hormonal imbalance or food allergies.
Neurological	Criminals and delinquents often suffer brain impairment. Attention deficit disorder and minimum brain dysfunction are related to antisocial behavior.
Genetic	Delinquent traits and predispositions are inherited. The criminality of parents can predict the delinquency of children.
Psychological Theories	
Psychoanalytic	The development of personality early in childhood influences behavior for the rest of a person's life. Criminals have weak egos and damaged personalities.
Social learning	People commit crimes when they model their behavior after others they see being rewarded for the same acts. Behavior is enforced by rewards and extinguished by punishment.
Cognitive	Individual reasoning processes influence behavior. Reasoning is influenced by the way people perceive their environment and by their moral and intellectual development.
Social Structure Theories	
Social disorganization	The conflicts and problems of urban social life and communities control the crime rate. Crime is a product of transitional neighborhoods that manifest social disorganization and value conflict.
Strain	People who adopt society's goals but lack the means to attain them seek alternatives, such as crime.
Social Process Theories	
Learning	People learn to commit crimes from exposure to antisocial behaviors. Criminal behavior depends on the person's experiences with rewards for conventional behaviors and punishments for deviant ones. Being rewarded for deviance leads to crime.
Social control	A person's bond to society prevents him or her from violating social rules. If the bond weakens, the person is free to commit crimes.
Conflict Theories	
Conflict	People commit crimes when the law, controlled by the rich and powerful, defines their behavior as illegal. The immoral actions of the powerful go unpunished.
Left realism	Crime is a function of relative deprivation; criminals prey on the poor.
Radical feminism	The capital system creates patriarchy, which oppresses women. Male dominance explains gender bias, violence against women and repression.
Peacemaking	Peace and humanism can reduce crime; conflict resolution strategies can work.
Integrated Theories	
Latent trait: general theory of crime	Crime and criminality are separate concepts. People choose to commit crime when they lack self-control. People lacking in self-control will seize criminal opportunities.
Developmental	Criminals go through lifestyle changes during their offending career. As people mature, the factors that influence their propensity to commit crime change. In childhood, family factors are critical; in adulthood, marital and job factors are key.
Victimization Theories	
Victim precipitation	Victims trigger criminal acts by their provocative behavior. Active precipitation involves fighting words or gestures. Passive precipitation occurs when victims unknowingly threaten their attackers.
Lifestyle	Victimization risk is increased when people have a high-risk lifestyle. Placing oneself at risk by going out to dangerous places results in increased victimization.
Routine activities	Crime rates can be explained by the availability of suitable targets, the absence of capable guardians and the presence of motivated offenders.

SOURCE: Joseph J. Senna and Larry J. Siegel. *Introduction to Criminal Justice*, 9th ed. Belmont, CA: Wadsworth Publishing Company, 2002, pp.102–103. Reprinted by permission.

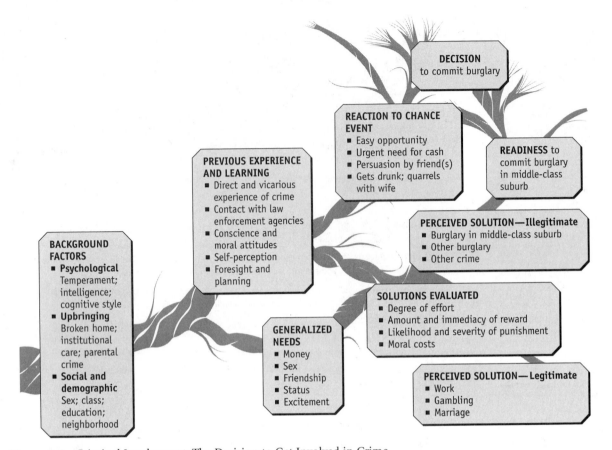

Figure 3.4 Criminal Involvement: The Decision to Get Involved in Crime

SOURCE: Joel Samaha. *Criminal Justice*, 3rd ed. St. Paul, MN: West Publishing Company, 1994, pp.58–59. Reprinted by permission. All rights reserved.

importance of the ways in which those goals are pursued, and it helps create and sustain social structures incapable of restraining criminogenic cultural pressures."

Because the concepts of crime, delinquency and deviancy apply to such a wide range of behaviors, having in common only the fact that they have been declared illegal, no single causal explanation is possible. The complex interplay of factors leading to the commission of a crime is illustrated in Figures 3.4 and 3.5.

Laub (2004, p.1) sees a turning point in addressing crime in the works of James Q. Wilson: "In my view, the work of the political scientist, James Q. Wilson, has had the largest impact on criminology. . . . Wilson's 1975 book *Thinking about Crime*, remains a tour de force that literally changed thinking about crime by focusing on the role of the criminal justice system . . . as a tool to influence the individual decision making of offenders." Laub notes: "Wilson, in collaboration with George Kelling, developed the idea of 'broken windows' and redirected attention to concepts such as physical and social disorder and their role in not only generating crime, but fear of crime, which in turn can generate more crime and affect quality of life, especially in urban communities."

Career Criminals or Recidivists

Of major concern are the **chronic** or **career criminals**—a small group of offenders arrested five or more times as juveniles. Such an offender is also considered a *repeat offender* or **recidivist**. Although most offenders "age out," chronic offend-

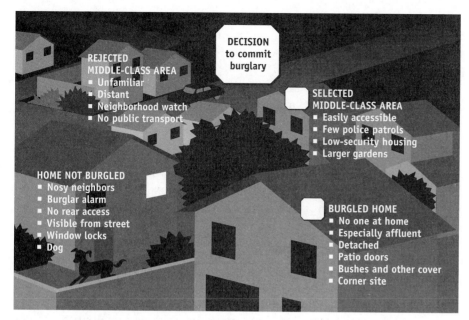

Figure 3.5 The Criminal Event: The Decision to Commit a Specific Burglary

SOURCE: Joel Samaha. *Criminal Justice*, 3rd ed. St. Paul, MN: West Publishing Company, 1994, pp.58–59. Reprinted by permission. All rights reserved.

ers continue a life of crime. Traditional programs aimed at rehabilitation have little effect on such criminals. Piquero et al. (2004) studied variables affecting criminal career length. They found that an early onset of criminal behavior is a marker and subsequent predictor of lengthy criminal careers (p.427). They also found that poor neuropsychological/cognitive ability scores relate to lengthy criminal careers. A third finding was that lengthy stays in prison/jail were associated with shorter criminal careers.

Some refer to our criminal justice system as a revolving door, with criminals getting out of prison faster than the authorities can convict and incarcerate others. Often those who were released are involved in more crime and are right back in prison. The Violent Crime Control and Law Enforcement Act of 1994 reflects the desire to deal with recidivism and the perpetual revolving door, calling for "mandatory life imprisonment without possibility of parole for federal offenders with three or more convictions for serious violent felonies or drug-trafficking crimes." Some states, such as California, have enacted similar "three strikes and you're out" legislation.

In addition to targeting career criminals, the criminal justice system must focus attention on youths, especially juvenile delinquents, because delinquency is often the beginning for the career criminal.

Juvenile Offenders

State specifications as to the age of a juvenile vary, but most state statutes define a juvenile as an individual under the age of 16 or 18. Juvenile delinquency, therefore, is considered behavior by a person not of legal age that violates a local, state or federal law. **Delinquency** refers to actions or conduct by a juvenile in violation of criminal law or constituting a status offense; an error or failure by a child or adolescent to conform to society's expectations of social order. A **delinquent** is a child adjudicated to have violated a federal, state or local law; a minor who has done an illegal act or who has been proven in court to have misbehaved seriously. A child may be found delinquent for a variety of behaviors not criminal for adults (status offenses).

According to ten Bensel (n.d., p.41), national expert on child abuse and neglect, studies have shown that virtually "all violent juvenile delinquents have been abused children," that "all criminals at San Quentin prison . . . studied had violent upbringings as children" and that "all assassins . . . in the United States during the past 20 years had been victims of child abuse."

Juvenile delinquency presents a serious challenge with an enormous number of youths involved. Self-report studies indicate approximately 90 percent of all young people have committed at least one act for which they could be brought to juvenile court. However many of these offenses are minor (for example fighting and truancy), and state statutes often define juvenile delinquency so broadly that virtually all youngsters could be classified as delinquent.

Status Offenders   A special category of offenses has been established for juveniles, designating certain actions as illegal for any person under the state's defined juvenile age of 16 or 18. These are **status offenses,** violations of the law applying to only those under legal age. They include absenting from home, truancy, drinking alcoholic beverages, smoking, violating curfew and incorrigibility. As noted by Hess and Drowns (2004, p.332): "Children and their families who are brought before the court for status offenses occupy a great share of the court's workload. Status offenders can try the patience of the court because such children often are considered as simply being in need of supervision."

Serious and Violent Offenders   The National Center for Juvenile Justice's "Crime Statistics" (2003) reports that the juvenile Violent Crime Index arrest rate in 2000 was at its lowest level since 1985—41 percent below the peak year of 1994. Nonetheless, serious and violent offenders pose a formidable problem.

 Most often violent offending begins among juveniles who have themselves been victimized.

Shaffer and Ruback (2002, pp.6–7) report: "Violent victimization is an important risk factor for subsequent violent offending. . . . Repeat offending is more common than repeat victimization. . . . Violent victimization is a warning signal for future violent offending."

Similar conclusions are reported in *The 8% Solution* (2001). The Orange County (California) Probation Department tracked a small group of first-time offenders for three years and found that a small percentage (8 percent) of the juveniles were arrested repeatedly (a minimum of four times within a three-year period) and were responsible for 55 percent of repeat cases. According to the report (p.1):

The characteristics of this group of repeat offenders (referred to as "the **8% problem**") were dramatically different from those who were arrested only once. These differences did not develop after exposure to the juvenile justice system, as some might expect; they were evident at first arrest and referral to juvenile court, and they worsened if nothing was done to alleviate the youth's problems. Unfortunately, in wanting to "give a break" to first-time offenders, the juvenile justice system often pays scant attention to those at greatest risk of becoming chronic offenders until they have established a record of repeated serious offending. [emphasis added]

The good news is that most of the small group of potentially serious, chronic offenders can be identified reliably at first contact with the juvenile justice system. The "8%" offenders enter the system with a complex set of problems or risk factors, which the study identified as (1) involvement in crime at an early age and (2) a multiproblem profile including significant family problems (abuse, neglect, criminal family members and/or a lack of parental supervision and control), problems at school (truancy, failing more than one course or a recent suspension or expulsion), drug and alcohol abuse and behaviors such as gang involvement, running away and stealing.

As noted, frequently those who have been victims become victimizers themselves.

Victims of Crime and Violence

Everyone expects law enforcement officers to know how to deal with criminals. Of equal importance, however, is officers' ability to deal with crime victims. This not only enhances the image of police officers as professionals but enhances communications that likely will result in officers' ability to obtain more crime-related information. Crime victims are often said to be the overlooked element of the criminal process, invisible and forgotten.

Types of Victims

Direct or **primary victims** of crime are those initially harmed by injury, death or loss of property as a result of crimes committed. When a violent crime occurs, the impact often goes further than the victim. Often the entire community suffers. **Indirect** or **secondary victims** of crime are all other community members who may be threatened or fearful as a result of the commission of crime. This can include family, relatives, friends, neighborhoods, the entire community and even police officers who must deal with the aftermath of violent crimes, such as battered children and grisly deaths.

If a small-town youth murders his entire family or opens fire in the neighborhood school, the community may go into shock. Everyone feels vulnerable. Fear sets in. Morale drops. Trust plummets. In addition convicted criminals sentenced to prison are financially supported by society while incarcerated. In short everyone pays the price as a victim of crime.

Victimization Factors—Who Is at Risk?

Distinct demographic and individual characteristics, called **risk factors,** influence the chance of being victimized. The degree of risk people face is affected by household factors related to how and where they live as well as by individual factors.

Household Factors   Using data from the NCVS, Klaus (2002, pp.6–7) reports the following:

- A greater proportion of households headed by Hispanics experienced at least one crime when compared with non-Hispanic households.
- Households in urban areas were significantly more likely to be victimized by crime than those in suburban or rural areas.

- Households in the West were significantly more likely to be victimized by crime than households in other regions of the country.
- In general, the more people in a household the greater the susceptibility to crime.

Individual Risk Factors   Data from the NCVS indicate certain individuals are at greater risk than others. "Those most vulnerable to violent victimization in the past—males, teens, and blacks, for example—continued to be the most vulnerable" (Rennison, 2002, pp.6–7):

- *Gender:* Men are more likely than women to be victims of crime.
- *Age:* In general, the younger the person, the higher the rate of violent victimization, regardless of the type of violence considered.
- *Race:* Blacks are more likely to be victims of violent crime—especially aggravated assaults and robberies—than whites or people of "other races."
- *Marital Status:* The divorced or separated and the never married are more likely than the married or the widowed to be victims of crime.

 Violent crime hits children, minorities and the poor hardest. Males are more often victimized than females. As income rises and as age increases, the victimization rate drops.

Other Factors in Victimization

Beyond statistics several other factors enter into understanding victimization, including the relationship between the victim and offender, the use of weapons and how victims protect themselves—or attempt to do so.

The Victim/Offender Relationship   When people worry about crime, they are most often worried about being attacked by strangers. This fear is often justified. With the exception of murder and rape, most violent crimes are committed by strangers. Males, African Americans and young people face the greatest risk of violent crime by strangers and are victimized by violent strangers at an annual rate almost triple that of women. African Americans are more than twice as likely as whites to be robbed by strangers.

Women are more vulnerable than men to assaults by acquaintances and relatives, with two-thirds of all assaults on divorced and separated women committed by acquaintances and relatives. Spouses or former spouses committed only 5 percent of the assaults by single offenders. In almost three-fourths of spouse-versus-spouse assaults, the victim was divorced or separated at the time of the incident.

More than half of all homicides are committed by someone known to the victim. Further, victims and offenders are usually of the same race.

How Victims Protect Themselves   Victims of violent crime can protect themselves by returning physical force, by verbal response, by attracting attention, by nonviolent evasion or by brandishing a weapon. Rape victims are more likely to use force, try a verbal response or attract attention and are less likely than others to do nothing to protect themselves. In contrast robbery victims are least likely to try to talk themselves out of being victimized and most likely to do nothing.

Effects of Victimization

Victims of violent crimes often suffer from the effects of the victimization for the rest of their lives. Shootings, knifings, acid throwings or beatings are traumatic, with long-lasting physical, emotional and psychological damage to victims and their families. Victims may also suffer financially through the loss or destruction of property (including irreplaceable property with only sentimental value), time lost from work, medical costs and the introduction of security measures to prevent future victimization. The greatest effect of victimization, however, is often psychological.

 Victims may suffer physical, economic and psychological harm that lasts their entire lives.

Fear of Victimization

Public opinion polls show that, while people do fear crime in general, they usually feel their own neighborhoods are relatively safe. If someone in the neighborhood is victimized, however, the entire neighborhood may feel much more vulnerable.

The people with the highest risk of being victimized, young males, do not express the greatest fear of victimization. Those who express the greatest fear of being victimized are women and the elderly, even though they are at lower risk than other groups. Whether they are at lower risk because they take measures to reduce their chances of being victimized is not known. If the elderly, for example, restrict their activities because they are afraid of becoming crime victims, this fear is, in itself, a sort of victimization.

The "Second Wound": Further Victimization by the Criminal Justice System

While feeling the impact of being victimized, many victims are subjected to a second victimization.

 A second victimization may occur as a result of insensitivity on the part of those in the criminal justice system.

Police are trained extensively in dealing with criminals but do not receive much training in communicating with victims. Victims are often the only ones who can identify the offender and the property stolen in the crime. The victim's property may be held for months until introduced as evidence in the trial. The victim is often called to testify in a trial and subjected to severe cross-examination, more than the person charged with the crime, since the defendant is not required to take the witness stand.

The investigative and prosecution process may require a number of trips to the court or county attorney's office, which is not only an expense but requires time off from employment. Victims often complain that once they make their initial contribution to the investigation, they are not kept informed of the progress of the case. They often are not notified when the offender is released from custody or incarceration, preventing them from taking safety precautions.

 Victims may also be victimized again by lack of release data and notification and by intimidation.

In one case a woman was brutally murdered by her former boyfriend, who had earlier been arrested and charged with her rape. However, he unexpectedly made bail, and two days after his release, the man ambushed her as she left work and shot her six times in the head at close range. She died instantly. No one had notified her, the police or the prosecutors in the case that the offender was out of jail.

One solution to this problem is the Victim Information and Notification Everyday (VINE) system that is spreading across the country, having already reached at least 300 communities in 26 states. The system is activated by calling a toll-free number and providing a prisoner's name or ID number. The user receives computerized information about where the prisoner is being held, the date of upcoming parole hearings and when the sentence expires. It also provides the phone number and address of the facility holding the prisoner.

Victims and witnesses are often further victimized by overt or covert intimidation, most commonly in gang and drug cases, as well as domestic violence cases. Intimidation may occur in the courtroom in the form of threatening looks or gestures or packing the courtroom with the defendant's friends. Such intimidation seriously hampers the efforts of law enforcement, prosecutors and the entire criminal justice system. One approach to countering such intimidation is to take a class of police cadets into courtrooms where intimidation is suspected.

Assisting Victims—Historical Overview

In 1965 California established the first crime victim compensation program. Since then, most states have established similar programs. In 1975 the first "Victim's Rights Week" was organized by the Philadelphia district attorney. In 1979 Frank G. Carrington, considered by many to be the father of the victims' rights movement, founded the Crime Victims' Legal Advocacy Institute, Inc.

Many support groups for victims of crime exist in each state and numerous municipalities or counties—rape crisis centers, family shelters, victims of crime groups, domestic violence groups, Mothers Against Drunk Drivers (MADD), the National Organization for Victim Assistance (NOVA) and other groups. Significant legislation has also been passed to assist crime victims.

The Crime Victims' Reparations Act passed in 1974, gives victims the right to be compensated for the cost of crimes, including medical and funeral costs, loss of income, counseling services and other expenses.

The Victim and Witness Protection Act of 1982 was passed to help victims cope with the labyrinth of police, courts and corrections, mandating that the U.S. Attorney General develop procedures to assist victims and witnesses through this legal process. The act provides for victim impact statements (VIS) at sentencing and parole hearings, discussed in detail shortly.

The Crime Victims' Bill of Rights was passed in 1983, recognizing for the first time the rights of victims to participate in criminal prosecutions. Until then, prosecutors were not obligated to inform victims about crucial decisions, such as plea bargain arrangements. Victims have acquired even more rights since then, including the opportunity to make a statement at the time of sentencing.

The Victims of Crime Act (VOCA) of 1984 established the Crime Victims' Fund, made up of federal criminal fines, penalties and bond forfeitures to support state victim compensation and local victim service programs. The fund provides grants to states for compensation to crime victims, crisis intervention, salaries of crime victim service personnel, child abuse and prevention, and victim assistance programs.

The Victim and Witness Protection Act of 1994 provides for compensation and other victim assistance from fines, penalties and forfeited bail bonds paid by convicted federal offenders. Courts often make restitution part of the sentence, depending on the circumstances and merits of each case.

Crime Victims' Rights

According to Hackett (2003, p.6):

> For more than 30 years, our nation has witnessed both a growing awareness of the plight of crime victims and the birth of a profession dedicated to serving crime victims within community-based organizations and the criminal and juvenile justice systems. Across the United States, the past three decades have seen enormous strides in establishing basic rights for crime victims concerning the emotional, physical and financial needs they experience in the aftermath of a crime.

Victims' Rights (1998) reports that every state has enacted laws that provide basic rights to crime victims. Over half the states have amended their constitutions to further protect the rights of crime victims. *The Crime Victim's Right to Be Present* (2002, p.1) states: "For crime victims and their families, the right to be present during criminal justice proceedings is an important one. Victims want to see justice at work."

 Victims' rights may include the right to appear at sentencing, the right to appear at plea bargaining, the use of victim impact statements prior to sentencing, the right to be informed of the status of their case, the right to be informed of an offender's release from prison and the right to receive restitution.

Victim Statements Since the late 1980s, victim impact statements have been included in the federal presentence investigation report to the court, as well as in many state court proceedings. The **victim impact statement (VIS)** includes information concerning the effect of the crime on the victim and the community. The victim impact statement itemizes economic losses directly related to and resulting from the offense, describes the necessity of any psychological services needed as a result of the offense, describes changes in family relationship as a result of the offense and identifies physical injuries, their severity and whether the injuries are temporary or permanent—factors that relate to the medical, financial, psychological and social impact on the victim. These impact statements provide victims an opportunity to participate in the judicial process in those cases that go to trial or a sentencing hearing. The **victim statement of opinion (VSO),** in contrast, is more subjective, allowing victims to tell the court their opinions as to what sentence a defendant should receive. The opinion may be presented verbally in court by the victim or delivered in a written statement to the judge.

Victim Restitution Victim restitution may result from a community justice approach described earlier or may be a condition of probation that requires offenders to compensate their victims for damages or loss incurred as a direct result of their crime. Restitution has widespread use in cases of larceny, burglary and other property crimes, as well as some crimes of violence.

Restitution may take several forms such as monetary payment equal to the loss incurred or other arrangements that do not directly benefit the victim but may compensate the state or community for prosecution costs. Orders to pay are adjusted to the ability to pay. Many payments are made in monthly installments. The judge may order the defendant to work in a community program. In addition to making payments to the victim, working and making these payments forces offenders to accept responsibility for their crimes.

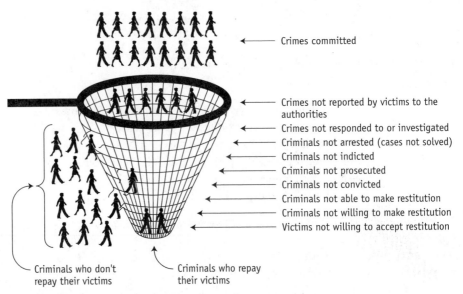

Crimes committed

Crimes not reported by victims to the authorities
Crimes not responded to or investigated
Criminals not arrested (cases not solved)
Criminals not indicted
Criminals not prosecuted
Criminals not convicted
Criminals not able to make restitution
Criminals not willing to make restitution
Victims not willing to accept restitution

Criminals who don't repay their victims

Criminals who repay their victims

Figure 3.6   Funneling or Shrinkage: The Leaky Net

SOURCE: Andrew Karmen. *Crime Victims: An Introduction to Victimology,* 3rd ed. Belmont, CA: Wadsworth Publishing Company, 1996, p.308. Reprinted by permission.

Ordering Restitution to the Crime Victim (2002, p.1) states: "Every state gives courts the statutory authority to order restitution. In addition, 18 of the 32 state crime victims' rights constitutional amendments give victims a right to restitution." The bulletin also states: "Regardless of whether restitution is mandatory, about one-quarter of all states require courts to state on the record the reason for failing to order restitution or for ordering only partial restitution." Figure 3.6 illustrates how few offenders actually make restitution to their victims.

Should the U.S. Constitution Be Amended to Include Victims' Rights?

Although the majority of states have victims' bills of rights, the push for amending the U.S. Constitution to include a victims' bill of rights has come up several times. Such a push was defeated in 1997, but was again presented in 2003 and was approved by the subcommittee studying it.

Arguments Favoring the Amendment   Co-sponsor of the current proposed amendment, Senator Dianne Feinstein (D-California), points out:

> Currently, while criminal defendants have almost two dozen separate constitutional rights—15 of them provided by amendments to the U.S. Constitution— there is not a single word in the Constitution to protect the rights of crime victims. This amendment will bring balance to the system by giving crime victims the rights to be *informed, present and heard* at critical stages throughout their case—the least that the system owes to those it failed to protect in the first place ("President Endorses New Version," 2002, p.1).

As *The Crime Victim's Right to Be Present* (p.1) notes: "Thirty-nine states give crime victims the right to attend criminal justice proceedings, including trials. However, most of these states impose limitations on that right. The restrictions stem from concern that a victim's rights to attend proceedings may conflict with the rights of the accused."

"Supporters argue that only a constitutional amendment will elevate the rights of crime victims and ensure that judges and prosecutors heed them" (Boyter, 2003, p.8). They are joined in their support by President Bush who stated: "The needs of victims are often an afterthought in our criminal justice system. It's not just; it's not fair; and it must change. As we protect the rights of criminals, we must take equal care to protect the rights of the victims" ("President Endorses New Version . . .," 2002, p.1).

Arguments against the Amendment   Critics of an amendment suggest that it would be better for Congress to enact victims' rights protections statutorily rather than by amending the Constitution. They also point out that the proposed amendment applies only to victims of violent crime and does not protect the millions of American who are victims of nonviolent crime each year.

Opponents argue such an amendment would impose a burden on prosecutors. A study by the Vera Institute found: "Most prosecutors believe that victim rights laws have imposed significant costs on their offices and other criminal justice agencies" ("Victim Rights Impose . . .," 2002, p.3). The survey also found that four out of five prosecutors believed that their states' victims' rights laws have affected the outcome of criminal cases in some way. Forty-two percent felt the laws had increased the number of prison sentences, and the same proportion reported that sentence lengths had increased because of victims' rights laws. Nearly one-third of the prosecutors believed that victims' rights laws increased case-processing time.

Further, a victim's rights amendment would impose costly and overwhelming duties on officials in the corrections field, requiring correctional administrators to notify victims of any parole proceeding, public or not. Regardless of whether the constitutional amendment setting forth victims' rights passes, states are still under an obligation to provide programs and services to victims of crime.

Programs and Services for Crime Victims

In addition to progress in victims' rights, including making victim impact statements, much progress has been made in the programs and services provided to victims. Table 3.9 identifies various victim and witness services that may be provided during eight stages of the criminal justice process. Not all services may be provided in every state.

Victim Compensation Programs   A majority of states have Victim Compensation Programs established by legislation. Names of applicable support groups should be provided to the victim, such as rape crisis centers. The victim should be provided the names of federal and state compensation centers and programs and any other support programs available. Contacts should be retained with the victim if dangerous or threatening circumstances follow the initial complaint. Information should be furnished concerning any civil actions against the offender or third parties that may be available. Any profits from books or other events by the offender should first go to satisfy victim costs and then to minimize prosecution costs to the state or local government. All reasonably possible profit should be eliminated from the commission of a crime.

Victim Advocate Programs   Victims' rights have been steadily increasing for four decades, but victims need more legal rights. They need assistance in understanding what has happened to them, directions throughout the legal

Table 3.9 Victim and Witness Services

Stage One: Emergency Response	Stage Two: Victim Stabilization	Stage Three: Resource Mobilization	Stage Four: After Arrest
When: First contact after crime **Who:** *By telephone:* 911 operator Crisis line Family and friends *Face-to-face:* On-scene crisis intervener Law enforcement Family and friends Public **What:** Trauma assessment Physical first aid Emotional first aid Crisis intervention Protection from further harm **Rights:** Protection Information Dignity and compassion	**When:** On scene, or upon report, or within 48 hours After victim reacts to trigger events **Who:** Crisis counselors Law enforcement patrol and investigators Family and friends **What:** *Crisis counselors or law enforcement:* Stabilizing interviews Crisis counseling Conflict management Shelter, transportation or protection Criminal justice orientation Referrals *Family and friends:* Personal assistance Emotional first aid Companionship and reassurance **Rights:** Protection Information Dignity and compassion	**When:** Until resolution of victimization experience **Who:** Victim service providers Law enforcement Compensation programs Family or friends **What:** *Victim services:* Outreach Supportive counseling Information, referrals *Aid with:* Financial claims Landlords, creditors Employers Property return Legal referrals Crime, violence, substance abuse information Advocacy *Law enforcement:* Fast property return Information, referrals *Compensation:* Outreach Assistance with claims Emergency aid *Family and friends:* Information Understanding Aid with crime prevention Advocacy **Rights:** Protection Information Reparations Property/employment Dignity and compassion	**When:** First contact after arrest **Who:** Prosecutors Victim service providers Law enforcement Family and friends **What:** *Prosecutors* *Information on:* Justice process Case status Reparations *Consultations on:* Charging decisions Release conditions Diversion Case scheduling *Aid with:* Restitution Intimidation reports Protection orders Relocation *Victim services:* Start/continue Stage 1–3 services Aid with media Supportive counseling *Law enforcement:* Protection order, bail enforcement Relocation *Family and friends:* Support in system **Rights:** Protection Information Counsel Reparations Property/employment Due process Dignity and compassion

SOURCE: Julie Esselman Tome and Daniel McGillis. *Serving Crime Victims and Witnesses,* 2nd edition. Washington, DC: National Institute of Justice, February 1997, pp.6–7.

Stage Five: *Pre-Court Appearance*	*Stage Six:* *Court Appearance*	*Stage Seven:* *Before Case Disposition*	*Stage Eight:* *After Case Disposition*
When: Before any appearance **Who:** Prosecutors Victim service providers Family and friends **What:** *Prosecutors:* Enforcement of protection orders, bail Protection of victim names, addresses *Information on:* Justice process Case status scheduling, continuances Testifying and the courtroom Consultation on plea Aid with landlord, creditor, employer Support on due process claims *Victim Services:* Start/continue Stage 1–4 services Justice orientation Aid with media Aid with victim impact statements Aid with transportation, child care, creditors, etc. *Family and friends:* Support in court **Rights:** Protection Information Counsel Reparations Property/employment Due process Dignity and compassion	**When:** Day of hearing or trial **Who:** Prosecutors Judiciary Victim service providers Family or friends **What:** *Prosecutors:* Protection from intimidation, media intrusion Aid with transportation, child care, creditors, etc. Consultation on unexpected events Aid with witness fees Aid with due process claims *Judiciary:* Ban badgering by defense, media Let victims, family attend all proceedings Provide information about court process *Victim service providers:* Start/continue Stage 1–5 services Help prosecutor provide services *Family and friends:* Support in court **Rights:** All victim rights involved	**When:** After verdict or entry of guilty plea **Who:** Judiciary Probation Prosecutors Victim service providers Family and friends **What:** *Judiciary:* Ban badgering by defense, media Allow victim impact statement, allocation Order restitution for all damages Address victim concerns at hearing *Probation:* Information on verdict, sentencing hearing Consultation on victim impact statement, restitution claims Explore VORP option *Prosecutor:* Parallel services with probation *Victim services:* Start/continue Stage 1–6 services Help prosecutor, probation provide services Information, referrals on civil entitlement *Family and friends:* Provide victim impact information Support in court **Rights:** All victim rights involved	**When:** After disposition **Who:** All corrections agencies Victim service providers Prosecutors Judiciary Family and friends **What:** *Probation:* Administer VORP Offender status info Enforce conditions, restitution orders *Corrections:* Offender status information Teach "victim impact" Enforce restitution *Parole:* Notice on hearings Allow victim input Order/enforce restitution, protection *Prosecution:* Invite victim input in revocation hearings *Judiciary:* Enforce conditions *Victim service providers:* Advocacy with, support to, others Start/continue Stage 1–7 services *Family or friends:* Ongoing support Protection of victim from further intimidation or harassment Provide victim impact information **Rights:** All victim rights engaged

processing and someone to talk to when they feel abandoned. The introduction of victims' advocates into the criminal justice system has filled a serious need.

Online Directory of Services for Crime Victims   The Justice Department's Office for Victims of Crime (OVC) has established an online directory of agencies that can provide services to crime victims. This directory, available at http://www.ncjrs.org/findvictimsservices, allows crime victims, within minutes, to find assistance in their own communities that meets their specific needs. Users can search for services by location, type of victimization and type of service needed. OVC does not endorse any of the listed services but has verified that all do provide direct services, have been doing so for at least 12 months or are receiving funds through the Victims of Crime Act, are open to the public, are administered by nonprofit or public agencies and have submitted accurate contact information.

A Parallel Justice System for Victims?

The National Center for Victims of Crime (NCVC) is launching a Parallel Justice Project: "an ambitious initiative designed to revolutionize our country's response to crime victims [by] forging a separate or parallel path to justice for victims" ("Victims' Group to Test . . .," 2003, p.1). NCVC Executive Director Herman says: "Far too many of the nearly 25 million Americans who become victims of crime each year must struggle on their own with the enormous emotional, financial and physical consequences of crime" (p.1).

Parallel Justice will undergo pilot testing in three sites: Burlington, Vermont; Redlands, California; and Winston-Salem, North Carolina. NCVC states: "With Parallel Justice, there would always be a second, parallel set of responses—a focused effort to help ensure the victim's safety, to help the victim recover from the trauma of crime and to provide resources to help victims get their lives back on track. . . . Honoring this separate social obligation to victims would be a critical part of providing a just response to crime" (p.1).

The NCVC also suggests that, unlike most victims' bills of rights and even the current proposed constitutional amendment, Parallel Justice would be available to *all* victims of crime, not just victims of violent crime: "Victims of crime are victims of crime. They all deserve justice from our society" (p.2).

The Role of the Police

The first and all-important contact between the police and a victim is made during the preliminary investigation. Police officers must be realistic with victims. If a police agency has an "early case closure system," victims should be told that nothing further can be done unless additional information comes to light. Victims should be given the case number and a phone number to call if they should obtain more information about the crime.

Victims should be told of any assistance available to them, and if applicable, reminded to call their insurance companies. If victims need legal advice, police officers should advise them about the legal aid office. If a case continues under investigation or will go to court, police officers should maintain contact with victims (and witnesses). If property is recovered, it should be returned to victims as soon as possible. If a case goes to court, victims should be briefed as to their roles and should be kept updated.

Truthfulness and embellishment are problems for the police and prosecution, and, indeed, some complaints are false, motivated by revenge, jealousy, monetary gain or other reasons. The victim's reluctance to follow through with prosecution is also a problem for police and prosecuting attorneys, especially in cases where the victim knows the offender. The victim may wish to cooperate but may be a poor witness due to personal physical appearance, mental or emotional instability, fear of reprisal, passage of time or reluctance to testify in court. As Herman (2002, p.34) stresses: "Victims who receive the support they need—from law enforcement's first responders and others—recover more quickly and are more likely to participate in the investigation and prosecution of the crime."

Police Officers as Victims

Police officers are not immune from being victimized. Officers are assaulted, robbed, burglarized and victimized in all the ways civilians are, including being killed. The National Law Enforcement Officers Memorial Fund (NLEOMF, *Law Enforcement Fatalities, 2002*) reports that in 2002, 147 law enforcement officers across the nation were killed in the line of duty, well below the decade-long average of 165 deaths annually and a major drop from 2001 when 230 officers were killed (including 72 officers in the September 11 attacks). The most common causes of death were being fatally shot (55 officers) and being in an automobile crash.

The most common way police officers become victims, however, is as secondary victims, dealing with the pain of victims and with the distress of seeing the "bad guys" get off easy or out of prison early.

AP/Wide World Photos

An injured New York City police officer is assisted by colleagues during a protest by union members. Police barriers could not contain protestors who clogged Fifth Avenue, blowing whistles, waving flags and chanting.

Summary

The most frequently used sources of information about crime are the media, official government statistics and self-reporting surveys. The crimes most frequently reported to police, the most serious crimes in the nation, are called Part I or Index Crimes. The eight Part I crimes are murder, aggravated assault causing serious bodily harm, forcible rape, robbery, burglary, larceny/theft, motor vehicle theft and arson. Other serious crimes include white-collar crime, computer-related crime, organized crime, bias or hate crime and ritualistic crime.

White-collar crime—occupational or business-related crime—includes fraud involving credit cards, checks, identity theft, securities, insurance, illegal competition and deceptive practices, as well as bankruptcy fraud, embezzlement and pilferage, bribes, kickbacks, payoffs and receiving stolen property.

Of growing concern is white-collar, computer-related crime. Computer crimes are relatively easy to commit and difficult to detect. Most are committed by insiders, and most are not prosecuted. A white-collar crime distinct from other types of crimes is organized crime, which is characterized by corruption and enforcement powers. Hate crimes may be motivated by bias against a person's race, religion, ethnic group or sexual orientation. A ritualistic crime is an unlawful act committed during a ceremony related to a belief system. It is the crime, *not* the belief system, that must be investigated.

Crimes are committed by youths and adults. Why? Two fundamental philosophies exist. The classical theory sees people as free agents with free will. People commit crimes because they want to. The positivist theory, in contrast, sees criminals as "victims of society" and of their own biological, sociological, cultural and physical environments. It is likely that criminal behavior is the result of both heredity and life experiences. No definitive answer exists as to why people commit crimes. Of the theories set forth, several suggest a combination of sociological, psychological and biological factors.

Most often, violent offending begins among juveniles who have themselves been victimized. Violent crime hits children, minorities and the poor hardest. Males are more often victimized than females. As income rises and as age increases, the victimization rate drops. Victims may suffer physical, economic and psychological harm that lasts for the rest of their lives. A second victimization may occur as a result of insensitivity on the part of those in the criminal justice system. Victims may also be victimized again by lack of release data and notification and by intimidation. Victims' rights may include the right to appear at sentencing, the right to appear at plea bargaining, the use of victim impact statements prior to sentencing, the right to be informed of the status of their case, the right to be informed of an offender's release from prison and the right to receive restitution.

Discussion Questions

1. Why are some crimes divided into categories or degrees?

2. Would a law that made the reporting of all crimes to the police mandatory be a good deterrent to future criminal activity?

3. Should computer hackers pay a heavy penalty for their misdeeds?

4. Should additional penalties be imposed on people found guilty of committing bias crimes?

5. How long does one remain a criminal—until the crime has been "paid for" or for a lifetime?

6. Have you ever known an adult convicted of a crime? A juvenile? If so what was he or she like?

7. Does your state have victim compensation laws? If so how do they compare with those provided in other states?

8. Have you ever been victimized? Has a member of your family? A friend or neighbor? What were the effects?

9. Do you feel that in most cases the police in your area are sensitive to crime victims' needs?

10. Discuss the current differences between the rights of the criminal and the rights of the victim. Should there be changes in these rights?

INFOTRAC COLLEGE EDITION ASSIGNMENTS

- Use InfoTrac College Edition to help answer the Discussion Questions as appropriate.

- Use InfoTrac College Edition to find *hate groups,* and particularly note Robert Stacy McCain's brief article on hate groups. Compare his opinions with those of at least two others. Be prepared to share your perspective with the class.

- Use InfoTrac College Edition to find and outline "The Seven-Stage Hate Model: The Psychopathology of Hate Groups" by John R. Schafer and Joe Navarro to share with the class.

- Use InfoTrac College Edition to find and outline "Best Practices of a Hate/Bias Crime Investigation" by Walter Bouman to share with the class.

INTERNET ASSIGNMENTS

- Using the key words *crime news,* bring up the category of crime news 2004. After reading about the various crimes, do you feel heinous crimes are on the increase?

- Select one topic covered in this chapter and research it using any of the Web sites listed in the resources on the book-specific Web site.

BOOK-SPECIFIC WEB SITE

The book-specific Web site at http://info .wadsworth.com/0534552803 hosts a variety of resources for students and instructors. Included are extended activities from each chapter in which students write a policy, use critical thinking skills to make choices in response to a given scenario, use InfoTrac College Edition with direct links to articles for participation in topical discussion forums and analyze court cases using Web links for research. Many activities can be printed or emailed to instructors. Plus, cited cases with Web links, interactive key term FlashCards, PowerPoint presentations, chapter objectives, and an extensive collection of chapter-based Web links provide additional information and activities to include in the curriculum.

REFERENCES

Albinsson, Mats. "Visual Route Helps Save the Children." *Law and Order,* December 2002, pp.39–42.

Bouman, Walter. "Best Practices of a Hate/Bias Crime Investigation." *FBI Law Enforcement Bulletin,* March 2003, pp.21–25.

Boyter, Jennifer. "Subcommittee Approves Victims' Rights Amendment." *The Police Chief,* July 2003, p.8.

Chiricos, Ted and Eschholz, Sarah. "The Racial and Ethnic Typification of Crime and the Criminal Typification of Race and Ethnicity in Local Television News." *Journal of Research in Crime and Delinquency,* November 2002, pp.400–420.

Crime in the United States, 2003. Uniform Crime Reports. Washington, DC: Federal Bureau of Investigation, 2003.

The Crime Victim's Right to Be Present. Washington, DC: U.S. Department of Justice Legal Series Bulletin #3, January 2002. (NCJ 189187)

The 8% Solution. Washington, DC: OJJDP Fact Sheet #39, November 2001. (FS 200139)

Fantino, Julian. "Hate Crime." *The Police Chief,* August 2003, pp.36–37, 93.

Farrington, David P.; Jolliffe, Darrick; Hawkinds, J. David; Catalano, Richard F.; Hill, Karl G.; and Kosterman, Rick. "Comparing Delinquency Careers in Court Records and Self-Reports." *Criminology,* August 2003, pp.933–958.

Finckenauer, James O. and Voronin, Yuri A. *The Threat of Russian Organized Crime.* Washington, DC: National Institute of Justice, June 2001. (NCJ 187085)

Fleck, Carole. "Stealing Your Life." *AARP Bulletin,* February 2004, pp.3–4.

Garrett, Ronnie. "Policing the Shadows." *Law Enforcement Technology,* March 2004, pp.62–67.

Griffith, David. "How to Investigate Cybercrime." *Police,* November 2003, pp.18–22.

Hackett, Frank A. "Victims' Rights." *The Law Enforcement Trainer,* March/April 2003, p.6.

Hansell, Saul. "Net Fraud Rising, Linked to Organized Crime Groups." The Associated Press, as reported in the (Minneapolis/St. Paul) *Star Tribune,* March 24, 2004, pp.D1, D7.

Herman, Susan. "Law Enforcement and Victim Services: Rebuilding Lives, Together." *The Police Chief,* May 2002, pp.34–37.

Hess, Kären M. and Drowns, Robert W. *Juvenile Justice,* 4th ed. Belmont, CA: Wadsworth Publishing Company, 2004.

Johnston, Richard L. "The National Cybercrime Training Partnership: Helping Your Agency Keep Pace with Electronic Crime." *The Police Chief,* January 2002, pp.52–54.

Juergensmeyer, Mark. "Cult." *Worldbook Online Americas Edition*, September 2002.

Klaus, Patsy A. *Crime and the Nation's Households, 2000*. Washington, DC: Bureau of Justice Statistics Bulletin, September 2002. (NCJ 194107)

Laub, John H. "The Life Course of Criminology in the United States: The American Society of Criminology 2003 Presidential Address." *Criminology*, February 2004, pp.1–26.

Law Enforcement Fatalities, 2003. Washington, DC: National Law Enforcement Officers Memorial Fund. Accessed http://www.nleomf.com/media

Lombroso, Cesare. *Crime: Its Causes and Remedies*. Montclair, NJ: Patterson Smith, 1968. Originally published in 1911.

Marketing Community Policing in the News: A Missed Opportunity? Washington, DC: National Institute of Justice Research for Practice, July 2003. (NCJ 200473)

Martin, Judith. "Electronic Crimefighting." *Law and Order*, December 2003, pp.52–55.

McEwen, Tom. "Information Management." In *Local Government Police Management*, 4th ed., edited by William A. Geller and Carrel W. Stephens. Washington, DC: International City/County Management Association, 2003, pp.391–421.

Menard, Scott; Mihalic, Sharon; and Huizinga, David. "Drugs and Crime Revisited." *Justice Quarterly*, June 2001, pp.269–299.

Messner, Steven F. and Rosenfeld, Richard. *Crime and the American Dream*, 3rd ed. Belmont, CA: Wadsworth Publishing Company, 2001.

National Center for Juvenile Justice. "Crime Statistics." Washington, DC, February 18, 2003.

Ordering Restitution to the Crime Victim. Washington, DC: U.S. Department of Justice Legal Series Bulletin #6. November 2002. (NCJ 189189)

Piquero, Alex R.; Brame, Robert; and Lynam, Donald. "Studying Criminal Career Length through Early Adulthood among Serious Offenders." *Crime & Delinquency*, July 2004, pp.412–435.

"President Endorses New Version of Constitutional Amendment." *Criminal Justice Newsletter*, May 8, 2002, pp.1–2.

Rantala, Ramona R. *Cybercrime against Businesses*. Washington, DC: Bureau of Justice Statistics Technical Report, March 2004. (NCJ 200639)

Rennison, Callie. *Criminal Victimization 2001: Changes 2000–01 with Trends 1993–2001*. Washington, DC: Bureau of Justice Statistics National Crime Victimization Survey, September 2002. (NCJ 194610)

Rennison, Callie Marie and Rand, Michael R. *Criminal Victimization, 2002*. Washington, DC: Bureau of Justice Statistics National Crime Victimization Survey, August 2003. (NCJ 199994)

Rogers, Donna. "Intercepting the Cybersleuth." *Law Enforcement Technology*, November 2003, pp.22–27.

Schafer, John R. and Navarro, Joe. "The Seven-Stage Hate Model: The Psychopathology of Hate Groups." *FBI Law Enforcement Bulletin*, March 2003, pp.1–8.

Shaffer, Jennifer N. and Ruback, R. Barry. *Violent Victimization as a Risk Factor for Violent Offending among Juveniles*. Washington, DC: OJJDP Juvenile Justice Bulletin, December 2002. (NCJ 195737)

Sourcebook of Criminal Justice Statistics 2003. Washington, DC: Bureau of Justice Statistics, 2003.

Sung, Hung-En. "State Failure, Economic Failure, and Predatory Organized Crime: A Comparative Analysis." *Journal of Research in Crime and Delinquency*, May 2004, pp.111–129.

ten Bensel, R. Testimony. Quoted in *Child at Risk*, 41. Office of Juvenile Justice and Delinquency Prevention, U.S. Department of Justice. Washington, DC: U.S. Government Printing Office (no date).

Thomas, Marcus C. "Study Group Workshops Bring IT Industry and Law Enforcement Together." *The Police Chief*, April 2003, p.14.

"Victim Rights Impose Burdens on Prosecutors, Study Shows." *Criminal Justice Newsletter*, June 5, 2002, pp.3–4.

"Victims' Group to Test Agencies 'Parallel' to Justice System." *Criminal Justice Newsletter*, December 1, 2003, pp.1–2.

Victims' Rights: Right for America. Washington, DC: Office for Victims of Crime, 1998.

Weitzer, Ronald and Kubrin, Charis E. "Breaking News: How Local TV News and Real-World Conditions Affect Fear of Crime." *Justice Quarterly*, September 2004, pp.497–520.

Wexler, Sanford. "The Nation's Fastest Growing Crime: Identity Theft." *Law Enforcement Technology*, April 2002, pp.28–32.

Widom, Cathy S. and Maxfield, Michael G. *An Update on the "Cycle of Violence."* Washington, DC: National Institute of Justice Research in Brief, February 2001. (NCJ 184894)

Wolak, Janis; Mitchell, Kimberly; and Finkelhor, David. *Internet Sex Crimes against Minors: The Response of Law Enforcement*. Washington, DC: National Center for Missing & Exploited Children, November 2003. http://www.missingkids.com.

Zhang, Sheldon and Chin, Ko-Lin. "Enter the Dragon: Inside Chinese Human Smuggling Organizations." *Criminology*, vol. 40, no. 4, 2002, pp.737–768.

CONTEMPORARY LAW ENFORCEMENT

Section I described the evolution of law enforcement from its historical roots to its development in the United States. Wuestewald (2004, pp.22–23),* in addressing the graduation ceremony of the Oklahoma Council of Law Enforcement Education and Training, describes the differences new officers of today will face compared to what they faced 30 years ago as rookies:

> Of all differences between my day and theirs, technology represents the greatest contrast and the supreme challenge. Consider this: when I began my career as an officer, technology was a 1977 Plymouth Fury with a 400-cubic inch, 4 bbi V-8, an old hickory nightstick and a .357 revolver. Now, compare that with the fact that these officers will drive a police car with more sophisticated electronics than the first Apollo moon shot—cars fully equipped with state-of-the-art mobile data computers, digital video cameras and 800 megahertz radios. They will wear lightweight ballistic vests made of space-age material that provide incredible new levels of protection. They will carry high-capacity, 40-caliber semiautomatic pistols, pepper spray and electronic impulse Tasers capable of stopping even the meanest and most determined attacker. They will have access to infrared and thermal-imaging devices to help them see into the darkness. They will use lasers to catch speeding motorists, and they will swipe a digital driver's license to produce an electronic ticket. They will use DNA to identify violent offenders and GPS tracking devices to follow drug dealers, and crime mapping will help them predict where the next burglary will occur.

This section looks at technology and more, beginning with an overview of contemporary policing (Chapter 4) followed by an in-depth discussion of community policing and its emphasis on partnership and problem solving in addition to providing services (Chapter 5). Next is a look at patrol, the backbone of policing, as well as traffic, often a major responsibility of patrol (Chapter 6). The section concludes with a description of specialized roles of police, including investigation, profilers, intelligence officers, juvenile officers, vice officers, SWAT officers, K-9 assisted officers and reserve officer (Chapter 7).

---

*Todd Wuestewald. "The X-Factor in Policing." *FBI Law Enforcement Bulletin*, June 2004, pp.22–23.

CHAPTER 4

Contemporary Policing: An Overview

As a law enforcement officer, my fundamental duty is to serve the community; to safeguard lives and property; to protect the innocent against deception, the weak against oppression or intimidation and the peaceful against violence or disorder; and to respect the constitutional rights of all to liberty, equality and justice.

—Law Enforcement Code of Ethics

 Do You Know . . .

- Why we have police?
- How police agencies relate to the people?
- What five traditional goals most law enforcement agencies set?
- What two concerns must be balanced by law enforcement?
- What additional goals are established by community policing?
- What two basic units exist in most police departments?
- What functions are handled in administration?
- How officers receive their information?
- What the NCIC is?
- What types of records are typically used in law enforcement?
- Why centralization of records is encouraged?
- What is required by a data privacy act?
- What functions are handled in field service?
- What basic styles of policing have been identified?
- How the police image arises?

Can You Define?

administrative services	E911	phantom wireless 911 calls	roll call
community policing	field services	police authority	subculture
discretion	image	reverse 911	typologies
	interoperability		

Introduction

A police funeral symbolizes six themes that illuminate the meanings of police in our contemporary society:

First, the police, to many audiences, represent the presence of the civil body politic in everyday life—they symbolize the capacity of the state to intervene and the concern of the state for the affairs of its citizenry. To many they symbolize as well the continuity and integrity of the society by their visibility and attachment to traditional values of patriotism, honor, duty, and commitment. . . .

Second, the mobilization in uniform of a large body of officers transmits messages about their mutual identification with the corporate body of police—it speaks to the reality of the occupation as formal social control. . . .

Third, the police role conveys a sense of *sacredness* or awesome power that lies at the root of political order, and authority, the claims a state makes upon its people for deference to rules, laws, and norms. . . .

Fourth, the police, and by inversion the death of a police officer, represent also the means by which the political authorities maintain the status quo. They act in the interests of the powerful and the authoritative against those without power and without access to the means to power. . . .

Fifth, the police represent the capacity to deter citizens from committing acts that threaten the order they are believed to symbolize. The police are expected to deter crime, to deter immorality, to deter evil thoughts, or conspiracies to commit crimes. The loss of a police life can be seen as an indication of the vulnerability of the society, of the weakness of the sacred moral binding of the society, and of the reduced capacity to deter such acts. . . .

AP/Wide World Photos

Police officers line the road from the Salem Baptist Church in McDonnough, Georgia, as other officers march alongside the funeral procession carrying the remains of Forest Park Police Officer Richard Cash. Representatives from over 100 law enforcement agencies from around the state attended the funeral service. Cash was shot during a traffic stop in Forest Park.

Finally, this drama with its associate public media coverage indicates and reaffirms the centrality of formal social control in everyday life, and it provides a legitimate occasion for the dramatization of the palpable police presence (Manning, 1997, pp.20–23).

This chapter begins with a look at why we have police and what police do. Next is a discussion of how policing relates to the people, followed by the basic goals of policing and the organization of law enforcement agencies. Then the police culture is examined, as are the styles of police work. The chapter concludes with a discussion of the police image.

Why We Have Police

Why does a modern society such as ours need police? Think about that. Why might you call the police? What if a neighbor's barking dog kept you awake night after night and the owner ignored your complaints? You might sue him, but that would involve time and expense. You might consider shooting the dog, but that could get you sued. Society offers you another option: call the police. Police sociologist Egon Bittner (1974, p.30) says we have this option because situations occur in which "something-ought-not-to-be-happening-and-about-which-something-ought-to-be-done-NOW!"

In our society it is the police who have the authority to do something and to do it now. That something may involve the use of coercive force. In fact Bittner (1980) suggests that this capacity to use force is the core of the police role: "In sum, the role of the police is to address all sorts of human problems when and insofar as their solutions do or may possibly require the use of force at the point of their occurrence. This lends homogeneity to such diverse procedures as catching a criminal, driving the mayor to the airport, evicting a drunk person from a bar, directing traffic, crowd control, taking care of lost children, administering medical first aid, and separating fighting relatives."

It is the police who can demand conformity to society's laws and expectations.

 Police are necessary when coercion is required to enforce the laws.

The widespread stereotyped image of the police, however, commonly overemphasizes their role as "crime fighters," often to the exclusion of all other roles.

What Police Do

What is it that makes the general public think of the law enforcement aspect of police work more often than the social service aspect, when approximately 90 percent of a police officer's time is spent in the social service function?

The cover of a major city's annual police report dramatically shows two police officers reaching for their guns as they burst through the doors of a massive black and white police car which is screeching to a halt . . . the flashing red lights and screaming siren complete the illustration. A less dramatic scene on an inside page of the report shows a police officer talking to a grateful mother whose lost child was returned. Which one of these illustrations most accurately describes the police role? . . . The *New York Times* reports that policemen like to think of themselves as uniformed soldiers in an extremely dangerous war against crime . . . in fact the police are more social workers and administrators than crime fighters (Webster, n.d., p.94).

Most people have ideas about what the police do. According to Manning (p.27):

"To police" means in the most general sense to control by political means the behavior and morality of the members of a politically organized unit. This sense of the word was derived early from the Greek word *polis,* meaning *city,* later roughly translated as *politics.* Policing in this sense means controlling, monitoring (in terms of correcting misguided behavior), tracking and altering, if required, public conduct.

Policing also refers . . . to the tasks that people expect the police individually and in the aggregate to perform for them.

So are the police primarily crime fighters or preservers of the peace? The answer varies by department, but in most departments, the police serve both of these functions. Where the emphasis is placed is increasingly influenced by the citizens within the jurisdiction. It is from them that the police derive their power and to them that they are accountable.

Policing and the People

Police authority comes from the people—their laws and institutions. Although the Tenth Amendment reserves police power for state and local governments, these governments must adhere to the principles of the Constitution and the Bill of Rights as well as to federal and state statutes. Police agencies are not only part of their local community, they are part of state and federal government which, through legislation, provides their formal base of authority. Police are also part of the state and federal criminal justice system which, through the court, determines society's course in deterring lawbreakers and rehabilitating offenders, as was illustrated in Figure 2.1.

To a large extent, the goals and priorities of a police agency are established by what the community wants. For example a community might want more patrols at night, stricter enforcement of traffic regulations during rush hour or reduced enforcement for certain violations such as speeding.

Priorities are often more influenced by the desires of the policed than by any other consideration. Because the success of policing depends heavily on public support, the citizens' wishes must be listened to and considered. Of interest is that one-third of the U.S. population is comprised of "baby boomers," who are generally conservative.

 The people largely determine the goals of policing and give law enforcement agencies their authority to meet these goals. Citizen support is vital.

Because law enforcement is a highly visible representative of local government whose officers are on duty 24/7, people often call upon police for services that they are not specifically required to perform. Other agencies might be providing these services, but people do not know of them. For example if a woman seeks help in dealing with a drunken husband (he is not abusing her; he is just drunk), a drug counselor, minister or social worker might be the appropriate person to call. The woman, however, often does not know this. Because the police agency's reactions to requests for help affect the amount of respect they receive and promote a cooperative relationship with the public, they usually respond as helpfully as possible, even when the matter is technically civil and outside their responsibility.

Traditional Goals of Policing

Because citizens have such a great influence on the goals of policing within the community, the goals of different police agencies vary. Traditionally, however, five basic goals have been established.

 Historically, the basic goals of most police agencies are to:
1. Enforce laws.
2. Preserve the peace.
3. Prevent crimes.
4. Protect civil rights and civil liberties.
5. Provide services.

These goals often overlap. For example officers intervening in a fight may not only enforce a law by arresting a suspect for assault, they may also maintain order; prevent others from becoming involved in the fight; protect the civil rights and civil liberties of the suspect, the victim and the bystanders; and provide emergency service to an injured victim.

Success or failure in meeting each goal directly affects the success or failure of fulfilling the other goals. Although five goals normally established by police are listed, in reality, policing is a single role comprised of numerous responsibilities. In addition any discussion of goals in law enforcement must consider the vast differences between small and large agencies, as well as between rural, suburban and urban departments. Small agencies, often located in rural or suburban areas, tend to have much less specialization, a closer relationship to the citizens being served and less diversity among those citizens and within the agency. Large agencies, often located in urban areas, are likely to have more specialization, a more distant relationship to the citizens being served and much greater diversity among those citizens.

Enforcing Laws

The designation *law enforcement agency* underscores the central importance of this long-accepted goal. Historically, enforcing laws has been a prime goal of policing. However this goal has become increasingly complex. Police not only must decide what laws to enforce, but they also must serve as an integral part of the criminal justice system, responsible for apprehending offenders and assisting in their prosecution.

Unfortunately, because police are in the closest contact with the public, they are often blamed for failures in the criminal justice system. For example an assault victim whose attacker is found innocent in court may feel resentment not only against the court but also against the department. The release of a suspect from custody for lack of sufficient evidence, the failure of a prosecutor to take a case to trial or the failure of the corrections system to reform a convict prior to parole or release all directly affect the public image of policing. The public image of policing is critical considering a large percentage of police work is in direct response to citizen complaints or reports. In fact public support may be the single most important factor in the total law enforcement effort.

Because each community and each state has numerous statutes and limited resources, full enforcement of all laws is never possible. Even if it were, it is questionable whether full enforcement would be in keeping with legislative intent or the people's wishes. **Discretion,** that is, judgment, must be exercised as to which laws to enforce. Both the department and the public must accept that not all laws can be enforced at all times.

Each department must decide which reported crimes to actively investigate and to what degree, and which unreported crimes to seek out and to what degree. The law does not set priorities; it simply defines crimes, classifies them as felonies or misdemeanors and assesses penalties for them. The department sets its own priorities based on citizens' needs.

Usually departments concentrate law enforcement activities on serious crimes—those that pose the greatest threat to public safety and/or cause the greatest economic losses. From that point on, priorities are usually determined by past department experience, citizen wishes and expectations and available resources.

Preserving the Peace

Preserving the peace has also long been accepted by police as an important goal. They have the legal authority to arrest individuals for disturbing the peace or for disorderly conduct.

Police are often called to intervene in noncriminal conduct such as that which occurs at public events (crowd control), in social relations (domestic disputes) and in traffic control (parking, pedestrians) to maintain law and order. They often help people solve problems that they cannot cope with alone.

Frequently such problems, if unresolved, could result in crime. For example loud parties, unruly crowds or disputes between members of a family, business partners, landlord and tenant, or a businessperson and customer might result in bodily harm—assault. Studies indicate that domestic violence often leads to homicide.

A department's effectiveness in actually preserving the peace will largely be determined by public acceptance of this role. Often if police officers simply ask a landlord to allow an evicted tenant access to his or her apartment to retrieve personal possessions or ask the host of a loud party to turn down the stereo, this is enough. Mere police presence may reduce the possibility of a crime—at least temporarily. Here, as in enforcing laws, public support is vital.

Preventing Crime

Crime prevention is closely related to law enforcement and peace preservation. If the peace has been kept, crime has, in effect, been prevented. Crime prevention differs from peacekeeping and law enforcing in that it attempts to eliminate potentially dangerous or criminal situations. It is proactive.

If police are highly visible in a community, crimes may be prevented. For example, a routine patrol might not only discover a crime in progress, but it might also prevent crimes from being committed. This connection is extremely difficult to prove, however, because it is not known what crimes might have been committed if the police were not present.

Crime prevention activities often undertaken by police departments include working with juveniles, cooperating with probation and parole personnel, educating the public, instigating operation identification programs and providing visible evidence of police authority. In addition many community services often provided by police departments aid in crime prevention.

Just as police officers cannot be expected to enforce all the laws at all times, they cannot be expected to prevent all crimes from occurring. Klockars (1991, p.244) suggests: "The 'war on crime' is a war police not only cannot win, but cannot in any real sense fight. They cannot win it because it is simply not within their power to change those things—such as unemployment, the age distribution of the population, moral education, freedom, civil liberties, ambitions, and the social and economic opportunities to realize them—that influence the amount of crime in any society." Regarding these "quality-of-life" issues, Klockars stressed (p.250): "[The police] cannot control economic conditions, poverty, inequality; occupational opportunity, moral, religious, family, or secular education; or dramatic social, cultural, or political change. These are the 'big ticket' items in determining the amount and distribution of crime. Compared to them what police do or do not do matters very little."

A study of resident/police relations in poor urban communities revealed: "The degree of trust that residents have in police is considered to be the degree to which community members believe that the police will share their priorities, act competently, behave dependably, and treat them with respect" (Stoutland, 2001, p.227). However (p.241):

> Many community members were not convinced that the police shared all of their priorities. They saw the police as focusing too narrowly on crime reduction for the short term and not enough on overall quality-of-life issues. Furthermore, a few community members were convinced the police shared so few of their priorities that they were unwilling to cooperate with them and in general avoided contact.

This is where the idea of **community policing** comes from—the need for the police and the people in a community to work together as "coproducers of crime prevention" (Klockars, p.251). The citizens know what the community's problems are and how they might be solved. Citizens are on the front lines and know the pain of victimization. Community policing is the focus of Chapter 5.

Protecting Constitutional Rights

Not only are departments charged with enforcing laws, preventing crime and providing services, they are expected to do so as specified by the U.S. Constitution and Bill of Rights.

The first paragraph of the *Law Enforcement Code of Ethics* concludes with the statement that law enforcement officers have a fundamental duty "to respect the constitutional rights of all to liberty, equality and justice." As noted by the National Advisory Commission on Criminal Justice Standards and Goals (1973, p.9) more than a quarter century ago: "Any definition of the police role must acknowledge that the Constitution imposes restrictions on the power of the legislatures to prohibit protected conduct, and to some extent defines the limits of police authority in the enforcement of established laws."

The commission, however, goes on to state (p.9): "Concern for the constitutional rights of accused persons processed by the police has tended to obscure the fact that the police have an affirmative obligation to protect all persons in the free exercise of their rights. The police must provide safety for persons exercising their constitutional right to assemble, to speak freely, and to petition for redress of their grievances."

Police officers are independent decision makers and have both personal and positional power. One tool officers have is discretion. Right or wrong, officers are often guided by the seriousness of the law violation, who committed it, and the person's age, race and social class.

Many citizens are angered when a suspect's rights prevent prosecuting a case. They begin to doubt the criminal justice system. However, should these same people find themselves suspected of a crime, they would expect their rights to be fully protected. As Sir John Fortescue said: "Indeed, one would rather twenty guilty persons should escape the punishment of death than one innocent person should be executed." The United States must guarantee all citizens, even those perceived as unworthy of such protection, their constitutional rights, or there is danger of a police state.

The authority, goals and methods of the police must promote individual liberty, public safety and social justice. Protecting civil rights and civil liberties is perceived by some as the single most important goal of policing. As a case in point, the National Advisory Commission on Criminal Justice Standards and Goals states (p.9): "If the overall purposes of the police service in today's society were narrowed to a single objective, that objective would be to preserve the peace in a manner consistent with the freedoms secured by the Constitution."

These civil rights and civil liberties also extend to juveniles. Juveniles are subjected to a conglomeration of laws and restraints that do not apply to adults, called status offenses. For example, juveniles are often arrested for liquor law violations, curfew violations, absenting from home, truancy, smoking and incorrigibility. Usually the police deal directly with status offenses, warning the youths or returning them to their parents unless the youth has been a habitual offender.

 Concern for crime control must be balanced by concern for due process—a large challenge for law enforcement.

Providing Services

In addition to enforcing laws, preserving the peace, preventing crime and protecting civil rights and liberties, the police are often called on to provide additional services to their community. This role is acknowledged in the first sentence of the *Law Enforcement Code of Ethics:* "As a law enforcement officer, my fundamental duty is to serve the community." Many police departments have as their motto: "To Serve and Protect."

As society has become more complex, so have the types of service requested. Many new demands are made including giving information, directions and advice; counseling and referring; licensing and registering vehicles; intervening in domestic arguments; working with neglected children; rendering emergency medical or rescue services; dealing with alcoholics and the mentally ill; finding lost children; dealing with stray animals; and controlling traffic and crowds. In addition many police departments provide community education programs regarding crime, drugs, safety and the like.

Considerable disagreement exists regarding what type and amount of services the police should provide. They are often inappropriately asked to perform functions that might better be performed by another government agency—usually because they are the only government representatives available around the clock and because they have the resources and the authority to use force if necessary. However in many small cities and towns the police services provided (even though considered by some as inappropriate "social services") could not be provided by any other agency.

Many police departments offer referral services to direct people in need to the proper agency. For example in Washington, DC, the department uses a *Referral Handbook of Social Services* that indexes available governmental and private services by problem and agency. Police in Milwaukee, Wisconsin, have a comprehensive directory of almost 500 community agencies and organizations.

Of primary importance is that people who need help receive it; who provides the help is secondary. Because many people are likely to turn first to the police for help, however, the department must be prepared either to provide the help or to refer the person to an agency that can provide it.

Contemporary Goals Resulting from Community Policing

Police departments that have implemented the community policing philosophy still place importance on the traditional goals of law enforcement. However most departments have also established two new important goals.

 Goals resulting from implementing community policing usually include forming partnerships with the community and a proactive, problem-solving approach to crime, fear of crime and crime prevention.

Community policing is the focus of the next chapter.

Organization of the Department

The nation's police departments vary greatly, from small, informally organized departments with few employees to highly organized metropolitan police departments with many subdivisions and thousands of employees. The specific organization of a police department is influenced by the department's size, location and the extent and type of crime with which it must deal. For example, small police departments often combine patrol, traffic, community services and investigative tasks in a single division; large police departments usually have separate divisions for each. A community with a major freeway running through its business section faces different problems than a community located on a coast or on a border between the United States and Canada or Mexico. Communities with large groups of minorities face different problems than those that are homogeneous. For some communities traffic control is a major problem; for others gambling, smuggling or racial unrest may be priorities.

Whatever an agency's size, the police organization seeks "strict accountability through a clear rank structure, military symbols and procedures, a rigid communicational hierarchy, and close supervision" (Manning, p.96). The chief of police oversees the operation of the entire department. Under the chief, depending on

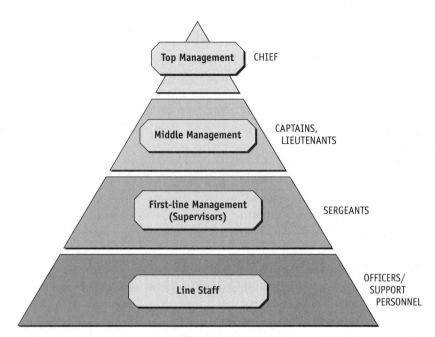

Figure 4.1   Typical Police Department Management Structure Pyramid

the size of the department, are captains, lieutenants, sergeants and police officers. Traditionally most departments have been structured in a militaristic pyramid, with the chief at the top, as depicted in Figure 4.1.

Many departments are moving away from a tall hierarchy to a more flattened structure with fewer officers in supervisory positions, more officers in the patrol division and an emphasis on teamwork rather than on strict obedience to higher authority.

Law enforcement administrators have two sets of obligations:

■ *Internal obligations*—concerned with running the organization: organizing, staffing, directing and controlling.
■ *External obligations*—concerned with the organization's "environment": dealing with important outside forces that affect the agency, such as politicians, the community, the media, judges, prosecutors and the like.

To meet these obligations the police chief must coordinate the efforts of two primary groups—administrative and field services.

 Most police departments are organized into two basic units: administrative services and field services. Tasks and personnel are assigned to one or the other.

Administrative services (also called staff or support services) include recruiting and training, planning and research, records and communications, and crime laboratories and facilities, including police headquarters and jail. Teamwork is essential within and between field services and administrative services. **Field services** (also called operations or line services) include patrol, traffic, community service and investigation. Whatever the size or configuration of the department, basic administrative and field services will be expected. The clear lines depicted in Figure 4.2 may become blurred as departments move to community policing and a team approach.

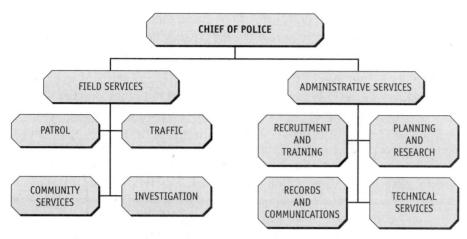

Figure 4.2   Typical Department Organization of Services

Administrative Services

 Administrative services include communications and records, recruitment and training and provision of special facilities and services.

Administrative services are those functions that occur "behind the scenes," away from the front line of the officer in the field. These services include clerical and technical efforts to support and manage the information needed and generated by those in field services. Administrative services' two areas that most directly affect the efficient provision of field services are communications and records.

Communications

To properly serve the community, police officers must be kept currently and completely informed. They must know where and how much of each type of crime occurs. They also have to know what services are needed.

 Current information is usually provided at roll call, by radio, phone and computer.

Roll Call   One of the most important functions of the administrative division in its support of the other units is keeping members informed of daily police operations and providing administrative instructions, special assignments and tasks to be performed. This is usually done at a **roll call** session before the officers on the next shift "hit the street."

Up-to-date information is usually provided in a daily bulletin, which contains brief summaries of what has transpired in the previous 24 hours. Officers are given a synopsis of each complaint received and acted on, as well as descriptions of missing and/or wanted persons, stolen personal property and stolen autos.

Radio and Phone Communications   The information provided at roll call is continuously updated by radio or cell phone. Data are available to officers in patrol cars or carrying portable radios or cell phones. The introduction of the small, hand-carried police radio, cell phone and beeper have extended the communications system so that officers on foot may be reached to assist mobile patrol units and vice versa. This immediate communication has improved law enforcement officers' safety and provided better allocation of resources. Radio transmission dependability has improved steadily over the years and has resulted in a great reduction in response time to calls for service or reported criminal activity.

Computers Computers have revolutionized law enforcement operations, including various administrative functions and communication avenues. According to McEwen (2003, p.391): "Since the 1970s computers have dropped significantly in cost while increasing in power and storage capacity. Moore's Law, which says that processing power will double every 18 months, has held since 1965 and shows no signs of abatement. . . . This revolution [in technology] has profoundly affected the organization and daily operations of police departments nationwide. Advances in technology provide the opportunity for improvements in virtually every departmental function."

Computers have also brought tremendous benefits to the communication efforts of law enforcement, whether occurring within a department, between agencies and departments or with the community. Going online allows officers to access vital data and share information with other officers and managers, locally, nationally and even globally. Furthermore, the Internet provides a forum in which a department can communicate with the community, not only to give the public information about police activities and events but also to get information by soliciting leads from citizens to help in crime prevention and detection efforts.

Interoperability **Interoperability,** or the capacity of various telecommunications and computing devices to "talk" to each other, has become an important issue because of the many companies independently producing PCs, mobile phones, pagers, printers, display monitors and other devices. In the absence of interoperability, these devices remain virtually isolated from each other, able to communicate only through the use of multiple proprietary, or product-specific, cables. Reliance on cable connections greatly limits a user's range of movement and decreases the portability of attached devices.

As Roskind (2002, p.82) points out: "On September 11, 2001, the nation got its first look at a 'Class A' terrorist act, and today we are still afraid to look at the communications failure that was knowingly present and how many hundreds of lives might have been saved if communications had been fixed." He (p.83) notes: "The failures in communications were fully documented. The primary communications failure occurred because of information overload on the incident-commander."

Rogers (2002b, p.48) reports: "On that fateful day [9/11] up to 1,000 fire-fighters, rather than the usual 10 or 20, were attempting to communicate with each other on one congested channel." In addition, fire, police and EMS could not communicate with each other. As Careless (2002, p.72) suggests: "When it comes to improving radio communications between police, fire and EMS, inter-agency coordination is the best way to solve the problem." Ake (2003, p.20) notes: "Interoperability can improve public safety by making it easier for first responders to do their jobs." First responders must be able to communicate and share information. Such information sharing is also of importance in criminal investigations. According to Garrett (2003, p.6): "Information in the hands of law enforcement is power—the power to solve and possibly prevent crime. In homeland security efforts, access to information is critical—the lives of officers, the public and even the country's welfare might be at stake." She also stresses that such sharing of information begins with interoperability.

The National Crime Information Center   One vital source of information for officers in the field is the FBI's online computerized National Crime Information Center (NCIC). In 1967 the FBI implemented this computerized crime information storage system dedicated to serving law enforcement and criminal justice agencies nationwide. Under this system each state has a number of computer terminals that interface with the FBI's main computer in Washington, DC, The computer contains records of stolen property, such as guns, autos and office machines and, in some cases, records of persons wanted on warrants. According to McEwen (p.400): "By 2002, NCIC handled more than 2 million transactions a day, contained more than 10 million records in 18 different files and had access to 24 million criminal history records. . . . NCIC averages about 20 inquiries per second. . . . The results from one year are noteworthy: 81,750 'wanted' persons were found, 113,293 individuals were arrested after NCIC hits, 39,268 missing juveniles and 8,549 missing adults were found, and 110,681 cars valued at over $70 million were found."

 The National Crime Information Center (NCIC) gives all police agencies in the country access to the computerized files of the FBI.

The NCIC computer receives information from other federal law enforcement agencies and from state and local law enforcement agencies. The NCIC makes it possible for a law enforcement officer in Texas who stops a suspicious person or car from California to make an inquiry, to the Washington NCIC terminal in a matter of seconds, on the status of the individual and/or the car. The officer can be quickly informed if the car has been stolen or if an arrest warrant is outstanding on the person in the car. Computers have also had a big impact on how calls are dispatched.

Dispatchers   Communication is the lifeline of the police department. As Rogers (2002a, p.46) suggests: "Call-takers and dispatchers are the first point of contact for the public at their greatest time of need. They are the silent, behind-the-scenes partners, the guiding force and underpinning for the success of all police, fire and EMS efforts." The police dispatcher receives all citizens' requests for police service. In some instances the calls come directly to the dispatcher, who must act upon them and determine their priority. Some agencies have telephone operators screen the calls before giving them to the dispatcher to segregate informational calls from service calls.

Dispatchers are responsible for knowing what patrol vehicles are ready for assignment and dispatching them to requests for service. They may also have some records responsibility, for example making out the original incident complaint report containing the time the call was received, the time the patrol was dispatched, the time it arrived, the time it cleared and the disposition of the call. In addition, dispatchers handle walk-in complaints. Some may also monitor jails through a closed-circuit television hookup. Such a system exists in many smaller and medium-sized departments.

In larger agencies several dispatchers handle incoming calls and assign priority according to seriousness and availability of officers to respond. Larger agencies may also have direct and complete integration of police radio with regular

Before giving calls to the dispatcher, some agencies have operators screen them to segregate informational calls from service calls.

telephone service. In this system any call to the police emergency number is automatically channeled to the dispatcher, who controls squad cars assigned to the area from which the caller is telephoning.

As noted by McEwen (p.395): "Since their introduction in the 1960s CAD [computer-aided dispatch] systems have been the supporting backbone for patrol operations. They operate in real time environments in police communications centers to (1) record information from citizens who call for police assistance, (2) assist dispatchers in sending patrol units and support units to scenes, (3) track the activities of all field units and (4) provide data to police managers to improve the deployment of patrol personnel."

Scott (2003, p.54) notes: "There is an endless array of CAD options available today. CAD features enhanced user interface for quicker data entry, storing and verifying location information entered. This can include such information as street names, intersections, addresses, blocks and common place names." In addition to implementing CAD, many cities have also implemented a 911 system.

911 Systems In a *911 system*, a person needing emergency police, fire or rescue service dials 911, and a central dispatching office receives the call directly. The eventual goal is to have 911 as the emergency number for police service in all U.S. cities. Sampson (2002, p.3) reports: "The U.S. 911 system handles 500,000 calls daily, or about 183 million annually." The 911 system is not without its problems. Sampson (p.2) explains that **phantom wireless 911 calls** occur when a cell phone is preprogrammed to call 911 if a 9 or 1 key is pressed, if the redial is pressed after a 911 call has been placed or when an older cell phone's batteries are low. The National Emergency Number Association reports that phantom wireless calls account for between 25 and 70 percent of all 911 calls in some communities (Sampson, p.3).

In 1996, in response to the proliferation of cell phones and the public's increasing reliance on them to reach out for help, the Federal Communications Commission (FCC) issued a mandate for all wireless service providers to implement E911 technology, which uses geolocation capabilities to quickly trace a caller's location. When fully implemented, **E911** (enhanced 911) service will require wireless carriers to identify the location of the caller within 125 meters at least two-thirds of the time. Thus, if a victim is carjacked and left on the street in an unfamiliar part of town, or is locked in the car's trunk and driven to unknown parts, armed with a cell phone he or she might be able to call 911 and have authorities pinpoint the victim's, and possibly the suspect's, location. However, as Gerber (2003, p.46) points out: "Doubts, delays and dollars hinder E911 implementation."

Sometimes confused with E911 is **reverse 911** (R911), which, as the name implies, allows agencies to alert the public in emergencies. As "Spreading the Word" (2003, p.48) explains: "Reverse 911 (R911) is an Interactive Community Notification system headquartered in Indianapolis, Indiana. Pioneered by Sigma Micro Corporation in 1993, the system is designed to quickly contact citizens in a specific geographic location to communicate urgent information."

With the enormous amount of information police departments must receive, transmit and be able to retrieve, an effective, efficient records system is imperative.

Records

The quality of records kept is directly related to the quality of communications and field services provided. To give proper direction, police agencies must have sound records systems as well as efficient communications systems. Police departments throughout the country vary in their reporting systems and their needs in management control and effective operational control. Their activities require keeping records not only of criminal activity but of all vital department activities.

Types of Records

 Police records may be categorized as (1) administrative records, (2) arrest records, (3) identification records and (4) complaint records.

Administrative records include inventories of police equipment, personnel records, evaluation reports, department memorandums and all general information that reflects correspondence or services rendered. *Arrest records* contain information obtained from arrested persons when booked and information about the control and/or release of prisoners and court procedures. *Identification records* contain fingerprints, photographs and other descriptive data obtained from arrested persons.

Complaint records contain information related to complaints and reports received from citizens or other agencies, as well as any actions initiated by the police. Because police work is public business, it requires accurate documentation of complaints received and the action taken by officers. Complaints may be criminal or noncriminal; they may involve lost or damaged property, traffic crashes, medical emergencies or missing persons. Requests for police assistance may also involve robberies, murders, burglaries, vandalism, children playing in the streets or cats up trees.

Most police agencies have a procedure for recording complaint information on either forms or data processing cards. Initial complaint records are filled out on all complaints or requests for service received by the dispatcher or a police officer. Information on the initial complaint record normally shows the complainant, victim, address of each, type of complaint, time of day, day of week, the officer handling the complaint or request, the area of the community where it occurred, the disposition, whether there was an arrest and whether follow-up reports or further investigation is justified.

Computerized Records Management   According to the *Survey of State Criminal History Information Systems, 2001* (2003, p.1), all 50 reporting states and Puerto Rico had automated name indexes. Forty-nine reporting states, the District of Columbia and Puerto Rico had automated at least some records in the criminal history record file, and 27 states and Puerto Rico had fully automated criminal history files.

Benefits of Efficient Records Systems   An efficient records system is a vital management tool that aids in assessing department accomplishments, developing budget justifications, determining additional workforce needs, evaluating the performance of officers and assessing whether objectives and goals have been met.

Evaluation of carefully kept records will generally reflect needs in training, recruitment, public relations and allocation of resources, as well as general effectiveness. Management's continual or periodic evaluation of records for planning and research has allowed police agencies to provide better service to the public, and, in turn, they have gained greater public support.

 Centralized, integrated, accurate systems of communication and records increase the effectiveness and efficiency of field services.

Privacy of Records   The most sensitive aspect of records on persons arrested is the possibility of including in the file unsubstantiated information that might be derogatory, incomplete or incorrect—information that disseminated to the wrong person could prove damaging and provide cause for a civil action against the police agency. In addition police agencies often tend to retain information longer than necessary.

The Department of Justice has issued regulations to assure that criminal history record information is collected, stored and disseminated in a way that ensures its completeness, integrity, accuracy and security while protecting individual privacy. The regulations apply to all state and local agencies and individuals collecting, storing or disseminating criminal history information either manually or by computer.

 A data privacy act regulates the use of confidential and private information on individuals in the records, files and processes of a state and its political subdivisions.

The *Compendium of State Privacy and Security Legislation: 2002 Overview* (2002, p.4) reports: "Today, virtually all states have enacted legislation governing at least the *dissemination* of criminal history records. Although the approaches differ considerably, virtually all states have followed the lead of the DOJ regulations in distinguishing between information referring to convictions and current arrests, on the one hand, and nonconviction data on the other (information referring to cases without recorded dispositions or with dispositions favorable to the accused). Most states have placed stricter limits on the release of nonconviction data for *noncriminal justice* purposes. All but two states have also established procedures to permit record subjects to review their records and to institute procedures to correct inaccuracies."

Administrative services are vital to the efficient functioning of any police department, but they are a *support* for the field services.

Field Services

Sometimes field services are performed by one division, sometimes by separate divisions. They may be further specialized by the type of individual involved: juveniles, gamblers, prostitutes, burglars, drug dealers and so on; by specific geographic areas (beats); by specific times when demand for service is highest, for example holiday traffic; or by abnormal conditions, such as strikes and protests.

 Field services include patrol, traffic, investigation and community services.

Traditionally police departments have been generalists. That is, most of their personnel is assigned to patrol, and each officer is responsible for providing basic law enforcement services of all types to a specified geographic area. General patrol has been and is the backbone of police work in smaller departments. Larger departments tend to be more specialist oriented.

Patrol

Usually 60 to 70 percent of a department's police officers are assigned to patrol operations, providing continuous police service and high visibility of law enforcement. Tasks include crime prevention, response to calls for service, self-initiated activity and completing administrative functions. Although other divisions may have more prestige, patrol officers are the first and primary contact between the public and the criminal justice system. They not only initiate the criminal justice system, they strongly influence the public's perception of this system. The patrol function is discussed in detail in Chapter 6.

Traffic

Traffic may be a responsibility of patrol, or it may be a separate function. A well-rounded traffic program involves many activities designed to maintain order and safety on streets and highways. Traffic officers enforce traffic laws, direct and control traffic, provide directions and assistance to motorists, investigate motor vehicle crashes, provide emergency assistance at the scenes of crashes, gather information related to traffic and write reports.

The most frequent contact between the police and the noncriminal public is through traffic encounters. Consequently the opportunity for improving community relations through the handling of traffic violations must be considered. Although the traffic responsibilities of a police officer may not have the glamour of a criminal investigation, they are critical not only to the safety of the citizens but also to the police image. In addition many criminal arrests result from traffic stops, for example wanted persons and discovery of contraband. The traffic function is discussed in detail in Chapter 6.

Investigation

Although some investigations are carried out by patrol officers, the investigation services division (also known as the detective bureau) has the responsibility for follow-up investigation. The success of any criminal investigation relies on the cooperative, coordinated efforts of both the patrol and the investigative functions.

The primary responsibilities of the investigator are to secure the crime scene, interview witnesses and interrogate suspects, photograph and sketch the crime scene, obtain and identify evidence and record all facts related to the case for future reference. Investigation is discussed in detail in Chapter 7.

Community Service/Community Relations

In essence every action of police officers affects community relations—either positively or negatively. Many larger departments have separate community relations divisions or community service divisions to strengthen communication channels between the public and its police department and/or to stress public education programs and crime prevention programs. The importance of community relations and community service is emphasized throughout this text.

Specialized Officers

In addition to the basic divisions within police departments, larger departments frequently train officers to perform highly specialized tasks. Specialized officers may include evidence technicians, identification officers, intelligence officers, juvenile officers, vice officers, K-9 assisted officers and tactical forces officers. Specialized officers are discussed in Chapter 7.

The vast array of required general and specialized functions performed by police presents a special challenge in rural areas.

Rural Policing

Many rural departments have only one officer on duty who may be backed up by an off-duty officer, an on-call officer or a neighboring department, and this backup may be more than 30 minutes away. That makes rural policing potentially more dangerous. In addition, uniformed patrol officers in rural environments must be better prepared than their counterparts in urban environments who can defer to specialists when needed.

In some areas of the country, rural policing is performed by a sheriff responsible for a given county. Often the county sheriff is an elected office, making it accountable to the local community. In the majority of states, it is a constitutional office rather than an agency created by state statute, so it can be abolished only through constitutional amendment, and none of its powers or responsibilities may be changed by a county board.

The office of county sheriff has existed for hundreds of years, with roots in ninth-century England. The sheriff's office has evolved into a multipurpose agency with more diverse legal responsibilities than most local police departments, including providing correctional services (transporting prisoners and administering the county jail), providing court security through the assignment of bailiffs, processing judicial writs and court orders, seizing property claimed by the county, collecting county fees and taxes, and selling licenses and permits.

Not all county agencies are rural. Many urban counties also have sheriffs' departments. For example San Diego County includes the city of San Diego and ranks 17th in population of all U.S. metropolitan areas. The San Diego County Sheriff's Department has more than 3,000 members and 31 facilities located throughout the county.

Within larger departments, urban, suburban or rural, a subculture is likely to exist.

The Police Subculture

A **subculture** is any group demonstrating specific patterns of behavior that distinguish it from others within a society. Policing has been identified as a subculture commonly referred to as "The Blue Brotherhood." Police officers work nights and weekends; deal with highly confidential material that cannot be shared with friends; must enforce the law impartially, even when a friend violates a law; and frequently face public hostility, abuse, name calling and biased reporting in the media. A combination of these factors largely accounts for the existence of a "police culture."

Individuals who become police officers commonly lose their nonpolice friends within a few years. In addition to working different hours, they may make some of their friends uneasy, especially those who drink and drive or who habitually speed. Police officers' friends often do not understand some of the actions police are forced to take in fulfilling their responsibilities.

In addition to losing their nonpolice friends, officers may also come to realize that they are now a part of a group isolated from the rest of society—a fellowship united by risk, hardship and fear. Although officers are highly visible, they are set apart. They may be feared, disliked, hated or even assaulted by citizens. Thus they keep close ranks for protection and security. The closer they become, the more citizens fear and distrust them, leading to even tighter ranks, and so the cycle goes. The police become the "in group," and everyone else is the "out group." To a police officer the world consists of cops and civilians, or perhaps better phrased as cops versus civilians.

This "us versus them" attitude, fairly common in some departments, leads to defensiveness exhibited in such ways as reluctance to give up traditional police responsibilities (for example traffic control on state highways) or reluctance to explain their actions to citizens. Official police silence is sometimes necessary to protect the rights of others or to safeguard an investigation, but sometimes it is, in reality, a defensive response. The "us versus them" mentality may also foster an unofficial "blue wall of silence":

> A "Code of Silence" exists today in the law enforcement profession. Those who would suggest that some law enforcement officers today no longer hide behind the banner of loyalty are either naïve or concealing reality, contributing to the problem and enabling others to do the same. Some progress has been made in tearing down this age-old problem, but in many ways a police culture that exalts loyalty over integrity still exists (McErlain, 2001, p.87).

Furthermore, according to Trautman (2001, p.71): "The Us vs. Them mentality is usually present within the minds of those who participate in the code of silence. The code of silence and the Us vs. Them phenomenon often bond together." Trautman (2002, p.17) also notes: "The development of loyalty and the code of silence among officers is a totally natural phenomenon among people who spend significant time together."

However, research conducted by Ferrell (2003, p.9) using statistics from 15 of the nation's 50 largest departments found that "the blue wall or code of silence exists only in the minds of Hollywood movie directors." Research by Paoline (2003) tends to support this assertion: "Recent police studies suggest that police culture is no longer monolithic in nature. With increasing diversity in police hiring practices, individual differences in the work force and in the corresponding culture of law enforcement are expected to emerge. . . . The consensus is that although many social and cultural similarities remain, the traditional 'blue' monolithic attitude and behavioral conceptualization of the police culture is a thing of the past" (p.205).

The subculture of a department or agency can directly affect the styles of police work within it.

Styles of Policing

Many studies have looked at styles of policing and have classified these styles into clusters called **typologies.** Few police officers fall completely into a single typology.

 Basic styles of policing include the following:
- Enforcer
- Crime fighter/zealot
- Social service agent
- Watchdog

The *enforcer* focuses on social order and keeping society safe. Enforcers are less concerned with individual rights and due process. Such officers are often critical of the Supreme Court, politicians, police administrators and minority interest groups. Enforcers have little time for minor violations of the law or for the social services aspect, seeing them as a waste of police time and resources. Officers of this typology are most likely to use excessive force.

The *crime fighter/zealot* is like an enforcer in that a primary goal is to keep society safe. These officers tend to deal with all laws and all offenders equally. The crime fighter/zealot is often relatively new, inexperienced or unable to see the gray areas associated with policing. Zealots are less critical of the social service aspects of policing than are enforcers.

The *social service agent* is more accepting of the social service roles and more attuned to due process. Such officers are often young, well educated and idealistic. Like the enforcer and the crime fighter, social service agents are also interested in protecting society but are more flexible in how this is approached.

The *watchdog* is on the opposite end of the spectrum from the enforcer. The watchdog is interested in maintaining the status quo, in not making waves. Watchdogs may ignore common violations, such as traffic offenses, and tolerate a certain amount of vice and gambling. They use the law more to maintain order than to regulate conduct. They also tend to judge the requirements of order dif-

Table 4.1   The Typologies of Policing Styles

James Q. Wilson (1968)	Robert Pursley (1987)	Joseph Senna and Larry Siegel (1993)
Legalistic	Enforcer	Law enforcer
	Zealot	Crime fighter
Service style	Social service agent	Social agent
Watchdog	Watchdog	Watchdog

ferently depending on the group in which the infraction occurs. Table 4.1 summarizes these typologies as described by three sources.

No officer is purely one type or another, and an officer may change from one style to another depending on the situation. In any given department, it is likely that a variety of policing styles with some combination of the preceding typologies can be found. Policing style is greatly influenced by an officer's personality.

Stereotypes

The police deal daily with criminals, complainants and citizens who may be cursing, yelling, lying, spitting, fighting, drunk, high, angry, irrational, demanding, manipulative or cruel. Some officers' reactions to these daily encounters and the negative personality traits displayed may result in *all* officers being stereotyped as suspicious, cynical, indifferent, authoritarian, bigoted and brutal.

Suspicious   Police work requires an officer to be wary of people and situations that are out of the ordinary, for example a person with an umbrella on a sunny day or a person wearing sunglasses at midnight. Not only is keen observation critical to effective investigation and crime prevention, it is critical to self-defense. Danger is always possible in any situation. Police officers develop a perceptual shorthand to identify certain kinds of people as potential assailants, that is, officers come to recognize certain gestures, language and attire as a prelude to violence.

Cynical   Because police officers deal with criminals, they are constantly on guard against human faults. Officers see people at their worst. They know that people lie, cheat, steal, torture and kill. They deal with people who do not like police, who even hate them, and they feel the hatred. In addition they may see people they firmly believe to be guilty of a heinous crime freed by a legal technicality. This cynicism may also lead to paranoia.

Indifferent   When police officers are called to the scene of a homicide, they are expected to conduct a thorough, impartial investigation. Their objectivity may be perceived by grieving relatives of the victim as indifference or coldness. Officers must remain detached, however; one of the grieving relatives might well be the murderer. Further, a certain amount of distancing is required to work with difficult situations.

Authoritarian   Effective law enforcement requires authority; authoritarianism comes with the job. Without authority and respect, an officer cannot effectively compel citizens of the community to obey the law. As noted by the French philosopher Pascal: "Justice without force is powerless; force without justice is tyrannical." The physical appearance of the police officer adds to this authoritarian image. The uniform, gun, baton and handcuffs project an image to which many people respond with uneasiness or even fear. However, this image projects the right of the police to exercise the lawful force of the state in serving and protecting as well as in enforcing laws. The difficulty arises when the power that comes with the position is transferred to "personal power."

Bigoted   Police are frequently victims of problems they have nothing to do with and over which they have no control. They are not to blame for the injustices suffered by minority groups: housing, educational and employment discrimination. Often, however, members of minority groups perceive the police as a symbol of the society that has denied them its privileges and benefits. Tension between minority groups and any representatives of "authority" has become almost a way of life in many parts of large cities. The minority group members vent their anger and frustration on the police, and some police come to feel anger and dislike for them.

Brutal   Sometimes force is required to subdue suspects. Unfortunately the crime-related aspects of a police officer's job are what frequently draw public attention. When police officers have to physically subdue a suspect, people notice. When they help people get into their locked cars, few notice.

Sometimes, however, more force is used than is required, crossing the line from justifiable force to police brutality. This, too, is easier to understand if one considers the other traits that often become part of the police "personality," particularly cynicism and authoritarianism. Police officers may use excessive force with a rapist if they believe that the probability is great that the rapist will never be brought to trial because of the prosecutor's policies on rape cases. They may also erroneously believe that violence is necessary to obtain respect from individuals who seem to respect nothing but force and power.

A person who dislikes police officers will probably perceive a specific behavior negatively, whereas the same behavior might be perceived positively by one who has a high regard for police officers. Consider, for example, the actions listed in Table 4.2 and the way each is described by a person who feels negatively about the police and one who feels positively about the police.

Two conflicting views exist today as to why these traits might occur more often among police officers than in the general population. One view, the *unique traits viewpoint,* suggests policing attracts individuals who already possess these

Table 4.2   Police Actions Seen Negatively and Positively

Action by Officer	*Negative Person*	*Positive Person*
Steps in to stop a fight in a bar	Interference	Preserving the peace
Questions a rape victim	Indifferent, cold	Objective
Uses a baton to break up a violent mob	Brutal	Commanding respect
Steadily watches three youths on a corner	Suspicious	Observant

traits. The opposing view, the *socialization viewpoint*, suggests that the traits are developed by the experiences the officers have as they become socialized into their departments.

Despite the contention that the police personality may include negative traits, the public image of the police remains high.

The Police Image

Each police officer is an individual. Police officers are fathers, mothers, sons, daughters, uncles, aunts, coaches of Little League teams, church members and neighbors. As people they like to be liked, but often their profession requires that they take negative actions against those who break the law. As a result they are often criticized and berated for simply doing their jobs. Although police officers are individuals just like those in the community they have sworn to "serve and protect," their behavior is very public. It may simply be that they are extraordinarily visible ordinary people.

The public's **image** of the police varies greatly. Some see police officers as protectors; others see them as militaristic harassers. The sight of a police officer arouses feelings of respect, confidence and security in some citizens; fear, hostility and hatred in others; and indifference in yet others. According to Johnson (2001, p.27): "The police officer's uniform has a profound psychological impact on others." He (p.31) asserts: "The uniform of a police officer conveys the power and authority of the person wearing it. . . . Citizens in the presence of a person in a police uniform cooperate more and curb their illegal or deviant behaviors."

The image of the police officer often portrayed on television has not been helpful. The "Dirty Harry" tactics, with violence and disregard for civil rights, are

Warrick (Gary Dourdan), Catherine (Marg Helgenberger), and Grissom (William Peterson) star in an episode of the CBS television crime drama "CSI: Crime Scene Investigation."

CBS/Landov

often presented as the way police officers behave. The effects of television on both the police image and the fight against crime cannot be accurately measured. Certainly it has an impact. Hardly an hour passes without an illegal search, a coerced confession, police brutality and general violence dealt out by television police officers. Many modern police "heroes" are shown blatantly indulging in illegal and unconstitutional behavior, which in effect instills in the public the opinion that police misconduct is acceptable and, in fact, sometimes the only way to apprehend criminals. The same criticisms may be applied to our movies.

 The police image results from the media portrayal of police officers and from everyday contacts between individual police officers and citizens.

In spite of what is written in books or portrayed on television and in movies, the abstraction called the "police image" is primarily the result of day-to-day contacts between police and citizens. Research by Schafer et al. (2003, p.462) on citizen perceptions of police concludes: "Although demographic factors matter, they are less important than being satisfied with police contacts."

It is the behavior of police officers at the patrol level rather than at the command level that is of greatest importance in establishing the police image. In turn the individual behavior of the police officer who creates the police image is the result of several factors, including length of service, the community served (ghetto or exclusive suburb), training and experience.

Factors Influencing Police Image

In addition to easily identifiable and predictable factors, such as experience, training and locality served, many subtle factors influence police behavior and image, including the nature of police work itself, the police officer's unique relation to the criminal justice system and the individual officer's appearance.

The Nature of Police Work Many demands are placed on police officers—they are under constant pressure and faced with rapidly changing conditions, sometimes life-threatening situations, with few guidelines and little supervision. They often must "play it by ear."

Police officers must interact with people from all walks of life who are involved in criminal and noncriminal activities and must use broad discretion in a wide variety of situations. They deal with crimes already committed and with people who are hurt, confused, angry and upset. Yet officers must remain neutral, calm and objective. They may appear indifferent or unsympathetic, but much like physicians, they cannot become personally involved and still do a professional job.

The image resulting from the nature of police work might easily be compared to the image of a football referee. It is readily accepted that referees are necessary to the game. Without them chaos would reign. Despite their importance, however, their image is often negative. No matter what call they make, a great many people are unhappy with them. They are usually perceived as being on the opponent's side. Defeats are often blamed on referees, but seldom is a referee given credit for a team's victory. It is often a thankless, sometimes dangerous job. Fans have tried to physically assault referees. They call them abusive names. It often makes one wonder what kind of person could work under such pressures.

Unique Relationship to the System Another factor influencing the police image is the officers' relationship to the law. Although police officers are many people's first contacts with the criminal justice system, they often feel like outsiders in the judicial system. They may feel their investigation and apprehension of criminals is hampered by legal restrictions and that suspects have more rights than victims.

Although police officers are frequently blamed for unacceptable crime rates, their participation in the legal system is often minimized. They may be made to feel as if they were on trial during the court proceedings as the defense attorney cross-examines them. They are seldom included in any plea bargaining, and many defendants are found not guilty because of loopholes or legal technicalities. When a confessed robber is acquitted on a technicality or a known rapist is not brought to trial by the prosecutor, police officers may take this as a personal affront, as a criticism of their investigative expertise. Citizens of the community may also blame the police for the unsuccessful prosecution of a suspect. Legal technicalities may even result in the police officer being sued for false arrest.

Officers' Appearance   Grooming standards have become somewhat controversial, with some employees arguing that appearance is part of personal liberty and to restrict it is unconstitutional. They also argue that society's standards for acceptable appearance have changed over the years. However, according to Tinsley et al. (2003, p.42): "Police administrators have responded to recent challenges of grooming standards by arguing that more liberal standards would erode public respect for police." Their (p.45) survey found that 95 percent of respondents saw police as a symbol of justice; 87 percent agreed that uniformed police should be governed by strict grooming standards; and 86 percent agreed that public view of the police is governed by their appearance. They conclude: "Relaxed grooming standards would erode public confidence in the police to the extent that respect, trust and pride would decline. The positive image that police currently benefit from has been developed over many years under current conservative grooming policies, and any changes may have long-term and unknown negative effects" (p.45).

The Importance of Image

Blum (2004, p.22) stresses: "Law enforcement administrators who ignore or misplace society's fetish with image are missing a huge point. Requiring personnel to maintain a steadfast agency image will promote officer health and safety, aid recruitment efforts, reduce employee turnover, save money and enhance public image. Leaders who fail to recognize the importance of image may actually hinder their ability to obtain higher salaries, procure needed equipment and elevate community respect for agency personnel and the profession overall."

How the Public Really Feels about the Police

General public support of and confidence in the police appears solid and favorable. Results of a Gallup poll reported in the *Sourcebook of Criminal Justice Statistics 2002* (2003, p.115) indicate the public has more confidence in the police than in the majority of other American institutions. The poll, which analyzed public confidence in 16 specific institutions, revealed that 61 percent of Americans have a great deal or quite a lot of confidence in the police, ranking them second after the military and well ahead of the church and organized religion (50 percent), the presidency (55 percent) and the criminal justice system (29 percent).

SUMMARY

Police are necessary when coercion is required to enforce the laws. The people largely determine the goals of policing and give law enforcement agencies their authority to meet these goals. Citizen support is vital.

One primary goal of police agencies is to enforce laws and assist in prosecuting offenders. A second important goal is to preserve the peace. A third goal is crime prevention. A fourth goal is to protect citizens' constitutional rights. In seeking this goal, law enforcement faces the challenge of balancing the concern for crime control with the concern for due process. A fifth goal of police agencies is to provide services.

Most police departments are organized into two basic units: field services and administrative services. Tasks and personnel are assigned to one or the other. Administrative services provide support for field services and include communications and records, recruitment and training and provision of special facilities and services. Current information is usually provided at roll call, by radio and phone and by computer.

In addition to direct communication, police officers also rely upon information contained in various records depositories. The National Crime Information Center (NCIC) gives all police agencies in the country access to the computerized files of the FBI. Among the types of records the police officer may use are administrative, arrest, identification and complaint records. Centralization of local police agencies' records allows the various line functions to be coordinated. Centralized, integrated, accurate systems of communication and records increase the effectiveness and efficiency of field services. Access to information is not always unlimited, however. A data privacy act regulates the use of confidential and private information on individuals in the records, files and processes of a state and its political subdivisions. Among the field services provided in a police department are patrol, traffic, community services and investigation. Sometimes these are specialized departments; sometimes the services are provided by a single department.

With the varying roles and responsibilities police officers have, it is not surprising that distinct styles of policing have developed. Four basic styles of policing are the enforcer, the crime fighter/zealot, the social service agent and the watchdog. The style of policing demonstrated by various officers contributes to their image. The police image results from the media portrayal of police officers and from everyday contacts between individual police officers and citizens.

DISCUSSION QUESTIONS

1. How has communication between the officer in the field and headquarters changed in the last 100 years?
2. How have the responsibilities of police officers changed over time?
3. What services should police officers provide? Which are provided in your community?
4. What style of policing will you probably lean toward? Why?
5. Have you witnessed firsthand police discretion? Explain.
6. Do you feel police agencies and officers have too little, too much or just the right amount of discretion?
7. What is your image of the police? What do you believe your community thinks of the police?
8. Have you seen examples of unethical behavior in police work? Of actual corruption?
9. What do you see as the greatest challenge for police officers in the twenty-first century?
10. What effect, if any, did the September 11, 2001, terrorist attacks in the United States have on your image of the police? Do you think that event changed how our country views the efforts of law enforcement?

INFOTRAC COLLEGE EDITION ASSIGNMENTS

■ Use InfoTrac College Edition to help answer the Discussion Questions as appropriate.
■ Use InfoTrac College Edition to locate articles on *truancy*. Outline how communities are dealing with this

problem. How are police assisting communities in addressing this problem? Be prepared to share your outline with the class.

- Use InfoTrac College Edition to compare the image of the police in the United States to that of the police in Singapore. Outline the main similarities and differences, and be prepared to share your findings with the class.

- The National Crime Information Center (NCIC) has a wealth of information. Use InfoTrac to find the NCIC and outline what it has to offer. Select one area of interest to explore and write a brief recap of what you learned. Be prepared to share your outline and recap with the class.

 ### INTERNET ASSIGNMENT

Use the Internet to search for *police culture*. Select a document that indicates how the police culture changes in or is affected by a multicultural society. Briefly outline the major changes, and be prepared to share your findings with the class.

 ### BOOK-SPECIFIC WEB SITE

The book-specific Web site at http://info .wadsworth.com/0534552803 hosts a variety of resources for students and instructors. Included are extended activities from each chapter in which students write a policy, use critical thinking skills to make choices in response to a given scenario, use InfoTrac College Edition with direct links to articles for participation in topical discussion forums, and analyze court cases using Web links for research. Many activities can be printed or emailed to instructors. Plus, cited cases with Web links, interactive key term FlashCards, PowerPoint presentations, chapter objectives, and an extensive collection of chapter-based Web links provide additional information and activities to include in the curriculum.

REFERENCES

Ake, George. "First Responder Communication across Jurisdictional Boundaries." *The Police Chief*, July 2003, p.20.

Bittner, Egon. "Florence Nightingale in Pursuit of Willie Sutton: A Theory of Police." In *The Potential for Reform of Criminal Justice*, edited by H. Jacob. Beverly Hills, CA: Sage Publications, 1974, pp.17–44.

Bittner, Egon. *The Functions of Police in Modern Society*. Cambridge, MA: Oelseschlager, Gunn and Hain, 1980.

Blum, Jon. "Image Is Not Everything—But It Helps." *The Law Enforcement Trainer*, January/February 2004, pp.19–22.

Careless, James. "Cooperation: Key to Interoperability." *Law and Order*, August 2002, pp.72–76.

Compendium of State Privacy and Security Legislation: 2002 Overview—Criminal History Record Information. Washington, DC: Bureau of Justice Statistics, November 2002. (NCJ 200030)

Ferrell, Craig E., Jr. "Code of Silence: Fact or Fiction?" *The Police Chief*, November 2003, pp.9–11.

Garrett, Ronnie. "Sharing Info Begins with Interoperability." *Law Enforcement Technology*, January 2003, p.6.

Gerber, Greg. "One Nation, One Number." *Law Enforcement Technology*, July 2003, pp.46–55.

Johnson, Richard R. "The Psychological Influence of the Police Uniform." *FBI Law Enforcement Bulletin*, March 2001, pp.27–32.

Klockars, Carl B. "The Rhetoric of Community Policing." In *Community Policing: Rhetoric or Reality*, edited by J. R. Greene and S. D. Mastrofski. New York: Praeger Publishers, 1991.

Manning, Peter K. *Police Work: The Social Organization of Policing*, 2nd ed. Prospect Heights, IL: Waveland Press, Inc., 1997.

McErlain, Ed. "Acknowledging the Code of Silence." *Law and Order*, January 2001, p.87.

McEwen, Tom. "Information Management." In *Local Government Police Management*, 4th ed., edited by William A. Geller and Carrel W. Stephens. Washington, DC: International City/County Management Association, 2003, pp.391–421.

National Advisory Commission on Criminal Justice Standards and Goals. *The Police*. Washington, DC: U.S. Government Printing Office (LEAA Grant Number 72-DF-99-0002, and NI-72-0200), 1973.

Paoline, Eugene A., III. "Taking Stock: Toward a Richer Understanding of Police Culture." *Journal of Criminal Justice*, vol. 1, no. 3, 2003.

Rogers, Donna. "Crisis in the Comm. Center." *Law Enforcement Technology*, January 2002a, pp.46–51.

Rogers, Donna. "Linking Communications for Interoperability." *Law Enforcement Technology*, August 2002b, pp.48–53.

Roskind, Michael. "Doubling Our Defenses." *Law Enforcement Technology*, June 2002, pp.82–86.

Sampson, Rana. *Misuse and Abuse of 911*. Washington, DC: Office of Community Oriented Policing Services, Problem-Oriented Guides for Police Series, No. 19, August 27, 2002.

Schafer, Joseph A.; Heubner, Beth M.; and Bynum, Timothy S. "Citizen Perceptions of Police Services: Race, Neighborhood Context and Community Policing." *Police Quarterly*, December 2003, pp.440–468.

Scott, Mike. "State-of-the-Art Dispatch Centers." *Law and Order*, August 2003, pp.52–58.

Sourcebook of Criminal Justice Statistics 2002. Washington, DC: Bureau of Justice Statistics, 2003.

"Spreading the Word." *Law Enforcement Technology*, November 2003, pp.48–51.

Stoutland, Sara E. "The Multiple Dimensions of Trust in Resident/Police Relations in Boston." *Journal of Research in Crime and Delinquency,* August 2001, pp.226–256.

Survey of State Criminal History Information Systems, 2001. A Criminal Justice Information Policy Report. Washington, DC: Bureau of Justice Statistics, September 2003. (NCJ 200343)

Tinsley, Paul N.; Plecas, Darryl; and Anderson, Gregory S. "Studying Public Perceptions of Police Grooming Standards." *The Police Chief,* November 2003, pp.42–45.

Trautman, Neal E. "Truth about Police Code of Silence Revealed." *Law and Order,* January 2001, pp.68–76.

Trautman, Neal E. "The Code of Silence Antidote: If Successful, Systemic Corruption Will Seldom Occur." *The Law Enforcement Trainer,* March/April 2002, pp.18–21.

Webster, J. A. "Police Task and Time Study." *Journal of Criminal Law, Criminology, and Police Science,* vol. 61 (no date).

CHAPTER 5

Community Policing, Problem-Solving Policing and Service

The vocation of every man and woman is to serve other people.

—Leo Tolstoy

 Do You Know . . .

- What community policing is?
- How citizens have become involved in and educated about what police do?
- What the two critical key elements of community policing are?
- What the core components of a successful partnership are?
- What problem solving requires police to do?
- What four strategies are involved in the SARA model of problem-oriented policing?
- What changes implementing community policing requires of a department?
- What community services a police department may provide its citizens?
- Who is ultimately responsible for successful police/community relations?
- What community programs have been developed for youths?
- What community crime prevention programs have been developed?
- How our population has changed in the past decades and how it is likely to continue to change?
- What special law enforcement challenges are presented by this changing population?

Can You Define?

American Dream	demographers	integrated patrol	SARA model
broken-window phenomenon	ghetto	medical model	social capital
	ghetto syndrome	paradigm shift	stereotype
CPTED	hot spots	participatory leadership	target hardening
de facto segregation	incident	problem-oriented policing	
deinstitutionalization	incivilities		

Introduction

Rosenthal et al. (2003, p.34) assert: "Community policing is one of the most significant trends in policing history." Police departments and, to a lesser extent, sheriffs' offices in the United States report that they are involved in community policing. Sixty-eight percent of local police departments and 55 percent of sheriffs' offices had a community policing plan in 2000. Two-thirds of all police departments (Hickman and Reaves, 2003a, pp.14–15) and nearly two-thirds (62 percent) of sheriffs' offices were using full-time community policing officers (Hickman and Reaves, 2003b, pp.14–15).

Wuestewald (2004, p.22) suggests: "Certainly, our communities expect much more from a police officer today than when I first pinned on the badge. It's not as simple as putting the bad guys in jail anymore. Citizens expect us to communicate and collaborate. They expect openness and access. They expect us to solve problems and form partnerships. Police work always has involved much more than enforcing the law. But, today, the social aspects of policing are center stage."

This chapter begins with community policing because the ramifications of the change from a professional model to a community-oriented model affect all aspects of police operations. Included within the discussion are the definitions currently applied to community policing, its historical roots, the importance of community, how citizens can be involved and educated and the key elements. This is followed by a discussion of the importance of partnerships and the types of partnerships that might be involved as well as problem-oriented policing, a vital component of community policing. Then a discussion of implementing community policing and its effects is provided. Next the role of community services and the importance of effective police-community relations are explored, including programs that have been implemented for youths and for crime prevention. The chapter concludes with a discussion of the challenges to community policing, including the changing population to be served.

Community Policing Defined

Numerous definitions of community policing exist, but a common thread runs through them. Consider the following definitions:

> Community policing is an organization-wide philosophy and management approach that promotes community, government, and police partnerships; proactive problem solving; and community engagement to address the causes of crime, fear of crime and other community issues (Upper Midwest Community Policing Institute, n.d.).

> The essence of community policing is to return to the day when safety and security are participatory in nature and everyone assumes responsibility for the general health of their community—not just a select few, not just the local government administration, not just the safety forces, but absolutely everyone living in the community (Brown, 2001, p.56).

> Community policing is . . . a belief that working together, the police and the community can accomplish what neither can accomplish alone (Miller and Hess, 2005, p.xix).

Community policing is a *philosophy* of full-service, *personalized policing* where the same officer *patrols* and works in the area on a *permanent basis* from a decentralized *place*, working in a *proactive partnership* with citizens to identify and solve *problems* (Allendar, 2004, pp.18–19).

 Community policing is a philosophy that stresses working proactively in partnership with citizens to prevent crime and to solve crime-related problems.

Community policing might be best understood by looking first at its historical roots, then the components of the philosophy and the four major dimensions it encompasses and, finally, its implementation, as well as impediments to implementation.

Historical Roots of Community Policing

While community policing is considered innovative, recall from Chapter 1 that its roots can be found in the Anglo-Saxon tithing system establishing the principle of collective responsibility for maintaining local law and order, and in the Norman Frankpledge system requiring all freemen to swear loyalty to the king's law and to take responsibility for maintaining the local peace. The importance of citizens in maintaining the peace was also recognized by Sir Robert Peel in 1829, whose central tenets of involvement with and responsiveness to the community were clearly stated when he asserted that ". . . the police are the public and the public are the police." However as the police evolved in the United States, they grew farther apart from the public they served. Social distancing was enhanced by the advent of patrol cars to replace traditional foot patrol.

Conventional police departments are insular organizations that respond to calls for service from behind the "blue curtain." This insular, professional approach began to change in many agencies in the late 1970s and early 1980s. Community policing is viewed by many as a **paradigm shift** from the traditional, professional model of policing. Table 5.1 summarizes the differences between these two approaches to policing.

The Importance of Community

Community has many definitions. It has been defined as a group of people living in an area under the same government. It can refer to a social group or class having common interests. Community may even refer to society as a whole—the public. This text uses a specific, admittedly simplistic, meaning for community. *Community* refers to the specific geographic area served by a police department or law enforcement agency and the individuals, organizations and agencies within that area.

Police officers must understand and be a part of this defined community if they are to fulfill their mission. The community may cover a very small area with a limited number of citizens, organizations and agencies, perhaps policed by a single officer. Or the community may cover a vast area and have thousands of individuals and hundreds of organizations and agencies and be policed by several hundred officers. And while police jurisdiction and delivery of services are based on geographic boundaries, a community is much more than a group of

Table 5.1   Traditional versus Community Policing: Questions and Answers

Question	Traditional	Community Policing
Who are the police?	A government agency principally responsible for law enforcement	Police are the public and the public are the police: the police officers are those who are paid to give full-time attention to the duties of every citizen
What is the relationship of the police force to other public service departments?	Priorities often conflict	The police are one department among many responsible for improving the quality of life
What is the role of the police?	Focusing on solving crimes	A broader problem-solving approach
How is police efficiency measured?	By detection and arrest rates	By the absence of crime and disorder
What are the highest priorities?	Crimes that are high value (e.g., bank robberies) and those involving violence	Whatever problems disturb the community most
What, specifically, do police deal with?	Incidents	Citizens' problems and concerns
What determines the effectiveness of police?	Response times	Public cooperation
What view do police take of service calls?	Deal with them only if there is no real police work to do	Vital function and great opportunity
What is professionalism?	Swift, effective response to serious crime	Keeping close to the community
What kind of intelligence is most important?	Crime intelligence (study of particular crimes or series of crimes)	Criminal intelligence (information about the activities of individuals or groups)
What is the essential nature of police accountability?	Highly centralized; governed by rules, regulations and policy directives; accountable to the law	Emphasis on local accountability to community needs
What is the role of headquarters?	To provide the necessary rules and policy directives	To instill organizational values
What is the role of the press liaison department?	To keep the "heat" off operational officers so they can get on with the job	To coordinate an essential channel of communication with the community
How do the police regard prosecutions?	As an important goal	As one tool among many

SOURCE: M. K. Sparrow. "Implementing Community Policing." *Perspectives on Policing.* U.S. Department of Justice, National Institute of Justice, November 1988, pp.8–9.

neighborhoods administered by a local government. The schools, businesses, public and private agencies, churches and social groups are vital elements of the community.

Also of importance are the individual values, concerns and cultural principles of the people living and working in the community and the common interests they share with neighbors. Where integrated communities exist, people share a sense of ownership and pride in their environment. They also have a sense of what is acceptable behavior, which makes policing in such a community much easier. Community also refers to a feeling of belonging—a sense of integration, a sense of shared values and a sense of "we-ness." Research strongly suggests that a sense of community is the "glue" that binds communities to maintain order and provides the foundation for effective community action.

Social Capital

Communities might also be looked at in terms of their **social capital.** Coleman (1990, p.302) developed this concept, which he defined as: "A variety of different entities having two characteristics in common: They all consist of some aspect of a social structure, and they facilitate certain actions of individuals who are within the structure." Coleman saw the two most important elements in social capital as *being trustworthiness,* that is, citizens' trust of each other, and their public institutions and *obligations,* that is, expectation that service to each other will be reciprocated.

Social capital exists at two levels: local and public. *Local social capital* is the bond among family members and their immediate, informal groups. *Public social capital* refers to the networks tying individuals to broader community institutions such as schools, civic organizations, churches and the like as well as to networks linking individuals to various levels of government—including the police.

Community Factors Affecting Social Capital   If citizens perceive low levels of physical disorder, they will feel safer. If citizens feel safe and trust one another, social capital is heightened. The higher the levels of public social capital, the higher the levels of collective action will be. It is likely that adequate levels of social capital are required for community policing to work. Unfortunately, the communities that most need community policing are often the ones with the lowest levels of social capital.

Lack of Community

Community implies a group of people with a common history and understandings, a sense of themselves as "us" and outsiders as "them." In reality, many communities lack this "we-ness." In such areas, the police and public have a "them-versus-us" relationship. Areas requiring the most police attention are usually those with the least shared values and limited sense of community. When citizens cannot maintain social control, the result is social disorganization. All entities within a community—individuals as well as organizations and agencies—must work together to keep that community healthy. Such partnerships are vital, for a community cannot be healthy if unemployment and poverty are widespread; people are hungry; health care is inadequate; prejudice separates people; preschool children lack proper care and nutrition; senior citizens are allowed to atrophy; schools remain isolated and remote; social services are fragmented and disproportionate; and government lacks responsibility and accountability.

Sociologists have described for decades the loss or breakdown of "community" in modern, technological, industrial, urban societies such as ours. Proponents of community policing in some areas may be missing a major sociological reality—the absence of "community"—in the midst of their optimism about police playing a greater role in encouraging community.

Broken Windows   In unhealthy communities, disorder and crime may flourish. In a classic article, "Broken Windows," Wilson and Kelling (1982, p.31) contend:

> Social psychologists and police officers tend to agree that if a window in a building is broken and is left unrepaired, all the rest of the windows will soon be broken. This is as true in nice neighborhoods as in run-down ones. Window-breaking does not necessarily occur on a large scale because some areas are inhabited by determined window-breakers whereas others are populated by window-lovers; rather, one unrepaired broken window is a signal that no one cares, and so breaking more windows costs nothing. (It has always been fun.)

The **broken-window phenomenon** suggests that if it appears "no one cares," disorder and crime will thrive.

© Tom Carter/PhotoEdit

Wilson and Kelling's classic broken window theory states that broken windows left unrepaired send a message that no one cares about the neighborhood. In such neighborhoods crime and disorder flourish.

Wilson and Kelling based their broken-window theory, in part, on research done in 1969 by a Stanford psychologist, Philip Zimbardo. Zimbardo arranged to have a car without license plates parked with its hood up on a street in the Bronx and a comparable car on a street in Palo Alto, California. The car in the Bronx was attacked by vandals within 10 minutes, and within 24 hours it had been totally destroyed and stripped of anything of value. The car in Palo Alto sat untouched. After a week Zimbardo took a sledgehammer to it. People passing by soon joined in, and within a few hours that car was also totally destroyed. According to Wilson and Kelling (1982, p.31): "Untended property becomes fair game for people out for fun or plunder, and even for people who ordinarily would not dream of doing such things and who probably consider themselves as law-abiding."

Broken windows and trashed cars are very visible signs of people not caring about their community. Other more subtle signs include unmowed lawns, piles of accumulated trash, litter, graffiti, abandoned buildings, rowdiness, drunkenness, fighting and prostitution, often referred to as **incivilities.** Incivilities and social disorder occur when social control mechanisms have eroded. Increases in incivilities may increase the fear of crime and reduce citizens' sense of safety. They may physically or psychologically withdraw, isolating themselves from their neighbors. Or increased incivilities and disorder may bring people together to "take back the neighborhood."

It is extremely difficult to implement community policing when the values of groups within a given area clash. Another factor that negates a sense of community is the prevalence of violence. We live in a violent society. The United States was born through a violent revolution. The media emphasizes violence, constantly carrying news of murder, rape and assault. Even children's cartoons contain more violence than most adults realize and teach children that violence is acceptable and justified. Citizens expect the police to prevent violence, but the police cannot do it alone. Individuals must come together to help stop violence and in so doing can build a sense of community. One way to promote community policing is by involving citizens and educating them about what police do.

Involving and Educating Citizens

Community members often have great interest in their local police departments and have been involved in a variety of ways for many years. This involvement, though it accomplishes important contacts, should not be mistaken for community policing.

 Citizen involvement in the law enforcement community and in understanding policing has taken the form of civilian review boards, citizen patrols, citizen police academies, ride-alongs and similar programs.

Civilian Review Boards

The movement for citizen review has been a major political struggle for over 40 years and remains one of the most controversial issues in police work today. Supporters of civilian review boards believe it is impossible for the police to objectively review actions of their colleagues and emphasize that the police culture demands that police officers support each other, even if they know something illegal has occurred. Opponents of civilian review boards stress that civilians cannot possibly understand the complexities of the policing profession and that it is demeaning to be reviewed by an external source.

Successful resolution of this issue requires that the concerns of both the community and the police be addressed. The desired outcome would be that the police maintain the ability to perform their duties without fear of being second-guessed, disciplined or sued by those who do not understand the difficulties of their job. The key, according to Walker (2001, p.1–21), is that successful oversight agencies do more than simply investigate complaints: "They take a proactive view of their role and actively seek out the underlying causes of police misconduct or problems with the complaint process."

Citizen Patrols

Community policing is rooted in law enforcement's dependence on the public's eyes, ears, information and influence to exert social control. Citizen patrols are not new. The sheriffs' posses that handled law enforcement in America's Wild West have evolved to present-day citizen patrols, reserve police programs and neighborhood watch groups. Some citizen patrols have formed as part of partnerships with the local police department, some independent of police partnerships and some in the face of police opposition. It is often difficult for citizen volunteers to win the respect, trust and support of the police. Police frequently have strong opinions about civilian involvement in what they consider police business or see them as critics of department efforts.

Many of the citizen patrols established throughout the country focus on the drug problem. Some citizen groups have exchange programs to reduce the chance of retribution by local drug retailers. Such exchange programs provide nearby neighborhoods with additional patrols while reducing the danger since local dealers are less likely to recognize a vigil-keeper who lives in another neighborhood.

Citizen Police Academies

Another type of community involvement is through citizens' police academies designed to familiarize citizens with law enforcement and to keep the department in touch with the community. Police academies, while popular with police departments and citizens, have the benefit of building community support for law enforcement and of helping citizens understand the police. They are not, however, community policing initiatives.

The first recorded U.S. citizen police academy (CPA) began in 1985 in Orlando, Florida, and was modeled after a citizen police academy founded in England in 1977. Such academies help a community's residents become more familiar with the daily operations of their police department and to understand the procedures, responsibilities and demands placed on their officers.

Citizen police academies are not without limitations. First, even if attendees sign hold-harmless waivers, the agency may still be sued if a participant is injured or killed while attending the academy. Second, officers and administrators may resist an academy, feeling law enforcement activities should not be open to the public. Third, an agency may feel its resources could be better used.

A variation of the citizens' academy is the Teen Citizen Academy of the Arroyo Grande (California) Police Department. Designed for youths 13 to 18 years old, the academy provides an overview of topics such as gangs, drugs, weapons safety and personal safety.

Ride-Along Programs

Ride-along programs are a popular, yet controversial, means to improve police-community relations and get citizens involved in the efforts of the department and its officers. These programs are designed to give local citizens a close-up look at the realities of policing and what police work entails while giving officers a chance to connect with citizens in a positive way.

Many ride-along programs permit any responsible juvenile or adult to participate, but other programs have restrictions and may limit ridership. Participation by officers in a ride-along program is usually voluntary. Whether riders are allowed to use still or video cameras during a ride-along varies from department to department. Many departments also require their riders to dress appropriately.

Despite the numerous benefits of ride-along programs, some departments do not get involved for legitimate reasons such as insurance costs, liability and concerns about the public's safety. Some departments ask participants to sign a waiver exempting the officer, the department and the city from liability.

CAUTION: Citizen involvement in understanding and helping to police their communities is very important, but it in itself is *not* community policing. At the heart of the community policing philosophy is an emphasis on partnerships and on problem solving.

 The two critical key elements of community policing are partnerships and problem solving.

Partnerships

Partnerships are a cornerstone of community policing. Officers and their departments may team up with citizens, businesses, private policing enterprises and other law enforcement agencies to achieve their community policing objectives.

Police/public partnerships exist on two levels. On a more passive level, the community assumes a compliant role and shows support for law and order by what they *don't* do—they don't interfere with routine police activities and they don't, themselves, engage in conduct that disrupts the public peace.

On an active level, citizens step beyond their daily law-abiding lives and get directly involved in projects, programs and other specific efforts to enhance their community's safety. Such participation may include neighborhood block watches, citizen crime patrols and youth-oriented educational and recreational programs. Citizens may respond independently or form groups, perhaps collaborating with the local police department.

However, today's heterogeneous communities often foster differing and conflicting interests, which are sometimes represented by competing interest groups. Clashes may result between the elderly and the youths within a community, or between various ethnic and cultural groups within a neighborhood.

Traditional policing expected the citizens to remain in the background. Crime and disorder were viewed as police matters, best left to professionals. That meant most citizen-police interactions were *negative contacts.* After all, people do not call the police when things are going well. Their only opportunity to interact with officers was either when they were victims of crime or were involved in some other emergency situation or were the subject of some enforcement action, such as receiving traffic tickets.

Some wonder why the police would consult the public about setting police priorities and why the police would ask for their assistance in solving neighborhood problems. Some believe that the police are paid to deal with crime and disorder and should not expect communities to take any responsibility or do their job for them. Others feel that until something is done about the "whole laundry list of community woes that social scientists tell us are the causes of crime (poverty, teen pregnancy, racism, homelessness, single-parent families, lousy schools, no jobs) the crime problem will never go away" (Rahtz, 2001, pp.35–36). To this Rahtz says: "They are flat-out wrong. Beat cops, working with the people in their neighborhoods, have proven that crime and community disorder can be reduced without waiting for the underlying problems to be solved. I am not saying that poverty, teen pregnancy, etc., are not important issues and do not deserve attention. But if we, as police officers and citizens, sit back in the belief that we are impotent in the face of crime until the problems are solved, we are doing a grave disservice to ourselves and our neighborhoods." Rahtz (p.35) calls partnerships "the glue of community policing."

Partnerships usually result in a more effective solution to a problem because there are shared responsibilities, resources and goals. Partnerships are often referred to as collaboration. Rinehart et al. (2001, p.7) explain: "Collaboration occurs when a number of agencies and individuals make a commitment to work together and contribute resources to obtain a common, long-term goal." When it works correctly, a successful problem-solving collaboration that results in a workable solution tends to be a positive experience for everyone involved.

Rinehart et al. (p.7) suggest: "Not all law enforcement relationships must be collaborative, nor should they strive to be. Under some circumstances it may be appropriate for law enforcement personnel just to establish a good communication plan. Under other circumstances cooperation between two individuals may be sufficient. Perhaps coordination between two agencies to avoid duplication of effort is all that is required. Collaboration is, however, critical for many community policing endeavors." They (p.6) cite the following reasons for developing law enforcement/community partnerships:

- Accomplish what individuals alone cannot.
- Prevent duplicating of individual or organizational efforts.
- Enhance the power of advocacy and resource development for the initiative.
- Create more public recognition and visibility for the community policing initiative.
- Provide a more systematic, comprehensive approach to addressing community or school-based crime and disorder problems.
- Provide more opportunities for new community policing projects.

To accomplish these results, several components of a partnership or collaboration are necessary.

 The core components of effective community partnerships are:
- Stakeholders with a vested interest in the collaboration.
- Trusting relationships among and between the partners.
- A shared vision and common goals for the collaboration.
- Expertise.
- Teamwork strategies.
- Open communication.
- Motivated partners.
- Means to implement and sustain the collaborative effort.
- An action plan (Rinehart et al., p.6).

Figure 5.1 illustrates these core components.

The September 11, 2001, terrorist attacks on the United States, while unquestionably horrific and devastating, had a positive effect by bringing even the most diverse, fragmented communities together in ways rarely seen before. The government's appeal to the nation's public to become "soldiers" in the effort to preserve our American way of life and to be increasingly vigilant about activities occurring in their neighborhoods is a direct application of the community policing philosophy. Everyone is made to feel they have a part to play, an implicit responsibility, in keeping themselves, their communities and their country safe from harm. As Carter and Holden (2003, p.299) stress: "Good communications increase awareness of security issues by the police and public alike and may improve the chance of an early warning of a terrorist attack."

Law enforcement can also partner with local businesses to help combat community problems. Broder (2001) reports on the recently launched "CEOs for Cities," a consortium of business leaders, university presidents and mayors of both parties. He (p.A31) explains:

"Partnership" is the key concept in the approach they are pushing, often built around community development corporations—locally led groups that leverage public and private funds into projects that upgrade housing, improve commercial and recreational facilities and organize neighborhoods to fight crime and demand better schools.

Herbert (2001, p.A23) adds that CEOs for Cities is "committed to the idea that vibrant cities are essential to the long-term health of the U.S. . . . [and contends]

Partnership

Figure 5.1 Core Components of a Successful Collaboration/Partnership

SOURCE: Tammy A. Rinehart, Anna T. Laszlo and Gwen O. Briscoe. *Collaboration Toolkit: How to Build, Fix and Sustain Productive Partnerships*. Washington, DC: U.S. Department of Justice, Office of Community Oriented Policing Services, 2001, p.7.

that the concentration of poverty in the cities, along with the related issues of racial isolation and social pathology, may well be the nation's number one problem."

Another partnership involves "The World's Largest Block Watch on Wheels"— Cab Watch. According to Haldar (2001, p.13): "Cab drivers in New York are eight times more likely than the average citizen to witness or be involved in crimes and emergencies." Taking advantage of the "sheer size, scope and potential" of the city's taxi industry, Haldar explains:

Cab Watch broadens the city's reach in law enforcement without spending a dime of tax money. With the help of the New York Police Department, Cab Watch trains cab drivers to report incidents and accidents without putting themselves or others at risk. Then, it outfits the drivers with 911-direct wireless phones, which are donated. . . .

In the last two years, Cab Watch has expanded from a 50-driver pilot program to more than 1,700 drivers outfitted with wireless phones and ready to dial 911 on the spot. Drivers have alerted police to hundreds of incidents, helping to lead to the arrest of suspects in slayings, hit-and-runs, burglaries, assaults, even incidents of pick-pocketing. The cabbies' quick calls have also helped save lives in car accidents and building fires (p.13).

Various partnerships may be formed to tackle specific community crime problems. For example, in the City Heights area of San Diego, a neighborhood challenged by a very culturally diverse population, widespread poverty and a violent crime rate more than double the citywide average, local residents had identified drug-related crime and juvenile delinquency as their primary concerns. Partnering members of law enforcement with community members was considered a potential solution to these problems. As Stewart-Brown (2001, p.10) describes: "The City Heights Neighborhood Alliance, comprised of a team of police officers and civilian community organizers, set out to solve drug-related crimes in partnership with community residents and to provide residents with the knowledge and skills to solve their own neighborhood quality-of-life problems."

The community benefits from partnerships by a commitment to crime prevention, public scrutiny of police operations, accountability to the public, customized police service and involvement of community organizations. The police benefit by greater citizen support and increased respect, shared responsibility and greater job satisfaction.

Partnerships are also a focal point of the **medical model** sometimes used to explain the relationship between the police and the community. In this model patients are primarily responsible for their own health, with physicians advising patients on how to be healthy, as well as assisting when health problems arise. So, too, in the community citizens are responsible for public safety and keeping their neighborhoods healthy, and they cannot expect the police to take sole responsibility for it. In this community wellness concept, the police and the public share responsibility for the causes of crime, the fear of crime and actual crime.

Another aspect of the medical model is an emphasis on prevention rather than cure, on being proactive rather than reactive and on treating causes rather than symptoms. The medical profession has found that rather than investing all its resources in curing disease, it is more effective to prevent disease in the first place. Such prevention requires the skill and expertise of the professional, as well as the willing, responsible cooperation of the patient.

Interestingly, one of the private-sector businesses that public law enforcement has begun forging partnerships with is private security. In years past, much competition and animosity existed between public and private police. Public law enforcement officers regarded private security personnel as police "wanna-be's," and those in the private sector considered public police officers trigger-happy, ego-inflated crime fighters who often held themselves to be above the law. Recently, however, these two groups have put aside their differences to focus on their common goal of ensuring public safety. One such partnership is the Private Sector Liaison Committee (PSLC) founded by the International Association of Chiefs of Police (IACP) in 1986. The committee's stated mission is to "develop and implement cooperative strategies for the enhancement of public law enforcement and private sector relationships in the interest of the public good."

In addition to partnerships with a community's citizenry and private sector businesses, police departments may also partner with other public law enforcement agencies at various jurisdictional levels.

Cooperative Policing

In the effort to make policing at the community level a success, agencies must not overlook the importance of the services provided at the county, state and federal levels, the basis of *cooperative policing*. Cooperative policing entails developing partnerships among various agencies of law enforcement and the publics they serve.

School/Law Enforcement/Community Partnerships

The differences between traditional policing in the schools and community policing in the schools is summarized in Table 5.2.

The International Association of Chiefs of Police has published a *Guide for Preventing and Responding to School Violence,* which includes the topic of developing partnerships with schools. One of the oldest and most commonly used partnerships is assigning police officers to schools—the school resource officer (SRO). Atkinson (2002, pp.10–11) describes characteristics of effective schools and how school-law enforcement partnerships contribute, as shown in Table 5.3.

Partnerships with the Media

The media can be a powerful ally or a formidable opponent in implementing the community policing philosophy. Positive publicity can enhance both the image and the efforts of a department. Conversely, negative publicity can be extremely

Table 5.2 Comparison between Traditional and Community Policing in Schools

Traditional Policing in Schools	Community Policing in Schools
Reactive response to 911 calls	Law enforcement officer assigned to the school "community"
Incident driven	Problem oriented
Minimal school–law enforcement interaction, often characterized by an "us vs. them" mentality	Ongoing school–law enforcement partnership to address problems of concern to educators, students and parents
Police role limited to law enforcement	Police role extended beyond law enforcement to include prevention and early intervention activities
Police viewed as source of the solution	Educators, students and parents are active partners in developing solutions
Educators and law enforcement officers reluctant to share information	Partners value information sharing as an important problem-solving tool
Criminal incidents subject to inadequate response; criminal consequences imposed only when incidents reported to police	Consistent responses to incidents is ensured—administrative *and* criminal, as appropriate
Law enforcement presence viewed as indicator of failure	Law enforcement presence viewed as taking a positive, proactive step to create orderly, safe and secure schools
Police effectiveness measured by arrest rates, response times, calls for service, etc.	Policing effectiveness measured by the absence of crime and disorder

SOURCE: Anne J. Atkinson. *Fostering School–Law Enforcement Partnerships.* Portland, OR: Northwest Regional Educational Laboratory, September 2002, p.7. Reprinted by permission.

Table 5.3 Characteristics of Effective Schools and How School–Law Enforcement Partnerships Contribute

Effective Schools Alone	*Effective Schools with Partnership*
Safe and Orderly Environment	
A safe and orderly environment is often referred to as "the number-one correlate of effective schools." In such schools there is an orderly, purposeful atmosphere free from the threat of physical harm. School climate is not oppressive but is conducive to teaching and learning. Teachers and students interact in a positive, cooperative manner.	SROs bring to the school setting the expertise of a public safety specialist. They provide an immediate response to life-threatening situations, ensure that laws are enforced when illegal activities occur and work collaboratively with schools to resolve problems that threaten the safety of schools. Their presence has a deterrent effect on illegal and disruptive behavior and communicates that the school and larger community have made school safety a priority.
High Expectations for Success	
In the effective school, there is a climate of expectation in which staff members believe and demonstrate that all students can master the essential content and school skills, and also believe that they have the capability to help all students achieve that mastery.	SROs reinforce clear expectations for appropriate behavior through enforcement of laws, law-related education, and involvement of students in crime prevention activities.
Clear School Mission	
In the effective school, there is a clearly articulated school mission through which the staff shares an understanding of and commitment to instructional goals, priorities, assessment procedures and accountability.	The school–law enforcement partnership helps schools to focus on their central mission—educating—by reducing the amount of time the staff must spend on disciplinary matters.
Instructional Leadership	
In an effective school, the principal and other staff members take an active role in instructional leadership with the principal becoming a "leader of leaders" (rather than a leader of followers), functioning as a coach or partner.	When crime and other disruptive behaviors are reduced, school leaders can focus more effectively on their central instructional leadership role.
Frequent Monitoring of Student Progress	
In the effective school, student academic progress is measured frequently using a variety of assessment procedures. The assessment results are used to improve individual student performance and the instructional program.	The school–law enforcement partnership uses data on crime and discipline to assess and improve school safety.
Opportunity To Learn and Student Time on Task	
In the effective school, teachers allocate a significant amount of classroom time to instruction in the essential skills.	Opportunity to learn and student time on task are increased when disruptive behavior is reduced.
Home–School Relations	
Effective schools have formed partnerships with parents who are given the opportunity to play important roles in the school. These schools have built trust and communicated with parents who understand and support the school's basic mission.	Partnership, characterized by trust and communication, is a central component of community policing. Law enforcement adds a public safety specialist to home–school partnerships.

SOURCE: Anne J. Atkinson. *Fostering School–Law Enforcement Partnerships.* Portland, OR: Northwest Regional Educational Laboratory, September 2002, pp. 10–11. Reprinted by permission.

School resource officers (SROs) are found throughout the country, helping to make schools safer and more conducive to learning and building positive relationships between students and law enforcement.

damaging. Therefore, police agencies can and should make every effort to build positive working partnerships with the media. The police and members of the media share the common goal of serving the public.

As Gardner (2001, p.8) stresses: "In reality, police and the media need each other. The news business needs law enforcement and its leaders as perhaps the single, biggest source of the stories the public wants to hear and see. The police executive, on the other hand, needs the access to his or her citizenry the press can provide. The wise law enforcement executive will take advantage of that access to recognize the good work done by the frontline troops, enlist the public's support in backing a new program or crime prevention effort and get the community's help in solving a tough case."

To improve police-media relations, the press should be informed of a department's policies and procedures regarding the media and crime scenes. Officers should avoid police jargon and technical terminology and respect reporters' deadlines by releasing information in a timely manner so the press has a chance to fully understand the situation. As police departments adopt the community policing philosophy and implement its strategies, public support is vital. The media can play an important role in obtaining that support—or losing it.

Community Policing, Partnerships and the Decrease in Crime

According to the Bureau of Justice Statistics National Crime Victimization Survey (NCVS), from 1999 to 2000 the violent crime rate declined 15 percent, reaching the lowest level in NCVS history, and property crime declined 10 percent, continuing a more than 20-year decline. Other data from the FBI's Uniform Crime Reports indicate the crime index rate fell for the ninth straight year in 2000, declining 3.3 percent from 1999, 18.9 percent from 1996 and 30.1 percent from 1991 (BJS Web site, http://www.ojp.usdoj.gov/bjs).

Many researchers report a direct correlation between the number of officers on the street and the decline in crime. The decrease in crime, however, cannot all be attributed to community policing efforts. Quality-of-life issues, a robust economy and a population with greater numbers of elderly and fewer juveniles also contribute to lower crime rates.

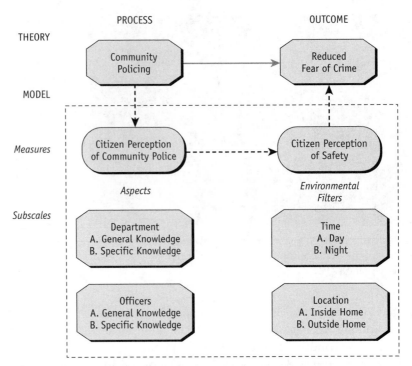

Figure 5.2 Theoretical Relationship between Community Policing and Fear of Crime and Model for Testing Theory

SOURCE: A. Steven Dietz. "Evaluating Community Policing: Quality Police Service and Fear of Crime." *Policing: An International Journal of Police Strategy and Management.* vol. 20, no. 1, 1997, p.88. Reprinted by permission.

Some have praised community policing efforts for their ability to reduce citizens' fear of crime. However, caution is needed when evaluating such results. Figure 5.2 presents the theoretical relationship between community policing and citizen fear of crime.

Acknowledging the impediments, criticisms and cautions concerning the community policing philosophy is a vital step in moving forward to true police/community partnerships. Another vital step is to adopt a problem-oriented approach to policing, which is, again, proactive rather than reactive.

Problem-Oriented Policing and Problem Solving

Problem-oriented policing and community-oriented policing are sometimes equated. In fact, however, problem-oriented policing is an essential component of community policing. Its focus is on determining the underlying causes of problems, including crime, and identifying solutions. Miller and Hess (p.17) explain:

> Where traditionally policing has been *reactive*, responding to calls for service, community policing is *proactive*, anticipating problems and seeking solutions to them. The term *proactive* is beginning to take on an expanded definition. Not only is it taking on the meaning of anticipating problems, but it is also taking on . . . that of accountability and choosing a response rather than reacting the same way each time a similar situation occurs. Police are learning that they do not obtain different results by applying the same methods. In other words, to get different results, different tactics are needed.

Community policing or variations of it that rely on problem solving are known by several names: community-oriented policing and problem solving (COPPS), neighborhood-oriented policing (NOP), problem-oriented policing (POP), community-based policing and the like. Eck and Spelman's classic *Problem Oriented Policing* (1987) defines **problem-oriented policing** as a "departmental-wide strategy aimed at solving persistent community problems. Police identify, analyze and respond to the underlying circumstances that create incidents." No matter what the approach is called, all use a problem-solving approach to crime and disorder. Throughout this text references to community policing infer that problem solving is involved.

Many practitioners equate community policing and problem solving. As Wilson and Kelling (1989, p.49) note: "Community-oriented policing means changing the daily work of the police to include investigating problems as well as incidents. It means defining as a problem whatever a significant body of public opinion regards as a threat to community order. It means working with the good guys, and not just against the bad guys." Wilson and Kelling suggest that community policing requires the police mission to be redefined "to help the police become accustomed to fixing broken windows as well as arresting window-breakers."

Goldstein (1990, p.20), who is credited with originating problem-oriented policing (POP) and coining the term, was among the first to criticize the professional model of policing as being incident driven: "In the vast majority of police departments, the telephone, more than any policy decision by the community or by management, continues to dictate how police resources will be used." The primary work unit in the professional model is the **incident,** that is, an isolated event that requires a police response. The institution of 911 has greatly increased the demand for police services and the public's expectation that the police will respond quickly.

As Rahtz (p.57) explains: "The emphasis on solving problems is what separates our two styles of policing [traditional policing and community policing]. Reactive Jack's day is dictated by the radio. Anyone in the community who picks up the phone and dials 911 has more control over Jack than his supervisor does. Jack's workday is not informed by any serious analysis of the problems on his beat. Instead, he runs willy nilly where the radio calls lead. He handles the calls as quickly as possible, and in the time between radio runs he cruises about with little purpose waiting for the next dispatch. For a lot of cops, that is the sum total of police work. For beat officers tired of the merry-go-round of reactive policing, for cops looking for a more intelligent approach to police work, community policing emphasizing problem solving will be a godsend."

Goldstein (p.33) also asserts: "Most policing is limited to ameliorating the overt, offensive symptoms of a problem." He suggests that police are more productive if they respond to incidents as symptoms of underlying community problems. He (p.66) defines a problem as "a cluster of similar, related, or recurring incidents rather than a single incident, a substantive community concern, and a unit of police business." Once the problems in a community are identified, police efforts can focus on addressing the possible causes of such problems.

 Problem solving requires police to group incidents and, thereby, identify underlying causes of problems in the community.

Although problem solving may be the ideal, law enforcement cannot ignore specific incidents. When calls come in, most police departments respond as soon as possible. Problem solving has a dual focus. First, it requires that incidents be linked to problems. Second, time devoted to "preventive" patrol must be spent proactively, determining community problems and their underlying causes.

Many law enforcement agencies have now combined the operational strategies of community-oriented policing and problem solving (COPPS) to address a broad range of crime problems and the quality-of-life issues associated with them. Problem-oriented policing, a vital component of the community policing philosophy, requires that police move beyond a law enforcement perspective in seeking solutions to problems.

As noted by Goldstein (p.2): "The dominant perspective of policing is heavily influenced by the primary method of control associated with the work—the authority to enforce the criminal law." He suggests that this view has "disproportionately influenced the operating practices, organization, training, and staffing of police agencies." It is like tunnel vision. Effective problem-oriented policing requires abandoning the "simplistic notion that the criminal law defines the police's role" and accepting that "policing consists of developing the most effective means for dealing with a multitude of troublesome situations." He suggests that "these means will often, but not always, include appropriate use of the criminal law."

Goldstein illustrates this change in perspective with the way the police have approached the drug problem, that is, with a law enforcement approach. Gradually the police and the public are coming to realize that this approach, arresting and prosecuting drug dealers, is ineffective. Goldstein contends:

> The challenge is to determine what use should be made by the police of the criminal law (given the difficulty of the process and limited resources); what other means are available to the police for dealing with the problem; and what the police (given their first-hand knowledge of the magnitude and complexity of the problem) should be urging others to do in responding to it (p.2).

Eck and Spelman (p.2) explain that problem-oriented policing is the result of 20 years of research into police operations converging on three main themes:
1. *Increased effectiveness* by attacking underlying problems that give rise to incidents that consume patrol and detective time.
2. *Reliance on the expertise and creativity of line officers* to study problems carefully and develop innovative solutions.
3. *Closer involvement with the public* to make sure that the police are addressing the needs of citizens.

Eck and Spelman developed the **SARA model** of problem-oriented policing.

 The four strategies of the SARA model of problem-oriented policing are:
1. **S**canning—grouping individual incidents into meaningful "problems."
2. **A**nalyzing—collecting information from all available sources (not just police data).
3. **R**esponding—selecting and implementing solutions.
4. **A**ssessing—evaluating the impact of the solution.

One proposed tool to help law enforcement use problem solving to tackle crime is the crime triangle.

The Crime Triangle

The crime triangle consists of an offender, a victim and a location. Crime is presumed amenable to suppression if any of the three legs of the triangle are removed, or neutralized. Figure 5.3 illustrates the crime triangle.

As illustrated in the crime triangle, one critical element of crime is location. Criminal justice researchers and practitioners have only recently begun to shift their focus from *people* who commit crimes to *places* where offenses occur. One result of this shift has been the identification of **hot spots,** specific locations with high crime rates. (The term is borrowed from geology in describing areas where hot magma rises toward the earth's surface, creating the potential for volcanic eruption.) A hot spot may be a single address or intersection, a group of addresses in close proximity to each other or an entire block or more.

Borrowing a concept from ecology, Braiden (1998, p.8) proposes another way to view the significance of location in the problem-solving efforts of policing—"the hunt and the habitat":

> I can't think of two special-interest groups more philosophically opposed to each other than hunters and animal rights activists, yet there are two things they totally agree upon: The species will survive the hunt; it will not survive loss of its habitat.
>
> What can policing learn from this basic principle of nature? Well, if the ultimate goal is to eliminate the criminal species forever, surely the best way to do that is to eliminate the habitat that spawns and sustains that species. Structured as it is, the criminal justice system puts 95 percent of its resources

Figure 5.3 The Crime Triangle

into the hunt while the habitat is left almost untouched. We can never win working that way, because the habitat never stops supplying new customers for the hunt.

So what is law enforcement to do if they hope to sharpen their problem-solving skills and maximize the effectiveness of their efforts? Several long-term solutions have been suggested.

Long-Term Solutions   Continuing with the ecological analogies, communities may be seen as fertile environments, or gardens, able to produce nearly anything if the proper conditions are present. However, like most gardens, weeds (criminals) inevitably crop up and need to be removed to allow the more desirable flowers (law-abiding citizens) the necessary room and resources to grow. The federal government's Weed and Seed program was intended to help "groom" communities, planting seeds to help rebuild urban neighborhoods and weeding out the elements of crime, but some have criticized that too much focus has been placed on weeding and not enough on seeding.

Common Mistakes in Problem Solving

As Bennett and Hess (2004, p.128) note: "Common mistakes in problem solving and decision making include spending too much energy on unimportant details, failing to resolve important issues, being secretive about true feelings, having a closed mind and not expressing ideas. . . . Inability to decide, putting decisions off to the last minute, failing to set deadlines, making decisions under pressure and using unreliable sources of information are other common errors in problem solving and decision making." Other mistakes commonly made during problem solving and decision making include making multiple decisions about the same problem, finding the right decision for the wrong problem (that is, dealing with symptoms rather than causes), failing to consider the costs, delaying a decision and making decisions while angry or excited.

Bennett and Hess (p.129) offer a checklist against which to evaluate decisions. Is the decision: consistent with the agency's mission, goals and objectives; a long-term solution; cost effective; legal; ethical; practical; and acceptable to those responsible for implementing it?

Implementing Community Policing

 Community policing will require a change in management style, mission statement and departmental organization.

Community policing usually requires a different management style. The traditional autocratic style effective during the industrial age will not have the same effect in the twenty-first century. One viable alternative to the autocratic style of management is participatory leadership. In **participatory leadership** each individual has a voice in decisions, but top management still has the ultimate decision-making authority. Table 5.4 summarizes the key concepts of and compares the authoritarian and participatory styles of management.

The leader must also have a vision for the department and the community. This vision should include the essential elements of the community policing phi-

Table 5.4 Authoritarian and Participatory Leadership Styles Compared

Authoritarian (Mechanistic) Style	Participatory (Organic) Style
Response to incidents	Problem solving
Individual effort and competitiveness	Teamwork
Professional expertise	Community orientation; ask customers what they want
Go by the "book"; decisions by emotion	Use data-based decision making
Tell subordinates	Ask and listen to employees
Boss as patriarch and order giver	Boss as coach and teacher
Maintain status quo	Create, innovate, experiment
Control and watch employees	Trust employees
Reliance on scientific investigation and technology rather than people	Reliance on skilled employees—a better resource than machines
When things go wrong, blame employees	Errors mean failed systems/processes—improve them
Organization is closed to outsiders	Organization is open

losophy: problem solving, empowering everyone, forming community partnerships and being proactive—making preventing crime as important as enforcing the law. Changes in the organization usually include the following:

- The bureaucracy is flattened and decentralized.
- Roles of those in management positions change to leaders and mentors rather than managers and supervisors.
- Patrol officers are given new responsibilities and are empowered to make decisions and problem solve with their community partners.
- Permanent shifts and areas are assigned.
- Despecialization reduces the number of specialized units, channeling more resources toward the direct delivery of police services to the public.
- Teams improve efficiency and effectiveness by pooling officer resources in groups.
- Civilianization replaces sworn personnel with nonsworn personnel to maximize cost effectiveness; reassigning sworn personnel to where they are most needed.

In addition to these organizational changes, the needs of the community must be assessed.

Analyzing the Community

"A survey sends a clear message to community stakeholders that their opinions matter. This is especially important in neighborhoods that are wary of government intervention and suspicious of outsiders. By conducting a survey, planners show that their project will be different: it will not be an unwanted government program. Rather, the project will be tailored to the community's needs and concern" (Palk, 2003).

The Effect of Implementing Community Policing

Researchers Zhao et al. (2003) examined changes in law enforcement organizational priorities related to three core policing functions—crime control, the maintenance of order and the provision of services—during the era of community policing. They analyzed the changes by using data from three national surveys of more than 200 municipal police departments conducted in 1993, 1996 and 2000. They found that police core-function priorities remained largely unchanged, but that the systematic implementation of COP programs reflects an all-out effort to address all three core functions at a higher level of achievement. They (p.716) conclude: "Our analysis showed that the extent of implementation of COP is a statistically significant predictor of all core functions of policing. On the basis of the analysis presented here, we argue that COP can be characterized as a comprehensive effort by local police simultaneously to control crime, to reduce social disorder and to provide services to the citizenry." A basic difference, however, is that they no longer seek to do it alone, but rather through partnerships and problem solving.

A Community Service Orientation

A key strategy of community policing is linking policing to the delivery of city services. Community service translates into customer service. If policing is viewed as a business, its product is service, and its customers are the citizens, businesses, organizations and agencies within its jurisdiction.

Taking a page from the business world, "customer oriented" means providing the best service possible; being courteous, honest, open and fair; treating each person as an individual, not as an inconvenience; listening and being responsive to what each person wants; keeping promises; knowing who to refer people to; and thanking people when they are helpful. Police officers should be "consumer friendly" as they serve and protect. The types of service provided by the police take a variety of forms.

 Police departments may provide a wide variety of services including giving information, directions and advice; counseling and referring; licensing and registering vehicles; intervening in domestic arguments; working with neglected and/or abused children; rendering emergency medical or rescue services; dealing with alcoholics and the mentally ill; finding lost children; dealing with stray animals; controlling crowds; and providing community education programs on crime prevention, drug abuse, safety and the like.

Although some police departments have a separate division assigned to the responsibilities of community service and some have made community service a responsibility of a patrol team, in reality, community service is a vital part of every police officer's job.

Many citizens use 911 as a local hotline, a number to call to get the right number to call. To help handle the barrage of such calls, some police agencies are going online with Web sites for citizen information and input.

Clearly, serving as a resource is one aspect of law enforcement's duty "to serve." As another part of their role to preserve the peace and safety of the public, police officers may be dispatched to handle calls regarding domestic violence, to intervene in disputes and disturbances, to quell civil disturbances and to maintain order in labor/management disputes and strikes.

A common and often dangerous type of call made to the police department is for assistance in settling *disputes or quarrels*, for example bar fights. Often alcohol is involved in such situations. Tempers are short, and the potential for violence is ever present. This potential for disputes and disturbances exists in a variety of situations—parties to traffic crashes, young people blasting stereos and other incidents where hostility may arise. The fine line between obnoxious behavior that infringes on other people's peace and harmless antics that merely defy standards of "good behavior" is easily crossed. Neighborhood residents may be annoyed when teenagers hang out on the streets, and people walking down a city sidewalk may be disturbed by activists passing out political or religious fliers, yet the teenagers and activists each have a legal right to be doing what they are doing.

Civil disturbances and riots present another challenge to police in preserving community peace and safety. The civil disturbances on campuses throughout the country in the 1960s highlighted the role of the police in controlling such disturbances. Although civil disturbances are not as prevalent today, demonstrations continue throughout the country—for example antiwar protests, demonstrations against legislative decisions, demonstrations for or against abortion and protests against industries engaged in manufacturing war materials.

In dealing with civil disturbances, the primary responsibilities of police officers are to maintain order and to protect lives and assets. In the event of sit-in demonstrations, it may be necessary to forcibly remove participants. However, police must also be aware of citizens' constitutionally protected right to *peacefully* assemble. Only when the assembly is no longer peaceful do officers have the responsibility to intervene. Determining what constitutes peaceful assembly places a large amount of discretionary power in the hands of police officers.

Labor/management disputes and strikes may also threaten community peace and safety. Strikes are legal, but as with the right to assemble, the strike must be peaceful. If strikers physically restrict others from crossing the picket line, they are acting illegally, and the police may be called to intervene. In such instances police officers must remain neutral. Their only responsibility is to prevent violence and property damage or loss.

Providing Emergency Services

Patrol officers are often the first on the scene of a situation requiring emergency services. For example, at the scene of a traffic crash, police are responsible for providing first aid to any injured persons. They may also be called to help people who have been injured in other ways or who become seriously ill. Police officers should be thoroughly trained and certified in CPR and advanced first aid, including measures to stop bleeding and to deal with fractures, shock, burns and epileptic seizures.

Police officers may be required to transport to the nearest medical facility accident victims or gravely ill or injured people. In fact, in some communities, the police department is the sole ambulance service, and patrol cars are specially equipped to serve as ambulances. This policy of providing ambulance service tends to make the public more appreciative of the police department and may foster citizen cooperation.

Natural disasters, such as floods, tornadoes, hurricanes, fires and earthquakes, can produce emergency conditions requiring police action. Police may need to provide first aid to victims, provide crowd control and protect the property of those

© Mark Richards/PhotoEdit

During civil disturbances or riots police are faced with not only controlling the crowds but protecting property.

involved. Furthermore, many departments are also actively involved in search-and-rescue operations that may or may not be necessitated by natural disasters.

In some departments police and fire fighting are combined into a public safety department. In such instances police officers must be trained in fire-suppression techniques. In departments where the police are not primarily responsible for fire-suppression activities, they may still be the first to arrive at the scene of a fire and can lend valuable assistance to the firefighters.

If a bomb threat is made or a bomb is actually found, the police are usually the ones notified. In such instances their main responsibility is to assure the safety of those in the bomb's vicinity and to call in experts to actually dispose of the bomb. Frequently a bomb disposal unit of a military installation is called. Larger departments may have their own bomb disposal teams. In the event of an actual explosion, be it intentional or accidental, the police are usually responsible for crowd control and for investigating the incident.

The heroism of law enforcement officers was graphically illustrated in the September 11, 2001, attacks on the United States when officers were rushing to the World Trade Center twin towers as citizens were rushing from it. Twenty-three

New York City police officers and 37 Port Authority officers lost their lives in addition to 356 emergency rescue workers who also perished (NYPD Web site, Port Authority Web site and http://www.vwtcmemorial.com).

Other Community Services

Police departments may or may not provide several other services, depending on local policy, including helping to locate missing persons; investigating damage-to-property incidents; providing a lost and found; dealing with missing and stray animals; providing escort services; assisting people who have locked themselves out of their vehicles or homes; transporting civilians on official business; licensing handguns, parade permits and the like; inspecting buildings for adherence to fire codes, health codes and building codes; inspecting trucks' weights; and answering alarms, which can be a tremendous drain on a police department given the false-alarm problem.

Hundreds of programs have aided the police not only by improving law enforcement efforts but also by enhancing community relations. As police officers' knowledge of the community and its citizens increases, so does their effectiveness as law enforcement officers. Their street contacts and sources of information are also vastly improved. While community acceptance of crime prevention programs depends on the overall effectiveness of all police operations, it is the individual police officer on the street who serves as the department's community relations officer. The officer's actions, demeanor, appearance and empathy translate into positive or negative community relations.

 The police officer on the street is ultimately responsible for the success of police-community relations.

Community relations is a responsibility of both the police and citizens. The majority of police departments in the country have implemented some type of community-oriented programs, the most common being programs for youths, educational programs, block watch programs, special task units and foot or mounted patrol. Other community-oriented programs include block meetings, volunteer programs, business watch, storefront stations, victim contact programs, citizen surveys and community newsletters.

Youth Programs

The youths of our country are of critical importance.

 Programs for youths may include PAL programs, school resource officers, McGruff, Explorer posts and the DARE program.

The PAL Program

Police Athletic League (PAL) programs have been in operation for more than 50 years. These programs were developed to give youths opportunities to interact with police officers in sports, providing positive alternative activities. In Portland, Oregon, the police department has adopted the program to deal with increasing gang violence and street sales of drugs. Sports in their program include boxing, wrestling, football, soccer, martial arts, basketball, racquetball, track and field, volleyball and speed and quickness training.

School Resource Officers

Girouard (2001, p.1) states: "Although research continues to show that schools are relatively safe places for children . . . the subject of school safety continues to concern families, school administrators, and communities." The response to this concern is not new; the first police-school liaison program was developed in Flint, Michigan in 1958. Atkinson (p.55) asserts: "Demand for school resource officers (SROs) has increased dramatically with heightened public concern about school safety."

The Omnibus Crime Control and Safe Streets Act of 1968 defines an SRO as "a career law enforcement officer, with sworn authority, deployed in community-oriented policing, and assigned by the employing police department or agency to work in collaboration with school and community-based organizations" (Girouard, p.1). Atkinson notes that, as public safety specialists, SROs contribute daily to the safety and security of the schools in which they work: "Experience has taught that the presence of an SRO has a deterrent effect on illegal and disruptive behavior" (p.57).

The COPS Office has awarded in excess of $715 million to more than 2,600 law enforcement agencies to fund over 6,000 school resource officers through its COPS in Schools (CIS) program. In addition, COPS has dedicated approximately $21 million to training COPS-funded SROs and the school administrator in the partnering school(s) or school district(s) to work more collaboratively through the CIS program (*Cops in Schools*, 2003, p.1). The COPS Secure Our Schools (SOS) initiative provides funds to help cover the cost of security measures such as metal detectors, locks and lighting as well as security assessments and training (*Secure Our Schools Initiative*, 2003).

Operation CleanSWEEP

One innovative response to school crime and violence is Operation CleanSWEEP (Success with Education/Enforcement Partnership), which treats students who have violated certain criminal codes on campus with a combination of retributive and rehabilitative measures. "In other words," Penrod (2001, p.64) explains, "they are both punished and given appropriate counseling to help them avoid problem behavior in the future." Penrod (p.65) continues:

> For many teens, Operation CleanSWEEP represents their first encounter with the notion of personal accountability, and they are meant to feel the sting of a reprimand to their actions. . . . Instead of suspending or expelling the student, the program keeps the offender in the classroom. This allows the student's education to proceed without interruption. . . .
>
> Operation CleanSWEEP is also made up of two other components: a security assessment that inspects schools for safety-related problems, and a speaker's bureau that provides participating campuses with presentations, demonstrations, and guest speakers on a wide variety of crime- and security-related issues.

McGruff

The "McGruff Takes a Bite Out of Crime" program began as a national media campaign using public service announcements from late 1979 to 1981. It was hoped that McGruff would become to crime prevention what Smokey Bear was to fire prevention. The campaign's four major objectives were to:

- Change citizen feelings about crime and the criminal justice system, particularly feelings of frustration and hopelessness.

- Generate an individual sense of responsibility for reducing crime among citizens.
- Encourage citizens, working within their communities and with local law enforcement agencies, to take collective crime prevention action.
- Enhance existing crime prevention programs at the local, state and national levels.

Police Explorers

Police Explorers are senior Scouts (boys or girls) who volunteer time with a police department. Most departments require three to six months' probation and provide extensive training in personal conduct, first aid, police procedures, weapons familiarization, crime scene investigation, traffic control, radio procedures, interpersonal communication, criminal law and specialized police duties.

Giordano (2001, p.148) describes how one community recruited local teens already involved in the Explorer program to help curb speeding and other traffic problems through an effort called CAN ID (Cadets Assisting Neighborhoods to Identify Driving Violations):

> After a brief training in traffic monitoring practices, including the use of handheld digital radar detectors, the students or cadets who sign up for CAN ID take to the streets in teams of two to watch for moving violations, which range . . . from "people who blow through stop signs" to those who ignore pedestrians in crosswalks. . . .
>
> The cadets, however, don't hand out tickets to delinquent drivers. Instead, they take their logs back to the department, where, with the help of police officers, they run the plate numbers to identify the drivers. A warning letter is sent out to each of the motorists . . . [advising that] future violations will be documented.

DARE

The well-known Drug Abuse Resistance Education (DARE) program was developed jointly by the Los Angeles Police Department and the Los Angeles Unified School District. Its purpose is to teach elementary school children to "say no to drugs," to resist peer pressure to experiment with drugs and to find alternatives to drug use. DARE places police officers in schools to teach kids about self-esteem, the dangers of drugs and how to resist peer pressure to try them.

Evaluation of DARE programs has met with mixed reviews. Supporters of DARE point out that such programs bring millions of children into positive contact with police officers. Other advocates claim it may not be the *content* of the program so much as the *nature* of the program that makes it a success.

Other Programs

Programs in the schools, such as lectures and videos about "Children and the Law," have aided police in their fight against vandalism and shoplifting. They reach a segment of society that represents future citizens, informing children of the crime problem in our society and how they might help reduce this problem.

In addition to community programs to help combat crime, many police departments have programs to promote safety and the general welfare of the public. Most such programs are aimed at children, such as bike safety programs.

Community Crime Prevention Programs

Many police departments have instituted programs aimed at preventing crime in the community.

 Crime prevention programs include neighborhood or block watch programs, operation identification programs, home security, store security and automobile security.

Neighborhood or Block Watch Programs

Block watch programs instruct homeowners to form cooperative groups to deter burglaries and thefts when homeowners are away and to provide safe places for children who might be threatened on their way to or from school. Such neighborhood watch programs bring neighbors together in an effort to reduce the incidence of crime in their neighborhood. The program helps homeowners know their neighbors and their neighbors' daily routines. They are encouraged to report suspicious activities or persons in their neighborhood to the police.

With the cooperation and involvement of all citizens, such as sharing the responsibility of checking neighbors' homes when they are on vacation, the neighborhood is a safer place to live. Most programs emphasize that residents should *not* try to apprehend suspects, so programs do not create "vigilante" actions.

These citizen crime-reporting programs (CCRPs) are the most widely used police-community crime prevention programs in the country. These groups serve as "eyes and ears" for the police. Signs stating that the neighborhood is involved in a CCRP are usually prominently displayed at curbside, as well as on the homes or apartments themselves. Often such programs lead to establishing property identification programs.

Operation Identification Programs

Police have also implemented operation identification programs in which citizens are loaned markers to identify their property with a permanent identification number. If these items are lost or stolen and recovered by the police, the identification number provides a method of identifying the rightful owner. If the items are found in the possession of a burglar or thief, the number can help police prosecute and convict the suspect. Stickers and decals are given to citizens so they can place warnings on their doors and windows to deter burglars from trying to steal that property (see Figure 5.4).

Figure 5.4   Operation I.D. Sticker
SOURCE: Courtesy of Minnesota Crime Watch—Department of Public Safety.

Home Security

Police officers may go to a citizen's home, evaluate its security and suggest methods for making the home a less inviting target for crime. Recommendations may be made to install deadbolt locks, improve lighting and so on. In some communities, a subsidy is available for making recommended changes.

Store Security

Police departments may also help store owners reduce losses from shoplifting by studying their stores and recommending action. Recommendations might include hiring store detectives; implementing educational campaigns; installing convex, wide-angle mirrors in isolated areas; installing closed-circuit television cameras; or installing electronic systems using special magnetic or microwave-sensitive tags. The tags require a deactivating device or a special tool to remove them without damaging the merchandise. If a customer leaves an area of the store before a salesperson removes the tag or deactivates it, a sensor sounds an alarm, and store personnel apprehend and detain the suspect for the police.

Often crime prevention through environmental design (CPTED) is an integral part of these programs. Based on Oscar Newman's concept of "defensible space," CPTED uses access control, lighting and surveillance as key strategies of **target hardening,** that is, making it more difficult for crime to occur.

Automobile Security

Because of the vulnerability of autos to theft, many antitheft programs and devices have been introduced to make it more difficult for a person to steal a car and more difficult for that person to use or sell it without its stolen nature being detected.

Automobile manufacturers have contributed by making the ignition switch mechanism lock the steering wheel and by having a separate steering-post lock key and door lock key. Some police agencies have placed on every parking meter a sticker asking, "Have you locked your car?" and provided dashboard stickers that remind motorists, "Have you taken your keys and locked your car?"

Some cities have encouraged used-car dealers to fence in their lots or chain their entrances and exits. Public education campaigns have also been instituted using newspaper, radio, television and placard publicity, as well as bumper stickers with slogans reminding motorists to lock their cars.

An innovative anti–auto-theft program using modern technology is the Lo-Jack Auto Recovery System (LARS), which uses a homing device installed in a customer's car that is automatically activated if the car is reported stolen.

A less expensive, less high-tech program is the Combat Auto Theft (CAT) program initiated in New York City in 1988. In this program a special decal is placed in the car's rear window. The police can stop any vehicle with this decal they see being driven between 1 A.M. and 5 A.M. without probable cause for the stop. In this voluntary program, car owners who normally do not operate their vehicles during these hours sign a consent form and are given the CAT decal to affix prominently on the inside of the car's rear window.

What Works/What Doesn't

According to Sherman et al. (1998, p.1), a systematic review of more than 500 scientific evaluations of crime prevention practices has led to the following conclusion: "Enough evidence is available . . . to create provisional lists of what works, what doesn't, and what's promising." The results of this review were presented in a 1997 report to Congress. Tables 5.5, 5.6 and 5.7 outline the findings.

Table 5.5　Crime Prevention Programs That Work

- **For infants:** Frequent home visits by nurses and other professionals
- **For preschoolers:** Classes with weekly home visits by preschool teachers
- **For delinquent and at-risk preadolescents:** Family therapy and parent training
- **For schools:**
  - —Organizational development for innovation
  - —Communication and reinforcement of clear, consistent norms
  - —Teaching of social competency skills
  - —Coaching of high-risk youth in "thinking skills"

- **For older male ex-offenders:** Vocational training
- **For rental housing with drug dealing:** Nuisance abatement action on landlords
- **For high-crime hot spots:** Extra police patrols
- **For high-risk repeat offenders:**
  - —Monitoring by specialized police units
  - —Incarceration
- **For domestic abusers who are employed:** On-scene arrests
- **For convicted offenders:** Rehabilitation programs with risk-focused treatments
- **For drug-using offenders in prison:** Therapeutic community treatment programs

SOURCE: Lawrence W. Sherman et al. *Preventing Crime: What Works, What Doesn't, What's Promising.* National Institute of Justice Research in Brief, July 1998, p.1.

Table 5.6　Crime Prevention Programs That Don't Work

- Gun "buyback" programs
- Community mobilization against crime in high-crime poverty areas
- Police counseling visits to homes of couples days after domestic violence incidents
- Counseling and peer counseling of students in schools
- Drug Abuse Resistance Education (DARE)
- Drug prevention classes focused on fear and other emotional appeals, including self-esteem
- School-based leisure-time enrichment programs
- Summer jobs or subsidized work programs for at-risk youths
- Short-term, nonresidential training programs for at-risk youths
- Diversion from court to job training as a condition of case dismissal
- Neighborhood watch programs organized with police
- Arrests of juveniles for minor offenses

- Arrests of unemployed suspects for domestic assault
- Increased arrests or raids on drug market locations
- Storefront police officers
- Police newsletters with local crime information
- Correctional boot camps using traditional military basic training
- "Scared Straight" programs whereby minor juvenile offenders visit adult prisons
- Shock probation, shock parole and split sentences adding jail time to probation or parole
- Home detention with electronic monitoring
- Intensive supervision on parole or probation (ISP)
- Rehabilitation programs using vague, unstructured counseling
- Residential programs for juvenile offenders using challenging experiences in rural settings

SOURCE: Lawrence W. Sherman et al. *Preventing Crime: What Works, What Doesn't, What's Promising.* National Institute of Justice Research in Brief, July 1998, p.7.

Table 5.7 Crime Prevention Programs That Are Promising

- **Proactive drunk driving arrests with breath testing** (may reduce accident deaths)
- **Community policing with meetings to set priorities** (may reduce perceptions of crime)
- **Police showing greater respect to arrested offenders** (may reduce repeat offending)
- **Polite field interrogations of suspicious persons** (may reduce street crime)
- **Mailing arrest warrants to domestic violence suspects who leave the scene before police arrive**
- **Higher numbers of police officers in cities** (may reduce crime generally)
- **Gang monitoring by community workers and probation and police officers**
- **Community-based mentoring by Big Brothers/Big Sisters of America** (may prevent drug abuse)
- **Community-based afterschool recreation programs** (may reduce local juvenile crime)
- **Battered women's shelters** (may help some women reduce repeat domestic violence)
- **"Schools within schools" that group students into smaller units** (may prevent crime)
- **Training or coaching in "thinking" skills for high-risk youths** (may prevent crime)
- **Building school capacity through organizational development** (may prevent substance abuse)
- **Improved classroom management and instructional techniques** (may reduce alcohol use)

- **Job Corps residential training programs for at-risk youths** (may reduce felonies)
- **Prison-based vocational education programs for adult inmates** (in federal prisons)
- **Moving urban public housing residents to suburban homes** (may reduce risk factors for crime)
- **Enterprise zones** (may reduce area unemployment, a risk factor for crime)
- **Two clerks in already-robbed convenience stores** (may reduce robbery)
- **Redesigned layout of retail stores** (may reduce shoplifting)
- **Improved training and management of bar and tavern staff** (may reduce violence, DUI)
- **Metal detectors** (may reduce skyjacking, weapon carrying in schools)
- **Street closures, barricades and rerouting** (may reduce violence, burglary)
- **"Target hardening"** (may reduce vandalism of parking meters and crime involving phones)
- **"Problem-solving" analysis unique to the crime situation at each location**
- **Proactive arrests for carrying concealed weapons** (may reduce gun crime)
- **Drug courts** (may reduce repeat offending)
- **Drug treatment in jails followed by urine testing in the community**
- **Intensive supervision and aftercare of juvenile offenders** (both minor and serious)
- **Fines for criminal acts**

SOURCE: Lawrence W. Sherman et al. *Preventing Crime: What Works, What Doesn't, What's Promising.* National Institute of Justice Research in Brief, July 1998, p.10.

Services and Programs That Implement Community Policing

The community policing movement has had a profound impact on community service, particularly on services in the "promising" category. Programs that have not succeeded have often been implemented in agencies whose approach was more traditional, where community policing was seen merely as a way of operating, not as an overall philosophy of policing. Providing services to a community is more complex now than in previous times.

Challenges to Community Policing

Despite the many advantages and benefits of community policing, its implementation is not without challenges. Critics and skeptics exist both internally, among officers and police managers, and externally, in the community at large. Furthermore, even when the community policing philosophy has the support of the department and the public, our increasingly diverse population presents an ever-expanding challenge to community policing efforts.

Resistance and Misguided Perceptions

Many officers have difficulty accepting or appreciating the community-oriented policing philosophy. Some wonder whether officers will or should readily accept the increased accountability that accompanies greater decision-making responsibilities. Others question the willingness of police administrators to embrace decentralization, to "loosen the reins" and empower officers with greater authority, responsibility and decision-making capabilities. These organizational impediments are some of the chief barriers to implementation.

Other challenges to implementation include community resistance, a concern that community policing is "soft" on crime and structural impediments involved with making the change from a reactive to a proactive policing mission. The impediment of limited resources is also a reality: how to simultaneously respond to calls for service, solve crimes and conduct activities involved with community policing. Another large obstacle is the difficulty of changing the police culture.

The perception that community policing goes against aggressive law enforcement practices is perhaps one of the most difficult impediments to overcome. No agency wishes to be perceived as "softies," and no community wants to place crime control and safety in the hands of "pushovers." However, the goals of community policing and aggressive enforcement are not mutually exclusive. The combination of these two elements has been termed **integrated patrol.**

Benefits of Community Policing to Officers

To help overcome doubts and misperceptions about the strength and virtue of the community policing philosophy, it is valuable to note studies that demonstrate that community policing benefits not only the community but the participating officers as well. Officers engaging in community policing have job enrichment, get to know the citizens with whom they work, have greater responsibility and authority, and can build their problem-solving skills.

Such benefits are vitally important for community policing officers faced with serving and protecting an increasingly diverse population.

Serving and Protecting Our Increasingly Diverse Population

Our society has changed tremendously over the past decades, as have the challenges facing law enforcement. Technology has made the task easier, but the increasing diversity of our population has made it more difficult. In addition, although poverty has always existed in the United States, the gap between those who live in poverty and those who are more affluent is widening. The **American Dream,** that anyone can succeed through hard work and sacrifice, is becoming much more difficult to attain, not only for members of minority groups but also for middle-class people of all ethnic and racial backgrounds. A college education, the traditional key to "getting ahead," is becoming prohibitively expensive for many youths. Jobs are harder to find. Many high-paying assembly line and factory jobs have been mechanized and computerized.

Our elderly population is increasing rapidly, as is our minority population. In addition hundreds of thousands of immigrants are pouring into the United

States, a great many of whom speak no English. The homeless population is growing at an alarming rate, and the number of people with infectious diseases is also escalating. Each of these populations presents a challenge to police.

 Our population is becoming older and has more minorities, more immigrants, more homeless people and more individuals with infectious diseases. In addition the gap between those who live in poverty and those who are more affluent is widening.

The Growing Elderly Population

Our elderly population is growing and will continue to do so. In 1996 the first wave of "baby boomers" turned 50. In the twenty-first century, the financial burden of caring for our elderly, the majority of whom are white, will fall to an increasing number of minority members who themselves may be struggling financially. Further, as the "graying of America" continues, more people with Alzheimer's disease will be in our communities, presenting an additional challenge to law enforcement.

The Growing Minority Population

Demographers, individuals who study the characteristics of human populations, predict that in less than 100 years, white dominance of the United States will end. **De facto segregation** continues to keep many minorities trapped in decaying crime- and drug-riddled, inner-city neighborhoods. Of particular concern is that many minority members live in ghettos. A **ghetto** is an area of a city in which people of a specific ethnic or racial group live in poverty. The frustrations, sense of futility and failure experienced by those who live in ghettos have been described as the **ghetto syndrome**—a vicious cycle of poverty and welfare dependency leading to inability to go to college or prepare for a good-paying job, leading to lack of motivation, further unemployment, poverty and welfare dependency.

Adding to the growing minority population is the ever-increasing number of immigrants.

The Growing Immigrant Population

White Anglo-Saxons were not the original inhabitants of North America. Aside from Native Americans, the settlers of this country were all immigrants, primarily of European descent. In fact, Europeans constituted more than 80 percent of all immigrants throughout the nineteenth century and remained the primary "type" of immigrant until the 1960s. However, during the 1970s, nearly 4.5 million immigrants entered the United States, and more than 7 million arrived in the 1980s. At least 80 percent of these immigrants came from Latin America or Asia. From 1994 to 1997, between 700,000 and 900,000 immigrants became permanent U.S. residents each year, the overwhelming majority of whom came from Mexico and Asia ("Immigration," 2001).

Recent immigrants tend to cluster in specific areas, often in poor neighborhoods that have high crime rates. Consequently the tendency is to **stereotype** them as being involved in crime, when as often as not they are victims rather than perpetrators. The majority of immigrants are law-abiding, trying to build a new life and fit into our society.

Many immigrants speak no English and fear the authorities. They are very likely to become victims, particularly of violent crime. Compounding this problem is the fear and lack of respect many immigrants hold for authorities of law. This distrust and unfamiliarity with our customs can result in volatile situations. For example the commonly used arrest position of having a suspect kneel, back to the officer with hands clasped behind the head, is the position used for executions in Vietnam. Distrust of law enforcement often leads to another problem—failure to report crime and victimization.

 Major challenges presented by immigrants are language barriers, unfamiliar customs and failure to report victimization.

In addition to problems of crime, problems also arise when others in the community believe the new immigrants are taking their jobs. For example, in St. Paul, Minnesota, blacks and whites have banded together to resist the competition from the influx of Hmongs.

Another challenge is that of the thousands of *illegal* immigrants entering the United States each year. These immigrants will avoid coming into contact with the police for fear of deportation. They are especially easy targets for those who would take advantage of them.

The Growing Homeless Population

The homeless problem can be found throughout the United States. Among the three million plus homeless people in the United States are veterans, the mentally ill, the physically disabled or chronically ill, the elderly, families, single parents, runaway children, alcoholics, drug abusers, immigrants and traditional tramps, hobos and transients. A large number of mentally ill people are homeless partially as the result of the **deinstitutionalization** policies of the mid-1960s and 1970s, by which hundreds of thousands of mentally ill patients were discharged from state psychiatric facilities. Where sleeping on the streets is illegal, what begins as a social problem becomes a law enforcement problem.

The public often pressures the police to "do something" about homeless people, yet often the only thing officers can do is persuade street people to move along. Until a homeless person breaks the law by panhandling, trespassing, breaking into buildings, shoplifting, dealing drugs or committing some other offense, police power to arrest that person is limited by statutes and laws.

 The challenge in dealing with homeless people is to balance compassion for them with the public's right to be free from interference.

As with the newly arrived immigrants, homeless people are also a challenge to law enforcement because they are often victims. What limited possessions they have may be stolen. They may be assaulted, and they have no phone from which to call 911.

The Growing Number of Individuals with AIDS and Other Infectious Diseases

AIDS is a spectrum of reactions to the human immunodeficiency virus (HIV), which infects and destroys specific white blood cells, undermining the body's ability to fight infection. A person can be infected with HIV and remain symptom-free for years, but even without symptoms that person can transmit the virus to others. Those at high risk of contracting HIV include intravenous drug users, homosexuals and individuals having sexual contact with people in these groups, including prostitutes.

The growing number of individuals with AIDS is of concern to law enforcement. An estimated 40,000 new HIV infections occur in the United States each year. In 2000, between 800,000 and 900,000 U.S. residents were HIV-positive and another 300,000 had full-blown AIDS ("Acquired Immunodeficiency Syndrome," 2001). Go to www.CDC.gov for the most current statistics.

Although the AIDS virus causes the most concern for most police officers, greater danger lies with tuberculosis (TB), hepatitis and meningitis. The hazards posed by infectious diseases can be avoided by not drinking, smoking, eating or chewing gum at a crime scene, and by wearing protective gloves.

The Growing Number of Individuals with Disabilities

An estimated 43 million people in the United States—more than one-sixth or 17 percent of our population—have physical or mental disabilities, making them the largest minority in the country. This includes the hearing impaired, the severely visually impaired, those who use wheelchairs and those with mental retardation. With the passage of the Americans with Disabilities Act of 1990, more people with disabilities are in the mainstream.

Further, those in law enforcement must learn to distinguish between behaviors resulting from disabling conditions and those resulting from excessive alcohol use or the use of drugs. Among the disabling conditions that might be mistaken for inebriation or a drug high are epilepsy, diabetes, Alzheimer's disease, carbon monoxide poisoning, mental retardation or certain types of head injury. Again education and training are vital.

The Widening Gap between the Rich and the Poor

Law enforcement must also be concerned with the dynamics of economics in this country because money, or lack of it, is often the basis for criminal activity. This widening gap and the increase in the number of people surviving below the poverty line translates into potentially more theft and the types of violence that accompany offenses motivated by economic gain.

 SUMMARY

Many law enforcement agencies are adopting community policing, a philosophy that stresses working proactively with citizens to prevent crime and to solve crime-related problems. Citizen involvement in the law enforcement community and in understanding policing has taken the form of civilian review boards, citizen patrols, citizen police academies, ride-alongs and similar programs. Such involvement is important, but community policing requires more.

Two critical elements of community policing are partnerships and problem solving. The core components of effective community partnerships are stakeholders with a vested interest in the collaboration, trusting relationships among and between the partners, a shared vision and common goals for the collaboration, expertise, teamwork strategies, open communication, motivated partners, means to implement and sustain the collaborative effort and an action plan.

Problem-oriented policing requires that police move beyond a law enforcement perspective in seeking solutions to problems. Problem-oriented policing (the SARA model) uses four strategies: (1) scanning—grouping individual incidents into meaningful "problems," (2) analyzing—collecting information from all available sources, (3) responding—selecting and implementing solutions and (4) assessing—evaluating the impact of the solution. Implementing community policing will require a change in management style, mission statement and departmental organization.

Community policing also promotes a community-service focus. Departments may provide a wide variety of services, including giving information, directions and advice; counseling and referring; licensing and registering vehicles; intervening in domestic arguments or in disputes and quarrels; working with neglected and/or abused children; rendering emergency medical or rescue services; dealing with alcoholics and the mentally ill; finding lost children; dealing with stray animals; controlling crowds; and providing community education programs on crime prevention, drug abuse, safety and the like. Such efforts are important, as the police officer on the street is ultimately responsible for the success of police-community relations.

Programs for youths may include PAL programs, school resource officers, McGruff, Explorer posts and the DARE program. Crime prevention programs include neighborhood or block watch programs, operation identification programs, home security, store security and automobile security.

Community policing requires much interaction with citizens, a particular challenge given the increasing diversity of our citizenry. Our population is becoming older and has more minorities, more immigrants, more homeless people and more individuals with infectious diseases. In addition the gap between those who live in poverty and those who are more affluent is widening. Major challenges presented by immigrants are language barriers, unfamiliar customs and failure to report victimization. The challenge in dealing with those who are homeless is to balance compassion for those "on the streets" with the public's right to be free from interference.

DISCUSSION QUESTIONS

1. What community services are available in your community? Which are most important? Which might be frivolous? Are any necessary services not provided?

2. What do you feel are the greatest strengths of community policing?

3. What is the relationship of problem-oriented policing to community policing?

4. What basic similarities and differences exist between community policing and such systems as the tithing system?

5. Might community policing dilute the power and authority of the police?

6. Which "growing population" discussed in this chapter do you feel is the greatest challenge to law enforcement? Why?

7. Are community policing and problem solving important in your police department?

8. What do you see as the greatest impediment to implementing community policing? Problem-oriented policing?

9. Which position do you favor for dealing with the homeless: strict enforcement, benign neglect or somewhere in between?

10. What do you see as the greatest benefit of community policing and problem-oriented policing?

INFOTRAC COLLEGE EDITION ASSIGNMENTS

- Use InfoTrac College Edition to help answer the Discussion Questions as appropriate.

- Use InfoTrac College Edition to find "What Taxpayers Need to Know about COPS," an article describing the intentions of the Violent Crime Control Act of 1994 designed to reinforce community policing. List the results of this act, and be prepared to discuss your list with the class.

- Read and outline one of the following articles:
  - "Lasting Impact: Maintaining Neighborhood Order" by Ronald W. Glensor and Kenneth Peak
  - "A Medical Model for Community Policing" by Joseph A. Harpold
  - "Community Policing: Exploring the Philosophy" by David M. Allendar
  - "Community Mobilization: The Foundation for Community Policing" by Rachel Stewart-Brown
  - "The X-Factor in Policing" by Todd Wuestewald

 INTERNET ASSIGNMENT

Use the search engine Google.com to find a number of community policing programs that failed. List them and comment on why they failed. Be prepared to share your comments with the class.

 BOOK-SPECIFIC WEB SITE

The book-specific Web site at http://info .wadsworth.com/0534552803 hosts a variety of resources for students and instructors. Included are extended activities from each chapter in which students write a policy, use critical thinking skills to make choices in response to a given scenario, use InfoTrac College Edition with direct links to articles for participation in topical discussion forums, and analyze court cases using Web links for research. Many activities can be printed or emailed to instructors. Plus, cited cases with Web links, interactive key term FlashCards, PowerPoint presentations, chapter objectives and an extensive collection of chapter-based Web links provide additional information and activities to include in the curriculum.

REFERENCES

"Acquired Immunodeficiency Syndrome." Microsoft® Encarta® Online Encyclopedia 2001. *Available at* http://encarta.msn.com.

Allendar, David M. "Community Policing: Exploring the Philosophy." *FBI Law Enforcement Bulletin*, March 2004, pp.18–22.

Atkinson, Anne J. "School Resource Officers: Making Schools Safer and More Effective." *The Police Chief*, March 2002, pp.55–63.

Bennett, Wayne W. and Hess, Kären M. *Management and Supervision in Law Enforcement*, 4th ed. Belmont, CA: Wadsworth Publishing Company, 2004.

Braiden, Chris. "Policing—The Hunt and the Habitat." *Law Enforcement News*, October 31, 1998, pp.8, 10.

Broder, David S. "Urban Renewal Even the GOP Could Love." *The Washington Post*, May 9, 2001, p.A31.

Brown, Jim. "Community Policing Reality Check." *Law and Order*, April 2001, pp.55–58.

Bureau of Justice Statistics Web site: http://www .ojp.usdoj.gov/bjs.

Carter, David L. and Holden, Richard N. "Terrorism and Community Security." In *Local Government Police Management*, 4th ed., edited by William A. Geller and Darrell W. Stephens. Washington, DC: International City/County Management Association, 2003, pp.291–311.

Coleman, J. *Foundations of Social Theory*. Cambridge: Harvard University Press, 1990.

Cops in Schools: The COPS Commitment to School Safety. COPS Fact Sheet. Washington, DC: Office of Community Oriented Policing Services, April 8, 2003.

Eck, John E. and Spelman, William. *Problem-Solving: Problem-Oriented Policing in Newport News*. Washington, DC: The Police Executive Research Forum, 1987.

Gardner, Gerald W. "Media Guidelines for the Law Enforcement Executive." *Subject to Debate*, October/November 2001, pp.8–11.

Giordano, Alice. "Teen Drivers Turn into Speed Busters." *Law and Order*, July 2001, pp.148–149.

Girouard, Cathy. *School Resource Officer Training Program*. Washington, DC: Office of Juvenile Justice and Delinquency Prevention, Fact Sheet #05, March 2001. (FS-200105)

Goldstein, Herman. *Problem-Oriented Policing*. New York: McGraw-Hill, 1990.

Guide for Preventing and Responding to School Violence. Arlington, VA: International Association of Chiefs of Police. http://www.theiacp.org

Haldar, Sujoy. "NYC Cabbies Extend Police Reach." *Community Links*, March 2001, p.13.

Herbert, Bob. "Championing Cities." *New York Times*, April 26, 2001, p.A23.

Hickman, Matthew J. and Reaves, Brian A. *Local Police Departments, 2000*. Washington, DC: Bureau of Justice Statistics, January 2003a. (NCJ 196002)

Hickman, Matthew J. and Reaves, Brian A. *Sheriffs' Offices, 2000*. Washington, DC: Bureau of Justice Statistics, January 2003b. (NCJ 196534)

"Immigration." Microsoft® Encarta® Online Encyclopedia 2001. http://encarta.msn.com.

Miller, Linda S. and Hess, Kären M. *Community Policing: Partnerships for Problem Solving*, 4th ed. Belmont, CA: Wadsworth Publishing Company, 2005.

Palk, Leslie. *Surveying Communities: A Resource for Community Justice Planners*. Washington, DC: BJS Monograph, May 2003. (NCJ 197109)

Penrod, Gary S. "Operation CleanSWEEP: The School Safety Program That Earned an A-Plus." *The Police Chief*, March 2001, pp.64–65.

Rahtz, Howard. *Community-Oriented Policing: A Handbook for Beat Cops and Supervisors*. Monsey, NY: Criminal Justice Press, 2001.

Rinehart, Tammy A.; Laszlo, Anna T.; and Briscoe, Gwen O. *Collaboration Toolkit to Build, Fix, and Sustain Productive Partnerships.* Washington, DC: U.S. Department of Justice, Office of Community Oriented Policing Services, 2001.

Rosenthal, Arlen M.; Fridell, Lorie A.; Dantzker, Mark L.; Fisher-Stewart, Gayle; Saavedra, Pedro J.; Makaryan, Tigran; and Bennett, Sadie. "Community Policing: Then and Now." *NIJ Journal,* Issue 249, 2003, p.34. (NCJ 187693)

Secure Our Schools Initiative. COPS Fact Sheet. Washington, DC: Office of Community Oriented Policing, April 24, 2003.

Sherman, Lawrence W.; Gottfredson, Denise C.; MacKenzie, Doris L.; Eck, John; Reuter, Peter; and Bushway, Shawn D. *Preventing Crime: What Works, What Doesn't, What's Promising.* National Institute of Justice Research in Brief, July 1998. (NCJ 171676)

Stewart-Brown, Racheal. "Community Mobilization: The Foundation for Community Policing." *FBI Law Enforcement Bulletin,* June 2001, pp.9–17.

Upper Midwest Community Policing Institute. *"Community Policing Defined."* No date.

Walker, Samuel. *Police Accountability: The Role of Citizen Oversight.* Belmont, CA: Thomson/Wadsworth Publishing, 2001.

Wilson, James Q. and Kelling, George L. "The Police and Neighborhood Safety: Broken Windows." *The Atlantic Monthly,* March 1982, pp.29–38.

Wilson, James Q. and Kelling, George L. "Making Neighborhoods Safe." *The Atlantic Monthly,* February 1989, pp.46–52.

Wuestewald, Todd. "The X-Factor in Policing." *FBI Law Enforcement Bulletin,* June 2004, pp.22–23.

Zhao, Jhong "Solomon"; He, Ni; and Lovrich, Nicholas P. "Community Policing: Did It Change the Basic Functions of Policing in the 1990s? A National Follow-Up Study." *Justice Quarterly,* December 2003, pp.697–724.

CHAPTER 6

Patrol: The Backbone of Policing

The difference between the ordinary and the extraordinary is the little extra.

—Anonymous

 DO YOU KNOW . . .

- What three major spheres of activity must be coordinated in the patrol function?
- What type of shift and beat staffing often lessens the effectiveness of preventive patrol?
- How patrol has traditionally functioned? What changes might make it more effective?
- What directed patrol does?
- How hot spots or specific problems might be identified?
- What activities officers typically engage in while on patrol?
- What methods of patrol may be used? Which are most effective?
- What the primary goal of traffic law enforcement is?
- What the responsibilities of the traffic officer are?
- What the most common violations of traffic law are?
- What implied consent laws are?
- How driving impairment can be detected?
- Why all uniformed officers should enforce traffic laws?
- What the most basic causes of motor vehicle crashes are?

CAN YOU DEFINE?

aggressive patrol	environmental	pretext stop	road rage
cold crimes	anomalies	racial profiling	saturation patrols
differential response	hot spots	random patrol	scofflaws
strategies	implied consent laws	residual deterrence	selective enforcement
diffusion of benefits	incident-driven	effect	
directed patrol	policing		

Introduction

The idea of uniformed officers patrolling the streets goes back at least to the Roman states in 400 B.C. A reliance on a visible, roaming presence of law enforcement officers has carried into present-day policing, largely unchanged in many jurisdictions. And in all jurisdictions, patrol is the most vital component of police work. All other units are supplemental to this basic unit.

Sweeney (2003a, p.89) contends: "Patrol officers remain 'master generalists' expected to handle competently a mind-boggling array of calls. . . . In addition to being varied, this master generalist's job is the most important in the police department." He suggests one reason for the importance of patrol: "The positive daily interactions of patrol officers on their beat with citizens places a human face on policing and builds that critical social capital necessary to carry a department and community through the difficult times that will occur when the inevitable negative incident or unfortunate mistake takes place."

Patrol can contribute to each of the common goals of police departments, including preserving the peace, protecting civil rights and civil liberties, enforcing the law, preventing crime, providing services and solving problems. Unfortunately in many departments, patrol officers not only have the position with the least prestige, but they also are the lowest paid, the least consulted and the most taken for granted. Patrol officers strive to move "up." According to Sweeney (2003a, p.90): "Challenging, important and hazardous though patrol work may be, the laborious routine, and onerous schedule prevent it from getting the prestige it deserves." He (p.131) suggests: "The police executive dedicated to improving patrol must take clear and consistent actions to demonstrate—both internally and externally—that patrol is the core function of the department." Sweeney advises that management modify its compensation and promotion practices to recognize the complexity of the patrol officer's role and central importance to accomplishing the department's mission. Management should find ways to encourage talented, experienced officers to remain with the patrol division.

This chapter begins with a discussion of the responsibilities of the patrol officer, the structure and management of patrol and the types of patrol most frequently used. This is followed by a description of common methods of patrol. Next, an important subset of patrol is described—the responsibilities of the traffic officer, including an in-depth look at the major responsibility of enforcing traffic laws against speeding, running red lights, not using seatbelts, aggressive driving and road rage, and driving under the influence of drugs or alcohol. Next is a description of responsibilities related to traffic crashes and the importance of crash reports and crash reconstruction. The chapter concludes with discussions of how patrol and traffic enforcement support community policing.

Patrol Officer Responsibilities

Traditionally, patrol has been responsible for providing continuous police service and high-visibility law enforcement to deter crime and maintain order. Progressive departments also emphasize partnering with the community to solve problems related to crime and disorder. In addition patrol officers must understand the federal, state and local laws they are sworn to uphold and use good judgment in enforcing them.

In recent years, our society has become more diverse, many social controls have broken down, and information technology has proliferated, making the patrol function increasingly complex and critical to accomplishing the police department's mission. Most officers in a department are assigned to the patrol function, and most of a department's budget is usually spent here. Patrol may cost an average jurisdiction half a million dollars a year in salary and benefits. Patrol officers have the closest contact with the public and have the most influence on how the public perceives the police in general. To those departments instituting community policing, the patrol is critical.

The patrol function is the most visible form of police activity, and individual patrol officers represent the entire police department. The tasks they are expected to accomplish are almost overwhelming. Patrol officers' specific responsibilities in most police departments are to enforce laws, investigate crimes, prevent criminal activity and provide day-to-day police services to the community. The specific duties involved in fulfilling these responsibilities are varied and complex. The size of the department often dictates what functions are assigned to patrol.

As protectors patrol officers promote and preserve order, respond to requests for services and try to resolve conflicts between individuals and groups. As law enforcers a key duty of patrol officers is to protect constitutional guarantees (as described in Chapter 8); a second duty is to enforce federal, state and local statutes. Patrol officers not only encourage voluntary compliance with the law but also seek to reduce the opportunity for crimes to be committed.

Patrol officers also serve important traffic control functions, described later in this chapter, and important investigative functions, described in Chapter 7. Patrol officers in any community are the most visible government representatives and are responsible for the safety and direction of hundreds of people each day.

Management of Patrol Operations

Management of patrol involves overseeing three major spheres of activity, which often occur simultaneously.

 The three major spheres of patrol activity are (1) responding to emergencies and calls for service, (2) undertaking activities to apprehend perpetrators of crime and (3) engaging in strategic problem-solving partnerships with the community to address long-standing or emerging problems of crime and disorder.

Traditionally, rapid response to calls for service has driven most departments, as discussed shortly. The law-enforcing, criminal-apprehending aspect of policing has also been a traditional focus of policing. In fact, the action taken by the patrol officer arriving at the scene of a crime is the single most important factor in the success of a criminal investigation, as discussed in the next chapter.

The third sphere of activity, partnering with the community to solve crime and disorder problems, goes full circle back to Peel's principles that the people are the police and the police are the people and an emphasis on crime *prevention.* Citizens are often more concerned about disorder and quality-of-life issues than they are about crime. As noted by Sweeney (2003a, p.106): "More than any other feature, it is the emphasis on systematic problem solving with the community that differentiates the modern patrol operation from earlier forms of policing."

In addition to overseeing these three spheres of activity, middle management and first-line supervisors must balance structure and authority with discretion and creativity. Management must also attend to infrastructure requirements such as training, performance evaluations, needed equipment and resources, and information support. Furthermore, management must determine how to deploy patrol officers.

 Traditionally patrol officers have been assigned a specific time and a specific geographic location, or beat, of equal geographic size, and these assignments have been rotated.

Beats set up to be of equal geographic size pose obvious problems because the workload is not the same at all hours of the day or in all areas. Several attempts have been made to overcome the problems inherent in equal-shift and beat-size staffing. Some departments, usually larger ones, assign officers according to the demand for services, concentrating the officers' time where it is most needed, although union contracts sometimes make this impossible. Computer programs are available to help with deployment of patrol. Sometimes beat lines are redrawn to match "natural" neighborhoods identified through profiling adjoining beats. Another important decision is what type of patrol to employ.

Types of Patrol

Patrol is often categorized as either general or specialized. Both general and specialized patrol seek to deter crime and apprehend criminals, as well as to provide community satisfaction with the services provided by the police department. General patrol does so by providing rapid response to calls for service. Specialized patrol does so by focusing its efforts on already-identified problems. Whether general or specialized patrol is used depends on the nature of the problem and the tactics required to deal with it most effectively.

General Patrol

General patrol is also referred to as preventive patrol, random patrol and routine patrol. The term *routine patrol* should not really be used, however, because there is nothing routine about it. The challenges of general patrol change constantly. The patrol officer may be pursuing an armed bank robber in the morning and giving a talk at an elementary school in the afternoon.

 Traditionally patrol has been random, reactive, incident driven and focused on rapid response to calls.

These characteristics can be seen in the main activities officers engage in during a typical patrol shift: random/preventive patrol, calls for service, directed patrol, self-initiated activities and administrative duties.

Random/Preventive Patrol

Traditionally patrol officers begin their shifts on **random patrol** in squad cars in hopes of detecting (intercepting) crimes in progress, deterring crime by creating an illusion of police omnipresence or being in the area and able to respond to crime-in-progress calls rapidly.

Preventive patrol is generally done by uniformed officers moving at random through an assigned area. Because officers usually decide for themselves what they will do while on preventive patrol, this time is sometimes referred to as "noncommitted" time. It comprises between 30 and 40 percent of patrol time, but it is often broken into small segments because of interruptions by self-initiated activities, service calls and administrative duties.

Often priorities for preventive patrol are identified and/or assigned during roll call. For example patrol officers may be told to watch for a known escaped criminal sighted in the area.

A serious challenge to random patrol came over 30 years ago in the findings of the often-cited Kansas City Experiment. Funded by a grant from the Police Foundation, the Kansas City Preventive Patrol Experiment of 1972 is often deemed the most comprehensive study of routine preventive patrol ever undertaken. The basic design divided 15 beats in Kansas City into three different groups:

- Group 1 Reactive Beats—five beats in which no routine preventive patrol was used. Officers responded only to calls for service.
- Group 2 Control Beats—five beats maintained their normal level of routine preventive patrol.
- Group 3 Proactive Beats—five beats doubled or tripled the level of routine preventive patrol.

The results of the study were that decreasing or increasing routine preventive patrol as done in this experiment had no effect on crime, citizen fear of crime, community attitudes toward the police on delivering services, police response time or traffic crashes. Klockars (1983, p.130) asserted that the results of the Kansas City Patrol Experiment indicated that "it makes about as much sense to have police patrol routinely in cars to fight crime as it does to have firemen patrol routinely in fire trucks to fight fire."

This landmark research provided powerful evidence that the traditional goals of random patrol were ineffective. The goal of *interception* was seldom accomplished, probably because two-thirds of Index Crimes are committed indoors, out of view of patrolling officers. The goal of *deterrence* was not reached, probably because deterrence depends on the certainty and swiftness of punishment. The goal of *rapid response* to crimes in progress was also not reached. This may be because fewer than 25 percent of dispatched calls involve crimes in progress, 75 percent of calls regarding Index Crimes are **cold crimes** (happened after the perpetrator had left the scene) and the fact that half of victims and witnesses wait five or more minutes before calling the police. The time elapsed between the commission of the crime and the call to dispatch is the most important factor in apprehending perpetrators at the scene. As Sweeney (2003a, p.93) observes: "Random preventive patrol was found to be a high-cost, low-pay-off strategy."

Although the Kansas City study found no significant differences in the incidence of crime resulting from varying the *level* of patrol, the results might have been different if they had varied the *form* of the patrol. For example, would the outcome differ if patrol officers more aggressively probed individuals, places and circumstances, being *proactive* rather than *reactive*, directed rather than random? Studies conducted in Syracuse, New York; San Diego, California; and Houston,

Texas found that patrol officers could expect to intercept fewer than 1 percent of street crimes, giving credence to the saying: "Random patrol produces random results."

Given that streetwise criminals study police patrol methods and select targets not likely to be detected, and given that many crimes are committed on the spur of the moment, particularly violent crimes such as murder and assault, and given that much crime is committed inside buildings, out of the patrols' sight, Goldstein (1990, p.35), the father of problem-oriented policing, suggests a different approach: "Focusing on the substantive, community problems that the police must handle . . . requires the police to go beyond taking satisfaction in the smooth operation of their organization; it requires that they extend their concern to dealing effectively with the problems that justify creating a police agency in the first instance." This approach is used in directed patrol.

Directed Patrol

Directed or **aggressive patrol** meshes well with problem-oriented policing and with community policing and focuses on high-crime areas or specific offense types.

 Directed patrol uses crime statistics to plan shift and beat staffing, providing more coverage during times of peak criminal activity and in high-crime areas.

Specific activities that qualify as "aggressive patrol" include saturation, crackdowns, field interrogation, aggressive traffic enforcement and detection of **environmental anomalies,** which are unusual activities that warrant further investigation. Covert tactics that might be used in crackdowns include stakeouts (the simplest form), plainclothes officers, decoys and surveillance.

Research by McGarrell et al. (2001) found that directed patrol, or patrol they call specific deterrence patrol, in high-violent-crime locations reduced violent firearms crimes. Scott (2003) likewise reports on research showing that law enforcement crackdowns—targeting certain crimes or certain locations—can significantly reduce crime and disorder without merely displacing it, at least in the short term. Scott (p.13) notes: "The positive effects of crackdowns sometimes continue after the crackdowns end . . . referred to as **residual deterrence effect.** In addition, crackdowns can reduce crime and disorder outside the target area or reduce offenses not targeted in the crackdowns, a phenomenon criminologists commonly refer to as a **diffusion of benefits.**" Scott suggests that crackdowns are most effective when used in combination with other responses that address the underlying conditions contributing to the problem.

A method that enhances the effectiveness of aggressive patrol is geographic permanence, that is, officers are regularly assigned the same beat. With a permanent assignment, officers get to know the normal activities of the beat, enhancing their ability to recognize what is unusual and thus requires investigation. Geographic permanence also fosters rapport between police and citizens, helping with the overall department mission.

A key to directed patrol is identifying the **hot spots** on the beat, the estimated 10 percent of locations that account for 60 to 65 percent of calls for service. The intent is to break the incident-call-response cycle illustrated in Figure 6.1.

 Crime analysis using mapping, geographic information systems (GIS) and CompStat can identify hot spots or specific problems to target through directed patrol.

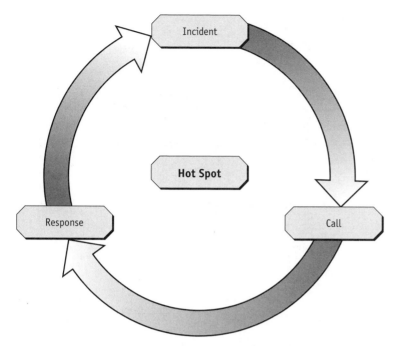

Figure 6.1 The Incident-Call-Response Cycle of Hot Spots

Crime Mapping/Geographic Information Systems (GIS) La Vigne and Wartell (2001, p.1) contend: "The case for mapping crime and criminal behavior is well founded in both research and practical applications." Rich (2001, p.1) observes: "Crime mapping has become increasingly popular among law enforcement agencies and has enjoyed high visibility at the federal level, in the media and among the largest police departments in the nation." Dees (2002, p.43) explains: "The modern-day equivalent of the pin map is the Geographic Information System (GIS) application. A GIS, in its simplest form, translates data into visual map displays that can make patterns and clusters far more apparent than would be the case from reading the lines of data. . . . GIS applications can merge layers of information in a visual form so that the relationships between places, times, events and trends become more evident than they would from analyzing the raw data."

Crime mapping can be used to determine where patrol is most needed. Groff and La Vigne (2001, p.257) note: "Law enforcement officers and civilian crime analysts have been mapping crime with push pins and paper maps virtually since the time that police agencies were established." However: "The recent introduction of user-friendly mapping software, designed primarily for environmental and planning purposes, offers new tools for examining and predicting crime and criminal behavior." Individual crimes show up as colored dots, and high-crime areas emerge as large, colored blobs.

GIS plays a vital role in data-driven decision making by enabling law enforcement to better use crime information and statistics to help guide policy and practice. Mapping can identify correlations between crime, demographics, societal issues and more, and can help departments deploy their resources more effectively. One police chief describes the impact mapping technology can have on targeting crime in a certain area (Rogers, 2001, p.65): "It's like if a health care

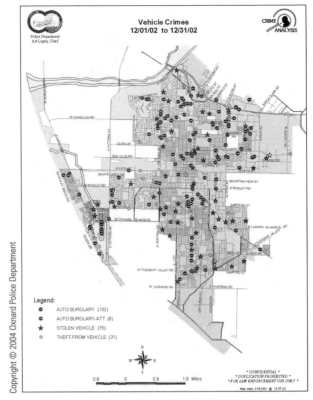

Crime mapping is becoming more popular with law enforcement agencies and can be used to determine where patrol is needed most. This map from the Oxnard (CA) Police Department shows vehicle crimes from 12/1/02 to 12/31/02.

professional said: 'Someone in this group has cancer. Let's give everyone chemotherapy.' That's how we have dispensed community resources in the past. Now we can tailor our response based on the community diagnosis."

Diamond (2003, p.42) suggests: "Crime mapping has emerged as a key crime-fighting tool across the nation." He notes: "Crime mapping technology gives agencies nationwide the intel to efficiently deploy officers and prevent crime." In addition, according to Lutz (2003, p.118): "Intranets offer a cost-effective and powerful means of intra-departmental communications that computer mapping is just now beginning to exploit." This ability to share information across juris-dictional lines can be invaluable not only in fighting crime locally but also in providing information vital for homeland security.

Furthermore, as Lutz (p.122) suggests: "Intranet mapping is not just about policing; it is also about community redevelopment and effectively coordinating governmental services and resources for both homeland security and economic development." Closely related to mapping and geographic information systems is CompStat, another crime analysis tool.

CompStat McDonald (2004, p.33) asserts: "CompStat represents a sea change in managing police operations, and perhaps the most radical change in recent history." Schick (2004, pp.17–18) notes: "CompStat, short for 'computer statistics' or 'comparison statistics,' is a multi-faceted system for managing police operations with a proven track record in several major police departments." Walsh and Vito (2004, p.57) add: "CompStat is a goal-oriented, strategic management process that uses information management technology, operational strategy and managerial accountability to guide police operations."

According to Anderson (2001, p.9): "William Bratton, who was New York City's police commissioner from 1994 to 1996, is credited with developing Compstat along with his deputy commissioner, Jack Maple, in an effort to get control of the city's huge police force." CompStat is based on four crime-reduction principles: (1) accurate and timely intelligence, (2) rapid deployment of personnel and resources, (3) effective tactics and (4) relentless follow-up and assessment (Shane, 2004, p.13). In addition, according to Anderson: "The appeal of the strategy extends beyond crime control. Information and accountability help police make better sense of their jobs. . . . [One officer] says that the sense of heightened focus and accountability is quickly felt at the patrol level. 'I like it,' he says. 'The captain knows a lot more about what's going on in the district, and that increases the police officer's awareness of what's going on. Everyone is more informed.' " CompStat and other forms of crime analysis can greatly enhance the efficiency and effectiveness of patrol. While on patrol, officers also engage in other activities.

Activities While on Patrol

 While on patrol officers respond to calls for service and emergencies, undertake self-initiated tasks and perform administrative duties.

Calls for Service

The two-way radio has made the service call an extremely important element of patrol. It has also made it necessary to prioritize calls. A radio dispatch almost always takes precedence over other patrol activities. For example if an officer has stopped a traffic violator (a self-initiated activity) and receives a call of an armed robbery in progress, most department policies require the officer to discontinue the contact with the motorist and answer the service call.

In most departments calls for service drive the department. This is known as **incident-driven policing.** Because 40 to 60 percent of patrol officers' time is spent responding to calls for service, the way police respond to such calls significantly affects every aspect of their function.

The response is usually reactive, incident driven and as rapid as possible. Many departments have found that **differential response strategies,** suiting the response to the call, are much more effective.

Call-related factors to consider include the type of incident and when it happened, that is, how much time has elapsed since it occurred. An in-progress major personal injury incident would be viewed differently than a minor noncrime incident that occurred several hours ago.

Calls for service may be answered by either sworn or nonsworn officers. The response time and nature of the response may vary considerably, from an immediate on-site response, to an on-site response within an hour, to a response when time permits. The caller may need to arrange an appointment for an officer to respond, or the officer may simply telephone a response without ever meeting the caller face-to-face. If it is determined the call for service does not require the dispatch of an officer, either sworn or nonsworn, the complainant may be told to come to the department to file a complaint, asked to mail in a complaint or be referred to another agency altogether. Although police response time is often a cause of citizen complaints, if citizens know what to expect, complaints can be reduced.

Patrol might also be more effective if it were proactive, directed and problem oriented and if it used differential response strategies.

The problem-oriented approach is often criticized as being unrealistic because it demands so much patrol officer time. However as Goldstein (p.152) suggests:

> The time now wasted between calls for help and in the limited number of self-initiated activities of officers can be put to better use. The value of many of the specialized and permanent jobs (other than patrol) to which officers are currently assigned can be challenged, with reassignment to more useful work. Many hours can be saved by using different responses to problems. Alternatives to arrest, when feasible, can greatly reduce the inordinate amount of time commonly consumed in processing an arrest. Calls to the police can be screened more effectively and, where appropriate, handled by telephone or diverted to another unit of the department or to another agency.

Self-Initiated Tasks

Officer-initiated activities usually result from officers' observations while on preventive or directed patrol; that is, they encounter situations that require their intervention. For example an officer may see a crime in progress and arrest the suspect. Usually, however, officer-initiated activities involve community relations or crime prevention activities, such as citizen contacts or automobile and building checks. Officers may see a large crowd gathered and decide to break it up, thereby preventing a possible disturbance or even a riot. Or they may see a break in a store's security, take steps to correct it, and thus prevent a later possible burglary.

Officers are sometimes hesitant to get involved in community services and preventive activities because such duties make them unavailable for radio dispatches and interfere with their ability to respond rapidly to service calls. Hand-held radios, beepers and cell phones have allowed patrol officers more freedom of movement and have allowed them to initiate more activity.

Too often little attention is paid to the officer's use of noncommitted time, which is commonly regarded as having no function other than to ensure that officers are available to quickly respond to service calls. Frequently noncrime service calls interrupt a patrol officer's self-initiated activity that could prevent or deter crime. Emphasis on rapid response to all service calls has sometimes retarded the development of productive patrol services. Obviously not all service calls require a rapid response.

The emphasis on problem solving in partnership with the community provides an excellent way for officers to use their noncommitted time, which has been estimated at 60 percent of total patrol time. This time could be better used talking with citizens to determine what they perceive as neighborhood problems and possible solutions. In addition, much of an officer's uncommitted time often involves administrative duties.

Administrative Duties

Administrative work includes preparing and maintaining the patrol vehicle, transporting prisoners and documents, writing reports and testifying in court. Efforts to make patrol more cost-effective have often been aimed at cutting time spent on administrative duties. Some departments have greatly reduced the time officers spend maintaining their vehicles. Other departments have drastically reduced the amount of paperwork required of patrol officers by allowing them to dictate reports, which secretaries then transcribe, or by using computer-generated reports.

The types of reports police officers frequently use include motor vehicle reports, vehicle recovery reports, offense reports, continuation reports, juvenile reports, missing persons reports, arrest/violation reports and record checks.

A Demanding Role

Whether general or specialized, the demands made on patrol officers are many. Patrol officers who are "swamped" responding to calls for service on a first-come, first-served basis have little or no time to perform in the other two major spheres of activity or to perform required administrative duties. Another factor influencing how patrol officers fulfill their responsibilities is the method of patrol they use.

Methods of Patrol

Patrol officers in the United States were originally on foot or horseback. Bicycles were introduced in policing in Detroit in 1897 and automobiles in 1910. Airplanes were first used by the New York City Police Department in 1930. At that time daredevil pilots were flying all over the city, sometimes crashing in densely populated areas. The New York Airborne police unit was created to control reckless flying over the city. These means of patrol and others can be found in the twenty-first century.

 Patrol can be accomplished by foot, automobile, motorcycle, bicycle, Segway, horseback, aircraft and boat. The most commonly used and most effective patrol is usually a combination of automobile and foot patrol.

Foot Patrol

The word *patrol* is derived from the French word *patrouiller,* which means, roughly, to travel on foot. Foot patrol, the oldest form of patrol, has the advantage of close citizen contact and is proactive rather than reactive. Its goal is to address neighborhood problems before they become crimes. Most effective in highly congested areas, foot patrol may help to deter burglary, robbery, purse snatching and muggings. Kelling (n.d., pp.2–3) reports the consistent findings of two foot patrol experiments:

- When foot patrol is added in neighborhoods, levels of fear decrease significantly.
- When foot patrol is withdrawn from neighborhoods, levels of fear increase significantly.
- Citizen satisfaction with police increases when foot patrol is added in neighborhoods.
- Police who patrol on foot have a greater appreciation for the values of neighborhood residents than police who patrol the same areas in automobiles.
- Police who patrol on foot have greater job satisfaction, less fear and higher morale than officers who patrol in automobiles.

The 1980s saw a significant trend back to foot patrol. In the 1990s it became almost synonymous with community policing. Foot patrol is relatively expensive and does limit the officer's ability to pursue suspects in vehicles and to get from one area to another rapidly. Used in conjunction with motorized patrol, foot patrol is highly effective. According to the National Neighborhood Foot Patrol Center, Michigan State University School of Criminal Justice (n.d.):

> Foot patrol is an exercise in communication—an attempt to develop rapport between the officer on the beat and the citizens he or she serves. Foot patrol officers constantly interact with the community. They instruct citizens in crime prevention techniques and link them to available governmental services. They are catalysts of neighborhood organizations.

The center notes that "motorized patrolling has proven ineffective in certain key areas. Crime rates continue to rise, and even in areas where they are not high, vagrants, abandoned cars and groups of juveniles on the street create an impression that the environment is violent and uncontrollable." The center cites a series of experimental programs conducted by criminal justice researchers to see if a modified version of foot patrol could contribute to modern policing. The intent was not to replace motorized patrol but rather to provide a combination of foot and motorized patrol, capitalizing on the strengths of each.

Automobile Patrol

Automobile patrol offers the greatest mobility and flexibility and is usually the most cost-effective method of patrol. It allows wide coverage and rapid response to calls; the vehicle radio provides instant communications with headquarters. The automobile also provides a means of transporting special equipment and prisoners or suspects.

However, while patrolling in a vehicle, officers cannot pay as much attention to details they might see if they were on foot, such as a door ajar, a window broken or a security light out. The physical act of driving may draw attention away from such subtle signs that a crime may be in progress. Furthermore, research on the effectiveness of preventive patrol indicates that a crime prevented by a passing vehicle can be, and usually is, committed as soon as the police are gone. In effect police presence prevents street crime only if the police can be everywhere at once.

Modern patrol cars are greatly enhanced by technology. Onboard computers are now commonplace, and global positioning systems (GPS) are also becoming standard in patrol cars. GPS can be used to track suspects, more efficiently monitor fleets and determine the whereabouts of undercover surveillance officers (Rogers, 2003, p.75). GPS is also invaluable in search and rescue missions, with searchers able to download each specific search area onto a map.

Another type of technology finding its way into patrol cars is the visual surveillance and imaging systems similar to those used by the military as well as thermal imaging. A third type of technology commonly used in patrol cars is the dashboard-mounted video camera. Such in-car videos (ICV) hold great promise, as described by Maghan et al. (2002, p.39): "Video technology could deter abuses by officers, limit frivolous complaints against officers about alleged abuses and help restore confidence in the fairness of police departments. It could also provide evidence of crimes or attacks against officers, streamline the truth-finding process by providing the best evidence and encourage the humane treatment of suspects and fairness and respect for civil rights and liberties."

Whitehead (2004b, p.82) describes another type of technology being used in patrol cars: facial recognition. Digital cameras installed in patrol cars allow officers to photograph a subject, place the camera on a docking station in the patrol car, and through wireless communication link to an image database to conduct a face recognition search to determine if the individual has been previously arrested. Ultimately it will give a name to the face, helping officers know how to handle a subject.

Ioimo and Aronson (2004, p.403) studied the effectiveness of technology in patrol cars. They conclude: "Field officers recognize the potential benefits mobile computing affords them . . . . Administrators, detectives and records personnel all experienced statistically significant improvements in the tasks they performed, directly resulting from the implementation of mobile computing."

One-Officer versus Two-Officer Squads One factor of importance when using automobile patrol is whether to have one or two officers assigned per squad. Circumstances should determine whether a one-officer or a two-officer unit is more appropriate. The single-officer unit is the rule rather than the exception, and one officer can handle most incidents. If two or more officers are required, multiple one-officer units can be dispatched to the scene. Two-officer units should be restricted to those areas, shifts and types of activities most likely to threaten the officers' safety, for example during the evening or in high-crime areas.

The one-officer unit offers several advantages, including cost-effectiveness in that the same number of officers can patrol twice the area, with twice the mobility and with twice the power of observation. In addition officers working alone are generally more cautious in dangerous situations, recognizing that they have no backup. Officers working alone also are generally more attentive to patrol duties because they do not have a conversational partner. The expense of two cars compared to one, however, is a factor.

Police unions usually support two-officer patrol units and may include provisions for two-officer units in their contracts, jeopardizing management's ability to best use available resources and to make rational decisions about personnel deployment and scheduling.

Motorcycle Patrol

According to Kariya (2004a, p.24): "The motorcycle police officer has been an American icon for more than half a century." In fact, motorcycle officers have patrolled our streets since their introduction in Pittsburgh, Pennsylvania, almost 100 years ago. Motorcycles are used for traffic enforcement, escort and parade duty. Motorcycles and automobiles have dominated traffic enforcement for the past seven or eight decades. They can also enhance community relations.

Among the disadvantages of motorcycles are their relatively high cost to operate, their limited use in adverse weather and the hazards associated with riding them.

Bicycle Patrol

Bicycle patrols were introduced in Detroit in 1897 and enjoyed great popularity until around 1910 with the introduction of the automobile and the emphasis on rapid response to calls. But they are making a comeback. Kariya (2004b, p.20) reports: "Today, more and more departments all over the world are adding bicycles

The Petersburg, Virginia, Bureau of Police formed a bicycle unit in 1993 to patrol some of the most crime-ridden areas of the city. Criminal activity decreased with roundups of street-level drug dealers. Why do you think bicycle patrols were effective in this situation?

to their arsenal of tools." He (p.21) suggests: "Bicycle patrols are good community-policing tools. They're also very inexpensive when compared to the costs of maintaining cars and motorcycles."

Bicycle patrol is sometimes used in parks and on beaches or in conjunction with stakeouts. Bike units are ideal for patrolling small areas and for performing directed patrol assignments. They may even be used to cover small areas some distance apart, with departments mounting bike racks on patrol cars for officers to transport their bikes to various patrol sites. In addition to mobility, bicycles provide a "stealth factor" and an "element of surprise" because they can be ridden very quietly and do not attract attention.

Heinecke (2004, p.81) points out: "One recent development for bicycle patrols is homeland security and disaster relief. On September 11, 2001, bicycle messengers, though not members of public service agencies, added to the relief effort by running messages, blood, first aid equipment and other supplies to and from Ground Zero. . . . Other areas bicycle patrols are expanding into include search and rescue, private security and airport security."

Clark (2003, p.78) reports on a study that compared the effectiveness of officers in a squad car and officers on bicycles, which found: "Bike patrol officers reported significantly more activity in many categories, including arrests, crimes discovered, warrants served and motorist assists." Table 6.1 summarizes the results of this study.

Bicycle patrols have been extremely successful on college campuses. Vonk (2003, p.86) reports: "Officers on bike patrol have pursued and caught armed robbers, home invasion criminals, car thieves, criminals breaking into cars and criminals in possession of stolen property including bicycles, computers, money and jewelry. They have assisted in searches for missing children and joggers." In addition, according to Hicks (2003, p.89): "When officers began patrolling the campus on mountain bikes, a new and special relationship developed between

Table 6.1 Weekly Average of Officer in Car versus on Bicycle

Officer's Weekly Average	Officer in Car	Officer on Bike
Hours on Duty	40.00	40.00
Arrest—Felony	01.00	02.25
Arrest—Misdemeanor	02.98	09.49
Juvenile Arrests & Referrals	00.88	02.11
Field Interview Report (FIR)	00.23	01.69
Vice Incidents	00.48	04.67
Property Recovery Incidents	01.22	02.87
Warrants Served	04.86	09.74
Crimes Discovered	00.44	01.55
Misdemeanor Cleared/Follow Up	00.51	02.55
Parking Violation	02.80	09.78
Motorist Assists	00.64	06.57

SOURCE: Wesley Clark. "Electric Bicycles: High-Tech Tools for Law Enforcement." *Law Enforcement Technology,* November 2003, p.76. Reprinted by permission.

the police and the public. A rapport was easily established through the common ground provided by the mountain bike."

Some departments have gone to electronic bicycles or e-bikes. Clark (p.80) notes: "The electronic bikes enable rapid response while conserving strength and energy. Officers are able to arrive at a scene quickly without becoming winded, even when riding up big hills or in hot weather. With an electric assist, officers can quickly apprehend suspects in pursuit situations, patrol larger areas for longer periods of time and carry more equipment and supplies."

Bicycle patrol remains very appealing to agencies, officers and the community, but it does require special training and conditioning. Vonk (2004) describes the International Police Mountain Bike Association (IPMBA) Police Cyclist Course, which is a difficult five-day, 40-hour training session focusing on physical skills, mind-set and safety. Beck (2004, p.43) cautions: "Bike training is a high-risk, high-liability activity. As with training in firearms, defensive tactics and emergency vehicle operation, officers can get injured, or even killed, if the training activities aren't tightly controlled and properly supervised."

According to Feavel (2003, p.95): "With a little bit of effort, the bike team will become an integral part of the department, one that officers want to be identified with and one that plays an important role in overall departmental operations."

Segways

A new form of patrol is the Segway Human Transporter, more commonly known as a Segway HT or simply a Segway. Segways were introduced in December 2001 and have been found to be ideal not only for transportation but also for interacting with citizens. Whitehead (2004a) explains: "Segway is an extremely intelligent technology that has gyroscopes and tilt sensors that monitor a rider's center of gravity. When a rider leans forward, the Segway follows the shift in gravity and moves forward. When a rider leans back, the Seg-

Mounted officers are especially effective in situations requiring crowd control. Notice advanced protection given the horses.

way moves backward. Turns are made by twisting the handlebar. The harder the turn of the handlebar, the harder and tighter the turn."

Mounted Patrol

Mounted patrol evolved from military antecedents and comprises some of the oldest and most varied police units in the United States. In 1871 the New York City Police Department was one of the first agencies in the country to establish a mounted patrol unit.

Mounted patrols function in a variety of capacities, from community relations, to park and traffic patrol, to crowd and riot control, to crime prevention. Mounted patrols have also been used to assist in evidence searches at crime scenes, round up straying livestock, search for lost children in tall corn or grass and apprehend trespassers. It has been estimated that one mounted officer is equal to 10 foot patrol officers in crowd-control situations. In addition, according to Sherman (2003, p.56): "One officer mounted on a horse can see as much as 10 to 15 officers on the ground." Says Sherman (p.55): "Horse-mounted patrols are an economical adjunct to more sophisticated law enforcement technologies."

Air Patrol

Air patrol is another highly effective form of patrol, especially when large geographic areas are involved, such as with a widespread search for a lost person, a downed plane or an escaped convict. According to Strandberg (2001, p.20): "Having police officers in helicopters, patrolling the city by air, results in quicker response times, safer methods of policing and overall better performance." A helicopter 500 feet in the air has 30 times the visual range of a unit on the ground, providing a patrol capacity equal to 15 squad cars. Furthermore a helicopter can arrive at a crime scene 5 to 10 times faster than street-level units.

Means (2003, p.24) emphasizes: "When operated by trained, professional pilots, aircraft can provide tremendous benefits to law enforcement agencies and the public—benefits that would cost a lot more to obtain by any other means." Helicopters and small aircraft are generally used in conjunction with police vehicles on the ground in criminal surveillance and in traffic control, not only to report tie-ups but to clock speeds and radio to ground units. Helicopters have also been used to rescue persons from tall buildings on fire and in other situations, such as floods. In addition air travel is a cost-effective means of transporting prisoners over long distances.

Helicopters, even when donated to an agency, are extremely expensive to maintain. A cost-effective alternative aircraft for law enforcement is the gyroplane, which carries a much lower operating cost, requires less training to fly and is generally safer in flight than a helicopter. Even less expensive, yet still in the experimental stage, are *personal* vertical takeoff and landing (VTOL) aircraft. According to Cowper (2004, p.36): "VTOL aircraft . . . bring with them capabilities that will allow the creation of new and innovative tactics vitally necessary for police to be successful in the future." He (pp.37–38) cautions, however: "Innovative criminals and terrorists might exploit the technology to commit crimes and threaten homeland security."

Water Patrol

Water patrol is used extensively on our coasts to apprehend weapons and narcotics smugglers. Inland, water patrols are used to control river and lake traffic. Water patrol units are very specialized and are used in relatively few cities in the United States. In those cities with extensive coasts and other waterways, however, they are a vital part of patrol.

Watercraft range in size from personal watercraft, such as wave runners, to fully equipped 30-foot cruisers. Cost-effective inflatable equipment is also being used by some departments. Water patrols are used for routine enforcement of such circumstances as vessels exceeding "no wake" speed limits, intoxicated operators and safety inspections, as well as search-and-rescue operations, emergency transportation in flooded areas, general surveillance and antismuggling operations. Close ties can develop between a boating community and the marine agencies that patrol it.

Special-Terrain Patrol

Some police departments may require special-purpose vehicles for patrol. For example areas that receive a lot of snow may have snowmobiles as part of their patrol fleet. These vehicles may be especially useful in rescue missions as well as on routine patrol. Police departments with miles of beaches or desert to patrol may use jeeps and dune buggies. Police departments in remote, rugged or mountainous parts of the country may use four-wheel-drive all-terrain vehicles (ATVs).

As Strandberg (2004, p.16) explains: "ATVs help law enforcement get to areas too remote to be accessed by any other mode of transportation. They allow police officers to patrol and pursue suspects over rough terrain that would damage or destroy regular vehicles. ATVs are beneficial for crowd control and parking enforcement. In addition, ATVs are easy to maintain, difficult to destroy and cost effective."

Table 6.2 Summary of Patrol Methods

Method	Uses	Advantages	Disadvantages
Foot	Highly congested areas Burglary, robbery, theft, purse snatching, mugging	Close citizen contact High visibility Develop informants	Relatively expensive Limited mobility
Automobile	Respond to service calls Provide traffic control Transport individuals, documents and equipment	Most economical Greatest mobility and flexibility Offers means of communication Provides means of transporting people, documents and equipment	Limited access to certain areas Limited citizen contact
Motorcycle	Same as automobile, except that it can't be used for transporting individuals and has limited equipment	Maneuverability in congested areas and areas restricted to automobiles	Inability to transport much equipment Not used during bad weather Hazardous to operator
Bicycle	Stakeouts Parks and beaches Congested areas	Quiet and unobtrusive	Limited speed Not used during bad weather Vulnerability of officer Physical exertion required
Mounted	Parks and bridle paths Crowd control Traffic control	Size and maneuverability of horse Build rapport with citizens	Expensive Limited carrying capacity Street litter
Air	Surveillance Traffic control Searches and rescues	Covers large areas easily	Expensive Noisy
Water	Deter smuggling Water traffic control Rescues	Access to activities occurring on water	Expensive
Special-terrain	Patrol unique areas inaccessible to other forms Rescue operations	Access to normally inaccessible areas	Limited use in some instances

Combination Patrol

Combination patrol provides the most versatile approach to preventing or deterring crime and apprehending criminals. The combination used will depend not only on the size of the police department but also on the circumstances that arise. Table 6.2 summarizes the most common methods of patrol, their uses, advantages and disadvantages.

High Visibility versus Low Visibility

High-visibility patrol is often used in high-risk crime areas in hopes of deterring criminal activity. In addition high-visibility patrol gives citizens a sense of safety, justified or not. Types of high-visibility patrol include foot patrol, especially with a canine partner; mounted patrol; marked police car and motorcycle patrol; and helicopter patrol.

Low-visibility patrol is often used to apprehend criminals engaged in targeted crimes. Many of the specialized patrol operations would fall into this category. Types of low-visibility patrol include unmarked police cars and bicycles.

The relative effectiveness of high-visibility and low-visibility patrol has not been determined. A combination of both high- and low-visibility patrol is often needed and most effective.

In addition to focusing efforts on crime hot spots and using creative problem-solving partnerships, another basic function of patrol officers is enforcing traffic laws. This duty is often met with mixed reaction from the community—favorably when the police stop neighborhood speeders and other "dangerous drivers," negatively when citizens themselves are the subjects of traffic stops.

The Traffic Division: An Overview

Traffic law enforcement, the most frequent contact between police and otherwise law-abiding citizens, is a critical responsibility of officers. In the United States the regulation of traffic and enforcement of related laws have existed for over a century. In 1901 Connecticut established the world's first speed statute limiting horseless carriage speeds to 12 mph in cities and 15 mph in rural areas.

The principal objectives of the traffic division are to obtain, through voluntary citizen compliance, the smoothest possible movement of vehicles and pedestrians consistent with safety and to reduce losses from crashes. Furthermore, because officers are on the streets so much of the time, they often are among the first to know of problems in the transportation system and can provide information as well as advice on overall system planning.

 The primary goal of traffic law enforcement is to produce voluntary compliance with traffic laws while keeping traffic moving safely and smoothly.

Traffic officers may be responsible for enforcing traffic laws, directing and controlling traffic, providing directions and assistance to motorists, investigating motor vehicle crashes, providing emergency assistance at the scene of a crash, gathering information related to traffic and writing reports.

Enforcing Traffic Laws

Police officers seek the compliance of motorists and pedestrians with traffic laws and ordinances, as well as driver license regulations and orders, and they may issue warnings or citations to violators. According to Rao (2003, p.223): "Traffic law should be enforced at a substantial level. The quantity or visibility of enforcement should be sufficient to deter drivers from committing offenses. The approach to enforcement is as important as the visibility of enforcement. Selective enforcement (the recommended approach) targets specific high-accident areas and accident-causing violations."

Selective Traffic Enforcement

Because traffic violations occur every hour of every day, police departments cannot enforce all traffic regulations at all times. It is impossible to achieve 100 percent enforcement and almost always unwise to try do so. Based on thorough investigations of crashes, summarization and careful analysis of the records, **selective enforcement** targets specific crashes and/or high-crash areas, such as excessive speed around a school yard or playground where young children are present. As Rao (p.226) explains: "Selective traffic law enforcement is part of a planned allocation of police personnel and equipment and is guided by a study of the kinds of violators and road conditions that contribute to collisions." Because of this, accurate records are essential to the overall effectiveness of the selective enforcement program.

Selective enforcement is not only logical, it is practical because most police departments' limited workforces require them to spend time on violations that contribute to crashes. Enforcement personnel, such as officers on motorcycles or officers assigned to a radar unit, are usually the officers assigned to selective traffic enforcement. The officers' activity is directed to certain high-crash areas during certain days of the week and certain hours of the day or night.

Studies in city after city have proven a definite relationship between crashes and enforcement. In analyzing crash reports, one finds at the top of the list year after year the same traffic violations contributing to crashes and the same group of drivers being involved. Crashes are discussed later in the chapter.

Almost everyone has heard in exhaustive detail a friend's version of getting an "unfair" speeding ticket. The person will tell several people about it. In terms of quality and selective enforcement, this has the effect of informing the general public that the police are doing their job. Chermak et al. (2001, p.365) examined citizens' perceptions of aggressive traffic enforcement and report: "Overall the findings suggest that citizens strongly support aggressive traffic enforcement practices and that the implementation of such strategies does not reduce their support." High-quality enforcement is not only supported by the public, it has an important effect on the would-be traffic violator when the public is informed of the police department's enforcement program and it is understood and believed to be reasonable.

 Among the most common violations of traffic laws are speeding, red light running, nonuse of seatbelts, aggressive driving and road rage, and driving under the influence of drugs or alcohol.

Speeding

Speeding—most everyone does it at one time or another, if not all the time, and many justify it as "just going with the flow of traffic." However speeding has become an increasing problem for law enforcement, as more cars travel the streets and people seem more in a hurry than ever before. In fact some do not even realize they are speeding until they see the flashing lights of the law in their rearview mirror. According to Scott (2001, p.1): "[Speeding] is often the chief concern of community groups, largely because of the perceived risks to children."

To combat the problem of lead-footed drivers, some agencies are using portable Speed Monitoring Awareness Radar Trailers (SMARTs) parked alongside the road. These trailers clock and digitally display motorists' speeds beneath a posted speed-limit sign in an effort to gain voluntary compliance with speed laws and reduce crashes.

Many motorists use radar detectors to avoid getting a speeding ticket. Such detectors are legal in all states except Virginia, Washington, DC, and U.S. military bases. Radar detectors are *not* legal in commercial vehicles. Fors (2004, p.30) notes: "Radar detection use in commercial vehicles was banned in all states per a directive of the U.S. Department of Transportation in February 1995." He explains: "With heightened concern for domestic terrorism and potentials of 18-wheelers transporting terrorists or dirty bombs coupled with present realities of smuggling illegal aliens, illegal drugs, avoidance of safety inspections, speeding and outstanding warrants, detecting radar detectors in commercial vehicles is crucial for public safety." Fors notes that detecting radar detectors has turned into a "chess game" because commercial vehicle drivers may also have radar detector detectors (RDD). So police need not only an RDD, but a detector to detect RDDs. So far law enforcement seems to be ahead in this quest. A problem related to speeding is red light running.

Red Light Running

Bolten (2002, p.114) notes: "Red light running is the leading cause of urban crashes in the United States." In addition, Helmick (2003, p.48) reports: "Red light running is currently one of the most frequent and least punished traffic offenses. Red light running was observed as frequently as once every five minutes in one intersection recently studied."

Many people think they simply do not have a spare minute to spend sitting at an intersection. Furthermore, traveling at 5 or 10 miles per hour, or more, over the posted speed limit makes stopping for red lights that much more difficult. The Insurance Institute for Highway Safety's Highway Loss Data Institute estimates more than 800 people die each year in crashes that involve red light running, and more than 200,000 are injured in such crashes (Highway Loss Data Institute).

Some jurisdictions are installing red light cameras to help enforce traffic laws. These cameras photograph red light runners, getting a shot of the license plate for identification, and typically stamp the date, time of day, time elapsed since the light turned red and the vehicle's speed. Dewey-Kollen (2003a, p.32) notes: "Red light camera enforcement has been effective and beneficial in many communities across the country. While the administrative and legal aspects of this automated enforcement program can be extensive, the recorded reductions in violations and crashes associated with red light photo enforcement make this program an important traffic safety tool."

Nonuse of Seat Belts

Cox (2004, p.14) reports that the number one priority of the National Highway Traffic Safety Administration (NHTSA) for 2004 to 2005 is increasing seat belt use. According to NHTSA studies, safety belts are 45 percent effective in preventing fatalities, 50 percent effective in preventing moderate-to-critical injuries, and 10 percent effective in preventing minor injuries. When safety belts are combined with air bags, injuries are reduced by 68 percent. Beginning in 1998 all new cars were required to have driver and passenger air bags along with safety belts.

Seven years and 13 waves of seat belt mobilization after the first national mobilization in 1997, seat belt use in the United States has increased from 71 percent to 79 percent. Fifty million more Americans are now buckled up (Dewey-Kollen, 2004, p.12). According to Ashton (2004, p.66): "Safety belts clearly save lives. Each percentage point increase in safety belt usage translates into 250 lives spared." Runge (2003b, p.12) says of the increase to 79 percent safety belt usage: "This is a historic level of belt use, representing a 4 percent increase over 2002. This difference will result in saving at least 1,000 lives each year we sustain the increase and preventing more than 16,000 serious injuries. Also this will result in saving the U.S. economy an estimated $3.2 billion, mostly in medical costs and lost productivity." He further notes: "The 2003 Click It or Ticket campaign was truly a nation-wide effort—all 50 states participated—involving more than 100,000 law enforcement agencies."

Bolton (2003, p.70) reports that use of safety belts for toddlers has increased to 94 percent, also up 4 percent from 2002. However, according to the NHTSA survey, too many children are still riding in the front seat of passenger vehicles. Despite public education campaigns to teach parents that children are safer in the back seat, 15 percent of infants under age one, 10 percent of children ages one to three and 29 percent of children ages four to seven are still riding in the front seat. Another area of traffic enforcement patrolling officers watch for is aggressive driving.

Aggressive Driving and Road Rage

A tailgater on the freeway veers into the next lane, speeds up to pass and then cuts back in front of the car it was once behind. The car now tailing speeds up so the two cars' bumpers nearly touch. Tempers flare, words fly, fingers flip. Both drivers wish they had a gun. Is this a case of aggressive driving or road rage? They are not the same. The NHTSA makes the distinction that aggressive driving is a traffic violation and **road rage** is a criminal offense, with aggressive driving often precipitating road rage incidents.

One well-publicized incident of road rage began in February 2001 as a two-car fender-bender that led to a confrontation in which one driver hurled the other driver's dog into traffic to its death and then sped away. It ended five months later with the dog-throwing driver receiving the maximum sentence allowed for his actions—three years behind bars ("Man Gets 3 Years . . .," 2001, p.A6). The judge rejected the defendant's plea for leniency, saying it was a case of rage-induced violence and that he feared the defendant could harm someone in the future.

According to the NHTSA, aggressive driving has emerged as one of the leading safety hazards on U.S. highways and, according to several recent studies, is considered to be more dangerous than drunk driving or driving without seatbelts by many American drivers. Common behaviors of aggressive drivers include tailgating, changing lanes unsafely, weaving in and out of traffic, exceeding speed limits, driving too fast for road conditions and ignoring traffic control devices such as stop lights and yield signs. A study by the American Automobile Association (AAA) found the most common reasons given for driving aggressively were lateness, slow traffic in the high-speed lane and frustration at traffic congestion. In many instances alcohol or drugs were also involved.

Driving under the Influence of Alcohol or Drugs

In the early 1970s, law enforcement gave contacts with drunk drivers a low priority, preferring to avoid such encounters. But the situation has changed, and reducing impaired driving is now the number two priority of the NHTSA for 2004 to 2005 (Cox, p.14). One reason is that, as noted by Dewey-Kollen (2003b, p.83): "An estimated 3 of every ten Americans will be involved in an alcohol-related traffic crash at some time in their lives." Data from the NHTSA estimates that in 2002 almost 17,500 people were killed in alcohol-related crashes. Dewey-Kollen (2003b, p.82) reports: "One alcohol-related fatality occurred every 30 minutes and one injury every two minutes for a total of an estimated 258,000 injuries. Approximately 1.4 million drivers were arrested in 2001 for driving under the influence of alcohol or narcotics. While this arrest rate is one for every 137 licensed drivers in the United States, only one arrest is made for every 772 impaired driving trips according to the NHTSA." In addition, according to Runge (2003a, p.10): "Impaired driving costs us $51 billion (in 2000 dollars)."

Because so many fatal automobile crashes involve drivers who have been drinking alcohol, legislators and law enforcement agencies have tried to find a valid way to determine if drivers are under the influence of alcohol. In 1953 New York enacted the first implied consent statute.

 Implied consent laws state that any person driving a motor vehicle is deemed to have consented to a chemical blood test of the alcohol content of his or her blood if arrested while intoxicated; refusal to take such a test can be introduced in court as evidence.

The alcohol content in a person's body can be determined through breath, urine or blood tests. The courts have held that this is *not* a violation of a person's Fifth Amendment privilege against self-incrimination. One of the first cases to test the constitutionality of forcibly taking blood from an arrested person was *Breithaupt v. Abram* (1957) in which the conviction was upheld. Then in 1966, in the landmark case of *Schmerber v. California*, the issue was greatly clarified. The U.S. Supreme Court upheld the conviction and stressed that taking a blood sample was not a violation of the privilege against self-incrimination:

> We hold that the privilege protects an accused only from being compelled to testify against himself, or otherwise provide the state with evidence of a testimonial or communicative nature, and that the withdrawal of blood and use of analysis in question in this case did not involve compulsion to these ends.

The Court did caution that the blood sample should be taken by medical personnel in a medical environment. The Court also ruled that the blood test did not violate the Fourth Amendment even though there was no warrant. The Court reasoned that the blood-alcohol content might have dissipated if the officer had been required to obtain a warrant before ordering the test.

State statute often defines illegal levels of blood-alcohol concentration (BAC), with the average at the .08 level. The National Institute on Alcohol Abuse and Alcoholism and the Clearinghouse on Alcohol Information both state that a BAC level above .05 is described as "driving while impaired." In the fall of 2000 President Clinton signed into law a measure that establishes a national 0.08 percent BAC standard for drunken driving. States that fail to comply with the national standard lost 2 percent of their federal highway grants, starting in fiscal year 2004. That penalty increases to 5 percent in fiscal 2005, 6 percent in fiscal 2006, and 8 percent in fiscal 2007.

Blood-alcohol concentration can be influenced by many factors, including physiological differences, food consumption, the amount of alcohol ingested and the time elapsed between drinking and testing.

Detecting Impairment

 Officers can detect impairment through standardized field sobriety tests (SFSTs) and drug recognition experts (DRE), as well as through testing for blood-alcohol concentration.

Paul (2002, p.34) states: "Today virtually every officer receives some training on DUI enforcement and administering the SFSTs." He (p.43) cautions: "The psychomotor tests (walk and turn test and one-legged stand) are not scientific tests. . . .

Some states require attending an additional class to be certified in administering HGN [horizontal gaze nystagmus] because of its status as a scientifically validated test." According to Paquette (2002, p.62): "SFSTs and DREs form a one-two punch that greatly enhances law enforcement's ability to detect and remove impaired drivers."

Garrett (2002, p.80) describes an innovation that can also detect driver impairment: "The Eyecheck Pupillometer . . . has harnessed the power of the pupil as a means to allow officers to inexpensively conduct sobriety checks in the field. This lightweight, handheld, binocular-type instrument measures absolute pupil dynamics to presumptively detect alcohol, drugs or fatigue in a suspect."

Getting impaired drivers off the road can be improved by using saturation patrols. According to Greene (2003, p.3): "**Saturation patrols** involve an increased enforcement effort targeting a specific geographic area to identify and arrest impaired drivers. . . . Saturation patrols concentrate their enforcement on impaired driving behaviors, such as driving left of center, following too closely, reckless driving, aggressive driving, and speeding [emphasis added]."

Getting impaired drivers off the road can also be assisted by instituting a Freeway Watch. Peterson (2002, p.18) describes this initiative: "[Freeway Watch] encourages people to call 911 to report drunk drivers. It is a neighborhood watch on wheels." In addition to focusing on detecting impaired drivers and getting them off the road, law enforcement also focuses on efforts to reduce impaired driving.

Efforts to Reduce Impaired Driving   One national effort to deter impaired driving is the You Drink and Drive, You Lose national initiative that occurs in December—the national Drunk and Drugged Driving Month (3D Month)—and into the first few days of January. As Cahill (2003, p.86) notes: "This holiday period is one of the most heavily traveled times on America's highways and represents an ideal opportunity for an agency to engage in sustained, high-visibility enforcement efforts."

Pitcher and Moore (2003, p.377) suggest that agencies: "Utilize the media to gain public support and approval for the jurisdiction's ABC [Alcohol Beverage Control] efforts. The media has been very successful in educating the public to the various law enforcement efforts to rid the community of ABC-related crimes and problems." Rao (p.232) emphasizes: "Improving public awareness of the dangers of driving while impaired is essential. Research indicates that deterring DWI violators can have a greater long-term safety effect than arresting limited numbers of actual offenders."

Garrett (2003, p.72) describes a way to deter repeat impaired drivers: "An ignition interlock helps offenders monitor how much they've had to drink; the vehicle simply won't start if they've had too much. The Intoxalock even gives drivers an exact readout of their BAC on its LED display."

Another effort aimed at repeat impaired driving offenders is the victim impact panel (VIP). According to Rojek et al. (2003, p.1319): "Victim Impact Panels (VIPs) were introduced by Mothers Against Drunk Driving (MADD) in 1982 and have since spread throughout the United States in an effort to reduce drunk driving. The objective of a VIP is to expose DUI offenders to the pain and suffering caused by drunk driving without necessarily condemning the DUI offender." Their research found that the VIP effect was strong in the first two years but then waned. Yet another attempt to address the problem of impaired drivers are sobriety checkpoints.

Sobriety Checkpoints   Many states use sobriety checkpoints to deter driving while under the influence of alcohol. In *Michigan Department of State Police v. Sitz* (1990), the Supreme Court ruled that "sobriety checkpoints are constitutional" because the states have a "substantial interest" in keeping intoxicated drivers off the roads and because the "measure of intrusion on motorists stopped at sobriety checkpoints is slight."

Safety for motorists and officers must be a primary consideration, including proper lighting, warning signs and clearly identifiable official vehicles and personnel. A neutral formula must be used to decide who to stop, for example, every third car. Finally, each motorist should be detained only long enough for officers to briefly question the driver and to look for signs of intoxication, such as the odor of an alcoholic beverage on the breath, slurred speech and glassy or bloodshot eyes.

Alcohol is not the only substance that may impair drivers. Drugs, whether legal over-the-counter prescription medications or illegal substances, can adversely affect a person's driving competency.

Drug Checkpoints   Citing the success and validity of sobriety checkpoints, some jurisdictions have tried implementing drug interdiction roadblocks as natural extensions of the acceptable DUI checkpoints.

The U.S. Supreme Court, in *City of Indianapolis v. Edmond* (2000), ruled 6 to 3 that such narcotics interdiction roadblocks were unconstitutional and violated the Fourth Amendment's protections against unreasonable search and seizure. Makholm (2001) states: "The Court, over the dissents of Justices Rehnquist, Scalia, and Thomas, determined that the Indianapolis checkpoints were unconstitutional in that the purpose behind these checkpoints was indistinguishable from the 'general interest in crime control.'"

Once an officer has probable cause, whether it is having clocked a driver exceeding the posted speed limit, witnessing a red light runner or an impaired driver, or some other traffic violation, a traffic stop can be made.

The Traffic Stop

Sweeney (2003b, p.38) says of traffic stops: "Neglect them at your peril." He suggests: "Even as serious traffic crashes are on the rise, street level enforcement is declining. . . . When budgets get tight as they are now, police executives often cut the traffic unit first. The message? Traffic enforcement is not as important as other police functions." Officers assigned to a traffic unit often feel they are not doing real police work. And when citizens are stopped, they often complain that the officers should be concentrating on real criminals, not on them. However, as Sweeney (2003b, p.42) notes: "Traffic stops are among the most dangerous tasks police officers take. Officers have been struck by passing vehicles as they are stopped alongside the violator's door, have had their cruisers struck in the rear end as they sit inside them writing a ticket and have been attacked without warning by motorists who feel they have nothing to gain and everything to lose if the officer discovers what they are up to." The importance of the traffic stop as a crime fighting tool is discussed shortly.

When traffic laws are consistently enforced, the department will receive fewer complaints. Sweeney (2003b, pp.40–41) cites the four primary reasons for a traffic stop: (1) to halt an ongoing violation, (2) to have a symbolic effect on other potential violators, (3) to discover evidence of any more serious crime and (4) to change the motorist's future driving behavior for the better.

Police are sometimes accused of making a **pretext stop,** using the traffic stop as an excuse to execute another agenda, such as searching a vehicle or driver for drugs. The question: Is the temporary detention of a motorist who the police believe has committed a civil traffic violation constitutional under the Fourth Amendment if the officer, in fact, had some other law enforcement objective? The Supreme Court's decision, through its ruling in *Whren v. United States* (1996), is yes:

> The temporary detention of a motorist upon probable cause to believe he has violated the traffic laws does not violate the Fourth Amendment's prohibition against unreasonable seizures, even if a reasonable officer would not have stopped the motorist absent some additional law enforcement objective.

In other words, the test for the validity and constitutionality of a stop is not whether police officers "would have" made the stop but rather whether the officers "could have" made the stop. In *Whren,* the officers could have made and did make a valid stop because the driver committed a traffic violation, even if the actual purpose for making the stop was to search for drugs. Consequently, the real purpose of a stop, even if ulterior, does not render the stop and subsequent search invalid if there was, in fact, a valid reason for the stop.

Electronic Citations   Miller (2003, p.78) states: "Electronic citations eliminate redundant data entry and can even be used in data analysis tools." Personal digital assistants (PDAs) equipped with printers, magnetic stripe readers and wireless modems can create these electronic citations (e-cites), taking away the drudgery of running a records check and then handwriting citations in triplicate. Some software automatically calculates fees and fines after the e-cite is completed. Often individuals receiving a citation believe they have been unfairly cited, especially if the person is a member of a minority group. That person may feel racial profiling has occurred.

Racial Profiling

Batton and Kadleck (2004, p.31) define **racial profiling** as "the use of discretionary authority by law enforcement officers in encounters with minority motorists, typically within the context of a traffic stop, that result in the disparate treatment of minorities." They (p.30) note: "Racial disparities in the justice system have long been of interest to researchers who have documented disproportionate numbers of racial ethnic minorities in virtually every stage of justice processing." Citing results from their study of contacts between the police and the public, Langan et al. (2001, p.2) report:

> In 1999 an estimated 10.3% of licensed drivers [19.3 million people] were pulled over by police one or more times in a traffic stop. . . . Blacks (12.3%) were more likely than whites (10.4%) to be stopped at least once, and blacks (3.0%) were more likely than whites (2.1%) to be stopped more than once. . . . During the traffic stop, police were more likely to carry out some type of search . . . on a black (11.0%) or Hispanic (11.3%) than a white (5.4%).

Interestingly, when examining data pertaining to the race of the officer involved in traffic stops, the study revealed that black drivers had a worse outcome than white drivers regardless of the officer's race, whether white or black (Langan et al., p.19).

Smith and Petrocelli's (2001, p.4) study of police traffic stops involving drivers of different races and ethnic backgrounds found:

> Minority citizens in general, and African Americans in particular, were disproportionately stopped compared with their percentage in the driving-eligible population. However, they were searched no more frequently than Whites; in fact, Whites were significantly more likely than minorities to be the subjects of consent searches. Compared with Whites, and after controlling for variables, minority drivers were more likely to be warned, whereas Whites were more likely to be ticketed or arrested. Examining officer race as a predictor revealed White officers were no more likely than minority officers to stop, search, or arrest minority drivers.

For departments seeking accreditation by the Commission of Accreditation for Law Enforcement Agencies (CALEA), the prohibition of racial profiling has been added to its list of more than 400 standards: "Agencies seeking accreditation will now be required to prohibit any traffic or field contact, asset seizure or forfeiture effort based on bias" ("CALEA Takes Stand on Racial Profiling," 2001, p.5). The accreditation standard concedes that profiling in itself can be a useful tool in law enforcement, but goes on to describe bias-based profiling as the selection of an individual based solely on race, ethnic background, sexual orientation, religion and economic status, among other characteristics that may lead to allegations of constitutional-rights violations, as well as undermining legitimate law enforcement efforts.

Jurisdictions across the country place racial profiling among the top most important law enforcement issues, and they are striving to develop policies to address this concern. Data analysis technology is available to help police managers make critical personnel and operational decisions in their efforts to prevent racial profiling: "The Police Foundation has announced that its Institute for Integrity, Leadership, and Professionalism in Policing has developed computer software for collecting and analyzing data on police officer–citizen contacts, including traffic stop data. The technology [is] called the Risk Analysis Management System and the Quality of Service Indicator" (http://www.policefoundation.org). Racial profiling is discussed further in Chapter 11 as an important issue facing police officers.

Traffic Enforcement and the Apprehension of Criminals

The standard traffic stop results in many arrests for more serious crimes. According to Hustmyre (2003, p.113): "All officers know America's highways are often haunted by criminals. They use them as escape routes, as a place to find victims and as a way to traffic their own nefarious brand of commerce—drugs, guns, property and stolen cash." Sweeney (2003b, pp.41–42) also notes:

> Burglars, by and large, do not walk to and from the jobs they pull; they ride in motor vehicles. . . . Drugs are transported in motor vehicles. And the September 11 terrorists didn't hitchhike up and down the eastern seaboard for a year before they hijacked those airplanes on that fateful day; they drove.
>
> Many criminals are easy pickings for alert officers who are constantly on the lookout for traffic violations. Criminals frequently pay little attention to

other laws, such as fastening their seat belts, registering their vehicles on time, obeying posted speed limits, abstaining from alcohol and drugs before getting behind the wheel and keeping their vehicle's equipment in shape. The annals of law enforcement are filled with cases of dangerous criminals apprehended as a result of a stop for a traffic violation.

A case in point: Oklahoma state trooper Charles Hanger stopping Timothy McVeigh's car because it did not have license plates. Trooper Hanger, unaware of the driver's involvement in the day's earlier terrorist bombing of the Alfred P. Murrah Building in Oklahoma City, cited McVeigh for, among other things, the absence of license tags and carrying a concealed gun. While McVeigh was sitting in a jail cell, being processed into the system for his offenses, investigators handling the immediate aftermath of the bombing were searching for suspects, including McVeigh. Their database search turned up a "hit," and the trooper was credited for apprehending, albeit unwittingly, a terrorist. McVeigh was later convicted and executed for his involvement in the bombing.

 All uniformed officers should enforce traffic laws because of the potential for apprehending a felon.

Directing and Controlling Traffic

"Traffic direction and control (TD&C) can be broadly thought of as facilitating the safe and efficient movement of vehicular traffic in hazardous conditions or special circumstances" (Rao, p.234). Police officers frequently are called on to direct traffic flow, control parking, provide escorts and remove abandoned vehicles. They often are asked to assist in crowd control at major sporting events. They also are responsible for planning traffic routing, removing traffic hazards and assuring that emergency vehicles can move quickly through traffic.

In many jurisdictions officers and other responders en route to an emergency, such as ambulances or fire trucks, can control traffic lights to their favor, eliminating the need to slow or stop at a red light and preventing crashes that may occur when a squad car or other emergency vehicle passes through an intersection against the light. In these systems a frequency-coded signal is emitted from the approaching vehicle to a signal controller device on the traffic light, providing a green light to the emergency vehicle.

Assisting at and Investigating Traffic Crashes

Motor vehicle crashes are a leading cause of death for people ages 1 to 44. During the hour in which you read this chapter, there will be some 200 crashes resulting in injury and 5 resulting in death. Billions of dollars are lost annually through motor vehicle crashes, and the cost in human suffering and loss is impossible to estimate.

Most crashes involve factors relating to the driver, the vehicle and the road. The interaction of these factors often sets up a series of events that culminate in the mishap.

 The basic causes of motor vehicle crashes are human faults, errors, violations and attitudes; road defects; and vehicle defects.

Good driving attitudes are more important than driving skills or knowledge, a fact frequently overlooked in driver education programs. Drivers who jump lanes, try to beat out others as they merge from cloverleafs, race, follow too closely or become angry and aggressive account for many of our serious motor vehicle crashes. Negative driver behavior, such as illegal and unsafe speed, failure to yield the right of way, crossing over the center line, driving in the wrong lane, driving while under the influence of alcohol or drugs and road rage, increases the number of crashes and causes traffic statistics to rise year after year.

Responsibilities of the Officer Called to a Crash Scene

Frequently police officers who are equipped, trained and legally responsible for providing services—perhaps lifesaving services if they act quickly and effectively—are the first to arrive on the scene of a traffic crash. In addition to rendering first aid to crash victims, police officers have several other duties to perform, such as protecting victims from further harm, reducing to the greatest extent possible the involvement of other cars as they arrive on the scene, summoning emergency services for victims and, if needed, towing services for the vehicles involved, protecting the victims' personal property, locating witnesses, securing evidence and in other ways investigating the crash and keeping traffic moving as though no crash had occurred.

Crash reports by police officers provide a guide for many other department activities. In addition a host of other agencies involved in traffic make use of the information in crash reports. Public information agencies, such as newspapers, television and radio disseminate information about traffic, traffic conditions, road conditions and crashes. Attorneys and the courts use crash reports to determine the facts about the crashes that result in lawsuits. The state motor vehicle department or state department of public safety, which has the power to suspend or revoke driver's licenses, also uses information contained in these reports. Legislative bodies in each state may rely on crash reports when they plan for providing funds, equipment and personnel to effectively enforce traffic safety programs and when they determine what laws must be passed to control traffic.

Traffic crash reports may be used by engineers, both federal and state, who research ways to improve highway systems and by the National Safety Council and state safety councils that compile statistics related to crashes: Who is having them? Where? When? How? The reports may be used by insurance companies that base their automobile insurance rates on the crash record of the community.

Crash reports serve as the basis of traffic law enforcement policy, crash prevention programs, traffic education, legislative reform of traffic laws, traffic engineering decisions and motor vehicle administrative decisions.

Crash Reconstruction

Crash reconstruction using videotape can establish the facts of crashes and help in lawsuits, insurance cases and vehicular criminal cases. In video reconstruction, scale models of the vehicles are used, often with a photo or video of the crash scene itself as the background. Speed calculations are made from the reporting officer's diagrams and notes.

Many computer software programs are also available to help crash investigators re-create the scene and determine some of the "unknowns," such as how fast the vehicles were traveling, if and how environmental elements factored into the crash and how stationary objects may have affected vehicle trajectory. According to Warren and Meyers (2004, p.28): "Cumbersome methods once used to map an accident scene and collect data have been replaced with the latest computer-aided diagramming programs and laser mapping systems. The result is more detailed and accurate crash scene diagrams that reveal more vividly than ever before the events that most likely occurred at the scene."

The Traffic Program

Violating traffic laws does not carry the social stigma attached to the violation of other laws, such as laws against murder and rape. Running a stoplight or speeding is not considered a crime, and people regularly and unconsciously violate laws designed to ensure safe use of the streets and highways. Recall the distinction between crimes that are *mala in se* (bad in themselves) and *mala prohibita* (bad because they are forbidden). Traffic laws are excellent examples of *mala prohibita* crimes.

A properly administered and executed police traffic law enforcement procedure is probably the most important component of the overall traffic program. If people obey the traffic laws, traffic is likely to flow more smoothly and safely, with fewer tie-ups and crashes. Effective traffic law enforcement usually consists of at least five major actions: (1) on-the-spot instructions to drivers and pedestrians, (2) verbal warnings, (3) written warnings with proper follow-up, (4) citations or summonses and (5) arrests. Traffic officers consider the circumstances of each incident and apply their discretion in determining which action is most appropriate.

The question inevitably arises as to how much enforcement is needed to control traffic and reduce crashes. This local issue must be determined for each jurisdiction.

Public Education Programs

The police also strive to educate the public in traffic safety. Although education is not their primary responsibility, they often participate in local school programs, private safety organizations, local service clubs and state safety councils. The police know these programs are important and that they can contribute to the community good.

Traffic safety education, including wearing seat belts, also has high public relations value. An officer on the school grounds supervising the school crossing guards (patrols) or teaching children bicycle safety contributes much to the police officers' image by reflecting their concern for the safety and welfare of the community's youths. Safety education, however, is a community responsibility.

Patrol and Community Policing

The support of patrol officers for community policing is vital. Some communities are making the patrol officer an integral part of the neighborhood. One inexpensive approach to integrating patrol officers into the neighborhood is found in Providence, Rhode Island, and Horry County, South Carolina, where McDonald's restaurants have provided reserved tables and telephone lines for officers to use. Signs reading "Police Work Station" are posted prominently. Weiss and Dresser (2001, p.117) note: "Small things like reclaiming shopping carts, removing drunks from park benches, discouraging panhandling and advocating street lighting can reduce a city's crime rate, allowing it to regain its ambiance and beauty." They describe how the city of St. Petersburg, Florida, approached the local crime problem from a community policing perspective.

"St. Pete" had been in seedy decline for many years, with a vacancy rate of 26 to 30 percent, until the implementation of the Downtown Deployment team in 1985. This unit patrols a 7-square-mile city center area from morning until bar closing time, focusing on the small things—the misdemeanor offenses—thus allowing police to "cut into the staging ground for larger crime." One of the methods used by this uniformed services task force is identifying local **scofflaws,** people who habitually violate the law. According to Weiss and Dresser (p.117): "By establishing a high profile and looking for scofflaw misdemeanors, the police take away the sense of lawlessness and discourages crime."

Another activity that has helped reduce neighborhood crime involves community policing patrol officers teaching landlords how to screen tenants (Weiss and Dresser, p.117): "If the police learn of a crack pusher, they call the landlord who will evict the tenant and even return the security deposit. Now, crack houses are closed down within a couple of days. The police work with the people of a community, urging them to report violations."

The unit has also engaged the business community in the effort to lower crime and disorder, and "business groups are actively aiding the police in enforcing statutes and gaining convictions" (Weiss and Dresser, p.118). Through the ongoing, high-profile efforts of the downtown task force, an overall 25 percent reduction in downtown crime has been achieved, and the city is now considered a center for arts, culture, sports and entertainment.

Sweeney (2003b, p.43) points out that when agencies embracing the community-policing philosophy survey citizens to find out what concerns them most, traffic problems head the list whether in a quiet suburban neighborhood or a crime-ridden inner-city neighborhood: "Citizens want to see police on the street, and they don't want to see them ignoring traffic violations. Traffic enforcement is not at odds with community policing; in fact, it helps police satisfy important objectives of community-oriented police services—namely, increasing the visibility of officers and improving the quality of life for every member of the community."

 SUMMARY

Of all the operations performed by the police, patrol is the most vital. The three major spheres of activity of patrol are (1) responding to emergencies and calls for service, (2) undertaking activities to apprehend perpetrators of crime and (3) engaging in strategic problem-solving partnerships with the community to address long-standing or emerging problems of crime and disorder.

Traditionally patrol officers have been assigned a specific time and a specific geographic location, or beat, of equal geographic size to patrol, and these assignments have been rotated. In addition, patrol has traditionally been random, reactive, incident driven and focused on rapid response to calls. Patrol might be more effective if it were proactive, directed and problem oriented and if it used differentiated response strategies. Directed patrol uses crime statistics to plan shift and beat staffing, providing more coverage during times of peak criminal activity and in high-crime areas. Crime analysis using mapping, geographic information systems (GIS) and CompStat can identify hot spots or specific problems to target through directed patrol.

While on patrol, officers respond to calls for service and emergencies, undertake self-initiated tasks and perform administrative duties. Patrol can be accomplished by foot, automobile, motorcycle, bicycle, Segway, horseback, aircraft and boat. The most commonly used and most effective patrol is usually a combination of automobile and foot patrol.

Many hours are spent in traffic-related police work. The primary goal of traffic law enforcement is to produce voluntary compliance with traffic laws while keeping traffic moving safely and smoothly. Traffic officers have many responsibilities and specific tasks to perform. Traffic officers may be responsible for enforcing traffic laws, directing and controlling traffic, providing directions and assistance to motorists, investigating motor vehicle crashes, providing emergency assistance at the scene of a crash, gathering information related to traffic and writing reports. Among the most common violations of traffic laws are speeding, red light running, nonuse of seat belts, aggressive driving and road rage, and driving under the influence of drugs or alcohol. Officers can detect impairment through standardized field sobriety tests (SFSTs) and drug recognition experts (DRE), as well as through testing for blood-alcohol concentration. All uniformed officers should enforce traffic laws because of the potential for apprehending a felon.

However effective a traffic program may be, motor vehicle crashes will occur. The three basic causes of crashes are (1) human faults, errors, violations and attitudes, (2) road defects and (3) vehicle defects.

Alcohol is often involved in traffic crashes. In an effort to determine if a driver is intoxicated, legislatures have enacted implied consent laws. These laws state that any person driving a motor vehicle is deemed to have consented to a chemical test of the alcohol content of his or her blood if arrested while intoxicated; refusal to take such a test can be introduced in court as evidence.

The responsibilities of the patrol/traffic officer in a mobile society are numerous, demanding and vital.

DISCUSSION QUESTIONS

1. What type of patrol is used in your community?
2. Why doesn't patrol have as much prestige as investigation?
3. Why is patrol considered a hazardous assignment by some and a boring assignment by others?
4. Which do you support, a one-officer or two-officer patrol unit? Why?
5. If you had your choice of patrol, what method would you select? Why?
6. What kind of traditional patrol do you feel is effective? Which of the suggested changes do you support?
7. Have you ever been involved in a traffic crash? How would you evaluate the performance of the officer(s) responding to the call?
8. What can the public do to make the traffic officer's job easier?
9. Does your state have a seat belt law? If so, when was it passed, and what kind of penalty does it impose?
10. When do you think police officers should issue warning tickets rather than citations for people who are speeding?

INFOTRAC COLLEGE EDITION ASSIGNMENTS

- Use InfoTrac College Edition to help answer the Discussion Questions as appropriate.
- Check *police patrol* on InfoTrac College Edition and note the Supreme Court case *Atwater v. City of Lago Vista* (arrest for minor traffic offenses). This case covers arrest, discretion and police punishment. It is historical and could be used as a guideline. Outline important points of the case, and be prepared to share and discuss your notes with the class.
- Read and outline one of the following articles:
  - "Police on Horseback: A New Concept for an Old Idea" by John C. Fine
  - "The Role of Race in Law Enforcement: Racial Profiling or Legitimate Use?" by Richard G. Schott
  - "Collecting Statistics in Response to Racial Profiling Allegations" by Karen J. Krajer
  - "Battling DUI: A Comparative Analysis of Checkpoints and Saturation Patrols" by Jeffrey W. Greene
  - "CompStat Process" by Jon M. Shane

INTERNET ASSIGNMENT

Go to http://www.ih2000.net/ira/copbook.htm and outline the article "Police on Patrol: The Other Side of the Story." This is a test of discretionary problems. Be prepared to discuss some of these problems with the class.

 BOOK-SPECIFIC WEB SITE

The book-specific Web site at http://info .wadsworth.com/0534552803 hosts a variety of resources for students and instructors. Included are extended activities from each chapter in which students write a policy, use critical thinking skills to make choices in response to a given scenario, use InfoTrac College Edition with direct links to articles for participation in topical discussion forums, and analyze court cases using Web links for research. Many activities can be printed or emailed to instructors. Plus, cited cases with Web links, interactive key term FlashCards, PowerPoint presentations, chapter objectives, and an extensive collection of chapter-based Web links provide additional information and activities to include in the curriculum.

REFERENCES

Anderson, David C. "Crime by the Numbers—Compstat Takes Off." *Law Enforcement News,* March 15, 2001, p.9.

Ashton, Richard J. "Saved by the Belt or Air Bag—Revisited." *The Police Chief,* March 2004, p.66.

Batton, Candice and Kadleck, Colleen. "Theoretical and Methodological Issues in Racial Profiling Research." *Police Quarterly,* March 2004, pp.30–64.

Beck, Kirby. "The IPMBA Instructor Course." *Law and Order,* June 2004, pp.42–46.

Bolton, Joel. "Red Light Running and Other Intersection Hazards." *The Police Chief,* August 2002, p.114.

Bolton, Joel. "Good News from NHTSA: Seat Belt Use Is Up." *The Police Chief,* May 2003, p.70.

Cahill, Patricia. "December Is National Drunk and Drugged Driving (3D) Prevention Month." *The Police Chief,* December 2003, p.86.

"CALEA Takes Stand on Racial Profiling." *Law Enforcement News,* April 15, 2001, p.5.

Chermak, Steven; McGarrell, Edmund F.; and Weiss, Alexander. "Citizens' Perceptions of Aggressive Traffic Enforcement Strategies." *Justice Quarterly,* June 2001, pp.365–391.

Clark, Wesley. "Electric Bicycles: High-Tech Tools for Law Enforcement." *Law Enforcement Technology,* November 2003, pp.78–82.

Cowper, Tom. "Vertical Takeoff and Landing Aircraft for the 21st Century." *Law Enforcement Technology,* September 2004, pp.36–39.

Cox, Otis. "NHTSA's Highway Safety Priorities." *The Police Chief,* April 2004, pp.14–16.

Dees, Tim. "Understanding GIS." *Law and Order,* August 2002, pp.42–46.

Dewey-Kollen, Janet. "Photo Red Light Enforcement." *Law and Order,* August 2003a, pp.28–32.

Dewey-Kollen, Janet. "Saturation Patrols and Sobriety Checkpoints." *Law and Order,* December 2003b, pp.82–83.

Dewey-Kollen, Janet. "National Seat Belt Enforcement Mobilization." *Law and Order,* April 2004, pp.12–14.

Diamond, Joe. "Connecting the Dots." *Police,* April 2003, pp.42–46.

Feavel, Kurt. "Sustaining a Bike Unit." *Law and Order,* April 2003, pp.91–95.

Fors, Carl. "Detecting Detectors." *Law and Order,* April 2004, pp.30–32.

Garrett, Ronnie. "Suspects Can't Hide Their Lying Eyes with EyeCheck." *Law Enforcement Technology,* May 2002, pp.80–85.

Garrett, Ronnie. "Turning the Key on Drunk Driving." *Law Enforcement Technology,* May 2003, pp.72–75.

Goldstein, Herman. *Problem-Oriented Policing.* New York: McGraw-Hill, 1990.

Greene, Jeffrey W. "Battling DUI: A Comparative Analysis of Checkpoints and Saturation Patrols." *FBI Law Enforcement Bulletin,* January 2003, pp.1–6.

Groff, Elizabeth R. and LaVigne, Nancy G. "Mapping an Opportunity Surface of Residential Burglary." *Journal of Research in Crime and Delinquency,* August 2001, pp.257–278.

Heinecke, Jeannine. "Super Heroes Swooping In." *Law Enforcement Technology,* July 2004, pp.72–81.

Helmick, D. O. "Spike." "CHP Addresses Two Highway Safety Problems: Running Red Lights and Senior Citizen Driving Safety." *The Police Chief,* July 2003, pp.44–50.

Hicks, Gary. "Campus Bike Patrol." *Law and Order,* April 2003, pp.87–90.

Highway Loss Data Institute, Insurance Institute for Highway Safety. http://www.hwysafety.org

Hustmyre, Chuck. "Catching Criminals on the Highway." *Law and Order,* December 2003, pp.113–117.

Ioimo, Ralph E. and Aronson, Jay E. "Police Field Mobile Computing: Applying the Theory of Task-Technology Fit." *Police Quarterly,* December 2004, pp.403–428.

Kariya, Mark. "Working on Two Wheels." *Police,* February 2004a, pp.24–28.

Kariya, Mark. "How to Start a Bicycle Patrol Unit." *Police,* May 2004b, pp.20–24.

Kelling, George L. *Foot Patrol.* Washington, DC: National Institute of Justice, no date.

Klockars, Carl B. *Thinking about Police: Contemporary Readings.* New York: McGraw-Hill, 1983.

Langan, Patrick A.; Greenfeld, Lawrence A.; Smith, Steven K.; Durose, Matthew R.; and Levin, David J. *Contacts between Police and the Public: Findings from the 1999*

National Survey. Washington, DC: Bureau of Justice Statistics, February 2001. (NCJ 184957)

La Vigne, Nancy G. and Wartell, Julie. *Mapping across Boundaries: Regional Crime Analysis.* Washington, DC: National Institute of Justice Crime Mapping Research Center and the Police Executive Research Forum, 2001.

Lutz, William. "The Powerful Combination of Intranets and Mapping." *Law Enforcement Technology,* June 2003, pp.118–122.

Maghan, Jess; O'Reilly, Gregory W.; and Chung Ho Shon, Phillip. "Technology, Policing and Implications of In-Car Videos." *Police Quarterly,* March 2002, pp.25–42.

Makholm, John A. "Legal Lights." *The Law Enforcement Trainer,* January/February 2001.

"Man Gets 3 Years for Tossing Dog to Its Death." Associated Press, as reported in (Minneapolis/St. Paul) *Star Tribune,* July 14, 2001, p.A6.

McDonald, Phyllis P. "Implementing CompStat: Critical Points to Consider." *The Police Chief,* January 2004, pp.33–37.

McGarrell, Edmund F.; Chermak, Steven; Weiss, Alexander; and Wilson, Jeremy. "Reducing Firearms Violence through Directed Patrol." *Criminology and Public Policy,* vol. 1, no. 1, 2001, p.119.

Means, Kevin P. "How to Start an Air Support Unit." *Police,* October 2003, pp.24–30.

Miller, Christa. "That's the Ticket." *Law Enforcement Technology,* October 2003, pp.78–83.

National Neighborhood Foot Patrol Center (pamphlet). East Lansing, MI: Michigan State University, no date.

Paquette, Douglas. "Detecting Impairment to Make Streets (and Schools) Safer." *The Police Chief,* July 2002, pp.51–62.

Paul, Eric T. "Standardized Field Sobriety Testing." *Law and Order,* September 2002, pp.32–34.

Peterson, Suzanne Farr. "Freeway Watch: Call 911 to Zap Drunk Drivers." *Community Links,* March 2002, p.18.

Pitcher, Kris and Moore, Stephen. "Operation ABC: Effective Alcoholic Beverage Control Planning, Enforcement and Education." *Law and Order,* February 2003, pp.372–378.

Rao, Angelo. "Transportation Services." In *Local Government Police Management,* edited by William A. Geller and Darrel W. Stephens. Washington, DC: International City/County Management Association, 2003, pp.221–238.

Rich, Thomas. *Crime Mapping and Analysis by Community Organizations in Hartford, Connecticut.* Washington, DC: National Institute of Justice Research in Brief, March 2001. (NCJ 185333)

Rogers, Donna. "The Rap on Mapping." *Law Enforcement Technology,* June 2001, pp.64–68.

Rogers, Donna. "GPS Gains a Stronger Position." *Law Enforcement Technology,* September 2003, pp.74–80.

Rojek, Dean G. "The Effect of Victim Impact Panels on DUI Rearrest Rates: A Five-Year Follow-Up." *Criminology,* November 2003, pp.1319–1340.

Runge, Jeffrey W. "Our Nation's Best Chance for Reducing Impaired Driving." *The Police Chief,* 2003a, pp.10–11.

Runge, Jeffrey W. "Increasing Safety Belt Use: A National Priority." *The Police Chief,* December 2003b, p.12.

Schick, Walt. "CompStat in the Los Angeles Police Department." *The Police Chief,* January 2004, pp.17–23.

Scott, Michael S. *Speeding in Residential Areas.* Washington, DC: Office of Community Oriented Policing Services, Problem-Oriented Guides for Police Series No. 3, August 14, 2001.

Scott, Michael S. *The Benefits and Consequences of Police Crackdowns.* Washington, DC: Office of Community Oriented Policing, Problem-Oriented Guides for Police Response Guide Series No. 1, September 30, 2003.

Shane, Jon M. "CompStat Process." *FBI Law Enforcement Bulletin,* April 2004, pp.12–21.

Sherman, Sue. "Police Units with Horse Sense." *Law Enforcement Technology,* September 2003, pp.55–59.

Smith, Michael R. and Petrocelli, Matthew. "Racial Profiling? A Multivariate Analysis of Police Traffic Stop Data." *Police Quarterly,* March 2001, pp.4–27.

Strandberg, Keith. "Setting Up an Air Unit." *Law Enforcement Technology,* September 2001, pp.20–25.

Strandberg, Keith. "Across Mountains and Beaches." *Law Enforcement Technology,* February 2004, pp.16–18.

Sweeney, Thomas J. "Patrol." In *Local Government Police Management,* edited by William A. Geller and Darrel W. Stephens. Washington, DC: International City/County Management Association, 2003a, pp.89–133.

Sweeney, Thomas J. "Traffic Stops: Neglect Them at Your Peril." *The Police Chief,* July 2003b, pp.38–43.

Vonk, Kathleen. "Bike Patrol Successes." *Law and Order,* April 2003, pp.82–86.

Vonk, Kathleen. "The IPMBA Police Cyclist Course." *Law and Order,* April 2004, pp.80–90.

Walsh, William F. and Vito, Gennaro F. "The Meaning of CompStat." *Journal of Contemporary Criminal Justice,* February 2004, pp.51–69.

Warren, Joe and Meyers, Duane. "PowerPoint for Crash Scenes." *Law and Order,* May 2004, pp.28–33.

Weiss, Jim and Dresser, Mary. "Cleaning Up the City." *Law and Order,* June 2001, pp.117–118.

Whitehead, Christy. "Segways and Community Interaction." *Law and Order,* August 2004a, pp.24–25.

Whitehead, Christy. "Facial Recognition for Patrol." *Law and Order,* September 2004b, pp.82–84.

CASES CITED

Breithaupt v. Abram, 352 U.S. 432 (1957)

City of Indianapolis v. Edmond, No.99-1080 (2000)

Michigan Department of State Police v. Sitz, 496 U.S. 444, 110 (1990)

Schmerber v. California, 384 U.S. 757 (1966)

Whren v. United States, 517 U.S. 806 (1996)

CHAPTER 7

Specialized Roles of Police

Knowledge is of two kinds. We know a subject ourselves, or we know where we can find information upon it.

—Samuel Johnson

 DO YOU KNOW . . .

- What the primary characteristic of an effective investigator is?
- What the primary responsibilities of the investigator are?
- What questions investigators seek answers to?
- Why both sketches and photographs of a crime scene are usually needed?
- How investigators must deal with evidence?
- What DNA profiling is?
- What the three basic types of identification are?
- In what two areas intelligence units work?
- Why all officers are juvenile officers much of the time?
- In what areas vice officers become involved?
- What characterizes SWAT team officers and what they seek to accomplish?
- How K-9s are used? In what categories they may be specifically trained?

CAN YOU DEFINE?

ballistics	DNA profiling	interrogate	riflings
chain of evidence	evidence	interview	solvability factors
complainant	field identification	involvement crimes	suppressible crimes
contamination	follow-up	latent fingerprints	totality of
criminalistics	investigation	modus operandi (M.O.)	circumstances
cyanoacrylate	forensic science	preliminary	undercover
discovery crimes	informant	investigation	witness

Introduction

In addition to the general function of patrol, including traffic assignments, a number of specialized functions are also required of law enforcement personnel. Sometimes all the functions are performed by a single person—a formidable challenge. In large departments, however, separate divisions may exist for each specialized function. Some patrol officers receive special training to deal with specific problems, such as hostage and sniper situations, VIP protection, riot or crowd control, rescue operations and control of suppressible crimes.

Suppressible crimes are crimes that commonly occur in locations and under circumstances that give police officers a reasonable opportunity to deter or apprehend offenders. Included among suppressible crimes are robbery, burglary, car theft, assault and sex crimes. Such problems often involve a need for covert surveillance and decoys, tactics that cannot be used by uniformed patrol officers.

Specialized operations are often used to saturate particular areas or to stake out suspects and possible crime locations. Countermeasures to combat street crimes have included police decoys to catch criminals—one of the most cost-effective and productive apprehension methods available. Officers have posed as cab drivers, old women, truck drivers, money couriers, nuns and priests. They have infiltrated drug circles as undercover agents. Usually operating in high-crime areas, decoy officers are vulnerable to violence and injury. The results are considered worth the risk because, an attack upon a decoy almost always results in the attacker's conviction.

This chapter begins with what is often considered the most glamorous aspect of policing—investigation. Next the specialized functions of profilers, psychics and intelligence officers are explored. This is followed by a discussion of juvenile officers, vice officers and SWAT officers. The chapter concludes with a discussion of K-9 assisted officers and reserve officers.

Investigation

To the general public, the term *criminal investigation* often brings to mind the detective as portrayed in novels, on the radio, in magazines and on television. The detective or investigator single-handedly digs out evidence, collects tips from informants, identifies criminals, tracks them down and brings them to justice. Investigation is a prestigious assignment.

The hit television series *CSI: Crime Scene Investigation* has added to this image. As Wexler (2003, p.44) contends: "[This series] portrays the crime scene investigator as a sort of a whiz-of-all-trades—a combination high-tech investigator, shrewd detective and encyclopedic forensic scientist." Technology and forensics have become important tools in investigations. However the two primary goals have not changed over time: (1) has a crime been committed and (2) who dunit?

Forensic Science

Forensic science deals with examining physical evidence to answer legal questions. Forensic experts can be found in a wide array of occupations, including forensic accountants, anthropologists, artists, chemists, dentists, entomologists, geologists, pathologists, psycholinguists, psychologists and toxicologists.

Criminalistics is a branch of forensic science that deals with physical evidence related to a crime. This may include fingerprints, firearms, tool marks, blood, hairs, documents and other types of physical evidence. According to Lundrigan (2001, p.40): "Like many aspects of forensic science, crime scene investigation is a true union of art and science."

The Investigator

Throughout this chapter, when the term *investigator* is used, it may refer either to a patrol officer performing investigative duties, to a detective or to a forensic specialist. In a great many departments throughout the country, the detective is a patrol officer—no special detective or investigative division exists. In other departments a crime scene investigation unit is available to assist in processing crime scenes, as discussed shortly. Investigators do *not* determine the suspects to be guilty; they remain objective in their investigation.

 The primary characteristic of an effective investigator is objectivity.

The investigator seeks the truth, not simply proof of the suspect's guilt. Article 10 of the *Canons of Police Ethics* (International Association of Chiefs of Police) states:

> The law enforcement officer shall be concerned equally in the prosecution of the wrongdoer and the defense of the innocent. He shall ascertain what constitutes evidence and shall present such evidence impartially and without malice. In so doing, he will ignore social, political and all other distinctions among the persons involved, strengthening the tradition of the reliability and integrity of an officer's word.
>
> The law enforcement officer shall take special pains to increase his perception and skill of observation, mindful that in many situations his is the sole impartial testimony to the facts of a case.

Strandberg (2001, pp.20–21) suggests: "Technology helps crime scene investigators gather the facts that help solve the crime. . . . The search for facts is what's behind today's forensic technology. And new technologies are making the investigator's quest for truth a bit easier. From DNA analysis to hair samples to 3D ballistics comparisons, things have never been better in the forensic world."

The Preliminary Investigation

The **preliminary investigation** consists of actions performed immediately upon receiving a call to respond to the scene of a crime and is usually conducted by patrol officers.

The importance of response time has been debated. Traditionally, rapid response has been stressed, but this has been called into question. Some studies have found that arrests are seldom attributed to fast police response to reported serious crimes because about 75 percent of all serious crimes are **discovery crimes,** crimes uncovered after they have been committed. Only the remaining 25 percent, the **involvement crimes,** require rapid response.

The National Institute of Justices's (NIJ's) Technical Working Group on Crime Scene Investigation (2000, pp.11–17) has developed a guide for law enforcement that sets forth the following prioritization of efforts for first responders arriving at a crime scene:

1. *Initial Response/Receipt of Information*—The initial response to an incident shall be expeditious and methodical. The initial responding officer(s) shall promptly, yet cautiously, approach and enter crime scenes, remaining observant of any persons, vehicles, events, potential evidence and environmental conditions.
2. *Safety Procedures*—The safety and physical well-being of officers and other individuals, in and around the crime scene, are the initial responding officer(s') first priority. The initial responding officer(s) arriving at the scene shall identify and control any dangerous situations or persons.
3. *Emergency Care*—After controlling any dangerous situations or persons, the initial responding officer(s') next responsibility is to ensure that medical attention is provided to injured persons while minimizing contamination of the scene.
4. *Secure and Control Persons at the Scene*—The initial responding officer(s) shall identify persons at the crime scene and control their movement.
5. *Boundaries: Identify, Establish, Protect and Secure*—The initial responding officer(s) at the scene shall conduct an initial assessment to establish and control the crime scene(s) and its boundaries.
6. *Turn Over Control of the Scene and Brief Investigator(s) in Charge*—The scene briefing is the only opportunity for the next in command to obtain initial aspects of the crime scene prior to subsequent investigation.
7. *Document Actions and Observations*—Documentation must be maintained as a permanent record.

The preliminary investigation results are written in an incident report containing the basic facts about the crime, the crime scene and any suspects. Some cases are solved during this phase. For those that are not, the decision must be made as to whether to pursue the case. Usually this decision is based on **solvability factors**, factors affecting the probability of successfully concluding the case, such as whether there are witnesses and/or physical evidence. If the solvability factors indicate the case might be successfully resolved, a follow-up investigation is conducted.

The Follow-Up Investigation

The **follow-up investigation** may be conducted by the investigative services division, sometimes also known as the detective bureau. Therefore successful investigation relies on cooperative, coordinated efforts of both the patrol and the investigative functions. In most smaller departments, the same officer handles both the preliminary and the follow-up investigations.

Investigative Responsibilities

The responsibilities of investigators are many and varied.

Investigative responsibilities include:
- Securing the crime scene.
- Recording all facts related to the case.
- Photographing, measuring and sketching the crime scene.

- Obtaining and identifying evidence.
- Protecting and storing evidence.
- Interviewing witnesses and interrogating suspects.
- Assisting in identifying suspects.

Securing the Crime Scene   Any area that contains evidence of criminal activity is considered a crime scene and must be secured to eliminate **contamination,** that is, the introduction of something foreign into the scene, moving items at the scene or removing evidence from it. The first officer on the scene must protect it from any change. This single responsibility may have far-reaching effects on solving the crime. Physical evidence must be properly protected to have legal and scientific validity. Unfortunately, as Lundrigan (p.38) notes: "All too often a crime scene is compromised by the presence of too many investigators. Items get moved, toilets get flushed and evidence is destroyed."

Recording Relevant Information   Investigators record all necessary information by photographing, sketching and taking notes to be used later in a written report and testifying in court.

 The investigator must obtain answers to the questions: Who? What? Where? When? How? and Why?

Answers to these questions are obtained by observation and by talking to witnesses, complainants and suspects, as discussed shortly. They are recorded in notes, photographs and sketches or are in the form of physical evidence.

Photographing, Measuring and Sketching the Crime Scene   The scene is usually photographed, measured and sketched. The photographs show the scene as it was found, taken in a series to tell a story. Close-up photographs of evidence, such as footprints, tire tracks and tool marks are also taken. In addition to traditional photography, other types of photography such as ultraviolet, infrared and aerial are used. Videotaping has become increasingly common in recording a crime scene.

The digital camera has made photography much more efficient and cost-effective. Garrett (2004, p.6) cites several benefits of digital photography including the fact that digital pictures are available for immediate viewing and printing, and they are easy to store. Digital photography can enhance obscured fingerprints, record crime scenes and take mug shots. Digital photographs can also be enlarged or manipulated; for example a mug shot showing a criminal with long hair and a mustache can be manipulated to shorten the hair and to remove the mustache.

In addition to photographs, a sketch is usually made of the scene. Sketches can be selective and can also show entire areas, for example an entire layout of a home or business. The sketch need not be an artistic masterpiece as long as it includes all relevant details and is accurate and clear. (See Figure 7.1.)

Computer programs based mostly on computer-aided design (CAD) have made crime scene sketching much easier. According to Dees (2001, p.12): "Crime scene drawing software . . . [makes] it possible for anyone who can use a keyboard and mouse to produce a top-flight drawing. . . . CAD software makes it as easy to produce a true scale drawing as it is to produce a rough sketch, and there is no limit to the size of the 'paper' on which the drawing is displayed. . . .

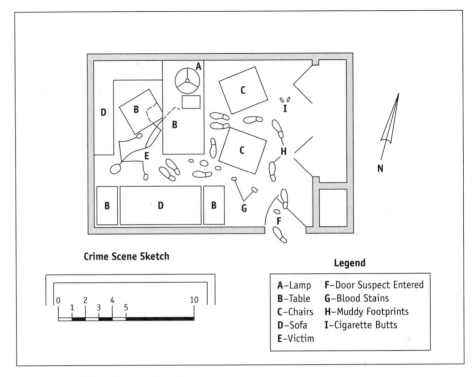

Crime Scene Sketch

Legend

A—Lamp   F—Door Suspect Entered
B—Table   G—Blood Stains
C—Chairs   H—Muddy Footprints
D—Sofa   I—Cigarette Butts
E—Victim

Figure 7.1   Crime Scene Sketch

SOURCE: Wayne W. Bennett and Kären M. Hess. *Criminal Investigation,* 7th ed. Belmont, CA: Wadsworth Publishing Company, 2004, p.56. Reprinted by permission.

CAD software also allows for the creation of layers that include certain objects but omit others." As Davis (2004, p.86) points out: "If there is any truth to that old adage [that a picture is worth a thousand words] then an easy-to-use 3D drawing application is easily worth a billion words or more to the average cop."

> Both photographs and sketches are usually needed. The photographs include all details and can show items close up. Sketches can be selective and can show much larger areas.

Obtaining and Identifying Physical Evidence   A large part of an investigator's role centers around obtaining information and **evidence**—proof that a crime has been committed, as well as proof that a particular person (the suspect) committed the crime. Locard's Principle of Exchange, developed in 1928, states that when any two objects come into contact, a transfer of material from each object to the other always occurs. Investigators use such material to build connections between objects, people and locations. All important decisions will revolve around the available evidence and how it was obtained.

> Investigators recognize, collect, mark, preserve and transport physical evidence in sufficient quantity for analysis and without contamination.

Some agencies have established the position of *evidence technician*. The evidence technician is usually a patrol officer who has received extensive classroom and laboratory training in crime scene investigation. In departments that have small detective bureaus and relatively inexperienced officers, this position fills a notable void. The officer has not been relieved of regular patrol duties but may be called on to conduct crime scene investigations.

The kind of evidence to be anticipated is often directly related to the type of crime committed. Scenes of *violent crimes* frequently contain such evidence as blood, hair, fibers, fingerprints, footprints and weapons. Scenes of property crimes are commonly characterized by forcible entry with tools leaving marks on doors, windows, safes, money chests, cash registers and desk drawers. Among the most common types of evidence found at the crime scene are fingerprints, blood, hair, fibers, documents, footprints or tire prints, tool fragments, tool marks, broken glass, paint, insulation from safes, bite marks, firearms and explosives.

Fingerprints are often found at crime scenes. According to Burger (2002, p.34): "The fingerprint has always been one of law enforcement's most solid, undefeatable bits of evidence. Matching prints can be as good as gold." **Latent fingerprints** are made by sweat or grease that oozes out of the pores from little wells under the ridges at the ends of the fingers. Fingerprint identification is an extremely important form of positive identification. *Identification officers* have specialized training in taking, identifying and filing fingerprints. They are skilled in using scanners and computers in their identification.

An important development in detecting and preserving fingerprints is the **cyanoacrylate,** or superglue, fuming process. When cyanoacrylate is heated, fumes are generated that adhere to fingerprints. This process can be used on items taken to a crime laboratory or items at the scene. Lighting can also help detect fingerprints and trace evidence.

One of the first uses of computers in law enforcement was to assist in identifying fingerprints. More and more departments are installing automated fingerprint identification systems (AFIS). Burger (p.34) notes: "Fingerprint technology has developed more in the past 15 years than it did in the first 100 years." He (p.36) explains: "The product with the greatest potential to impact officers in the short-term is IBIS, a revolutionary mobile identification system that captures forensic quality fingerprints and photographs."

Unfortunately, as Kanable (2003, p.48) states: "Thousands of latent fingerprints recovered from crime scenes languish in police department files. . . . Many large agencies don't submit all automated identification system (AFIS) quality fingerprints to an AFIS. Many smaller agencies do not have access to an AFIS or their own resources to compare fingerprints." In addition: "Twenty states currently do not electronically submit latent fingerprints to the FBI's Integrated Automated Fingerprint Identification System (IAFIS)."

Individuality is not limited to a person's fingertips. Palm prints are now being recognized as valuable evidence when found at a crime scene; in fact, sometimes such prints are the only evidence. One crime lab associate director (Kanable, 2001, p.42) states: "If you process a large amount of evidence, about 25 to 30 percent of the latent impressions are going to be palm prints or partial palm prints." An officer of a company that manufactures and sells AFIS technology estimates 30 percent of cases have nothing but palms (Kanable, 2001, p.43).

But because palm prints can have 1,000 minutiae, or 8 to 12 times more minutiae than fingerprints, manual comparison of suspect palm prints is extremely tedious. However: "Palm print technology is starting to catch up with fingerprint technology . . . [and] there may come a day when automated palm print identification systems spread throughout the U.S. as AFIS technology did" (Kanable, 2001, p.42). The capability exists in many European countries, where palm print technology is a requirement.

A specialized form of "fingerprinting" is DNA profiling. Deoxyribonucleic acid (DNA) is the basic building block comprising each person's genetic code. DNA is found in virtually every cell in a person's body, including blood, semen, hair and skin cells; and it provides a blueprint for the various characteristics that make each person unique. A person's distinctive DNA composition remains the same throughout life, making it a powerful investigative tool: "DNA evidence collected from a crime scene can link a suspect to a crime or eliminate one from suspicion in the same way that fingerprints are used" (Turman, 2001, p.1).

 DNA profiling uses the material from which chromosomes are made to positively identify individuals. No two individuals, except identical twins, have the same DNA structure.

A major difficulty with DNA profiling is the massive backlog of untested cases. The *National Forensic DNA Study Report* (Lovrich et al., 2004) estimates approximately 542,700 cases with biological evidence still await DNA testing, including 52,000 homicides, 169,000 rapes and 264,000 property cases. According to the report, only 10 percent of these cases are backlogged at crime laboratories; 90 percent are still in possession of local law enforcement agencies.

In addition, DNA profiling is expensive and very labor intensive; however the implications for law enforcement are tremendous. To enhance DNA's evidentiary value to criminal investigations, a database similar in concept to AFIS has been developed. Known as CODIS, the FBI's **C**ombined **D**NA **I**ndex **S**ystem is an electronic national database and searching mechanism containing hundreds of thousands of DNA profiles obtained from evidence samples from unsolved crimes and from known offenders ("DNA Evidence: What Law Enforcement Officers Should Know," 2003, p.11).

DNA evidence has also been used to free persons wrongly convicted of and imprisoned for serious crimes, such as rape or homicide: "As a result of DNA testing, more than 70 persons previously convicted of capital crimes and frequently having served long prison terms have been exonerated" (National Commission, 2000, p.1). In light of such findings, the National Commission on the Future of DNA Evidence was created in 1998 to examine the potential of such evidence and how the National Institute of Justice could encourage its most effective use as a crime-fighting tool. Commission members include representatives from the prosecution, the defense bar, law enforcement, the scientific and medical communities, academia and victims' rights organizations.

One of the Commission's technology projections regarding the future of DNA evidence has direct applications to the officer or investigator in the field: "Within 10 years we expect portable, miniaturized instrumentation that will provide analysis at the crime scene with computer-linked remote analysis. This should permit rapid identification and, in particular, quick elimination of innocent suspects" (p.3). However, such technology will likely place law enforcement under further scrutiny regarding their competence in investigative techniques. Indeed, *People v. Simpson* (1995) made apparent the need for thorough, professional processing of a crime scene and the importance of focusing on proper evidence collection procedures rather than on the reliability of evidence.

In addition to assisting in current criminal investigations: "Throughout the nation, criminal justice professionals are discovering that advancements in DNA technology are breathing new life into old, cold or unsolved criminal cases. Evidence that was previously unsuitable for DNA testing because a biological sample was too small or degraded may now yield a DNA profile" (*Using DNA to Solve Cold Cases,* 2002, p.v).

Another type of evidence often found at crime scenes is a *firearm.* A firearm left at a crime scene may be traced to its owner through the serial number, the manufacturer's identification or the dealer who sold it. The firearm might also contain the suspect's fingerprints or other marks that could lead to identification.

The make of the weapon is usually determined by the **riflings,** spiral grooves cut into the gun's barrel during its manufacture. The riflings vary considerably from manufacturer to manufacturer. **Ballistics** deals with the "internal (within the weapon), external (after the projectile leaves the muzzle and before impact), terminal (after the bullet impacts and comes to rest) and forensic (examining comparisons of projectiles/cases and their relationship to firearms)" (Petrone, 2004, p.38). As with fingerprints and DNA, a communications network to link crimes through ballistic evidence has been developed by the Bureau of Alcohol, Tobacco, Firearms and Explosives (AFT): The National Integrated Ballistic Information Network (NIBIN; Budden, 2002, p.51).

Protecting and Storing Evidence   All evidence collected is marked to identify who collected it. It is then packaged and placed in the evidence room until needed. If it is removed from the evidence room for any reason, strict check-out and check-in procedures are followed to maintain the **chain of evidence,** that is, documentation of who has had possession of the evidence from the time it was discovered and taken into custody until the present time. A computerized evidence tracking system (ETS) can prevent countless problems. Many such systems are available. Often they incorporate barcodes, such as those used on merchandise in grocery stores.

Interviewing and Interrogating   A large part of any investigation is talking with people to obtain information. The community policing philosophy stresses the importance of communicating with citizens to identify problems and concerns. Investigators **interview** those with information about a crime. They talk with victims, witnesses and friends, coworkers, neighbors or immediate members of victims' and suspects' families. As Reece (2003, p.66) asserts: "The quality of an investigation's interviews is often the deciding factor in its solvability and the likelihood of a successful prosecution." He suggests:

> The rewards of a quality interview are numerous. It promotes the victims' and public's confidence in law enforcement and increases the likelihood of guilty pleas, reducing time spent testifying and saving tax dollars by reducing court costs and public defender fees. It reduces the man-hours often spent re-interviewing witnesses, due to an earlier officer's inexperience. It directs investigators to additional suspects, evidence of the crime, additional victims and the recovery of property. A quality interview reduces the likelihood of false arrests and improves morale among the department and the investigating officers.

A **witness** is a person other than a suspect who has helpful information about a specific incident or a suspect. A witness may be a **complainant** (the person reporting the offense), an accuser, a victim, an observer of the incident, an eye-witness, an expert or a scientific examiner of physical evidence. Danaher (2003, p.133) points out:

> The main evidence presented during our 300,000 annual jury trials is eyewit-ness testimony. Therein lays the problem. When there is an eyewitness to a crime, and that person identifies the suspect, that evidence alone can and usu-ally is enough to place the suspect under arrest. When the suspect goes to trial and the only evidence is the eyewitness testimony, that alone in most cases is enough to convict the individual. . . .
>
> Relying only on eyewitness identification may result in arrest and detention based on mistaken identity and malicious prosecution under Section 1983. There is now a preponderance of empirical evidence from legal, psychological, media demonstrating that eyewitness identifications are often unreliable.
>
> There are many reasons for incorrect eyewitness identification. One rea-son, the eyewitness is lying. . . .
>
> Another reason for incorrect identification is that the witness' perception of the event was somehow impaired.

In such cases as robbery, assault or rape, eyewitness testimony of the victim or a witness may be all that is necessary for a conviction. It is always preferable, how-ever, to have physical evidence to corroborate the eyewitness testimony, that is, to support or confirm the testimony.

Officers may also use an **informant,** an individual who did not witness the offense but knows something about who committed it. What motivates people to inform? While an informant might receive money as a reward, most informants cooperate with law enforcement to receive a reduced sentence for a pending crimi-nal matter. According to Hendrie (2003, p.10): "It is reasonable to believe that an informant has a motive to be truthful when he is expecting some leniency for pend-ing charges." Other common motives include revenge and civic duty. Hendrie (p.12) notes: "Concerned citizen informants usually give police information out of a sense of civic duty. To be considered a concerned citizen informant by the courts, an informant must not be involved in the criminal milieu." In addition to receiving information from witnesses and informants, investigators also talk with suspects.

When investigators talk with suspects, they technically **interrogate** suspects, although the questioning may also be called an interview. In 2002 the Center for Interviewer Standards and Assessment (CISA) was formed to create professional interview standards and to provide an exam covering the most important aspects of an investigative interviewer's job. Officers who pass the exhaustive 15-section test become certified forensic interviewers (CFIs). "As CFI becomes engrained in law enforcement interviewing and interrogation, it will become meaningful to governmental bodies, to businesses and, possibly most importantly of all, to the legal community. Since you can count on liability to become more and more of an issue, CFI will help law enforcement organizations mitigate liability accusa-tions in the first place, and more easily disprove liability cases that do come up. Having attained a recognized professional standard will make investigators more valuable in front of lawyers and the court, making it easier to prosecute suspects" ("Certified Forensic Interviewer Program," 2003, p.44). As an additional protec-tion against liability, many departments videotape interviews and interrogations.

Identifying Suspects   If officers do not witness a crime, eyewitness identification plays an important part in the arrest, as well as in the trial proceedings. Very specific questions and use of an identification diagram may aid witnesses in identifying suspects. Other information related to the suspect is also obtained: for example how the suspect left the scene—running, walking, in a vehicle—and in what direction.

If the witness knows the suspect, the investigator asks about the suspect's personal associates, habits and where he or she is likely to be found. Usually, however, the witness does not know the suspect. In such cases investigators must obtain identification in other ways.

The three basic types of identification are:
- Field identification.
- Photographic identification.
- Lineup identification.

Each type of identification is used in specific circumstances, and each must meet certain legal requirements to be admissible in court. Sometimes more than one type of identification is used.

Field identification is at-the-scene identification, made within a short time after a crime has been committed. Generally the suspect is returned to the crime scene for possible identification, or the witness may be taken to where the suspect is being held. Field identification is used when a suspect matches the description given by a witness and is apprehended close to the crime scene. The critical element in a field identification is time.

Field identification is based on a **totality of circumstances,** taking into consideration the witness's concentration on the suspect when the crime was committed, the accuracy of the description, the certainty at the time of the confrontation and the length of time between crime commission and the field identification. A reasonable basis for believing that immediate identification is needed must exist because the suspect does not have the right to have counsel present (*United States v. Ash, Jr.,* 1973).

Photographic identification is another option. Most people are familiar with the procedure of having victims and witnesses go through mug books in hopes of finding a picture of the person they saw commit a particular crime. This type of identification is time consuming and is profitable only if the suspect has a record.

Mug shots are not the only types of photographs used in suspect identification. Frequently officers know, or have a strong suspicion about, who committed a given crime. If the suspect is not in custody, or if it is not possible to conduct a fair lineup, officers may present photographs of people of similar general descriptions to victims or witnesses, who may identify the suspect from among the photographs.

A third option is a lineup, allowing witnesses to observe several individuals, one of whom is the suspect, to see if the witnesses can identify the suspect. A suspect may be asked to speak, walk, turn, assume a stance or make a gesture. If for any reason a suspect refuses to cooperate in a lineup, photographic identification may be used. The suspect's refusal to participate may be used against him or her in court.

Another way to identify a suspect may be the **modus operandi** or **M.O.** Computer software is useful for managing large volumes of data in M.O. files.

AP/World Wide Photos

Searching a crime scene requires meticulous attention to detail. Each officer at a crime scene should have a specific task such as photographing, measuring, sketching and the like. The more officers at the scene, the greater the chance of contaminating evidence.

Crime Scene Investigation Units

The crime scene investigator (CSI) has been briefly introduced. Some departments have an entire unit to assist in processing the crime scene. According to Weissberg (2001, p.45): "The Crime Scene Investigations Unit (CSU) provides support services in the form of crime scene processing, fingerprint identification and forensic photography. The Crime Scene Unit responds to major crime scenes to detect, preserve, document, impound and collect physical evidence. The Unit assists in the identification of unknown subjects, witnesses and victims involved in criminal investigations. . . . The Crime Scene Unit will work closely in conjunction with the Detective Bureau in providing assistance in follow-up investigations."

Just as officers may become certified forensic interviewers, they may also become certified CSIs. According to Wexler (p.44): "Besides adding credibility to a crime scene investigator's testimony, certification also provides the necessary background for conducting more accurate and thorough investigations." One of the few organizations that certifies CSIs is the International Association for Identification (IAI), founded in 1919 and now consisting of over 5,000 members from the United States and 70 other countries.

Case Management/Investigation

Sophisticated software packages have been developed to help with case management—receiving, processing, organizing and interrelating all aspects of information on a case. These programs can also keep track of ongoing progress in an investigation. As discussed in detail in Chapter 6, computerized crime mapping technology has allowed even small agencies to get big-city crime analysis.

The Internet

The Internet has revolutionized the way law enforcement gathers and shares information. Not only does the Internet provide access to unlimited general information, it also presents a forum in which a department can reach out to the community. With many households online, and more sure to follow, a department's Web page may post requests for tips regarding certain crimes, inform the community about local public safety issues and increase awareness of law enforcement activities and achievements.

Community Policing and Investigation

In many departments, the detective squad is seen as the "country club" unit, segregated from the other divisions. Investigators have a reputation of being "prima donnas," reluctant to seek help from or share information with officers in other units. Interaction with one another may be infrequent, even within the detective squad itself. Such a culture effectively isolates investigators from a sea of information held by other officers, resources that could be vital to solving a case.

In line with the community policing philosophy, investigators are now recognizing the benefits to developing partnerships with various community members as well as with other units in the department. This approach makes investigation more proactive and fosters problem solving among detectives. According to Singh (2001, p.4): "A shift to community-oriented investigations is an acknowledgement that crime is a complex phenomenon that requires a balanced response. Adopting a balanced approach means that detectives must collaborate better among themselves and with other community stakeholders." Partners that may be enlisted to enhance investigative efforts include the department's community policing unit, the crime prevention unit, crime victims and local businesses.

Singh (p.7) explains how such initiatives should not be thought of as "programs," which have a beginning and an end, but rather as cultural changes in the way police do their work. The intention of these initiatives is not to create a community investigation unit but "to create an entire department equipped to use problem solving in its everyday police work" (p.8).

Profilers

Since the first police investigation, detectives have focused on relatively superficial characteristics to identify suspects, such as height, weight, race, gender, age, accent, type of car driven, M.O., and so on. While these descriptors remain valid and are still considered when searching for suspects, profilers have begun delving deeper into suspects' personalities, psyches, pathologies and resultant behaviors to develop more complete portraits of serial criminals. Such profiles can and often do exist in the absence of any physical descriptors. The Hollywood version of a profiler was seen in the movie *The Silence of the Lambs*, but was a rather unrealistic picture.

Gallo (2003, p.19) explains how profiling works: "The purpose of profiling is to provide a scientific method for focusing resources. . . . As a scientific method, profiling can be viewed as pattern recognition through systematically collecting, organizing and analyzing information collected by observation or measurement; drawing conclusions in assessing criminal suspicion; and sharing data with others. The method demands that procedures be objective or free from personal bias and emotion."

Gorman (2001, p.8) cautions: "It is absolutely essential to thoroughly understand and distinguish between racial profiling and criminal profiling. The former is a crime and violation of civil rights, while the latter is an essential tool for an effective police officer and crime fighter." According to Sharpe (2002, p.9):

"Criminal profiling is easy to understand. If 90 percent of all murders were committed by clowns, is it not fair to say that the first likely suspect in a murder case would have a rubber nose?"

A major source of research and development on criminal profiling is the Investigative Support Unit of the National Center for the Analysis of Violent Crime (NCAVC). An additional resource is the Web site for Criminal Profiling Research, http://www.criminalprofiling.ch/research.htm/

Psychics

The use of psychics in investigations has also been popularized by the media. Many investigators place absolutely no faith in psychics, but other investigators have found them to be helpful, especially in cold cases. According to Martinez (2004, p.52), who has successfully used psychics: "A psychic can be a tool in the investigator's toolbox, but it wouldn't be the first tool you'd look for."

Hibbard et al. (2002) recommend asking other officers for referrals. They also suggest contacting local health food stores and metaphysical bookstores and churches to request names. Within a few days of interviewing, officers will find that the same names keep coming up because there are underground networks of psychics, most of whom know each other. According to Hibbard et al.: "The investigator's theory should be primary and should only be replaced by a psychic's theory on its merits and not because of its paranormal origin."

Intelligence Officers

Most large departments have an intelligence division whose top officer reports directly to the chief and whose activities are kept from the rest of the department. Intelligence units work in two areas.

 Intelligence officers may be undercover officers investigating crime or internal affairs officers investigating complaints against officers within the department.

Undercover Officers

Undercover work involves ongoing investigations into such criminal activity as illegal sale of guns, payoffs to politicians, major drug cases and organized crime activities. Undercover employees (UCEs) often work on cases in cooperation with county, state and federal investigators. The goal of undercover officers is to identify suspects and gather evidence for prosecution.

Given the nature of such assignments and their reliance on anonymity and obscurity, undercover intelligence officers do not wear uniforms or drive marked cars, and they may use assumed names and fictitious identities. To avoid identification problems, some large agencies use officers who have just graduated from rookie school because they are not known on the street.

Two broad categories of undercover work are the light cover and the deep cover. Light undercover officers may have a fake ID, but usually go home to their families and real life, most likely in another city. They may pose as a utility worker or phone company repair person to gain access to a suspect's living quarters or place of work. They might plant listening devices or look for signs of illegal activity.

One approach to light undercover work is the sting operation or ruse, where police deceive criminals into openly committing illegal acts. According to Miller (2001, p.28): "The ruse has evolved as a necessary and important tactic in law enforcement. A strategically planned deception as to a law enforcement officer's identity or purpose can save months of investigative work and be just as effective." Miller suggests four purposes served by ruses or stings:

- To net fugitives from justice. The Kenton County (Kentucky) Sheriff's Office used a lure of "unclaimed tax money" to arrest more than 200 people on outstanding warrants.
- To establish probable cause to arrest or search. The Portland (Maine) Police Department set up a "massage parlor" as part of an effort to crack down on prostitution. Twenty-six "Johns" were arrested for soliciting sex from undercover police officers.
- To access a person or property without use of force during warrant execution. Police typically pose as utility workers or package delivery personnel.
- To interview a subject who might otherwise be uncooperative, usually by pretending to investigate a different crime or a different person.

Such operations, however, carry legal risks for law enforcement. Officers must adhere to department policies and procedures, and accurately document their activity, lest the undercover agents and the agency be accused of entrapment.

Deep undercover officers live their roles 24/7, with a false ID and a false personal history. The first name is usually kept so answering to the name comes naturally, and the personal history will be as close to the truth as possible to avoid slipups. These officers usually have actual employment, own a house or rent an apartment and establish a role that provides them access inside whatever group or organization they wish to infiltrate. Deep undercover operations are usually designed to target big-time drug dealers, gangs or crime bosses.

While undercover operations are often perceived as mysterious and glamorous assignments, psychological and physical dangers abound. Family and social relationships may suffer from such assignments, as officers are precluded from sharing what they are involved in with those closest to them. In addition, intense, long-term operations may also lead to officer burnout, which may couple with complacency, causing an agent to lose focus, not pay attention to important details or misread a potentially threatening situation. Furthermore many undercover officers find it difficult to return to routine police work once the covert operation is over.

Even the most cautious undercover officers may find themselves unavoidably immersed in the violence that defines the criminal world, victims of assault, shootings and worse, sometimes at the hands of other officers who are unaware of their undercover status. As Floyd (2001, p.58) notes: "Behind enemy lines . . . undercover cops pay the ultimate price." He gives the following example: "A search of the records kept by the National Law Enforcement Officers Memorial Fund shows that 60 federal, state and local officers made the ultimate sacrifice while working undercover."

The second area of intelligence work is investigating officers in the department.

Internal Affairs

Griffith (2003, p.76) states: "Among more polite officers, internal affairs is thought of as a necessary evil. In less polite, more candid circles it's thought of in less savory terms like 'the secret police' and 'the rat squad.' Since the 1950s when the first internal affairs units were established, policing the police has not been an easy job. It was never intended to be." According to Griffith: "The job of internal affairs investigators is to find the truth about charges levied by civilians against fellow cops and to protect the department from systemic corruption." He suggests: "Internal affairs investigators tread the fine line of protecting the public from abusive police, individual officers from unfounded allegations and their agencies from corruption."

Marko (2004, p.84) contends: "The key to being proactive with citizen complaints is a timely response to the complainant and equipping the office with a well-founded internal affairs program. Even in agencies that do not have a dedicated internal affairs division or officer, in-depth training in this area will enable agencies to present strong cases for the innocence of their officer and to recognize problem employees and deal with them accordingly."

Both the International Association of Chiefs of Police (IACP) and the Commission on Accreditation for Law Enforcement Agencies (CALEA) have developed policies and standards addressing the need for effective, efficient methods for receiving and processing all complaints of misconduct involving law enforcement personnel. Kelly (2003, p.6) cautions: "It remains critical to the integrity of an agency that it accept and fully investigate all complaints." According to Thurnauer (2002, p.73): "A simple declaration that all complaints against any member of the police department will be received and investigated leaves little room for dispute." As Lober (2002, p.57) points out: "Internal affairs can impact the cultural values and the core values of a department. . . . If internal affairs . . . decides not to open investigations into alleged use of excessive force, sexual misconduct or police shootings, then the message is sent loud and clear that such conduct is acceptable."

Colaprete (2003, p.100) contends: "The internal affairs investigation is the most complex and sensitive investigation conducted by a police organization. Insurmountable barriers of attitudes, politics and egos block the road. The daunting task then is to overcome these ulterior motives to search for the truth. . . . In doing so, the rights of the complainant should be equal to and not overshadow the rights of the accused officer."

Dees (2003, p.88) offers further insight into the role of internal affairs officers: "Internal affairs sections, sometimes also referred to as professional standards, policy compliance and quality assurance officers, have traditionally been reactive operations, responding to complaints from citizens and reports of misconduct and policy violations from other department employees. The litigious nature of American society, as well as a citizenry that is increasingly intolerant of transgressions by police, has required that agencies assume a more proactive role." This more proactive role often involves establishing some sort of early warning system to identify officers who have the *potential* for unacceptable behavior.

Mills-Senn (2004, p.86) describes software for an internal affairs/early intervention program to help internal affairs (IA) departments identify a variety of performance problems. It might, for example, red flag an officer or unit with an excessive number of complaints compared to peers.

IA officers must be aware of the ruling in *Garrity v. New Jersey* (1967). In *Garrity* the U.S. Supreme Court held that the government violates the Fourteenth Amendment if it uses a police officer's statement in a criminal trial against that officer if the statement resulted from his being told if he refused to answer the question it might cost him his job. As Brooks (2002, p.27) observes: "The *Garrity* ruling imposes significant restraints on law enforcement administrators investigating misconduct allegations within an agency."

Yet another specialized assignment is that of the juvenile officer.

Juvenile Officers

Police officers are often the first contact for youths in legal trouble. Therefore it is justifiable and logical to have juvenile police specialists. Because most juvenile work is informal and officer discretion plays a critical role, such as determining whether to release, refer or detain, juvenile officers must be chosen from the most qualified officers in the department. The usual flow of how police interact with youths in the juvenile justice system is illustrated in Figure 7.2.

Because juveniles commit a disproportionate number of local crimes, all officers are juvenile officers much of the time. Also, the police usually are youths' initial contact with the juvenile justice system. They have broad discretion and may release juveniles to their parents, refer them to other agencies, place them in detention or refer them to a juvenile court.

Whether a juvenile is actually taken into custody usually depends on a number of factors, the most important of which is the seriousness of the offense. Other considerations include age, attitude, family situation, previous record and the attitudes of the school and the community. Figure 7.3 illustrates the discretionary decision points in police handling of juveniles. The probation department may or may not be part of a juvenile division.

The police may also be responsible for some specific services involving children, such as helping to locate missing or runaway children, conducting fingerprinting programs and investigating reports of neglected or abused children.

On October 12, 1982, President Ronald Reagan signed into law the Missing Children Act, requiring the attorney general to "acquire, collect and preserve any information which would assist in the location of any missing person (including children . . .) and provide confirmation as to any entry (into FBI records) for such a person to the parent, legal guardian or next of kin." Though this law does not require that the FBI investigate the case, it does give parents, legal guardians or the next of kin access to the information in the FBI National Crime Information Center's (NCIC) Missing Person File.

Because of this law, it is important that children be fingerprinted. Many schools have instituted such a program in conjunction with the local police department. The same procedures used to search for a missing child might be used to locate a runaway child.

Police are also called on to investigate reports of neglected or abused children. In most jurisdictions parental abuse or neglect of children is a crime, but jurisdictions vary in what constitutes abuse or neglect. Usually neglect includes failure to feed and clothe a child or provide adequate shelter.

A special type of juvenile officer is the school resource officer (SRO), discussed in detail in Chapter 5. Benigni (2004, p.24) notes: "SRO programs offer

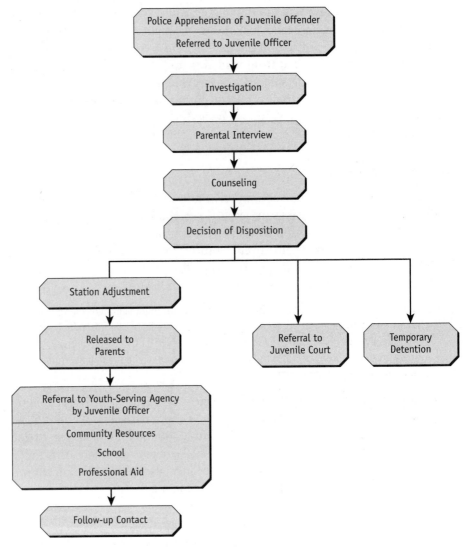

Figure 7.2 Police Responsibility for Juveniles

SOURCE: Reprinted by permission of the International Association of Chiefs of Police.

an opportunity for school officials to proactively protect their schools and improve their educational environment." Many schools have turned to SROs to help address the problems of gang violence, drug use, property crime, assaults and other crimes committed on school grounds. SROs are enhancing their effectiveness through specialized training in such areas as critical incident response, legal issues for SROs and school administrators, identifying adolescent drug use, and bullying prevention and intervention. Like officers on the streets, officers in schools are now using crime prevention through environmental design (CPTED) to identify, prevent and solve crime problems.

Vice Officers

 Vice officers usually concentrate their efforts on illegal gambling, prostitution, pornography, narcotics and liquor violations.

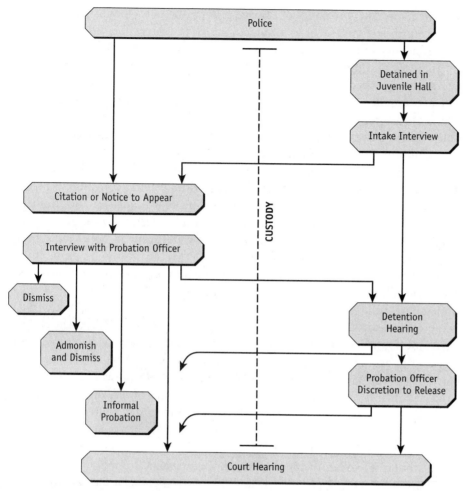

Figure 7.3   Decision Points in Police Handling of Juveniles
SOURCE: Reprinted by permission of the International Association of Chiefs of Police.

Vice problems vary from community to community. Sometimes the work is coordinated with that of intelligence officers.

Illegal and Legal Gambling

Some people view gambling as a vice; others view it as a harmless form of entertainment. Within the gambling industry, the term *gambling* has fallen into disfavor and has been replaced with the term *gaming,* perhaps to make it more socially acceptable. The most significant forms of illegal gambling in the United States are numbers betting with bookmakers or bookies and sports pools or sports cards. The Internet is a rapidly growing source of gambling with an estimated 300 gambling-related sites, some set up offshore.

Charitable gaming, pari-mutuel betting, casino gaming and lotteries are *legal* in most states. However, Moffett and Peck (2001, p.16) contend: "Gambling and gamblers attract many of the traditional vices (e.g., prostitution, pornography, loan-sharking and extortion). . . . In addition to crimes at the casinos, the [Biloxi, Mississippi] police department experienced an increase in the investigations of robberies, check and credit card fraud, property crimes, domestic abuse and alcohol-related violations." They (p.17) conclude: "Legal gambling will attract an unsavory element that can jeopardize the safety and well-being of the city's residents and the many visitors who come to gamble."

The view that the presence of casinos increases crime is called into question by researchers Stitt et al. (2003, p.253), who found that crime does not inevitably increase with the introduction of a casino into a community, but rather the effects of casinos on crime appear to be related to a variety of variables that are only poorly understood. They (pp.282–283) report: "When a casino opens in a community, it often changes the nature of the community in a multitude of ways, both positively (e.g., stimulating the economy and adding employment and entertainment options) and negatively (e.g., adding traffic congestion, altering traditional patterns of interaction and introducing large numbers of nonresidents into a community). The interplay of these and other factors (location, size and number of casinos; state gaming regulations; law enforcement policies; etc.) vary by jurisdiction and may well determine the effect of the casino on crime in the community. . . . Crime does not appear to be an inevitable or necessary product of casino presence."

Similar findings are reported by Wilson (2001, p.610), who conducted an empirical investigation of riverboat gambling and crime in Indiana: "The casinos were not found to increase crime in Hammond but were associated with increases in aggravated assaults and thefts in Rising Sun. These somewhat attenuated effects on crime suggest the enhanced criminal opportunity created by riverboat casinos did not increase the overall frequency of individual offenses as might be expected from routine activities theory and related tourism literature."

Prostitution and Pornography

Some areas of the country allow prostitution, but most do not. For areas where prostitution is illegal, it often seems to law enforcement as if they are fighting a losing battle. Scott (2001, p.1) notes: "Street prostitution accounts for perhaps only 10 to 20 percent of all prostitution, but it has the most visible negative impact on the community." It is also the type of prostitution citizens complain the most about. In addition to complaints from citizens, Scott (pp.1–3) gives several other reasons police should be concerned about prostitution: moral concerns, public health concerns, personal safety concerns, economic concerns, civil rights concerns and spillover effect concerns. Spillover effect concerns include the following (p.3):

- Street prostitution and street drug markets are often linked.
- Prostitution may provide the seedbed for organized crime.
- Prostitutes create parking and traffic problems where they congregate.
- Prostitution attracts strangers and criminals to a neighborhood.

Some jurisdictions publish the names of people arrested for soliciting prostitutes in hopes of deterring the activity. For agencies that post their lists on the Web and can track the number of "hits," such pages are proving to be very popular sites.

Surratt et al. (2004, p.54) studied the subculture of violence of "female street sex workers" and found that: "These women's historical and current life experiences are replete with episodes of victimization and violence." They (p.55) also report: "Nearly 45 percent of those in the sample are homeless, the majority have limited education, and very few possess any sort of social or professional ties with the larger community. . . . Virtually all of the women encountered in this project indicated that prostitution is not a chosen career. Rather, for most it is *survival sex*, and for almost all it is the result of a drug habit combined with the lack of other skills or resources."

Another challenge facing vice workers is pornography. Of great concern is the proliferation of child pornography on the Internet. According to Fantino (2003, p.28): "The Internet has not only become a limitless library of child pornography but it has opened a new arena for offenders' secret clubs." He reports that more than 100,000 Web sites contain child pornography. Vice officers investigating pornography usually work covertly behind the scenes. Much more visible and often the center of media attention are tactical forces or SWAT officers.

SWAT Officers

Special Weapons and Tactics (SWAT) teams began in 1967 when the Los Angeles Police Department organized such a unit to respond to critical incidents. Scoville (2003, p.28) observes: "[Such teams] have been a part of the public consciousness since 'S.W.A.T.' made its television debut in 1975."

Ramirez (2003, p.68) provides the definition of a SWAT team approved by the California SWAT Commission: "A SWAT team is a designated unit of law enforcement officers who are specifically trained and equipped to work as a coordinated team to respond to critical incidents, including, but not limited to, hostage taking, barricaded suspects, snipers, terrorist acts and other high-risk incidents. As a matter of agency policy, such a unit may be used to serve high-risk warrants, both search and arrest, where public and officer safety issues compel the use of such a unit."

 SWAT team officers are immediately available, flexible, mobile officers used to deploy against critical incidents. They seek to contain and neutralize dangerous situations.

Williams and Westall (2003, p.469) report: "Today, 90 percent of cities with more than 50,000 in population have SWAT teams, and 66 percent of smaller cities also have them." Sometimes the teams are full time, but more typically the teams are drawn from the officers on the force who, for the most part, perform more traditional assignments.

SWAT team members are highly trained in marksmanship, guerrilla tactics, night operations, camouflage and concealment, and use of chemical agents. They often participate in field exercises to develop discipline and teamwork. Scoville (p.28) notes: "To the appreciative hostage whose life they have saved, SWAT team members are knights in shining ballistic armor. To their critics, they are gung-ho macho men, prone to wrong house entries and preemptive shootings. Somewhere between these images, the perceptions and accusations lies a truth: if ever an entity embodied the philosophy of 'hope for the best, but plan for the worst,' it is the SWAT unit."

Some have criticized the overemphasis on physical assault and combat techniques by tactical teams, yet such aggressive measures are becoming more necessary as today's street gangs and drug traffickers become better armed, stocking

AP/Wide World Photos

Miami Beach SWAT team members move into position in front of a houseboat on the Intracoastal waterway where an armed suspect had been discovered. SWAT team members are trained to contain and neutralize high-risk situations.

arsenals of semiautomatic and assault weapons that would make many law enforcement agencies envious. Most studies of SWAT activity show that such teams are rarely deployed in an offensive situation; rather they are almost always called out for defensive purposes.

Williams and Westall studied the use of force by trained SWAT officers and non-SWAT officers and found that there was no statistically significant difference between the two groups of officers in terms of the frequency or the type of force used. They (p.469) concluded: "The results may indicate that regular department-wide training on the use of force is a more significant influence on behavior than an officer's part-time assignment to SWAT duties."

The question has also been raised as to how SWAT teams can coexist with officers operating in a community-policing mind-set. SWAT team officers are by definition reactive; community policing officers seek to be proactive. The challenge is to teach officers to function in either mode, depending on the circumstances.

If a search is involved in a SWAT deployment, many departments find that K-9s can greatly enhance the safety of their officers as well as enhance the search itself. However, as Smith (2003, p.38) stresses: "The K-9 handlers must learn that the SWAT team is in charge of the search . . . Once the dog has located the suspect for the SWAT team, the dog's job is done." K-9s can be invaluable assets to a department.

K-9 Assisted Officers

The first organized K-9 unit in the United States began in 1907 in New York City. According to Hamilton (2003, p.18): "Knowing that canines will save time and money is just common sense. A dog could search a building in 10 minutes while it might take two or three officers an hour to do that same search. . . . A dog's sense of smell is about 700 times greater than a human's."

Although police K-9 programs, unlike police officers, do not have any national reporting base, Russ Hess (2001), national executive director of the United States Police Canine Association, Inc., observes: "There are more police K-9 units today than ever before and, in light of the events of September 11, 2001, we are likely to see a worldwide increase in the number and use of explosive detector dogs."

 K-9s are used to detect concealed suspects, drugs, weapons and explosives; find evidence discarded by fleeing suspects; control crowds and break up fights; recover lost articles; and locate distressed persons and dead bodies.

Police dogs are often used in place of a second officer on automobile and foot patrols. Service K-9s can run down a suspect, jump barricades and maneuver through confined spaces more readily than a human officer, thereby significantly decreasing the risks to their two-legged counterparts. Today's police dog has intensive schooling with one officer—the dog's partner. Both spend many weeks under a special trainer and receive instruction specific to one of five general categories.

 K-9s may be specifically trained in search, attack and capture, drug detection, bomb detection and crime deterrence.

As noted by McEntire (2002, p.32), a decade ago the Maine Criminal Justice Academy helped pioneer the use of accelerant-sniffing dogs to investigate cases of suspected arson. Some overlap and cross-training of K-9s does occur, although rarely is one dog trained or expected to perform in all capacities.

A variety of detector scents are available to help train these K-9s, including narcotics (cocaine, heroin, LSD, marijuana), powder explosives, injured people and cadaver scent. Various breeds of dogs are used, but the most popular is the German shepherd.

The cost of training such dogs can be a major deterrent to small departments. While some agencies are fortunate enough to receive donated dogs, many must purchase their canines, which can be quite costly. Whatever the cost, the benefits of K-9 units are numerous. Detector dogs can be used in airports and on planes, in schools, in the workplace and at border checkpoints.

In addition to functioning in active crime fighting and prevention duties, K-9 units have helped in search and rescue (SAR) efforts to locate victims of bombings and plane crashes and are also used to enhance community relations as well as to enhance SWAT efforts as discussed previously.

The police dog is being held to a higher standard than ever before, just like their human counterparts in law enforcement. While dogs are still dogs, officers must answer to any complaint lodged regarding the actions of their canine partners. Officers should also be familiar with legal issues when using K-9s.

On day 2 of the 9/11 World Trade Center disaster police and search and rescue dogs are on their way to "Ground Zero" in the WTC restricted area in lower Manhattan. K-9s are effective helpers in the efforts to locate victims at disaster scenes.

K-9 Case Law

Green (2004, p.39) stresses: "Administrators and trainers need to be very familiar with case law as it pertains to the specialty of canines." Most issues revolve around the Fourth Amendment's right to be free from unreasonable search and seizure. In *United States v. Place* (1993) the U.S. Supreme Court ruled that the exposure of luggage to a canine sniff did not constitute a search. According to Walker (2001, p.28): "Most courts addressing cases involving a dog sniff of the exterior of a warehouse or garage from a public location have found that it is not a search."

The courts have also usually sided with law enforcement on use-of-force issues. Devanney and Devanney (2003, p.12) report: "Several courts . . . have already held that the use of properly trained police dogs does not constitute deadly force." In fact, according to Smith (2004, p.32): "The courts have ruled many times that dogs are considered reasonable force, not deadly force." A source of current information on K-9–related case law is the Web site of Terry Fleck, an expert in canine legalities: www.k9fleck.org.

Reserve Officers

Some departments have reserve units to help achieve departmental goals. Reserve officers, also called auxiliary police, patrol in uniform and are visible symbols of law enforcement, although they cannot write citations. Reserve officers also help in public education programs, informing the public about such things as drugs, bike safety and Operation Identification, in which valuables are marked for identification in case of theft. When a crime does occur, reserves can guard the crime scene while the officers continue with their routine or specialized patrol.

Besides performing traditional street patrol, reserves may be found on bicycles, in the water and in the air. Volunteer aviators may extend the resources of law enforcement agencies. While departments of all sizes across the country supplement their policing efforts with reserve officers, Weinblatt (2001, p.30) observes: "Reserves in the United States have a much larger presence in smaller, rural agencies . . . [which] have been forced to do more with less." The sheriff of Union County, North Carolina, acknowledges that volunteers engaged in search-and-rescue missions and other reserve activities are really an extension of community policing. Reserve officers are not always welcomed with open arms, however, and controversy often accompanies their use.

Heuston (2002, p.260) describes a new type of reserve officer, the police reserve specialist (PRS), which was prompted by the attacks on the World Trade Center and the Pentagon on September 11, 2001: "The PRS program evolved from an initial concept—to train private sector experts for use in emergencies—to the notion that the best manner of preparing for emergencies is to assimilate them as a volunteer force in active investigations." He (p.261) describes the needed areas of expertise, including computer forensics, telecommunications, information technology and security, computer network and system analysis, intellectual property investigations, and identity theft and Internet fraud cases.

 SUMMARY

A large part of an investigator's role centers around *objectively* obtaining and presenting information and evidence. Investigative responsibilities include securing the crime scene; recording all facts related to the case; photographing, measuring and sketching the crime scene; obtaining and identifying evidence; interviewing witnesses and interrogating suspects; and assisting in identifying suspects.

Investigators must obtain answers to the questions: Who? What? Where? When? How? and Why? Usually they must obtain both photographs and sketches because although photographs include all details and can show items close up, sketches can be selective and can show much larger areas.

A primary responsibility of investigators is to recognize, collect, mark, preserve and transport physical evidence in sufficient quantity for analysis and without contamination. DNA profiling uses the material from which chromosomes are made to positively identify individuals. No two individuals, except identical twins, have the same DNA structure.

If officers do not witness a crime, eyewitness identification plays an important part in the arrest, as well as in the trial proceedings. The three basic types of identification are field identification, photographic identification and lineup identification.

Most large departments have an intelligence division whose top officer reports directly to the chief and whose activities are kept secret from the rest of the department. Intelligence officers may be undercover officers investigating crime or internal affairs officers investigating officers within the department.

Because juveniles commit a disproportionate number of local crimes, all officers are juvenile officers much of the time. Larger departments often have several types of specialized officers. Vice officers usually concentrate their efforts on illegal gambling, prostitution, pornography, narcotics and liquor violations. SWAT officers are immediately available, flexible and mobile, deployed during critical incidents. K-9s have been used to detect concealed suspects, drugs, weapons and explosives; find evidence discarded by fleeing suspects; control crowds and break up fights; recover lost articles; and locate distressed persons and dead bodies. K-9s may be specifically trained in search, attack and capture, drug detection, bomb detection and crime deterrence.

DISCUSSION QUESTIONS

1. What are the goals of an investigating officer?
2. What does a preliminary investigation consist of?
3. What differences exist between a studio photographer and a crime scene photographer?
4. Why is DNA profiling not more commonly used in criminal investigations?
5. Why and how are computers being used in investigations?
6. Why would people not want to help put a stop to crime by being witnesses?
7. How do empathy and perception interact? Why are they important to an interviewer/interrogator?
8. Does your police department use reserve officers? If so, how many are there and what are their main duties? Should they have authority to write citations? Make arrests?
9. Does your police department have a SWAT team? If so, when is it used?
10. Does your police department use K-9s? If so, what are they used for?

INFOTRAC COLLEGE EDITION ASSIGNMENTS

- Use InfoTrac College Edition to help answer the Discussion Questions as appropriate.
- Using InfoTrac College Edition, find *criminal investigation*. Then find the article "The Post-Columbo Era: How the Courts Killed Good Detective Work," discussing how laws limit methods of criminal investigation. Outline the article, and be prepared to share and discuss your outline with the class.

- Read and outline one of the following articles:
  - "Managing Undercover Stress: The Supervisor's Role" by Stephen R. Band and Donald C. Sheehan
  - "When an Informant's Tip Gives Officers Probable Cause to Arrest Drug Traffickers" by Edward M. Hendrie
  - "Statements Compelled from Law Enforcement Employees" by Michael E. Brooks
  - "Internal Affairs Issues for Small Police Departments" by Sean F. Kelly
  - "When Casino Gambling Comes to Your Hometown: The Biloxi Experience" by Tommy Moffett and Donald L. Peck
  - "Using Drug Detection Dogs: An Update" by Jayme S. Walker
  - "The Need for School Resource Officers" by Mark D. Benigni

 ### INTERNET ASSIGNMENT

Search for the key words *undercover officer*. Find the article "Undercover Police Work" and outline it. Again, be prepared to discuss your outline with the class.

 ### BOOK-SPECIFIC WEB SITE

The book-specific Web site at http://info .wadsworth.com/0534552803 hosts a variety of resources for students and instructors. Included are extended activities from each chapter in which students write a policy, use critical thinking skills to make choices in response to a given scenario, use InfoTrac College Edition with direct links to articles for participation in topical discussion forums, and analyze court cases using Web links for research. Many activities can be printed or emailed to instructors. Plus, cited cases with Web links, interactive key term FlashCards, PowerPoint presentations, chapter objectives, and an extensive collection of chapter-based Web links provide additional information and activities to include in the curriculum.

REFERENCES

Benigni, Mark D. "The Need for School Resource Officers." *FBI Law Enforcement Bulletin*, May 2004, pp.22–24.

Brooks, Michael E. "Statements Compelled from Law Enforcement Employees." *FBI Law Enforcement Bulletin*, June 2002, pp.26–31.

Budden, Jennifer. "Linking Crimes through Ballistic Evidence." *Law and Order*, November 2002, pp.51–52.

Burger, Dan. "New Fingerprint Technology IDs Bad Guys Faster Than Ever." *Police*, January 2002, pp.34–39.

"Certified Forensic Interviewer Program." *Law and Order*, May 2003, pp.42–45.

Colaprete, Frank. "The Necessary Evil of IA." *Law and Order*, May 2003, pp.96–100.

Danaher, Larry. "The Investigative Paradigm." *Law and Order*, June 2003, pp.133–134.

Davis, Bob. "The CAD Zone: Law Enforcement Drawing Software." *Police*, March 2004, pp.86–87.

Dees, Tim. "Crime Scene Drawing Programs." *Law and Order*, August 2001, pp.12–14.

Dees, Tim. "Internal Affairs Management Software." *Law and Order*, May 2003, pp.88–95.

Devanney, Joe and Devanney, Diane. "Canine Case Law." *Law and Order*, September 2003, pp.12–14.

"DNA Evidence: What Law Enforcement Officers Should Know." *NIJ Journal*, July 2003, pp.10–15.

Fantino, Julian. "Child Pornography on the Internet: New Challenges Require New Ideas." *The Police Chief*, December 2003, pp.28–30.

Floyd, Craig W. "Behind Enemy Lines . . . Undercover Cops Pay the Ultimate Price." *American Police Beat*, March 2001, pp.58–59.

Gallo, Frank J. "Profiling vs. Racial Profiling: Making Sense of It All." *The Law Enforcement Trainer*, July/August 2003, pp.18–21.

Garrett, Ronnie. "Is It Time to Solve the Digital Mystery?" *Law Enforcement Technology*, February 2004, p.6.

Gorman, Michael J. "Draw Line between Criminal, Racial Profiling." *American Police Beat*, July/August 2001, p.8.

Green, Bernie. "Well Trained and Reliable Canine." *Law and Order*, April 2004, pp.38–40.

Griffith, David. "Policing the Police." *Police*, October 2003, pp.76–79.

Hamilton, Melanie. "How to . . . Start a K-9 Unit." *Police*, February 2003, pp.18–23.

Hendrie, Edward M. "When an Informant's Tip Gives Officers Probable Cause to Arrest Drug Traffickers." *FBI Law Enforcement Bulletin*, December 2003, pp.8–21.

Hess, Russ. National Executive Director, United States Police Canine Association, Inc., Springboro, OH. Personal e-mail correspondence: December 4, 2001.

Heuston, George Zell. "Police Reserve Specialists." *Law and Order*, September 2002, pp.260–263.

Hibbard, Whitney; Worring, Raymond; and Brennan, Richard. *Psychic Criminology: A Guide for Using Psychics in Investigations*, 2nd ed. Springfield, IL: C. C. Thomas, 2002.

Kanable, Rebecca. "Palmprint Technology Catches Up to Fingerprint Technology." *Law Enforcement Technology*, March 2001, pp.42–45.

Kanable, Rebecca. "Fingerprints Making the Case." *Law Enforcement Technology*, March 2003, pp.48–53.

Kelly, Sean F. "Internal Affairs Issues for Small Police Departments." *FBI Law Enforcement Bulletin*, July 2003, pp.1–6.

Lober, Richard E. "Value-Based Leadership and the Role of Internal Affairs." *The Police Chief*, May 2002, pp.54–57.

Lovrich, Nicholas P.; Pratt, Travis C.; Gaffney, Michael J.; Johnson, Charles L.; Asplen, Christopher H.; Hurst, Lisa H.; and Schellberg, Timothy M. *National Forensic DNA Study Report*. Washington, DC: U.S. Department of Justice, 2004. http://www.ojp.usdoj.gov/nik/pdf/dna_studyreport_final.pdf

Lundrigan, Nicole. "Crime Scene Priorities." *Law and Order*, May 2001, pp.38–42.

Marko, Jennifer. "IPTM's Internal Affairs Course." *Law and Order*, June 2004, pp.84–86.

Martinez, Liz. "Looking into the Crystal Ball." *Law Enforcement Technology*, July 2004, pp.52–59.

McEntire, Gwen. "Accelerant Dogs Make 'Scents' at Some Fire Scenes." *The Law Enforcement Trainer*, November/December 2002, pp.32–35.

Miller, Christa. "The Art of the Ruse." *Law Enforcement Technology*, November 2001, pp.26–32.

Mills-Senn, Pamela. "Tracking Officer Behavior." *Law Enforcement Technology*, April 2004, pp.86–93.

Moffett, Tommy and Peck, Donald L. "When Casino Gambling Comes to Your Hometown: The Biloxi Experience." *FBI Law Enforcement Bulletin*, January 2001, pp.12–18.

National Commission on the Future of DNA Evidence. *The Future of Forensic DNA Testing: Predictions of the Research and Development Working Group*. Washington, DC: National Institute of Justice, November 2000. http://www.ojp.usdoj.gov/nij/dna (NCJ 183697)

Petrone, Frank. "Firearms, Ammunition and Related Terminology." *The Law Enforcement Trainer*, June 2004, pp.37–40.

Ramirez, Eugene P. "SWAT and the Law." *Police,* May 2003, pp.58–60.

Reece, Hunter. "The Keys to Quality Interview Techniques." *Law and Order,* November 2003, pp.66–69.

Scott, Michael S. *Street Prostitution.* Washington, DC: Office of Community Oriented Policing Services Problem-Oriented Guides for Police Series No. 2, August 6, 2001.

Scoville, Dean. "How to . . . Start a SWAT Team." *Police,* March 2003, pp.28–33.

Sharpe, R. E. "Practicing Realism, Not Racism." *Law Enforcement News,* June 15, 2002, p.9.

Singh, David. "Community-Oriented Investigation at the North Miami Beach Police Department." *Practitioner Perspectives.* Washington, DC: Bureau of Justice Assistance, April 2001. (NCJ 185367)

Smith, Brad. "K9 Interacting with SWAT." *Tactical Response,* Spring 2003, pp.38–42.

Smith, Brad. "Is the Bite Too Long?" *Tactical Response,* Spring 2004, pp.32–35.

Stitt, Grant B.; Nichols, Mark; and Giacopassi, David. "Does the Presence of Casinos Increase Crime? An Examination of Casino and Control Communities." *Crime & Delinquency,* April 2003, pp.253–284.

Strandberg, Keith W. "The Facts Don't Lie." *Law Enforcement Technology,* June 2001, pp.20–24.

Surratt, Hilary L.; Inciardi, James A.; Kurtz, Steven P.; and Kiley, Marion C. "Sex Work and Drug Use in a Subculture of Violence." *Crime & Delinquency,* January 2004, pp.43–59.

Technical Working Group on Crime Scene Investigation. *Crime Scene Investigation: A Guide for Law Enforcement.* Washington, DC: National Institute of Justice, January 2000. http://www.ojp.usdoj.gov/nij

Thurnauer, Beau. "Internal Affairs: Practice and Policy Review for Smaller Departments." *The Police Chief,* October 2002, pp.73–82.

Turman, Kathryn M. *Understanding DNA Evidence: A Guide for Victim Service Providers.* Washington, DC: Office for Victims of Crime, April 2001. (NCJ 185690)

Using DNA to Solve Cold Cases. Washington, DC: NIJ Special Report, July 2002. (NCJ 194197)

Walker, Jayme S. "Using Drug Detection Dogs: An Update." *FBI Law Enforcement Bulletin,* April 2001, pp.25–32.

Weinblatt, Richard B. "Reserves Aid Rural Counties." *Law and Order,* January 2001, pp.30–32.

Weissberg, Michael. "Recent Directions in Crime Scene Investigations." *The Law Enforcement Trainer,* March/April 2001, pp.44–48.

Wexler, Sanford. "Making the Case for Crime Scene Certification." *Law Enforcement Technology,* March 2003, pp.42–46.

Williams, Jimmy J. and Westall, David. "Study Finds No Use of Force Difference between SWAT and Non-SWAT Officers." *Journal of Criminal Justice,* vol. 31, no. 5, 2003, p.469.

Wilson, Jeremy M. "Riverboat Gambling and Crime in Indiana: An Empirical Investigation." *Crime & Delinquency,* October 2001, pp.610–640.

CASES CITED

Garrity v. New Jersey, 385 U.S. 493 (1967)
People v. Simpson, Super. Ct. No. BA097211 (1995)
United States v. Ash, Jr., 413 U.S. 300 (1973)
United States v. Place, 462. U.S. 696 (1983)

CHALLENGES TO THE PROFESSION

Section II presented how contemporary law enforcement fulfills its mission through administrative and field services. The evolving importance of community policing and its influence on patrol and the other specialized roles of police were explored. This section examines challenges facing law enforcement. A major challenge in everything officers do is policing within the law. Officers must be knowledgeable of and perform within the limits set by our Constitution and by their respective state constitutions and local ordinances (Chapter 8).

Two persistent, often interlinked challenges are combating gangs and illegal drugs in our country. Billions of dollars and personnel hours are spent in this effort (Chapter 9). A challenge that has always been present but, until September 11, 2001, had not been a priority, is terrorism. The threat of terrorism is now a top priority at the local, county, state and national level (Chapter 10). In addition to these very specific challenges, issues related to officer conduct must be addressed. Such issues include discrimination, use of force, pursuits, civil liability, corruption, ethics and integrity (Chapter 11). The last major series of challenges are found within law enforcement agencies throughout the country: recruiting, selecting and retaining the best qualified officers; use of civilian review boards; sexual harassment; unionization; privatization; moonlighting; accreditation; and professionalization of law enforcement.

CHAPTER 8

Policing within the Law

The patrol officer is the first interpreter of the law and in effect performs a quasi-judicial function. He makes the first attempt to match the reality of human conflict with the law; he determines whether to take no action, to advise, to warn, or to arrest; he determines whether he must apply physical force, perhaps sufficient to cause death. It is he who must discern the fine distinction between a civil and a criminal conflict, between merely unorthodox behavior and a crime, between a legitimate dissent and disturbance of the peace, between the truth and a lie. As the interpreter of the law, he recognizes that a decision to arrest is only the first step in the determination of guilt or innocence. He is guided by, and guardian of, the Constitution.

—Task Force on the Police

DO YOU KNOW . . .

- The major provisions of the Fourth Amendment?
- On what sources probable cause can be based?
- What basic principles underlie stop and frisk and what differences distinguish them?
- What significance the *Terry* case has in relation to the Fourth Amendment?
- When roadblocks and checkpoints are constitutional?
- What principal justifications are set forth by the courts for reasonable searches? What limitations are placed on them?
- What a search warrant is and what it must contain? What may be seized?
- When warrantless searches are justified and the conditions placed on each?
- How a warrantless search can be challenged?
- What authorities and restrictions are provided by the following cases: *Chimel? Carroll? Chambers? Coolidge? Maryland v. Wilson?*
- What special conditions apply to searches of vehicles?
- Whether open fields, abandoned property or trash can be searched without a warrant?
- Whether using thermal imaging to view inside a house without a warrant is constitutional?
- When general searches are constitutional?
- What the authorities for lawful arrest are?
- When the *Miranda* warning must be given?
- What the public safety exception provides?

CAN YOU DEFINE?

administrative
  warrant
affidavit
arrest
consent
contraband
curtilage
custody
de facto arrest
dual motive stop
emergency situations
entrapment
exigent circumstances
extenuating
  circumstances

field detention
field inquiry
forced entry
frisk
immediate control
inevitable discovery
  doctrine
inspection warrant
instruments of a
  crime
magistrate
mobility
nightcap warrants
nighttime search
  warrants

no-knock search
  warrant
open fields doctrine
ordinary care
pat down
plain feel/touch
  doctrine
plain view
pretext stop
probable cause
protective sweep
public offenses
public safety
  exception

reasonable
  search
search warrant
seizure
stop
stop and frisk
threshold inquiry
totality of the
  circumstances
waiver
wingspan

Introduction

> Decency, security and liberty alike demand that governmental officials shall be subjected to the same rules of conduct that are commands to the citizen. In a government of laws, existence of the government will be imperiled if it fails to observe the law scrupulously. Our government is the potent, the omnipresent teacher. For good or ill, it teaches the whole people by its example. Crime is contagious. If the government becomes a lawbreaker, it breeds contempt for the law; it invites every man to become a law unto himself; it invites anarchy. To declare that in the administration of the criminal law the end justifies the means—to declare that the government may commit crimes in order to secure the conviction of a private criminal—would bring terrible retribution. Against this pernicious doctrine this court should resolutely set its face.

This synopsis was delivered by Supreme Court Justice Louis D. Brandeis in *Olmstead v. United States* (1928) and says, in effect, that government agents, including police officers, are subjected to certain restrictions in enforcing the laws. Those who are entrusted with the responsibility of protecting life and property must understand the principles of the federal and state constitutions and the duties that flow from their application, as well as the many laws and statutes that have been enacted. In short, police officers must know the law without the benefit of having gone to law school. Any violations of the law can result in evidence being disallowed under the Exclusionary Rule, as discussed in Chapter 2.

This chapter begins with a discussion of the Fourth Amendment, which governs searches and seizures. This is followed by explanations of sources of probable cause and the principle of stop and frisk. Next lawful searches are described, including when roadblocks and checkpoints are constitutional, the principal justifications for searching, gaining entrance, nighttime and no-knock search warrants, what may be seized, administrative warrants and warrantless searches. Also discussed under lawful searches are warrantless searches of vehicles, plain view searches, plain feel/touch searches and searching open fields, abandoned property and trash. The discussion of lawful searches concludes with a look at aerial searches, use of thermal imaging and limitations on searches.

Next lawful arrests are discussed, covering the elements of a criminal arrest, arrest warrants and arresting without a warrant, and concluding with a segment on protecting suspects' rights (*Miranda*), including waiver of rights, the public safety exception, the rights of foreign nationals, involuntary confessions and the issue of entrapment. The chapter concludes with a summary of the key cases presented.

The Fourth Amendment

> The right of the people to be secure in their persons, houses, papers, and effects, against unreasonable searches and seizures, shall not be violated, and no warrants shall issue, but upon probable cause, supported by oath or affirmation, and particularly describing the place to be searched, and the persons or things to be seized.

Arbitrary searches and/or seizures have no place in a democratic society. In fact colonial grievances against unreasonable searches and seizures, in part, led to the revolt against English authority. The Fourth Amendment to the Constitution guarantees the right of citizens to be secure from such arbitrary searches and seizures.

 The constitutional standards for searches and seizures, including arrests, are contained in the Fourth Amendment, which requires that searches and seizures be reasonable and based on probable cause.

The terms *reasonable* and *probable cause* provide a very fine, but significant, weight to balance the scales of justice, which measure the conduct of all people. Without what is referred to as probable cause, the laws that govern us might easily become unbalanced, that is, too permissive or too restrictive.

The second part of the Fourth Amendment, called the "warrant clause," states: "No warrants shall issue but upon probable cause." In other words all warrants (search and arrest warrants) must be based on probable cause.

Reasonable

The rules for determining what constitutes a reasonable search or reasonable seizure result from interpretation of the first part of the Fourth Amendment, called the "reasonable search and seizure clause," which states, in part: "The right of the people to be secure in their persons, houses, papers, and effects, against unreasonable searches and seizures shall not be violated." **Reasonable** means sensible, justifiable, logical, based on reason. A key determinant in whether an officer's actions are lawful is whether the officer has reasonable suspicion that criminal activity is occurring. In a fairly recent pivotal case a U.S. Border Patrol agent stopped a vehicle near Douglas, Arizona, suspecting the operator was smuggling aliens or drugs because it was traveling a usually deserted road and set off a sensor. A search of the vehicle turned up over 100 pounds of marijuana for which Arvizu, the driver, was convicted. However the U.S. Court of Appeals reversed the district court decision, holding that each factor of reasonable suspicion should be reviewed independently. In *United States v. Arvizu* (2002), the U.S. Supreme Court reversed this decision, relying on past Court decisions that reasonable suspicion is based on the **totality of the circumstances.** The facts on which the suspicion is based must be reviewed as a whole. They are not to be examined individually.

Probable Cause

The concept of probable cause is one of the oldest and most important in criminal law, having existed for more than 2,000 years and occurring in both Roman law and the common law of England. **Probable cause** requires more than mere suspicion; it requires facts or proof that would lead a person of reasonable caution to believe a crime has been committed or that premises contain evidence of a crime.

In *Draper v. United States* (1959), the U.S. Supreme Court stated: "Probable cause exists where the facts and circumstances within their (the arresting officers') knowledge and of which they had reasonable trustworthy information are sufficient in themselves to warrant a man of reasonable caution in the belief that an offense has been or is being committed." *Smith v. United States* (1949) defines probable cause as: "The sum total of layers of information and the synthesis of what the police have heard, what they know, and what they observe as trained officers. We [the courts] weigh not individual layers but the laminated total." According to Hendrie (2002, p. 23): "No exposition of probable cause would be complete without a discussion of *Illinois v. Gates* (1983)." In this case the Court stated that the test for probable cause should be a totality of the circumstances.

This view was reflected in *United States v. Arvizu,* discussed previously. As Whalen (2002, p. 11) notes: "The U.S. Supreme Court's recent ruling in *United States v. Arvizu* continues a series of decisions that recognize the inexact science of determining probable cause and reasonable suspicion and the importance of teaching officers to document all of the facts leading to their decision to make a stop or conduct a search." Wood (2002, p. 22) suggests: "Some constitutional scholars believe that the opinion may also reflect a new attitude by the Court, in the wake of the terrorist attacks that occurred on September 11, 2001, in favor of less stringent standards for investigatory stops."

Probable cause may be based on:
- Observation by officers.
- Expertise of officers.
- Circumstantial factors.
- Information communicated to officers.

Often more than one source is involved.

Observational Probable Cause Observational probable cause is what officers see, hear or smell, that is, evidence presented directly to the senses. This is similar to eyewitness testimony and is the strongest form of probable cause. The courts have generally recognized certain types of events as being significant in determining probable cause.

Suspicious activities contribute to probable cause. For example a car being driven slowly can be suspicious when (1) the car has circled a block several times, (2) the people in the car are carefully observing a building, (3) the building is closed and (4) the building is located in a high-crime area. All four factors contribute to probable cause. *Familiar criminal patterns* also contribute to probable cause. A person's conduct can indicate a familiar pattern associated with the sale of stolen property or narcotics or of someone casing a building. Any one fact by itself may not be sufficient, but collectively they provide justification— probable cause.

Expertise and Circumstantial Probable Cause   Expertise and circumstantial probable cause are often tied to observational probable cause. Police officers' knowledge of criminal traits and their ability to "put the pieces together" may also contribute to probable cause. For example two police officers questioned two men seen driving from an alley at 2:00 A.M. The officers noted the license number and occupants' names and questioned the driver and passenger. The two men were allowed to continue, but a short time later, when the officers learned there had been a burglary in a nearby town, they forwarded the description of the car and its occupants to the local police, who apprehended the suspects. A search of the vehicle revealed burglary tools, as well as the property taken in two burglaries.

In the original confrontation with the suspects, the two officers were not satisfied with the suspects' explanation of why they were in the alley at such an early hour, and even though they did not have sufficient evidence to establish probable cause for an arrest, their investigation of the suspicious circumstances eventually led to the suspects' arrests and convictions.

Informational Probable Cause   Informational probable cause covers a wide range of sources. In the case previously described, the information about the two suspects forwarded by the police to the nearby town constituted informational probable cause. The major categories of informational probable cause are official sources, victims of crimes, informants and witnesses.

Official sources include police bulletins, police broadcasts and roll-call information. This information can be relied on because it is received through official police channels. As in any other case, the original source must be reliable. For instance if police officers make an arrest based on information obtained from other police officers, the original officers may be required to testify about *their* information source. It is that source that must establish probable cause. The source may be a victim of a crime, an informant or a witness. Complete and otherwise credible information from an eyewitness, based on personal knowledge, is generally sufficient to establish probable cause.

Stop and Frisk

One basic responsibility of police officers, and one heavily reliant on reasonableness and probable cause, is investigating suspicious behavior. Officers may simply talk to someone acting suspiciously and decide no crime seems to be in progress or about to be committed, or they may confirm their suspicions and investigate further. The simple act of stopping someone may lead to a **stop and frisk**. The stop is also called a **field inquiry** or **threshold inquiry**.

The basic legal considerations in a stop and frisk situation were set forth in the landmark U.S. Supreme Court decision *Terry v. Ohio* (1968). Detective McFadden, a veteran police officer with 39 years of experience, saw two men standing near a jewelry store. They seemed to be just talking to each other, but to McFadden, "they just didn't look right." Based on his experience, he suspected they were casing the store and were possibly armed. He watched for a while as the men went through the routine of walking around, looking into the store window, walking to the corner and returning to the original spot to talk with each other. A third man joined them, went inside the store for a moment and came back out. The routine continued.

Deciding to act, McFadden approached the three men and identified himself as a police officer. He asked for their names and then grabbed one of the men, later identified as John Terry. McFadden made a quick pat down of Terry's outer clothing and felt what he thought might be a gun in Terry's coat pocket. It turned out to be a .38 caliber revolver; another gun was removed from the coat of a man named Chilton. Terry and Chilton were formally charged with carrying concealed weapons.

The defense lawyers argued the guns could not be used as evidence, claiming they were illegally seized. The trial judge, however, found both men guilty. Terry and Chilton appealed their conviction to the U.S. Supreme Court, but before the Court's decision was handed down in 1968, Chilton had died. Therefore its review applied only to Terry.

The issue: Is it always unreasonable for a police officer to seize a person and conduct a limited search for weapons unless there is probable cause for arrest? Recognizing McFadden as a man of experience, training and knowledge, certainly "a man of reasonable caution," the Supreme Court answered "no," upholding the trial court verdict. The Court noted that McFadden, as a man of "**ordinary care and prudence**" (boldface added), had waited until he had strengthened his suspicions, making his move just prior to what he believed would be an armed robbery. He had to make a quick decision when he saw the three gathered at the store, and his actions were correct.

The Supreme Court (*Terry v. Ohio*) said there is a **seizure** whenever a police officer restrains an individual's freedom to walk away, and there is a search when an officer explores an individual's clothing even though it is called a "**pat down**" or "**frisk.**"

 A **stop** is a seizure if physical force or a show of authority is used. A frisk is a search.

In June 2004, the Supreme Court ruled in *Hiibel v. Sixth Judicial District Court of Nevada, Humboldt County* that police may require a person to identify themselves unless their name would be incriminating. In this case police stopped Hiibel during an investigative stop involving a reported assault. Nevada's "stop and identify" statute requires a person detained by an officer under suspicious circumstances to identify himself. Hiibel argued that his Fourth Amendment right against unreasonable search and seizure and his Fifth Amendment right against compelled self-incrimination were violated by the Nevada law. Hiibel refused 11 times to identify himself, so he was arrested, charged with the misdemeanor of refusing to identify himself. The Nevada Supreme Court upheld his conviction, as did the U.S. Supreme Court (Greenhouse, 2004, p. A8).

Although stopping and frisking fall short of an arrest, they are definitely forms of search and seizure. Police officers stop citizens daily, but most encounters cannot be considered "seizure of the person" because the officers do not restrain the individual's liberty. Defining the term *frisk*, however, leaves no other alternative than to consider it a search. As the Supreme Court (*Terry*) cautioned:

"It is simply fantastic to urge that such a procedure, performed in public by a police officer, while the citizen stands helpless, perhaps facing a wall with his hands raised, is a 'petty indignity'. . . . It is a serious intrusion upon the sanctity of the person, which may inflict great indignity and arouse strong resentment, and it is not to be undertaken lightly." The Court gave its own definition of stop and frisk by calling it a "protective search for weapons."

Stop and frisk is a protective search for weapons in which the intrusion must be limited to a scope reasonably designed to discover guns, knives, clubs and other hidden instruments that may be used to assault a police officer or others. *Terry* established that the authority to stop and frisk is independent of the power to arrest. A stop is *not* an arrest, but it is a seizure within the meaning of the Fourth Amendment and, therefore, requires reasonableness.

Several key court cases have clarified when police can and cannot execute a lawful stop and frisk. The decision in *Florida v. J. L.* (2000) established that reasonable suspicion for an investigative stop does not arise from a mere anonymous tip. In this case, police acted solely on a tip describing a man carrying a gun and, with no other reason to suspect the individual of criminal involvement, frisked the man. Although the frisk did yield a firearm and the man was charged with carrying a concealed weapon, in reviewing the case, the Supreme Court upheld lower court rulings that granted the trial court action to suppress the gun as evidence as a result of an unlawful search, noting that reliance solely on an anonymous tip would create a vulnerability to pranks, grudges and other unreliable information.

When police receive an anonymous tip, they must take steps to verify its reliability before taking action. This is easier if the tipster provides predictive information about what the suspect is about to do.

Stop and frisk is a protective search for weapons in which the intrusion must be limited to a scope reasonably designed to discover guns, knives, clubs and other hidden instruments that may be used to assault a police officer or others. A stop is not an arrest, but it is a seizure and therefore requires reasonableness.

© AP/World Wide Photos

Another case that focused on the justification for a stop and frisk is *Illinois v. Wardlow* (2000), in which the Supreme Court ruled that a person's sudden flight upon seeing a police officer can be used to establish reasonable suspicion for a stop. In this case, Wardlow was seen holding an opaque bag in a Chicago neighborhood known for drug activity. When a group of police cars drove past him, he fled swiftly. The officers, acting on reasonable suspicion, pursued, stopped and frisked Wardlow, finding a loaded gun.

The trial court convicted Wardlow of possession of a firearm, but the appellate court overturned the conviction, stating the discovery of the gun was the result of an unjustified stop and frisk and, thus, that evidence should have been suppressed. The Supreme Court reversed, with Chief Justice Rehnquist writing: "Headlong flight—wherever it occurs—is the consummate act of evasion; it is not necessarily indicative of wrongdoing, but it is certainly suggestive of such." The Court noted the officers had based their reasonable suspicion on three facts, not just one—the suspect's flight, the location of the incident as a known drug area and the opaque bag in the suspect's hand. Basing reasonable suspicion on only one fact, such as the flight alone, is less likely to hold up if challenged in court.

Plain View and Plain Feel/Touch

Plain view refers to evidence that is not concealed and is seen by an officer engaged in a lawful activity. Vision can be augmented with binoculars and flashlights, but it is not proper to move or pick up items without probable cause to believe the items are contraband.

Closely related to the plain view doctrine is the **plain feel/touch doctrine** used in several states. A pivotal case in the plain feel/touch doctrine is *Minnesota v. Dickerson* (1993). Two officers saw Dickerson leave a known crack house and, upon seeing their marked squad car, abruptly turn and walk in the opposite direction. This aroused the officers' suspicions, so they followed Dickerson into the alley and ordered him to stop and be patted down. They found no weapons, but they did find a suspicious small lump in Dickerson's jacket. Dickerson was arrested and charged with drug possession. The officer testified in court that during the pat down, he felt a small lump in Dickerson's front pocket and, after manipulating it with his fingers, determined it felt like a lump of crack cocaine but never thought it was a weapon. The trial court found the search to be legal under the Fourth Amendment, stating:

> To this Court, there is no distinction as to which sensory perception the officer uses to conclude the material is contraband. An experienced officer may rely upon his sense of smell in DUI stops or in recognizing the smell of burning marijuana in an automobile. . . . The sense of touch, grounded in experience and training, is as reliable as perceptions drawn from the other senses. "Plain feel," therefore, is no different than "plain view."

The Minnesota Supreme Court, however, overturned the conviction stating that the sense of touch is less immediate and less reliable than the sense of sight and is far more intrusive into the personal privacy that is at the core of the Fourth Amendment. A frisk that goes beyond that allowed under *Terry* is not valid. In this case, the search went beyond the pat down search allowed in *Terry* because the officer manipulated the packet's content before knowing it was cocaine. The U.S. Supreme Court granted review of *Dickerson* and upheld the ruling of the Minnesota Supreme Court that the cocaine seizure was invalid:

> This goes beyond *Terry*, which authorizes a patdown for only one purpose: officer safety. That was absent here because the officer admitted that what he felt was not a weapon. The Court's decision might have been different, however, had the officer testified that he knew it was not a weapon when he felt the lump, but that he had probable cause to believe—from his experience as a police officer and the circumstances of this case—that the lump was cocaine. If those were the circumstances, the seizure may have been valid, not under stop and frisk, but under probable cause.

This ruling is significant because it supports limited plain touch or plain feel probes during frisks and, if contraband is plainly felt by the officer in good faith, allows any discovered evidence to be admissible in court.

The Court has applied the *Dickerson* logic to extend to luggage searches, ruling that police can visually inspect a bus passenger's luggage but cannot squeeze or otherwise manipulate baggage to determine whether it contains contraband (*Bond v. United States,* 2000). Chief Justice Rehnquist stated: "A bus passenger fully expects that his bag may be handled. He does not expect that other bus passengers or bus employees will feel the bag in an exploratory manner." It is unlikely, particularly in the wake of the September 11, 2001, terrorist attacks, that the ruling will extend to air travel, where the public has a lesser degree of expectation of privacy because of security issues.

In addition to this ruling, in *United States v. Drayton* (2002), as Makholm (2002, p. 77) explains: "The Supreme Court dealt with the question of whether or not law enforcement officers MUST advise bus passengers of their right not to cooperate during an otherwise legitimately structured, consensual, bus interdiction. The Court answered: 'NO.' The passengers do not have to be advised of their legal right to not cooperate."

Road Blocks and Checkpoints

Border checkpoints, because they serve a broad social purpose, have been declared constitutional. Rutledge (2004b, p. 89) notes: "For many years, the court has upheld the constitutionality of briefly stopping vehicles at fixed checkpoints at or near international borders to check immigration status." In *U.S. v. Martinez-Fuerte* (1976) the Court affirmed that "a vehicle may be stopped at a fixed checkpoint for brief questioning of its occupants even though there is no reason to believe the particular vehicle contains aliens."

A similar ruling was handed down in 2004 in *United States v. Flores-Montano,* which involved a search of a vehicle fuel tank at the Mexican border ("Court Allows Routine Search of Vehicle Fuel Tank at Border," 2004, p. 6). Speaking for the Court, Chief Justice Rehnquist said:

> Complex balancing tests to determine what is a "routine" search of a vehicle . . . have no place in border searches of vehicles. The government's interest in preventing the entry of unwanted persons and effects is at its zenith at the

international border. Time and again, we have stated that searches made at the border, pursuant to the longstanding rights of the sovereign to protect itself by stopping and examining persons and property crossing into this country, are reasonable simply by virtue of the fact that they occur at the border.

Sobriety checkpoints, serving the broad social benefit of protecting motorists from drunk drivers, are another form of stop that have been declared constitutional, provided they are conducted fairly and do not pose a safety hazard (*Michigan Department of State Police v. Sitz,* 1990).

Informational roadblocks have also been declared constitutional. As Devanney and Devanney (2004, p. 20) note: "The Court, in the case of *Illinois vs. Lidster* [2004], allowed roadblocks to be used in situations when police are merely seeking witnesses who may have information about earlier and unrelated crimes." As Makholm (2004b, p. 60) explains: "As so often happens during a 'checkpoint,' along comes an under-the-influence driver (Robert S. Lidster) who gets snagged in the checkpoint, almost strikes an officer and goes to jail for DUI." Lidster challenged the constitutionality of the checkpoint, and the case went all the way to the Supreme Court, which upheld its constitutionality.

 The Supreme Court has upheld roadblocks at national borders, sobriety checkpoints and informational checkpoints.

Recall from Chapter 6, however, that *drug checkpoints* have been found to violate the Fourth Amendment. In *City of Indianapolis v. Edmond* (2000), the Supreme Court deemed drug interdiction roadblocks an unconstitutional means to a valid law enforcement end, with Justice O'Connor writing for the majority: "We cannot sanction stops justified only by the generalized and ever-present possibility that interrogation and inspection may reveal that any given motorist has committed some crime." Interpreting *Edmond* as an exception to the Fourth Amendment would set a precedent allowing authorities to construct roadblocks for almost any conceivable law enforcement purposes and permitting police to make such "intrusions . . . a routine part of American life." This ruling makes *general crime control checkpoints* unconstitutional. In addition, *driver's license checkpoints* are not permitted. According to Risher (2004, p. 10): "The Fourth Amendment reasonableness standard prohibits officers from randomly stopping vehicles to check driver's licenses and registration."

 The Supreme Court has held that drug checkpoints, general crime control checkpoints and driver's license checkpoints are not constitutional.

Field Detention

The courts have upheld police officers' right to detain suspects with less than probable cause. Such **field detention** occurred in the case of *Michigan v. Summers* (1981), in which police officers arrived at Summers's home to execute a search warrant. They encountered Summers coming down the steps and asked him to let them in and wait while they conducted their search. They found narcotics in the basement and then searched Summers, finding heroin in his pocket. The court ruled that it was legal to require the suspect to reenter his house and remain there until evidence establishing probable cause was found.

More recently, in *Illinois v. McArthur* (2001), the Supreme Court ruled that police did not violate the Fourth Amendment when they detained a man outside his trailer home for several hours while officers sought a warrant to search the residence for drugs ("Brief Seizure of Premises . . .," 2001, p. 13). McArthur's estranged wife, in the process of moving her belongings out of their home, informed police that her husband had "dope" hidden under a couch inside the home ("Supreme Court Allows . . .," 2001, p. 130). When police knocked on the door, told McArthur what his wife had said, and asked for consent to search the home, McArthur refused. While one officer left to get a search warrant, McArthur stepped out of the house onto the porch. Suspecting McArthur would destroy the evidence if allowed back inside the trailer, police told McArthur he could not reenter the residence unless accompanied by an officer until the search warrant was obtained. Two hours later, the search warrant was acquired and police searched the trailer, finding less than 2.5 grams of marijuana ("Court Lets Police . . .," 2001, p. 3).

The trial court suppressed the evidence as a result of an unlawful police seizure, but the U.S. Supreme Court, in an 8-to-1 ruling, reversed:

> The Court determined that this search and seizure was "reasonable" in light of four conditions: (1) the police had "probable cause" to believe contraband was in the home; (2) the police had good reason to believe McArthur would destroy the contraband before they could return with a warrant; (3) the police made "reasonable efforts to reconcile their law enforcement needs with the demands of personal privacy," i.e., they did not search without a warrant, did not immediately arrest him, and did allow him some access to his home in the interim period; and (4) "the police imposed the restraint for a limited period of time, namely, two hours" (Makholm, 2001, p. 13).

Lawful Searches

A **search,** in the context of the Fourth Amendment, involves governmental invasion of privacy. Searches are intended to obtain incriminating evidence. The questions most often asked by prosecutors and courts before admitting evidence are: Was the search justified and therefore legal? Was the arrest, if there was one, legal?

 The principal justifications established by the courts for the right to search are when:
- A search warrant has been issued.
- No warrant has been issued but:
  - Consent to search was given.
  - Exigent circumstances exist.
  - There is no expectation of privacy and, thus, no requirement for a search warrant.

These circumstances are the preconditions for a reasonable, legal search.

Searches Conducted with a Warrant

A **search warrant** is an order issued by a judge, a **magistrate,** with jurisdiction in the area where the search is to be made. The Fourth Amendment states that warrants must particularly describe "the place to be searched and the persons or things to be seized." To get a search warrant, police officers must first prepare an **affidavit,** a written statement about a set of facts establishing probable cause to search. The officer then presents the affidavit to a magistrate and swears under oath that the statement is truthful. If the magistrate determines, based on the facts presented, that probable cause to search exists, a search warrant is issued. The warrant must contain the reasons for requesting the search warrant, the names of the persons presenting affidavits, what specifically is being sought and the signature of the judge issuing it.

 Technically all searches are to be made under the authority of a search warrant issued by a magistrate. A search warrant is a judicial order, based on probable cause, directing a police officer to search for specific property, seize it and return it to the court. The search must be limited to the specific area and specific items delineated in the warrant.

What May Be Seized   A search warrant must clearly specify or describe the things to be seized. The prosecution must accept the burden of proof when items not specified in the warrant are seized. Such items can be seized if a reasonable relationship exists between the search and the seizure of materials not described—that is, they are similar in nature to the items described, they are related to the particular crime described or they are contraband. **Contraband** is anything illegal to own or have in possession, such as heroin or a machine gun. It is not necessary that the contraband be connected to the particular crime described in the search warrant.

Gaining Entrance   Police officers are usually required to announce their authority and purpose before entering a home. In *Wilson v. Arkansas* (1995), a unanimous Supreme Court held that, absent exigent circumstances, officers are required to "knock and announce" to meet the reasonableness requirements of the Fourth Amendment. Devanney and Devanney (2003, p. 72) give three reasons for this requirement: (1) to protect the citizen's right to privacy, (2) to reduce the risk of possible violence to both police and household occupants and (3) to prevent unnecessary destruction of private property.

The Court also stressed, however, that the "Fourth Amendment's flexible requirement of reasonableness should not be read to mandate a rigid rule of announcement that ignores countervailing law enforcement interests." Such interests include threats of physical harm to police or others, pursuit of recently escaped arrestees and when evidence is likely to be destroyed if police announced their presence.

Sometimes the suspect will not allow entrance, or there may be no one home. In such cases police officers may forcibly enter the house by breaking an inner or outer door or window. If the dwelling is an apartment, they could get a passkey from a caretaker, but this would still be considered a **forced entry.** Opening a closed but unlocked door or window is also considered a forced entry.

According to Hopper (2004, p. 22): "The U.S. Supreme Court handed down a unanimous decision in the landmark knock-and-announce case, *United States v. Banks* (2003). The Court has determined that 15–20 seconds is a sufficient amount of time for law enforcement officers to wait before forcibly entering a dwelling to execute a search warrant." Rutledge (2004a, p. 75) suggests that when possible an audio or video recording of the knock-notice announcement provides evidence of compliance with the knock-notice as well as the amount of time elapsed before forcing entry. Makholm (2004a, p. 64) called this ruling "a present to law enforcement officers throughout the United States. . . . This ruling provides much needed guidance to law enforcement officers/entry teams, heretofore wondering just how long they need to wait before forcing entry into a residence."

Nighttime and No-Knock Search Warrants   A search warrant is normally issued to be served during daylight hours and requires the officers to knock and announce themselves. As just discussed, however, circumstances sometimes exist when these procedures could render the police less effective. In such instances special warrants may be issued. Two types of search warrants, nighttime and no-knock, must be authorized by a judge as special provisions of a search warrant.

Nighttime search warrants (also called **nightcap warrants**) must state the reasons, based on facts, for fearing that unless the search is conducted at night the objects of the search might be lost, destroyed or removed. Justifications for a nighttime search include the imminent consumption or movement of drugs, information that the drug trafficking occurs only at night, darkness is essential to officer safety or when a nighttime search would be less intrusive than a daytime search, for example, in a business open to the public during the day.

Unannounced entries to execute search warrants must also receive prior judicial authorization. The **no-knock search warrant** is reserved for situations where the judge recognizes that normal citizen cooperation is unlikely and that an announced entry may result in loss, destruction or removal of the objects of the search. For example surprise entries are often used in searches for narcotics and gambling equipment. In either instance the court usually acknowledges that evidence can easily be destroyed during the time required to give notice, demand admittance and accept denial of entry.

Administrative Warrants   An **administrative** or **inspection warrant** is issued by a court to regulate building, fire, plumbing, electrical, health, safety, labor or zoning codes if voluntary compliance cannot be obtained. It does not justify a police entry to make an arrest.

Public safety personnel may enter structures that are on fire to extinguish the blaze. After the fire has been extinguished, officials may remain for a reasonable length of time to investigate the cause of the blaze (*Michigan v. Tyler*, 1978). After this time, if the police want to return to the scene to conduct an investigation into the cause of the fire, they may need an administrative warrant. Such warrants require an affidavit stating the location and legal description of the property; the purpose, area and time of the search; and the use of the building. Searches are limited to items specified in the warrant. Evidence found may be seized, but once officers leave after finding evidence, they must have a criminal warrant to return for a further search.

Searches Conducted without a Warrant

The courts have recognized certain situations and conditions in which officers may conduct a search without first obtaining a warrant.

 Warrantless searches are justified when consent to search is given, when exigent circumstances exist or when no right to privacy exists.

Warrantless Searches with Consent   As Holcomb (2004, p. 22) asserts: "The U.S. Supreme Court has stated that a search conducted pursuant to lawfully given consent is an exception to the warrant and probable cause requirements of the Fourth Amendment." In a search where **consent** is given, the consent must be free and voluntary. It cannot be given in response to a claim of lawful authority by the officer to conduct the search at the moment.

 Consent must be free and voluntary, and the search must be limited to the area for which the consent is given.

As noted by the Maine Supreme Court in *State v. Barlow, Jr.* (1974): "It is a well established rule in the federal courts that a consent search is unreasonable under the Fourth Amendment if the consent was induced by deceit, trickery or misrepresentation of the officials making the search." A recognized exception to this general rule is when undercover operations are involved. According to Hendrie (2003, p. 25): "An officer who is working in an undercover capacity can use deception to obtain valid consent to enter premises. Once an undercover officer obtains the initial consent to enter, that consent can be transferred to officers who later enter the premises to arrest the suspects."

When a court is asked to determine if consent to search was "free and voluntary," it considers such things as the subject's age, background, mental condition and education. Officers must not show weapons when making the request, as the courts have considered such displays coercive. The number of officers involved should not be a factor if no aggressiveness is shown.

The time of day might also be a consideration. Officers should generally avoid seeking voluntary consent to search at night. In *Monroe v. Pape* (1961), Justice Frankfurter said: "Modern totalitarianisms have been a stark reminder, but did not newly teach, that the kicked-in door is the symbol of a rule of fear and violence fatal to institutions founded on respect for the integrity of man. . . . Searches of the dwelling house were the special object of this universal condemnation of official intrusion. Nighttime search was the evil in its most obnoxious form."

Perhaps most important is the way the request to search is made. It must be a request, not a command. Furthermore, the consent may be withdrawn at any time, requiring officers to end the search immediately.

Warrantless Searches under Exigent Circumstances   The implicit right to privacy contained within the Fourth Amendment provides the rationale to guide law enforcement in obtaining search warrants whenever possible. When police officers secure a search warrant, they receive an advance court decision that probable cause exists, therefore justifying an intrusion on a subject's privacy. However, there are situations when **exigent circumstances—emergency situations** or **extenuating circumstances**—exist to justify a degree of police infringement on personal privacy to achieve a legitimate and overriding law enforcement objective, such as securing public safety or the safety of the officer.

As Stephen (2002, p. 66) cautions: "The 'exigent circumstances' exception only applies if there is a compelling need for immediate action and delay will cause substantial risk." In situations where police officers believe they have established probable cause but have no time to secure a warrant, they can act without a warrant, but a defense lawyer can challenge the search's legality. Although a number of challenges can be raised, two occur most frequently.

When police officers conduct a warrantless search, they may be challenged on the basis that:

- Probable cause was not established—in other words, given the facts, a magistrate would not have issued a warrant.
- The officers did have time to secure a warrant and had no justification to act without one.

Courts have recognized that there are times when exigent circumstances justify reasonable, yet warrantless, searches and seizures based on police officers' decisions. Such circumstances include (1) searches incidental to a lawful arrest, (2) searches of automobiles and other conveyances and (3) plain view and plain feel/touch situations.

Warrentless Searches Incidental to a Lawful Arrest   In a search incidental to a lawful arrest, the search must be made simultaneously with the arrest and must be confined to the immediate vicinity of the arrest (*Chimel v. California*, 1969). In *Chimel*, officers went to the suspect's home with a warrant to arrest Ted Chimel on a charge of burglarizing a coin shop. After the officers were let in, they handed Chimel the arrest warrant and told him they wanted to "look around." Chimel objected but was told the officers had a right to search because it was a lawful arrest.

The officers opened kitchen cabinets, searched through hall and bedroom closets, looked behind furniture in every room and even searched the garage. (Prior to this case, the courts had accepted extensive searches incidental to an arrest.) On several occasions the officers had Mrs. Chimel open drawers and move contents so they could look for items removed in the burglary. The search took nearly an hour and turned up numerous stolen coins.

Chimel was convicted in a California court but appealed his burglary conviction on the grounds that the evidence—the coins—had been unconstitutionally seized. The U.S. Supreme Court studied the principle of search incidental to arrest and determined:

> When an arrest is made, it is reasonable for the arresting officer to search the person arrested in order to remove any weapons that the latter might seek to use in order to resist arrest or affect his escape.
>
> It is entirely reasonable for the arresting officer to search for and seize any evidence on the arrestee's person in order to prevent its concealment or destruction and the area from within which the arrestee might gain possession of a weapon or destructible evidence.

In the *Chimel* case, the Supreme Court specified that the area of search can include only the arrestee's person and the area within his or her immediate control. The Court defined **immediate control** as being that area within the person's reach, also called the person's **wingspan**.

Limitations on a search made incidental to an arrest are found in the *Chimel* Rule, which states that the area of the search must be within the immediate control of the suspect, that is, it must be within his or her reach.

The court noted that if an arrest is used as an excuse to conduct a thorough search, such as in the *Chimel* case, the police would have power to conduct "general searches," declared unconstitutional by the Fourth Amendment more than 200 years ago.

In addition to allowing a limited search of suspects and the area within their reach, the Supreme Court has also allowed the **protective sweep,** defined as "a quick and limited *search of premises,* incident to an arrest and conducted to protect police officers and or others" (*Maryland v. Buie,* 1989). A protective sweep might include quick checks of closets or behind doors to see if anyone who may pose a threat is present. As Rutledge (2003c, p. 67) notes: "If you do have a reasonable suspicion that a potential assailant is present in a premises where you are making a lawful arrest, you can make a *'Buie* sweep' of possible hiding places throughout the premises." He notes that such a sweep must be limited to places that could contain a person.

Warrantless Searches of Automobiles and Other Conveyances   Officers who conduct searches without a warrant must prove an emergency or extenuating circumstance existed that did not allow them time to secure a search warrant. Such circumstances often involve automobiles and other conveyances, and the rules of reasonableness are quite different. The courts have long recognized the need for separate exemptions from the requirement of obtaining a search warrant where **mobility,** the capability of being moved quickly and with relative ease, is at issue.

The precedent for a warrantless search of an automobile resulted from *Carroll v. United States* (1925), a bootlegging case that occurred during Prohibition. Two undercover federal agents, posing as buyers, met with bootleggers George Carroll and John Kiro to discuss a transaction. Although the meeting seemed to go well and arrangements were made, the bootleggers became suspicious and backed out of the deal. The agents resumed watching a section of road known to be used by bootleggers. Within a week after their unsuccessful "buy," the agents recognized Carroll and Kiro driving by and gave chase, but eventually lost the car.

Two months later they again recognized Carroll's car and pursued, this time overtaking it. Having reason to believe the automobile contained bootleg liquor, the agents searched the car and found 68 bottles of whiskey and gin, most behind the seats' upholstery where the padding had been removed. The contraband was seized, and the two men were arrested.

Carroll and Kiro were charged with transporting intoxicating liquor and convicted in federal court. Carroll's appeal, taken to the U.S. Supreme Court, led to a landmark decision defining the rights and limitations for warrantless searches of vehicles. The agents' knowledge of the two men and their operation, combined with the recognition of Carroll's car and the belief it was being used to transport liquor, produced the probable cause necessary to justify a search.

 The *Carroll* decision established that the right to search an automobile does not depend on the right to arrest the driver or an occupant. It depends on the officer's probable cause for believing (1) the automobile's contents violated the law and (2) the conveyance would be gone before a search warrant could be obtained.

The requirement of mobility is also present in *Chambers v. Maroney* (1970), which involved the armed robbery of a service station. The station attendant described to officers the two men who held guns on him, and two boys gave a description of a car they had seen the men in circling the block before the robbery and later speeding out of the area. Within an hour officers spotted the vehicle and identified the occupants as the men the three witnesses had described. Police stopped the car and arrested the men. Officers took the car to the police station and searched it, finding two revolvers and a glove filled with change stolen from the service station. The evidence was seized and later used to convict Chambers and the other man.

Chambers appealed, with the defense contending the search was illegal because it was not made simultaneously with the arrest. The defense was right; as a search incidental to an arrest, it would have been illegal. However the Court observed the same set of circumstances in relation to the warrantless search of a vehicle; the seizing officers had probable cause to believe the contents of the automobile violated the law. Therefore it was the right to search, not the right to arrest, that provided the officers with authority for their actions.

The Supreme Court added another opinion to *Chambers* when it held it was not unreasonable under the circumstances to take the vehicle to the police station to be searched. Based on the facts, there was probable cause to search, and because it was a fleeing target, the Chambers vehicle could have been searched on the spot where it stopped. The Court reasoned that probable cause still existed at the police station and so did the car's mobility.

 Chambers established that a car may retain its mobility even though it is impounded.

A case that tested mobility requirements was *Coolidge v. New Hampshire* (1971), involving the disappearance of a 14-year-old girl. Her body was found eight days after she disappeared and revealed she had been shot. A neighbor's tip led police to E. H. Coolidge, whom officers admitted was fully cooperative, even to the point of agreeing to a polygraph examination. The examination was conducted several days after Coolidge was first questioned. During the next two and a half weeks, evidence against Coolidge began to accumulate. The evidence included what the prosecution said was the murder weapon, which officers had obtained from Mrs. Coolidge.

The arrest and search warrants based on this evidence, however, were drawn up and signed by the man who became chief prosecutor in the case. The search warrant specifically designated Coolidge's car, which was in the driveway in plain view of the house at the time of the arrest. Mrs. Coolidge was told she was not allowed to use the car, and it was impounded before other officers took Mrs. Coolidge to a relative's home. During the next 14 months, the car was searched three times, and vacuum sweepings from the car were introduced as evidence.

Coolidge was convicted of the girl's murder. He appealed, challenging the legality of the evidence seized from the car based on invalid warrants. With the warrants declared void and unable to prove the search of the car was incidental to an arrest, the prosecution was left with only the contention that the seizure of the car should be allowable based on the standards established by *Carroll* and *Chambers*.

The Court considered the principles of the *Coolidge* case and weighed them against those of the precedent cases. Because testimony from witnesses and from

Coolidge indicated that his car was at the murder scene, the Court accepted that probable cause to search had been established. However was there sufficient cause to fear that the automobile might be moved?

The Court said no. Coolidge could not have gained access to the automobile when the officers came to arrest him, and in fact, he had received sufficient warning that he was a prime suspect to have already fled. The only other adult occupant, Mrs. Coolidge, was driven to a relative's home by other officers who were with her after the vehicle was actually taken to the station.

 Coolidge v. New Hampshire established that the rule of mobility cannot be applied unless there is actually a risk the vehicle will be moved.

Vehicles may also be searched without a warrant when they are used in committing felonies. Such **instruments of a crime** include getaway vehicles as well as automobiles, trailers or similar conveyances used to hide or transport stolen items.

The right to search vehicles incidental to an arrest was upheld in *New York v. Belton* (1981), when the Supreme Court ruled that officers can search a vehicle's interior and all its contents if an occupant has been lawfully arrested and the vehicle search is subsequent to the arrest. In May 2004, in *Thornton v. United States,* the Supreme Court ruled that when police arrest a motorist, they may search his car—even if the arrestee has gotten out of the car and is walking away when confronted by the police. As Rutledge (2004a, p. 142) explains: "The Supreme Court extended the search incident to arrest to cases in which the arrested person was a 'recent occupant' of the vehicle." In other words, in *Thornton* the Supreme Court held that *Belton* governs even when an officer does not make contact until the person arrested has left the vehicle. *United States v. Ross* (1982) held that the police may search a car, including containers in the car, without a warrant as long as they have probable cause to believe contraband is somewhere in the car.

Florida v. Jimeno (1991) extended the *Ross* decision in examining whether a person's consent to a vehicle search allowed the searching officer to open a container in the vehicle. In this case a police officer overheard Jimeno, who was using a public phone, arranging what sounded like a drug deal. When Jimeno drove off, the officer followed him, saw him make an illegal right turn at a red light, and pulled him over. The officer explained why he had stopped the car and also said that he suspected there were narcotics in the car. He requested permission to search, which was granted. The officer found a brown sack on the passenger-side front seat, opened it and found a kilogram of cocaine. Jimeno was arrested and convicted. The Supreme Court upheld the decision, stating: "A criminal suspect's Fourth Amendment right to be free from unreasonable searches is not violated when, after he gives police permission to search his automobile, they open a closed container found within the car that might reasonably hold the object of the search."

Finally *Colorado v. Bertine* (1987) ruled that police can inventory the contents of an impounded vehicle. Police often routinely inventory the contents of impounded vehicles to accurately record an arrestee's possessions so they may be safely returned at the appropriate time. If during such a routine inventory, police find contraband or evidence of a crime, it is admissible in court. In this case Bertine was arrested for drunk driving, and the van he was driving was impounded. During a routine inventory search, police found canisters of cash and drugs, which were admitted in evidence, and Bertine was convicted. On appeal the Supreme Court ruled that a warrant was not required because it was a routine inventory search.

A relatively new issue related to vehicle stops is the **pretext stop,** also called a **dual motive stop,** in which a vehicle is stopped for a traffic violation, but the intent is to search the vehicle for contraband or evidence of a crime. For example if an officer sees a driver who he believes acts suspiciously, the officer may follow the car hoping the driver will violate a traffic law so the officer may lawfully stop the car and make an inquiry. This issue has come up in several state courts, and case law on this issue is building. The question of pretext stops was addressed in *Whren v. United States* (1996) when the Supreme Court stated: "The temporary detention of a motorist upon probable cause to believe he has violated the traffic laws does not violate the Fourth Amendment's prohibition against unreasonable seizures, even if a reasonable officer would not have stopped the motorist absent some additional law enforcement objective." In effect, the validity and constitutionality of a stop does not depend on whether police officers "would have" made the stop but rather whether the officers "could have" made the stop. The real purpose of a stop, even if ulterior, does not render the stop and subsequent search invalid if there was, in fact, a valid reason for the stop, such as a traffic violation in the *Whren* case. The dangers of "routine" traffic stops are high. This danger increases when the vehicle has more than one occupant, as affirmed in *Maryland v. Wilson* (1997).

 Maryland v. Wilson established that, given the likelihood of a traffic stop leading to either violence or the destruction of evidence when passengers are in the vehicle, officers may order passengers out of the car pending completion of the stop.

It was noted that passengers outside the vehicle are denied access to any weapons that might be inside the car. The Court also recognized the possibility of violence if a traffic stop reveals further evidence of a more serious crime.

Warrantless Searches Where No Reasonable Expectation of Privacy Exists

In some situations, officers may lawfully conduct a warrantless search even in the absence of an incidental arrest or exigent circumstances, simply because the Fourth Amendment protection against unreasonable searches and seizure is not at issue—there is no reasonable expectation of privacy. *Katz v. United States* (1967) established that: "The Fourth Amendment protects people, not places. What a person knowingly exposes to the public, even in his own home or office, is not a subject of Fourth Amendment protection. But what he seeks to preserve as private, even in an area accessible to the public, may be constitutionally protected." As Hunsucker (2003, p. 10) summarizes: "Anywhere a law enforcement officer has a right to be, he has a right to see—through the use of any of his unaided senses."

In *Katz*, law enforcement officers tape recorded Katz's conversation with his bookie. They did not have a warrant for the wiretap, which the court found to be illegal as Katz had an expectation of privacy in the phone booth. Following the *Katz* decision Congress passed the Omnibus Crime Control and Safe Streets Act of 1968. Title III of that act governs interception of wire, electronic and oral communications by the government and private parties. Title III mandates that communications intercepted in violation of Title III may not be received in evidence during any trial, hearing or other proceeding.

Schott (2003, p. 27) points out: "Surreptitious recording of telephone conversations is not prohibited by Title III when one party consents." He (p. 30) also notes: "Surreptitious recording of individuals in a police agency's interrogation room is not prohibited by the Fourth Amendment." Situations involving right to privacy concerns also include (1) workplace privacy; (2) open fields, abandoned property and trash; (3) aerial searches and (4) use of thermal imaging.

Workplace Privacy   The issue of workplace privacy and whether public employees have a reasonable expectation of privacy at their jobs is complex. It is generally held that employees' personal effects are subject to full Fourth Amendment protection, even within the workplace, and that searches of items such as purses, wallets, briefcases and personal mail require probable cause and a warrant. However, in *O'Connor v. Ortega* (1987), the Supreme Court, observing that facilities within government and other public agencies are generally shared by and accessible to many, ruled that a public employee's position, by its very nature, allows a degree of intrusion into privacy that would otherwise violate the Fourth Amendment. In *Ortega* the Court held that all an employer needs for a work-related intrusion to qualify as reasonable under the Fourth Amendment is a reasonable suspicion that the investigative search will uncover evidence of an employee's work-related misconduct. A workplace search is also justified if it serves a valid noninvestigatory, work-related purpose, such as retrieving a needed file.

One controversial area is whether employers have a right to monitor how employees use the company's computers, including tracking an employee's online activities. Can employers reprimand employees who use email for personal use or who visit non–work-related Web sites during office hours?

Open Fields, Abandoned Property and Trash

 If something is open to the public and therefore has no expectation of privacy, it is not protected by the Fourth Amendment. This includes open fields, abandoned property and trash.

The principles governing search and seizure of open fields and trash were established in *Hester v. United States* (1924). In this case police were investigating bootlegging operations and went to Hester's father's home. As police approached the residence, they saw a man identified as Henderson drive up to the house, so they hid. When Hester came out and gave Henderson a bottle, the police sounded an alarm. Hester ran to a car parked nearby, took out a gallon jug, and he and Henderson ran across an open field. One officer chased them. Hester dropped his jug, and it broke, but about half its contents remained. Henderson threw his bottle away. Police found another broken jar containing liquid that appeared to be illegal whiskey. The officers seized the jars, even though they had no search warrant, and arrested Hester, who was convicted of concealing "distilled spirits." On appeal his lawyer contended that the officers conducted an illegal search and seizure. The Court disagreed, saying:

> It is obvious that even if there had been a trespass, the above testimony was not obtained by an illegal search and seizure. The defendant's own acts, and those of his associates, disclosed the jug, the jar and the bottle—and there was no seizure in the sense of the law when the officers examined the contents of each after it had been abandoned. . . .
>
> The special protection accorded by the Fourth Amendment to the people in their "persons, houses, papers, and effects," is not extended to the open fields.

The **open fields doctrine** holds that land beyond what is normally associated with use of that land, that is, undeveloped land, can be searched without a warrant. **Curtilage** is the term used to describe the portion of property generally associated with the common use of land, for example buildings, sheds, fenced-in areas and yards. A warrant is required to search the curtilage. In *Oliver v. United States* (1984), the Supreme Court described the curtilage as "the area to which extends the intimate activity associated with the 'sanctity of a man's home and the privacies of life.'" The courts have generally regarded driveways, walkways to a house's front door and unfenced front yards as areas commonly accessed by neighbors, visitors, postal carriers, delivery drivers, salespeople and other members of the public. As such, these areas receive a lower level of protection in issues of privacy, and courts have upheld police officers' right to enter onto a property's "public access" areas without a warrant.

In *United States v. Dunn* (1987), the Supreme Court specified four factors to consider in determining if an area is within a home's curtilage:

- The proximity of the area to the home
- Whether the area is within the same enclosure as the home
- The nature of the use to which the area is put
- Measures taken by the home's occupant to protect the area from the view of passersby

Oliver v. United States strengthened the open fields doctrine by ruling that "No Trespassing" signs and locked gates do not constitute a "reasonable expectation of privacy":

> The test of a reasonable expectation of privacy is not whether the individual attempts to conceal criminal activity, but whether the government's intrusion infringes upon the personal and societal values protected by the Fourth Amendment. Because open fields are accessible to the public and because fences or "No Trespassing" signs, etc. are not effective bars to public view of open fields, the expectation of privacy does not exist and police are justified in searching these areas without a warrant.

Once a person throws something away, the expectation of privacy is lost. *California v. Greenwood* (1988) established that garbage left outside the curtilage of a home for regular collection could be inspected: "Here we conclude that respondents exposed their garbage to the public sufficiently to defeat their claim to Fourth Amendment protection. It is common knowledge that plastic garbage bags left on or at the side of a public street are readily accessible to animals, children, scavengers, snoops, and other members of the public." If no expectation of privacy exists, Fourth Amendment protection does not exist either.

Some states, however, do not allow such searches. A New Jersey Court ruled 5–2 that garbage left on a curb is private property that police officials cannot search through without a warrant:

> Garbage reveals much that is personal. We do not find it unreasonable for people to want their garbage to remain private and to expect that it will remain private from the meddling of the state.
>
> A free and civilized society should comport itself with more decency [than to allow] police to pick and poke their way through garbage bags to peruse without cause the vestiges of a person's most private affairs.

This case illustrates how critical it is that police officers know not only the federal laws, but also the laws of their respective states, which often can be more restrictive than federal laws.

Aerial Searches   Another area closely related to the plain view doctrine and the open fields doctrine is that of aerial searches. *California v. Ciraola* (1986) expanded the police's ability to "spy" on criminal offenders. In this case police received a tip that marijuana was being grown in the defendant's backyard. The yard was surrounded by two fences, one 6 feet tall, the other 10 feet tall. Since the height of the fences precluded visual observation from the ground, the officers decided to fly over the curtilage at an altitude of 1,000 feet to confirm that it contained marijuana plants. Based on this information, a search warrant was obtained and executed, and the evidence was used to convict Ciraola on drug charges. On appeal the Supreme Court found that the defendant's privacy had not been violated since officers traveling in a navigable airspace are not required to avert their eyes when passing over homes or yards.

In *Florida v. Riley* (1989), the Court expanded this ruling when it stated that police do not need a search warrant to conduct even low-altitude helicopter searches of private property.

Thermal Imaging   The subject of searches, as an applied law enforcement procedure, has received close scrutiny by the courts and remains, in the public eye, an avenue vulnerable to invasion of privacy by the government. When technology is added to the picture, public concern takes on more of a "Big Brother" uneasiness, especially when the technology is aimed at someone's home. An example of how advancing technology affects Fourth Amendment privacy issues is seen in *Kyllo v. United States* (2001), a case involving thermal imaging.

During the course of a drug investigation, a federal agent used a thermal imager to scan the exterior of the home of a man suspected of growing marijuana. The scan, conducted without a search warrant, revealed abnormally high amounts of heat coming from the home, relative to neighboring residences. Investigators believed this data, combined with previously developed information, provided probable cause to secure a search warrant for the property. The search revealed not only marijuana plants but also drug paraphernalia and weapons, and Kyllo was convicted of manufacturing marijuana.

Kyllo appealed, arguing that targeting his home with a thermal imager was an unreasonable Fourth Amendment search. The appeal went all the way to the U.S. Supreme Court, which reversed the circuit court's ruling. In a 5-to-4 decision, the Supreme Court asserted that using a thermal imager to surveil a home is a search under the Fourth Amendment and, as such, requires a search warrant based on probable cause.

 The Supreme Court has ruled that using thermal imaging to view inside a home without a warrant is unconstitutional.

"In *Kyllo v. United States*, the U.S. Supreme Court drew a bright line around the home and announced a rule that warrantless police use of technology stops at the front door" (Colbridge, 2001, p. 31). Worrall (2003, p. 221) disagrees. He notes that the Court said using devices "not in general public use" to view "details of home" is a search under the Fourth Amendment; however: "The Court's decision is anything but bright line. Rather, it is muddy and gray. It is unclear what technologies are not in general public use. There is also little agreement over what can be considered details of the home. Furthermore, the Court placed significant restrictions on the ability of law enforcement officers to make inferences about criminal activity, and it flatly ignored the philosophy of judicial restraint." Woessner and Sims (2003, p. 224) question the implications of this ruling for the ongoing fight against international terrorism.

Limitations on Searches

After establishing the right to search, police officers must determine the limitations on that right—limitations imposed by law and interpreted by the courts.

 The most important limitation imposed on any search is that the scope must be narrowed. General searches are unconstitutional.

Often what is found during a search provides the probable cause to make an arrest. As with searches, in an arrest the general rule is that a warrant is required.

Lawful Arrests

Laws of arrest are generally uniform in all 50 states and in federal criminal proceedings. Statutes throughout the United States generally define **arrest** as the taking of a person into custody by the actual restraint of the person or by his or her submission to the custody of the officer so that he or she may be held to answer for a public offense before a judge.

Elements of Criminal Arrest

Four elements of a criminal arrest are:
1. An *intent* by an officer to make an arrest
2. *Authority* to arrest
3. A *seizure* or *restraint*
4. An *understanding* by the person that he or she is being arrested

Arrest Warrants

All states have a statute authorizing law enforcement officers to make arrests, but the Constitution stipulates that lawful arrests require an arrest warrant. From a practical point of view, police officers should obtain arrest warrants to protect themselves against civil liability for false imprisonment, in case it is later determined the arrest was unjustified. Like a search warrant, an arrest warrant requires an affidavit stating the facts supporting probable cause and sworn to by the officer presenting the affidavit. The judge determines if probable cause exists and, if so, issues the warrant. The warrant itself must name the person to be arrested, the offense and the officer(s) directed to make the arrest. The warrant must be signed by an impartial judge.

Arrests without a Warrant

Police officers may make lawful arrests without a warrant for felonies or misdemeanors committed in their presence, called **public offenses.** Walker and McKinnon (2003, p. 239) note: "Supreme Court decisions in the 1990s had the effect of expanding the authority of police [including] . . . strengthening of police powers in warrantless arrests." This trend continued in *Atwater v. City of Lago Vista*

© Mark Reinstein/Index Stock Imagery

When an arrest is made, the suspect is usually handcuffed for the officer's safety. An arrest is a critical discretionary action, never to be taken lightly as it may change a person's life forever.

(2001) when a police officer arrested a woman who was driving her pickup truck with her two young children in the front seat, none of them wearing a seat belt. Atwater filed a civil suit under 42 U.S.C. § 1983 against the officer and the city. The case found its way to the Supreme Court, which ruled that the Fourth Amendment does not forbid a warrantless arrest for a minor offense punishable only by a fine.

Officers can also make arrests for felonies not committed in their presence if they have probable cause. They may not, however, enter a dwelling to arrest without a warrant. In *Payton v. New York* (1980), the Supreme Court ruled that the Fourth Amendment prohibits warrantless entry into a dwelling to arrest in the absence of sufficient justification for the failure to obtain a warrant. Since then, "dwelling" has been expanded to include temporary residences including motels and hotels, tents in public campgrounds and migrant farm housing on private property.

If, however, an emergency situation exists and officers have probable cause to believe a person has committed a crime, they may make a warrantless arrest. The courts will determine its legality.

 If there is probable cause and an emergency situation exists, an officer may make an arrest without a warrant. The courts will determine whether the arrest was lawful.

The Fourth Amendment was intended to protect citizens from unjust arrests. The courts must balance this protection against the justice system's charge to protect society against those who violate its laws.

An arrest is never to be taken lightly. It can change a person's life forever. Officer discretion is critical when arrest decisions are made. It is also vital that officers clearly differentiate between a simple stop and frisk situation and an arrest. Sometimes a stop and frisk situation leads to an arrest situation. Table 8.1 summarizes the important differences between the two.

Table 8.1 Stop and Arrest

	Stop	*Arrest*
Justification	Reasonable suspicion	Probable cause
Intent of officer	To resolve an ambiguous situation	To make a formal charge
Search	Possibly a "pat down" or frisk	Complete body search
Record	Minimal	Fingerprints, photographs and booking

Right to Resist Arrest

Sometimes when an arrest is made, the person being arrested resists, and the officer must use force to make the arrest, an issue discussed in Chapter 11. It should be noted here, however, that American courts adopted the common law right to resist arrest until the mid-twentieth century. The trend during the past 50 years has been to eliminate that right. The decision of whether to continue or eliminate this right rests on the degree to which we value liberty rather than order.

De Facto Arrests

A **de facto arrest** occurs when officers who lack probable cause to arrest take a suspect in for questioning. If the officers' actions have the appearance of an arrest—that is, the suspect is not free to refuse—it is a detention tantamount to arrest. Rutledge (2003b, p. 77) asserts: "If police take someone from one location and transport him or her involuntarily to a police facility for investigation, this will be considered a *de facto* arrest. Without probable cause, that arrest will be unlawful, with predictable consequences for both evidence suppression and civil liability."

Kaupp v. Texas (2003) involved this issue. Police suspected Kaupp of involvement in the murder of a 14-year-old girl. Three plainclothes detectives and three uniformed officers went to his house at 3 A.M. His father let them in, and they proceeded to Kaupp's bedroom, awakened him and told him they needed to talk. They handcuffed him and led him shoeless and dressed only in a T-shirt and boxer shorts to their patrol car. At the police station, after 10 or 15 minutes of denying involvement, he admitted he had taken part in the crime. As Holtz (2003, p. 118) notes: "The Court remanded the case to the lower court directing that Kaupp's confession be suppressed unless the prosecution can 'point to testimony undisclosed on the record' and 'weighty enough' to demonstrate a break in the causal connection between the illegal arrest and the confession."

Protecting a Suspect's Rights—The Miranda Warning

Before interrogating any suspect, police officers must give the Miranda warning, as established in *Miranda v. Arizona* (1966). The U.S. Supreme Court asserted that suspects must be informed of their rights to remain silent, to have counsel present, to state-appointed counsel if they cannot afford one and to be warned that anything they say might be used against them in a court of law. Many investigators carry a card that contains the Miranda warning to be read before interrogating a suspect. (See Figure 8.1.)

> **Miranda Warning**
> 1. You have the right to remain silent.
> 2. If you give up the right to remain silent, anything you say can and will be used against you in a court of law.
> 3. You have the right to speak with an attorney and to have the attorney present during questioning.
> 4. If you so desire and cannot afford one, an attorney will be appointed for you without charge before questioning.
>
> **Waiver**
>
> 1. Do you understand each of these rights I have read to you?
> 2. Having these rights in mind, do you wish to give up your rights as I have explained them to you and talk to me now?

Figure 8.1 Miranda Warning Card

On the evening of March 3, 1963, an 18-year-old girl was abducted and raped in Phoenix, Arizona. Ten days after the incident, Ernesto Miranda was arrested by Phoenix police, taken to police headquarters and put in a lineup. He was identified by the victim and shortly thereafter signed a confession admitting the offenses. Despite the defense attorney's objections to the statement, the trial court admitted the confession. Miranda was convicted and sentenced 20 to 30 years on each count.

Miranda appealed on the grounds that he had not been advised of his constitutional rights under the Fifth Amendment. The Arizona Supreme Court ruled in 1965 that because Miranda had been previously arrested in California and Tennessee, he knowingly waived his rights under the Fifth and Sixth Amendments when he gave his confession to the Phoenix police. In 1966, upon appeal, the U.S. Supreme Court reversed the supreme court of Arizona in a 5–4 decision and set up precedent rules for police custodial interrogation. Chief Justice Warren stated: "The mere fact that he signed a statement which contained a typed-in clause stating that he had 'full knowledge of his legal rights' does not approach knowing the intelligent waiver required to relinquish constitutional rights."

 The Miranda warning must be given to a suspect who is interrogated in police **custody,** that is, when the suspect is not free to leave.

Two terms are key in this situation: *interrogated* and *in custody.* The circumstances involved in an interrogation and whether it requires a Miranda warning were expanded in *Oregon v. Mathiason* (1977) when the Court said:

> Any interview of one suspected of a crime by a police officer will have coercive aspects to it, simply by virtue of the fact that the police officer is part of a law enforcement system which may ultimately cause the suspect to be charged with a crime. But police officers are not required to administer Miranda warnings to everyone whom they question. Nor is the requirement of warnings to be imposed simply because the questioning takes place in the station house, or because the questioned person is one whom the police suspect. Miranda warnings are required only where there has been such a restriction on a person's freedom as to render him "in custody." It was that sort of coercive environment to which Miranda by its terms was made applicable, and to which it is limited.

As Rutledge (2003a, p. 140) explains: "In *Miranda v. Arizona* the Supreme Court created a judicial presumption that any police interrogation conducted

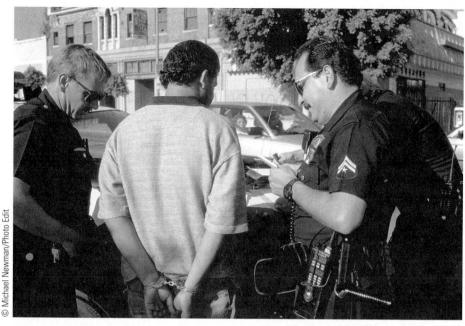

An L.A. police officer reads a suspect his Miranda rights. Failure to do so can result in important statements or even a confession being inadmissible in court.

while the subject is in custody inherently urges the person to talk. That meant that any statement obtained through a police interrogation while a person was in custody, without a declaration of his rights, could not be admitted in his criminal prosecution because of the Fifth Amendment privilege against compelling a person to testify against himself."

Custodial interrogation takes place in two situations: (1) when a suspect is under arrest or (2) when a suspect is not under arrest, but is deprived of freedom in a significant way. Miranda warnings are not required if questioning witnesses, in "stop and frisk" cases, or before fingerprinting and/or photographing during the arrest or booking process. Police who conduct DUI stops and ask routine questions need not give the Miranda warning (*Pennsylvania v. Muniz*, 1990).

Another case significant to the protection of suspects' rights actually resulted in two separate trials with two different prosecutors, yet both trials involved the same defendant, Robert Williams, and the same case, the Christmas Eve disappearance and suspected homicide of a 10-year-old girl. During the investigation, police developed information leading to suspect Williams and obtained a warrant for his arrest. Williams eventually turned himself in to police in a town 160 miles from where the girl disappeared, and Williams's lawyer agreed to have police return the suspect to the case's city of origin.

All agreed that Williams would not be interrogated in any way during the long car trip. However, during the drive, aware that Williams possessed a strong religious faith, one officer said the following to Williams, in what has become known as the "Christian Burial Speech":

I want to give you something to think about while we're traveling down the road. . . . It's going to be dark early this evening. They are predicting several inches of snow for tonight, and I feel that you yourself are the only person that knows where this little girl's body is, that you yourself have only been there once, and if you get snow on top of it, you yourself may be unable to find it. And since we will be going right past the area on the way [back], I feel that we could stop and locate the body, that the parents of this little girl should be entitled to a Christian burial for the little girl who was snatched away from them on Christmas Eve and murdered.

The detective said he was not looking for an answer but that he just wanted Williams to think about it as they drove. Shortly after, Williams directed the officers to the girl's body. The lower courts admitted Williams's damaging statements into evidence, but the Supreme Court in *Brewer v. Williams* (1977) reversed, holding that any statements made by Williams were inadmissible because the way they were elicited violated his constitutional right to counsel:

> The pressures on state executive and judicial officers charged with the administration of the criminal law are great, especially when the crime is murder and the victim a small child. But it is precisely the predictability of those pressures that makes imperative a resolute loyalty to the guarantees that the Constitution extends to us all.

The Court granted Williams a second trial with a different prosecutor (*Nix v. Williams*, 1984). Again, Williams's statements were suppressed, but the Court allowed the body to be admitted as evidence not because it was found through the improper questioning by police but because an independent search party would have eventually discovered it. This is the **inevitable discovery doctrine.** Former Chief Justice Warren E. Burger wrote in the majority opinion: "Exclusion of physical evidence that would inevitably have been discovered adds nothing to either the integrity or fairness of a criminal trial." The point of the inevitable discovery doctrine, he said, was to put the police in the same, not a worse, position than they would have been in if no police error or misconduct occurred.

The Miranda warning survived a challenge to its validity in *Dickerson v. United States* (2000). The case involved Charles Dickerson, who voluntarily confessed to several bank robberies and waived his rights in writing. At trial, the defendant moved to suppress his confession because he had waived his rights before being given the Miranda warning. The Federal District Court granted his motion to suppress, but the U.S. Court of Appeals reversed the decision, stating that the lower court had used the wrong standard in judging the confession's admissibility.

The higher court noted that two years after the Miranda decision, Congress enacted 18 U.S.C. § 3501, which effectively attempted to nullify the Supreme Court's decision in Miranda by changing the test for the admission of confessions in federal court from the stricter Miranda rule to the less stringent judicial standard of totality of circumstances. The appellate court interpreted that Miranda was not a "Constitutional Holding" and Congress's later law superceded Miranda.

In *Dickerson*, the Court, by a 7-to-2 margin, refused to strike down *Miranda* and upheld it as a constitutional decision that cannot be overruled by an Act of Congress. The Court added it could find no compelling reason to overturn a 43-year-old decision that "has become embedded in routine police practice to the point where the warnings have become part of our national culture." The Court's ruling in *Dickerson* also struck down § 3501 as unconstitutional: "Experience suggests that the totality-of-the-circumstances test which § 3501 seeks to revive is more difficult than *Miranda* for law enforcement officers to conform to, and for courts to apply in a consistent manner."

Thus, the *Dickerson* decision affirmed the "bright line rule," stating that in any custodial interrogation where a confession is made by a suspect, the confession will be presumed involuntary and, therefore, inadmissible in court *unless* the police officer first provides the suspect with the four specific warnings spelled out in *Miranda*. Petrowski (2001, p. 30) observes: "The critical impact of the *Dickerson* decision is that intentional violations of the requirements of *Miranda*, commonly known as questioning 'outside *Miranda*,' now may provide the basis for a lawsuit alleging a federal constitutional violation."

Waiving the Right

Suspects can *waive* their rights against self-incrimination and talk to police officers, but the **waiver** must be voluntary and must be preceded by the Miranda warning. The suspect must fully understand what rights are being given up and the possible consequences. If after hearing a police officer read the Miranda warning, suspects remain silent, this is *not* a waiver. To waive their rights, suspects must state, orally or in writing, that (1) they understand their rights and (2) they will voluntarily answer questions without a lawyer present. Officers are allowed to ask more than once if a suspect would like to waive his or her rights.

Special care must be taken with individuals who do not speak English well, who are under the influence of drugs or alcohol, who appear to be mentally retarded or who appear to be hampered mentally in any way. It is preferable to get the waiver in writing.

The Public Safety Exception

The **public safety exception** is an important consideration when discussing the *Miranda* decision. On June 12, 1984, in a landmark 5–4 decision in *New York v. Quarles*, the U.S. Supreme Court announced that in certain cases police may question suspects in custody without first advising them of their right not to incriminate themselves.

Writing for the Court's majority, Justice Rehnquist cited the Court's decision in *Michigan v. Tucker* (1974) and made the distinction that the Miranda warnings are "not themselves rights protected by the Constitution, but are measures to insure that the right against compulsory self-incrimination is protected. . . . On some facts there is a 'public safety' exception to the requirement that Miranda warnings be given before a suspect's answers may be admitted into evidence, and that the availability of that exception does not depend upon the motivation of the individual officers." Although the Court set forth the "public safety exception," no attempt was made to determine in what situations this exception might apply.

 The public safety exception allows police officers to question suspects without first giving the Miranda warning if the information sought sufficiently affects the officer's and the public's safety.

In *Quarles*, a young woman stopped two police officers and said she had been raped. She described her rapist who, she said, had just entered a nearby supermarket armed with a gun. The officers located the suspect, Benjamin Quarles, and ordered him to stop, but Quarles ran, and the officers momentarily lost sight of him. When they apprehended and frisked him, the officers found an empty shoulder holster. When the officers asked Quarles where the gun was, he nodded toward some cartons and said, "The gun is over there." The officers retrieved the gun, arrested Quarles and read him his rights. Quarles waived his rights and answered questions.

At the trial the court ruled that the statement, "The gun is over there," and the subsequent discovery of the gun resulting from that statement were inadmissible at the defendant's trial. However, the Supreme Court, after reviewing the case, ruled that if Miranda warnings had deterred the response to the officer's question, the cost would have been more than just the loss of evidence that might lead to a conviction. As long as the gun remained concealed in the store, it posed a danger to public safety.

The Court ruled that in this case the need to have the suspect talk took precedence over the requirement that the defendant be read his rights. The Court ruled that the material factor applying this public safety exception is whether a public threat could possibly be removed by the suspect making a statement. In this case the officer asked the question only to ensure his and the public's safety. He then gave the Miranda warning before continuing questioning. Numerous other court decisions have favored public and officer safety over the right of suspects to be immediately read their rights and have recognized that this reasonable precaution should not compromise the admissibility of evidence. Although every law enforcement officer knows about *Miranda*, many are not familiar with the rights of foreign nationals arrested by federal, state or local law enforcement officers.

Protecting the Rights of Foreign Nationals

Similar to the Miranda warning card, the U.S. Department of State's *Consular Notification and Access Reference Card* contains consular rights warnings that must be given to arrested or detained foreign nationals. In addition, as Clark (2002, p. 22) points out: "Under appropriate circumstances, they [law enforcement officials] must notify the foreign nationals' consular officials who are posted in the United States." Clark (p. 23) explains: "Most countries of the world, including the United States, are parties to or otherwise obligated by the *Vienna Convention on Consular Relations and Optional Protocol on Disputes* (VCCR). Consistent with the Constitution, this multilateral treaty is the 'supreme law of the land' within the United States." Clark (p. 30) cautions: "Officers failing to give VCCR rights conceivably may be subject to civil liability."

Involuntary Confessions

Arizona v. Fulminante (1991) established that the "harmless error" doctrine applies to cases involving the admissibility of involuntary confessions. In this case Fulminante was suspected of murdering his stepdaughter, but evidence was insufficient to charge him. Later he was arrested and jailed on a federal charge of possession of a firearm. While in prison a fellow inmate, Sarivola, a paid FBI informant, told Fulminante that the other inmates considered him a child killer and that if he would admit to the crime, Sarivola would protect him from the inmates. Fulminante did confess. When he was released from prison, he also confessed to Sarivola's wife.

Fulminante was charged with the murder, and at the trial his confession was challenged as being coerced and therefore excluded by the Fifth and Fourteenth Amendments. His confession to the wife was also challenged as "fruit" of the first confession. The confessions were admitted, however, and Fulminante was convicted and sentenced to death. On appeal the Arizona Supreme Court declared that Fulminante's confession was coerced because he feared for his safety and needed Sarivola to protect him.

The question then became, did allowing the confessions to be admitted into evidence harm the defendant's case or was it a "harmless error"? In this case a majority of the court said the error was not harmless. If the error is harmful or if the prosecution fails to establish beyond reasonable doubt that the error is harmless, the conviction is reversed. Situations in which suspects feel they have been tricked into confessing may also use entrapment as a defense.

Entrapment

Entrapment is an act of government agents to induce a person to commit a crime that is not normally considered by the person to institute a criminal prosecution against him or her. Many Supreme Court cases in which entrapment was at issue have led to rulings that help define the boundaries for law enforcement. In *Sorrells v. United States* (1932), the Court stated:

> Society is at war with the criminal classes, and the courts have uniformly held that in waging this warfare the forces of prevention and detection may use traps, decoys and deception to obtain evidence of the commission of a crime. Resort to such means does not render an indictment thereafter found a nullity nor call for the exclusion of evidence so procured. . . . Entrapment is the conception and planning of an offense by an officer, and his procurement of its commission by one who would not have perpetrated it except for the trickery, persuasion or fraud of the officer.

The Court's ruling in *Grossman v. State* (1969) helped delineate police conduct constituting entrapment to include appeals to sympathy, guarantees that the act is legal and inducements making the crime unusually attractive. The Court further defined entrapment in its ruling in *Sherman v. United States* (1958): "Entrapment occurs only when the criminal conduct was 'the product of the creative' activity of law-enforcement officials. To determine whether entrapment has been established, a line must be drawn between the trap for the unwary innocent and the trap for the unwary criminal."

The line between "unwary innocents" and "unwary criminals" was clarified in *United States v. Russell* (1973): "There are circumstances when the use of deceit is the only practicable law enforcement technique available. It is only when the government's deception actually implants the criminal design in the mind of the defendant that the defense of entrapment comes into play." The Court elaborated on this ruling in *Jacobson v. United States* (1992), when it held government has the burden of proving "beyond a reasonable doubt" the defendant's predisposition to commit the offense. If the government fails to prove predisposition, the defense wins on the presumption that the defendant is an "unwary innocent" instead of an "unwary criminal."

A Recap of the Landmark Cases

The challenge of policing within the law is formidable, but critical. Officers must know constitutional restrictions on their powers at both the federal and state levels. Although statutes vary from state to state, several generalizations usually apply. The most important of these are summarized in Table 8.2.

Table 8.2   Summary of Major Court Rulings Regarding the Fourth Amendment (Search and Seizure), Fifth Amendment (Self-Incrimination), Entrapment and Exclusions to These Clauses

Doctrine	Case Decision	Holding
Fourth Amendment		
Probable Cause	*Smith v. United States* (1949)	Probable cause is the sum total of layers of information and the synthesis of what the police have heard, what they know, and what they observe as trained officers. The courts weigh not the individual layers but the laminated total.
	Draper v. United States (1959)	Probable cause exists where the facts and circumstances within the arresting officers' knowledge are sufficient to warrant a person of reasonable caution in the belief that an offense has been or is being committed.
Stop and Frisk	*Terry v. Ohio* (1968)	The authority to stop and frisk is independent of the power to arrest. A stop is not an arrest, but it is a seizure within the meaning of the Fourth Amendment and therefore requires reasonableness.
	Florida v. J. L. (2000)	Reasonable suspicion for an investigative stop does not arise from a mere anonymous tip.
	Illinois v. Wardlow (2000)	A person's sudden flight upon seeing a police officer can be used to establish reasonable suspicion for a *Terry*-type stop.
Sobriety Checkpoints	*Michigan Department of State Police v. Sitz* (1990)	Sobriety checkpoints are a form of stop and are constitutional if they are conducted fairly and do not pose a safety hazard.
Drug Interdiction Roadblocks	*City of Indianapolis v. Edmond* (2000)	Narcotics checkpoints are unconstitutional and violate the Fourth Amendment's protections against unreasonable search and seizure in that their purpose is indistinguishable from the general interest in crime control.
Field Detention	*Michigan v. Summers* (1981)	Police officers may detain suspects with less than probable cause and may legally require suspects to reenter their houses and remain there until evidence establishing probable cause is found.
	Illinois v. McArthur (2001)	Police did not violate the Fourth Amendment when they detained a suspect outside his home for several hours while officers sought a warrant to search the premises for drugs.
Search with a Warrant—Gaining Entrance	*Wilson v. Arkansas* (1995)	Whether police "knock and announce" their presence before executing valid search warrants is part of the Fourth Amendment inquiry into the reasonableness of a search.
	United States v. Espinoza (2001)	A failure to knock and announce does not require suppression of evidence if the target resists.
	District of Columbia v. Mancouso (2001)	Officers who disregard the knock-and-announce rule while serving a search warrant on an empty house, even if the occupants are standing outside the premises "within earshot" of the officers, have violated statutory requirements, thus providing standing for the residents to move to suppress any evidence recovered inside.
Administrative Warrants	*Michigan v. Tyler* (1978)	Public safety personnel may enter structures that are on fire to extinguish the blaze, after which officials may remain a reasonable length of time to investigate the cause of the blaze.
Warrantless Search with Consent	*State v. Barlow, Jr.* (1974)	Consent must be free and voluntary, and the search must be limited to the area for which the consent is given.
Time of Day of Search	*Monroe v. Pape* (1961)	Officers should generally avoid seeking voluntary consent to search at night.

Table 8.2   *(Continued)*

Doctrine	Case Decision	Holding
Fourth Amendment, *cont.*		
Search Incidental to Lawful Arrest	*Chimel v. California* (1969)	When making an arrest, it is reasonable for an officer to search the person arrested to remove any weapons the latter might use to resist arrest or affect an escape. The search must be made simultaneously with the arrest and must be confined to the area within the immediate control of the suspect—that is, within his or her reach (wingspan).
Protective Sweeps	*Maryland v. Buie* (1989)	A protective sweep is legal and protects the arresting officer from danger posed by unknown third parties. The duration of the sweep is limited and can last no longer than necessary to dispel the suspicion of danger.
Warrantless Searches of Vehicles	*Carroll v. United States* (1925)	The right to search a vehicle is not dependent on the right to arrest the driver or an occupant. It depends on the probable cause the officer has for believing (1) the vehicle's contents violate the law and (2) the conveyance would be gone before a search warrant could be obtained (mobility).
	Chambers v. Maroney (1970)	A car may retain its mobility even though it is impounded.
	Coolidge v. New Hampshire (1971)	The rule of mobility cannot be applied unless there is actually a risk that the vehicle will be moved.
	New York v. Belton (1981)	Officers can search a vehicle's interior and all its contents if an occupant has been lawfully arrested and the vehicle search is subsequent to the arrest.
	United States v. Ross (1982)	Police may search a car, including containers in the car, without a warrant as long as they have probable cause to believe contraband is in the car.
	Colorado v. Bertine (1987)	Police can inventory the contents of an impounded vehicle.
	Florida v. Jimeno (1991)	A criminal suspect's Fourth Amendment right to be free from unreasonable searches is not violated when, after he gives police permission to search his automobile, they open a closed container found within the car that might reasonably hold the object of the search.
Pretext/Dual Motive Traffic Stops	*United States v. Millan* (1994)	If an officer's original intent in stopping a vehicle is to "check it out" and not for a specific violation, any subsequent search will be illegal.
	Whren v. United States (1996)	The real purpose of a stop, even if ulterior, does not render the stop and subsequent search invalid if there was, in fact, a valid reason for the stop, such as a traffic violation.
Danger of Traffic Stops	*Maryland v. Wilson* (1997)	Given the likelihood of traffic stops leading to either violence or destruction of evidence when passengers are in the vehicle, officers making traffic stops may lawfully order all of a vehicle's occupants, including passengers, to get out of the car pending completion of the stop, extending a previous Court decision applicable only to drivers.
Plain Feel/Touch	*Minnesota v. Dickerson* (1993)	Supporting limited "plain touch" or "plain feel" probes in frisk situations, if contraband is plainly felt by the officer in good faith, what he finds will not be suppressed. Under the Plain Feel Doctrine, an officer must determine simultaneously that an item is not a weapon and is, in fact, contraband.
	Bond v. United States (2000)	Extended *Dickerson*, ruling police can visually inspect passengers' luggage but cannot squeeze or otherwise manipulate baggage to determine whether it contains contraband.

(continued)

Table 8.2   *(Continued)*

Doctrine	Case Decision	Holding
Fourth Amendment, *cont.*		
Workplace Privacy	*O'Connor v. Ortega* (1987)	As a general rule, searches of employees' private property (purses, wallets, personal mail) in their workspaces are subject to full Fourth Amendment protection, requiring probable cause and a search warrant. But the nature of a public employee's position allows some intrusion into privacy. All an employer needs for a work-related intrusion to be "reasonable" under the Fourth Amendment is reasonable suspicion the search will reveal evidence of an employee's work-related misconduct or that the search is necessary for a noninvestigatory, work-related purpose, such as retrieving a needed file.
Open Fields, Abandoned Property and Trash Curtilage	*Hester v. United States* (1924)	If something is open to the public and has no expectation of privacy, it is not protected by the Fourth Amendment.
	Oliver v. United States (1984)	A warrant is required to search the curtilage, the area to which extends the intimate activity associated with the "sanctity of a man's home and the privacies of life." "No Trespassing" signs and locked gates do not constitute a reasonable expectation of privacy.
	United States v. Dunn (1987)	Four factors to consider in determining if an area is within a home's curtilage are (1) the proximity of the area to the home, (2) whether the area is within the same enclosure as the home, (3) the nature of the use to which the area is put and (4) measures taken by the home's occupant to protect the area from the view of passersby.
	California v. Greenwood (1988)	Garbage left outside the curtilage of a home for regular collection may be inspected without a warrant. If no expectation of privacy exists, Fourth Amendment protection does not exist either.
Aerial Searches	*California v. Ciraola* (1986)	A defendant's privacy is not violated when officers traveling in a navigable airspace observe illegal activity or contraband.
	Florida v. Riley (1989)	Expands *California v. Ciraola* by stating police do not need a search warrant to conduct even low-altitude helicopter searches of private property.
Thermal Imaging	*Kyllo v. United States* (2001)	Using a thermal imager to surveil a home is a search under the Fourth Amendment and, as such, requires a search warrant based on probable cause.
Inevitable Discovery Doctrine	*Nix v. Williams* (1984)	Illegally obtained evidence may be admitted at trial if the prosecution can prove the evidence would "inevitably" have been discovered by lawful means.
Arrest without a Warrant	*People v. Ramey* (1976)	The Fourth Amendment prohibits a warrantless entry into a dwelling to arrest in the absence of sufficient justification for the failure to obtain a warrant (California Supreme Court).
	Payton v. New York (1980)	Extended *People v. Ramey* to apply to all states.
Fifth Amendment		
Self-Incrimination	*Miranda v. Arizona* (1966)	Before questioning, police must inform suspects in custody of their rights to remain silent, to have counsel present, to state-appointed counsel if they cannot afford their own attorney and to be warned that anything they say may be used against them in a court of law.

Table 8.2 *(Continued)*

Doctrine	Case Decision	Holding
Fifth Amendment, *cont.*		
Self-Incrimination, *cont.*	*Oregon v. Mathiason* (1977)	Police are not required to give Miranda warnings to everyone whom they question, nor is the requirement imposed simply because questioning takes place in the station house or because the questioned person is one whom the police suspect. Miranda warnings are required only where there has been such a restriction on a person's freedom as to render him or her "in custody."
Custodial Interrogation	*United States v. Mesa* (1980)	Incriminating statements in a suspect's recorded conversation are not obtained in violation of the suspect's rights if the Miranda warning is not first given.
DUI Stops	*Pennsylvania v. Muniz* (1990)	Officers conducting DUI stops who ask routine questions do not need to give the Miranda warning.
Right to Counsel	*Brewer v. Williams* (1977)	A suspect's incriminating statements were inadmissible because the way they were elicited violated his constitutional right to counsel.
Constitutionality of *Miranda*	*Dickerson v. United States* (2000)	Affirmed *Miranda* as a constitutional decision that cannot be overruled by an Act of Congress and upheld the "bright line rule": any confession made during a custodial interrogation will be presumed involuntary and, thus, inadmissible *unless* the police officer first provides the suspect with the four specific warnings spelled out in *Miranda*.
Public Safety Exception	*Michigan v. Tucker* (1974)	Miranda warnings are not themselves rights protected by constitution, but are measures to ensure that the right against compulsory self-incrimination is protected. On some facts there is a "public safety" exception to the requirement that Miranda warnings be given before a suspect's answers may be admitted into evidence, and the availability of that exception does not depend upon the motivation of the individual officers.
	New York v. Quarles (1984)	The public safety exception allows police to question suspects without first giving the Miranda warning if the information sought sufficiently affects the officer's and the public's safety.
Involuntary Confessions (Harmless Error)	*Arizona v. Fulminante* (1991)	When involuntary confessions are admitted into evidence, the question is:" Did the allowance harm the defendant's case or was it a 'harmless error' "? If the error is harmful or if the prosecution fails to establish beyond reasonable doubt that the error is harmless, the confession is inadmissible and any conviction based on it must be reversed.
Entrapment	*Sorrells v. United States* (1932)	Law enforcement may use traps, decoys and deception to obtain evidence of the commission of a crime. Resort to such means does not render an indictment thereafter found a nullity nor call for the exclusion of evidence so procured.
	Grossman v. State (1969)	Police conduct constituting entrapment includes appeals to sympathy, guarantees that the act is legal and inducements making the crime unusually attractive.
	Sherman v. United States (1958)	Entrapment occurs only when the criminal conduct was "the product of the creative" activity of law enforcement officials.
	United States v. Russell (1973)	Only when government deception actually implants the criminal design in the mind of the defendant does the defense of entrapment come into play.
	Jacobson v. United States (1992)	Government has the burden of proving "beyond a reasonable doubt" the defendant's predisposition to commit an offense. Failing to prove such a predisposition, the defense wins on the presumption the defendant is an "unwary innocent" instead of an "unwary criminal."

SOURCE: © Innovative Systems—Publishers Inc., 2001. Reprinted by permission of the publisher.

SUMMARY

The constitutional standards for searches and seizures, including arrests, are contained in the Fourth Amendment, which requires that searches and seizures be reasonable and be based on probable cause. Probable cause requires more than mere suspicion. It requires facts or proof that would lead a person of reasonable caution to believe a crime has been committed by a specific individual or that premises contain evidence of a crime. Probable cause may be founded on (1) observation, (2) expertise, (3) circumstantial factors and (4) information conveyed to the officers, including official sources, victims of crimes and informants.

Stop and frisk is a form of search and seizure and, as such, is governed by the intent of the Fourth Amendment. A stop is not an arrest, but it is a seizure if physical force or a show of authority is used. A frisk, however, is a search. Stop and frisk is a protective search for weapons in which the intrusion must be limited to a scope reasonably designed to discover guns, knives, clubs and other hidden instruments that may be used to assault a police officer or others; it is not a search for evidence of a crime. *Terry* established that the authority to stop and frisk is independent of the power to arrest. A stop is *not* an arrest, but it is a seizure within the meaning of the Fourth Amendment and, therefore, requires reasonableness.

The Supreme Court has upheld roadblocks at national borders, sobriety checkpoints and informational checkpoints. The Supreme Court has held that drug checkpoints, general crime control checkpoints and driver's license checkpoints are not constitutional.

Reasonable searches must also meet the standards set forth in the Fourth Amendment. The principal justifications established by the courts for the right to search are (1) a search warrant has been issued, (2) no warrant has been issued but consent to search was given, (3) no warrant has been issued but exigent circumstances exist or (4) no warrant has been issued because there is no expectation of privacy and, thus, no requirement for a search warrant.

Technically all searches are to be made under the authority of a search warrant issued by a magistrate. A search warrant is a judicial order directing a police officer to search for specific property, seize it and return it to the court. The search must be limited to the specific area and specific items delineated in the warrant. Probable cause is required for issuance of all warrants.

Police officers may conduct a search without a warrant if consent is given, exigent circumstances are present or no reasonable expectation of privacy exists. The limitations to a search made with consent are that the consent must be free and voluntary, not in response to an implied right to search, and the scope must be limited to the area for which consent has been given. The Supreme Court has ruled that using thermal imaging to view inside a home without a warrant is unconstitutional. When police conduct a warrantless search, they may be challenged on the basis that probable cause was not established (i.e., a magistrate would not have issued a warrant) or that the officers had time to secure a warrant and had no justification to act without one. The limitations placed on searches incidental to lawful arrest come from *Chimel v. California,* which states that the scope of the search must be narrowed to the area within the suspect's immediate control—that is, it must be within his or her reach.

Special provisions have been made for warrantless searches of cars and other conveyances due to their mobility. The *Carroll* decision established that the right to search an automobile is not dependent on the right to arrest the driver or an occupant. It depends on the probable cause the officer has for believing (1) the automobile's contents violate the law and (2) the conveyance would be gone before a search warrant could be obtained. *Chambers* established that a car may retain its mobility even though impounded. *Coolidge* established that the rule of mobility cannot be applied unless there is actually a risk the vehicle will be moved. *Maryland v. Wilson* established that, given the likelihood of a traffic stop leading to either violence or the destruction of evidence when passengers are in the vehicle, officers may order passengers out of the vehicle pending completion of the stop.

If something is open to the public and, therefore, has no expectation of privacy, it is not protected by the Fourth Amendment. This includes open fields, abandoned property and trash.

Even when the required conditions are met, certain limitations are placed on the search. The most important limitation imposed on any search is that the scope must be narrowed. General searches are unconstitutional.

U.S. citizens are also protected against unreasonable arrest (seizure) by the Fourth Amendment. The Fourth Amendment requires that arrests be made by having a magistrate issue an arrest warrant, but police officers may make an arrest without an arrest warrant in certain circumstances. For example if there is probable cause and an emergency situation exists, an officer may make an arrest without a warrant. The courts will determine whether the arrest was lawful.

The Miranda warning must be given to a suspect who is interrogated in police custody, that is, when the suspect is not free to leave. The public safety exception allows officers to question suspects without first giving the Miranda warning if the information sought sufficiently affects the officer's and the public's safety.

DISCUSSION QUESTIONS

1. In popular television programs, how are police officers portrayed in relation to their duty to protect citizens' Fourth Amendment rights?

2. Why are the police not given total freedom to help stop crime? Why are they not allowed to use evidence that clearly establishes a person's guilt, no matter how they obtained this evidence?

3. In a state where stop and frisk is legal, can a police officer be sued for stopping and frisking someone?

4. What are the most important factors in determining if and when an arrest occurred?

5. Must all elements of probable cause exist before a lawful arrest can be made?

6. Why is the presence of 10 officers not considered intimidation when a request to search is made?

7. Have you ever been involved in a search and seizure situation? How was it handled?

8. From what you have learned about search and seizure, do you feel the restrictions placed on police officers are reasonable?

9. Do you support the plain touch/feel doctrine? Why or why not?

10. Is it too easy for criminals to allege entrapment? How can officers protect against this?

INFOTRAC COLLEGE EDITION ASSIGNMENTS

■ Use InfoTrac College Edition to help answer the Discussion Questions as appropriate.

■ Use InfoTrac College Edition to search for articles on the *bright line rule* and zero in on the *Fourth Amendment* and *traffic stops*. Describe the bright line rules in conjunction with the totality-of-circumstances test. Be prepared to discuss your findings with the class.

■ Read and outline one of the following articles:

  ■ "Anonymous Tips and Frisks: Determining Reasonable Suspicion" by Michael J. Bulzomi

  ■ "Civil Liability for Violations of Miranda: The Impact of *Chavez v. Martinez*" by Kimberly A. Crawford

  ■ "Consent Once Removed" by Edward M. Hendrie

- "Consent Searches Scope" by Jayme Walker Holcomb
- "Inferring Probable Cause: Obtaining a Search Warrant for a Suspect's Home without Direct Information That Evidence Is Inside" by Edward Hendrie
- "*Kyllo v. United States*: Technology versus Individual Privacy" by Thomas D. Colbridge
- "*Miranda* Revisited: *Dickerson v. United States*" by Thomas D. Petrowski
- "Protective Sweeps" by Thomas D. Colbridge
- "Providing Consular Rights Warnings to Foreign Nationals" by M. Wesley Clark
- "Warrantless Entries to Arrest: Constitutional Considerations" by Edward M. Hendrie
- "Warrantless Interception of Communications: When, Where and Why It Can Be Done" by Richard G. Schott

INTERNET ASSIGNMENT

Go to *Dickerson v. United States* (http://supct.law .cornell.edu/supct/html/99-5525.ZS.html) and review this Supreme Court case. Note the dissents of Justices Scalia and Thomas. Outline the arguments on both sides (majority rule versus dissenting opinions), and be prepared to discuss your findings with the class and which position you agree with.

BOOK-SPECIFIC WEB SITE

The book-specific Web site at http://info .wadsworth.com/0534552803 hosts a variety of resources for students and instructors. Included are extended activities from each chapter in which students write a policy, use critical thinking skills to make choices in response to a given scenario, use InfoTrac College Edition with direct links to articles for participation in topical discussion forums, and analyze court cases using Web links for research. Many activities can be printed or emailed to instructors. Plus, cited cases with Web links, interactive key term FlashCards, PowerPoint presentations, chapter objectives, and an extensive collection of chapter-based Web links provide additional information and activities to include in the curriculum.

REFERENCES

"Brief Seizure of Premises to Obtain a Search Warrant Permissible under the Fourth Amendment." *NCJA Justice Bulletin*, March 2001, p. 13.

Clark, M. Wesley. "Providing Consular Rights Warnings to Foreign Nationals." *FBI Law Enforcement Bulletin*, March 2002, pp. 22–32.

Colbridge, Thomas D. "*Kyllo v. United States*: Technology versus Individual Privacy." *FBI Law Enforcement Bulletin*, October 2001, pp. 25–32.

"Court Allows Routine Search of Vehicle Fuel Tank at Border." *Criminal Justice Newsletter*, April 14, 2004, pp. 6–7.

"Court Lets Police Bar Suspect from House Pending Warrant." *Criminal Justice Newsletter*, February 26, 2001, pp. 3–4.

Devanney, Joe and Devanney, Diane. "An Analysis of the Knock and Announce Rule." *Tactical Response*, Spring 2003, pp. 72–73.

Devanney, Joe and Devanney, Diane. "Supreme Court Rules in Roadblock Case." *Law and Order*, May 2004, p. 20.

Greenhouse, Linda. "Justices Rule Police May Properly Request a Name." *New York Times*, as reprinted in the (Minneapolis/St. Paul) *Star Tribune*, June 22, 2004, p. A8.

Hendrie, Edward. "Inferring Probable Cause: Obtaining a Search Warrant for a Suspect's Home without Direct Information That Evidence Is Inside." *FBI Law Enforcement Bulletin*, February 2002, pp. 23–32.

Hendrie, Edward M. "Consent Once Removed." *FBI Law Enforcement Bulletin*, February 2003, pp. 24–32.

Holcomb, Jayme Walker. "Consent Searches Scope." *FBI Law Enforcement Bulletin*, February 2004, pp. 22–32.

Holtz, Larry. "Transporting Suspects for Questioning." *Law Enforcement Technology*, August 2003, p. 118.

Hopper, Joan. "Every Second Counts in the U.S. Supreme Court." *Law and Order*, January 2004, pp. 22–24.

Hunsucker, Keith. "Right to Be, Right to See: Practical Fourth Amendment Application for Law Enforcement Officers." *The Police Chief*, September 2003, pp. 10–13.

Makholm, John A. "Legal Lights: *Illinois v. McArthur*." *The Law Enforcement Trainer*, May/June 2001, p. 13.

Makholm, John A. "Legal Lights: *United States v. Drayton*." *The Law Enforcement Trainer*, July/August 2002, pp. 77–78.

Makholm, John A. "Legal Lights: *United States v. Banks*." *The Law Enforcement Trainer*, January/February 2004a, pp. 64–65.

Makholm, John A. "Legal Lights: *Illinois v. Lidster*." *The Law Enforcement Trainer*, March/April 2004b, pp. 60–61.

Petrowski, Thomas D. "*Miranda* Revisited: *Dickerson v. United States*." *FBI Law Enforcement Bulletin*, August 2001, pp. 25–32.

Risher, Julie A. "New U.S. Supreme Court Decision Approves 'Informational' Checkpoint." *The Police Chief*, March 2004, pp. 10–12.

Rutledge, Devallis. "Demystifying Miranda: Know When to Read 'em Their Rights." *Police*, July 2003a, pp. 140–141.

Rutledge, Devallis. "Avoiding De Facto Arrests." *Police*, 2003b, pp. 74–77.

Rutledge, Devallis. "Officer Safety Searches." *Police*, November 2003c, pp. 66–67.

Rutledge, Devallis. "Knock before Entry." *Police*, February 2004a, pp. 74–75.

Rutledge, Devallis. "Vehicle Checkpoints." *Police,* March 2004b, pp. 89–91.

Schott, Richard G. "Warrantless Interception of Communications: When, Where and Why It Can Be Done." *FBI Law Enforcement Bulletin,* January 2003, pp. 25–32.

Stephen, John A. "Emergency Entry without a Warrant." *Police,* September 2002, pp. 66–69.

"Supreme Court Allows Police to Ban Suspect from Home while Seeking Search Warrant." *The Law Officers' Bulletin,* March 29, 2001, pp. 130–131.

Walker, Jeffery T. and McKinnon, Kristi M. "*Atwater v. City of Lago Vista:* Police Authority to Make Warrantless Misdemeanor Arrests." *Journal of Contemporary Criminal Justice,* May 2003, pp. 239–252.

Whalen, Michael J. "Supreme Court Rulings Acknowledge Practical Considerations of Law Enforcement." *The Police Chief,* April 2002, p. 11.

Woessner, Matthew C. and Sims, Barbara. "Technological Innovation and the Application of the Fourth Amendment: Considering the Implications of *Kyllo v. United States* for Law Enforcement and Counterterrorism." *Journal of Contemporary Criminal Justice,* May 2003, pp. 224–238.

Wood, Scott. "Totality of Circumstances: Analysis for Reasonable Suspicion Reaffirmed by the Supreme Court." *The Law Enforcement Trainer,* March/April 2002, pp. 22–26.

Worrall, John L. "*Kyllo v. United States:* Why the Supreme Court Has Not Laid the Thermal-Imaging Debate to Rest." *Journal of Contemporary Criminal Justice,* May 2003, pp. 205–223.

CASES CITED

Arizona v. Fulminante, 499 U.S. 279 (1991)

Atwater v. City of Lago Vista, 532 U.S. 295 (2001)

Bond v. United States, 120 S.Ct. 1462 (2000)

Brewer v. Williams, 430 U.S. 387 (1977)

California v. Ciraolo, 476 U.S. 207 (1986)

California v. Greenwood, 486 U.S. 35 (1988)

Carroll v. United States, 267 U.S. 132 (1925)

Chambers v. Maroney, 339 U.S. 42 (1970)

Chimel v. California, 395 U.S. 752 (1969)

City of Indianapolis v. Edmond, 531 U.S. 32, 41 (2000)

Colorado v. Bertine, 479 U.S. 367 (1987)

Coolidge v. New Hampshire, 403 U.S. 443 (1971)

Dickerson v. United States, 530 U.S. 428 (2000)

Draper v. United States, 358 U.S. 307 (1959)

Florida v. Jimeno, 499 U.S. 934 (1991)

Florida v. J. L., 120 S.Ct. 1375 (2000)

Florida v. Riley, 109 S.Ct. 693 (1989)

Grossman v. State, 457 P.2d 226 (1969)

Hester v. United States, 265 U.S. 57, 44 (1924)

Hiibel v. Sixth Judicial District Court of Nevada, Humboldt County, No. 03-5554 (June 21, 2004)

Illinois v. Gates, 462 U.S. 213 (1983)

Illinois v. Lidster, 540 U.S. 419 (2004)

Illinois v. McArthur, 121 S.Ct. 946 (2001)

Illinois v. Wardlow, 528 U.S. 119 (2000)

Jacobson v. United States, 503 U.S. 540 (1992)

Katz v. United States, 389 U.S. 347, 351 (1967)

Kaupp v. Texas, 123 S.Ct. 1843 (2003)

Kyllo v. United States, 121 S.Ct. 2038 (2001)

Maryland v. Buie, 109 S.Ct. 2447 (1989)

Maryland v. Wilson, 117 S.Ct. 882 (1997)

Michigan Department of State Police v. Sitz, 496 S.Ct. 444 (1990)

Michigan v. Summers, 452 U.S. 692 (1981)

Michigan v. Tucker, 417 U.S. 433 (1974)

Michigan v. Tyler, 436 U.S. 499 (1978)

Minnesota v. Dickerson, 113 S.Ct. 2130 (1993)

Miranda v. Arizona, 384 U.S. 436 (1966)

Monroe v. Pape, 365 U.S. 167 (1961)

New York v. Belton, 453 U.S. 454 (1981)

New York v. Quarles, 104 S.Ct. 2626 (1984)

Nix v. Williams, 104 S.Ct. 2501 (1984)

O'Connor v. Ortega, 107 S.Ct. 1492 (1987)

Oliver v. United States, 466 U.S. 170 (1984)

Olmstead v. United States, 277 U.S. 438 (1928)

Oregon v. Mathiason, 429 U.S. 492, 332 (1977)

Payton v. New York, 445 U.S. 573 (1980)

Pennsylvania v. Muniz, 496 U.S. 582 (1990)

Sherman v. United States, 356 U.S. 369 (1958)

Smith v. United States, 337 U.S. 137 (1949)

Sorrells v. United States, 287 U.S. 435 (1932)

State v. Barlow, Jr., 320 A.2d 895 (Me. 1974)

Terry v. Ohio, 392 U.S. 1 (1968)

Thornton v. United States, No. 03-5165 (U.S. May 24, 2004)

United States v. Arvizu, 122 S.Ct. 744 (2002)

United States v. Banks, 124 S.Ct. 521 (2003)

United States v. Drayton, 536 U.S. 194 (2002)

United States v. Dunn, 480 U.S. 294, 301 (1987)

United States v. Flores-Montano, No. 02-1794 (2004)

United States v. Martinez-Fuerte, 428 U.S. 543, 566, 546 (1976)

United States v. Ross, 456 U.S. 798 (1982)

United States v. Russell, 411 U.S. 423 (1973)

Whren v. United States, 517 U.S. 806 (1996)

Wilson v. Arkansas, 115 S.Ct. 1914 (1995)

CHAPTER 9

Gangs and Drugs: Threats to Our National Security

Gangs are now spreading through our society like a violent plague.

—Jackson and McBride, LAPD

Drug use and the crime it generates are turning the American dream into a national nightmare for millions of Americans.

—Lee P. Brown

DO YOU KNOW . . .

- Whether gangs, gang membership and the gang problem are increasing or decreasing?
- What the distinguishing characteristics of gangs are?
- How gang members might be identified?
- What the most common reasons for joining gangs are?
- What factors contribute to the formation of a gang?
- What the most important risk factor for becoming a gang member probably is?
- What act made it illegal to sell or use certain narcotics and dangerous drugs?
- What federal law prohibits in relation to narcotics and dangerous drugs?
- What the most commonly observed drugs on the street, in possession of users and seized in drug raids are and what the most frequent drug arrest is for?
- What common effects of the various narcotics and other dangerous drugs are?
- What the most widely abused drug in the United States is?
- If drug use and alcohol abuse are linked to crime?
- What approaches to the drug problem have been suggested?

CAN YOU DEFINE?

amphetamines	civil injunction	drug-defined offenses	instrumental gangs
barbiturates	corporate gangs	drug-related offenses	interdiction
Bloods	crack	gang	methamphetamine
broken-window theory	Crips	graffiti	monikers
choloization	deliriants	hallucinogens	mules
	drug gangs	hedonistic gangs	narcotics

Introduction

Drugs and gangs are often mentioned in the same sentence. Gordon et al. (2004, p.56), for example, note research showing that: "Drug selling, drug use, violent behaviors and vandalism of property increase significantly when a youth joins a gang." This chapter begins by discussing the threat of gangs. First gangs are defined and the various types of gangs that have developed in the United States are described, including various racial and ethnic gangs and the increasing presence of females in gangs. This is followed by a discussion of specific characteristics of gangs, including the gang subculture and how gang members might be identified. Next reasons for joining a gang are discussed, followed by a look at problems in prosecuting gang members, various gang control strategies, the role drugs and drug addiction play in the world of gangs and differences between street gangs and drug gangs.

The link between gangs and drugs provides the transition into the next section—the threat of drugs. Discussion of this topic begins with a look at the various narcotics and other dangerous drugs under federal regulation regarding their prescription, distribution and possession. Next, alcohol, the most widely abused drug in the country, is discussed, followed by an examination of the links between crime and illicit drug and alcohol use. This section concludes by exploring the impact drug use and abuse have had on society and the various drug control strategies being used in the war on drugs, ranging from incarceration to legalization.

The Threat of Gangs

Gangs have existed in nearly every civilization throughout recorded history. Street gangs probably started in our country in Los Angeles at about the turn of the last century. According to Walter Miller (2001, p.iii):

> The last quarter of the 20th century was marked by significant growth in youth gang problems across the United States. In the 1970s, less than half the states reported youth gang problems, but by the late 1990s, every state and the District of Columbia reported youth gang activity. In the same period, the number of cities reporting youth gang problems mushroomed nearly tenfold—from fewer than 300 in the 1970s to more than 2,500 in 1998.

Miller's report (p.x) concludes: "The data provide considerable support for a prediction that the rate of growth that prevailed during the later 1990s will decrease in the early 2000's and some support for a prediction that the actual number of gang localities in the United States will decrease." This prediction is supported by key findings of the *2002 National Youth Gang Survey* (Egley and Major, 2004, p.2):

- In 2002, there were an estimated 721,500 gang members and 21,500 gangs active in the United States. The estimated number of gang members between 1996 and 2002 decreased 14 percent, and the estimated number of jurisdictions experiencing gang problems decreased 21 percent.
- All cities with a population of 15,000 or more reported gang activity in 2002, as did 38 percent of suburban counties, 27 percent of smaller cities and 12 percent of rural counties. Based on survey results it is estimated that nearly 3,000 jurisdictions across the United States experienced gang activity in 2002.
- Forty-two percent of respondents indicated their youth gang problem was "getting worse" in 2002 compared with 2001 and 16 percent indicated it was "getting better." In the 2001 survey, these statistics were 27 percent and 20 percent, respectively, indicating an appreciable increase in the proportion of respondents who regarded their gang problem as worsening.

 Gangs and gang membership are both decreasing, but the problem is perceived as worsening.

Despite the decrease in numbers, gangs still pose a significant challenge to law enforcement. In testimony before a Senate committee in October 2003, McBride, president of the California Gang Investigators Association, urged that the United States focus on reducing gang violence because Los Angeles County gangs, numbering more than 1,100 with a membership of nearly 100,000, have spread across the country: "These gangs began migrating across this country in the mid-1980s and have established their presence in nearly every state of the union. They freely cross state lines transporting firearms and narcotics, but possibly what may be even more important is that they bring their street-gang mentality with them, a mentality that depends on inane gang violence to establish their rule. The most important weapon in the gang's arsenal is fear. . . . After a time, physical threats are not needed; the threat is unspoken but part of the community culture" ("California Law Enforcement Praises School Anti-Gang Program," 2003, p.5).

Gangs Defined

As Weisel (2003, p.275) points out: "The police and the public use the term [*gang*] to refer to organized groups of young adults engaged in a wide variety of criminal behavior, including drug dealing, assaults, drive-by shootings and a host of other violent and property crimes."

The Chicago Police Department (*Gang Awareness*, n.d., p.1) defines a gang as "a group which has an organizational structure, leadership and . . . exists or benefits substantially from the criminal activity of its members." A **gang** is a group of individuals with a recognized name and symbols who form an allegiance for a common purpose and engage in unlawful activity.

A definition commonly accepted by law enforcement is that a gang is any group gathering continuously to commit antisocial behavior. But as Esbensen et al. (2001b, p.124) caution: "Obviously the definition used greatly affects the perceived magnitude of the gang problem. By restricting gang membership status to gangs that are involved in delinquent activity and have some level of organization, we reduce the size of the gang problem substantially." According to Weisel

(2003, p.275): "Although increasingly defined by statute, the terms 'gang,' 'gang member' and 'gang-related crime' mean different things to different police departments. The selection of definitions may result in over- or underestimation of the nature and extent of the local gang problem."

Langston (2003, p.8) urges: "Adoption of a uniform [definition] would benefit the entire law enforcement community in several ways." In addition to differing definitions for gangs, understanding the threat of gangs is made more complex because of the numerous categories that have been established.

Types of Gangs

Shelden et al. (2004, pp.42–43) describe the major types of gangs identified in various studies by different researchers nationwide:

- **Hedonistic/social gangs**—only moderate drug use and offending, involved mainly in using drugs and having a good time; little involvement in crime, especially violent crime.
- **Party gangs**—commonly called "party crews"; relatively high use and sale of drugs, but only one major form of delinquency—vandalism; may contain both genders or may be one gender; many have no specific dress style, but some dress in stylized clothing worn by street gang members, such as baseball caps and oversize clothing; some have tattoos and use hand signs; their flexible turf is called the "party scene"; crews compete over who throws the biggest party, with alcohol, marijuana, nitrous oxide, sex and music critical party elements.
- **Instrumental gangs**—main criminal activity is property crimes (most use drugs and alcohol but seldom sell drugs).
- **Predatory gangs**—heavily involved in serious crimes (robberies, muggings) and the abuse of addictive drugs such as crack cocaine; may engage in selling drugs but not in organized fashion.
- **Scavenger gangs**—loosely organized groups described as "urban survivors"; prey on the weak in inner cities; engage in rather petty crimes but sometimes violence, often just for fun; members have no greater bond than their impulsiveness and need to belong; lack goals and are low achievers; often illiterate with poor school performance.
- **Serious delinquent gangs**—heavy involvement in both serious and minor crimes, but much lower involvement in drug use and drug sales than party gangs.
- **Territorial gangs**—associated with a specific area or turf and, as a result, often involved in conflicts with other gangs over their respective turfs.
- **Organized/corporate gangs**—heavy involvement in all kinds of crime, heavy use and sale of drugs; may resemble major corporations, with separate divisions handling sales, marketing, discipline and so on; discipline is strict, and promotion is based on merit.
- **Drug gangs**—smaller than other gangs; much more cohesive; focused on the drug business; strong, centralized leadership with market-defined roles.

Many of the preceding gangs can also be classified as street gangs in contrast to the last category above, the drug gang. Table 9.1 summarizes the common differences between street gangs and drug gangs.

Table 9.1 Common Differences between Street Gangs and Drug Gangs

Characteristic	Street Gangs	Drug Gangs
Crime focus	Versatile ("cafeteria-style")	Drug business exclusively
Structure	Larger organizations	Smaller organizations
Level of cohesion	Less cohesive	More cohesive
Leadership	Looser	More centralized
Roles	Ill-defined	Market-defined
Nature of loyalty	Code of loyalty	Requirement of loyalty
Territories	Residential	Sales market
Degree of drug selling	Members may sell	Members do sell
Rivalries	Intergang	Competition controlled
Age of members	Younger on average, but wider age range	Older average, but narrower age range

SOURCE: *The American Street Gang* by Malcolm Klein © 1995 by Oxford University Press, Inc. Used by permission of Oxford University Press, Inc.

Racial or Ethnic Gangs

Most gangs are racially or ethnically homogeneous, comprised of members who share the same language, cultural background and, frequently, heritage.

Hispanic Gangs

Between 1910 and 1925, a great influx of immigrants arrived from Mexico. These immigrants tended to live with others from their native areas of Mexico, and rivalries developed that eventually resulted in the formation of gangs, such as Bunker Hill, Mara Villa and San Fernando. These Hispanic gangs lived in barrios that often could trace their heritage back several generations. They had a strong system of tradition and became known as **traditional gangs.**

The depression of the 1930s brought Latino families from Arizona, New Mexico and Texas to Los Angeles. They fragmented into groups, each claiming its own territory and forming such gangs as Happy Valley, HoyoSoto, Alpine Hazard and White Fence. In the 1960s freeway displacement drove families from the central city eastward, where they created more new gangs, such as Lomas and Bassett.

Today, Hispanic gangs are comprised of not only Chicanos, a term reserved for those from Mexico, but also Puerto Ricans, Cubans and individuals from various Central and South American countries. Despite the diversity within the Hispanic gang community as a whole, individual gangs tend to remain ethnically homogeneous. Researchers Lopez and Brummett (2003, p.627) report on empirical evidence supporting **choloization,** that is, asserting a Chicano identity, having pride in this identity and denying being Americanized. According to their research, gang members have more of a Mexican orientation than nongang members. Valdez (2001b, p.49) notes Hispanic street gangs are the fastest-growing type of gang in the United States today.

African American Gangs

African American street gangs also existed in the Los Angeles area for many years. They began as groups of young high school "thugs" who extorted money from students and terrorized teachers. One gang, calling itself the Crips, had the reputation of being the toughest African American gang in Los Angeles, so other gangs began incorporating the word "Crip" into their names. Although these gangs shared a common name, they were in reality independent, and rivalries developed. Another group of African American youths began to get together for protection from attacks by Crip sets. They called themselves the Compton Pirus and are believed to be the first gang to borrow the term *blood brothers* and apply it to their gang name. Thus began the division of African American gangs into the **Crips** and the non-Crips or **Bloods.** According to Shelden et al. (p.54) Crips currently outnumber Bloods by about three to one in Los Angeles.

Asian Gangs

In the early 1900s, secret fraternal organizations called the Tongs used boys called Wah Chings as lookouts. As the Tongs became more legitimate and established, they no longer needed the Wah Chings. The Wah Chings, however, refused to disband, taking up where the Tongs left off.

Although the Tongs are now primarily benevolent societies, when necessary they will resort to violence through the Wah Chings. Eventually differences developed within the Wah Chings, and they split into two groups, with the older members becoming known as Yu Li, while the younger members retained the name Wah Ching.

A member of the Yu Li named Joe Fong became disenchanted with the Yu Li and broke off into another gang called the Joe Fong gang or Joe Boys. The massacre at the Golden Dragon restaurant in 1967 occurred when the Joe Fong gang attacked the Wah Ching gang. All three gangs, the Wah Chings, Yu Lis and Joe Boys, exist today and have spread to most major cities of the United States and Canada.

As with Hispanic gangs, ethnic diversity exists among Asian gangs. For example, Vietnamese gangs, described by Krott (2001, p.100), are a "small, but noticeably vicious minority of the Vietnamese community." Says Krott: "Vietnamese gangs are well known for their mobility and the typical gang consists of males and females, usually runaways, 13 to 25 years old with a propensity towards violence." Further: "They are survival criminals with no long-term goals, and no attachments or allegiances to anything except each other. These are some of the most violent criminals on the American streets."

A new breed of Asian gang is the home invaders, whose well-armed and well-organized members specialize in home robberies of other Asians. The targeting of Asian victims by Asian gang members is relatively common, because of a general unwillingness among the Asian community to report victimization to the police.

Another relatively new Asian gang is the Hmong gang. Straka (2003, p.12) reports: "Throughout the United States, the number of Hmong gangs and the level of their criminal activity is increasing in severity. Their participation in criminal activity has evolved over time. During that evolution, they have become involved in a wide range of crimes, such as homicides, gang rapes, prostitution, home invasions, burglaries, auto thefts and, most recently, the sale and distribution of illicit drugs. The crime of rape, however, with its violent nature, its strong incorporation into the gang's operational structure and the serious implications for the victim and the overall Hmong community, represents a particular concern to the law enforcement profession." Straka (p.16) stresses: "Networking among law enforcement agencies throughout the country is imperative due to the mobility of Hmong gangs."

White Ethnic Gangs

Valdez (2002b, p.90) notes: "White supremacist 'gangs' have been around in the United States since the Ku Klux Klan was founded in 1866." White ethnic gangs are composed primarily of European American members. Neo-Nazi skinheads are perhaps the best known white ethnic gang, with members who are militantly racist and advocate white supremacy. The Aryan Youth Movement (AYM) and White Aryan Resistance (WAR) are groups also aligned by racism. White "stoner" gangs emphasize the occult and satanic rituals. White ethnic gangs typically engage in hate crimes directed at other ethnic and religious groups and those with "alternative" lifestyles. They may attack blacks, Hispanics, Jews or homosexuals. According to Walker et al. (2004, p.58): "Skinheads are unique in the sense that they use violence not to protect turf, protect a drug market, or commit robberies but rather for the explicit purpose of promoting political change by instilling fear in innocent people."

Motorcycle Gangs

Weisel (2003, p.285) notes: "Outlaw motorcycle gangs originated in California after World War II. Today there are four primary gangs: Hell's Angels, Outlaws, Pagans and Bandidos with an estimated 8,000 members in 850 chapters throughout the nation." Valdez (2001a, p.46) describes outlaw motorcycle gangs as among the "most dynamic gangs worldwide," influencing the drug trade and using extortion, white slavery and money laundering. He estimates there are more than 1,000 motorcycle gangs in the United States and Canada. They have become "prolific traders in the drug market," and, as Valdez (p.48) cautions: "Motorcycle gangs involved in meth trafficking are going to be organized and will exhibit a willingness to use violence to accomplish their objectives." While the image of the biker gang member remains one of a leather-and-denim rough-and-tough guy, the reality today is that many members of such gangs are well-educated, some holding college-level degrees in finance, business and law to improve the gang's profitability.

Prison Gangs

According to Weisel (2003, p.285): "Prison-based gangs, such as the Mexican Mafia, Nuestra Familia, Aryan Brotherhood, Black Guerilla Family, Texas Syndicate and Consolidated Crip Organization, have close ties to street gangs. Their leaders may serve as 'shot callers' for street gangs, coordinating drug trafficking, extortion, intimidation, gambling and other activities from prison." Weisel reports: "The dangerous link between the prison gang and the community is furthered when gang members are released. Prison gangs traffic in drugs in and out of the prison system. These gangs are also active in prostitution, extortion, protection and murder for hire."

Other Types of Gangs

Filipino neighborhood street gangs are similar to Hispanic gangs and may gravitate toward Mexican gangs. The most common Filipino gangs are the Santanas, the Tabooes and Temple Street. The Korean community also has active gangs, the most well known being the Korean Killers. Furthermore it has been noted that Native American gangs are also spreading throughout the country. Table 9.2

Table 9.2   Criminal Organizations

Type of group	Groups	Criminal activity
Chinese street gangs, Tongs and Triads	Ghost Shadows, Flying Dragons, Wah Ching, United Bamboo, Ping On, Fuk Ching, White Tigers, Taiwan Brotherhood	Heroin distribution, smuggling of humans and exploitation of new immigrants; extortion of Chinese businesses, street taxes; gambling.
Drug-trafficking gangs	Bloods, Crips, Gangster Disciples, Latin Kings and many others	Trafficking of heroin, cocaine, crack and other drugs; violence; arson; indirect prostitution; vandalism, property crime; strong-arm robbery. African American gangs known for crack; Chicano gangs known for heroin and crack.
Graffiti or tagger crews (also tagger posses, mobs, tribes and piecers)	Known by three-letter monikers such as NBT (Nothing But Trouble) or ETC (Elite Tagger Crew)	Graffiti vandalism; tag-banging in which violence occurs.
Hate groups (terrorist groups, including militias, are closely related to hate groups. All share a focus on ideology.)	Aryan Nation, Ku Klux Klan, skinheads (White Aryan Resistance), American Nazi Party, Christian Defense League	Violence; counterfeiting; bombings; loan fraud; armored car and bank robberies; theft rings.
Japanese gangs (Yakuza or Boryokudan)	Yamaguchi Gumi, Kumiai, Sumiyoshi Rengo	Gambling; prostitution and sex trade; trafficking in weapons and narcotics; management of foreign criminal investments in American corporations; money laundering.
Jamaican posses	Shower posse, Spangler posse	Trafficking of cocaine, crack and marijuana; weapons trafficking; known for gratuitous violence; trafficking green cards.
Korean gangs	Flying Dragons, Korean Power, Junior Korean Power, AB (American Burger), KK (Korean Killers)	Prostitution, massage parlors, exploitation of women for nude and topless bars; extortion of Korean businesses, especially green grocers, produce markets and restaurants; gambling; loansharking.
La Cosa Nostra	Families such as Bonnano, Gambino and Genovese	Gambling, loansharking, corrupting public institutions and officers; money laundering; theft of precious metals, food and clothing; fencing stolen property; labor racketeering; stock manipulation; murder; securities fraud.
Latin American gangs (Cuban, Mexican, Colombian, Peruvian, El Salvadoran and others)	Medellin, Cali cartels; Arellano-Felix organization, Amezcua Contreras brothers, Amado Carillo Fuentes group, Caro Quintero organization	Trafficking of cocaine, crack, heroin, marijuana; counterfeiting; pickpocketing; murder; money laundering into real estate.
Nigerian gangs	NCE (Nigerian Criminal Enterprise)	Use of mules for heroin smuggling and heroin dealing; infiltrate private security: planned bankruptcy of companies; credit card fraud; exploitation of other Africans.
Outlaw motorcycle gangs	Hell's Angels, Outlaws, Pagans, Bandidos	Trafficking in methamphetamine (crank), speed, ice, PCP angel dust, LSD; chop shops; massage parlors; strip bars; prostitution; weapons trafficking; arson.
Prison gangs	Mexican Mafia, Nuestra Familia, Consolidated Crip Organization, Aryan Brotherhood, Black Guerilla Family, Texas Syndicate	Drug trafficking; prostitution; extortion; protection; murder for hire.
Russian (or Soviet) gangs	Odessa Mafia, Evangelical Russian Mafia, Malina/Organizatsiya, Gypsy gangs	Theft of diamonds, furs, gold and fencing stolen goods; extortion; insurance fraud; export and sale of stolen Russian religious art and gold; counterfeiting; daisy chain tax evasion schemes; credit card scams; smuggling illegal immigrants; drug trafficking; money laundering.
Street gangs (African American, Hispanic, Caucasian, and others)	Variants of Bloods/Crips such as Westside or Rolling Crips, Latin Kings, Disciples, Vice Lords, Dog Pound and many others	Motor vehicle theft; drug sales (especially crack and marijuana); weapons trafficking; assaults; drive-by shootings; robbery; theft and fencing stolen property; vandalism, graffiti; and burglaries.
Vietnamese gangs	Born to Kill (BTK)	Strong arm and violent crimes related to business extortion; home invasion for theft of gold, jewelry and money coupled with rape to deter reporting; prostitution.

Note: Although nationality and ethnicity are often unifying characteristics of criminal organizations and used to identify them, this view is overly narrow and promotes ethnic stereotypes. The organization of criminal groups by nationality and ethnicity in this table is not intended to suggest that criminal behavior is characteristic of any group; ethnicity, however, is often a marker to police.

SOURCE: Deborah Lamm Weisel. "Criminal Investigation." In *Local Government Police Management,* edited by William A. Geller and Darrel W. Stephens. Washington, DC: International City/County Management Association, 2003, p.270. Reprinted by permission.

describes several types of criminal organizations, most of which are gangs, listing their names and the types of criminal activity they engage in.

While a majority of gangs remain ethnically or racially homogeneous and limited to members of the same gender, hybrid gangs are growing in number.

Hybrid Gangs

Beginning in the early 1990s, it was noted that some gangs in Southern California were admitting females and persons of other races as members. Valdez (2001b, p.49) affirms: "Hybrid gangs are encountered with increasing frequency. These gangs often have a mixed race or multi-ethnic membership which can include female members."

Starbuck et al. (2001, p.1) describe the hybrid gang: "Hybrid gang culture is characterized by mixed racial and ethnic participation within a single gang, participation in multiple gangs by a single individual, vague rules and codes of conduct for gang members, use of symbols and colors from multiple—even rival—gangs, collaboration by rival gangs in criminal activities and the merger of smaller gangs into larger ones. Thus, hybrid gang customs are clearly distinguished from the practices of their predecessors."

Howell et al. (2002, p.7) also note: "Many of the gangs that have sprung up relatively recently throughout the country may not follow the same traditional rules or methods of operation as their predecessors from Los Angeles or Chicago. For example, these newer gangs may adopt symbols from both Chicago- and Los Angeles-based gangs, they may not have an allegiance to a traditional 'color,' they may change the gang name, members may change their affiliation from one gang to another or belong to more than one gang, and two or more gangs may suddenly merge and form a new gang."

Females and Gangs

Females may be part of an entirely female gang, participants in a coed gang or auxiliary members of a predominantly male gang. A female gang may have a name affiliated with its male counterpart, such as the Vice Ladies (from the Vice Lords). These auxiliaries usually consist of sisters and girlfriends of the male gang members. The females often assist the male gang, serving as decoys for rival gang members, as lookouts during the commission of crimes or as carriers of weapons when a gang war is impending. They may also carry information in and out of prison and provide sexual favors (they are often drug dependent and physically abused).

Research by Jody Miller (2001) found that compared to nongang girls, gang girls commit significantly more crime, but significantly less than their male counterparts. Only one-third of the gang girls in Miller's study reported an ongoing engagement in serious crime. Although guns are the preferred weapon of male gang members, female gang members prefer knives and fists. For the gang girls who choose to participate in criminal activity, the reasons for their involvement and the circumstances in which crime is committed mirror those of their male counterparts. Miller also found that gang girls have a significantly higher rate of exposure to violence than nongang girls, with the rate twice as high for gang girls. Further, the rate of being victimized was 250 to 300 percent higher for gang girls than for nongang girls.

Characteristics of Gangs

Five general characteristics are often associated with gangs.

 Distinguishing characteristics of gangs include leadership, organization, associational patterns, domain identification and illegal activity.

Leadership

In some gangs leadership is quite well defined and may be one of three types: (1) key personality, (2) chain of command or (3) collective. In the key personality leadership gang, one gang member, often older than the others and from the ranks of the hard-core membership, is a strong, influential leader. He becomes a role model for other gang members.

In a gang with a chain-of-command form of leadership, the gang functions like a military unit or even a police department. Each member within the group has a specific rank, with authority going from the top down.

In a gang with a collective leadership style, leaders change depending on the gang activity. If the gang is planning a crime, the best criminal mind is leader. If they are planning an attack on a neighboring gang, the best fighter is leader.

Organization

Some gangs are quite formally organized. One common organizational element is age, with many gangs typically having two to four age divisions. Another common organizational element is location; two or more gangs may have localized versions of the same gang name, for example the Southside Warriors and the Tenth Street Warriors. Gangs also tend to have a hierarchical authority, as described in the "Leadership" section. Miller and Hess (2002, p.249) note: "The hard-core members who hold leadership positions pose a threat to the community and the police because (1) they typically possess guns and other weapons, and (2) they tend to be aggressively anti-social and are encouraged to be so by the gang as long as their behavior does not violate gang rules or discipline."

In addition to hard-core members, most gangs have a *marginal membership*, a much larger group that surrounds the hard-core members. Hard-core members are recruited from the marginal membership.

Another term for those on the fringes of gangs are **wannabes**—youths who aspire to become gang members, who dress and talk like gang members, but who have not yet been accepted by the gang. Gangs are also on the lookout for "potentials" or "could be's," youths with dysfunctional families, those failing in school, those in trouble with the law and those living in impoverished neighborhoods born into an environment of street gang activity. Figure 9.1 illustrates the typical progression of youths in becoming hard-core members. It is from this group that the leaders emerge. They are the oldest group members and usually have extensive criminal records. They expect unquestioned obedience from all gang members.

Gang organization may vary considerably from gang to gang and from region to region. Many street gangs have a prison affiliate, and vice versa. Weisel (2003, p.77) studied whether street gangs were "metamorphosing into criminal

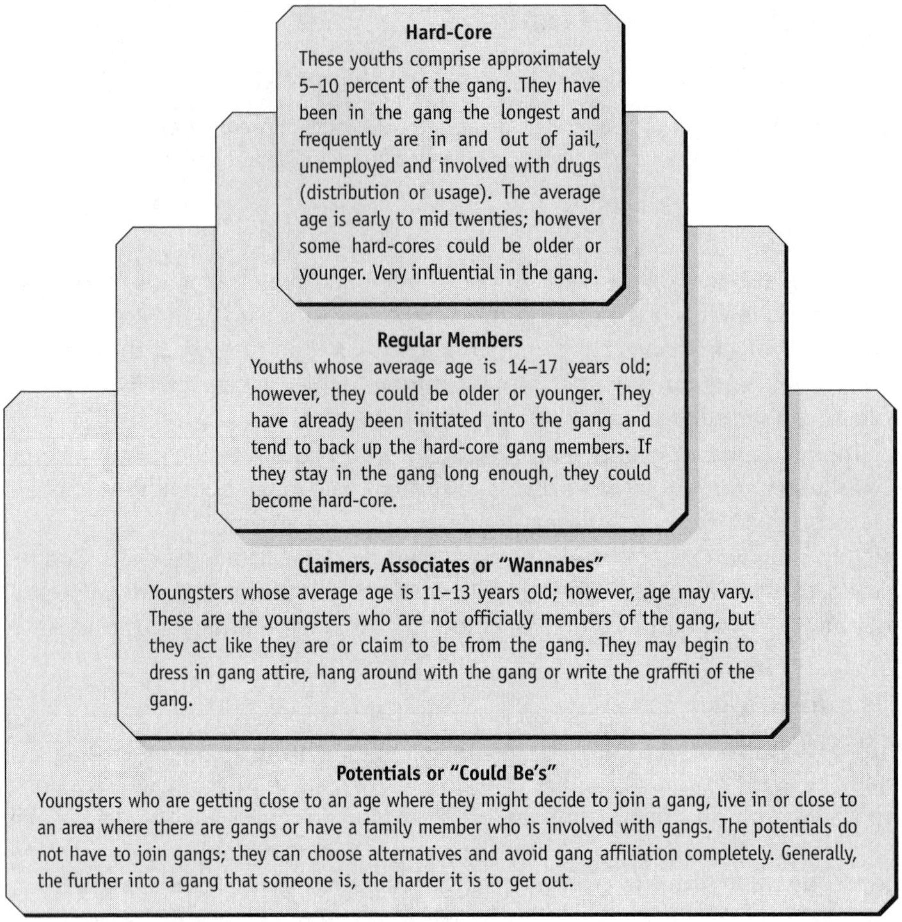

Hard-Core
These youths comprise approximately 5–10 percent of the gang. They have been in the gang the longest and frequently are in and out of jail, unemployed and involved with drugs (distribution or usage). The average age is early to mid twenties; however some hard-cores could be older or younger. Very influential in the gang.

Regular Members
Youths whose average age is 14–17 years old; however, they could be older or younger. They have already been initiated into the gang and tend to back up the hard-core gang members. If they stay in the gang long enough, they could become hard-core.

Claimers, Associates or "Wannabes"
Youngsters whose average age is 11–13 years old; however, age may vary. These are the youngsters who are not officially members of the gang, but they act like they are or claim to be from the gang. They may begin to dress in gang attire, hang around with the gang or write the graffiti of the gang.

Potentials or "Could Be's"
Youngsters who are getting close to an age where they might decide to join a gang, live in or close to an area where there are gangs or have a family member who is involved with gangs. The potentials do not have to join gangs; they can choose alternatives and avoid gang affiliation completely. Generally, the further into a gang that someone is, the harder it is to get out.

Figure 9.1   Progression into a Hard-Core Gang Member

enterprises and large, highly organized structures." In her study of Chicago and San Diego gangs, she reported:

> Little specialization of roles and organization in the gangs was identified. Instead there was a wide range of gang types with various structures and a great variety of criminal activities. Even though some gangs were large and had existed for many years, and even though some gangs exhibited some features of highly structured organizations, overall there was little evidence of evolution into formal organizations resembling traditional organized crime. Instead, the gangs appeared to represent an adaptive or organic form of organization, featuring diffuse leadership and continuity despite the absence of hierarchy. Gangs in both cities experienced considerable organizational change over time—consolidating, merging, acquiring smaller gangs, reorganizing and splintering. Their "generalist" orientation may have contributed to their ability to adapt to these changes and survive in a volatile environment. The criminal versatility of gangs suggests that law enforcement directed at particular criminal behavior will work primarily for gangs that are specialized, but most are not; and enforcement and prosecution directed at targeting gang leadership may be suitable only to the few gangs that have distinctive leadership patterns.

Domain Identification

Typically gangs stake out a geographic territory, or **turf,** as their domain. This may be a specific facility, such as a school, or it may be an entire neighborhood. If one gang trespasses on another gang's turf, gang violence is likely. Some gangs claim exclusive control over certain activities in an area, such as the right to collect fees from students for using the restrooms or "insurance" payments from local merchants in exchange for protection.

Criminal Activity

Research indicates that most gang members already were committing crimes before they joined a gang, but their delinquency rates increase dramatically after joining a gang. Gang-related crimes are typically violent and often involve firearms. Violence may be used against members within a gang if it is feared that a member will betray the gang's code of silence by talking to police. Drive-by shootings are also relatively common.

Weisel (2002, p.35) conducted a national survey of police departments and found that specific gang types tended to favor certain types of crime: "Entrepreneurial gangs were reported to have the highest involvement in motor vehicle theft and theft in general, whereas violent gangs had the highest involvement in assault, intimidation, graffiti and vandalism. As expected, drug-dealing gangs were the most involved in selling crack, powder cocaine, marijuana and other drugs." Table 9.3 summarizes Weisel's findings regarding criminal gang activity.

Identifying Gangs and Gang Members

Walker (Gangs OR Us Web site) suggests: "The presence of gangs may be seen everywhere. Gang members do not represent an invisible empire. They thrive on recognition and are constantly seeking ways to make their presence known or felt. They only go unseen when law enforcement personnel, as well as educators and parents, fail to recognize the signs of gang activity and an individual's involvement."

 Gangs and gang members might be identified by their names; their symbols (clothing, colors and tattoos); how they communicate, including graffiti and sign language; and their activities.

Indicators of gang activity have already been described, including drive-by shootings, intimidation assaults, murders and the open sale of drugs.

Names

Gang *names* vary from colorful and imaginative to straightforward. They commonly refer to localities, Tenth Streeters; animals, Cobras; royalty, Kings; rebellion, Rebels; leaders, Garcia's Boys; or a combination of these elements, West Side Warlords. Individual gang members also often have colorful street names or **monikers.**

Symbols

Gang *symbols* are common. Clothing, in particular, can distinguish a particular gang. Sometimes "colors" are used to distinguish a gang. Gang members also use

Table 9.3   Criminal Activity by Gang Type

Crime	Percent of Police Who Report That Violent Gangs Commit the Offense Very Often or Often (n = 223)	Percent of Police Who Report That Drug-Dealing Gangs Commit the Offense Very Often or Often (n = 148)	Percent of Police Who Report That Entrepreneurial Gangs Commit the Offense Very Often or Often (n = 75)
Motor vehicle theft	25	25	44
Arson	1	1	1
Assault	87	69	57
Burglary	36	25	37
Drive-by shooting	42	49	32
Crack sale	55	80	39
Powder cocaine sale	23	46	29
Marijuana sale	35	54	33
Other drug sale	17	26	25
Graffiti	67	50	38
Home invasion	10	11	27
Intimidation	81	72	74
Rape	7	4	8
Robbery	33	30	36
Shooting	37	41	38
Theft	49	37	52
Vandalism	57	38	37

Note: Reflects aggregation of police estimates of participation in criminal activity by a gang of that type in the jurisdiction.

SOURCE: Deborah Lamm Weisel. "The Evolution of Street Gangs: An Examination of Form and Variation." In *Responding to Gangs: Evaluation and Research.* Washington, DC: National Institute of Justice, July 2002, p.36 (NCJ 190351)

jerseys, T-shirts and jackets with emblems. However, some gangs, such as Asian gangs, seldom have a particular dress code, making identification difficult.

Tattoos are also used by some gangs, particularly outlaw motorcycle gangs and Hispanic gangs. African American gang members seldom have tattoos.

Communication

Graffiti is a common form of communication used by gang members, frequently to stake out a gang's turf. Graffiti is sometimes called the "newspaper of the street." Defacing, erasing or substituting one gang's graffiti by a rival gang constitutes a challenge and usually results in violence and gang warfare:

> Much valuable information relative to police work may be gained from gang graffiti. For instance, one may be able to determine what gang is in control of a specific area by noting the frequency of the unchallenged graffiti. . . . Writing left unchanged reaffirms the gang's control. As one moves away from the center or core area of a gang's power and territory, the more rival graffiti and cross-outs are observed (*Street Gangs of Los Angeles County,* n.d.).

Gang members communicate via graffiti and hand signals. They also often wear certain colors or items of clothing to identify themselves as members of a particular gang.

This Los Angeles White Paper also notes that African American and Latino styles of graffiti are vastly different, with the African American graffiti lacking the flair and attention to detail evidenced by the Latino gang graffiti. Much of the African American gang wall writing is filled with profanity.

Graffiti artists, known as *taggers,* may act individually or be part of tag crews, which are separate from traditional street gangs. As the number of taggers and crews has grown, competition for "wall space" has increased. Once crews begin placing their graffiti within turf claimed by traditional gangs, violent confrontations occur, and taggers, once a relatively peaceful group, find themselves in need of protection from street gang violence.

Another form of communication typical of gang members is hand signals. A person often uses these signs to indicate that he is with a specific gang.

Criteria for Identifying Gang Members

Lists of criteria are often used to determine if an individual is a gang member. An individual usually must meet a certain number of criteria to be certified as a gang member. In Minnesota, for example, at least three of the following eight elements are necessary to classify someone as a gang member:

- Admitted gang membership, regular association with gang members or being arrested with known gang members
- Tattoos indicating gang membership or clothes with symbols associated with specific gangs
- Appearance in photographs with known gang members
- Appearance in photographs showing use of gang-related hand signs
- Name presence in gang-related graffiti or in gang documents
- Identification by a reliable source
- Correspondence with known gang members
- Being mentioned in writing about gangs (Weisel, 2003, pp.275–276)

Table 9.4   Criteria for Defining Gangs

Criteria Used	Large Cities* (Percent)	Smaller Cities* (Percent)
Use of symbols	93	100
Violent behavior	81	84
Group organization	81	88
Territory	74	88
Leadership	59	78
Recurrent interaction	56	80

*Of the cities surveyed 70 (89 percent) of the large cities and 25 (58 percent) of the smaller cities indicated the criteria used to define gangs.

SOURCE: G. David Curry et al. *Gang Crime and Law Enforcement Recordkeeping*. Washington, DC: National Institute of Justice Research in Brief, August 1994, p.7. Data from NIJ: Gang Survey.

Table 9.4 shows the criteria some departments use to identify the presence of gangs.

Stereotypes

While generalized descriptions and categorization of gangs and gang members help law enforcement deal with the gang problem, Howell (2000, pp.49–50) says studies have produced findings that contradict many of the traditional stereotypes of youth gangs:

- The gangs, drugs and violence connection appears to apply more to adult drug and criminal gangs than to youth gangs.
- The seemingly intractable connection of gangs, drugs and violence is not as strong among youth gangs as suggested by traditional stereotypes.
- It is not as difficult for adolescents to resist gang pressures as commonly believed. In most instances, adolescents can refuse to join gangs without reprisal.
- Gang members (especially marginal members) typically can leave the gang without serious consequences.
- At least in emerging gang areas, most adolescents do not remain in gangs for long periods, suggesting that members can be drawn away from gangs with attractive alternatives.
- Contemporary legends about gangs, especially initiation rites, are without scientific basis.
- Modern gangs make less use of symbols, including gang names, clothing and traditional initiation rites, than gangs of the past, and the meaning of their graffiti is sometimes murky or unclear.
- Drug franchising is not the principal driving force behind gang migration.

The Gang Subculture

Taken together, the many characteristics of gangs just described form a gang subculture. According to Miller and Hess (p.250): "A gang member's lifestyle is narrow and limited primarily to the gang and its activities. . . . Members develop fierce loyalty to their respective gang and become locked into the gang's lifestyle, values, attitudes and behavior."

Shelden et al. (p.69) state: "Youth gangs constitute a unique subculture in modern society. . . . They have their own unique set of values, norms, lifestyles and beliefs." These values, norms, lifestyles and beliefs are often found in a gang code of behavior, which may include the requirement to always wear gang colors, to get a tattoo representing the gang, and, if arrested, to never reveal anything about the gang, as there is no lower life form than a "snitch." To the gang members themselves, the idea of a gang is quite simple. As one gang member said: "Well, in my words, a gang ain't nothing but people come together to do crime and make money and be a family to each other. That's the original idea" (Weisel, 2003, p.47). This simple explanation provides insight into why people join gangs.

Why People Join Gangs

Domash (2001, p.49) contends: "Why children join gangs is a complicated combination of social, political, family, educational and community factors." The most frequently cited reason for people joining gangs is to *belong*. The close ties of gang members are a major motive for membership. Most gang members are underachievers who come from broken homes or homes with no strong male authority figure, and membership provides both psychological and physical security.

 The most common reasons for joining a gang are for belonging, identity or recognition, protection, fellowship and brotherhood or to make money.

According to Shelden et al. (p.151), the literature confirms that females become involved in gang life for generally the same reasons as males: "A sense of belonging (family-like), power, protection, respect, fear and, sometimes paranoia." They (p.157) say: "What emerges from a review of research on girl gangs is a portrait of young women who, just like their male counterparts, find themselves trapped in horrible social conditions, characterized by widespread poverty and racism." Moore and Hagedorn (2001, p.3) add that the gang is often a refuge for young women victimized at home.

In our society of instant gratification, where happiness and success are often measured by the amount of money one has, it is hard to convince a youth who's making $1,000 a week guarding a crack house that he ought to be getting up at 4 A.M. every day to deliver newspapers. Shelden et al. have an entire chapter entitled: "Gangs in Context: Inequality in American Society," which states (pp.228–229): "Under American capitalism, the 'free market' is largely a myth, and a 'surplus population' is constantly being created and reproduced. Most criminal activity of gang members is consistent with basic capitalist values, such as the law of supply and demand, the need to make money (profit), and the desire to accumulate consumer goods." They identify other factors contributing to the formation of gangs as changes in the labor market, the development of an underclass and isolation in inner cities. They (p.208) conclude:

 Unemployment, poverty and general despair lead young people to seek out economic opportunities in the growing illegal marketplace, often done within the context of gangs.

Criminologists have proposed other theoretical reasons for why people join gangs, summarized in Table 9.5.

In addition to looking at *why* people join gangs, predisposing or risk factors should be considered.

Table 9.5   Theories Regarding Why Gangs Exist

Theory	*Major Points/Key Factors*
1. Social disorganization	Crime stems from certain community or neighborhood characteristics, such as poverty, dilapidated housing, high density, high mobility and high rates of unemployment. Concentric zone theory is a variation that argues that crime increases toward the inner city area.
2. Strain/anomie	Cultural norms of "success" emphasize such goals as money, status and power, while the means to obtain such success are not equally distributed. As a result of blocked opportunities many among the disadvantaged resort to illegal means, which are more readily available.
3. Cultural-deviance	Certain subcultures, including a gang subculture, exist within poor communities, which contain values, attitudes, beliefs, norms and so on that are often counter to the prevailing middle class culture. An important feature of this culture is the absence of fathers, thus resulting in female-headed households which tend to be poorer. Youths get exposed to this subculture early in life and become embedded in it.
4. Control/social bond	Delinquency persists when a youth's "bonds" or "ties" to society are weak or broken, especially bonds with family, school and other institutions. When this occurs a youth is apt to seek bonds with other groups, including gangs, in order to get his/her needs met.
5. Learning	Delinquency is learned through association with others, especially gang members, over a period of time. This involves a process that includes the acquisition of attitudes and values, the instigation of a criminal act based on certain stimuli and the maintenance or perpetuation of such behavior over time.
6. Labeling	Definitions of delinquency and crime stem from differences in power and status in the larger society, and those without power are the most likely to have their behaviors labeled as "delinquency." Delinquency may be generated, and especially perpetuated, through negative labeling by significant others and by the judicial system. One may associate with others similarly labeled, such as gangs.
7. Rational choice	People freely choose to commit crime based on self-interest because they are goal oriented and want to maximize their pleasure and minimize their pain. A variation is known as routine activities theory, which suggests that criminals plan very carefully by selecting specific targets based on such things as vulnerability (e.g., elderly citizens, unguarded premises, lack of police presence) and commit their crimes accordingly. However, choices are often based not on pure reason and rationality.
8. Critical/Marxist	Gangs are inevitable products of social (and racial) inequality brought about by capitalism itself. Power is unequally distributed, and those without power often resort to criminal means to survive.

SOURCE: Randall G. Shelden, Sharon K. Tracy and William B. Brown. *Youth Gangs in American Society,* 3rd ed. Belmont, CA: Wadsworth Publishing Company, 2004, p.178. Reprinted by permission.

Risk Factors

Shelden et al. (p.224) identify what they believe to be the most critical factor related to crime and delinquency:

> Nearly every criminologist agrees that the family is probably the most critical factor related to crime and delinquency. In fact, for over 50 years, research has shown that three or four key family-related factors best distinguish the habitual delinquent from the rest of his or her peers. These factors include the affection of the parents toward the child (the lower the level of affection, the higher the rate of delinquency), the kind of discipline the parents use (those who use consistently harsh and physical discipline will produce the most habitual and violent delinquent), the prolonged absence of one or both parents (those from single parent households are more likely to become delinquent), and the degree of supervision provided by the parents (the lesser the amount of supervision, the higher the rate of delinquency).

 Family structure is probably the most important risk factor in the formation of a gang member.

Investigators have found certain common threads running through most families having hard-core gang members. The family is often a racial minority receiving some form of government assistance. It often lacks a male authority figure, or the male figure may be a criminal or drug addict and, therefore, a negative role model. Children live with minimal adult supervision.

When one child first encounters law enforcement authorities, the dominant figure (usually the mother) makes excuses for the child, often accusing society. Thus children are taught early that they are not responsible for their actions and are shown how to transfer blame to society.

A second common family structure is one with two strong family leaders in a mother and father. Usually graduates from gangs themselves, they see little wrong with their children belonging to gangs. This is known as assembly-line production of gang members.

A third common family structure is where the parents are non-English speaking. The children tend to adapt rapidly to the American way of life and, in doing so, lose respect for their parents and the "old ways." They become experts at manipulating their parents, and the parents lose all control. Many of these structures overlap. Hill et al. (2001, p.4) summarize the risk factors for youth gang membership. (See Table 9.6.)

Miller (2002, p.69) reports: "Research has shown that young women join gangs to solve myriad problems in their lives, but gang involvement tends to exacerbate the situation, increasing the likelihood they will engage in delinquency and exposing them to victimization by rival gangs and fellow gang members." Miller's study revealed three themes regarding girls joining gangs (p.76):

> The first theme was girls' neighborhood contexts and their exposure to gangs through neighborhood peer networks. A second theme was the existence of severe family problems, such as violence and drug abuse, which decreased parental supervision and led young women to avoid home and to meet their social and emotional needs elsewhere. Finally, many young women described

Table 9.6 Childhood Predictors of Joining and Remaining in a Gang, SSDP Sample

Risk Factor	Odds Ratio*	Risk Factor	Odds Ratio*
Neighborhood		**Individual**	
Availability of marijuana	3.6	Low religious service attendance	ns[‡]
Neighborhood youth in trouble	3.0	Early marijuana use	3.7
Low neighborhood attachment	1.5	Early violence[§]	3.1 (2.4)
Family		Antisocial beliefs	2.0
Family structure[†]		Early drinking	1.6
One parent only	2.4	Externalizing behaviors[§]	2.6 (2.6)
One parent plus other adults	3.0	Poor refusal skills	1.8
Parental attitudes favoring violence	2.3		
Low bonding with parents	ns[‡]	
Low household income	2.1	
Sibling antisocial behavior	1.9	
Poor family management	1.7	
School		
Learning disabled	3.6	
Low academic achievement	3.1	
Low school attachment	2.0	
Low school commitment	1.8	
Low academic aspirations	1.6	
Peer group		
Association with friends who engage in problem behaviors[§]	2.0 (2.3)	

* Odds of joining a gang between the ages of 13 and 18 for youth who scored in the worst quartile on each factor at ages 10 to 12 (fifth and sixth grades), compared with all other youth in the sample. For example, the odds ratio for "availability of marijuana" is 3.6. This means that youth from neighborhoods where marijuana was most available were 3.6 times more likely to join a gang, compared with other youth.

† Compared with two-parent households.

‡ ns = not a significant predictor.

§ These factors also distinguished sustained gang membership (i.e., more than 1 year) from transient membership (1 year or less). For each factor, the number in parentheses indicates the odds of being a sustained gang member (compared with the odds of being a transient member) for youth at risk on that factor.

SOURCE: Karl G. Hill, Christina Lui and J. David Hawkins. *Early Precursors of Gang Membership: A Study of Seattle Youth*. Washington, DC: OJJDP Juvenile Justice Bulletin, December 2001. (NCJ 190106)

the strong influence of gang-involved family members, particularly older siblings . . . on their decisions to join gangs.

Table 9.7 presents the risk factors for girls joining gangs.

Gang Control Strategies

Both short- and long-term solutions are needed for dealing with gangs and gang violence. Short-term approaches would rely on law enforcement efforts, including stiffer penalties for hard-core gang members, and on special training for police, prosecutors and judges. Long-term solutions would emphasize preventive and community-based counseling for both gang members and their parents. The criminal justice system, a host of social service agencies, schools and the community at large all play an important role in addressing the gang problem.

Spergel and Curry (1990) studied strategies being used to deal with the gang problem and identified four basic approaches: (1) community organization, (2) social intervention, (3) opportunities provision and (4) suppression or law

Table 9.7 Risk Factors for Female Gang Membership

Risk Factor	Number Answering Yes		Percent Answering Yes	
	Gang Members (N = 48)	Non-members (N = 46)	Gang Members (N = 48)	Non-members (N = 46)
Neighborhood Exposure to Gangs				
There is a lot of talk about gangs around the neighborhood	38	31	80	67
There is a lot of gang activity around the neighborhood	40	25	83	54
There are other gang members living on the same street	39	21	81	46*
There are rival gangs close by	35	26	73	57
Family Problems				
Witness to physical violence between adults	27	12	56	26*
Abused by family member	22	12	46	26*
Regular alcohol use in home	27	17	56	37
Regular drug use in home	28	8	58	17*
Family member in prison/jail	35	31	29	11*
More than three of the above	29	11	60	24*
More than four of the above	21	6	44	13*
Gang-Involved Family Members				
Gang member(s) in family	38	25	79	54*
Sibling(s) in gangs	24	8	50	17*
Multiple gang members in family	29	13	60	28*

*$p < .05$

SOURCE: Jody Miller. "Young Women in Street Gangs: Risk Factors, Delinquency and Victimization Risk." In *Responding to Gangs: Evaluation and Research*, edited by Winifred L. Reed and Scott H. Decker. Washington, DC: National Institute of Justice, July 2002, p.77. (NCJ 190351)

enforcement efforts. Although the study is dated, the findings still apply. These four approaches remain the basic areas being used. Table 9.8 summarizes law enforcement strategies used and their perceived effectiveness.

The most frequently used strategies were in-state information exchanges, local agency operational coordination and selected violations. Judged most effective were suppression efforts, street sweeps and crime prevention efforts.

Table 9.8 Law Enforcement Strategies and Perceived Effectiveness*

Strategy	Used	Judged Effective (if used)
Some or a Lot of Use		
Targeting entry points	14%	17%
Gang laws	40	19
Selected violations	76	42
Out-of-state information exchange	53	16
In-state information exchange	90	17
In-city information exchange	55	18
Federal agency operational coordination	40	16
State agency operational coordination	50	13
Local agency operational coordination	78	16
Community collaboration	64	54
Any Use		
Street sweeps	40%	62%
Other suppression tactics	44	63
Crime prevention activities	15	56

*Percentage of cities, n = 211. The number of cities responding to each question varied slightly.

SOURCE: James C. Howell. *Youth Gang Programs and Strategies.* Washington, DC: OJJDP, August 2000, p.46. (NCJ 171154)

Police Gang Units

The United States has seen a dramatic increase in specialized gang units in the last 15 years, most of which have been established to gather intelligence on gangs. Webb and Katz (2003, p.17) explain: "A police gang unit is a secondary or tertiary functional division within a police organization, which has at least one sworn officer whose sole function is to engage in gang control efforts." According to a study by Katz (2001, p.37), among large agencies with 100 or more sworn officers, special gang units existed in 56 percent of all municipal police departments, 50 percent of all sheriffs' departments, 43 percent of all county police agencies and 20 percent of all state law enforcement agencies. These findings suggest an estimate of 360 police gang units in the United States.

Weisel (2003, p.280) reports: "A study of 261 gang units discovered that gang sweeps are the most common form of suppression. Gang sweeps are highly concentrated law enforcement activities carried out in small areas where gangs are known to be prevalent. Police focus on gang-related crimes of concern to the public, such as drive-by shootings, drug sales, graffiti and assaults. These sweeps, often termed 'zero tolerance,' incorporate differing enforcement tactics, including traffic enforcement, weapons searches and checks on probation and ordinance violations."

Injunctions and Legislation

Sometimes communities pass legislation, such as loitering ordinances, or take other legal measures, including injunctions, to bring gang problems under con-

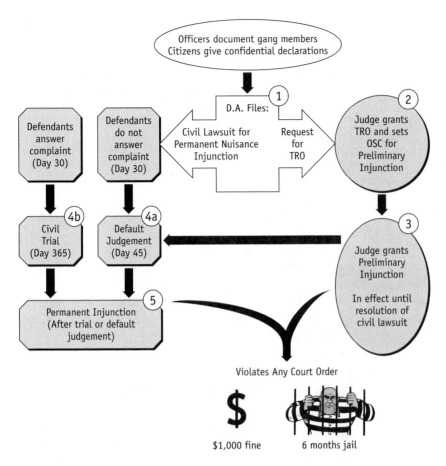

Figure 9.2 The Gang Injunction Process

SOURCE: Used by permission of San Diego Deputy District Attorney Susan Mazza.

trol. A **civil injunction** is a court order prohibiting a person or group from engaging in certain activities. Figure 9.2 illustrates how the civil injunction process works.

However, injunctions and ordinances may be challenged as unconstitutional violations of the freedom of speech, the right of association and due process rights if they do not clearly delineate how officers may apply such orders.

For example, Chicago passed a gang congregation ordinance to combat the problems created by the city's street gangs. During the three years following passage of the ordinance, Chicago police officers issued over 89,000 dispersal orders and arrested more than 42,000 people. However, in *City of Chicago v. Morales* (1999), the Supreme Court struck down the ordinance as unconstitutional because its vague wording failed to provide adequate standards to guide police discretion. The lesson here is that any civil injunctions a city passes must be clear in what officers can and cannot do when they observe what they believe to be gang members congregating in public places.

Tougher legislation is also being used as a gang control approach. Because some gangs use their younger members to commit serious crimes, relying on the more lenient juvenile sentencing laws, some jurisdictions have allowed courts to raise the penalties for teenagers convicted of gang-related offenses.

While injunctions, ordinances and legislation offer ways to help communities handle problems associated with gangs, they also raise serious issues regarding how to balance public safety with individual rights. In addition, as Miethe and McCorkle (2002, p.171) contend: "When gang cases were compared before and after enactment of the [antigang] legislation, no significant difference in conviction rates were found."

Gang Intelligence

In the war against gangs, information and intelligence are vital. Some states are taking advantage of the ever-expanding network of online computer services to enhance information sharing. For example, a national database called RISS-GANGS is a partnership involving more than 4,500 federal, state and local law enforcement agencies used to track and share gang intelligence. Another computer technology used to track gangs is the General Reporting, Evaluation and Tracking (G.R.E.A.T.) system—a combination hot sheet, mug book and file cabinet.

Meeker et al. (2002) describe the Gang Incident Tracking System (GITS) developed in Orange County, California, to track and monitor gang activity and report (p.291): "Of particular concern to community activists was whether the police overestimated gang crime. The evaluation revealed that, far from overestimating this type of crime, the police tended to underreport it. The GITS system above all demonstrated the usefulness of multijurisdictional efforts to understand and ultimately prevent gang crime. Output has been used by law enforcement to deploy personnel, allocate resources and evaluate gang intervention activities. The GITS system has made it possible to use GIS technology to create computerized maps that analyze the spatial and temporal distribution of gang activity." Table 9.9 summarizes the methods departments use to gather information on gangs.

In addition, many street gangs have Web sites law enforcement can monitor to learn about upcoming events, times and meeting places. According to "Underworld Dot-Coms" (2001, p.7): "Tens of thousands of gang-related sites have been posted over the past few years."

School Programs

Warning signs schools might use as gang identifiers include graffiti, colors, tattoos, initiations, hand signs, language and sudden changes in behavior such as an increasing number of violent, racially based incidents. Whether a school has a gang problem or not, it can still be instrumental in prevention efforts.

One such effort is the Gang Resistance Education and Training (GREAT) program that targets middle school students. As Esbensen (2004, p.1) explains, the nine-hour program is taught in schools by uniformed officers: "Students are taught to set positive goals, resist negative pressure, resolve conflicts and understand how gangs impact the quality of their lives." According to Esbensen et al. (2001a, p.87): "Over the past 10 years, the GREAT program has been incorporated into school curricula in all 50 states and the District of Columbia." They studied the effectiveness of the program using self-report surveys of several thousand students from six cities who had participated in the GREAT program and a similar number of students who had not participated. They found: "Over time, GREAT students exhibited more pro-social attitudinal changes than did non-GREAT stu-

Table 9.9   Methods Used for Gathering Information
on Gangs, Ranked by "Often Used" Category

	Never Used	Sometimes Used	Often Used
Internal contacts with patrol officers and detectives	1	22	64
Internal departmental records and computerized files	4	22	62
Review of offense reports	2	25	60
Interviews with gang members	5	26	56
Obtain information from other local police agencies	1	35	51
Surveillance activities	6	37	44
Use of unpaid informants	2	44	42
Obtain information from other criminal justice agencies	3	43	42
Obtain information from other governmental agencies	3	47	37
Provision of information by schools	2	50	35
Reports from state agencies	11	63	14
Use of paid informants	28	46	13
Reports from federal agencies	16	62	9
Obtain information from private organizations	27	51	9
Infiltration of police officers into gangs or related groups	75	11	2

SOURCE: James W. Stevens. "Youth Gangs' Dimensions." *The Encyclopedia of Police Science*, 2nd ed., edited by William G. Bailey. New York: Garland, 1995, p.832. Reprinted by permission.

dents. However, there were no significant differences in the behavioral outcomes of gang membership, delinquency and drug use." Esbensen's study found "modest positive results" from an evaluation of the program.

Another school-based program is the Gang Resistance Is Paramount (GRIP) program, which teaches second-, fifth- and ninth-grade students about gangs and territory, gangs and vandalism, peer pressure, drugs, alcohol, guns and family, self-esteem, gang violence, gangs and the police, alternatives to gang membership and related topics. A University of Southern California research team evaluated two decades of experience with GRIP and found a number of positive trends, including a significant decrease in the activity of major gangs, gang members and the ratio of gang members to residents in Paramount, California, since 1982. A survey of 735 ninth-grade students found that those who had participated in the GRIP program were less likely to report involvement with gang activity than nonparticipants, were more likely to have negative perceptions of gang activities and were more likely to believe that drugs and alcohol were a big part of gang life ("California Law Enforcement Praises School Anti-Gang Program," pp.4–5).

Gangs and Community Policing

The police cannot combat the gang problem alone. In addition to help from the schools, involvement of the entire community is needed. One source of such assistance is America's Promise. America's Promise was founded after the 1997 Presidents' Summit for America's Future attended by Presidents Clinton, Bush,

Carter and Ford with First Lady Nancy Reagan representing her husband. Colin Powell was the founding chairman of the alliance, which has grown to more than 400 national partner organizations and 400 local initiatives. The alliance focuses on five promises:

1. *Ongoing relationships with caring adults,* such as parents, other caregivers, extended family members, neighbors, teachers and even probation and parole officers.

2. *Safe places and structured activities* that nurture youths' social skills, vocational interests and sense of civic responsibility.

3. A *healthy start,* making fundamental resources available from birth to age 20, to prepare youths not only for school but also for adulthood.

4. *Marketable skills through education,* providing a solid foundation in reading, writing, mathematics, science, technology and communications; cultivating thinking skills, creativity, decision making, problem solving and reasoning; developing positive attitudes, sense of responsibility, integrity, self-motivation and management—all to create "work ethic."

5. *Opportunities to serve,* providing service learning experiences that enhance self-esteem, a sense of personal confidence and social responsibility for others.

The Five Promises Checklist identifies age-appropriate actions for each promise along with service providers who can address the action ("The Five Promises Checklist: Helping Communities Help Youths," 2003, p.5). The America's Promise Web site is www.americaspromise.org.

Another source of assistance is a new program of the Office of Juvenile Justice and Delinquency Prevention (OJJDP): the Gang Reduction Program (GRP). In introducing the new program to support community antigang efforts, then Attorney General Ashcroft stated:

> We must focus on the immediate priority of safeguarding the public, while at the same time attacking the underlying causes that attract young people to gangs in the first place. We must work to offer our youths a viable alternative to gangs by providing opportunities for success as productive citizens, and we must also prepare those young people who have been held in confinement to return to their communities—not to their gangs ("New Program Supports Community Anti-Gang Efforts," 2003, p.1).

The OJJDP's Gang Reduction Program uses a five-pronged approach:

1. *Primary prevention* targets the entire population in high-crime, high-risk communities. The key component is a one-stop resource center that makes services accessible and visible to community members. Services include prenatal and infant care, after-school activities, truancy and dropout prevention, and job programs.

2. *Secondary prevention* identifies young children (ages 7 to 14) at high risk and, drawing on the resources of schools, community-based organizations and faith-based groups, intervenes with appropriate services before early problem behaviors turn into serious delinquency and gang involvement.

3. *Intervention* targets active gang members, close associates and gang members returning from confinement and involves aggressive outreach and recruitment activity. Support services for gang-involved youths and their families help youths make positive choices.

4. *Suppression* focuses on identifying the most dangerous and influential gang members and removing them from the community.
5. *Reentry* targets serious offenders who are returning to the community after confinement and provides appropriate services and monitoring. Of particular interest are "displaced" gang members who may cause conflict by attempting to reassert their former gang roles.

The program is being pilot tested in Los Angeles, California; Miami, Florida; Milwaukee, Wisconsin; and Richmond, Virginia.

Gangs and the Criminal Justice System

Shelden et al. (p.265) identify four components of the criminal justice system that deal with the gang problem: (1) law enforcement, (2) prosecution, (3) courts and (4) corrections. They note: "Law enforcement represents society's first line of defense against crime. Consequently, law enforcement is the first segment of the criminal justice system that responds to the youth gang dilemma." In addition, according to Shelden et al., prosecutors have a tremendous amount of discretionary power and can be quite political when dealing with gang members. The courts, in contrast, continue to have their options decreased when dealing with gang members as the result of established guidelines jurists must follow. And finally, Shelden et al. (p.290) suggest that many politicians and legislative bodies have taken a "get tough on crime" stance, and this has often included gangs.

Prosecution Problems

Prosecution of gang-related crimes is often made difficult because victims and witnesses are reluctant to cooperate. One reason for the reluctance is a sense of futility in trying to rid an area of all gang activity—why bother getting involved and risk personal harm to put one gang away when another is poised to move right into the vacancy?

Another reason for victim and witness reluctance is gang intimidation and fear of reprisal. Other obstacles to prosecution include uncertain victim and witness credibility, inadequate police reports and a lack of appropriate sanctions for juvenile gang members involved in criminal activities. In fact, some older gang members refer to their younger members as "minutemen" because if they do get "busted," they'll be out in a minute. Adults hire juveniles to run their drugs for them, knowing that if the juveniles get caught, not much will happen to them. Table 9.10 illustrates some of the problems involved in prosecuting gangs.

As has been noted frequently during the discussion of gangs, drugs are often an additional problem facing law enforcement. For example, Valdez and Sifaneck (2004, p.82) found: (1) many gang members are user/sellers and are not profit-oriented dealers, (2) gangs commonly do extend "protection" to drug-selling members and (3) proximity to Mexican drug markets, adult prison gangs and criminal family members may play important roles in whether these gang members have access and the profit potential to actually deal drugs. Their research contributes to understanding the "complex intersections between gangs, drug using and drug selling."

The FBI has recognized this link between gangs and drug using/selling and has developed a strategy known as the Enterprise Theory of Investigation.

Table 9.10 Problems in Prosecuting Gang Cases—Views of Criminal Justice Officials in Clark and Washoe Counties, in Percent

	Gang D.A.s	Track D.A.s	Public Defenders	Judges	Police
Obtaining the Cooperation of Victims/Witnesses					
Not a problem/minor problem	0.0	0.0	27.6	33.3	8.3
Moderate problem	12.5	9.1	44.8	16.7	37.5
Major problem	87.5	90.9	27.6	50.0	54.2
Victim/Witness Credibility					
Not a problem/minor problem	12.5	9.1	10.3	25.0	25.0
Moderate problem	12.5	27.3	41.1	50.0	50.0
Major problem	75.0	63.6	48.3	25.0	25.0
Victim/Witness Intimidation					
Not a problem/minor problem	0.0	0.0	48.2	33.3	13.0
Moderate problem	37.5	45.5	34.5	41.7	39.1
Major problem	62.5	54.5	17.2	25.0	47.8
Heavy Caseloads					
Not a problem/minor problem	47.5	40.0	39.3	25.0	43.5
Moderate problem	62.5	20.0	32.1	41.7	30.4
Major problem	0.0	40.0	28.6	33.3	26.1
Inadequate Police Preparation of Crime Reports					
Not a problem/minor problem	87.5	40.0	51.7	66.6	87.0
Moderate problem	12.5	60.0	37.9	16.7	8.7
Major problem	0.0	0.0	10.3	16.7	4.3
Difficult Proof Requirement to Show That the Offense Was Committed to Further the Gang					
Not a problem/minor problem	25.0	11.1	48.1	25.0	30.4
Moderate problem	62.5	44.4	29.6	50.0	34.8
Major problem	15.5	44.4	22.2	25.0	34.8

SOURCE: Terance D. Miethe and Richard C. McCorkle. "Evaluating Nevada's Antigang Legislation and Gang Prosecution Units." In *Responding to Gangs: Evaluation and Research,* edited by Winifred L. Reed and Scott H. Decker. Washington, DC: National Institute of Justice, July 2002, p.190. (NCJ 190351)

The Enterprise Theory of Investigation

Weisel (2003, p.40) describes the goal of the FBI's Enterprise Theory of Investigation (ETI) as being "to identify, disrupt and ultimately dismantle violent gangs whose activities constitute criminal enterprises." According to Weisel: "The strategy is for the FBI, in conjunction with other federal, state and local law enforcement agencies, to combat major domestic violent street gang/drug gang enterprises as significant threats to American society through sustained, multidivisional, coordinated investigations that support successful prosecution."

The FBI defines a violent street gang/drug enterprise as a criminal enterprise that has an organizational structure and that functions as a continuing criminal conspiracy, employing violence and any other criminal activity to sustain itself. The ETI strategy also works with gangs that are not involved with drugs as well as with drug dealers who are not part of a gang.

The Threat of Drugs

American history is filled with drug use, including alcohol and tobacco. As the early settlers moved west, one of the first buildings in each frontier town was a saloon. Cocaine use was also common by the 1880s. At the beginning of the twentieth century, cocaine was the drug of choice, said to cure everything from indigestion to toothaches. It was added to flavor soft drinks like Coca-Cola.

In 1909 a presidential commission reported to President Theodore Roosevelt that cocaine was a hazard, leading to loss of livelihoods and lives. As the public became increasingly aware of the hazards posed by cocaine and other drugs, it pressed for legislation against use of such drugs.

 In 1914 the federal government passed the Harrison Narcotics Act, which made the sale or use of certain drugs illegal.

In 1920 every state required its students to learn about narcotics' effects. In 1937 under President Franklin Delano Roosevelt, marijuana became the last drug to be banned. For a quarter of a century, the drug problem lay dormant.

Then came the 1960s, a time of youthful rebellion, of Haight Ashbury and the flower children, a time to protest the Vietnam War. A whole culture had as its theme: tune in, turn on and drop out—often through marijuana and LSD. By the 1970s marijuana had been tried by an estimated 40 percent of 18- to 21-year-olds and was being used by many soldiers fighting in Vietnam. Many other soldiers turned to heroin. At the same time, an estimated half million Americans began using heroin back in the States.

The United States became the most drug-pervaded nation in the world, with marijuana leading the way. The 1980s saw a turnaround in drug use, with celebrities advocating, "It's not cool to do drugs," and "Just say no to drugs." At the same time, however, other advertisements suggested that alcohol and smoking are where the "fun is." The United States remains a culture of pill poppers. In fact, according to Ericson (2001, p.1): "Research has long shown that the abuse of alcohol, tobacco and illicit drugs is the single most serious health problem in the United States, straining the health care system, burdening the economy and contributing to the health problems and death of millions of Americans every year."

Studies on Current Drug Use

Three national studies of drug use in the United States shed light on the current threat of drugs: the *National Drug Threat Assessment 2004*, *Pulse Check: Trends in Drug Abuse* and *Monitoring the Future*.

National Drug Threat Assessment 2004   The Justice Department's National Drug Intelligence Center (NDIC) provides an annual report describing the availability and distribution of common drugs. According to the *National Drug Threat Assessment 2004* (2004), law enforcement agencies identified either powder or crack cocaine (37 percent) as their greatest drug threat, followed by methamphetamine at 36 percent, marijuana at 13.1 percent, heroin at 7 percent and MDMA or Ecstasy at 0.9 percent. Law enforcement and public health agencies consistently identified marijuana as the most commonly used illicit drug in the country in 2003, but saw it as posing a relatively low threat. Half of law enforcement agencies identified cocaine as the drug that most contributes to violent crime, and 42 percent reported that it is the prime drug associated with property offenses. Approximately 30 percent of the agencies named methamphetamine as the drug contributing most to violent crimes and property offenses.

Pulse Check: Trends in Drug Abuse (2004)   The Justice Department's Office of National Drug Control Policy (ONDCP) follows drug trends in 25 large cities, as shown in Figure 9.3.

Of the agencies surveyed, 77 percent believe the drug problem is "very serious" while the rest label it as "somewhat serious." The majority (66 percent) perceive the drug problem has not changed much. Key findings of this report (p.5) include the following:

- Marijuana remains the country's most widely abused illicit drug.
- Crack remains a serious problem in 18 cities. It is considered the most commonly used drug by 16 sources in 12 cities.
- Methamphetamine is reported as an emerging or intensifying problem in 15 cities.
- MDMA or Ecstasy continues to emerge or intensify as a problem in 16 cities.
- Heroin is the drug associated with the most serious consequences—such as overdose deaths and involvement in emergency department episodes.
- Illicit drug prices generally remained stable between the spring and fall of 2002.

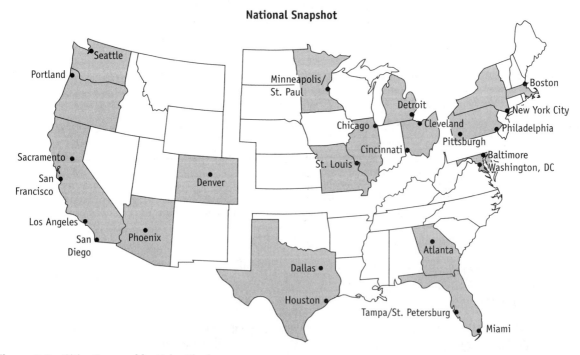

National Snapshot

Figure 9.3   Cities Surveyed by *Pulse Check*

SOURCE: *Pulse Check: National Trends in Drug Abuse.* Washington, DC: Office of National Drug Control Policy, January 2004, p. 5. (NCJ 210398) http://www.whitehousedrugpolicy .gov.

Monitoring the Future: National Results on Adolescent Drug Use: Overview of Key Findings, 2003   *Monitoring the Future* (Johnston et al., 2003) is a report issued by the University of Michigan's Institute for Social Research. The researchers survey 8th-, 10th- and 12th-grade students annually. Their most important finding (p.4) was that a number of illicit drugs showed broad declines in 2002 to 2003, most notably marijuana and Ecstasy. The report states: "The Partnership for a Drug-Free America, in conjunction with the Office of National Drug Control Policy, launched an anti-Ecstasy advertising campaign in January 2002. In addition to the normal news coverage of some consequences of Ecstasy use by young people, this campaign may well have contributed to the important downturn in the use of the drug."

Narcotics, Marijuana and Other Dangerous Drugs

The Controlled Substances Act (CSA) of 1984 placed all federally regulated substances into one of five schedules based on the substance's effects, medical use, potential for abuse, and safety or dependence liability. Drugs in Schedule I have the highest potential for abuse, unpredictable effects and no generally accepted medical use. Schedule I drugs include heroin, LSD, GHB and marijuana. At the other end of the scale, Schedule V drugs have the lowest potential for abuse, may lead to limited physical or psychological dependence and have many accepted medical uses. Drugs in this category include Lomotil, Robitussin A-C and over-the-counter or prescription drugs containing codeine. Drugs falling between these two extremes include the Schedule II substances of morphine, PCP, cocaine and methamphetamine; Schedule III substances such as anabolic steroids, codeine and some barbiturates; and Schedule IV substances including Valium, Xanax and Rohypnol.

Narcotics are drugs that produce sleep, lethargy or relief of pain and include heroin, ~~cocaine and crack~~. Other dangerous drugs are addicting, mind-altering drugs, such as marijuana, depressants, stimulants and hallucinogens. Methamphetamine and "club drugs" such as Ecstasy, GHB and Rohypnol are included in this category.

 In most states narcotics and other dangerous drugs may not be used or sold without a prescription. Federal law prohibits sale or distribution not covered by prescription.

Narcotics

Prohibited narcotics include heroin, cocaine and crack. *Heroin*, a commonly abused narcotic, is synthesized from morphine and is up to 10 times more potent. Heroin is physically addictive and expensive. It causes an easing of fears, followed by euphoria and finally stupor. While this drug can be smoked, snorted or eaten, injecting is the most common route of heroin administration.

Cocaine is a central nervous system stimulant narcotic derived from the South American coca bush. Cocaine smuggling is big business, run primarily by Colombians. They often are assisted by tourists and students, called **mules.** Larger quantities are brought in by professional smugglers, often using private planes and boats. Cocaine may be inhaled or injected, producing euphoria, excitation, anxiety, a sense of increased muscular strength, talkativeness and reduced feelings of fatigue. The pupils often become dilated, and the heart rate and blood pressure usually increase. Psychological dependence can be extreme.

Crack is a form of cocaine usually sprinkled on a marijuana or tobacco cigarette or mixed with marijuana or tobacco and then smoked in a pipe. Crack produces the same intense rush and euphoria that cocaine does but at a greatly reduced cost. Pellet-size chunks of crack are often sold in small glass or plastic vials, film canisters or small zippered baggies, with prices much lower than for a similar amount of cocaine. Because of its low price, crack has been called the "equal opportunity drug."

Marijuana

"Marijuana is the most widely available and abused illegal drug in the United States" (Strong, 2001, p.58). It is almost certainly the most socially accepted illegal drug; legislation lessening penalties for its use has frequently been proposed. Although it has been known for nearly 5,000 years, it is one of the least understood, yet most versatile, of all natural drugs.

Marijuana, derived from the cannabis plant, is a hardy weed adaptable to most climates. It still grows wild in many parts of the United States. It grows at a phenomenal rate from a seedling to a 20-foot plant in one year. The leaves are then picked and dried in the sun, a stove or even a clothes dryer. Many domestic marijuana growers are switching from outdoor to indoor cultivation. Home-grown marijuana is called **sinsemilla.**

Marijuana is most commonly rolled into a cigarette (joint) and smoked, producing a distinctive odor. The drug's effects on the user's mood and thinking vary widely, depending on the marijuana's strength and the amount used, as well as the social setting and the anticipated effects.

According to Bennett and Hess (2004, p.483): "Whether marijuana abusers progress to hard narcotics or other controlled substances has not been totally researched. The vast majority of hard-narcotics users once used marijuana, but how many marijuana users proceed to hard drugs is unknown." Data from Columbia University's National Center on Addiction and Substance Abuse shows that a young person who smokes marijuana is 85 times more likely to try cocaine (*National Drug Control Strategy,* 2003, p.1).

 The most commonly observed drugs on the street, in possession of users and seized in drug raids are heroin, opium, morphine, codeine, cocaine, crack and marijuana. Arrest for possession or use of marijuana is the most frequent drug arrest.

Other Dangerous Drugs

Other dangerous drugs include depressants, stimulants, hallucinogens, club drugs and deliriants.

Depressants (Barbiturates)   Depressants, or **barbiturates,** are sedatives taken orally as a small tablet or capsule to induce sleep or to relieve tension. Small amounts of barbiturates make the user relaxed, sociable and good-humored. Heavy doses cause sluggishness, depression, deep sleep or coma. A barbiturate addict often shows symptoms of drunkenness: speech becomes slurred and indistinct, physical coordination is impaired, and mental and emotional instability occurs. Overdoses are common and frequently cause intentional or accidental death.

Stimulants (Amphetamines)   Stimulants, or **amphetamines,** are taken orally as a tablet or capsule, or intravenously, to reduce appetite and/or relieve mental depression. Normal doses produce wakefulness, increased alertness and initiative, and hyperactivity. Large doses produce exaggerated feelings of confidence, power and well-being.

Heavy users may exhibit restlessness, nervousness, hand tremors, pupil dilation, mouth dryness and excessive perspiration. They may be talkative and experience delusions and/or hallucinations. Handling this deviant behavior has always been a source of concern and danger for law enforcement officers.

One stimulant posing a major problem for law enforcement is **methamphetamine,** or "meth," also known as *speed, ice* and *crystal.* Like cocaine, meth is a potent central nervous system stimulant that the Drug Enforcement Administration (DEA) calls "a dangerous, sometimes lethal and unpredictable drug" (DEA Web site, www.dea.gov, 2001). Meth is typically a white, odorless, bitter-tasting powder that easily dissolves in water. It can be smoked, snorted, injected or taken orally. Methamphetamine use frequently results in violent and erratic behavior. As Garrett (2004, p.38) reports: "Meth labs are a danger to all who encounter them." Meth labs contain ignitable, corrosive, reactive and toxic chemicals often in the presence of an open flame or heat source. Scott (2002, p.1) stresses: "Dealing with clandestine drug labs requires an extraordinarily high level of technical expertise. Responders must understand illicit drug chemistry; how to neutralize the risk of explosions, fires, chemical burns and toxic fumes; how to handle, store and dispose of hazardous materials; and how to treat medical conditions caused by chemical exposure."

Hallucinogens   **Hallucinogens** may produce distortion, intensify sensory perception and lessen the ability to discriminate between fact and fantasy. The unpredictable mental effects include illusions, panic, psychotic or antisocial behavior and impulses toward violence and self-destruction.

Although hallucinogens are usually taken orally as a tablet or capsule, their physical characteristics allow them to be disguised as various commonly used powders or liquids. Probably the best-known hallucinogen is LSD (lysergic acid diethylamide).

Another hallucinogen, PCP (phencyclidine), was developed as an anesthetic and is still used as such by veterinarians. It appeared in San Francisco in the 1960s and was called the "Peace Pill." As its use spread across the country, it was called by various other names, including angel dust. Symptoms of PCP intoxication vary greatly from person to person, depending on the dosage, previous use and how it was ingested. A symptom almost always present in PCP intoxication is **nystagmus,** an uncontrolled bouncing or jerking of the eyeball when the intoxicated person looks to the extreme right or left, and up or down. Much of the concern over the widespread use of PCP is the drug's ability to produce bizarre, sometimes tragic, *aggressive, violent behavior.* Users often have hallucinations and disturbed thought patterns that may produce panic, which triggers aberrant or aggressive behavior. Police officers have been injured attempting to subdue a person under the influence of PCP. Overwhelming evidence shows that some users "freaked out" on PCP exhibit *superhuman strength* while showing aggression. One explanation is that users believe their hallucinations are real. The adrenalin flows, and they fight desperately for survival using any method to escape the terror. The superhuman strength is also directly related to the drug's analgesic qualities under which users feel little or no pain.

"Club Drugs"   LSD and meth have also fallen into a growing category of drugs called "club drugs," named for their emerging presence in nightclub and rave scenes. Other substances included in this group are Ecstasy, GHB, Rohypnol, ketamine and nitrous oxide. According to Valdez (2002a, p.74): "Gangs control much of the flow of dangerous recreational drugs at raves."

Perhaps the most prolific club drug currently attracting law enforcement's attention is *MDMA* (3, 4-Methylenedioxymethamphetamine), also called *Ecstasy*. MDMA is a synthetic, psychoactive drug with both stimulant (amphetamine-like) and hallucinogenic (LSD-like) properties that create feelings of emotional closeness to others and break down any personal communication barriers that may exist (*MDMA*, 2002, p.1). "Found at raves, concerts, bars, clubs, in schools of all levels and on the streets, Ecstasy is used by a large array of people" (Streit, 2001, p.24). MDMA comes in tablet or capsule form and is almost always taken orally, although it can be snorted or dissolved in water and injected.

GHB, or gamma hydroxybutyrate, is a central nervous system depressant commonly sold as an odorless, colorless liquid in water bottles or as a powder mixed with beverages. Abused by high school and college students and rave-party attendees for its euphoric and hallucinatory properties, GHB is often combined with alcohol to magnify its intoxicating effect.

Rohypnol (flunitrazepam), also called roofies or the "date rape" drug, is not approved for medical use in the United States but is legally prescribed in over 50 other countries to treat insomnia and as a preanesthetic. According to DePresca (2003, p.210), Rohypnol "looks a lot like aspirin. When dropped in a drink, usually an alcoholic beverage, it is colorless and odorless." Rohypnol's effects include sedation, muscle relaxation and reduction in anxiety. It is fast-acting, with effects appearing 15 to 20 minutes after administration and typically lasting four to six hours. Because Rohypnol causes partial amnesia, users often cannot remember events that occurred while under the influence of the drug. This effect is particularly dangerous when the drug is used to commit a sexual assault because victims may not be able to clearly recall the assault, the assailant or the events surrounding the assault.

Ketamine, sometimes referred to as "K" or "special K," is used primarily in the veterinary field as an anesthetic but also presents hallucinogenic and dissociative properties when used by humans. Distributors acquire their product through veterinary office break-ins and pharmacy diversion. As with the other club drugs, ketamine is used at raves, nightclubs and in private residences.

Nitrous oxide, often referred to as "laughing gas," is an inhalant and a common propellant ingredient in many products. It is most typically used by white, suburban adolescents at raves and outdoor concerts. Inhalants are alternatively called deliriants.

Deliriants   Deliriants are volatile chemicals that generally produce a "high" and loss of inhibition similar to that produced by alcohol. Deliriants are composed of substances frequently found in more than 1,000 common household products, such as glues, hair spray, air fresheners, lighter fluid and paint products.

The inhalant high is usually followed by depression. Users may also experience headaches, wheezing, nausea, slurred speech, diminished motor coordination and distortion in perceptions of time and space. A characteristic redness or irritation called "glue sniffer's rash" commonly occurs around the nostrils and lips. Inhalant abuse is common among children and adolescents.

Although the various narcotics and other dangerous drugs produce different effects, they have certain common effects.

 Common effects of the various narcotics and other dangerous drugs include: (1) they are mind altering, (2) they may become addicting—either physically or psychologically, and (3) overdosage may result in convulsions and death.

Abuse of Prescription Drugs Burke (2004, p.17) reports: "Conservative estimates are that prescription drug abuse represents approximately 25 to 30 percent of the overall drug problem in America." According to Schanlaub (2003, p.93): "The abuse of prescription drugs is certainly not a new crime in the law enforcement arena. However, with drug technology improving by leaps and bounds and newer and more potent drugs hitting the streets, this is a good time to take another look at an ever-changing drug scene." He (p.95) contends: "Although there are hundreds of schedule drugs on the market, there may be one that deserves special mention, and that would be OxyContin®." This pain killer has heroin-like effects that can last up to 23 hours. According to Schanlaub (p.95): "Since 1996, the number of OxyContin® prescriptions has risen to approximately 5.8 million, becoming the number one prescribed Schedule II narcotic in the United States." The article "National Drug Control Strategy Targets Prescription Drug Abuse" (2004, p.1) notes: "'The nonmedical use of prescription drugs has become an increasingly widespread and serious problem in this country—one that calls for immediate action,' said John P. Walters, director of the Office of National Drug Control Policy (ONDCP). 'The federal government is embarking on a comprehensive effort to ensure that potentially addictive medications are dispensed and used safely and effectively.'"

According to *Pulse Check* (p.5): "Marijuana and crack are the illicit drugs most easily purchased by users and undercover police across the country." Figure 9.4 shows the ease of purchase of various drugs.

Alcohol

Many do not think of it as such, but alcohol is a drug. Although drinking alcohol is legal, laws have been established that regulate the age at which it becomes legal to drink, as well as the amount a person can drink and then operate a vehicle. The widespread abuse of alcohol is partly due to its legality but also to its social acceptance. Many people, although they know it is wrong and illegal, continue to drive after drinking. Drunk drivers are a life-threatening menace to themselves and others. Furthermore alcohol is the drug of choice among teenagers.

 Alcohol, a depressant, is the most widely abused drug in the United States.

Alcohol is often a factor in accidents and crime—traffic fatalities, pedestrian accidents, home accidents, fire deaths, drownings, skiing accidents, boating fatalities, murders, assaults, rapes, sex crimes against children, domestic violence and suicides.

 Alcohol use is clearly linked to criminal activity.

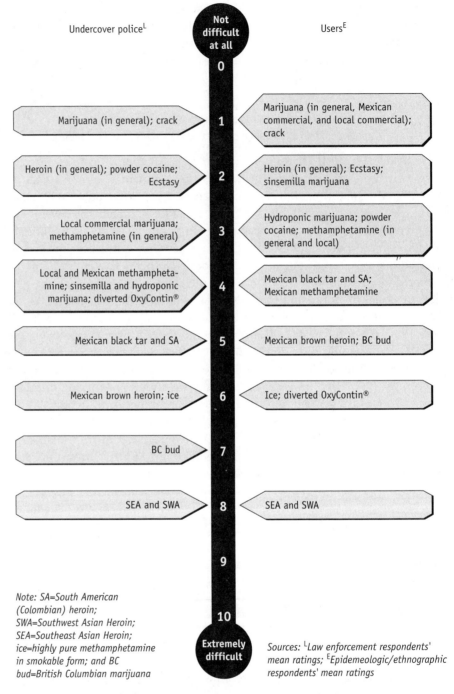

Undercover police[L]

Users[E]

Not difficult at all

0

Marijuana (in general); crack — 1 — Marijuana (in general, Mexican commercial, and local commercial); crack

Heroin (in general); powder cocaine; Ecstasy — 2 — Heroin (in general); Ecstasy; sinsemilla marijuana

Local commercial marijuana; methamphetamine (in general) — 3 — Hydroponic marijuana; powder cocaine; methamphetamine (in general and local)

Local and Mexican methamphetamine; sinsemilla and hydroponic marijuana; diverted OxyContin® — 4 — Mexican black tar and SA; Mexican methamphetamine

Mexican black tar and SA — 5 — Mexican brown heroin; BC bud

Mexican brown heroin; ice — 6 — Ice; diverted OxyContin®

BC bud — 7

SEA and SWA — 8 — SEA and SWA

9

10

Extremely difficult

Note: SA=South American (Colombian) heroin; SWA=Southwest Asian Heroin; SEA=Southeast Asian Heroin; ice=highly pure methamphetamine in smokable form; and BC bud=British Columbian marijuana

Sources: [L]Law enforcement respondents' mean ratings; [E]Epidemeologic/ethnographic respondents' mean ratings

Figure 9.4 How Difficult It Is for Undercover Police and Users to Buy Drugs (Fall 2002)

SOURCE: *Pulse Check: National Trends in Drug Abuse.* Washington, DC: Office of National Drug Control Policy, January 2004. (NCJ 210398) Available online at http://www.whitehousedrugpolicy.gov

North Carolina officers participate in a roadblock on a Saturday night to check for drunk drivers as part of the state's "Booze It and Lose It" campaign. Sixty-nine people were charged with DUI, and six vehicles were seized.

A study by the Harvard School of Public Health found that college students who frequently engaged in binge drinking were far more likely to experience alcohol-related problems than students who drank alcohol but did not binge drink. The study defined binge drinking as consuming at least five drinks in a row for men and at least four in a row for women two weeks before the survey. According to the study, approximately 44 percent of students were binge drinkers in 2003, the same rate as in 1993 ("Harvard Study Reveals . . .," 2003).

Researchers have found that children of alcoholics are 70 percent more likely than children of nonalcoholics to abuse drugs and alcohol at some point in their lives. Many children under age 12 say they learned to drink or do drugs from older brothers and sisters. During adolescence, fitting in is extremely important to teens. They are self-conscious and uncertain as to just who they are. Using alcohol and drugs helps anxious, awkward youths escape from a frightening world and gives them the illusion of membership, energy and confidence. Unfortunately many "innocent" drug users become involved in crime.

Illicit Drug Abuse and Crime

The relationship between illicit drugs and crime is complex: "Drugs and drug-using behavior are linked to crime in many ways. It is a crime to use, possess, manufacture or distribute illegal drugs. In addition the effects of drug-related behavior—violence as the effect of drug use, robberies to get money to buy drugs, violence against rival traffickers—influence society daily" (*Drug Treatment in the Criminal Justice System*, 2001, p.1).

Walker (2001, p.262) draws four lessons from history about the limits of criminal law in controlling products or services that a large number of people want:

1. If a large number of people want a product or service, someone will try to supply it.
2. Efforts to suppress that supply will result in massive evasion and the creation of criminal syndicates.

3. The enforcement effort itself will generate secondary crime (e.g., turf wars between gangs, corruption of law enforcement), abuse of individual rights (e.g., illegal searches and seizures) and loss of respect for the law.

4. Intensifying the enforcement effort encourages adaptations, either substitution of products (as in the case of some drugs) or transfer of the service to people more willing to take the increased risks.

Some acts involving drugs are illegal and are termed *systemic,* or **drug-defined offenses** in which violent crime occurs as a part of the drug business or culture. Examples of these offenses include marijuana cultivation, methamphetamine production and cocaine distribution. Other acts involve offenses in which the *effect* of the drug or the *need* for the drug is a contributing factor. These are called **drug-related offenses,** examples of which might include a user high on PCP who becomes violent and commits an assault because of the drug's pharmacologic effects, or an addict stealing to get money to buy drugs. Finally the *interaction* of drugs, crime and those involved with the drug culture may come into play, as when drug users and other deviants are exposed to situations that encourage crime, when criminal opportunities arise because of a drug user's contact with illegal markets and other offenders, or when offenders exchange criminal knowledge and learn criminal skills from each other.

The National Institute of Justice (NIJ) has implemented a Drug Use Forecasting (DUF) system to detect and track drug-use trends among people arrested for serious crimes. In this voluntary program, arrestees in several major cities are interviewed four times a year and asked to provide urine specimens, which are tested for illicit drugs. Initial tests showed a high level of drug use among the arrestees, with 50 to 80 percent of those arrested for serious crimes testing positive. The research also showed that criminals commit four to six times as much crime when they are actively using drugs as they do when they are drug free. According to the NIJ, most of those tested were charged with street crimes, such as burglary, grand larceny and assault. The most frequently found drugs were marijuana, cocaine, heroin, PCP and amphetamines.

 Clearly, illicit drug use is linked to criminal activity.

Incarcerated adults and youths report high levels of drug use. Among those incarcerated for violent crimes, one-third of state prisoners and more than one-third of the incarcerated youths said they had been under the influence of an illegal drug at the time of their offense. In addition major drug use (cocaine, heroin, PCP, LSD and methadone) is related to the number of prior convictions for state prisoners: the greater the use of major drugs, the more prior convictions the inmate was likely to report. Peyton and Gossweiler (2001, p.xi) report: "The use of illicit drugs and alcohol is a central factor in the soaring rate of incarceration in the United States." Researchers King and Mauer (2004, p.6) found that: "Fifty-eight percent of the persons currently incarcerated in state prisons for drug offenses—an estimated 124,885 persons—are nonviolent and [were] not engaged in high-level drug activity. They represent a pool of appropriate candidates for diversion to treatment programs or some other type of community-based sanctions."

Drugs and guns have also been linked. When crack became a major drug of choice, those recruited to distribute it were mainly youths. Fearing for their safety because they often carried large quantities of money, these youths also carried guns. Youths are apt to resort to violence to settle arguments rather than resolving disputes verbally. When guns are available, the outcome can be deadly.

Drugs and Society

The total economic costs to society of illegal drug use in 2000 was an estimated $160 billion, a 57 percent increase from 1991. Americans spent approximately $64 billion for illegal drugs in 2000—more than eight times the total federal outlays for research on HIV/AIDS, cancer and heart disease (*National Drug Control Strategy*, p.25).

Although drug abusers may claim it is their right to do whatever they want with their own bodies, the results of such actions have serious implications for society. Users no longer control what they think, say or do and often pose a threat to others.

An estimated 50 percent of intravenous drug abusers are infected with HIV. Intravenous drug abusers comprise 17 percent of AIDS victims and, among new reported cases of AIDS, approximately one-third were intravenous drug abusers. According to the Centers for Disease Control and Prevention (AIDS Policy and Law, n.d.): "Researchers now see intravenous drug abuse as the major vehicle for the AIDS virus to be spread to the general public." States have enacted more than 600 pieces of AIDS-related legislation dealing with employment, health care, insurance liability and criminal conduct. Some states are applying criminal punishment to those who knowingly spread HIV.

The costs of illicit drug use are high, and not only in financial terms. As noted in the transmittal letter for *The National Drug Control Strategy* (Bush, 2002):

> Illegal drug use threatens everything that is good about our country. It can break the bonds between parents and children. It can turn productive citizens into addicts, and it can transform schools into places of violence and chaos. Internationally, it finances the work of terrorists who use drug profits to fund their murderous work. Our fight against illegal drug use is a fight for our children's future, for struggling democracies and against terrorism.

This message is repeated in the Introduction to the *National Drug Control Strategy* (pp.1–2):

> Democracies can flourish only when their citizens value their freedom and embrace personal responsibility. Drug use erodes the individual's capacity to pursue both ideals. It diminishes the individual's capacity to operate effectively in many of life's spheres—as a student, a parent, a spouse, an employee—even as a coworker or fellow motorist. And, while some claim it represents an expression of individual autonomy, drug use is in fact inimical to personal freedom, producing a reduced capacity to participate in the life of the community and the promise of America.

Drug Control

The Office of National Drug Control Policy (ONDCP) has set forth clear goals to control drugs in this country. Its action plan is based on two basic rights of all citizens: the right to feel safe in one's home and community and the right to have one's children learn, grow and prosper in a safe and drug-free school and neighborhood. The current priorities set forth in the *National Drug Control Strategy* are (1) stopping use before it starts: education and community action; (2) healing America's drug users: getting treatment resources where they are needed; and (3) disrupting the market: attacking the economic basis of the drug trade.

In an interview with Scott Burns, ONDCP deputy director, Strandberg (2003, p.67) asks: "What do you have to say to law enforcement, the frontline officers?" The reply: "We are working every day to support you. We are fighting cynicism; every arrest, every major destruction counts. People are saying that we have lost the drug war—that's a lie. Every day, women and men of state and local law enforcement are making a difference."

Walters (2002a, p.1), director of the ONDCP, stresses: "More than any other group of Americans, our nation's law enforcement officers understand how drug use frays the fabric of our communities. . . . Every day, law enforcement officers across America risk their lives as they invest time and resources attempting to thwart the violence and depravity wrought by drugs. As the Director of the Office of National Drug Control Policy, I commend the efforts of these valiant guardians of our neighborhoods." He (p.3) asserts: "Through our collective experience we have learned one steadfast lesson: when we push back against the drug problem it recedes." Law enforcement might push back in several ways.

 The drug problem might be approached with the following methods:
- Crime control
- Punishment
- Rehabilitation
- Prevention
- Legalization

Figure 9.5 presents an overview of drug-control strategies.

Crime Control

Crime control includes source control at the international level, interdiction at the national level and enforcement at the local level.

Source Control   With the reigning drug lords living and working far from the scenes of their crimes, U.S. law enforcement faces a difficult challenge in controlling these sources of illegal drugs. Some drug sources have the open support of their national governments, with export of drug-related crops bringing substantial revenue to the countries. An example is opium production, the prevention of which, as Kaplan (n.d.) notes, would require controlling poppy cultivation and international cooperation. It is anticipated that the fall of the Taliban regime in Afghanistan and the de facto end to its national ban on poppy cultivation will return the country to its prior status as one of the world's leading opium producers, providing much needed economic relief for struggling poppy farmers but adding to the global supply of drugs. Such regionally sanctioned drug sources are very difficult, if not impossible, to control.

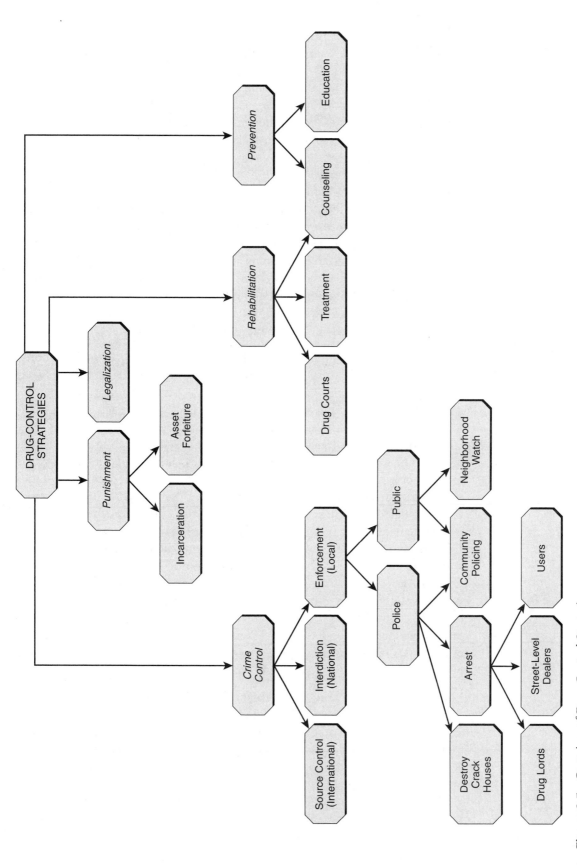

Figure 9.5 Overview of Drug-Control Strategies

International drug rings also pose a significant challenge to U.S. law enforcement. For example DEA agents have identified a Bangkok heroin cartel that is as powerful as the notorious Medellin and Cali Colombian rings. Difficulties in prosecuting the cartel include Thailand's reluctance to crack down on drug trafficking and the ingenious smuggling used by the cartel. In fact, some narcotics kingpins are virtually ignored by the government of the country in which they reside, whether out of intimidation and fear or because they have formed clandestine partnerships with such drug lords to profit from the business.

While the U.S. government cannot dictate how a foreign government should handle its resident drug lords, it can impose legislation aimed at preventing individuals and organizations from conducting illegal narcotics business within our national borders and prosecuting those who do so or attempt to do so. The Foreign Narcotics Kingpin Designation Act requires federal officials to compile an annual list of suspected drug kingpins and take steps to freeze their U.S. assets and bar them from entering the country. It also subjects anyone who knowingly does business with drug kingpins to criminal penalties.

After international drug sources have been addressed, the focus narrows in on ways to keep the drugs that are produced from getting into our country.

Interdiction   **Interdiction** is cutting off or destroying a line of communication—in the case of drug control, halting the flow of drugs into the United States. According to Steffen and Candelaria (2004, p.40): "The illicit drug market in the United States is one of the most profitable in the world. It attracts aggressive and sophisticated drug traffickers and organizations. Many diverse groups from around the globe distribute and traffick narcotics." American drug users pay drug traffickers an estimated $140 billion a year. Some dealers hand out free drug samples to hook new buyers. Illegal drugs, from marijuana to cocaine, are readily available. Preventing smuggling is difficult given the United States' more than 12,000 miles of coastline. Kaplan suggests, for example, that the total heroin requirement of all American addicts for an entire year is probably less than 10 tons, yet 100 million tons of freight come into the United States yearly, and more than 200 million people cross American borders yearly.

However, as Walters (2002b, p.i) notes: "Technology advancements are steadily enhancing our ability to interdict illicit drugs at our borders and on the high seas. Our overall goal is to attain the capability to nonintrusively inspect cargo containers and vessels in an efficient manner consistent with the free flow of legitimate trade and commerce." Once drugs pass into our country, the focus narrows further, turning to enforcement.

Enforcement   The Drug Enforcement Administration (DEA) is the federal agency charged with enforcing our nation's drug laws. In 1992 the DEA was assigned to develop a system to help federal, state and local law enforcement agencies investigate drug trafficking organizations, and in October 1997, the National Drug Pointer Index (NDPIX) became operational across the United States.

One approach to handling the drug problem is to attack street-level drug markets. However, street drug rings can be quite sophisticated, with a kingpin purchasing narcotics from foreign smugglers. Under the kingpin are leaders who oversee drug packaging and distribution. Runners take the drugs to the street sellers. Lookouts can earn several hundred dollars a day just watching for the police.

Enforcers, as the name implies, carry out the kingpin's orders, including killing people who get in the way of drug trafficking. Another approach to the drug problem is to simply bulldoze known crack houses.

Karchmer (2003, p.248) contends: "The low effectiveness of national efforts to control drug abuse puts increased emphasis on local police strategies. Local control of drug dealing requires a range of tactics. The following are three broad categories of police action that have produced, at best, limited results around the country:

1. *Investigative strategies,* targeted above the street level, are designed to disrupt networks of drug wholesalers, thereby increasing the risk and cost of the business of drug trafficking. Investigative strategies address the supply of drugs.
2. *Education strategies* are designed to keep children from turning to drugs, whether through experimentation or more serious use. These strategies address the demand side of the drug equation.
3. *Patrol strategies* are designed to reduce drug problems in small geographical neighborhoods, communities and blocks. They affect the market, where supply and demand come together. This has produced the most positive results if only of short duration."

Karchmer (p.256) describes three special kinds of patrol: saturation patrolling, street sweeps and street-level stings:

> Saturation patrolling involves the use of many officers to deter drug dealers from selling in open markets and to deter drug buyers from making contacts with dealers. . . . Like saturation patrolling, street sweeps involve the use of many officers in an area for a short period. But instead of trying to deter drug dealers and users, the objective is to arrest as many as possible. . . . In reverse buys, or "stings," undercover officers sell drugs (or drug look-alikes) to purchasers and then arrest the purchasers on a charge of attempted drug purchasing. The purpose of reverse buys is to deter users from making drug purchases in an area.

Karchmer (p.260) suggests: "Despite its special requirements, a problem-oriented approach to patrol drug enforcement by regular patrol officers has some distinct advantages over exclusive reliance on special units and foot patrols."

Drug raids are also conducted occasionally, an approach that has received much media attention. Cohen et al. (2003, p.257) studied the effectiveness of police raids in reducing drug dealing in and around nuisance bars and report: "Results indicate that the police intervention suppresses levels of drug dealing during periods of active enforcement, but the effects largely disappear when the intervention is withdrawn."

Punishment

Another way to handle the drug problem is to punish those involved in selling or using drugs, either through community service, incarceration or via asset forfeiture, in hopes such sanctions will deter future criminal behavior.

Community Service   For youthful first-time drug offenders, some communities are taking a "kinder, gentler approach . . .," calling for teenagers to sit down with parents or lawyers and work out a punishment that fits the crime. Said one chief: "I would rather take these first-time offenders and work their fannies off during community service" ("Taking a Different Road . . .," 2001, p.5). The community service would preferably be done alongside a police officer.

Incarceration   Spending time behind bars has been a consequence of illegal activity for thousands of years. During the 1970s, many citizens and legislators advocated a "get tough" approach to the growing drug-use crisis, viewing imprisonment of drug offenders as the best solution to the problem. Since the passage of mandatory drug sentencing laws during the 1970s, millions of substance abusers have been incarcerated by the nation's criminal justice system. This nondiscretionary sentencing policy has filled our nation's correctional institutions with drug offenders, leaving less room for what many consider the "real" criminals—murderers, rapists and other violent offenders.

With our correctional facilities overflowing, and the increasing number of violent offenders requiring prison space, courts have become more reluctant to incarcerate drug offenders. Adding to this reluctance is the growing body of evidence that tougher sentencing laws have not had much impact on reducing criminality in most drug offenders. Given the many shortcomings of incarceration as an effective punishment for drug offenders, another solution gaining popularity is asset forfeiture.

Asset Forfeiture   Asset forfeiture was introduced in the United States through passage of the Racketeer Influenced and Corrupt Organization (RICO) Act in 1970 and the Continuing Criminal Enterprises Act in 1984. The Asset Forfeiture Program, enacted in 1984, allows the Justice Department to share seized assets with state and local law enforcement agencies that participate in the investigations and arrests.

This type of response is intended to deprive drug offenders of ill-gotten gain, material possessions and wealth obtained through the sale or distribution of illegal drugs. Such forfeitures have included a recording studio; a Chevrolet dealership; a one-thousand-acre plantation; a horse farm with 210 Appaloosas, including a stallion worth $1.5 million; luxury homes; cars; boats; and planes.

Two key cases in the 1990s set a stronger foundation for issues involving forfeiture. In *United States v. Ursery* (1996), the Court held that civil forfeiture does not constitute double jeopardy, under the rationale that the prohibition against double jeopardy applies only if both proceedings are criminal and not when one is civil. In *United States v. Bajakajian* (1998), the Court held that the Eighth Amendment *does* apply in civil forfeitures. In this case the offense was failing to make a report to customs agents when taking more than $10,000 out of the country. The Court ruled that the forfeiture of $357,144 was grossly disproportionate to the offense and required Bajakajian to forfeit only $15,000.

Rehabilitation

Another approach taken with criminals for many centuries has been that of rehabilitation, attempting to change offenders' behavior—to "cure" them—so they no longer wish to engage in unlawful activities. Today rehabilitation of drug and alcohol offenders is a major focus of many communities, social service agencies, medical establishments and law enforcement agencies. Rehabilitation may be accomplished through drug courts, treatment programs and counseling.

Drug Courts   Drug courts are one attempt to deal with the drug problem and its resultant prison overcrowding. Since the first drug court began in 1989, almost 200,000 defendants have been placed in such courts across the nation. Several

© Joel Gordon

The Asset Forfeiture Program allows the Justice Department to share seized assets with state and local law enforcement agencies when they have participated in the investigations and arrests. Many police departments and sheriffs' departments use seized vehicles to convey a message to drug dealers and the public.

studies indicate that drug courts have higher retention rates, lower recidivism rates and are more cost effective than traditional drug treatment programs. According to a Drug Court Clearinghouse and Technical Assistance Project, felons are not only required to become clean and sober, they also must earn a GED, obtain and maintain employment, be able to pay their debts, such as child support and drug court fees, and have a sponsor who helps them assimilate back into the community. Another common requirement of drug courts is for offenders to submit to regular drug screens through urinalysis. Drug courts are discussed further in Chapter 13.

Treatment   Common therapeutic goals include getting past denial; changing attitudes toward offending, specifically toward one's primary offense; building morality; victim awareness, contrition and understanding of effects on victims; and relapse prevention. Many experts suggest drug treatment programs should be instituted in jails and prisons or as an alternative to incarceration. Inciardi et al. (2004) studied the impact of a multistage community treatment program on drug-involved offenders after their release from prison and found that therapeutic community treatment program participants were significantly less likely to relapse and recidivate.

Innovative attempts have been made at treating drug users, with the goal not necessarily the curing of drug addiction but the removal of the need to commit crime to get funds with which to buy drugs. For example under a two-market approach, drugs are supplied to addicts at clinics or other types of health facilities but are not available for nonaddicts. In Britain, methadone, a synthetic opiate, is provided as a maintenance drug to addicts at clinics specifically set up for that purpose.

One difficulty with sentencing offenders to treatment rather than prison is that often law enforcement officers see this as being soft on crime. As one officer stated: "Why should cops work so hard to arrest drug users if they're just going to get treatment anyway?" (Snyder, 2001, p.52).

Counseling A common element of drug treatment programs is counseling focused on trying to understand the cause(s) of the addictive or criminal behavior. Addressing these underlying causes can result in changes that eliminate the need to "escape" into drugs or alcohol. Counseling may also be used proactively as a prevention strategy for those at risk of using and becoming addicted to drugs and/or alcohol.

Prevention

Prevention attempts to stop drug use before it starts. Prevention is the first line of defense against drug- and alcohol-related crime.

Education The place to begin alleviating the problem of criminality is with our youths. It is vital to steer our nation's youths away from the devastation caused by drug use. Recall that the first priority of the *National Drug Control Strategy* (p.9) is stopping use before it starts. Educating youths about the dangers of drug use has become a common tool in the overall strategy to fight the drug problem. Chapter 5 discussed some youth programs currently operating in this capacity, such as Police Athletic Leagues and the DARE program.

The DARE (Drug Abuse Resistance Education) program has strong advocates such as Schennum (2001, p.103): "At present, it is refreshing to see DARE is still alive and effective. Today DARE is taught in more than 80% of all U.S. school districts, benefiting over 26 million students. DARE is an excellent program to assist parents and society as a whole in the fight against the influences of drugs, alcohol and tobacco on children and young adults."

However, research has not substantiated these claims. *Law Enforcement News* ("Truth, DARE & Consequences . . .," 2001, p.1) reports on a University of Illinois study that tracked 1,800 students over six years and found that by the end of high school, any impact of the program had worn off. In fact, an increase in drug use was detected in suburban students who had gone through the DARE program. Similar findings were reported by a 10-year University of Kentucky study. Walker p.265) also flatly asserts: "There is no evidence that DARE or other drug education programs reduce illegal drug use."

In response to these findings, DARE has revised its curriculum. As noted by Brown (2001, p.76): "The new program was developed in 1999 after the U.S. Departments of Education and Justice brought researchers and DARE officials together to resolve the ongoing controversy about the ineffectiveness of DARE." One key change is that the revised version of DARE will use police officers more as facilitators and less as instructors, helping children explore their own beliefs about drugs and develop their skills in asserting themselves and refusing drugs ("Drug Abuse Resistance Education . . .," 2001, p.2). Karchmer (p.255) says of DARE: "DARE must be viewed in its proper context—that is, compared not with ideal results but with other drug control efforts that almost uniformly fall short of even modest expectations. When viewed in this context, DARE has merit. The program can point to fairly widespread short-term effects—an improvement over the hundreds of millions of dollars in federal and nonfederal drug control efforts that have had no measurable impact at all. Moreover, the promising results from the new curriculum suggest that DARE can play a significant future role in national drug education."

Public media campaigns have also focused on educating teens and preteens on the realities of drug use—how smoking causes bad breath and makes hair stink, or how getting drunk can become embarrassing if it leads to vomiting or having parents revoke driving privileges.

"Operation Broken Windows"   Another strategy used to prevent gangs and drugs from moving into a community or to drive out gangs and drugs that have already crept in is based on the **broken-window theory**—that if a window is broken in a building and is left unrepaired, it will signal that no one cares and that more damage can be caused without fear of punishment. It is an open invitation to crime. Strategies used to repair "broken windows" have included undercover operations, a uniformed police presence, a crackdown on trafficking by assigning K-9 units to local bus stations, and attention to social conditions: cutting the grass, removing the trash, repairing or installing streetlights and inspecting buildings for code violations.

Community mobilization can be a valuable asset in the effort to control drug use. Greenberg (2001, p.9) suggests: "The problem of substance abuse, including alcohol, is enormous. An entirely new corps of police professional is needed to serve as 'drug control specialists.' " He further asserts: "The regular and systematic use of auxiliary [volunteer] police personnel would appear to be a natural component of a community policing anti-drug strategy."

Simonson (2001, p.1) describes another approach emphasizing citizen cooperation: the drug-free communities support program. In June 1997, the Drug Free Communities Act became law. This act is "a catalyst for increased citizen participation in efforts to reduce substance use among youths, and it provides community anti-drug coalitions with much-needed funds to carry out their important missions." Through this program, an estimated $143.5 million was authorized to support the program over five years. The two major goals of the Drug-Free Communities Support Program are (1) to reduce substance abuse among youths and, over time, adults and (2) to establish and strengthen community collaboration, including working with federal, state, local and tribal governments and private nonprofit agencies.

Legalization

Legalization of drugs has been a topic of debate in the United States since the passage of the Harrison Narcotics Act in 1914. Some advocate making marijuana and other drugs legal, just as alcohol is, claiming this would reduce the cost of maintaining a drug habit and, consequently, reduce the amount of crime committed to obtain money to support the habit.

Legalization proponents say the prohibition on drug use has resulted in enormous profits for drug dealers, jail overcrowding and urban terrorization by gangs. Opponents, however, claim legalization will provide a "green light" for drug use, leading to addiction and, consequently, to increases in crime.

Arguments for Legalization   Proponents of drug legalization provide the following arguments:

- *Costs.* Dollars now spent on enforcement could be used for education and treatment.
- *Organized crime.* Legalization would eliminate the drug lords' major source of funds.
- *Revenues.* Taxes on drugs, like taxes on alcohol and tobacco, could be used to finance treatment programs.

Many believe the way some drug users are currently treated—incarcerated and criminalized for no other reason than that they use drugs—is leading our nation on a downward spiral toward the status of a prison state.

Arguments against Legalization   Those opposed to legalization of drugs give the following reasons for their objection:

- *Increased drug use and addiction.* Inexpensive, widely available drugs would increase addiction.
- *Increased crime.* Because of the proven link between drug use and crime, more drug users/addicts would lead to increased levels of crime.

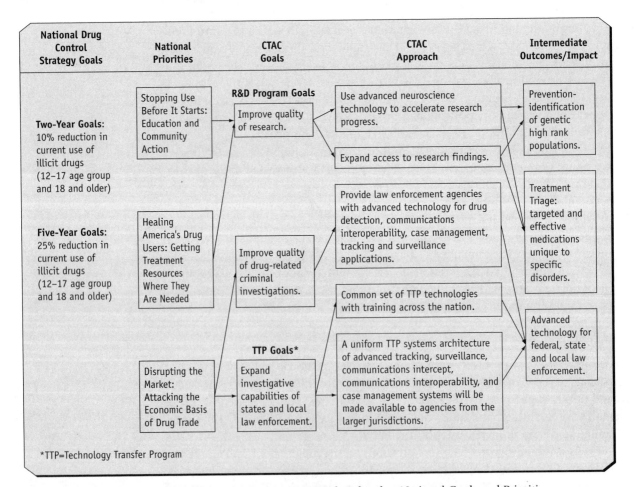

Figure 9.6   Counterdrug Technology Assessment Center Goals Related to National Goals and Priorities

SOURCE: *National Drug Control Strategy: 2003 CTAC Research and Development Blueprint Update 2003.* Washington, DC: Office of Drug Control Policy, February 2003.

- *Medical costs.* Health costs of drug abuse would increase.
- *Social values.* Legalizing drugs would make them socially acceptable.

The Need for a Combined Effort

The Counterdrug Technology Assessment Center (CTAC) within the Office of National Drug Control Policy is the central counterdrug enforcement research and development organization of the United States. The research goals of the CTAC were formulated to match the goals of the National Drug Control Strategy (*National Drug Control Strategy: CTAC Research and Development Blueprint,* 2003, p.1). These goals as they relate to national goals and priorities are illustrated in Figure 9.6.

SUMMARY

A major threat facing our nation today is gangs. Distinguishing characteristics of gangs include leadership, organization, associational patterns, domain identification and illegal activity. Gang members might also be identified by their names, their symbols (clothing and tattoos) and how they communicate, including graffiti and sign language. The most common reasons for joining a gang are for belonging, identity or recognition, protection, fellowship and brotherhood or from being intimidated to join. Unemployment, poverty and general despair lead young people to seek out economic opportunities in the growing illegal marketplace, often within the context of gangs. However, family structure is probably the most important risk factor in formation of a gang member. Many believe the fight against gangs will be in vain unless equal efforts are made at wiping out drug use.

Drug use and abuse pose another serious threat to our nation. In 1914 the federal government passed the Harrison Narcotics Act, which made the sale or use of certain drugs illegal, including narcotics and other dangerous drugs. In most states narcotics and other dangerous drugs may not be used or sold without a prescription. Federal law prohibits sale or distribution not covered by prescription. The most commonly observed drugs on the street, in possession of users and seized in drug raids are heroin, opium, morphine, codeine, cocaine, crack and marijuana. Arrest for possession or use of marijuana is the most frequent drug arrest.

Common effects of the various narcotics and other dangerous drugs include: (1) they are mind altering, (2) they may become addicting—either physically or psychologically, and (3) overdosage may result in convulsions and death. Although legal, alcohol, a depressant, is the most widely abused drug in the United States. Alcohol use is clearly linked to criminal activity, as is illicit drug use. The drug problem might be approached by crime control, punishment, rehabilitation, prevention or legalization.

DISCUSSION QUESTIONS

1. Do you think the gang problem is as serious as authorities claim?

2. Are there gangs in your area? If so, in what criminal activities are they involved?

3. What do you think might be done to reduce the gang problem? Is a hard or soft approach to gang activity the best approach to curtail criminal activity?

4. Which drugs pose the greatest problem for law enforcement?

5. If drugs were legalized, would law enforcement agencies benefit?

6. Should alcohol be banned in the United States?

7. What is the best approach to combat drugs?

8. Should nonviolent drug offenders be incarcerated or be diverted to treatment or some other form of community corrections?

9. Which poses the greater threat: gangs or drugs?

10. What law enforcement strategies might work equally well in suppressing gangs and drugs?

 INFOTRAC COLLEGE EDITION ASSIGNMENTS

- Use InfoTrac College Edition to help answer the Discussion Questions as appropriate.

- Use InfoTrac College Edition to research *alcohol* and *teen drinking*. Find and take the alcohol self-test. Did any of the results surprise you? If you feel comfortable doing so, be prepared to share your results with the class.

- Use InfoTrac College Edition to read and outline one of the following articles to share with the class.
  - "The Gangs behind Bars" by Tiffany Danitz
  - "Preventing Street Gang Violence" by Allen L. Hixon
  - "Safe Streets Task Force: Cooperation Gets Results" by David M. Allender
  - "Connecting Drug Paraphernalia to Drug Gangs" by Robert D. Sheehy and Efran A. Rosario
  - "Addressing the Need for a Uniform Definition of Gang-Involved Crime" by Mike Langston
  - "The Violence of Hmong Gangs and the Crime of Rape" by Richard Straka
  - "Gang Congregation Ordinance: Supreme Court Invalidation" by Daniel L. Schofield

INTERNET ASSIGNMENTS

Select two assignments to complete.

- Search for the key words *youth gangs*. Locate information on gangs in the United States and in foreign countries. Outline the similarities and differences between these gangs. Be prepared to discuss your findings with the class.

- Go to http://www.whitehousedrugpolicy.gov and outline the *president's drug policy*. Be prepared to share and discuss your outline with the class.

- Go to http://www.whitehousedrugpolicy.gov/drugfact/pulsechk/midyear2000/midyear2000.pdf for more current data on *drug use* to update your text. Be prepared to share with the class the updated data you found.

- Go to http://www.zonezero.com/exposiciones/fotografos/rodriguez for a photographic history of *gang life* seen from the street. Take notes on this photo essay, and be prepared to share your notes with the class.

- Go to http://www.usdoj.gov/ndic and find the National Drug Intelligence Center's *State Drug Threat Assessments*. Find your state and outline what the assessment for your state is.

BOOK-SPECIFIC WEB SITE

The book-specific Web site at http://info.wadsworth.com/0534552803 hosts a variety of resources for students and instructors. Included are extended activities from each chapter in which students write a policy, use critical thinking skills to make choices in response to a given scenario, use InfoTrac College Edition with direct links to articles for participation in topical discussion forums, and analyze court cases using Web links for research. Many activities can be printed or emailed to instructors.

Plus, cited cases with Web links, interactive key term FlashCards, PowerPoint presentations, chapter objectives, and an extensive collection of chapter-based Web links provide additional information and activities to include in the curriculum.

REFERENCES

AIDS Policy and Law (letter to "Executives"). Washington, DC: Buraff Publications, a division of The Bureau of National Affairs, Inc. (no date).

Bennett, Wayne W. and Hess, Kären M. *Criminal Investigation*, 7th ed. Belmont, CA: Wadsworth Publishing Company, 2004.

Brown, Cynthia. "DARE Officials, Responding to Critics, Come Up with New Program." *American Police Beat*, April 2001, p.76.

Burke, John. "Prescription Drug Diversion." *Law Enforcement Technology*, May 2004, pp.16–21.

Bush, George W. Transmittal Letter for the *National Drug Control Strategy*. Washington, DC: Office of National Drug Control Policy, February 2002.

"California Law Enforcement Praises School Anti-Gang Program." *Criminal Justice Newsletter*, November 2, 2003, pp.4–5.

Cohen, Jacqueline; Gorr, Wilpen; and Singh, Piyusha. "Estimating Intervention Effects in Varying Risk Settings: Do Police Raids Reduce Illegal Drug Dealing at Nuisance Bars?" *Criminology*, May 2003, pp.257–292.

DePresca, John. "Date Rape Drugs." *Law and Order*, October 2003, pp.210–213.

Domash, Shelly Feuer. "Stolen Dreams." *Police*, June 2001, pp.46–51.

"Drug Abuse Resistance Education Plans Test of a New Curriculum." *Criminal Justice Newsletter*, February 26, 2001, pp.2–3.

DEA Web site, www.dea.gov, 2001.

Drug Treatment in the Criminal Justice System. Washington, DC: ONDCP Drug Policy Information Clearinghouse Fact Sheet, March 2001. (NCJ 181857)

Egley, Arlen Jr. and Major, Aline K. *Highlights of the 2002 National Youth Gang Survey*. Washington, DC: OJJDP Fact Sheet #01, April 2004. (FS 200401)

Ericson, Nels. *Substance Abuse: The Nation's Number One Health Problem*. Washington, DC: OJJDP Fact Sheet #17, May 2001. (FS-200117)

Esbensen, Finn-Aage. "Evaluating GREAT: A School-Based Gang Prevention Program."*NIJ Journal*, 2004, pp.1–8. (NCJ 198604)

Esbensen, Finn-Aage; Osgood, D. Wayne; Taylor, Terrance J.; Peterson, Dana; and Freng, Adrienne. "How Great Is G.R.E.A.T.? Results from a Longitudinal Quasi-Experimental Design." *Criminology and Public Policy*, vol. 1, no. 1, 2001a, p.87.

Esbensen, Finn-Aage; Winfree, L. Thomas, Jr.; He, Ni; and Taylor, Terrance J. "Youth Gangs and Definitional Issues: When Is a Gang a Gang, and Why Does It Matter?" *Crime & Delinquency*, January 2001b, pp.105–130.

"The Five Promises Checklist: Helping Communities Help Youths." *OJJDP News @ a Glance*, September/October 2003, p.5. http://www.americaspromise.org.

Gang Awareness. Chicago: City of Chicago, Department of Human Services, no date.

Garrett, Ronnie. "Turning up the Heat on Meth Cooks." *Law Enforcement Technology*, May 2004, pp.36–42.

Gordon, Rachel A.; Lahey, Benjamin B.; Kawai, Eriko; Loeber, Rolf; Stouthamer-Loeber, Magda; and Farrington, David P. "Antisocial Behavior and Youth Gang Membership: Selection and Socialization." *Criminology*, February 2004, pp.55–84.

Greenberg, Martin A. "A Drug Strategy for the New Millennium." *Law Enforcement News*, September 28, 2001, pp.9–10.

"Harvard Study Reveals That College Binge Drinking Continues to Be a Problem." *NCJA Justice Bulletin*, 2003, pp.4–5.

Hill, Karl G.; Lui, Christina; and Hawkins, J. David. *Early Precursors of Gang Membership: A Study of Seattle Youth*. Washington, DC: OJJDP Juvenile Justice Bulletin, December 2001. (NCJ 190106)

Howell, James C. *Youth Gang Programs and Strategies*. Washington, DC: National Youth Gang Center, August 2000. (NCJ 171154)

Howell, James C.; Egley, Arlen, Jr.; and Gleason, Debra K. *Modern-Day Youth Gangs*. Washington, DC: OJJDP Juvenile Justice Bulletin, June 2002. (NCJ 191524)

Inciardi, James A.; Martin, Steven S.; and Butzin, Clifford A. "Five-Year Outcomes of Therapeutic Community Treatment of Drug-Involved Offenders after Release from Prison." *Crime and Delinquency*, vol. 50, no. 1, 2004, p.88.

Johnston, Lloyd D.; O'Malley, Patrick M.; Bachman, Jerald G.; and Schulenberg, John E. *Monitoring the Future: National Results on Adolescent Drug Use—Overview of Key Findings, 2003*. Bethesda, MD: National Institute on Drug Abuse, 2003. (NIH 04-5506) http://www.monitoringthefuture.org

Kaplan, J. *Heroin*. Washington, DC: National Institute of Justice, Crime File Study Guide. U.S. Department of Justice, no date. (NCJ 97225)

Karchmer, Clifford L. "Local Drug Control." In *Local Government Police Management*, 4th ed., edited by William A. Geller and Darrel Stephens. Washington, DC: International City/County Management Association, 2003, pp.241–266.

Katz, Charles M. "The Establishment of a Police Gang Unit: An Examination of Organizational and Environmental Factors." *Criminology*, February 2001, pp.37–74.

King, Ryan S. and Mauer, Mark. *Distorted Priorities: Drug Offenders in State Prisons*. Washington, DC: The Sentencing Project, 2004. http://www.sentencingproject.org

Krott, Rob. "Vietnamese Gangs in America." *Law and Order*, May 2001, pp.100–194.

Langston, Mike. "Addressing the Need for a Uniform Definition of Gang-Involved Crime." *FBI Law Enforcement Bulletin*, February 2003, pp.7–11.

Lopez, D. A. and Brummett, Patricia O'Donnell. "Gang Membership and Acculturation: ARSMA-II and Choloization." *Crime & Delinquency*, October 2003, pp.627–642.

MDMA (Ecstasy). Washington, DC: ONDCP Fact Sheet, April 2002. http://www.whitehousedrugpolicy.gov.

Meeker, James W.; Parsons, Katie J. B.; and Vila, Bryan J. "Developing a GIS-Based Regional Gang Incident Tracking System." In *Responding to Gangs: Evaluation and Research*, edited by Winifred L. Reed and Scott H. Decker. Washington, DC: National Institute of Justice, July 2002, pp.289–329. (NCJ 190351)

Miethe, Terance D. and McCorkle, Richard C. "Evaluating Nevada's Antigang Legislation and Gang Prosecution Units." In *Responding to Gangs: Evaluation and Research*, edited by Winifred L. Reed and Scott H. Decker. Washington, DC: National Institute of Justice, July 2002, pp.169–195. (NCJ 190351)

Miller, Jody. *One of the Guys: Girls, Gangs and Gender*. New York: Oxford University Press, 2001.

Miller, Jody. "Young Women in Street Gangs: Risk Factors, Delinquency and Victimization Risk." In *Responding to Gangs: Evaluation and Research*, edited by Winifred L. Reed and Scott H. Decker. Washington, DC: National Institute of Justice, July 2002, pp.67–105. (NCJ 190351)

Miller, Linda S. and Hess, Kären M. *The Police in the Community: Strategies for the 21st Century*, 3rd ed. Belmont, CA: Wadsworth Publishing Company, 2002.

Miller, Walter B. *The Growth of Youth Gang Problems in the United States: 1970–98*. Washington, DC: Office of Juvenile Justice and Delinquency Prevention, April 2001. (NCJ 181868)

Monitoring the Future. See Johnston et al.

Moore, Joan and Hagedorn, John. *Female Gangs: A Focus on Research*. Washington, DC: OJJDP Juvenile Justice Bulletin, March 2001. (NCJ 186159)

National Drug Control Strategy: CTAC Research and Development Blueprint, Update 2003. Washington, DC: Office of National Drug Control Policy, February 2003.

"National Drug Control Strategy Targets Prescription Drug Abuse." *Drug Enforcement Report*, March 8, 2004, pp.1–2.

National Drug Threat Assessment 2004. Washington, DC: National Drug Intelligence Center, 2004. http://www.usdoj.gov/ndic/products.htm.

"New Program Supports Community Anti-Gang Efforts." *OJJDP News @ a Glance*, September/October 2003, pp.1–2.

Peyton, Elizabeth A. and Gossweiler, Robert. *Treatment Services in Adult Drug Courts: Report on the 1999 National Drug Court Treatment Survey*. Washington, DC: National Treatment Accountability for Safer Communities, May 2001. (NCJ 188085)

Pulse Check: National Trends in Drug Abuse. Washington, DC: Office of National Drug Control Policy, January 2004. (NCJ 210398) http://www.whitehousedrugpolicy.gov.

Schanlaub, Russell. "A Prescription for Abuse." *Law and Order*, November 2003, pp.93–96.

Schennum, Tim. "Unfair Rap for DARE." *Law and Order*, August 2001, p.103.

Scott, Michael S. *Clandestine Drug Labs*. Washington, DC: Office of Community Oriented Policing Services Problem-Oriented Guides for Police Series No. 16, April 2002. http://www.cops.usdoj.gov.

Shelden, Randall G.; Tracy, Sharon K.; and Brown, William B. *Youth Gangs in American Society*, 3rd ed. Belmont, CA: Wadsworth Publishing Company, 2004.

Simonson, James M. *The Drug-Free Communities Support Program*. Washington, DC: OJJDP Fact Sheet #08, April 2001. (FS-200108)

Snyder, Nina. "Decriminalization of Dope Cases." *Police*, May 2001, pp.52–55.

Spergel, I. A. and Curry, G. D. "Strategies and Perceived Agency Effectiveness in Dealing with the Youth Gang." In *Gangs in America*, by C. Ronald Huff, 1990.

Starbuck, David; Howell, James C.; and Lindquist, Donna J. *Hybrid and Other Modern Gangs*. Washington, DC: OJJDP Juvenile Justice Bulletin, December 2001. (NCJ 189916)

Steffen, George and Candelaria, Samuel. "Currency Seizures during Interdiction Investigations." *Law and Order*, March 2004, pp.40–47.

Straka, Richard. "The Violence of Hmong Gangs and the Crime of Rape." *FBI Law Enforcement Bulletin*, February 2003, pp.12–16.

Strandberg, Keith. "The Nation's Drug Control Policy." *Law Enforcement Technology*, May 2003, pp.62–67.

Street Gangs of Los Angeles County: A White Paper. No date.

Streit, Corinne. "The Increasingly Popular Club Drug: Ecstasy." *Law Enforcement Technology*, May 2001, pp.24–28.

Strong, Ronald L. "The National Drug Intelligence Center: Assessing the Drug Threat." *The Police Chief*, May 2001, pp.55–60.

"Taking a Different Road with First-Time Drug Violators." *Law Enforcement News*, February 28, 2001, p.5.

"Truth, DARE & Consequences: Anti-Drug Program Officials Say Curriculum Needs a Makeover." *Law Enforcement News*, February 28, 2001, pp.1, 10.

"Underworld Dot-Coms: Gangs Staking Out Turf in Cyberspace." *Law Enforcement News*, October 31, 2001, p.7.

Valdez, Al. "Biker Gangs: Crime on Wheels." *Police*, January 2001a, pp.46–48.

Valdez, Al. "East to West Gang Trends." *Police*, February 2001b, pp.49–50.

Valdez, Al. "Club Drugs." *Police*, April 2002a, pp.74–78.

Valdez, Al. "White Supremacist Groups (crossed out) Gangs: From the Aryan Nation to the Posse Comitatus, White Racist Groups Are Still Recruiting and Spreading an Often Violent Message." *Police*, October 2002b, pp.90–93.

Valdez, Avelardo and Sifaneck, Stephen J. "'Getting High and Getting By': Dimensions of Drug Selling Behaviors among American Mexican Gang Members in South Texas." *Journal of Research in Crime and Delinquency*, February 2004, pp.82–105.

Walker, Robert. Gangs Or Us Web site. http://www.gangsorus.com/law.html.

Walker, Samuel. *Sense and Nonsense about Crime and Drugs: A Policy Guide*, 5th ed. Belmont, CA: Wadsworth Publishing Company, 2001.

Walker, Samuel; Spohn, Cassia; and DeLone, Miriam. *The Color of Justice: Race, Ethnicity, and Crime in America*, 3rd ed. Belmont, CA: Wadsworth Publishing Company, 2004.

Walters, John P. *National Drug Control Strategy: Counter-Drug Research and Development Blueprint Update*. Washington, DC: Office of National Drug Control Policy, February 2002a. (NCJ 192263)

Walters, John P. "Local Law Enforcement's Role in the National Drug Control Strategy." *Subject to Debate*, March 2002b, pp.1, 3.

Webb, Vincent J. and Katz, Charles M. "Policing Gangs in an Era of Community Policing." In *Policing Gangs and Youth Violence*, edited by Scott H. Decker. Belmont,

CA: Thomson/Wadsworth Publishing Company, 2003, pp.17–49.

Weisel, Deborah Lamm. "The Evolution of Street Gangs: An Examination of Form and Variation." In *Responding to Gangs: Evaluation and Research*, edited by Winifred L. Reed and Scott H. Decker. Washington, DC: National Institute of Justice, July 2002, pp.25–65. (NCJ 190351)

Weisel, Deborah Lamm. "Criminal Organizations." In *Local Government Police Management*, 4th ed., edited by William A. Geller and Darrel Stephens. Washington, DC: International City/County Management Association, 2003, pp.267–290.

CASES CITED

City of Chicago v. Morales, 119 S.Ct. 1849 (1999)
United States v. Bajakajian, 524 U.S. 321 (1998)
United States v. Ursery, 518 U.S. 267 (1996)

ADDITIONAL RESOURCES

Following are gang Web sites recommended for additional study:

Gangs and Security Threat Group Awareness: http://www.dc.state.fl.us/pub/gangs/index.html
This Florida Department of Corrections Web site contains information, photographs and descriptions on a wide variety of gang types, including Chicago- and Los Angeles-based gangs, prison gangs, nation sets and supremacy groups.

GangsorUs: www.gangsorus.com
This site offers a broad range of information, including a state-by-state listing of all available gang laws, gang identities and behaviors applicable to all areas of the United States as well as links to other sites that provide information to law enforcement, parents and teachers.

Southeastern Connecticut Gang Activities Group (SEGAG): www.segag.org
This coalition of law enforcement and criminal justice agencies from southeastern Connecticut and New England provides information on warning signs that parents and teachers often observe first, along with a large number of resources and other working groups that are part of nationwide efforts to contain gang violence.

National Gang Crime Research Center (NGCRC): www.ngcrc.com
This nonprofit independent agency carries out research on gangs and gang members and disseminates the information through publications and reports.

CHAPTER 10

Terrorism: The Newest Threat to Our National Security

Tonight we are a country awakened to danger and called to defend freedom. Our grief has turned to anger, and anger to resolution. Whether we bring our enemies to justice, or bring justice to our enemies, justice will be done. . . . Our war on terror begins with al-Qaeda, but it does not end there. It will not end until every terrorist group of global reach has been found, stopped, and defeated.

—President George W. Bush
in an address to Congress, September 20, 2001

DO YOU KNOW . . .

- What most definitions of terrorism include?
- What three elements are common in terrorism?
- How the FBI classifies terrorist acts?
- What motivates most terrorist attacks?
- What domestic terrorist groups exist in the United States?
- What methods terrorists may use?
- What federal office was established as a result of 9/11?
- What the lead federal agencies in combating terrorism are?
- What major act was legislated as a result of 9/11? How it enhances counterterrorism efforts by the United States?
- What the three-tiered model of al-Qaeda terrorist attacks consists of?
- What the key to successfully combating terrorism is?
- What four obstacles to intelligence effectiveness are?
- What two concerns are associated with the current "war on terrorism"?

CAN YOU DEFINE?

asymmetric warfare	cyberterrorism	interoperability	sleeper cell
bioterrorism	eco-terrorism	jihad	terrorism
contagion effect			

Introduction

The "war on drugs" has been a top priority for the past decade; however, on September 11, 2001, as a result of the terrorist attacks on America, this priority changed. The war on drugs, at least for the moment, has taken a backseat to the new war on terrorism, as both the FBI and the U.S. Customs Service have made terrorism their top priority. Commissioner of Customs Bonner stated: "The battle against terrorism is and will be the highest priority for the U.S. Customs Service" ("Terrorism Fight Is Top Priority . . .," 2001, p.1). In May 2002 the FBI announced that more than 500 of the agency's 11,500 agents were being transferred from law enforcement duties, mainly drug enforcement, to counterterrorism. The Bureau also undertook a rapid hiring effort to bring in 900 additional linguists, computer experts and other specialists to bolster antiterrorism activities ("Domestic Law Enforcement Given Lower Priority at FBI," 2002, p.1).

This chapter begins by defining terrorism, examining the various motivations for terrorism and classifying terrorism as domestic or international. Next is a look at the various motivations for terrorism, identifying the major domestic terrorist groups and the methods used by terrorists. This is followed by a brief chronology of major terrorist events that have occurred around the world from the first century to the present. The events of the September 11 terrorist attacks on America are then covered, including possible answers to the questions "Why did it happen?" and "Who is responsible?" Next is a look at the critical role of local law enforcement in the national response to terrorism and efforts to detect, prepare for, prevent, protect against, respond to and recover from terrorist attacks. Then the new type of war terrorism presents, asymmetric warfare, is explained. Next an important homeland initiative is described, the Center for Food Protection and Defense. The chapter concludes with a discussion of the role of the media in the war on terrorism and two major concerns related to that war: erosion of civil liberties and retaliation against people of Middle Eastern descent.

The Threat of Terrorism

Analyses of Gallup Polls over the past few years reveal that the American public has been significantly affected by terrorist events in the United States. For example, in a poll conducted January 10–14, 2001, respondents were asked, "What do you think is the most important problem facing the country today?" The question was open-ended, meaning respondents were not given a list of possible responses and asked to pick one, but instead were allowed to respond with whatever came to mind. In this poll, ethics and morality topped the chart of most important problems (13 percent), followed by education (12 percent), crime/violence (9 percent) and dissatisfaction with the government (9 percent). No responses of "terrorism" were noted (Newport, 2001). However, in a November 8–11, 2001, poll that asked the same open-ended question, 37 percent of respondents stated terrorism was the country's most important problem, with concerns about the economy in general a distant second (16 percent) and fear of war (13 percent) coming in third (Jones, 2001).

Similarly, in an April 7–9, 2000, poll that asked: "How worried are you that you or someone in your family will become a victim of terrorism?", 4 percent responded "very worried," 20 percent were "somewhat worried," and 75 percent were "not too worried" or "not worried at all." A September 11, 2001, poll, however, yielded vastly different results: 23 percent were "very worried," 35 percent were "somewhat worried," 24 percent were "not too worried," 16 percent were "not worried at all," and 1 percent reported knowing a victim of terrorism (Jones).

In June the State Department reported: "Significant acts of terror world-wide reached a 21-year high in 2003" (Schweld, 2004, p.A1). In 2002, 205 terrorist incidents occurred compared to 208 in 2003. Fewer people were killed in 2003, 625 compared to 725 killed in 2002. However, many more were injured in 2003, 3,646 compared to 2,013 injured in 2002. Thirty-five U.S. citizens were killed in international terror attacks in 2003. The deadliest was a suicide bombing in Riyadh, Saudi Arabia, which included nine Americans among the 26 victims (Schweld). The department's report did not include U.S. troops wounded or killed in Iraq as they were directed at "combatants."

Law enforcement has necessarily been called on to respond to the threat of terrorism and to help quell the public's heightened state of alarm by restoring peace and security to our free country. Then attorney general, John Ashcroft, announced plans for "a wartime reorganization and mobilization of the nation's justice and law enforcement resources" to meet the new "first and overriding" priority for the Justice Department: preventing additional terrorist attacks on America ("Ashcroft Announces Plan . . .," 2001, p.1).

Terrorism Defined

No single definition of terrorism is universally accepted because, as The Terrorism Research Center notes: "One man's terrorist is another's freedom fighter." The Center defines **terrorism** as "the use of force or violence against persons or property in violation of the criminal laws of the United States for purposes of intimidation, coercion or ransom." This is similar to the FBI's definition: "Terrorism is the unlawful use of force or violence against persons or property to intimidate or coerce a government, the civilian population, or any segment thereof, in furtherance of political or social objectives." The U.S. Code Title 22 defines terrorism as the "premeditated, politically motivated violence perpetrated against non-combatant targets by subnational groups or clandestine agents, usually intended to influence an audience." A more graphic definition is provided by James Poland: "Terrorism is the premeditated, deliberate, systematic murder, mayhem, and threatening of the innocent to create fear and intimidation in order to gain a political or tactical advantage."

 Most definitions of terrorism include the systematic use of physical violence, either actual or threatened, against noncombatants to create a climate of fear and cause some religious, political or social change.

Carter and Holden (2003, p.300) suggest: "Terrorism may be seen as a tactic, strategy, philosophy or pejorative label to describe the activities of one's enemies." They contend: "The most useful definition of terrorism is a form of political or religious militancy that uses violence or the threat of violence in an attempt to change behavior through fear." According to McVey (2002, p.174): "Terrorist acts can be identified as being criminal in nature, symbolically targeted and always aggressive. They seek to achieve political goals and communicate a message."

Three elements of terrorism are: (1) it is criminal in nature, (2) targets are typically symbolic and (3) the terrorist actions are always aggressive and often violent.

Classification of Terrorist Acts

 The FBI categorizes terrorism in the United States as either domestic or international terrorism.

Domestic Terrorism

The 1995 bombing of the Alfred P. Murrah Federal Building in Oklahoma City and the pipe bomb explosions in Centennial Olympic Park during the 1996 Summer Olympic Games highlight the threat of domestic terrorists. They represent extreme right- or left-wing and special interest beliefs. Many are antigovernment, antitaxation and engage in survivalist training to perpetuate a white, Christian nation. The right-wing militia or patriot movement is a law enforcement concern because of the potential for violence and criminal behavior. Some states have passed legislation limiting militias, including types of training they can undergo. Domestic terrorism is examined in depth under the later discussion of motivations for terrorism.

International Terrorism

International terrorism is foreign-based or directed by countries or groups outside the United States against the United States. The FBI divides international terrorism into three categories. The first threat is foreign state sponsors of international terrorism using terrorism as a tool of foreign policy, for example Iraq, Libya and Afghanistan. The second threat is formalized terrorist groups such as Lebanese Hezballah, Egyptian Al-Gamm's Al-Islamiyya, Palestinian HAMAS and Osama bin Laden's al-Qaeda. The third threat comes from loosely affiliated international radical extremists who have a variety of identities and travel freely in the United States, unknown to law enforcement or the government.

The Dual Threat

As Pitcavage (2003, p.35) stresses: "As America goes forward in its war on terrorism, those who wage that war must always remember that there are fronts. Even as the United States seeks to eradicate international terrorist groups such as al-Qaeda, it must never forget to protect its citizens from those among them who would like nothing better but to tear it apart and recast it in their own, warped image. America's police officers are on the front lines of that battle." Garrett (2002, p.22) also urges: "In the war against terrorism, it's important that all law enforcement—local, state and federal—keep as close an eye on domestic terrorists as they do on the international variety." One approach to understanding terrorism is to examine the motivations that produce it.

Motivations for Terrorism

 Most terrorist acts result from dissatisfaction with a religious, political or social system or policy and frustration resulting from an inability to change it through acceptable, nonviolent means.

Religious motives are seen in Islamic extremism. Political motives include such elements as the Red Army Faction. Social motives are seen in single-issue groups such as antiabortion groups, animal rights groups and environmentalists.

Borum (2003, pp.7–8) describes a four-stage process in the ideological development of terrorism: "To begin with, an extremist individual or group identifies some type of undesirable event or condition ('it's not right'). . . . Next they frame the undesirable condition as an 'injustice'; that is, it does not apply to everyone ('it's not fair'). . . . Then, because injustice generally results from transgressive (wrongful) behavior, extremists hold a person or group responsible ('it's your fault'), identifying a potential target. . . . Last, they deem the person or group responsible for the injustice as 'bad' ('you're evil'); after all, good people would not intentionally inflict adverse conditions on others." This four-stage process is illustrated in Figure 10.1.

 Domestic terrorist groups include white supremacists, black supremacists, militia groups, other right-wing extremists, left-wing extremists, pro-life extremists, animal rights activists and environmental extremists.

White Supremacists

Scoville (2003, p.48) notes: "One of the oldest American terrorist organizations is the Ku Klux Klan. Formed by Confederate veterans following the Civil War, the goal of the original Klan was to terrorize freed blacks and exert political influence over the Reconstruction south." He asserts: "The Klan is still out there. Members of local and regional Klan groups have been blamed for church burnings, intimidation and harassment of minorities and minority advocates, and other crimes."

Neo-Nazi groups also espouse white supremacy. Skinheads, discussed in Chapter 8, fall into this category. Pitcavage (p.33) notes: "Perhaps the greatest blow to white supremacists was the death in July 2002 of William Pierce, founder of the National Alliance (NA), the largest and most well-organized neo-Nazi group in the United States, and author of *The Turner Diaries*, a fictionalized blueprint for white revolution that inspired terrorists such as Timothy McVeigh."

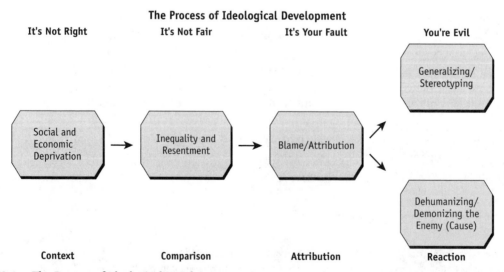

Figure 10.1 The Process of Ideological Development

SOURCE: Randy Borum. "Understanding the Terrorist Mind-Set." *FBI Law Enforcement Bulletin*, July 2003, p.9. Reprinted by permission.

Black Supremacists

The Black Panther Party for Self-Defense was established in 1966 during a time of racial turmoil. According to Scoville (p.46): "Today, a newly reconstituted Black Panther Party for Self-Defense has been organized, and it qualifies as a hate group. These contemporary Panthers are heavily armed, advocate violence against whites, and like their 1960's predecessors, see cops as the enemy."

The Militia Movement

White (2003, p.228) notes: "Research conducted by the Strategic Intelligence Division of the Bureau of Alcohol, Tobacco and Firearms suggests the militia movement is far from monolithic. ATF analysts believe militias tend to be issue oriented. Groups gather around taxes, abortion, gun control and/or Christian Identity. My own research reflects the ATF findings." Militia groups are usually heavily armed and practice their sharp-shooting skills. According to White: "Many militia members are frustrated, overwhelmed, and socially unable to cope with the rapid pace of change in the modern world. They may be extremists, but they are not terrorists. This is not to say that the militia movement is not related to domestic violence—far from it. Many militia groups provide the rhetoric for violence." White (p.229) contends: "Paramilitary groups come in a variety of shapes and sizes, and most of their action is rhetorical. The Arizona Vipers and the Freemen of Montana are exceptions. Rhetoric turns to violence when small detached groups emerge from larger extremist groups."

Other Right-Wing Extremists

The preceding groups might also be described as right-wing extremists. According to White (2003, p.223): "The appearance of right-wing extremism came to fruition around 1984 and has remained active since that time." He (p.224) cites three issues that rejuvenated the extreme right: the Brady Bill, Ruby Ridge and Waco. The Brady Bill caused militia groups to fear federal gun control legislation. Says White (p.225): "By stressing the fear of gun control, right-wing extremists hoped to appear to be mainstream."

The Ruby Ridge incident involved an attempt to arrest Randy Weaver, a white supremacist charged with selling illegal firearms to undercover ATF agents. A shootout ensued, resulting in the death of a U.S. marshal and Weaver's young son. The FBI laid siege to Weaver's Ruby Ridge cabin and killed his pregnant wife before Weaver surrendered.

White (p.225) describes the third galvanizing incident, the federal siege of the Branch Davidian compound near Waco, Texas:

> In 1993, ATF agents attempted to serve a search warrant on the compound, but they were met with a hail of gunfire. Four agents were killed, and several were wounded. After a three-month siege, FBI agents moved in with tear gas. Unknown to the agents, the compound was laced with gasoline. When the FBI moved in, the Branch Davidians burned their fortress, killing over 70 people, including several young children held inside the compound.

Figure 10.2 illustrates the interaction of the various groups within the right-wing terrorist movement.

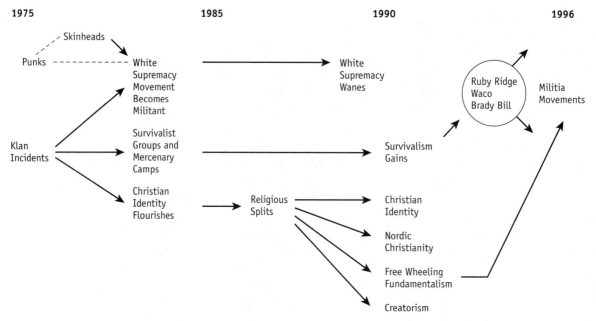

Figure 10.2   American Right-Wing Terrorism, 1979–1996

SOURCE: Jonathan R. White. *Terrorism: An Introduction,* 4th ed. Belmont, CA: Wadsworth Publishing Company, 2003, p.227. Reprinted by permission.

Left-Wing Extremists

Brinkley (2003, pp.33–34) explains: "The left wing believes in a Pro-Marxist stance where the rich must be brought down and the poor elevated. Presently the largest groups of supporters for this cause are Anarchists. . . . This group believes that one receives according to one's needs."

Pro-Life Extremists

Although many pro-life, antiabortion advocates stay within the law in promoting their beliefs, some groups do not. One such group is an active terrorist organization called the Army of God. According to Scoville (p.48): "Abortion clinics and their staffs are common Army of God targets, with zealots committing crimes, ranging from arson, to assault, to assassination. Like many domestic terrorist groups, Army of God practices leaderless resistance with no set structure, membership or command chain." Scoville cautions: "Army of God and other terrorist groups targeting abortion clinics are extremely dangerous to law enforcement personnel. Law enforcement officers working security for clinics on- and off-duty have been injured and even killed in pro-life terrorist attacks."

Animal Rights Activists

As Scoville (p.46) notes: "One of the most active domestic terrorist groups is the Animal Liberation Front (ALF). This clandestine and decentralized group has claimed credit for attacks on meat packing plants, furriers and research labs. Founded in England in 1976, ALF's influence spread to the United States in 1982. The succeeding two decades have seen the group cause millions of dollars in damages and medical research setback through its acts of vandalism, arson and the 'liberation' of laboratory animals."

ALF supposedly strives to avoid hurting people in its attacks, but another animal rights group, Stop Huntingdon Animal Cruelty (SHAC), believes differently. Members of this group feel that people who make animals suffer should be made to suffer. According to Scoville: "SHAC was organized in England to harass Huntingdon Life Sciences, one of the world's largest animal testing and research companies. SHAC makes death threats, carries out violent attacks and sends letter bombs to people they label 'collaborators with animal torture.' "

Scoville (p.46) describes another animal rights group called the Justice Department: "If ALF is bad and SHAC dangerous, a newer animal rights group, called the 'Justice Department' is just plain mean. Justice Department likes to send nasty little surprises to people it calls 'animal killing scum.' " One such surprise is envelopes sent to researchers and hunting guides that contain razor blades dipped in rat poison positioned to cut the fingers of anyone opening the envelopes without a letter opener.

Environmental Extremists

Environmental extremists are often referred to as eco-terrorists, with *eco* being derived from *ecology*—the study of the interrelationships of organisms and their environment. **Eco-terrorism** seeks to "inflict economic damage to those who profit from the destruction of the natural environment" (Vallee, 2001, p.40). Vallee (p.1) cautions: "Lately so-called 'eco-terrorist' movements have become increasingly violent and dangerous." According to Nilson and Burke (2002, p.1): "Ecological-terrorism is used as a tactic to stop companies, institutions, organizations and governments from damaging or altering the environment."

One such group is the Earth Liberation Front (ELF), often working with the Animal Liberation Front (ALF). Arson is a favorite weapon, responsible for tens of millions of dollars of property damage, including a U.S. Department of Agriculture building, a U.S. Forest Service ranger station and a Colorado ski resort. The group claims responsibility for releasing 5,000 mink from a Michigan fur farm, 600 wild horses from an Oregon corral and burning Michigan State University's genetic engineering research offices. In 2000 it claimed responsibility for torching a $2-million home in Colorado. In 2002, ELF claimed responsibility for arson at a research lab under construction on the St. Paul campus of the University of Minnesota to protest genetic engineering on plants (Sanow, 2002, p.5).

Nilson and Burke (p.3) contend that eco-terrorists commit many criminal acts in their fight to save nature, including equipment vandalism, package bombs or pipe bombs, destruction of research data, arson of buildings, obliteration of experimental plants and animals and the like. According to the FBI, ELF was responsible for more than $43 million in property damage from 1996 to 2002.

Methods Used by Terrorists

 Terrorists may use arson, explosives and bombs, weapons of mass destruction (biological, chemical or nuclear agents) and technology.

The use of arson has already been discussed.

Explosives and Bombs

According to Haber (2004, p.14): "Pipe bombs and other improvised explosive devices (IEDs) pose a serious threat to federal, state and local government facilities, considering how easily and inexpensively they can be put together. Schools, shopping malls, stadiums and other public places people can freely walk around and through are also potential targets for terrorist attacks." Directions for making pipe bombs and other incendiary devices can be found on the Internet. According to "The Shape of Things to Come" (2003, p.20): "Car and truck bombs will continue to be the modus operandi for terrorists."

From 1978 to 1996 Theodore Kaczynski terrorized the country as the Unabomber, through a string of 16 mail bombings that killed three people, apparently in protest against technology. Ramzi Ahmed Yousef, found guilty of masterminding the first World Trade Center bombing in 1993, declared that he was proud to be a terrorist and that terrorism was the only viable response to what he saw as a Jewish lobby in Washington. The car bomb used to shatter the Alfred P. Murrah Federal Building in 1995 was Timothy McVeigh's way to protest the government and the raid on the Branch Davidians at Waco. In 2002 Lucas Helder terrorized the Midwest with 18 pipe bombs placed in mailboxes across five states, leaving antigovernment letters with the bombs. Six exploded, injuring four letter carriers and two residents. And the most horrific act of terrorism against the United States occurred on September 11, 2001, when two airplanes were used as missiles to explode the World Trade Center twin towers, another plane was used as a missile to attack the Pentagon, and a fourth plane crashed in a Pennsylvania field before it could reach its intended target.

Gips (2003, p.16) describes one terrorist tactic, using a secondary explosive device after a first one is set off. This tactic was used in Bali, Indonesia, in October 2003 when a hand grenade was tossed into a nightclub, causing patrons to flee to the streets where they encountered a Jeep bomb. The attack, which killed almost 200 people, was attributed to Muslim extremists in Indonesia with links to al-Qaeda.

Suicide Bombers According to "Suicide Terrorism" (2003, pp.20–21): "Terrorists are ever willing to sacrifice themselves for their cause." Most believe the act makes them martyrs and assures them a place in their version of heaven. Their families are usually held in reverence and taken care of. Suicide bombers try to kill as many people as possible. "Confronting the Suicide-Bomber Threat" (2003, p.16) notes: "Although the United States has yet to be plagued by the type of routine belt-bomb suicide attacks that Israel experiences, many experts believe that it is only a matter of time before this tactic makes its way across the Atlantic."

Weapons of Mass Destruction (WMD)

Symonds (2003, p.19) contends: "Weapons of mass destruction (WMD) are not the result of any recent technological developments. Biological WMD have actually been in use since the 1300s. The advent of the 20th century brought with it the first use of artificially produced WMD—or chemical agents—during World War I. Today the world faces the major problem of how to get the genie back into the bottle. The means and recipes for the development of nuclear, radiological, biological and chemical weapons are well known and documented."

Guida (2002, p.54) suggests: "Terrorism through the release of biological, chemical and radiological agents is predicated upon use of the environment as a medium or weapon of mass harm and destruction. As a group, such acts can be referred to as enviroterrorism (this term should be distinguished from ecoterrorism, which has frequently been used to describe crimes committed allegedly to protect the environment)." Lesce (2001, p.90) notes: "Nuclear, chemical and biological threats have been known for decades; acceptance that the threats are real has been sluggish and preparations lacking."

Nuclear, biological or chemical agents are also referred to as "NBC" agents in the literature. "Safety on the Scene" (2002, p.6) notes that at NBC scenes, telemetry"data transmission to a remote location via radio, satellite, wireless or other communication"—can assist responders in several ways:

- It can relay weather data (including wind direction and speed, barometric pressure, relative humidity, etc.) to incident command (IC), allowing IC to assess the hazard's spread and to plan evacuations.
- It also can be combined with robotic detection and identification technology to warn IC of NBC agents' presence and strength.
- It can work with global positioning systems (GPS) to transmit the coordinates of an NBC release relative to the position of IC responders, residential or other civilian centers or other critical location information.
- It can track vehicles charged with transporting NBC materials to and from the site.

Some experts suggest that bioterrorism is the third most likely terrorist act to occur. Incendiary devices and explosives are most likely to be used because they are easy to make. Chemical devices are next in likelihood because the raw materials are easy to get and easy to use.

Biological Agents   **Bioterrorism** involves such biological weapons of mass destruction (WMD) as anthrax, botulism and smallpox. Hanson (2004, p.18) cautions: "The potential for a bioterrorist attack in the United States has become an unfortunate reality following the events of 9/11 and the anthrax scares." Martinez, unit chief of the FBI's Weapons of Mass Destruction Operations, says: "The advances in biotechnology, the open-source literature and the availability of the materials have made producing a bio-weapon a viable concern" (Strandberg, 2001, p.89). Biological agents include natural poisons, viruses, salmonella, botulism and anthrax.

The Central Intelligence Agency (CIA) reports that at least 10 countries are believed to possess or to be conducting research on biological agents for use as WMDs. In October 2001, a photo editor in Florida died from inhalation anthrax. Several weeks later, anthrax-laced letters were delivered to several major media networks and numerous government offices around Washington, DC. Environmental sampling also indicated massive amounts of anthrax spores at several post offices and mailroom facilities. While no cases of anthrax have been linked to the September 11 terrorist attacks or the al-Qaeda network, the incidents are regarded as terrorism, perhaps domestic in origin, and were investigated as crimes.

A survey of 2,000 hospitals conducted by the U.S. General Accounting Office (GAO) found that although 80 percent had written emergency response plans for large-scale infectious disease outbreaks, fewer than half had conducted training related to bioterrorism ("Bioterrorism," 2003, pp.24–25). Especially susceptible to bioterrorism are the nation's food and water supply, which might also be attacked using chemical agents.

Chemical Agents   Nason (2003, p.44) notes: "The Aum Shinrikyo event in the Tokyo subway in 1995 initially focused the security industry's efforts on detecting and mitigating chemical agent threats. That incident confirmed what all of us in this industry had long feared. A non-state entity could manufacture a viable chemical agent and deliver it in a public location." As White (2003, p.240) explains: "Members of a religious cult, the Aum Shinrikyo released a poisonous gas, sarin, into the crowded subway system. The act involved criminal terrorism for psychological gratification, but it had a deadly twist. The terrorists were not individuals seeking social release or some nebulous form of political events; they were members of an organized religious cult trying to destroy the Japanese government." Unfortunately, anyone with access to the Internet can obtain the chemical formula for sarin in less than 40 minutes through a Web search and can produce it inexpensively.

According to White (2003, p.251): "Chemical agents are not as lethal as biological agents, and they are easier to control." The four common types of chemical weapons are nerve agents, blood agents, choking agents and blistering agents.

Nuclear Terrorism   Stanton (2002, p.156) warns: "The United States finds itself at greater risk of an attack by nuclear-based weaponry today than at the height of the Cold War." According to the U.S. Nuclear Regulatory Commission (NRC) an average of approximately 375 devices of all kinds containing radioactive material are reported lost or stolen each year. Stanton reports: "Analysts say that this new nuclear threat will never be eliminated, only minimized. They point to the quantities of lost or stolen (called 'orphaned') radioactive waste in the United States and around the world that would be easy for terrorist groups to obtain. They also point to the arsenal of loosely guarded Russian tactical nuclear weapons (TNWs), some of which are also already missing." According to Stanton: "The successful detonation of a low-yield nuclear device or RDD [radiological dispersion device] would far surpass the aftermath of the terrorist attacks on September 11, 2001."

Technological Terrorism

White (2003, p.273) notes: "Technological terrorism is one of the more frightening scenarios one can imagine. Modern societies are susceptible to two methods of technological terror. The first is the employment of mass destruction weapons or the conversion of an industrial site—for example, a chemical plant—into a massively lethal instrument through sabotage. The other method is to attack a source that supplies technology or energy. The results of either type of attack could be catastrophic. Technology looms as a potentially sinister partner in the evolution of terrorism."

White (p.244) suggests: "The United States is the most technologically advanced superpower in the world. . . . The irony of U.S. success with technology is that the country has become vulnerable to attacks on technology and by technology." White (p.247) notes: "The United States relies on energy to support its technology, and the interruption of energy supplies could be construed as a national security threat. If a nation or terrorist group could shut off U.S. energy, it could close down major portions of the economy. Secure energy production, transportation and storage are all critical to the United States."

In 2000, President Clinton announced a billion-dollar plan to fight **cyberterrorism,** defined by the FBI as "terrorism that initiates, or threatens to initiate, the exploitation of or attack on information systems." Uner (2003, p.26) cautions: "The threat of cyberterrorism is real; it's only a matter of when." White (p.255), however, suggests: "Cyberterrorism is probably a misused term. Terrorists may use computers in terrorist acts. Such acts include the disruption of services, attacks on infrastructures including the defense system and placing cyberbombs in selected information systems." Damage to our critical computer systems can put our safety and our national security in jeopardy.

A Brief Chronology of Terrorism—Past to Present

Terrorism dates back to at least the first century when the Zealots, a Jewish sect, fought against Roman occupation of what is now Israel. In twelfth-century Iran, a group of Shiite Muslims committed terrorist acts against religious and political leaders of Sunni Islam. Through the eighteenth century most terrorist movements were based on religious beliefs. However, the word *terrorism* first appeared during the French Revolution (1789–1799) when revolutionaries who seized power in France used violence against their enemies. Their period of rule was called the Reign of Terror (Bassiouni, 2001).

During the nineteenth century, and into the twentieth, terrorist movements continued to be politically based. In the 1930s Germany's Adolf Hitler, Italy's Benito Mussolini and the Soviet Union's Joseph Stalin all used terrorism to discourage opposition to their governments. In 1945 conflict between Arab nations and Israel resulted in waves of terrorism throughout the Middle East. Since 1960 Palestinian groups have carried out acts of terrorism to establish an independent Palestinian state. According to Van Etten (2004, p.31): "The modern era of terrorism—that is, terrorism as we know it today—began in the late 1960s. . . . Worldwide there were 14,000 terrorist attacks from 1968 through 1999, and they resulted in more than 10,000 deaths."

In the United States, during the late 1800s and 1900s, the Ku Klux Klan advocated violence to terrorize blacks and their sympathizers. From 1978 to 1995, the anarchist and terrorist known as the Unabomber, using homemade bombs either mailed or planted, killed 3 people and wounded 23 others. Arrested in 1996, Theodore Kaczynski claimed allegiance to radical environmentalists and those opposed to the effects of industrialization and technology, targeting university professors, computer professionals and corporate executives.

The United States' support of Israel has resulted in several acts of terrorism against Americans by Palestinian radicals or supporters, including the 1983 attack by Shiite Muslim suicide bombers on the U.S. embassy in Beirut, Lebanon, and on the U.S. Marine barracks in Beirut, killing nearly 300, mostly Americans. In 1988 a bomb destroyed Pan American Flight 103 over Scotland, killing 259, including 189 Americans, and two Libyan terrorists were later charged with the act. One was found guilty of murdering the 259 passengers and crew. The court concluded it had insufficient evidence against the second suspect.

In the late 1980s the Animal Liberation Front used arson to terrorize in Davis, California; Tucson, Arizona; and Lubbock, Texas, and in 1990 the Popular Liberation Party used arson and bombs in Puerto Rico. Islamic radicals used a crude bomb made with agricultural fertilizer in a 1993 attack on the World Trade Center in New York that killed 6, injured nearly 1,000 and caused an estimated $600 million in damage. This blatant, foreign-sponsored terrorism was viewed with alarm and disbelief, yet because the towers still stood, Americans went on with life with a suppressed sense of invulnerability, and the fear of terrorism faded rapidly.

Then in 1995 a 4,800-pound truck bomb exploded in front of the Alfred P. Murrah Federal Building in Oklahoma City, killing 168 and injuring 500. Not only was this the deadliest terrorist attack the United States had ever endured up to that day, it was carried out by two Americans, Timothy McVeigh and Terry Nichols, both espousing the beliefs of a right-wing militia. The United States now faced the threat of both domestic and international terrorism. That same year the derailment of an Amtrak train in an Arizona desert was linked to terrorists.

In 1996 another truck bomb destroyed a barracks housing American military personnel in Dhahran, Saudi Arabia, killing 19 servicemen. In 1998 two U.S. embassies in East Africa were bombed, killing more than 200 people, including 12 Americans. Twenty-two people were charged with the crime. At the end of 2000, one had pled guilty to conspiring in the attacks, 5 were in custody in New York awaiting trial, 3 were in England awaiting extradition to the United States, and 13 were fugitives, including Osama bin Laden. Bin Laden was put on the FBI's 10 Most Wanted List, wanted in connection with the August 7, 1998, bombings of U.S. embassies in Dar Es Salaam, Tanzania, and Nairobi, Kenya.

Terrorism continued into the twenty-first century, and on October 12, 2000, 17 sailors died when two suicide bombers attacked the USS Cole while it was refueling in the Yemeni port of Aden. Then came September 11, 2001, the worst terrorist attack in the history of the United States, when terrorists hijacked four commercial airliners shortly after their take-offs and still carrying great amounts of fuel. Two of the planes were purposely crashed into the twin towers of the World Trade Center in New York, leaving 4,815 people missing and 417 confirmed dead, including the 157 passengers aboard Flight 11 and Flight 175. An hour later Flight 77 crashed into the Pentagon, leaving 189 believed dead, including everyone on board. Soon after that, another hijacked airliner presumed to be en route to either the White House or U.S. Capitol building crashed into a rural area in Pennsylvania, killing the 44 people aboard Flight 93 ("Lost But Not Forgotten," 2001). Among those missing or confirmed dead were 311 firefighters and 65 police officers ("IACP Response . . .," 2001, p.14).

September 11, 2001

"September 11, 2001, will go down as the bloodiest day in U.S. history with more deaths than the 4,000 plus who died in one day at Antietam or the 2,400 who died at Pearl Harbor" (Hackett, 2001, p.9). The Terrorism Research Center declared: "The attack of September 11 will be the precipitating moment of a new kind of war that will define a new century. This war will be fought in shadows, and the adversary will continue to target the innocent and defenseless." The Center outlined the effects of this attack:

> The President of the United States made it very clear in his September 20th speech to the Congress, the nation and the world, that this threat has not achieved its objectives of fear. Rather, it has galvanized the United States into action. The U.S. now sees a national security threat raised to an unprecedented level. However, the U.S. also sees an opportunity to solidify international support and national unity to combat this threat. . . .

This threat is not directed solely against the United States—it is a threat directed against all countries that seek freedom, peace and stability. The world's response to terrorism will change not only international efforts with respect to terrorism; it will change geopolitics as countries take sides and see mutual interests where few were apparent before. . . .

Adversaries of the United States will increasingly avoid direct confrontation with American interests. They will attack the soft underbelly of American society. They will exploit the benefits of a free society and remind the world of the risks that come with liberty, of the price of freedom. They will try to lessen the luster of America, but they will only succeed in fueling the flame of inspiration and opportunity the U.S. offers to people of the world. In their attempt to diminish the American spirit, they will find the best of what America and her allies have to offer, coming right at them.

Indeed, the horrific events of September 11 pulled together and unified the American people in a way most had never seen. Patriotism was suddenly popular again—Wal-Mart alone sold 88,000 American flags on September 12. Thousands of volunteers helped search for victims and donated blood and money. New York Governor George Pataki ordered nearly 3,000 National Guard troops and 200 state troopers into New York City, and an estimated 300 search-and-rescue dogs were flown in with their handlers from dozens of agencies ("A New 'Date Which Will Live in Infamy,' " 2001).

Why Did It Happen?

In 1996 the FBI established a Counterterrorism Center to combat terrorism. Also in 1996 the Antiterrorism and Effective Death Penalty Act was passed, including several specific measures aimed at terrorism. It enhanced the federal government's power to deny visas to individuals belonging to terrorist groups and simplified the process for deporting aliens convicted of crimes.

In 1999 then–FBI Director Louis Freeh announced: "Our No. 1 priority is the prevention of terrorism." The FBI added a new Counterterrorism Division with four subunits: the International Terrorism Section, the Domestic Terrorism Section, the National Infrastructure Protection Center and the National Domestic Preparedness Office. But this was not enough to avert the tragic events of September 11. As Anderson (2001, p.4) states: "Unthinkable is a word that describes the recent terrorist attacks. Many other words—gut-wrenching sadness and bitter

Attack on the World Trade Center.

Attack on the Pentagon.

anger, dull shock and utter disbelief—also come to mind. How could it happen? And who? And why? Definitely why?"

For one thing, U.S. immigration policies make it relatively easy for terrorists to enter the country and move freely within it. In fact, several people with connections to Osama bin Laden's al-Qaeda group received pilot training in the United States. In addition, Vincent (2001, p.26) contends that the terrorists took advantage of two major holes in the U.S. aviation security system: (1) a system fault in the FAA's Computer Assisted Passenger Profile System (CAPPS) and (2) its permissiveness in allowing knives and small cutting instruments on board in planes. Both American and United Airlines used the CAPPS system, which should have singled out some, perhaps all, of the hijackers. But the security measures applied only to checked baggage. No process was in place to notify screeners at screening points when a person met the CAPPS profile. As Vincent notes: "The hijackers probably did not know that this hole existed, but they did know that knives with less than four-inch blades were permitted."

In addition, those doing the screening are usually undertrained, underpaid and tired, many having to work two jobs to support themselves. To maintain the steady flow of hurried travelers trying to make their flights, screeners are instructed to spend only three to six seconds on each item passing through x-ray. Any distractions make this task more difficult.

Who Was Responsible?

The FBI, the lead agency investigating the attacks, undertook what Attorney General John Ashcroft describes as "the largest investigation in the history of the United States, probably in the history of the world" ("September 11 Terrorism . . .," 2001, p.1). Approximately 4,000 FBI agents and 3,000 support personnel were assigned to the case nationwide, and by early October, the FBI was handling more than a quarter-million potential leads and tips. It sent 18,000 law enforcement agencies a list of more than 190 witnesses, suspects and others they wanted to interview and, in the two months following the attack, the Justice Department had arrested more than 1,000 people suspected of having links to terrorist groups ("Ashcroft Announces Plan . . .," p.2).

The United States government, with concurrence from Britain and other United Nations member countries, believes it has an airtight case against bin Laden and several other suspects. Although no direct evidence links bin Laden with drug trafficking, ample evidence implicates the Afghanistan Taliban government, which provided sanctuary and other aid to bin Laden, in receiving much of its funding from the opium trade.

On September 20, 2001, in an address to Congress, President Bush said: "Al-Qaeda is to terror what the mafia is to crime. But its goal is not making money; its goal is remaking the world and imposing its radical beliefs on people everywhere. The terrorists' directive commands them to kill Christians and Jews, to kill all Americans, and make no distinctions among military and civilians, including women and children."

On November 13, 2001, the *Washington Post* reported that Britain would release more evidence implicating bin Laden in the September 11 attacks. The new dossier, updating charges laid out by Prime Minister Tony Blair on October 4, relied heavily on bin Laden's statements made in videotapes since military strikes began in Afghanistan ("Britain to Release More Evidence . . .," 2001, p.A13). In one videotape bin Laden is reportedly shown saying the September 11 hijackers were "blessed by Allah to destroy America's economic and military landmarks." He is also quoted as saying: "Yes, we kill their innocents, and this is legal religiously and logically." Another video shows bin Laden talking with associates in a relaxed atmosphere, reveling in the success of the deadly attacks and bragging he had known about them beforehand. Saying the attacks "benefited Islam greatly," bin Laden expressed pleasure that the destruction had exceeded his expectations. According to White (2003, pp.164–165): "Osama bin Laden redefined the meaning of terrorism in the modern world. . . . In 1996, Osama bin Laden officially 'declared war' on the United States."

The U.S. Response—Detect, Prepare, Prevent, Protect, Respond and Recover

In addition to an intense investigation, the United States initiated military action against Afghanistan after the Taliban government repeatedly refused to turn over Osama bin Laden. Furthermore, security was heightened at U.S. airports and throughout the country. As Sanow (2001, p.4) cautions: "While this is the boldest, least expected and most costly terrorist attack on U.S. soil, it is not the first and will not be the last."

The Department of Homeland Security

In September, then Attorney General Ashcroft announced that every U.S. attorney was establishing an antiterrorism task force to be conduits between federal and local agencies regarding information about suspected terrorists ("U.S. Antiterrorism Organization . . .," 2001, p.7). On October 8, 2001, President Bush signed Executive Order 13228 establishing the Department of Homeland Security (DHS) to be headed by Governor Tom Ridge.

 As a result of 9/11 the Department of Homeland Security was established, reorganizing the departments of the federal government.

How establishment of this department reorganized the federal government was explained in Chapter 1. The mission of the Department of Homeland Security is "to develop and coordinate the implementation of a comprehensive national strategy to secure the United States from terrorist threats or attacks" ("President Signs Homeland . . .," 2001, p.8). As noted by Rohen (2001, p.148): "Command and control of a terrorist threat or incident is a critical emergency management function that demands an integrated and unified framework for the preparation and execution of plans and orders."

 At the federal level, the FBI is the lead agency for responding to acts of domestic terrorism. The Federal Emergency Management Agency (FEMA) is the lead agency for consequence management (after an attack). The Department of Homeland Security (DHS) serves in a broad capacity, facilitating collaboration between local and federal law enforcement to develop a national strategy to detect, prepare for, prevent, protect against, respond to and recover from terrorist attacks within the United States.

In addition, the Office for Victims of Crime (OVC) has available the Terrorism and International Victims Unit (TIVU) to help victims of terrorism and mass violence (*Terrorism and International Victims Unit*, 2002). This organization provides training and technical assistance to first responders. It provided support to Oklahoma City in 1995 following the bombing of the Murrah Federal Building. After the attack on America September 11, 2001, the TIVU played a key role in the OVC's response to victims and their families in New York. Another effort to enhance national security was passage of the PATRIOT Act.

The USA PATRIOT Act

On October 26, 2001, President Bush signed into law the Uniting and Strengthening America by Providing Appropriate Tools Required to Intercept and Obstruct Terrorism (USA PATRIOT) Act, giving police unprecedented ability to search, seize, detain or eavesdrop in their pursuit of possible terrorists, saying: "This government will enforce this law with all the urgency of a nation at war." Bush asserted that the nation had little choice but to update surveillance procedures "written in the era of rotary telephones" to combat today's sophisticated terrorists ("Bush Signs Law . . .," 2001, p.A17). The law expands the FBI's wiretapping and electronic surveillance authority and allows nationwide jurisdiction for search warrants and electronic surveillance devices, including legal expansion of those devices to email and the Internet.

 The USA PATRIOT Act significantly improves the nation's counterterrorism efforts by:
- Allowing investigators to use the tools already available to investigate organized crime and drug trafficking.
- Facilitating information sharing and cooperation among government agencies so they can better "connect the dots."
- Updating the law to reflect new technologies and new threats.
- Increasing the penalties for those who commit or support terrorist crimes.

In defending the viability and constitutionality of "roving wiretaps," then Attorney General Ashcroft stated: "We are not asking the law to expand, just to grow as technology grows. . . . Terrorist organizations have increasingly used technology to facilitate their criminal acts and hide their communications from law enforcement. Terrorists are trained to change cell phones frequently, to route email through different Internet computers in order to defeat surveillance" ("Congress Debates Terror Bill's Effect on Criminal Justice," 2001, p.3).

The PATRIOT Act also includes money laundering provisions and sets strong penalties for anyone who harbors or finances terrorists. Senate Banking Committee Chairman Paul Sarbanes calls the PATRIOT bill the most significant money laundering legislation "since money laundering was first made a crime" in 1986, adding: "Osama bin Laden may have boasted 'Al-Qaeda includes modern, educated youths who are as aware of the cracks inside the Western financial system as they are aware of the lines in their hands,' but with [the PATRIOT legislation], we are sealing up those cracks" ("Congress Debates Terror . . .," p.3).

The 1984 Act to Combat International Terrorism (ACIT) established a monetary reward program for information involving terrorism. As Kash (2002, p.27) points out: "The recently enacted PATRIOT Act amended the reward program's authority by increasing the amount of money offered or paid to an informant." The PATRIOT Act also establishes new punishments for possessing biological weapons and makes it a federal crime to commit an act of terrorism against a mass transit system. However, according to Boyter (2003, p.17):

The law [the PATRIOT Act] has come under increasing attack from groups across the political spectrum. Some members of Congress and civil liberties groups say the act has given federal agents too much power to pursue suspected terrorists, threatening the civil rights and privacy of Americans.

Attorney General Ashcroft has defended the law, arguing that repealing it would endanger lives and aid terrorists. He said that any attempt to strip law enforcement agents of their expanded legal powers could open the way to further terrorist attacks.

He said that the law had been essential in preventing another terrorist attack in the United States. Expanding the powers of federal agents to use wiretaps, surveillance and other investigative methods and to share intelligence information "gives us the technological tools to anticipate, adapt and outthink our terrorist enemy," he said.

The Justice Department has launched a Web site, www.lifeandliberty.gov, devoted to the PATRIOT Act to dispel some of the myths about the act.

As Devanney and Devanney (2003, p.10) explain: "The intent of the PATRIOT Act, when it was passed in 2001 as an immediate response to the 9/11 attacks, was to provide *federal* law enforcement with better means to defend against terrorism" (emphasis added). They note: "Even in the first days after 9/11, federal officials recognized the importance of local officers in defense against terror. In October 2001, President Bush signed executive Order 12321, which called for federal agencies to reach out to state and local agencies." The concern about local involvement was later incorporated into the Homeland Security Act (HSA) in November 2002. But again, this act focused on reorganizing 22 agencies to defend against terrorism. Devanney and Devanney suggest: "At present, the exact relationship between these local entities and the federal government is still evolving, particularly as it concerns funding issues." Unquestionably, the efforts of local law enforcement agencies are critical in the fight against terrorism.

The Critical Role of Local Law Enforcement in Homeland Security

Bodrero (2002, p.43) notes: "Every terrorist event, every act of planning and preparation for that event (if conducted inside the United States) occurs in some local law enforcement agency's jurisdiction. No agency is closer to the activities within its community than the law enforcement agency that has responsibility and jurisdiction for protecting that community." The importance of partnerships between law enforcement agencies at all levels cannot be overstated as they apply to the war on terrorism:

- The nation is embarking upon a new and vigorous fight against terrorism, and local police agencies must be full partners in these efforts (C. Wexler, 2001b, p.1).
- The officer in the field, perhaps by transmitting the details of a seemingly routine traffic stop to a centralized data system, could potentially help avert a national disaster (Hickman and Reaves, 2002, p.83).
- It is vital that patrol officers correctly see themselves as the country's first line of defense against terrorist attacks (Gardner, 2003, p.6).

- "When it comes to homeland security, every law enforcement officer can play a vital role. . . . A single law enforcement officer can indeed foil a devastating terrorist attack" (S. Wexler, 2003, p.30).
- The 600,000 American law enforcement officers could become the eyes and ears of intelligence agencies, the first line in homeland defense (White, 2004, p.5).

In October, Glasscock (2001), then president of the International Association of Chiefs of Police (IACP), sent a letter to the membership, which stated, in part:

> The United States has begun air and group strikes against the Taliban in Afghanistan, taking the war against terrorism home to its instigators.
>
> But the war against terrorism isn't limited to actions overseas, or even restricted to military actions. The fight against terrorism begins in our own back yards—our own communities, our own neighborhoods—and police chiefs need to prepare themselves, their officers, and their communities—the people they've sworn to protect—against terrorism.

Needed Training

S. Wexler (p.35) stresses:

> The only way to successfully fight terrorism in the United States is for law enforcement to gain a clear understanding of the adversary and to establish meaningful inroads with the Arab community. Local law enforcement has to be brought up to speed as to who the adversary is, their thinking processes, their tactics and their mindset. . . . Local law enforcement must try to establish a good foothold in the Arab and Muslim communities so that they can obtain assistance in developing assets that can root out these individuals. It's not going to be done by the INS, the FBI or NSA satellites. It's going to be done by local law enforcement.

The importance of knowing one's enemy cannot be overemphasized. One critical dimension of this knowledge is differentiating the street criminal from the terrorist. Polisar (2004, p.8) observes: "Suddenly agencies and officers who have been trained and equipped to deal with more traditional crimes are now focused on apprehending individuals operating with different motivations, who have different objectives and who use much deadlier weapons than traditional criminals." Table 10.1 summarizes the most basic differences.

Cid (2003, p.33) urges: "The al-Qaeda training manual should be required reading for anyone with counterterrorism responsibilities at any level of law enforcement." White (2004, pp.99–101) describes the lessons taught in the al-Qaeda manual seized by the Manchester Constabulary in the United Kingdom (available online at http://www.fbi.gov).

The *first lesson* is a general introduction beginning with a lamentation on the state of the world and ending with a call to holy war *(jihad).* The *second lesson* focuses on the qualities of individual al-Qaeda members. The *third lesson* teaches forgery. The *fourth lesson* focuses on safe houses and other hiding places, including instructions for establishing a clandestine terrorist network. The *fifth lesson* concentrates on secret transportation and communication. Contacts are to be quick and to the point, and only commanders are authorized to initiate communication.

Table 10.1 Differences between the Street Criminal and the Terrorist

Typical Criminal	*Terrorist*
Crimes of opportunity	Fighting for political objective
Uncommitted	Motivated by ideology or religion
Self-centered	Group-focused—even berserkers or lone wolves
No cause	Consumed with purpose
Untrained	Trained and motivated for the mission
Escape-oriented	On the attack

SOURCE: Adapted from D. Douglas Bodrero. "Law Enforcement's New Challenge to Investigate, Interdict and Prevent Terrorism." *The Police Chief*, February 2002, p.44.

The *sixth lesson* discusses training and security during training. The *seventh lesson* covers weapons, one of the keys to terrorism, including building an arsenal and safely storing explosives. The *eighth lesson* discusses secrecy and member safety. It emphasizes the need to maintain family and neighborhood ties in the operational area. The *ninth lesson* is a lengthy discussion of security, emphasizing planning and operations. Secrecy is stressed time and again. The *tenth* and *eleventh lessons* focus on reconnaissance, including methods for clandestine spying and capturing prisoners.

The *twelfth lesson* continues the discussion of intelligence gathering, but focuses specifically on covert methods. It also provides information on counterintelligence. *Intermediate sections* between lessons twelve and eighteen give tips on handling recruited agents and dealing with countermeasures. Operatives are taught to watch for booby traps and when to assassinate potential enemies. The *eighteenth lesson* provides instructions about behavior when arrested. Al-Qaeda appears to have a working knowledge of the rights of prisoners in Western justice systems.

White (2004, p.98) also describes the three-tiered model of al-Qaeda terrorist attacks using sleeper cells. A **sleeper cell** is a group of terrorists who blend into a community.

The three-tiered model of al-Qaeda terrorist attacks consists of sleeper cells attacking in conjunction with the group's leaders in Afghanistan, sleeper cells attacking on their own apart from centralized command and individuals supported by small cells.

The centralized attacks such as those on 9/11 are the most effective. White notes: "In late 2001 the United States launched a devastating offensive against al-Qaeda, destroying its central command. . . . The second and third tiers of al-Qaeda are alive and well, surviving on every continent except Antarctica."

Investigating Terrorist Acts

The key to combating terrorism lies with the local police's investigation of terrorist acts and the intelligence they obtain to help prevent future attacks.

Fortunately, investigating terrorist acts is very similar to investigating other crimes: "The good news is that the investigation of terrorism is not really any different from the investigation of any other kind of criminal activity" (Strandberg, 2002, p.13). Baveja (2002, p.30) suggests that the war on drugs offers lessons for the fight against terrorism:

> Despite their differences, terrorism and illicit drug activity have several commonalities in their delivery and control, making a compelling case for exploring further to decipher any shared lessons. For example, drugs and terrorism involve covert illegal activities that call for sophisticated undercover enforcement operations. Both terrorism and drug activity do have a domestic component, but the threat from the organized and international component of these activities is far more devastating. In addition, there is evidence to suggest that terrorist cells and networks have structures similar to those of drug cartels.
>
> Further, both counterterror and counterdrug strategies require coordination among various law enforcement agencies, and strategic cooperation and information sharing with other partner countries. Finally, an overall policy for both these problems involves careful weighing of different strategies that reach beyond U.S. borders and span the globe. . . .
>
> Terrorism, like illicit drugs, is likely to be a long-term problem, and the war metaphor may indeed represent only a subset of strategies needed to address it.

Bridges (2002, p.35) suggests: "Suspected terrorist crimes will require investigations to determine suspects' identifications and possible links to crime networks. Disposable cell phones, Internet cafés, public library computers and even a Kinko's copy store were some of the instruments of communications used by terrorists associated with the terrorist acts committed on September 11, 2001."

Community Policing and Homeland Security

"In order to truly protect our communities from terrorism we must enlist them as partners in our fight to prevent the next attack. If we are to be successful, it is imperative that we have the full cooperation of the communities we are trying to serve. The onus is on law enforcement to expand our community policing capabilities and continue to build relationships with our citizens, so that we can work together to reduce crime, violence and fear" (C. Wexler, 2003, p.2). Or, as one chief of police asserted: "Community policing could well be our number-one line of defense [against terrorism]" (Nislow, 2001, p.1).

Olin (2002, p.28) likewise urges: "Every law enforcement agency in the United States should continue with its community–policing emphasis to strengthen the connections between citizens and the government." According to Wexler (2001c, p.vii):

> The events of September 11, 2001, have changed the role of local police in America—perhaps forever. Local law enforcement faces the challenges of assuming more responsibility in countering domestic terrorism threats while continuing to address crime and disorder. Success will depend on their ability to build on strong community-policing networks of information exchange and to maintain a collaborative problem-solving approach to crime amid high anxiety and crisis. Now more than ever, departments need to adhere to com-

munity problem-solving principles to decrease crime and disorder in their communities, increase their departments' efficiency and strengthen their relationships with citizens.

Carter and Holden (p.293) point out: "Community policing activities help police departments observe factors that could contribute to terrorism, identify individuals who may pose a threat or have information about terrorists' plans and lessen citizens' fears associated with terrorism."

Being Proactive "Homeland Security Funding Sources" (2004, p.27) describes Citizen Corps, a component of the USA Freedom Corps focusing on opportunities for people across the country to participate in a range of measures to make their families, homes and communities safer from the threats of terrorism, crime and disasters of all kinds. In addition, Citizen Corps brings together a community's first responders, firefighters, emergency health care providers, law enforcement and emergency managers with its volunteer resources.

The New York City police are providing antiterrorism training to building superintendents and doormen to be the department's eyes and ears. Plans call for training 28,000 building employees through 2005 (Butler, 2004, p.A7). Giannone and Wilson (2003, p.37) describe the CAT Eyes Program, the Community Anti-Terrorism Training Initiative, designed to enlist community members in the fight against terrorism: "The CAT Eyes program was designed to help local communities combat terrorism by enhancing neighborhood security, heightening the community's powers of observation, and encouraging mutual assistance and concern among neighbors."

Intelligence Gathering and Sharing

Many of the day-to-day duties of local law enforcement officers bring them into proximity with sources of information about terrorism. Runge (2002, p.96), administrator of the National Highway Traffic Safety Administration (NHTSA), for example, stresses the role of traffic law enforcement in homeland security: "Patrol operations—and specifically traffic law enforcement—provides a way to track down information related to terrorism. . . . If they are properly trained in what to look for and what questions to ask when interacting with citizens, they can be a tremendous source of intelligence for their state and federal homeland security counterparts."

Heinecke (2004, p.80) describes what she calls "another layer to the security blanket"—Behavior Pattern Recognition (BPR): "BPR is a security methodology based on two components: observation of irregular behaviors for the environment and targeted conversations with suspects. . . . BPR is an extension of trained observation. Officers, whether they are in an airport, sports arena or convention center, need to look for behaviors that are irregular for that location."

The community can also be instrumental in providing information, especially in those communities in which community policing is used. Figure 10.3 illustrates a model to help local police implement their new antiterrorism responsibilities.

Hoover (2002, p.1) describes four challenges to local police participation in intelligence effectiveness.

 Four obstacles to intelligence effectiveness are technological, logistical, political and ethical.

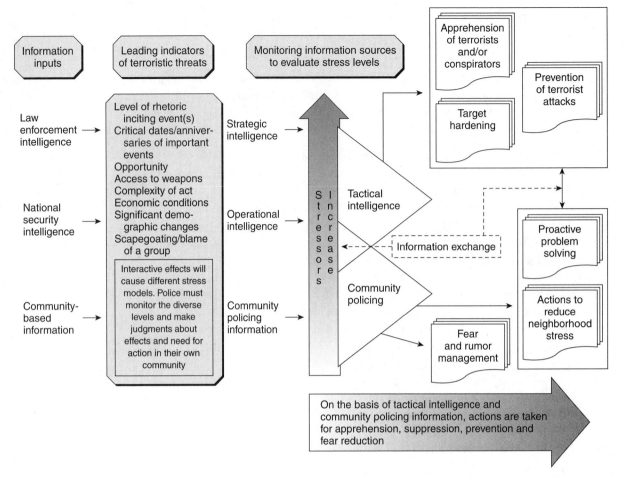

Figure 10.3   Implementation Model

SOURCE: David L. Carter and Richard N. Holden. "Terrorism and Community Security." *Local Government Police Management*, 4th ed., edited by William A. Geller and Darrel W. Stephens. Washington, DC: International City/County Management Association, 2003, p.307. Reprinted by permission.

Hoover (p.1) says: "The technological issue that most challenges state and local participation in any national anti-terrorism intelligence effort can be summarized by one word—**interoperability** [the ability to exchange information seamlessly]. The inability to exchange information on a regional and statewide level is overwhelmingly the primary issue." Logistical obstacles include data entry. "If intelligence officers spend all day entering data, they are not doing very much intelligence analysis" (Hoover, p.4). Political obstacles include finances, roles, relationships with the FBI and with the state police. According to Hoover (p.4): "By far the most serious impediments to establishing a national interconnected anti-terrorism database are political. . . . First and foremost . . . is the issue of 'who pays for this.'" The ethical obstacles include the issue of profiling and open records legislation. Profiling is discussed later in the chapter.

Withholding Information   As Pilant (2004, p.34) explains: "Counterterrorism and anti-terrorism are difficult tasks made even harder by the operational style that exists at almost every level of policing and in nearly every agency—that of withholding, rather than sharing, intelligence." A report by the Senate Governmental Affairs Committee (Lieberman, 2003, pp.38–41) states:

The frontline "first preventers" in the war against terrorism lack simple, streamlined access to the federal databases that are most valuable in the effort to identify and apprehend terrorists. . . .

States and localities still operate far too much as information islands, in relative isolation from their neighbors. Cities, counties and states also have few resources to learn what their counterparts around the country are doing to effectively protect their localities. . . .

Many state and local officials who need high-level information access lack the necessary federal security clearances to do what their job—and our safety—demands. . . .

States lack a single point of contact for both receiving "downstream" information needs and pushing intelligence and other information "upstream."

According to White (2004, p.17): "On the surface it seems simple: Defense and intelligence communities gather information concerning possible terrorist activities in the United States. . . . Under the surface, however, a complex network of interagency rivalries, laws, security clearance issues and turf protection reduces the possibility of shared information." Polisar (p.8) also asserts: "For far too long efforts to combat crime and terrorism have been handicapped by jurisdictional squabbles and archaic rules that prevented us from forging cooperative working relationships with our counterparts in local, regional, tribal and federal law enforcement. This must end."

Weiss and Davis (2002, p.80) note some sharing problems and limitations: "Sometimes information received by an agency such as the FBI is classified. . . . Rules of federal procedure and Grand Jury classified material are two other limitations to what or how much information can be shared."

The National Criminal Intelligence Sharing Plan (NCISP)   A subtitle of the Homeland Security Act of 2002, called the Homeland Security Information Sharing Act, required the president to develop new procedures for sharing classified information as well as unclassified but otherwise sensitive information with state and local police. This charge was fulfilled in May 2002 when the International Association of Chiefs of Police (IACP), the Department of Justice, the FBI, the Department of Homeland Security and other representatives of the federal, state, tribal and local law enforcement communities endorsed the National Criminal Intelligence Sharing Plan (NCISP). In releasing the plan, Attorney General John Ashcroft said: "The NCISP is the first of its kind in the nation, uniting law enforcement agencies of all sizes and geographic locations in a truly national effort to prevent terrorism and criminal activity. By raising cooperation and communication among local, state and federal partners to an unprecedented level, this groundbreaking effort will strengthen the abilities of the justice community to detect threats and protect American lives and liberties" ("Justice Dept. Announces Plan for Local Police Intelligence Sharing," 2004, p.5).

Wexler (2001b, p.1) asserts that success in this war will "require an improved relationship between local and federal law enforcement with respect to intelligence sharing and target hardening. . . . If we are to truly mount a major preemptive offensive then this relationship must evolve to one that recognizes the significant role of both local and federal agencies working collaboratively, sharing intelligence and developing joint strategies."

AP/Wide World Photos

On December 17, 2004, President Bush signed the Intelligence Reform and Terrorism Prevention Act, the largest overhaul of U.S. intelligence gathering in 50 years.

A New Kind of War—An Asymmetric War

"This is a different type of battle. We can't see the enemy. He hides in the shadows" (Rogers, 2001, p.16). An **asymmetric war** is one in which a much weaker opponent takes on a stronger opponent by refusing to confront the stronger opponent head on. As Choudhury (2002, p.183) explains: "The weaker side selects as its main axis of battle those areas where the adversary does not expect to be hit and where the attack will cause a huge psychological shock. The use of asymmetrical measures is conceived of as creating power for the powerless and rendering the stronger adversary unable to use its conventional resources."

Lasky (2002, p.4) suggests: "An asymmetric foe is an Osama bin Laden, international terrorist group, drug cartel or Mafiosi-type. We've recently found our military in other asymmetrical situations like those in Somalia, Kosovo and Lebanon where rogue states have disintegrated into such anarchy that conventional military parameters disappear. But this is now the reality of warfare."

Another Homeland Security Initiative: The Center for Food Protection and Defense

In July 2004 the University of Minnesota was awarded a $15 million grant for a national Center for Food Protection and Defense. It won the grant because it is one of only a few universities in the country with experts in agriculture, public health, veterinary medicine and medicine on the same campus. The university will partner with General Mills, Cargill, 3M and Hormel. Frank Busta, professor emeritus of food science and nutrition who will direct the grant, asserts: "Our charge is to protect and defend safe food from intentional contamination. The vulnerability of food is immense. . . . We hope we can make it sufficiently difficult [so] if and when terrorists decide to look at [attacking the food supply], they will say, 'We'll try something else'" (Smetanka, 2004a, p.A4).

In announcing the new Center for Food Protection and Defense, Homeland Security Secretary Ridge noted: "Government can't do it alone. . . . Partnerships between government and our great research universities, businesses and scientists will produce together what would be impossible individually" (Smetanka, 2004b, p.B1).

The Role of the Media in the War on Terrorism

According to White (2003, p.256): "One of the most controversial current topics of terrorism analysis is the way print and electronic media cover terrorist acts. Police and other government forces operate with a set of objectives diametrically opposed to the goals of reporters covering an event. In addition, experts have heatedly debated the effects of electronic coverage on terrorism, and there are several competing schools of thought on the effectiveness and impact of newspaper coverage. Regardless of which side one favors, reporting terrorism will remain controversial because the media has become part of the terrorist event."

The Terrorism Research Center suggests: "Terrorism and the media have a symbiotic relationship. Without the media, terrorists would receive no exposure, their cause would go ignored, and no climate of fear would be generated. Terrorism is futile without publicity, and the media generates much of this publicity."

White (2003, p.257) suggests: "Members of the media have two competing and often contradictory roles. They control the flow of information while simultaneously making the news entertaining enough to 'sell.' " White (p.259) raises the question of the **contagion effect,** that is, the coverage of terrorism inspires more terrorism. It is, in effect, contagious. This controversial issue leads to discussions about censorship in the war on terrorism.

Emerson (2002, p.35) contends: "The media need not become a tool of terrorism, by inadvertently spreading misinformation and escalating panic. Instead, state and local governments should learn to look at the mass media as partners in responding effectively to an attack."

Concerns Related to the War on Terrorism

 Two concerns related to the "war on terrorism" are that civil liberties may be jeopardized and that people of Middle Eastern descent may be discriminated against or become victims of hate crimes.

Concern for Civil Rights

Civil libertarians are concerned that valued American freedoms will be sacrificed in the interest of national safety. For example, the Justice Department has issued a new regulation giving itself the authority to monitor inmate-attorney communications if "reasonable suspicion" exists that inmates are using such communications to further or facilitate acts of terrorism ("Justice Dept. Moves . . .," 2001, p.2). However, criminal defense lawyers and members of the American Civil Liberties Union (ACLU) have protested the regulation, saying it effectively eliminates the Sixth Amendment right to counsel because, under codes of professional responsibility, attorneys cannot communicate with clients if confidentiality is not assured. The ACLU has vowed to monitor police actions closely to see that free-doms protected under the Constitution are not jeopardized.

According to Melekian (2002, p.1): "In the post-September 11 world, our greatest challenge is not dealing with terrorists. Rather it is finding the balance between enhancing security and maintaining liberty." Bulzomi (2003, p.26) stresses: "The government must use its new tools in a way that preserves the rights and freedoms guaranteed by America's democracy, but, at the same time, ensures that the fight against terrorism is vigorous and effective."

Retaliation or Discrimination against People of Middle Eastern Descent

Another concern is that some Americans may retaliate against innocent people of Middle Eastern descent, many of whom were either born in the United States or are naturalized citizens. According to Peed and Wexler (2004, p.vii): "America's multicultural neighborhoods, particularly Arab and Muslim communities, were initially affected by backlash violence and hate crimes following the terrorist attacks." Davies and Murphy (2004, p.1) likewise note: "Within hours of the Twin Towers' collapse and the attack on the Pentagon, U.S. residents and visitors, particularly Arabs, Muslims and Sikhs, were harassed or attacked because they shared—or were perceived to share—the terrorists' national background or religion. . . . Law enforcement's challenge since then has been to maintain an appropriate balance between the security interests of our country and the consti-tutional rights of every American."

We must remember the Japanese internment camps during World War II and make sure we do not repeat that mistake. As one police officer said on the Internet:

> I want to remind all of you that those residents of our neighborhoods who are Muslim share in the horror of Tuesday's events. They too are our American brothers and sisters. They were our neighbors and friends when we went to sleep on Monday night and the events of Tuesday morning did not change that. They are still our neighbors and friends today. . . . Our fears and sad-ness and anger are theirs as well, but they must also have a fear all their own, a fear of how they will now be perceived and treated. Let us show them that we will not be ruled by fear and anger, but instead by compassion. . . . We are still a land of many cultures, a land founded on idealistic principles that has always tried to welcome any who come to her shores. That's what we do here in America. . . . Should we choose to forget who we are as Americans, the terrorists win.

Closely related concerns are the rights of citizens detained as enemy combat-ants and the rights of detained foreign nationals. In *Hamdi v. Rumsfeld* (2004) the Supreme Court ruled that a citizen detained in the United States as an enemy combatant must be afforded the opportunity to rebut such a designation. Peti-tioner Hamdi was captured in an active combat zone in Afghanistan following the September 11, 2001, attack on the United States and surrendered an assault rifle. The U.S. District Court found that the declaration from the Defense Department did not support Hamdi's detention and ordered the government to turn over numerous materials for review. The U.S. Court of Appeals for the Fourth Circuit reversed, stressing that, because it was undisputed that Hamdi was cap-tured in an active combat zone, no factual inquiry or evidentiary hearing allowing Hamdi to rebut the government's assertions was necessary. A 6–3 Supreme Court vacated and remanded, concluding that Hamdi should have a meaningful opportunity to offer evidence that he was not an enemy combatant.

In *Rasul v. Bush* (2004) the Supreme Court ruled that U.S. courts have jurisdiction to consider challenges to the legality of the detention of foreign nationals captured in Afghanistan in a military campaign against al-Qaeda and the Taliban regime that supported it. The petitioners, 2 Australians and 12 Kuwaitis, were being held in Guantanamo Bay, Cuba, without charges. These and other legal issues regarding civil rights will be debated as the country seeks to balance the need for security with civil rights.

SUMMARY

The threat of terrorism has become a reality in the United States. Most definitions of terrorism have common elements, including the systematic use of physical violence, either actual or threatened, against noncombatants to create a climate of fear to cause some religious, political or social change. Three elements of terrorism are: (1) it is criminal in nature, (2) targets are typically symbolic and (3) the terrorist actions are always aggressive and often violent. The FBI classifies terroristic acts as either domestic or international. It is the lead agency for responding to terrorism. Most terrorist acts result from dissatisfaction with a religious, political or social system or policy and frustration resulting from an inability to change it through acceptable, nonviolent means. Domestic terrorist groups include white supremacists, black supremacists, militia groups, other right-wing extremists, left-wing extremists, pro-life extremists, animal rights activists and environmental extremists. Terrorists may use arson, explosives and bombs, weapons of mass destruction (biological, chemical or nuclear agents) and technology.

As a result of 9/11 the Department of Homeland Security was established, reorganizing the departments of the federal government. The Federal Emergency Management Agency (FEMA) is the lead agency for consequence management (after an attack). The Department of Homeland Security facilitates collaboration between local and federal law enforcement to develop a national strategy to detect, prepare for, prevent, protect against, respond to and recover from terrorist attacks within the United States.

The USA PATRIOT Act significantly improves the nation's counterterrorism efforts by:

- Allowing investigators to use the tools already available to investigate organized crime and drug trafficking.
- Facilitating information sharing and cooperation among government agencies so they can better "connect the dots."
- Updating the law to reflect new technologies and new threats.
- Increasing the penalties for those who commit or support terrorist crimes.

The three-tiered model of al-Qaeda terrorist attacks consists of sleeper cells attacking in conjunction with the group's leaders in Afghanistan, sleeper cells attacking on their own apart from centralized command and individuals supported by small cells. The key to combating terrorism lies with the local police and the intelligence they can provide to federal authorities. Four obstacles to intelligence effectiveness are technological, logistical, political and ethical.

Two concerns related to the "war on terrorism" are that civil liberties may be jeopardized and that people of Middle Eastern descent may be discriminated against or become victims of hate crimes.

DISCUSSION QUESTIONS

1. Which is the greater threat—domestic or international terrorism? Why?

2. Does your police department have a counterterrorism strategy in place? If so, what?

3. What type of terrorist attack would you fear most? Why?

4. Do you feel Americans have become complacent about terrorism?

5. What provision of the PATRIOT Act do you think is most important?

6. What barriers to sharing information among the various local, state and federal agencies do you think are most problematic?

7. Does media coverage of terrorist acts lead to more terrorism—that is, do you think the contagion effect is in operation?

8. Should Americans expect to give up some civil liberties to allow law enforcement officers to pursue terrorists?

9. Do you think a terrorist sleeper cell could operate in your community? What signs might indicate that such a cell exists?

10. Do you believe this subject warrants an entire chapter in this text?

INFOTRAC COLLEGE EDITION ASSIGNMENTS

- Use InfoTrac College Edition to help answer the Discussion Questions as appropriate.

- Use InfoTrac College Edition to read and outline one of the following articles to share with the class:

  - "Confronting Terrorism on the State and Local Level" in the *FBI Law Enforcement Bulletin*

  - "Fighting Terrorism in the 21st Century" by John F. Lewis, Jr.

  - "'Baseline' Training for Terrorism" by Gary J. Rohen

  - "Understanding the Terrorist Mind-Set" by Randy Borum

  - "Foreign Intelligence Surveillance Act: Before and after the USA PATRIOT Act" by Michael J. Bulzomi

  - "Hunting Terrorists Using Confidential Informant Reward Programs" by Douglas A. Kash

  - "Amnesty Boxes: A Component of Physical Security for Law Enforcement" by Charles Mesiah, Mark Henych and Randy Mingo

INTERNET ASSIGNMENTS

Select two assignments to complete.

- Go to the Web sites of the DEA (www.dea.gov), the FBI (www.fbi.gov), the Department of Justice (www.usdoj.gov) and the Department of the Treasury (www.ustreas.gov) and note how the different agencies are addressing the issue of *terrorism*. How do their focuses differ? Be prepared to share your findings with the class.

- Search for *USA PATRIOT Act (2001)*. List specific applications of the act to law enforcement practices and explain how they might differ from conventional practices. Do you believe the phrase "extraordinary times demand extraordinary measures" justifies "bending the rules," so to speak, in the war on terrorism? In other words, do the ends justify the means? Should law enforcement be permitted to use roving wiretaps and breach privileged inmate-attorney communications in the name of national security, or is this the beginning of the end of our civil liberties? Be prepared to discuss your answers with the class.

- Go to the Department of Justice Web site devoted to the PATRIOT Act and list the myths the site dispels.

- Go to http://www.policeforum.org and find "Local Law Enforcement's Role in Preventing and Responding to Terrorism." Read and outline the article. Be prepared to share your outline with the class.

- To learn what the U.S. Department of Homeland Security is doing to keep America safe go to http://www.ready.gov/.

- Go to the Terrorism Research Center's Web site, http://www.terrorism.com/ and select one of the links related to the U.S. Homeland Attack on 9/11.

- Go to the Counterterrorism Training and Resources Web site at http://www.counterterrorismtraining.gov and outline what resources are available for local police departments.

- Go to the Office for Domestic Preparedness (ODP) at http://www.osldps.ncjrs.org and outline what this site says regarding weapons of mass destruction.

REFERENCES

Anderson, Larry. "The Next Challenge: Defining the Industry's Post-Catastrophic Role." *Access Control & Security Systems*, October 2001, p.4.

"Ashcroft Announces Plan for DOJ 'Wartime Reorganization.'" *Criminal Justice Newsletter*, November 14, 2001, pp.1–2.

Bassiouni, M. Cherif. "Terrorism." *World Book Online Americas Edition*, 2001. http://www.aolsvc.worldbook.aol.com/wbol/wbPage/na/ar/co/551940.

Baveja, Alok. "War on Illicit Drugs May Offer Lessons for Fight against Terrorism." *The Police Chief*, March 2002, pp.30–33.

"Bioterrorism." *Security Management*, July 2003, pp.24–25.

Bodrero, D. Douglas. "Law Enforcement's New Challenge to Investigate, Interdict and Prevent Terrorism." *The Police Chief*, February 2002, pp.41–46.

Borum, Randy. "Understanding the Terrorist Mind-Set." *FBI Law Enforcement Bulletin*, July 2003, pp.7–10.

Boyter, Jennifer. "Attorney General Ashcroft Defends PATRIOT Act." *The Police Chief,* September 2003, p.17.

Bridges, Dennis. "It's a Police Problem: The Terrorist Threat's Impact on State and Local Law Enforcement." *The Police Chief,* February 2002, pp.35–37.

Brinkley, Larry. "Present Threats." *The Law Enforcement Trainer,* November/December 2003, pp.30–35.

"Britain to Release More Evidence Implicating Bin Laden in Attacks." *Washington Post,* as reported in the (Minneapolis/St. Paul) *Star Tribune,* November 13, 2001, p.A13.

Bulzomi, Michael J. "Foreign Intelligence Surveillance Act: Before and after the USA PATRIOT Act." *FBI Law Enforcement Bulletin,* June 2003, pp.25–32.

"Bush Signs Law That Expands Police Powers." Associated Press, as reported in the (Minneapolis/St. Paul) *Star Tribune,* October 27, 2001, p.A17.

Butler, Desmond. "Building Supers Standing Watch." Associated Press as reported in the (Minneapolis/St. Paul) *Star Tribune,* June 23, 2004, p.A7.

Carter, David L. and Holden, Richard N. "Terrorism and Community Security." In *Local Government Police Management,* Washington, DC: International City/County Management Association, 2003, pp.291–311.

Choudhury, Jayanto N. "Asymmetric Warfare: The 21st Century Challenge to U.S. Law Enforcement Executives." *The Police Chief,* April 2002, pp.183–188.

Cid, David. "Preventing Terrorism: The Intelligence Dimension." *The Police Chief,* March 2003, pp.30–35.

"Confronting the Suicide-Bomber Threat." *Security Management,* November 2003, p.16.

"Congress Debates Terror Bill's Effects on Criminal Justice." *Criminal Justice Newsletter,* October 30, 2001, pp.1–4.

Davies, Heather J. and Murphy, Gerard R. *Protecting Your Community from Terrorism: The Strategies for Local Law Enforcement Series Vol. 2: Working with Diverse Communities.* Washington, DC: The Office of Community Oriented Policing Services and the Police Executive Research Forum, 2004.

Devanney, Joe and Devanney, Diane. "Homeland Security and PATRIOT Acts." *Law and Order,* August 2003, pp.10–12.

"Domestic Law Enforcement Given Lower Priority at FBI." *Criminal Justice Newsletter,* June 5, 2002, pp.1–2.

Emerson, Peter Van D. "Utilizing the Mass Media." In *Beyond the Beltway: Focusing on Hometown Security: Recommendations for State and Local Domestic Preparedness Planning a Year after 9–11.* A Report of the Executive Session on Domestic Preparedness, John F. Kennedy School of Government, Harvard University, September 2002.

Gardner, Gerald W. "Getting Ready for the Big One: Terrorism Can Happen Anywhere, at Any Time." *Police,* October 2003, p.6.

Garrett, Ronnie. "Terrorism on the Homefront." *Law Enforcement Technology,* July 2002, pp.22–26.

Giannone, Donald and Wilson, Robert A. "The CAT Eyes Program: Enlisting Community Members in the Fight against Terrorism." *The Police Chief,* March 2003, pp.37–38.

Gips, Michael A. "Secondary Devices a Primary Concern." *Security Management,* July 2003, pp.16–20.

Glasscock, Bruce D. Letter to IACP Colleagues, October 16, 2001.

Guida, Joseph F. "Enviroterrorism: A Long-Range View." *Security Products,* October 2002, p.54.

Haber, Grant. "Facing the Threat of Improvised Explosives." *Law Enforcement News,* May 2004, pp.13–14.

Hackett, Frank A. "The Horror and the Heroes." *The Law Enforcement Trainer,* September/October 2001, p.9.

Hanson, Doug. "The Nation's Food and Water Supply: A New Target for Terrorists?" *Law Enforcement Technology,* January 2004, pp.18–24.

Heinecke, Jeannine. "Adding Another Layer to the Security Blanket." *Law Enforcement Technology,* March 2004, pp.78–85.

Hickman, Matthew J. and Reaves, Brian A. "Local Police and Homeland Security: Some Baseline Data." *The Police Chief,* October 2002, pp.83–85.

"Homeland Security Funding Sources." *The Police Chief,* February 2004, pp.23–27.

Hoover, Larry T. "The Challenges to Local Police Participation in the Homeland Security Effort." *Subject to Debate,* October 2002, pp.1, 3–10.

"IACP Response to the September 11 Terrorist Attacks." *The Police Chief,* October 2001, pp.14, 182–184.

Jones, Jeffrey M. "The Impact of the Attacks on America." *Gallup News Service.* September 25, 2001. Online at http://www.gallup.com.

"Justice Dept. Announces Plan for Local Police Intelligence Sharing." *Criminal Justice Newsletter,* June 1, 2004, p.5.

"Justice Dept. Moves to Monitor Inmate-Attorney Communications." *Criminal Justice Newsletter,* November 14, 2001, pp.2–3.

Kash, Douglas A. "Hunting Terrorists Using Confidential Informant Reward Programs." *FBI Law Enforcement Bulletin,* April 2002, pp.26–31.

Lasky, Steve. "Confronting an Enemy with No Face." *Security Technology & Design,* January 2002, p.4.

Lesce, Tony. "WMD Training." *Law and Order,* December 2001, pp.99–104.

Lieberman, Senator Joseph I. *State and Local Officials: Still Kept in the Dark about Homeland Security.* Washington, DC: A Report by the Senate Governmental Affairs Committee, August 13, 2003.

"Lost But Not Forgotten." *USA Today,* October 8, 2001.

McVey, Philip M. "Homeland Defense: An Effective Partnership." *The Police Chief,* April 2002, pp.174–180.

Melekian, Bernard. "Balancing Act: Security vs. Liberty." *Subject to Debate,* June 2002, pp.1, 4.

Nason, Randall R. "Chemical Agent Terrorism: A Refresher in Strategic Approach." *Security Technology & Design,* February 2003, pp.44–46.

"A New 'Date Which Will Live in Infamy.'" *Law Enforcement News*, September 15, 2001, pp.1, 12.

Newport, Frank. "Morality, Education, Crime, Dissatisfaction with Government Head List of Most Important Problems Facing Country Today." *Gallup News Service*, February 5, 2001. http://www.gallup.com.

Nilson, Chad and Burke, Tod. "Environmental Extremists and the Eco-Terrorism Movement." *ACJS Today*, January/February 2002, pp.1–6.

Nislow, Jennifer. "Secret Weapon against Terrorism? Chiefs Say Community Policing Is an Ace in the Hole." *Law Enforcement News*, October 15, 2001, pp.1, 11.

Olin, W. Ronald. "Why Traditional Law Enforcement Methods Cannot Win the War on Terrorism." *The Police Chief*, November 2002, pp.27–31.

Peed, Carl R. and Wexler, Chuck. "Foreword." In *Protecting Your Community from Terrorism: The Strategies for Local Law Enforcement Series Vol. 2: Working with Diverse Communities*, edited by Heather J. Davies and Gerard R. Murphy, Washington, DC: The Office of Community Oriented Policing Services and the Police Executive Research Forum, 2004, pp.vii–viii.

Pilant, Lois. "Strategic Modeling: Los Angeles County's Counterterrorism Program Is Being Duplicated Nationwide." *Police*, May 2004, pp.34–38.

Pitcavage, Mark. "Domestic Extremism: Still a Potent Threat." *The Police Chief*, August 2003, pp.32–35.

Polisar, Joseph M. "The National Criminal Intelligence Sharing Plan." *The Police Chief*, June 2004, p.8.

"President Signs Homeland Security EO and Ridge Sworn In as Its Director." *NCJA Justice Bulletin*, October 2001, pp.8–10.

Rogers, Donna. "A Nation Tested: What Is the Terrorist Threat We Face and How Can We Train for It?" *Law Enforcement Technology*, November 2001, pp.16–22.

Rohen, Gary J. "WMD Response." *The Police Chief*, October 2001, pp.148–163.

Runge, Jeffrey W. "The Role of Traffic Law Enforcement in Homeland Security." *The Police Chief*, October 2002, pp.90–98.

"Safety on the Scene." *First Responder Forum*, April 2002, pp.6–7.

Sanow, Ed. "WTC: Where We Go from Here." *Law and Order*, October 2001, p.4.

Sanow, Ed. "Vandalism? Terrorism." *Law and Order*, May 2002, p.5.

Schweld, Barry. "Corrected Terror Report Shows More Attacks, More Injured." The Associated Press as reported in the (Minneapolis/St. Paul) *Star Tribune*, June 23, 2004, p.A1.

Scoville, Dean. "The Enemies Within." *Police*, September 2003, pp.44–50.

"September 11 Terrorism Brings Changes in Law Enforcement." *Criminal Justice Newsletter*, October 15, 2001, pp.1–3.

"The Shape of Things to Come." *Security Management*, March 2003, p.20.

Smetanka, Mary Jane. "'U' Studies Terrorism at Your Table." (Minneapolis/St. Paul) *Star Tribune*, July 6, 2004a, pp.A1, A4.

Smetanka, Mary Jane. "'U' Center Safeguards Food Supply." (Minneapolis/St. Paul) *Star Tribune*, July 7, 2004b, pp.B1, B4.

Stanton, John J. "Is the U.S. Prepared for Nuclear Terrorism?" *Security Management*, March 2002, pp.154–156.

Strandberg, Keith. "Bioterrorism: A Real or Imagined Threat?" *Law Enforcement Technology*, June 2001, pp.88–97.

Strandberg, Keith. "Protecting the People: Law Enforcement's Role in the War against Terrorism." *Law Enforcement Technology*, January 2002, pp.12–16.

"Suicide Terrorism." *Security Management*, August 2003, pp.20–22.

Symonds, Daniel R. "A Guide to Selected Weapons of Mass Destruction." *The Police Chief*, March 2003, pp.19–29.

Terrorism and International Victims Unit. OVC Fact Sheet, January 2002. (FS-000276).

"Terrorism Fight Is Top Priority, Customs Commissioner Says." *Drug Enforcement Report*, vol. 16, no. 24, 2001, p.1.

The Terrorism Research Center. http://www.terrorism.com/index.html.

Uner, Eric. "Cyber Terrorism: Count on It." *Security Products*, February 2003, pp.26–28.

"U.S. Antiterrorism Organization under Review; New Laws Being Considered." *NCJA Justice Bulletin*, September 2001, pp.1, 7–10.

Vallee, Sarah. "Slash and Burn." *American Police Beat*, March 2001, pp.1, 40.

Van Etten, John. "Impacts of Domestic Security on Law Enforcement Agencies." *The Police Chief*, February 2004, pp.31–35.

Vincent, Billie H. "What Went Wrong?" *Access Control & Security Systems*, October 2001, pp.1, 26–27.

Weiss, Jim and Davis, Mickey. "Information Partnering and the FBI." *Law and Order*, January 2002, pp.80–81.

Wexler, Chuck. "Terrorism and Local Law Enforcement." *Subject to Debate*, September 2001a, pp.1–2, 4, 6, 11.

Wexler, Chuck. *Local Law Enforcement's Role in Preventing and Responding to Terrorism*. Washington, DC: Police Executive Research Forum, October 2001b.

Wexler, Chuck. "Foreword." In *Solving Crime and Disorder Problems: Current Issues, Police Strategies and Organizational Tactics*, edited by Melissa Reuland, Corina Sole Brito and Lisa Carroll. Washington, DC: Police Executive Research Forum, 2001c, p.vii.

Wexler, Chuck. "Policing a Multicultural Community." *Subject to Debate*, July 2003, p.2.

Wexler, Sanford. "Homeland Security: Think Locally." *Law Enforcement Technology*, January 2003, pp.30–35.

White, Jonathan R. *Terrorism: An Introduction*, 4th ed. Belmont, CA: Wadsworth Publishing Company, 2003.

White, Jonathan R. *Defending the Homeland: Domestic Intelligence, Law Enforcement and Security*. Belmont, CA: Wadsworth Publishing Company, 2004.

CASES CITED

Hamdi v. Rumsfeld, No.03-6696, U.S. (June 28, 2004)

Rasul v. Bush, No. 03-334, U.S. (June 28, 2004)

CHAPTER 11

Issues Concerning
Police Conduct

No one is compelled to choose the profession of a police officer, but having chosen it, everyone is obliged to perform its duties and live up to the high standards of its requirements.

—Calvin Coolidge

 DO YOU KNOW . . .

- Whether police discretion is positive or negative?
- Whether minorities' encounters with police are proportional to their numbers in the general population? Whether discrimination or disparity may account for any disproportionality?
- When force should or should not be used?
- If use of deadly force is justifiable?
- The effectiveness or safety level of high-speed police pursuits?
- Whether civil liability is of much concern for modern police agencies and officers?
- What constitutes police corruption and whether it is common?
- What three areas can enhance police integrity and reduce corruption?

CAN YOU DEFINE?

balancing	ethics	gratuities	litigaphobia
corruption	excessive force	homophobia	pursuit
deadly force	exculpatory evidence	integrity	racial profiling
discrimination	force	less-lethal force	reasonable force
disparity	ghosting	liability	

Introduction

Policing has several vital issues facing it in the twenty-first century. Some have existed for decades; others are relatively new. Each "Do You Know" presents more than facts—each presents major issues that face policing because the questions have no correct answers. They are controversial. Notice also that some subjects, such as discretion, have been introduced earlier.

This chapter focuses on issues related to how officers police—how they behave on the job—beginning with a discussion of police discretion. Next is a look at discrimination in enforcing the law based on a subject's gender, class or race. The critical issue of racial profiling is then examined, followed by discussions on use of force, police pursuits and civil liability issues associated with specific police conduct. The chapter concludes with a look at the issues of officer corruption, ethics and integrity.

Discretion

Discretion has been a theme throughout this text. Just as citizens can decide to obey the laws or not, police agencies and their officers can decide which offenses to actively seek to control and which offenses to simply ignore, which services to provide and at what level.

 Police discretion is the freedom of an agency or individual officer to choose to act or not. Whether such discretion is positive or negative is an issue.

Any speeder who has talked a traffic officer out of issuing a ticket probably thinks police discretion is good. The person who receives a ticket, however, probably thinks the officer has erred in spending time chasing speeders rather than catching criminals.

Discretion might be viewed on a continuum from low to high. Low-discretion situations include those involving routine activities such as executing a search warrant, responding to a citizen complaint or seeing an obvious violation of the law, for example, a motorist running a red light. The officer usually need not ponder what action to take. High-discretion situations, in contrast, are less clear cut, for example, responding to a call from a citizen reporting a fight going on next door. Upon arrival, the officers must determine what the situation is and sort out who is the victim and who is the perpetrator, or if both are at fault. It is the high-discretion incidents that invite both intentional and unintentional abuses of discretionary police power.

Richard Sheinwald/AP/Wide World Photos

The person receiving this traffic citation might be inclined to believe that this officer's discretion is not good. He may feel officers should be spending their time chasing "real criminals."

Table 11.1 Opportunities for Discretion

These Criminal Justice Officials	*Must Often Decide Whether or Not or How to*
Police	Enforce specific laws
	Investigate specific crimes
	Search people, vicinities, buildings
	Arrest or detain people
Prosecutors	File charges or petitions for adjudication
	Seek indictments
	Drop cases
	Reduce charges

SOURCE: *Report to the Nation on Crime and Justice.* U.S. Department of Justice, Bureau of Justice Statistics, March 1988, pp.56–60.

As noted, one of the most important discretionary options police officers have is whether to arrest someone. If that decision is to arrest, then the discretionary power of the prosecutor comes into play, as summarized in Table 11.1.

The ability to use discretion is, indeed, a vital element of contemporary American policing and is at the heart of the issues discussed in this chapter. Chief Justice Warren Burger has stated: "The officer working the beat makes more decisions and exercises broader discretion affecting the daily lives of people everyday and to a greater extent than a judge will exercise in a week" (Strong, 2004, p.65). Any discussion of discretion would be incomplete without recognizing the awesome power of citizen discretion. The less serious a crime is to the public, the less pressure is placed on police for enforcement. In addition, the wishes of complainants greatly influence police selective enforcement, often more than any other factor. Police discretion is frequently at the center of issues involving discrimination, racial profiling, use of force and pursuit.

Discrimination or Disparity in Policing: Gender, Class and Race Issues

The guarantee of equal protection under the law to all citizens is a fundamental principle of our democracy. When officers fail to treat equals equally because of economic status, race, religion, sex or age biases, discrimination occurs. Miller and Hess (2005, p.139) define **discrimination** as "showing a preference in treating individuals or groups or failing to treat equals equally, especially illegal unequal treatment based on race, religion, sex or age. Some male traffic officers, for example, are known to issue warnings to females who violate traffic laws and to issue tickets to males for the same violation." Is this a matter of discrimination or of disparity? **Disparity** refers to a simple difference, not necessarily caused by any kind of bias. For example, if there are more male drivers and if they more frequently break traffic laws, the difference in the number of traffic tickets issued to male drivers would be a function of disparity, not discrimination. Another example: in a high school, the vast majority of students will be between 16 and 18 years of age; this reflects disparity, not discrimination.

This same issue arises when the numbers of individuals involved in the criminal justice system are examined. Are more minorities arrested, processed and sentenced to prison because of discrimination or because they commit crimes in disproportionate numbers because of the numerous economic and social factors discussed in Chapter 3?

Gender Issues

The differential treatment of men and women by police is seldom raised as an issue. Why is it that so many more men than women are arrested and incarcerated? Do women commit fewer crimes, or are they given preferential treatment? Limited research has addressed this issue.

In examining contacts between the police and the public, Langan et al. (2001, p.2) found that males (12.5 percent) were more likely than females (8.2 percent) to be stopped at least once, and males (2.9 percent) were more likely than females (1.4 percent) to be stopped more than once. They also found that during a traffic stop, police were more likely to carry out some type of search on a male (9.4 percent) than a female (2.3 percent).

A gender-related issue that lacks much research is that of police attitudes toward gay individuals. Friction between the police and the gay community has been reported since the 1960s. Olivero and Murataya (2001, p.271) note: "Homicide in the gay community is a significant problem, with few law enforcement programs willing to address these problems. Moreover, those in the gay community are subject to assaults based solely upon their sexual orientation. . . . Currently there are calls for better police services for the gay community. This includes both better protection of gays and hiring members of the gay community as police officers."

What limited research is available has suggested police officers hold higher levels of **homophobia** than other sectors of society, that is, they are fearful of gays and lesbians (Olivero and Murataya). Based on such data, a line might then be drawn connecting officers who are homophobic to greater instances of discriminatory policing. Such officers may even engage in discrimination unconsciously. Of course, the research has not explored the issue this far, and such correlations remain pure speculation.

Consider one transgender woman's account of being abused by her boyfriend: "He'd punch me and tell me to take it like a man. When I told him to stop, he'd scream at me and hit harder. The neighbors called the police more than once, but they never arrested him because they said that fighting between two men wasn't domestic violence. They usually warned us to stop disturbing the peace and left. One officer actually said that if I was arrested they wouldn't know where to put me" (*Partner Abuse/Domestic Violence* . . ., 2002, p.21). According to the National Coalition of Anti-Violence Programs (2003, p.14):

> Police officers in general are more apt to view violence between LGBT [lesbian, gay, bisexual and transgender] individuals, especially partners of the same gender, as mutual or consensual abuse. Even among those well-meaning officers, few police receive the training necessary to distinguish the actual abuser in incidents of LGBT domestic violence, such that the arrest of the victim or of both parties is not an infrequent occurrence. In addition, many police officers continue to express homophobia themselves or at least act as its instruments

in other contexts. Many LGBT people are aware of long histories of negative associations between the LGBT community and the police and hold long-internalized and affirmed fear and mistrust that police will create safety rather than harm. The consequent fear of the police prevents many LGBT victims of domestic violence from seeking the assistance of law enforcement themselves.

Class Issues

Another area receiving limited attention is discriminatory policing based on a person's economic level. A half century ago, in *Griffin v. Illinois* (1956), Justice Hugo Black declared: "There can be no equal justice where the kind of trial a man gets depends on the amount of money he has." To many people, the O.J. Simpson double-murder trial was a blatant example of unlimited financial resources being able to "buy" a not guilty verdict.

At the law enforcement level, those who are poor are much more likely to come to the attention of the police simply because they are on the streets more than those who are not poor. Many are homeless, and some of their behaviors, such as sleeping on park benches, have been made illegal, changing a social problem into a law enforcement problem. And if a poor person does have a vehicle, it is often in need of repair, resulting in the person being ticketed for faulty equipment. Unfortunately, as Cox (2001, p.64) suggests: "Poverty is correlated with race and vehicle equipment violations so it can be expected that some police departments will disproportionately stop minority drivers for a lack of proper equipment."

Many poor people ride buses or trains—frequent targets of police sweeps for drugs. In West Palm Beach, bus sweeps over a 13-month period netted 300 pounds of cocaine, 800 pounds of marijuana, 24 handguns and 75 suspected drug "mules." In *Florida v. Bostick* (1991) a 28-year-old black man, Terrance Bostick, on his way from Miami to Atlanta, was asleep on a bus that had stopped in Ft. Lauderdale. Police officers boarded to work the bus looking for drugs. Wearing raid jackets with the Broward County Sheriff's Office insignia and displaying badges, one holding a gun, the officers awakened Bostick and asked to search his bag. Bostick agreed, and the officers found a pound of cocaine. Had Bostick been traveling in a private vehicle instead of a public transit vehicle, it is much more likely his illicit drugs would have gone undiscovered.

Bostick was convicted, and on appeal the case found its way to the Florida Supreme Court, which overturned the conviction. His lawyer argued that given the circumstances, most reasonable people would not feel free to ignore the police's request. Further, no reasonable person would agree to allow a search of a bag containing cocaine. The case then went to the U.S. Supreme Court, which overturned the Florida Supreme Court decision. The consequence of this ruling is that police can conduct dragnet-like searches of buses and trains, settings where it is difficult for any citizen to refuse cooperation.

Racial Issues

Walker et al. (2004, p.16) examine the issue of disparity and discrimination as it relates to racial and ethnic minorities.

 There is much controversy over whether study results indicate a pattern of systematic *discrimination* or a *disparity* that is related to other factors such as involvement in crime.

Systematic Discrimination	Institutionalized Discrimination	Contextual Discrimination	Individual Acts of Discrimination	Pure Justice

Definitions

Systematic discrimination—Discrimination at all stages of the criminal justice system, at all times, and all places.

Institutionalized discrimination—Racial and ethnic disparities in outcomes that are the result of the application of racially neutral factors, such as prior criminal record, employment status and demeanor.

Contextual discrimination—Discrimination found in particular contexts or circumstances (for example, certain regions, particular crimes, or special victim-offender relationships).

Individual acts of discrimination—Discrimination that results from the acts of particular individuals but is not characteristic of entire agencies or the criminal justice system as a whole.

Pure justice—No racial or ethnic discrimination at all.

Figure 11.1 Discrimination—Disparity Continuum

SOURCE: Samuel Walker, Cassia Spohn and Miriam DeLone. *The Color of Justice: Race, Ethnicity and Crime in America*, 3rd ed. Belmont, CA: Wadsworth Publishing Company, 2004, p.17.

They describe a discrimination-disparity continuum illustrating different kinds of discrimination, going from systematic discrimination to pure justice, as shown in Figure 11.1.

When discussing discrimination within the criminal justice system, it is important to differentiate among the various types of discrimination that might exist and, as previously stressed, to differentiate discrimination from disparity. Discrimination based on a person's race has come to the forefront of policing in the issue of racial profiling.

Racial Profiling

Novak (2004, p.65) notes: "An emerging controversial topic in American policing is the issue of racial profiling. Perhaps no other subject has recently stimulated such passionate debate among citizens, police administrators, policy makers and legislators at all levels of government."

Batton and Kadleck (2004, p.31) define **racial profiling** as "the use of discretionary authority by law enforcement officers in encounters with minority motorists, typically within the context of a traffic stop, that result in the disparate treatment of minorities." They (p.30) suggest: "Racial disparities in the justice system have long been of interest to researchers who have documented disproportionate numbers of racial and ethnic minorities at virtually every stage of justice processing." Gallo (2003, p.19) notes: "Today the term racial profiling is quite common and usually implies that the disproportionate involvement of minorities in traffic stops reflects police racism."

According to the National Criminal Justice Association ("The Racial Profiling Controversy . . .," 2001, pp.8, 13):

Racial profiling is a hot button issue for law enforcement today. Extensive media coverage of alleged use of racial profiling by police officers has not only caused many to believe the practice is deeply rooted, it has also helped to tarnish the minority community's trust in law enforcement. . . .

Law enforcement officials say that honest discussion on the issue of racial profiling cannot take place without acknowledging that police officers are under tremendous pressure to crack down on drug use and trafficking. In addition, according to several federal intelligence reports, minority groups do, in fact, dominate cocaine and marijuana trafficking and often transport narcotics on highways.

The perception of racial profiling has become so common that in Orange County, California, the phenomenon is being called DWA—"driving while Asian"; in El Paso, Texas, it's DWM—"driving while Mexican"; and nationwide the practice is called DWB—"driving while black." Langan et al. (p.2) found that blacks (12.3 percent) were more likely than whites (10.5 percent) to be stopped at least once, and blacks (3.0 percent) were more likely than whites (2.1 percent) to be stopped more than once. In addition, during a traffic stop, police were more likely to carry out some type of search on a black (11.0 percent) or Hispanic (11.3 percent) than a white (5.4 percent).

The Police Executive Research Forum (PERF) surveyed more than 1,000 agency executives nationwide, reviewed materials of over 250 agencies, reviewed published literature and conferred with subject-matter experts to generate a report on the issue of racial profiling, which concluded: "According to recent national surveys, the majority of white, as well as black, Americans say that racial profiling is widespread in the United States today" (Fridell et al., 2001, p.3). The report replaces the term *racial profiling* with *racially biased policing,* stating that use of the word *profiling* creates confusion about an "otherwise legitimate policing term." As Labbe (2001, p.25) insists: "Police have a mandate to battle crime. They use the tools they know work and profiling is one of them."

Sharpe (2002, p.9) explains: "Criminal profiling is easy to understand. If 90 percent of all murders were committed by clowns, is it not fair to say that the first likely suspect in a murder case would have a rubber nose?" Engel and Calnon (2004, p.54) assert: "Some scholars and police officials still embrace the informal use of profiles as an effective and efficient policing strategy. Advocates of profiling practices stress that given the distribution of criminal behavior in this country, it is reasonable for police to consider race in their decision making." Nowicki (2002, p.16) likewise notes: "It may be borderline incompetence to not use race if intelligence information points to a particular race. Race may be a factor, and it would be ludicrous to ignore the obvious."

Novak (p.66) states: "Police officers have suggested disproportionate contacts between officers and citizens may be an unanticipated byproduct of the war on drugs, the get-tough-on-crime movement, zero-tolerance policies or perhaps efficient operational policies." Researchers Meehan and Ponder (2002) found that racial profiling by police was a function of both race and place. As African Americans move farther away from predominantly black neighborhoods into more affluent white communities, racial profiling increases. Tomaskovic-Devey et al. (2004, p.3) also found a connection between profiling and geographic location: "If police are deployed more heavily in minority communities, this will produce high rates of minority stops."

Data analysis technology is available to help police managers make critical personnel and operational decisions in their efforts to prevent racial profiling. A press release on February 12, 2004, announced that the Police Executive Research Forum (PERF) was issuing a comprehensive guide on analyzing and interpreting vehicle stop data ("PERF Releases . . .," 2004). *By the Numbers: A Guide for*

Analyzing Race Data from Vehicle Stops is available as a free download from http://www.policefoundation.org.

This guide may help eliminate two problems associated with collecting data on race and traffic stops: balancing and ghosting. **Balancing** occurs when officers unfairly stop unoffending motorists to make the numbers come out right. As Buerger (2002, p.392) explains: "The issue is reduced to simple terms: 'If I stop a Black guy, I have to stop X number of White guys to make the numbers come out right.'" **Ghosting** is explained by Buerger (p.393) as "falsifying patrol logs to 'make the numbers come out right.'"

Labbe (p.37) says the nation's war on drugs is the number one culprit behind accusations of racial profiling and quotes the director of the Criminal Justice Center for Policy Analysis as saying: "It's an unpleasant fact that blacks are disproportionately involved in the drug trade. Cops aren't out to get blacks so much as to get drug dealers, creating collateral damage for black motorists." Labbe concludes: "To allow political correctness to disarm police of an important law enforcement tool on the grounds of unfounded claims of racism is criminal."

The more recent war on terrorism has again highlighted the conflict law enforcement faces when using race to identify criminal suspects. Rojek et al. (2004, p.145) report: "Since September 11, 2001, racial and ethnic profiling has assumed a different meaning for the American public, most of whom now approve of profiling to combat terrorism."

Nislow (2001, p.11) contends: "After years of enduring harsh criticism and suspicion from the public for alleged racial profiling practices, law enforcement in the aftermath of the World Trade Center disaster has suddenly found itself on the high road, as some who once considered the practice taboo are now eager for police to bend the rules when it comes to Middle Easterners." To illustrate, a *Los Angeles Times* poll conducted shortly after September 11, 2001, showed 68 percent of respondents favored law enforcement "randomly stopping people who may fit the profile of suspected terrorists."

Yet, despite the pronounced shift in the public's apparent tolerance for profiling, police remain bound by the Constitution and the requisite cause for making a stop. According to one scholar: "You can't say all of a sudden that the wrongness of making stops based purely on ethnicity, race, color or age isn't true anymore. It's still true" (Nislow, p.11). A police chief contends: "We are a nation under attack at the moment, and we are preparing for war, but the values of a police department don't change" (Nislow, p.11). Another police administrator asserts: "Racial profiling has never been right, and it's not right now. There is no circumstance where you do away with someone's individual rights, because that leads to chaos" (Nislow, p.11).

In PERF's model policy for responding to race-based policing, consideration of Arab ethnicity is acceptable within the context of current circumstances as long as reasonable suspicion and probable cause exist (Nislow, p.11):

> Along a continuum of approaches, the policy goes a step beyond the more restrictive suspect-specific approach, which says race and ethnicity can be used only when police have a particular description. . . .
>
> [The PERF policy] "would allow you to take into consideration [that] we've just had terrorism, every person involved was of Middle Eastern descent, we don't know who we're looking for but we have some key behavioral cues and we know these people are overwhelmingly Middle Eastern."

In the PERF report foreword, Wexler (2001, pp.x–xi) outlines the three themes behind the recommendations made: "First, racially biased policing is at its core a human rights issue . . . antithetical to democratic policing. . . . Second, racially biased policing is not solely a 'law enforcement problem,' but rather a problem that can be solved only through police-citizen partnerships based on mutual trust and respect." The final theme, and the reason underlying publication of the report, is that "police personnel around the country want to respond effectively to local and national concerns regarding racially biased policing."

In October 2001, the Supreme Court refused to hear the only remaining case docketed for the year concerning an equal protection claim in a case where police officers stop persons based primarily on racial or ethnic descriptions, in effect, upholding the ruling of the U.S. Court of Appeals for the Second Circuit in *Brown v. City of Oneonta* (2001). As Spector (2002, p.10) explains: "The court held that where law enforcement officials possess a description of a criminal suspect that consists primarily of the suspect's race and gender, and where they do not have other evidence of discriminatory intent, they can act on the basis of that description without violating the Equal Protection Clause of the Fourteenth Amendment."

The Court noted that subjecting officers to an equal protection strict-scrutiny analysis in making investigative detentions or arrests could hinder police work. Officers fearful of personal liability might fail to act when they are expected to. The Court held: "Police work, as we know it, would be impaired and the safety of all citizens compromised. . . . The most vulnerable and isolated would be harmed the most. And, if police effectiveness is hobbled by special racial rules, residents of inner cities would be harmed most of all."

One way departments are approaching the problem is through data collection, and more than a dozen states have legislation requiring law enforcement agencies to record data on traffic stops (Carrick, 2001, p.79). However, as Rivera (2001, p.85) cautions: "The broadest issue with data collection is one that is often missed: collection is simply a process focusing on a symptom and not a solution to the problem. Data collection is a crucial first step in the right direction." Furthermore, data collection and *effective analysis* can be costly. In addition, all policies and procedures and all training materials should be reviewed for bias, and citizens should be involved in both the review and the data collection and analysis.

Closely related to the issue of racially biased policing is the perception that police use force more often with minorities than with whites. Indeed, police use of force on any citizen can become an issue.

Use of Force

English philosopher Herbert Spencer proclaimed in 1851: "Policemen are soldiers who act alone; soldiers are policemen who act in unison." As solitary soldiers the police are justified in using force when required to control crime and keep the peace in our society. The IACP defines **force** as "that amount of effort required by police to compel compliance from an unwilling subject" (*Police Use of Force . . .*, 2001, p.1).

 If there is no resistance, no force should be used.

Langan et al. (p.2) note that force includes contacts in which police officers pushed, grabbed, kicked or hit a citizen. Force also includes police dog bites, unconsciousness-rendering holds, handcuffs and leg restraints, chemical agents (pepper spray, Cap-Stun), electrical devices (Taser) and a firearm pointed in a citizen's direction or the threat to carry out any of these types of force. It goes without saying that the killing of a subject by an officer is the most extreme use of police force.

The IACP (*Police Use of Force . . .*, p.i) reports: "Police used force at a rate of 3.61 times per 10,000 calls-for-service. This translates to a rate of 0.0361% use of force. Expressed another way, police did *not* use force 99.9639% of the time." According to this report (p.ii), from 1999 to 2000 the most common force used by officers was physical force, followed by chemical force and then impact. Arrests were the most frequent circumstance in which force was used, followed by disturbances, as shown in Figure 11.2.

The IACP (*Police Use of Force*, p.iv) also notes that, from 1995 to 2000, 8,148 reported incidents included racial descriptors for both the involved officers and subjects, of which:

- 44 percent involved white officers using force on African American subjects.
- 39 percent involved white officers using force on white subjects.
- 7 percent involved African American officers using force on African American subjects.
- 3.4 percent involved African American officers using force on white subjects.

According to the IACP (*Police Use of Force*, p.iv): "Subject intoxication appears to be a substantial predictor of police use of force during traffic stops. . . . 46% of all use of force incidents occurred where the subject was intoxicated or under the influence of drugs." Research by Reisig et al. (2004) examined officers' use of force and suspect disrespect. They found: "Most encounters in which officers are not shown respect involve suspects who are not altogether rational because they are emotionally overwrought, intoxicated or mentally impaired." They also found: "African American suspects were no more likely to behave disrespectfully once neighborhood context was taken into account. Based on our findings and extant research, we conclude that suspect disrespect among African Americans is likely fostered by economic and social disadvantage, not something unique to

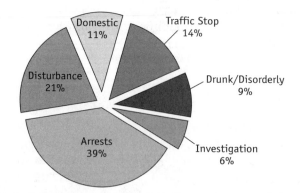

Figure 11.2   Percent of Officer Use of Force by Circumstance of Encounter (1999–2000)

race." They note: "If officers can be trained to appreciate the dynamics of such encounters, they may feel less offended or threatened by such displays and therefore be less inclined to punish suspects for their 'bad attitude.' " Finally, they (p.264) suggest: "Another practical implication of these findings is the usefulness of the common police practice of dispersing bystanders when tensions run high, a strategy that should prove especially effective at public disorders."

Researchers Garner et al. (2002) found that the characteristics most associated with police use of force were resistance by the suspect, demeanor and, to a lesser extent, race. They found that when suspects were uncivil to police, for example, talking back, the odds of force being used in their arrest increased by 163 percent. Research by Terrill (2003) also found that police use of force increases with suspect resistance. A study by Terrill and Reisig (2003) found that police officers are significantly more likely to use higher levels of force when suspects are encountered in disadvantaged neighborhoods and those with higher homicide rates.

Use of force was also influenced by the officer's age, education and training. The IACP (*Police Use of Force*, p.18) found that officers with a college education tended to use less force of all types than officers with only a high school education. Use of force exists along a continuum that officers may move up or down upon, depending on the situation or the totality of circumstances.

The Use of Force Continuum

The amount of force used can be placed on a continuum: no force—used with a cooperative person; to ordinary force—used with a person who is resisting; to extraordinary force—used with a person who is assaultive. One use of force continuum is shown in Figure 11.3.

The Use of Force Model currently used by the Federal Law Enforcement Training Center (FLETC) closely parallels the continuum in Figure 11.3 (Nowicki, 2001b, p.35). The first level is the Compliant Level where the subject is cooperative.

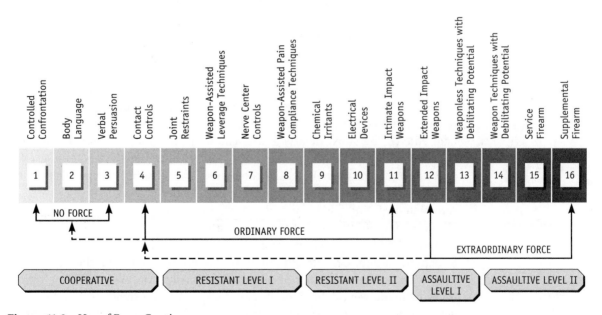

Figure 11.3 Use of Force Continuum

SOURCE: Adapted from G. Connor. "Use of Force Continuum: Phase II." *Law and Order*, March 1991, p.30. Reprinted by permission of *Law and Order* magazine.

At the second level (Resistive Passive), no physical energy is expended by the subject, but the subject does not follow the officer's commands. The third level (Resistive Active) is where the subject expends energy to actively resist the arrest, for example grabbing hold of something and refusing to let go. The fourth level is the Assaultive (Bodily Harm) Level, where the subject physically attacks the officer or others. The fifth level is the Assaultive (Serious Bodily Harm or Death) Level where officers believe serious bodily injury or death is threatened. As Rogers (2001, p.82) stresses: "Agencies need to have a continuum, and officers need to be able to articulate it."

Critics of use of force continuums argue that incidents when force must be used are not linear, that points along the continuum may, of necessity, be skipped, leaving an officer open to a lawsuit. Williams (2002, p.14) contends: "Force continuums often represent an unrealistic, almost wishful ideal." He (p.15) suggests: "Self-imposed requirements of a force continuum can cause various consequences. While sincerely attempting to adhere to the policies and training that they have received about employing force continuums, officers can encounter threats to their personal safety, and can face departmental, as well as civil, liability."

Aveni (2003, p.75) suggests: "As policing has evolved, so should force continuums being employed. . . . We've seen a paradigm shift in continuum design from linear to non-linear models:" He (pp.75–76) notes: "Since little about policing is linear, non-linear force continuums would seem to be a better fit. . . . The perceived advantages of non-linear continuums are that (1) they flow from the suspects' actions DIRECTLY to the most appropriate response, rather than through a linear chain of options that might not be applicable, (2) they seem to offer more latitude to officers dealing with threats that might not always be as quantifiable as we'd like them to be, and (3) the very nature of a non-linear force continuum lends itself to incorporation of one of the most neglected continuum options, DISENGAGEMENT from untenable situations."

Although officers are authorized to use force, including deadly force, they must use only that level and amount of force *reasonably* necessary to accomplish a legitimate law enforcement objective.

Reasonable Force

What constitutes **reasonable force** was established in *Graham v. Connor* (1989). In this case Graham, a diabetic, asked a friend to drive him to a store for some orange juice to counteract an insulin reaction. The friend agreed, but when Graham entered the store, he saw a long checkout line and, concerned about the delay, hurried out of the store to ask the friend to take him someplace else. Officer Connor, seeing Graham hastily enter and leave the store, grew suspicious and followed their car. Half a mile from the store, Connor made an investigative stop. Although the friend told Connor that Graham was simply suffering from a "sugar reaction," the officer ordered the two men to wait while he found out what, if anything, had happened at the store. When the officer returned to his patrol car to request backup, Graham got out of the car and passed out on the curb.

Moments later a number of other officers arrived on the scene. One officer rolled Graham over on the sidewalk and cuffed his hands tightly behind his back, ignoring the friend's pleas to get Graham some sugar. Several officers then lifted Graham up, carried him over to the friend's car, and placed him face down on its hood. Regaining consciousness, Graham asked the officers to check his wallet for a diabetic decal. One officer told him to "Shut up" and shoved Graham's face against the hood of the car. Four officers grabbed Graham and threw him head-first into the police car. Another friend of Graham's brought some orange juice to the car, but the officers refused to let him have it. Finally Officer Connor received a report that Graham had done nothing wrong at the store, and the officers drove him home and released him.

During this encounter Graham sustained a broken foot, cuts on his wrists, a bruised forehead and an injured shoulder. He also claimed to have developed a loud, permanent ringing in his right ear. Graham filed a lawsuit under 42 U.S.C. § 1983 against the individual officers involved in the incident, alleging they had used excessive force in making the investigatory stop. The Court, however, ruled that the officers did not use excessive force, explaining:

> The calculus of reasonableness must embody allowance for the fact that police officers are often forced to make split-second judgments—in circumstances that are tense, uncertain, and rapidly evolving—about the amount of force that is necessary in a particular situation. . . . The reasonableness of a particular use of force must be judged from the perspective of a reasonable officer on the scene, rather than with the 20/20 vision of hindsight.

According to del Carmen and Walker (2001, p.174): "This case gives police officers a 'break' in civil liability cases involving the use of force . . . [by recognizing] that police officers often make split-second judgments in situations that involve their own lives and must, therefore, be judged in the context of 'a reasonable officer at the scene.' This is a test most police officers welcome."

Excessive Force

The IACP (*Police Use of Force*, p.1) defines **excessive force** as "the application of an amount and/or frequency of force greater than that required to compel compliance from a willing or unwilling subject." According to their study excessive force was used only 0.42 percent of the time; excessive force was not used in 99.583 percent of all reported cases.

The IACP reports that from 1990 to 1999, men accounted for 80 percent of patrol officers but accounted for 95 percent of use-of-force settlements over $100,000 (Lonsway, 2001, pp.110–111). Women accounted for 20 percent of the patrol officers but for only 5 percent of the settlements. Put another way, the ratio of male to female officers on patrol was 4:1, while the ratio of payouts for excessive force was about 19:1. Lonsway (p.111) concludes: "Female officers are not reluctant to use force, but they are not nearly as likely to be involved in the use of excessive force."

Excessive force is synonymous with police brutality. An extreme example of such unprofessional conduct was the brutalization of Abner Louima, a Haitian immigrant who was sodomized at the police department with a broomstick. Louima received $9 million in a settlement for the incident ("NY Police, Louima Reach Tentative $9 Million Deal," 2001, p.A4).

Less-Lethal Force

As law enforcement technology expands, a wider variety of response options are becoming available to officers. For instances where an increased level of force is necessary but deadly force is too extreme, there are now a variety of **less-lethal**

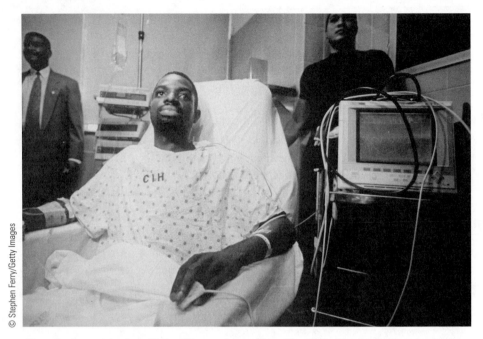

Abner Louima received an $8.7 million settlement from New York City. Louima was arrested in a brawl outside a Brooklyn nightclub in 1997 and taken to the 70th Precinct stationhouse, where Officer Volpe sodomized Louima with a broomstick. Louima sued for $155 million, claiming that officers conspired to create a "wall of silence and lies to obstruct justice."

force alternatives. Common less-lethal options include mace, CN and CS tear gas, oleoresin capsicum (OC) pepper spray, the Taser, projectile launchers and specialty impact munitions such as beanbags and flexible baton rounds, designed to deliver blunt trauma.

According to Heal (2001, p.93): "When compared to the historical evolution of lethal munitions, the less lethal munitions in use today are the functional equivalent to the blunderbuss age: short-range, inaccurate and awkward." Nonetheless, use of these projectiles, commonly called extended-range impact munitions, continues to grow. James (2001, p.17) notes: "The twelve-gauge pump shotgun and 'bean bag' round is the most common less-lethal system on the streets of America today."

Chemical agents such as CS and CN (tear gas) are less-lethal weapons effective for crowd control. Another effective chemical agent is OC or pepper spray. According to Nowicki (2001a, p.28), it is effective in 80 to 90 percent of the situations in which it is used. OC can be delivered as a cone-shaped spray, a fogger, a stream, a splatter stream or foam. In many departments' force options, pepper spray is allowed when verbal commands are ineffective, even before control holds and impact weapons are suggested. Current efforts to increase airline security include arming sky marshals with pepper ball guns that incapacitate a subject yet, unlike conventional bullets, will not puncture the plane's fuselage.

Capture nets are yet another less-lethal option, but they are difficult to deploy inside buildings or if a suspect is near a wall or other obstacle. In addition, once a suspect is ensnared, handcuffing and searching are difficult if not impossible.

A popular less-lethal weapon that has been in use for over 25 years is the stun gun, now called an electronic immobilization device (EID). One commonly used

EID is the Taser, an acronym for Thomas A. Swift Electric Rifle (named after Tom Swift in the popular children's adventure series of the 1920s and 1930s). As Nielsen (2001, p.57) explains:

> Tasers are conducted energy weapons that fire a cartridge with two small probes (darts) that are connected to the weapon by high-voltage, insulated wire. When the probes contact the target, they transmit very short duration, high energy, electrical pulses along the wires to overwhelm the sensory nervous system, stunning the target. . . .
>
> Recognizing that even a single failure to stop is one failure too many, Taser International set out in early 1996 to create a less-lethal system that can stop focused combatants. The ADVANCED TASER was the result. . . .
>
> The 18 to 26 watt T-Waves cause an immediate, uncontrollable contraction of the muscle tissue. They're capable of physically debilitating the subject regardless of his mental focus or pain tolerance. . . .
>
> The accuracy of the advanced Taser is excellent. . . . In all cases, there has been virtual 100% instant incapacitation when the advanced Taser has been employed within its intended design parameters.

According to Jones (2001, p.70), the courts have approved use of this technology: "In *Caldwell v. Moore* the court evaluated evidence and ruled EID technology is less-lethal, non-injurious and represents a 'safety factor for all involved in comparison to hands-on tactics.' " And as Sanow (2001, p.4) contends: "Electronic force holds the greatest amount of technological promise for the future to halt violent conflicts with the least chance of injury to anyone."

K-9s as Less-Lethal Force   Dogs have been of tremendous help to law enforcement officers in locating and apprehending criminal suspects. This use, however, often requires the dog to apply force, at the handler's command, on the suspect and thus falls under the Fourth Amendment's requirement of reasonableness. Several court decisions around the country have indicated that law enforcement–trained K-9s are to be considered a less-lethal alternative—and safer—means of applying force.

In *Mendoza v. Block* (1994), the court ruled that the specific circumstances of a situation determine if the use of a K-9 is reasonable. For example, it is reasonable to send a K-9 after a fleeing suspect if that subject is believed to be armed and has ignored an officer's warning that a dog will be used unless the suspect surrenders. It is not reasonable, however, to sic a K-9 on a suspect who has fully surrendered or is already under complete control.

In *Robinette v. Barnes* (1988), in which claims of unlawful use of deadly force were made after a suspect died as the result of a dog bite, the court held: "We do not dispute the fact that trained police dogs can appear to be dangerous, threatening animals. The dogs' ability to aid law enforcement would be minimal if they did not possess this trait. However, the mere recognition that a law enforcement tool is dangerous does not suffice as proof that the tool is an instrument of deadly force."

Less-Lethal Can Still Be Lethal   Debate has centered over the terminology applied to these weapons—should they be called *less-than-lethal, less-lethal, defensive, intermediate* or something else? Some use-of-force experts prefer the term *less-lethal* to *less-than-lethal* because of liability implications and misrepresentation of a weapon's lethality. Dorsch (2001, p.102) explains the dilemma such weapons pose for police: "If less lethal means are used, the officer can be sued; if an officer has less lethal ammunition but chooses not to use it, he can be sued."

The problem may be in the terminology. What does *less-lethal* mean? Can someone be less dead? The terms *less-lethal* and *less-than-lethal* create a trap for police officers and the agencies they serve and can be used for them or against them depending on the situation. The weapons might be called an intermediate weapon or a defensive weapon instead.

Whatever term is used, it must be recognized that many of these alternatives *can* inadvertently cause death. While officers acknowledge the fatal possibilities that may accompany use of less-lethal force, at times officers are justified in using force they *know* will likely result in a subject's death.

Deadly Force

Authority of law enforcement officers to use deadly force is an awesome responsibility. When considering the justifiable use of **deadly force,** two interrelated rights are important: the legal right to use such force and the moral right compelling the officer to do so.

State legislators have generally given the police very broad discretion in this area, with most politicians fearful of being labeled as "soft on criminals" if they did otherwise. Many state statutes authorize use of deadly force to prevent commission of a felony. Yet, to balance the legal and moral rights involved, several states have adopted penal codes that do not rely solely on a crime being classified as a felony. They focus instead on the danger the suspect poses to the officer and society.

 Justification for use of deadly force must consider not only the legal right, but also the need to apprehend the suspect compared to the arresting officer's safety and the value of human life.

To help officers make sound judgments in when to use this extreme level of force, a deadly force decision model was created (Figure 11.4). All three factors—ability, opportunity and jeopardy—must be present to justify use of deadly force.

Figure 11.5 presents a nonlinear description of a lethal force event from an assigned officer's expectations and on-scene arrival to the three possible outcomes: fight, flight or freeze, and the aftermath.

The landmark Supreme Court ruling, *Tennessee v. Garner* (1985), bars police from shooting to kill fleeing felons unless there is an imminent danger to life. This ruling invalidated state laws (passed in almost half the states) that allowed police officers to use deadly force to prevent the escape of a suspected felon.

The case involved a 1974 incident in which a Memphis police officer shot and killed an unarmed 15-year-old boy fleeing from the police after having stolen $10 in money and jewelry from an unoccupied home. The officer testified that he shot the boy to prevent him from escaping. He had been trained to do so, and Tennessee law permitted him to do so. The Supreme Court ruled that the Tennessee "fleeing felon" statute was unconstitutional because it authorized use of deadly force against unarmed fleeing suspects who posed no threat to the officer or third parties. In effect, taking a life is a "seizure," which the Fourth Amend-

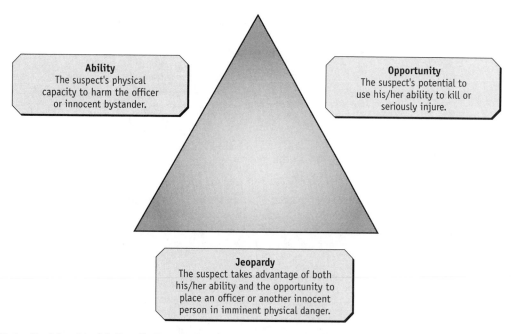

Ability
The suspect's physical capacity to harm the officer or innocent bystander.

Opportunity
The suspect's potential to use his/her ability to kill or seriously injure.

Jeopardy
The suspect takes advantage of both his/her ability and the opportunity to place an officer or another innocent person in imminent physical danger.

Figure 11.4   Decision Model: Deadly Force Triangle

SOURCE: Dean T. Olson. "Improving Deadly Force Decision Making." *FBI Law Enforcement Bulletin,* February 1998, p.4. Reprinted by permission.

ment states must be reasonable. A summary of the law on the use of force is given in Table 11.2.

One controversial type of force used by police is pursuit, which may result in injury or death for fleeing suspects, pursuing officers and/or innocent bystanders.

Police Pursuits

According to Nugent et al. (n.d., p.iv): "Police throughout the country engage in hundreds of high-speed automobile chases every day. Enough of these result in serious property damage, personal injury, and death to make police pursuit a major public concern." They (p.1) define **pursuit** as: "An active attempt by a law enforcement officer on duty in a patrol car to apprehend one or more occupants of a moving motor vehicle, providing the driver of such vehicle is aware of the attempt and is resisting apprehension by maintaining or increasing his speed or by ignoring the law enforcement officer's attempt to stop him."

While this definition limits pursuits to actions involving vehicles and, indeed, most people think of high-speed vehicle chases when they hear a pursuit is in progress, the majority of "pursuits" are on foot. Few departments have policies on foot pursuits and even fewer train in this area, instead focusing primarily on the execution and hazards of high-speed vehicle pursuit and whether such a pursuit should even be initiated. Klugiewicz and Smith (2004, p.120) contend: "Any officer who has ever had to run after a suspect knows that a foot chase is extremely hazardous. Running after a suspect can place you in a situation where you can be easily attacked, injured by accident or even have a heart attack. Real life is not a movie, and the decision to hoof it after the bad guy should never be made lightly. It can be a life and death decision."

Anatomy of a Lethal Force Event©

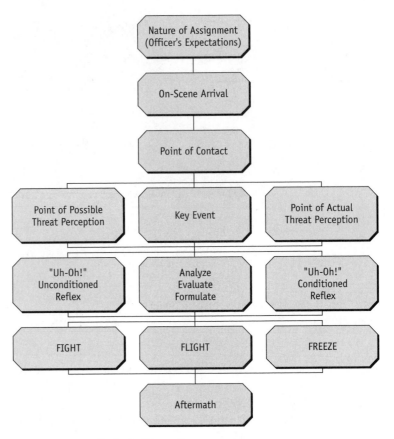

Figure 11.5   Anatomy of a Lethal Force Event

SOURCE: Thomas J. Aveni. "The Force Continuum Conundrum." *Law and Order,* December 2003, p.75. Reprinted by permission.

Vehicle pursuits also can become deadly. Hill (2002, p.15) reports: "Research indicates that pursuits become dangerous quite quickly. For example 50 percent of all pursuit collisions occur in the first 2 minutes of the pursuit, and more than 70 percent of all collisions occur before the sixth minute of the pursuit."

To Pursue or Not to Pursue

Witczak (2003, p.131) describes this issue: "The controversy over pursuits seems never-ending. One group says pursuits should be banned totally. Others feel that pursuits should only be allowed under certain circumstances. A third option is that pursuits should be left to the discretion of the officer involved in the incident. All of the groups appear to have valid reasoning and justification behind their convictions." The basic dilemma of pursuits is whether the benefits of potential apprehension outweigh the risks posed to police officers, the public and the suspects.

 High-speed pursuits are both effective and dangerous.

Because of the high probability of damage to property and people not connected with the pursuit, many advocate discontinuing a policy of police pursuit.

Table 11.2 Summary of the Law on the Use of Force

Situation	Less-Than-Deadly Force	Deadly Force
In self-defense or in the defense of others	"The use of (reasonable) force upon or toward another person is justified when the actor (reasonably) believes that such force is immediately necessary for the purpose of protecting himself or herself (or another) against the use of unlawful force by such other person on the present occasion."[a]	"The use of deadly force is not justified . . . unless such force is necessary to protect . . . against death, serious bodily harm, kidnapping, or sexual intercourse compelled by force or threat."[b]
In the defense of property	"Only such degree of force or threat thereof may intentionally be used as the actor reasonably believes is necessary to prevent or terminate the interference."[c]	Under the old common law, deadly force could be used in the defense of property. All states now forbid the use of intentional deadly force in the defense of property.
To apprehend a person who has committed a crime	"When an officer is making or attempting to make an arrest for a criminal offense, he is acting for the protection of public interest and is permitted even greater latitude than when he acts in self-defense, and he is not liable unless the means which he uses are clearly excessive."[d]	*Misdemeanor:* NEVER *Fleeing Felon:* Deadly force could be used when officers "have probable cause . . . to believe that the suspect (has committed a felony and) poses a threat to the safety of the officers or a danger to the community if left at large." *Tennessee v. Garner*
To stop a person for investigative purposes when only "reasonable suspicion" exists	Only such force that is reasonable and necessary under the circumstances that then exist	NEVER
Disciplining children (corporal punishment)	Only parents and other people having a status of *in loco parentis* to a child may use reasonable force "reasonably believed to be necessary for (the child's) proper control, training, or education."[e] Other persons (such as strangers or neighbors) may not discipline a child.	NEVER

[a]Sections 3.04(1) and 3.05(1) of the Model Penal Code.
[b]Section 3.04(2)(b) of the Model Penal Code.
[c]Section 939.49(1) of the Wisconsin Statutes.
[d]Restatement of Torts, Section 132(a).
[e]Restatement of Torts, Section 147(2), as quoted by the U.S. Supreme Court in *Ingraham v. Wright*, 429 U.S. 975,97 S.Ct. 481 (1976).

SOURCE: Thomas J. Gardner and Terry M. Anderson. *Criminal Law, Principles and Cases,* 7th ed. Belmont, CA: Wadsworth Publishing Company, 2000, p.127. Reprinted by permission.

Suspects who flee the police can be caught later without the risks of a high-speed pursuit. Other people, however, contend that police pursuit serves a vital purpose, arguing that if lawbreakers knew they could simply drive away and the police would not pursue, why would anyone ever stop? Many believe that with proper policies and increased officer training, pursuits should be allowed to continue.

Since the 1960s, researchers have focused on two opposing positions in this debate—first, support for pursuit because of the need to enforce laws and apprehend violators, and second, opposition to pursuit because of the risk to public safety. Three aspects of pursuit are agreed upon by law enforcement: (1) pursuits are dangerous, (2) pursuits must be controlled and (3) involvement in a pursuit increases the participants' adrenaline and excitement.

Pursuit Policies

As might be expected, pursuit policies range from a total ban on them to allowing officers complete discretion. Most policies suggest that factors to be considered include the offense, traffic conditions and weather conditions. Many departments' pursuit policies include use of a pursuit continuum, similar to those established for use of force. Figure 11.6 illustrates a pursuit continuum going from simply trailing a suspect vehicle to ramming and use of firearms, depending on the known threat posed by the suspect as indicated by the behavior observed.

Notice in Figure 11.6 that "disengage as an option" is always present along the continuum. Such continuums make sense considering a large number of pursuits result from minor traffic law violations. Despite the possibility of such pursuits ending in a collision, the fact also remains that many pursuits result in the arrest of a felon.

Many pursuit policies use situational elements as the determining criteria in whether to initiate a pursuit, differentiating between serious offenses where officers have little or no discretion and a sworn duty to act and minor offenses where pursuit may be more discretionary. Two classes of pursuit should be considered in the policy: imperative (Class I) and elective (Class II), the differences between which are explained in Figure 11.7.

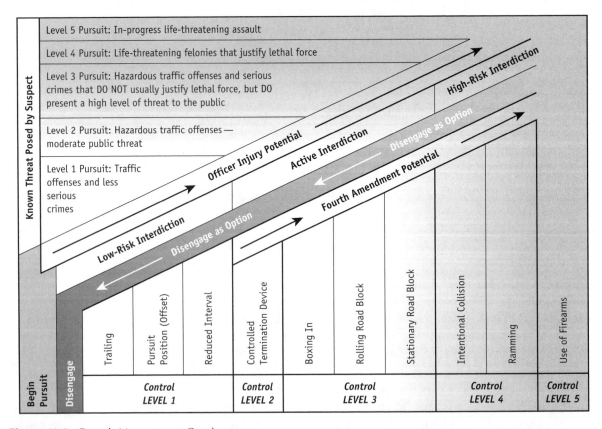

Figure 11.6   Pursuit Management Continuum

SOURCE: Steven D. Ashley. "Pursuit Management Implementing a Control Continuum." *Law and Order,* December 1994, p.60. Reprinted by permission.

Agencies often employ technology to make high-speed pursuits safer or eliminate them altogether. The most popular options are spike strips (tire-puncturing devices) and retractable barrier strips that can be remotely deployed so as to affect only the subject's vehicle. Other technology may also reduce the risks of high-speed pursuits, including GPS tracking systems, aircraft intervention, vehicle-to-vehicle communication technology and traffic light warning systems to shut down an intersection through which the pursuit might pass.

In addition to sound pursuit policies, departments must provide training in use of the policy as well as in executing it. Without such training, departments increase their vulnerability to lawsuits.

Liability in Police Pursuits

Because so many police vehicle pursuits end in crashes, and some in fatalities, lawsuits are inevitable. Departments can, however, minimize the risk of lawsuits by creating a pursuit policy that balances the need to apprehend offenders in the interest of justice with the need to protect citizens from the risks associated with such pursuits (Pipes and Pape, 2001, p.16). Departments must also know what limitations and allowances state and federal statutes provide. For example, *Galas v. McKee* (1986) held that police pursuits were allowed to capture traffic violators. More recently, *County of Sacramento v. Lewis* (1998) set the standard for liability in police pursuits.

In the latter case 16-year-old Philip Lewis was a passenger on a motorcycle driven by 18-year-old Brian Willard. When Willard committed a traffic violation,

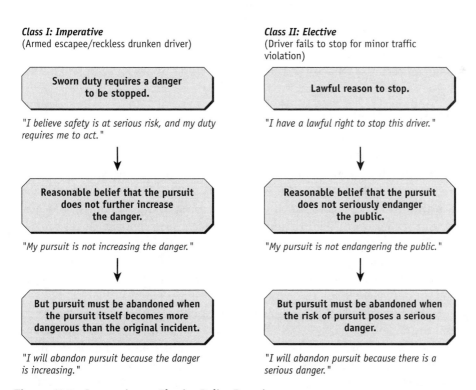

Figure 11.7 Imperative vs. Elective Police Pursuit

SOURCE: Phil Wright and Les McCarthy. "Why Do We Make Pursuit Policies?" *The Police Chief*, July 1998, p.52. Reprinted by permission. Copyright held by The International Association of Chiefs of Police, Inc. Further reproduction without express written permission is prohibited.

a Sacramento County sheriff 's deputy tried to stop the motorcycle, but the driver sped away. The deputy followed, and during the pursuit, the chase reached speeds of up to 100 miles per hour. The pursuit ended when the motorcycle tipped over and Lewis was struck and killed by the patrol car. The 9th Circuit Court ruled that the deputy was liable for Lewis's death by showing "deliberate indifference to, or reckless disregard for, a person's right to life and personal security."

The Supreme Court, however, overturned this ruling and held: "Only conduct that shows an intent on the part of the officer to cause harm unrelated to the legitimate object of making the arrest will meet the test of shocking and arbitrary conduct actionable as a deprivation of substantive due process." As a result of *Lewis*, "In high-speed vehicle pursuit cases, liability in Section 1983 cases ensues only if the conduct of the officer 'shocks the conscience.' The lower standard of 'deliberate indifference' does not apply" (del Carmen and Walker, p.270).

For over half a century, the Supreme Court has applied a "shocks-the-conscience" test to analyze claims similar to the one made in this case, and the Court considers *Rochin v. California* (1952) to be the benchmark case explaining this standard. In the years between *Rochin* and *Lewis,* the Court explained that conduct that "shocks the conscience" is conduct so brutal and offensive that it does not comport with traditional ideas of fair play and decency. Through this ruling, the Supreme Court recognizes that law enforcement officers are not to blame for police pursuits, and therefore, should not be held liable for accidents that result from them. The fault lies with drivers who endanger their own lives and the lives of others by fleeing police. Says Bellah (2003, p.29): "The real culprit is the rabbit. The motorist has the legal obligation to yield and stop when lawfully signaled by a police officer. The driver who fails to stop and elects to flee is the one responsible for placing his or her life in danger, placing the officers' lives in danger and is a menace to the civilian population." Despite the Court's ruling, officers may still be sued civilly under state statutes for wrongful death.

Civil Liability

As discussed, many aspects of police work (e.g., use of force, high-speed pursuits) leave officers and their departments vulnerable to possible lawsuits. Searches and arrests have the potential for lawsuits, as do failures to investigate or arrest. According to a survey by Vaughn et al. (2001), the most common allegations in lawsuits involved excessive use of force, false arrest or imprisonment, or unlawful searches/seizures. Slightly more than one-half of the police chiefs surveyed thought that police did not excessively or irrationally fear civil litigation, but a similar percentage indicated that lawsuits or the threat of litigation made it more difficult for police to do their job. Seventy-six percent believed that most lawsuits against police were frivolous.

Liability is a legal obligation incurred for an injury suffered/complained that results from failure to conduct a specific task/activity within a given standard. As discussed in Chapter 2, the U.S. Constitution and the Bill of Rights define the civil rights and civil liberties guaranteed each citizen by the government. Other civil rights protections with specific relevance to law enforcement are granted under 42 U.S.C. § 1983.

Civil liability suits, however, have not always been an issue for law enforcement. Until 1978, a public entity was not a "person" who could abuse official power and authority to deprive constitutionally protected civil rights or act in a conspiracy to violate otherwise constitutionally protected rights. This changed in 1978 when the Supreme Court decided *Monell v. Dept. of Social Services of the City of New York.* This case and several subsequent cases effectively removed the absolute sovereign immunity previously enjoyed by governmental entities and their employees.

 Today concern for civil liability is quite evident in law enforcement agencies' policies and practices.

"Lawsuit paranoia" has also been called **litigaphobia,** or the fear of litigation. Fear of being sued can cause confusion regarding which action to take in a given situation—the "damned if you do, damned if you don't" dilemma. As an example, for a while citizens in need of lifesaving assistance were filing and winning lawsuits against those who responded to their needs for injuries sustained during the assistance or other more ludicrous reasons. So people grew reluctant to "get involved," and lawsuits were then filed for failure to assist. To protect well-intentioned assistants, Good Samaritan laws were passed that required a showing of gross, wanton or willful negligence.

A police duty more commonly the subject of lawsuits is making arrests. High-risk warrantless arrest situations include drunk and disorderly arrests, escalating to excessive force claims and arrests under pro-arrest domestic violence statutes. In contrast is the officer sued for failing to arrest. This most often occurs when an officer fails to arrest an intoxicated driver.

The leading case in this area of "ministerial duties" is *Irwin v. Town of Ware* (1992). In this case an officer pulled over a vehicle that had "peeled out" of a bar's parking lot. The officer had the car's occupant get out, and an eyewitness said the driver was unsteady, holding his head and then holding onto the door. No sobriety tests were done, and the driver was sent on his way. Ten minutes later he was involved in a head-on collision that killed Misty Irwin. The court said the decision to arrest was not up to the officer. Because the state had enacted a statute authorizing police to arrest drunk drivers, this was their sworn duty.

The concept of "public duty" was reaffirmed in *Carleton v. Town of Framingham* (1993). In this case an officer talked with an obviously drunken person in a store. He waited until the driver got into his car and drove off before attempting to stop and arrest him. The driver did not stop and was involved in a head-on collision. Citing *Irwin* the court said the officer had a duty "to enforce the statutes with respect to intoxicated operators of motor vehicles and could anticipate that his failure to take action to remove the drunk driver from the highway could result in immediate and foreseeable physical injury to a member of the public."

Investigative procedure is another area of police work commonly brought up in lawsuits. Almost every investigation gives officers discretion to decide what evidence should be included in prosecutor reports and warrant applications, and what evidence should be omitted. Newbold (2001, p.10) notes: "The landmark case of *Brady v. Maryland* (1968) places on a prosecutor an affirmative constitutional duty to disclose **exculpatory evidence** (favorable to the accused) to a defendant: We now hold that the suppression of evidence by the prosecution of evidence favorable to an accused upon request violates due process where the evidence is material either to guilt or to punishment, irrespective of the good faith or bad faith of the prosecution" (bold added).

Leaving out exculpatory evidence may lead to liability for false arrest, malicious prosecution, and illegal search and seizure claims. To support such liability claims, a plaintiff must show that the affiant knowingly and deliberately, or with reckless disregard for the truth, omitted facts that are material or necessary to a finding of probable cause [*Franks v. Delaware*, 1978].

The constitutional protections extended to police officers while performing their duties "under color of law" were affirmed in *Saucier v. Katz* (2001). According to Makholm (2001, p.57): "It is mildly ironic that 'saucier' is defined, at least in part, as 'impossible to repress or control' . . . for military police officer Donald Saucier apparently was able to do just that, i.e., control and arrest the plaintiff/protestor Elliot M. Katz." Katz, president of Defense of Animals, during an appearance by then–Vice-President Gore, attempted to confront Gore with a banner that read: "Please Keep Animal Torture Out of Our National Parks." The military police, charged with keeping protestors at bay, had been alerted to the probable presence of Katz, and Officer Saucier and a sergeant picked Katz up and delivered him to a military vehicle. Katz claimed he was "thrown" into the vehicle and had to catch himself to avoid being injured. Katz filed an excessive force suit against Saucier. The District Court denied Saucier qualified immunity, and at the Ninth Circuit of Appeals, Saucier fared no better. However, the Supreme Court overturned the Ninth Circuit Court's holding.

The Supreme Court held that courts must take a two-step approach: The first inquiry must be whether a constitutional right would have been violated on the facts alleged; second, assuming the violation is established, the question of whether the right was clearly established must be considered on a more specific level. The Court explained that the privilege of qualified immunity is "an immunity from suit rather than a mere defense to liability; and like an absolute immunity, it is effectively lost if a case is erroneously permitted to go to trial. . . . We repeatedly have stressed the importance of resolving immunity questions at the earliest possible stage in litigation." In other words, the court is to resolve the issue of qualified immunity early and not put an officer through an entire trial.

Officer ignorance and disrespect for diversity may also lead to civil lawsuits. According to Rosenbaum (2001, p.68) chances of a lawsuit increase when officers fail to understand those who are different from themselves—different race, culture or background. They also increase when officers deal with persons with mental illness. Cultural awareness courses and sensitivity training are among the many ways departments can reduce officers' civil liability.

Reducing Civil Liability

What can an agency and its officers do to reduce the risk of being named in a civil suit? When police chiefs were asked what steps could prevent lawsuits, the most frequent answers were treating people fairly, better training, better supervision, better screening and early identification of problem officers—in that order. To help with the increasing tangle of legal issues, many police agencies now employ part-or full-time legal advisors.

While many departments cannot afford permanent, in-house legal counsel, it is vital that they develop a sound working relationship with such an advisor.

Another way departments are reducing civil liability is by modifying administrative policy decisions.

As discussed in Chapter 5, community policing takes a proactive approach to combating crime and other problems that plague a community by encouraging and supporting partnerships between law enforcement agencies and officers and the citizens and organizations within the community they serve. This fundamental shift in policing philosophy is still resisted by some agency administrators who are skeptical about the effectiveness and benefits of such an approach. While agencies and their officers continue to struggle with the question "Is it legal?" another question often posed is "Is it ethical?"

Corruption, Ethics and Integrity—Where to Draw the Line

Son and Rome (2004, p.179) suggest: "Police misconduct has been a social issue in the United States for much of the 20th century." As noted by Trautman: "More nationwide research was conducted on police corruption and integrity during the last five years than was completed throughout the preceding century. In spite of these advancements, scandals flourish and corruption continues to undermine America's trust in policing" (2001, p.91).

Swope (2001, pp.80–81) chronicles the commissions assigned to examine police corruption, beginning with the 1890s Lexow Commission and Mazet Commission and the 1910s Curan Committee to handle corruption in the New York City Police Department. The 1931 Wickersham Commission report documented corruption and brutality in the criminal justice system throughout the United States. The 1960s Knapp Commission again uncovered bribery and kickbacks throughout the NYPD. In 1974 the Philadelphia police were accused of engaging in criminal practices throughout the force. In the 1980s more than 70 Miami police officers were arrested for serious acts of corruption.

In 1993 the Mollen Commission report again found large-scale corruption in the NYPD including extortion, bribery and theft. From 1993 to 1995 more than 50 New Orleans police officers were arrested, indicted or convicted on charges including rape, aggravated battery, drug trafficking and murder. The Christopher Commission, investigating the Los Angeles Police Department after the Rodney King beating, found that significant numbers of LAPD officers "repetitively use excessive force against the public and persistently ignore the written guidelines of the department regarding force." In the late 1990s the Rampart Commission again found serious problems within the LAPD.

According to Griffith (2003, p.69): "Since 1993 major cities nationwide, including Los Angeles, Miami, Detroit and New Orleans, have been rocked by revelations of officer misconduct. Internal and external investigations of these departments led to lurid evidence of officers dealing drugs, stealing evidence, hiring themselves out for contract killings, planting guns on suspects after police-involved shootings and covering up for fellow officers."

As Fuller (2001, p.6) notes: "The police service in this country is more closely scrutinized and subject to more uninformed, biased criticism than any other occupational group, with the possible exception of presidential candidates." Because of this close scrutiny, it is imperative that officers avoid corruption.

What Constitutes Corruption?

 Police **corruption** occurs when an officer misuses authority for personal gain. It includes accepting gratuities and bribes as well as committing theft or burglary. The most common and extensive type of corruption is accepting small gratuities or tips.

Although discounts and free service are usually not considered important, cash payments to police officers are quite another matter. It is a serious issue when an officer accepts an outright bribe to refrain from making an arrest or imposing a fine. Another form of extremely serious police corruption occurs when officers appropriate material or money that comes into their possession in the line of duty, for example detectives dividing their "scores" of narcotics and cash, sometimes amounting to thousands of dollars, or property being taken from the property room and then mysteriously "disappearing."

The Knapp Commission, in its 1972 investigation of corruption among New York City police, distinguished between "grass eaters" and "meat eaters," with the grass eaters being officers who passively accepted gratuities offered to them, in contrast to the meat eaters who aggressively solicited payments. The commission also discovered another problem—officers who were not directly involved in corruptive practices but who tolerated or ignored such activities by their colleagues, thereby allowing an environment of corruption to flourish.

History has shown that some police officers have come to value results over duty and principle, and the standard measurement of good police work has become goal achievement, with all else being secondary. This tendency to place ends over means is one reason corruption can arise and perpetuate, but the problem is much more complex. This progression is illustrated in Figure 11.8.

The Corruption Continuum   Just as with the use of force and pursuits, a continuum exists to describe the transition from honest to corrupt cop—the continuum of compromise. O. W. Wilson referred to it as "the slippery slope hypothesis." Something seemingly insignificant can put an officer on a slippery slope, leading to major crimes. Most officers will travel down and up the continuum many times during their careers.

The "slippery slope" often begins with an officer accepting **gratuities,** tokens of appreciation. Withrow and Dailey (2004, p.159) note: "Very few issues cause more heated debate among police scholars and practitioners than gratuities." As White (2002, p.23) observes: "Police officers often face the dilemma of accepting gratuities. Some officers view the acceptance of free coffee and free or discounted meals as an entitlement, while others view it as an unethical act." Table 11.3 presents arguments for and against gratuities.

Withrow and Dailey developed a model of circumstantial corruptibility that considers the motivation of both the giver and the receiver of an exchange, no matter what the value of that exchange (Figure 11.9). They (p.171) contend that: "When the giver assumes the role of the presenter and the receiver assumes the role of the acceptor, the result is a *giving* exchange. A giving exchange is defined as the voluntary act of offering something of value without any expectation of prior or future reciprocity to another person as a symbol of affection, respect or appreciation. At this level, the giver voluntarily offers a gift without any expectation of a return from the receiver. The receiver, exerting no influence on the giver,

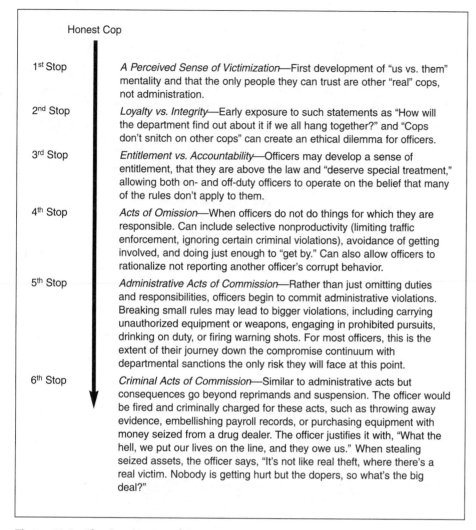

Honest Cop

1st Stop   *A Perceived Sense of Victimization*—First development of "us vs. them" mentality and that the only people they can trust are other "real" cops, not administration.

2nd Stop   *Loyalty vs. Integrity*—Early exposure to such statements as "How will the department find out about it if we all hang together?" and "Cops don't snitch on other cops" can create an ethical dilemma for officers.

3rd Stop   *Entitlement vs. Accountability*—Officers may develop a sense of entitlement, that they are above the law and "deserve special treatment," allowing both on- and off-duty officers to operate on the belief that many of the rules don't apply to them.

4th Stop   *Acts of Omission*—When officers do not do things for which they are responsible. Can include selective nonproductivity (limiting traffic enforcement, ignoring certain criminal violations), avoidance of getting involved, and doing just enough to "get by." Can also allow officers to rationalize not reporting another officer's corrupt behavior.

5th Stop   *Administrative Acts of Commission*—Rather than just omitting duties and responsibilities, officers begin to commit administrative violations. Breaking small rules may lead to bigger violations, including carrying unauthorized equipment or weapons, engaging in prohibited pursuits, drinking on duty, or firing warning shots. For most officers, this is the extent of their journey down the compromise continuum with departmental sanctions the only risk they will face at this point.

6th Stop   *Criminal Acts of Commission*—Similar to administrative acts but consequences go beyond reprimands and suspension. The officer would be fired and criminally charged for these acts, such as throwing away evidence, embellishing payroll records, or purchasing equipment with money seized from a drug dealer. The officer justifies it with, "What the hell, we put our lives on the line, and they owe us." When stealing seized assets, the officer says, "It's not like real theft, where there's a real victim. Nobody is getting hurt but the dopers, so what's the big deal?"

Figure 11.8   The Continuum of Compromise

SOURCE: Adapted from Kevin M. Gilmartin and John J. Harris. "The Continuum of Compromise." *The Police Chief,* January 1998, pp.25–28.

accepts the gift. As long as the giver and receiver continue to assume these roles, corruption does not occur." Withrow and Dailey (p.171) suggest: "If the giver and receiver assume other roles, corruption progresses to higher levels of social harm along a *hierarchy of wickedness,*" summarized in Table 11.4.

How Corruption Arises and Perpetuates

Every occupation has a learning process or socialization to which its new members are subjected. The socialization process makes most newcomers in the occupation adopt the prevailing rules, values and attitudes of their colleagues. Often, however, some existing informal rules and attitudes are at odds with the formal rules and attitudes society as a whole expects members of the occupation to follow. Officers may be taught to plant evidence, lie in court, shake people down or beat them up. They may be taught that since they are underpaid, it is all right to accept gratuities

394 Section III: Challenges to the Profession

Table 11.3   Arguments for and against Gratuities

Allowing Gratuities

- They help create a friendly bond between officers and the public, thus fostering community-policing goals.

- They represent a nonwritten form of appreciation and usually are given with no expectation of anything in return.

- Most gratuities are too small to be a significant motivator of actions.

- The practice is so deeply entrenched that efforts to root it out will be ineffective and cause unnecessary violations of the rules.

- A complete ban makes officers appear as though they cannot distinguish between a friendly gesture and a bribe.

- Some businesses and restaurants insist on the practice.

Banning Gratuities

- The acceptance violates most departments' policies and the law enforcement code of ethics.

- Even the smallest gifts create a sense of obligation.

- Even if nothing is expected in return, the gratuity may create an appearance of impropriety.

- Although most officers can discern between friendly gestures and bribes, some may not.

- They create an unfair distribution of services to those who can afford gratuities, voluntary taxing, or private funding of a public service.

- It is unprofessional.

SOURCE: Mike White. "The Problem with Gratuities." *FBI Law Enforcement Bulletin,* July 2002, p.21. Reprinted by permission.

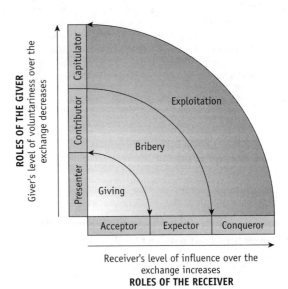

Figure 11.9   A Model of Circumstantial Corruptibility

SOURCE: Brian L. Withrow and Jeffrey D. Dailey. "A Model of Circumstantial Corruptibility." *Police Quarterly,* June 2004, p.171. Reprinted by permission.

or even share in cash confiscated during a drug raid. And above all, they may be taught that loyalty to one another is the prime duty; their lives depend on one another and they must protect each other no matter what is being done.

In addition to socialization influences, other elements act to create and perpetuate officer corruption, such as officer personality and ego, police unions and lack of ethical guidance by police administration.

Table 11.4 Hierarchy of Wickedness

Circumstances	Result
Giver assumes a Contributor role. Receiver assumes an Expector role.	**Bribery** The act or practice of exchanging something of value wherein the giver expects something in return for his or her gift, and the receiver, in violation of prior responsibilities, agrees to conform his or her behavior to the desires of the giver. The giver maintains control over the behavior of the receiver. However, the giver's level of voluntariness diminishes as more severe levels of corruption are reached.
Giver assumes a Capitulator role. Receiver assumes a Conqueror role.	**Exploitation** The act or practice of using another person for one's own profit or advantage through the illegal use of power. The receiver gains increasingly more control over the giver as more severe levels of corruption are reached.

SOURCE: Brian L. Withrow and Jeffrey D. Dailey. "A Model of Circumstantial Corruptibility." *Police Quarterly,* June 2004, p.173. Reprinted by permission.

Sometimes corruption is the result of personality. Green (2001, p.87) describes four basic types of individuals: (1) the person of good character, (2) the person who has excellent self-control, (3) the person who is uncontrolled and (4) the person who is criminal or of evil character. The fourth type of person probably would not be hired by an agency with sound selection practices. It is the third type of individual, the one lacking self-control, who is most likely to become corrupt. If only one or two individuals in a department are corrupt, they are sometimes referred to as a "few rotten apples." Failure to expose a few "bad apples" may allow them to spoil the whole barrel. As Swope (p.80) notes: "It is the unethical breeding environment of the barrel that generates the major difficulties. It is the barrel, the culture of the police organizations, that can cause the root shaking scandals that periodically face some police organizations."

Police corruption may arise from officers thinking they are "above the law." As Thompson (2001, p.77) notes: "The American public readily understands and recognizes that the police are entitled to special privileges and exceptions relative to obeying the laws. Police officers are allowed to exceed the speed limits and violate traffic controls in the interest of law enforcement. They are allowed to carry concealed weapons, and they often own or have access to weaponry that is prohibited or at least greatly restricted to private citizens." Unfortunately, says Thompson: "Early in the indoctrination into policing, some officers receive the message that they are special and they are above the law." Thompson (p.79) stresses: "Equality under the law is the foundation of American criminal justice. If law enforcement officers believe they are above the law, then this subverts the very essence of law enforcement and criminal justice in our society."

Bayley (2002, p.133) also suggests that there is a common presumption among police officers that "circumstances often justify cutting legal corners in the interest of public safety." He (pp.141–143) asserts: "Violating the rule-of-law impairs crime control by alienating the public. This occurs in two ways. First, violating the rule-of-law lessens the willingness of the public to assist the police in carrying out their assigned role. Research has shown again and again that the police are almost wholly dependent on the public to provide the information needed to provide safety and deter crime. . . . Second, when the police violate the rule-of-law, they not only forfeit the cooperation they need, but they also raise the likelihood that encounters with the public will generate hostility and violence." Bayley (p.145) also thinks violating the rule-of-law places police officers at risk: "Most obvious of all, the personal cost to officers who are caught violating the rule of law can be catastrophic."

One area in which officers may place themselves above the law is in the use of deception or lying. As Noble (2003, p.95) points out: "In the performance of their duties, police officers frequently engage in a significant amount of deceptive conduct that is essential to public safety. Consider lying to suspects, conducting undercover operations and even deploying unmarked cars. Presenting a suspect with false evidence, a false confession of a crime partner or a false claim that the suspect was identified in a lineup are but a few of the deceptive practices that police officers have used for years during interrogation."

In contrast to lies justified by necessity are what Noble calls "malicious lies." This includes the practice known as *testilying,* testifying falsely to bring about a conviction: "The officer's intent may be a worthy objective to the public; removing a criminal from society and the officer may validate his intent in his own mind by believing that he is engaging in a greater good. But this lie would violate the standard by which we would say the lie was reasonable and appropriate under the circumstances given the status obligations of the person engaging in the lie" (Noble, p.97).

Lying by police officers may be quite minor or can be deadly serious. Perjury, a criminal offense, is seen by many officers who have traveled down the continuum of compromise as a legitimate way to fight slippery criminals who hire even more slippery lawyers.

Another reason corruption can exist is the "code of silence" described in Chapter 4. According to Nowicki and Punch (2003, p.330): "To some officers, the most serious aspersion that can be cast upon another officer is to say that he or she breached the code of silence and provided information to internal affairs investigators." Griffith (p.74) suggests: "Police loyalty known as the 'blue wall' or the 'code of silence' has forced many officers to jeopardize their careers and their liberty to cover up another officer's misconduct. The results are often tragic." Griffith quotes Trautman, head of the National Institute of Ethics, as saying: "Misconduct and the code of silence are the most destructive forces in law enforcement. It is far more likely that an officer's career will be cut short by these things than by a bad guy with a knife in the alley" (p.27). Quinn (2004) also cautions:

> As terrible as it is, there is no escaping the Code. It is as inevitable as your childhood diseases and just as necessary. Each stinging battle with the Code will be either an inoculation of the spirit and an opportunity to grow stronger or a crippling injury to your integrity. Regardless of the outcome there will be vivid images you can't erase from your memory. There will always be the mental and physical scars to remind you of your battles.
>
> But, each encounter can leave you better prepared both physically and mentally for the tough challenges ahead, if you are willing to admit you're not superman, and you recognize your "dark side" for what it is. Because only when we know the Code of Silence for what it is can we gain some control over it. Either way, you won't escape unscathed because at some point in time you are going to "Walk with the Devil" in order to get the job done (p.27).

Every day is a new challenge and ethical police conduct is often an uphill battle. Even the best of cops have days when they want to give up and do whatever it takes to put a child molester, baby murderer, or other lowlife in prison. When you sit inches away from these scum and they brag about the truly horrific things they have done to an innocent it's easy to abide by the Code—if that's what it takes. When the evidence isn't perfect, you just use a little creative report writing and this guy will never harm another person again. Illegal searches, physical abuse, or even perjury, you know you will be in the company of many good cops who have done the same. But are they really good cops? (pp.13–14).

The choice of being a "Peace Officer" means there will be many battles in solitary combat with other cops and with yourself. You will not win them all—you cannot—the cards are stacked against you. There will be no medals, awards ceremonies or cheering crowds for the battles you do win. But there will be honor and integrity—in your life and in your work (p.14).

Yet another reason corruption can perpetuate, according to Diop Kamau, executive director of the nonprofit Police Complaint Center, is the unions: "There's an abuse-denial misconduct pattern. Police unions are out of control. They want police protected in any and all circumstances. . . . Even with clear evidence of problems, police unions claim they're being picked on and treated unfairly by the media" (Pederson, 2001, p.139). Corruption may also arise and perpetuate because departments fail to emphasize ethical behavior.

How Police Learn about Ethics

Ethics involves moral behavior, doing what is considered right and just. According to Swope (p.83): "An officer's behavior is influenced more directly by the actions or lack of actions in response to ethical shortcomings of his superiors than by the states' directives or written ethical code of an organization." Police managers may provide ethical leadership by helping officers develop their ethical decision-making skills.

The International Association of Chiefs of Police has developed a code of ethics and "Police Code of Conduct" to guide police administrators and officers through the ethical standards expected. They include the primary responsibilities of a police officer, how the duties are to be performed, use of discretion, use of force, confidentiality, integrity, cooperation with other police officers and agencies, personal-professional capabilities and even private life. The Law Enforcement Code of Ethics is on the book website.

The Importance of Police Integrity and Core Virtues

Integrity is a series of concepts and beliefs that provide structure to officers' professional and personal ethics. These concepts and beliefs include honesty, honor, morality, allegiance, principled behavior and dedication to mission. Avoiding bad behavior is not the same as having integrity any more than avoiding grammatical errors can make one a Pulitzer prize–winning author. Having integrity is more than simply playing by the rules. To develop officers with integrity, police departments need not only a formal code of ethics but also a statement of core values. Many internal and external forces interact to influence police integrity. The dynamics of these forces are illustrated in Figure 11.10.

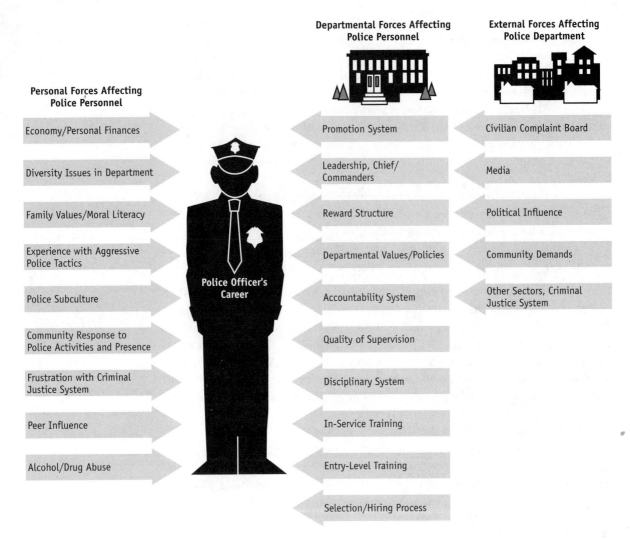

Figure 11.10 Dynamics of Police Integrity

SOURCE: *Police Integrity: Public Service with Honor.* Washington, DC: National Institute of Justice, January 1997, p.92.

Given the wide variety of forces influencing officer integrity, the challenge of building an ethical police department has never been greater.

Building an Ethical Department

For administrators struggling to build an ethical department, it may come as small consolation to know that while corruption has been a persistent problem in American policing, it is not a unique phenomenon, nor is it one that can ever be beaten down completely and permanently.

While acknowledging that corrupt officer behavior will likely never be eradicated entirely, administrators must not stop trying to achieve an ethical department. To help in this effort, administrators should focus on three areas to enhance police integrity.

 Three areas in which to enhance police integrity and reduce corruption are:
- The applicant selection process
- Consistent reinforcement of values
- Anticorruption posture of checks and balances

In the applicant selection process, prior behavior, arrest records, drug use and integrity must be aggressively researched. Consistent reinforcement of values is also vital. Department personnel should regularly discuss and analyze conduct standards to strengthen their understanding of and commitment to such principles. Management's most important task is to create an environment in which every police officer can perform with integrity and professionalism. In an anti-corruption posture of checks and balances, management can reinforce integrity, detect corruption and limit the opportunity for wrongdoing. The chief sets the level of integrity for the entire department. Supervisors provide leadership and guidance when needed.

Cline (2003, p.61) contends: "Training time and resources are spent showing officers how to stay alive in confrontations, but little or nothing is being spent on how to stay alive in confrontations with themselves." McNeff (2001, p.10) stresses: "In today's police environment, the incorporation of ethics into all aspects of police agency training and operations may yield wide-ranging benefits, including reduced exposure to liability." Many departments are establishing early warning systems (EWS). As Arnold (2001, p.85) states: "Proactive approaches must be explored and expanded where some type of intervention is introduced prior to misconduct." Examples of early warning signs include poor performance, hostility and anger, unnecessary risk-taking, increases in use of force and insubordinate conduct. Arnold (p.86) stresses: "EWS must be developed and utilized to their utmost in order to identify those employees who have the potential for future misconduct. Quality intervention steps must be taken to modify and hopefully eliminate problem behavior. Efforts spent on these endeavors can have a lasting positive impact on an agency, its members and the communities it serves."

As agencies seek to build ethical departments and officers with integrity, the newly organized National Commission on Law Enforcement Integrity may be of help. Information about this commission may be found at http://www.policeintegrity.org.

 ## SUMMARY

Policing has several vital issues facing it in the twenty-first century. Some have existed for decades, others are relatively new, and most are quite controversial. One of the most controversial issues surrounds police discretion, the freedom of an agency or individual officer to choose whether or not to act. Whether such discretion is positive or negative is a debatable issue.

Closely related to discretion is the issue of discrimination versus disparity. Minorities are arrested, stopped and questioned, and shot and killed by the police out of proportion to their representation in the population. There is much controversy over whether study results indicate a pattern of systematic *discrimination* or a *disparity* related to other factors such as poverty, socio-economic class and involvement in crime.

Use of force has been an issue of increasing concern for police agencies. When making an arrest, if there is no resistance, no force should be used. Justification for use of deadly force must consider not only the legal right but also the need to apprehend the suspect compared to the arresting officer's safety and the value of human life.

One form of use of force is the police pursuit. High-speed pursuits are both effective and dangerous. They also raise serious liability issues. Today concern for civil liability is quite evident in law enforcement agencies' policies and practices.

The issues of corruption, ethics and integrity are also of concern. Police corruption occurs when an officer misuses authority for personal gain. It includes accepting gratuities and bribes as well as committing theft or burglary. The most common and extensive type of corruption is accepting small gratuities or tips. Three areas in which to enhance police integrity and reduce corruption are the applicant selection process, consistent reinforcement of values and an anticorruption posture of checks and balances.

DISCUSSION QUESTIONS

1. Are police officers allowed too much discretion?
2. Do you see any problems with use of force continuums or pursuit continuums?
3. Should officers and their departments be shielded from civil liability as was previously allowed under "sovereign immunity"? Why or why not?
4. What roles can K-9s assume in dealing with fleeing suspects?
5. Do you believe the phrase *excessive force* has different meanings to different people in the criminal justice system? If so, why?
6. Do you believe racial profiling is occurring in your police department? Your state? Give reasons for your answer.
7. Do you think chemical agents are appropriate to use in dealing with uncooperative, violent suspects?
8. Do police pursuits fulfill a vital purpose?
9. What is the most important characteristic of police integrity?
10. How prevalent do you think corruption is in law enforcement agencies?

INFOTRAC COLLEGE EDITION ASSIGNMENTS

- Use InfoTrac College Edition to help answer the Discussion Questions as appropriate.
- Use InfoTrac College Edition to research *police pursuits*. Notice the many cases reviewed, how they initially started, how they ended and what implications the court decisions had on liability. Many standards are recommended in dealing with police pursuits. Outline these and pick one standard you feel could be the best with the least officer liability. Be prepared to share your selection and reasoning with the class.
- Use InfoTrac College Edition to read and outline one of the following articles to share with the class:
  - "Establishing a Foot Pursuit Policy: Running into Danger" by Edward E. Davis and Thomas J. Garrity, Jr.

- "Use of Force: A Systematic Approach" by Sam W. Lathrop
- "Improving Deadly Force Decision Making" by Dean T. Olson
- "Police Pursuits and Civil Liability" by Chris Pipes and Dominick Pape
- "Ensuring Officer Integrity and Accountability: Recent Court Decisions" by Daniel L. Schofeld
- "The Role of Race in Law Enforcement: Racial Profiling or Legitimate Use?" by Richard G. Schott
- "Force Continuums: A Liability to Law Enforcement?" by George T. Williams
- "High-Speed Police Pursuits: Dangers, Dynamics and Risk Reduction" by John Hill
- "Repairing Broken Windows: Preventing Corruption within Our Ranks" by Frank L. Perry
- "Suit Accuses Newark Police of Retaliatory Search and Cover-Up" by Mary P. Gallagher
- "Law Enforcement and the Holocaust" by William McCormack
- "Institutional Integrity: The Four Elements of Self-Policing" by John H. Conditt, Jr.
- "Making Ethical Decisions: A Practical Model" by John R. Schafer
- "The Problem with Gratuities" by Mike White
- "Opportunities and Expectations" by Russell J. Rice, Jr.

INTERNET ASSIGNMENTS

- Use the Internet to research *corruption in law enforcement*. Note the many uncomplimentary articles. Do these articles give you the idea there is another side to some police officers? Explain.
- Download *Racially Biased Policing* at http://www.PoliceForum.org and outline one chapter. Be prepared to share your outline with the class.

BOOK-SPECIFIC WEB SITE

The book-specific Web site at http://info.wadsworth.com/0534552803 hosts a variety of resources for students and instructors. Included are extended activities from each chapter in which students write a policy, use critical thinking skills to make choices in response to a given scenario, use InfoTrac College Edition with direct links to articles for participation in topical discussion forums, and analyze court cases using Web links for research. Many activities can be printed or emailed to instructors. Plus, cited cases with Web links, interactive key term FlashCards, PowerPoint presentations, chapter objectives, and an extensive collection of chapter-based Web links provide additional information and activities to include in the curriculum.

REFERENCES

Arnold, Jon. "Early Misconduct Detection." *Law and Order,* August 2001, pp.80–86.

Aveni, Thomas J. "The Force Continuum Conundrum." *Law and Order,* December 2003, pp.74–77.

Batton, Candice and Kadleck, Colleen. "Theoretical and Methodological Issues in Racial Profiling Research." *Police Quarterly,* March 2004, pp.30–64.

Bayley, David H. "Law Enforcement and the Rule of Law: Is There a Tradeoff?" *Criminology and Public Policy,* November 2002, pp.133–154.

Bellah, John L. "Special Report: High-Speed Pursuits. Cutting Out the Chase." *Police,* April 2003, pp.28–31.

Buerger, Michael. "Supervisory Challenges Arising from Racial Profiling Legislation." *Police Quarterly,* September 2002, pp.380–408.

By the Numbers: A Guide for Analyzing Race Data from Vehicle Stops. Washington, DC: Police Executive Research Forum, 2004.

Carrick, Grady. "A Police Response to Racial Profiling." *Law and Order,* October 2001, pp.79–82.

Cline, Thomas J. "Tough and Most Dangerous Battles." *Law and Order,* January 2003, pp.61–64.

Cox, Stephen M. "Racial Profiling: Refuting Concerns about Collecting Race Data on Traffic Stops." *Law and Order,* October 2001, pp.61–65.

del Carmen, Rolando V. and Walker, Jeffery T. *Briefs of Leading Cases in Law Enforcement,* 4th ed. Cincinnati, OH: Anderson Publishing Company, 2001.

Dorsch, Don. "Opened Door for Lawyers, Burden for Officers." *Law and Order,* September 2001, p.102.

Engel, Robin Shepard and Calnon, Jennifer M. "Examining the Influence of Drivers' Characteristics during Traffic Stops with Police: Results from a National Survey." *Justice Quarterly,* March 2004, pp.50–90.

Fridell, Lorie; Lunney, Robert; Diamond, Drew; and Kubu, Bruce with Scott, Michael and Laing, Colleen. *Racially Biased Policing: A Principled Response.* Washington, DC: Police Executive Research Forum, 2001. http://www.policeforum.org.

Fuller, John J. "Street Cop Ethics." *The Law Enforcement Trainer,* May/June 2001, pp.6–7.

Gallo, Frank J. "Making Sense of It All." *The Law Enforcement Trainer,* July/August 2003, pp.19–21.

Garner, Joel H.; Maxwell, Christopher D.; and Heraus, Cedric. "Characteristics Associated with the Prevalence and Severity of Force Used by the Police." *Justice Quarterly,* December 2002.

Green, Don. "Calculating Ethics." *Law and Order,* August 2001, pp.87–90.

Griffith, David. "Cracking Down on Bad Cops." *Police,* October 2003, pp.68–72.

Heal, Sid. "An Evaluation of Less Lethal." *Law and Order,* September 2001, pp.88–93.

Hill, John. "High-Speed Police Pursuits: Dangers, Dynamics and Risk Reduction." *FBI Law Enforcement Bulletin,* July 2002, pp.14–18.

James, Steve. "Impact in the Field." *Police,* July 2001, pp.16–20.

Jones, Tony. "Electronic Immobilization Devices." *Law Enforcement Technology,* October 2001, pp.70–75.

Klugiewicz, Gary T. and Smith, James G. "Think before You Run." *Police,* July 2004, pp.120–125.

Labbe, J.R. "Get It Straight! Profiling Is Not Racism." *American Police Beat,* October 2001, pp.25, 37.

Langan, Patrick A.; Greenfeld, Lawrence A.; Smith, Steven K.; Durose, Matthew R.; and Levin, David J. *Contacts between Police and the Public. Findings from the 1999 National Survey.* Washington, DC: Bureau of Justice Statistics, February 2001. (NCJ 184957)

Lonsway, Kim and the Law and Order Staff. "First Topic: Police Women and the Use-of-Force." *Law and Order,* July 2001, pp.109–114.

Makholm, John A. "Legal Lights." *The Law Enforcement Trainer,* November/December 2001, p.57.

McNeff, Michael. "One Agency's Effort to Reduce Liability Risk through Emphasis on Ethics." *The Police Chief,* August 2001, p.10.

Meehan, Albert J. and Ponder, Michael C. "Race and Place: The Ecology of Racial Profiling and African-American Motorists." *Justice Quarterly,* vol. 19, no. 3, 2002, p.399.

Miller, Linda S. and Hess, Kären M. *Community Policing: Partnerships for Problem Solving,* 4th ed. Belmont, CA: Wadsworth Publishing Company, 2005.

National Coalition of Anti-Violence Programs. *Lesbian, Gay, Bisexual and Transgender Domestic Violence in 2002: A Report of the National Coalition of Anti-Violence Programs.,* 2003. http:www.avp.org/publications/reports/2002NCAVPdvrpt.pdf.

Newbold, Mark. "Officer Liability for Failure to Disclose Exculpatory Evidence." *The Police Chief,* May 2001, pp.10–13.

"NY Police, Louima Reach Tentative $9 Million Deal." The Associated Press as reported in the (Minneapolis/St. Paul) *Star Tribune,* July 12, 2001, p.A4.

Nielsen, Eugene. "The Advanced Taser." *Law and Order*, May 2001, pp.57–62.

Nislow, Jennifer. "Are Americans Ready to Buy into Racial Profiling?" *Law Enforcement News*, October 15, 2001, p.11.

Noble, Jeff. "Police Officer Truthfulness and the *Brady* Decision." *The Police Chief*, October 2003, pp.92–101.

Novak, Kenneth J. "Disparity and Racial Profiling in Traffic Enforcement." *Police Quarterly*, March 2004, pp.65–96.

Nowicki, Dennis E. and Punch, Maurice E. "Fostering Integrity and Professional Standards." *Local Government Police Management*, 4th ed., edited by William A. Geller and Darrel W. Stephens. Washington, DC: International City/County Management Association, 2003, pp.315–352.

Nowicki, Ed. "OC Spray Update." *Law and Order*, June 2001a, pp.28–29.

Nowicki, Ed. "Use of Force Options." *Law and Order*, February 2001b, pp.35–37.

Nowicki, Ed. "Racial Profiling Problems and Solutions." *Law and Order*, October 2002, pp.16–18.

Nugent, Hugh; Connors, Edward F., III; McEwen, J. Thomas; and Mayo, Lou. *Restrictive Policies for High-Speed Police Pursuits*. Washington, DC: National Institute of Justice, no date. (NCJ 122025)

Olivero, J. Michael and Murataya, Rodrigo. "Homophobia and University Law Enforcement Students." *Journal of Criminal Justice Education*, Fall 2001, pp.271–281.

Partner Abuse/Domestic Violence Resource Guide for Los Angeles County. Los Angeles: L.A. Gay and Lesbian Center's STOP Partner Abuse/Domestic Violence Program, 2002. http://www.laglc.org/section05/DVResource.pdf.

Pedersen, Dorothy. "Rising above Corruption." *Law Enforcement Technology*, October 2001, pp.136–142.

"PERF Releases Comprehensive Guide on Collecting and Analyzing Racial Profiling Data." Press Release from the Police Executive Research Forum, February 12, 2004.

Pipes, Chris and Pape, Dominick. "Police Pursuits and Civil Liability." *FBI Law Enforcement Bulletin*, July 2001, pp.16–21.

Police Use of Force in America 2001. Alexandria, VA: International Association of Chiefs of Police, 2001.

Quinn, Michael W. *Walking with the Devil: The Police Code of Silence (What Bad Cops Don't Want You to Know and Good Cops Won't Tell You)*. Minneapolis, MN: Quinn and Associates, 2004.

"The Racial Profiling Controversy in America." *NCJA Justice Bulletin*, April 2001, pp.8, 13–15.

Reisig, Michael D.; McCluskey, John D.; Mastrofski, Stephen D.; and Terrill, William. "Suspect Disrespect toward the Police." *Justice Quarterly*, June 2004, pp.241–268.

Rivera, Richard G. "Nine Ways to Prevent Racial Profiling." *Law and Order*, October 2001, pp.85–88.

Rogers, Donna. "Use of Force." *Law Enforcement Technology*, March 2001, pp.82–86.

Rojek, Jeff; Rosenfeld, Richard; and Decker, Scott. "The Influence of a Driver's Race on Traffic Stops in Missouri." *Police Quarterly*, March 2004, pp.126–147.

Rosenbaum, Steven H. "Patterns and Practices of Police Misconduct." *Law and Order*, October 2001, pp.67–71.

Sanow, Ed. "Impact and Electronic Force." *Law and Order*, September 2001, p.4.

Sharpe, R. E. "Practicing Realism, Not Racism." *Law Enforcement News*, June 15, 2002, p.9.

Son, In Soo and Rome, Dennis M. "The Prevalence and Visibility of Police Misconduct: A Survey of Citizens and Police Officers." *Police Quarterly*, June 2004, pp.179–204.

Spector, Elliot B. "Stopping Suspects Based on Racial and Ethnic Descriptions." *The Police Chief*, January 2002, pp.10–12.

Strong, Paul. "Ethics." *Law and Order*, January 2004, p.65.

Swope, Ross. "Bad Apples or Bad Barrel?" *Law and Order*, January 2001, pp.80–85.

Terrill, William. "Police Use of Force and Suspect Resistance: The Micro Process of the Police-Suspect Encounter." *Police Quarterly*, March 2003, pp.51–83.

Terrill, William and Reisig, Michael D. "Neighborhood Context and Police Use of Force." *Journal of Research in Crime and Delinquency*, August 2003, pp.291–321.

Thompson, David. "Above the Law?" *Law and Order*, January 2001, pp.77–79.

Tomaskovic-Devey, Donals; Mason, Marcinda; and Zingraff, Matthew. "Looking for the Driving while Black Phenomena: Conceptualizing Racial Bias Processes and Their Associated Distributions." *Police Quarterly*, March 2004, pp.3–29.

Trautman, Neil. "National Commission on Law Enforcement Integrity." *Law and Order*, August, 2001, pp.91–93.

Vaughn, Michael S.; Cooper, Tab W.; and del Carmen, Rolando V. "Does Threat of Lawsuits Detract from or Improve Police Work? Assessing Legal Liabilities in Law Enforcement: Police Chiefs' Views." *Crime and Delinquency*, vol. 47, no. 1, 2001.

Walker, Samuel; Spohn, Cassia; and DeLone, Miriam. *The Color of Justice: Race, Ethnicity, and Crime in America*, 3rd ed. Belmont, CA: Wadsworth Publishing Company, 2004.

Wexler, Chuck. "Foreword." In *Racially Biased Policing: A Principled Response*, by Lorie Fridell et al. Washington, DC: Police Executive Research Forum, 2001, pp.ix–xi.

White, Mike. "The Problem with Gratuities." *FBI Law Enforcement Bulletin*, July 2002, pp.20–23.

Williams, George T. "Force Continuums: A Liability to Law Enforcement?" *FBI Law Enforcement Bulletin*, January 2002, pp.14–19.

Witczak, Tom. "Proactive Pursuit Policies." *Law and Order,* July 2003, pp.131–133.

Withrow, Brian L. and Dailey, Jeffrey D. "A Model of Circumstantial Corruptibility." *Police Quarterly,* June 2004, pp.159–178.

CASES CITED

Brady v. Maryland, 373 U.S. 89 (1968)

Brown v. City of Oneonta, 221 F.3d 329 (2nd Cir. 2000), *cert.denied,* 122 S.Ct.44 (2001)

Caldwell v. Moore, 968 F.2d 595 (6th Cir. 1992)

Carleton v. Town of Framingham, 615 N.E.2d 588 (Mass. App. Ct. 1993)

County of Sacramento v. Lewis, 523 U.S. 833 (1998)

Florida v. Bostick, 501 U.S. 429 (1991)

Franks v. Delaware, 438 U.S. 154 (1978)

Galas v. McKee, 801 F.2d 200 (1986)

Graham v. Connor, 490 U.S. 386, 396 (1989)

Griffin v. Illinois, 351 U.S. 12 (1956)

Irwin v. Town of Ware, 467 N.E.2d (1992)

Mendoza v. Block, 27 F.3d 1357 (9th Cir. 1994)

Monell v. Dept. of Social Services of the City of New York, 436 U.S. 658 (1978)

Robinette v. Barnes, 854 F.2d 909 (6th Cir. 1988)

Rochin v. California, 342 U.S. 165 (1952)

Saucier v. Katz, 121 S.Ct. 2151 (2001)

Tennessee v. Garner, 471 U.S. 1 (1985)

CHAPTER 12

Departmental Issues

No great advance has ever been made without controversy.

—Lyman Beecher

 DO YOU KNOW . . .

- What qualities are essential for good police officers?
- What the benefits of racially balanced and integrated police departments are?
- What advantages exist for law enforcement agencies that hire and retain more women?
- What steps are usually involved in officer selection?
- What basic requirements officer candidates must meet?
- Whether a college education is required of most police officer candidates?
- If police officers are required to live in the same community in which they work?
- What most physical fitness tests are like?
- What information is sought during interviews?
- What occurs during the background investigation?
- What is most important in the medical examination?
- What legal considerations in hiring practices are mandated by the Equal Employment Opportunity Act and the Americans with Disabilities Act?
- What the length and purpose of probation are?
- How stressful police work may be?
- Whether civilian review boards are positive or negative?
- How unions are viewed by line officers and administrators?
- How public and private law enforcement differ?
- Whether moonlighting is accepted?
- If accreditation for law enforcement is worth the time and expense?
- What the three key elements of professionalism are?

CAN YOU DEFINE?

accreditation	bona fide occupational	burnout	civilian review board
affirmative action	qualification	civilian review	credentialing
	(BFOQ)		

CAN YOU DEFINE? (CONTINUED)

moonlighting	post-traumatic stress	reverse discrimination	stress
multiple hurdle	disorder (PTSD)	sexual harassment	union
procedure	privatization	situational testing	union shop

Introduction

For years society has sought more effective law enforcement and a criminal justice system to meet its needs. At the same time criminologists, psychologists, sociologists, police practitioners and scientists have worked to solve America's crime problem. Despite some disillusionment and cynicism, progress has been made, and the future offers hope.

The most visible signs of progress in the vast criminal justice system have been in the field of law enforcement, and the most notable advancement in this field has been the professionalization of the police officer. This is, in part, because 80 to 90 percent of most police agencies' budgets are allocated for personnel, and therefore they are demanding higher quality performance from them. This is sometimes difficult to obtain, however, because most police departments are understaffed. The attrition rate throughout the United States—approximately 100,000 officers per year—compounds this problem and creates a constant demand for training.

An equally important force behind the professionalization of the police officer is the realization that, to a large degree, the future success of law enforcement is contingent on its police officers' quality and effectiveness, their status in the community and their ability to serve its residents. Women and members of minority groups are now considered necessary and valuable members in most departments. Although members of minority groups and women have had a long, difficult battle in achieving equal employment rights, excellent opportunities exist today for all who are interested in a law enforcement career.

This chapter begins with some suggestions on how to evaluate and select a law enforcement agency for employment. This is followed by a look at recruiting and selection and the federal guidelines and regulations affecting employment, including the Equal Employment Opportunity Act, affirmative action initiatives and the Americans with Disabilities Act. After examining who is selected and how, the chapter turns to what happens next, typically probation and training. The importance of retaining officers is discussed, including how factors such as salary, benefits, promotional opportunities, stress and burnout affect officer retention. This is followed by a look at several "hot button" topics in law enforcement—some controversial, some that police agencies seem eager to bring to the public's attention and others that agencies prefer to handle discreetly in hopes of avoiding publicity—including civilian review boards, sexual harassment, unions, privatization, moonlighting and accreditation. The chapter concludes with a discussion of law enforcement as a profession.

Evaluating and Selecting an Agency for Employment

Before an agency can screen and select an officer candidate, the candidate must first select the agency. This is done by researching the available options, assessing one's own professional goals and then evaluating and selecting specific agencies to apply to. Several factors are important to those seeking employment in law enforcement, including, but not limited to, the advantages and disadvantages of the following:

- Employment with municipal, county, state or federal agencies
- Working in a small, medium or large agency
- Working in an environment with a high rate of crime versus an environment with little crime and, therefore, limited police enforcement activity
- Working in a community where one was raised or currently resides

Other factors to consider include the salary, pension and fringe benefits; the opportunities to work varied assignments in the broad spectrum of law enforcement and the potential for promotion. What are the agency's current needs? Is there a hiring freeze? Does it have serious budget constraints?

Often, interested applicants may request either in person at the department, over the phone or online a fact sheet containing a brief job description, the salary range and fringe benefits, and an application. They may also be notified of the time and location of the next written examination.

How does a law enforcement candidate find an open position to evaluate? If the law enforcement agencies in the area are progressive, they will have a successful recruiting program. Many departments also recruit online by posting job openings on their Web sites.

While all departments seek "the best" candidates to hire, they must first specify which characteristics are most important. Finding individuals qualified to become police officers is no easy task. Recruiting, screening and selecting candidates are continuous, critical functions of all police agencies.

The Recruiting Process

Some departments are already beginning to feel the pinch of not having enough applicants to replace the growing number of officers who are leaving. Butterfield (2001, p.1) states: "Police departments in cities across the nation are facing what some call a personnel crisis, with the number of recruits at record lows." Domash (2002, p.35) notes that "a large number of officers nationwide who are reaching or passing their 20-year or 25-year retirement point may result in a potentially unprecedented crisis in law enforcement." Some agencies have seen the number of job applicants drop by more than 50 percent.

Among the reasons given are the relatively low starting pay, competition among departments and, as Bratton (2001, p.32) suggests, "the intense scrutiny and criticism for corruption, racial profiling, racial insensitivity, brutality, unresponsiveness to community concerns and professional incompetence." Nichols (2001, p.44) suggests: "Observers have noticed that the difference between departments that are able to find recruits and those that aren't is almost always tied to wages and benefits."

In addition to falling numbers of applicants, departments face other recruiting problems. One is the need for those who see policing as a calling, not just a job and who can be trusted to enforce the law without violating it themselves. Finding that ideal police recruit, one who seeks a long-term career as one of society's peacekeepers, is increasingly difficult. Furthermore, as Olson (2001, p.2) notes: "The real challenge we are facing is not just finding the most qualified candidates, but at the same time attracting a much more diverse workforce."

Desired Qualities of Law Enforcement Officers

If citizens were asked what traits they felt were desirable in police officers, their responses might go something like this: police officers should be able to work under pressure, to accept direction, to express themselves orally and in writing. They should have self-respect and the ability to command respect from others. They should use good judgment; and they should be considerate, compassionate, dependable, enthusiastic, fair, flexible, honest, humble, industrious, intelligent, logical, motivated, neat, observant, physically fit, prompt, resourceful, self-assured, stable, tactful, warm and willing to listen and to accept change.

Furthermore, with our society becoming increasingly diverse, the ideal officer would be able to police without bias or discrimination and be sensitive to the needs and concerns of various populations within a community. Unfortunately, no one has all these traits, but the more of these traits police officers have, the more effective they will be in dealing with not only the citizens of the community but lawbreakers as well.

In most states law enforcement candidates must also be U.S. citizens and must meet rigorous physical and personal qualifications. Personal qualities, such as honesty, good judgment and a sense of responsibility, are especially important.

 Qualities of a good police officer include reliability, leadership, judgment, persuasiveness, communication skills, initiative, integrity, honesty, ego control, intelligence, sensitivity and problem-solving ability.

Conroy and Placide (2003, p.10) conducted a survey in St. Paul, Minnesota, to determine what character traits that city's citizens wanted in their police officers. The following traits were identified in no particular order: enthusiastic, good judgment, creative, self-motivated, understanding, self-confident, independent, courageous, tenacious, respectful, compassionate, honest, loyal, interactive and responsible.

Finding Qualified Applicants

Most departments recruit through traditional avenues such as handouts, media advertisements (newspapers, radio, TV), job fairs and visits to colleges. Kanable (2001, p.66) suggests: "Advertising in two or three local papers might not be enough. Advertising in a newspaper with circulation throughout the state, ethnic newspapers and law enforcement publications or newsletters might help." In addition, many agencies use their Web sites to provide information about the agency, job opportunities, how to apply and the like. The IACP has a job Web site, www.iacppolicejobs.com, where departments list job openings for a fee. Job searches, however, are free.

Some departments are focusing on recruiting second-career officers. For example a recent rookie class in the Appleton (Wisconsin) Police Department included a car salesman, a former teacher, a juvenile counselor, a dental technician, a nurse, a paramedic, a businessman and an assistant district attorney.

Nevertheless colleges remain a fundamental source of police recruits. One way departments are avoiding the obstacle of recruiting inexperienced college graduates is by accessing participants in the College Law Enforcement Internship Program. Although specific programs vary, student interns are generally placed with an agency and must complete a certain number of credit hours per term.

Yearwood and Freeman (2004, p.43) studied police officer recruitment in North Carolina and found that the most frequently used recruitment technique was word-of-mouth, used by 95 percent of the agencies surveyed. The least frequently used technique was radio/TV ads, used by 25.4 percent. The other recruitment techniques included newspaper ads (83.1 percent), community college visits (71.8 percent), Internet (62.9 percent), personnel listings (61.3 percent), auxiliary/reserve force (57.3 percent), job fairs (49.2 percent) and Police Corps (35.5 percent). Respondents also rated the effectiveness of recruiting techniques on a scale of 0 to 9. Word-of-mouth received the highest rating: 6.83, followed by community colleges, 5.62; newspaper ads, 5.38; and auxiliary/reserve force, 5.32. Rated lowest were radio/TV ads, 0.85.

Whichever avenues an agency selects for recruiting officer candidates, the target audience should be diverse.

Recruiting Minorities

To gain the community's general confidence and acceptance, police departments seek personnel to represent the community. An integrated department helps reduce stereotyping and prejudice. Firman, research coordinator for the IACP, says: "A diverse department is a department with a much stronger capacity to understand issues and respond effectively to those issues." He adds: "A diverse department is a creative and dynamic department" (Streit, 2001, p.70).

Minority officers provide a department with an understanding of minority groups, their languages and their subcultures, all with practical benefits to successful law enforcement. For example a police officer who speaks Spanish can help to prevent conflicts between the police and the community's Spanish-speaking residents. A minority officer may also have insight into a particular population's cultural or behavioral idiosyncrasies, such as the reluctance of those in the Asian community to report victimization to the police.

 A racially balanced and integrated police department fosters community relations and increases police effectiveness.

Strandberg (2004, p.40) points out: "The widespread distrust of law enforcement in many minority communities, whether a result of cultural predispositions or bad experiences, compounds the problem of recruiting minorities." Although many minorities view police as the "enemy" and would never consider joining their ranks, others view law enforcement as a way to a better life. An African-American police lieutenant from Atlanta explains why he became a police officer: "You got out of my neighborhood without ending up dead or in prison by either becoming a minister or a cop. I always fell asleep in church so I decided to become a cop."

Another issue related to minority officers is where they should be assigned. Many believe that minority neighborhoods should be policed by officers of the same background. Others, however, view this as a form of segregation. In addition to minorities, another group gaining representation in law enforcement is women.

Recruiting Women

Garcia (2003, p.330) notes: "Recruitment of women into the gendered organization of policing has been slow." In 2000, according to the National Center for Women and Policing (2001), 13 percent of all sworn officers were women compared to 9 percent in 1990, a 4.9 percent increase during a decade. Women held only 7.3 percent of top command positions.

Lonsway and Campbell (2002, p.107) contend: "Credible research shows both that female officers are equally competent as their male colleagues, and that they bring a number of unique advantages to the field of law enforcement." Lonsway et al. (2002, p.60) report: "Data drawn from seven major police departments indicate women officers cost substantially less than their male counterparts in terms of civil liability payouts for excessive force lawsuits. Women officers are also significantly underrepresented compared to male officers in both citizen complaints of all kinds and sustained allegations of excessive force."

Recruiting and Retaining Women (2001, pp.22–27) lists six advantages, based on research, for law enforcement agencies that hire and retain more women:

- Female officers are proven to be as competent as their male counterparts.
- Female officers are less likely to use excessive force.
- Female officers can help implement community-oriented policing.
- More female officers will improve law enforcement's response to violence against women.
- Increasing the presence of female officers reduces problems of sex discrimination and harassment within an agency.
- The presence of women can bring about beneficial changes in policy for all officers.

 Studies show that women perform as well as men in police work, are less apt to use excessive force, can help implement community-oriented policing and can improve an agency's response to violence against women. In addition, an increased female presence among officers can reduce problems of sex discrimination and harassment and foster policy changes that benefit all officers.

Despite the many benefits women officers bring to law enforcement, they still are not accepted in many departments. The growing presence of females in a traditionally male-dominated profession has undoubtedly led to conflict between the genders.

So what can departments do to improve their recruitment efforts? Prussel and Lonsway (2001, p.95) state: "Women go on-line in massive numbers, especially when they are searching for career opportunities. To attract these potential applicants, it is important that law enforcement agencies develop a 'woman-friendly' Web site." In addition, Lonsway (2001, p.16) says police need to dismantle their "warrior image" that is often so important in the selection process. The emphasis on upper-body strength often washes out qualified candidates, especially women, despite the fact that a survey of law enforcement agencies found physical ability to be the *least* important of 10 dimensions of "being a successful peace officer." The highest-ranking characteristic was integrity.

Jones (2004, p.165) suggests: "To successfully increase the number of women in policing, law enforcement agencies should develop a specific plan of action that targets women in the recruiting process and emphasizes the agency's desire to significantly increase the number of women in their ranks." Maglione (2002, p.21) describes the efforts of the Charlotte-Mecklenburg (North Carolina) Police Department: "The recruiting staff has made trips to military bases to talk with prospects, set up booths at women's professional basketball games and produced television commercials and pamphlets targeted toward women."

The Selection Process

Spawn (2003, p.20) notes: "The officer candidate selection process—from the written test to the agility test, to background investigations, psychological evaluations and polygraph examinations—is intensive and expensive." The person wanting to become a police officer must usually go through several steps in the selection process, called the **multiple hurdle procedure.** Although procedures differ greatly from agency to agency, several elements are common to most selection processes.

 Police officer selection usually includes:
- A formal application.
- A written examination.
- A physical fitness test.
- A psychological examination.
- An interview.
- A background investigation.
- A medical examination.

The order in which these steps occur may vary from department to department. Figure 12.1 illustrates a typical selection process. Failure at any point in the selection process may disqualify a candidate.

The Formal Application—Basic Requirements to Become a Police Officer

Usually a police officer candidate completes a formal application, which includes driving record; any criminal record; visual acuity; physical, emotional and mental condition; and education. Most police agencies and civil service commissions accept applications even when no openings are listed. The application is placed on file, and when an examination is to be conducted, the applicant is notified by mail or phone.

 Most agencies require that a police officer:
- Be a U.S. citizen.
- Have or be eligible for a driver's license in the state.
- Not have been convicted of a felony.

Requirements related to education and residency are also frequently stated.

Education   Educational requirements for officers have long been a source of controversy in law enforcement. Opinions differ greatly as to how much education a police officer candidate should have or how much should be a prerequisite for advancement.

 Most police agencies require a minimum of a high school education or equivalency certificate, and some require a two- or four-year degree. Many police agencies are now requiring some college education for employment and/or promotion. Whether such education helps officers perform better has not been documented.

Armstrong and Polk (2002, p.24) note: "The question of the importance of education for the police is a question that has been part of the police movement toward professionalism for almost a full century now. The debate was started in 1905 when August Vollmer began his career in law enforcement administration

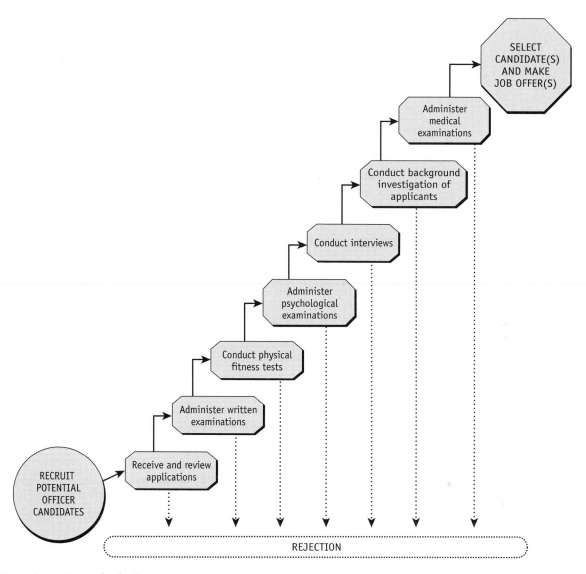

Figure 12.1   Typical Selection Process

SOURCE: Adapted from J. Scott Harr and Kären M. Hess. *Seeking Employment in Criminal Justice and Related Fields,* 4th ed. Belmont, CA: Wadsworth Publishing Company, 2003, p.176. Reprinted by permission. All rights reserved.

at Berkeley, California." And, as Sullivan (2003, p.25) points out: "A police officer's job is diverse—so diverse, a special Presidential Commission recommended that every officer have the minimum of a Bachelor's degree for entry into the field." That was in 1931.

According to Bowman (2002, p.11): "Only about 50 state and local police agencies nationwide require officers to have a four-year degree. That's a small number considering that in most other professions a college education is practically inherent." However, as Armstrong and Polk (p.25) suggest, although not many departments require it, the idea of an educated cop "has taken off like a rocket, reflecting to some extent the increase in higher education among the population in general." They report:

Between 1960 and 1990 the percentage of law enforcement officers with a four-year degree increased from 2.7 percent to 22.6 percent. The college-educated cop is now the rule, not the exception. It is estimated that 70 percent of all police officers in the United States have some college experience. In addition, more than 1,000 criminal justice programs are in existence at colleges and universities across the nation, and the discipline of criminal justice is the fastest growing program on many campuses. This is in spite of the fact that less than 15 percent of the law enforcement agencies in the U.S. require any education beyond the high school level.

They contend: "Higher education leads to more rapid advancement and movement within the officer's career path, particularly at the early stages."

The basic issue is, *Does more "formal" education make for better police officers?* The topic has been the source of litigation. For example in *Davis v. City of Dallas* (1978), the department's requirement that applicants have completed 45 semester hours of college credit with a "C" average was challenged. In this case the court ruled in favor of the police department:

> The City introduced evidence which supports the educational requirement. Numerous nationwide studies have examined the problem of setting the education requirement for police departments with favorable conclusions. A college education as a condition of hiring as a police officer has been recommended by the National Commission on Law Observance in 1931; by the President's Commission on Law Enforcement and Commission on Intergovernmental Relations in 1971; by the American Bar Association in 1972; and by the National Advisory Commission on Criminal Justice Standards and Goals in 1973. Defendant's experts established the relationship between college education and performance of police officers. A study by one expert relied upon factual data from two large metropolitan areas that took two years to complete, showing significantly higher performance rates by college-educated officers. A persuasive point was made that a high-school diploma today does not represent the same level of achievement which it represented 10 years ago.

Proponents of higher education for officers contend college-educated officers are less biased, less authoritarian and less likely to use force than non–college-educated officers. Advocates of advanced learning also believe college-educated officers hone their ability to flexibly handle difficult situations and develop an increased empathy and tolerance for minorities and persons with different lifestyles and ideologies. Completing occupation-specific courses provides a more complete understanding of the "big picture" of the criminal justice system and a better appreciation for the prosecutorial, courts and corrections roles. Furthermore the entire college experience allows time for the individual to mature and develop a general sense of responsibility.

Despite all the supposed advantages, many contend that good officers could be lost if educational levels are set too high. Critics of a college education requirement assert college graduates would be unlikely to seek employment in law enforcement, particularly women and minority college graduates, which would undermine the progress being made in recruiting them.

Some police chiefs believe that too much education makes social service officers of personnel who ought to be fighting crime in the streets. Others feel that requiring a degreed officer to perform such mundane tasks as issuing traffic tickets and parking tickets, making money runs and carding juveniles in liquor stores is demeaning. These opponents contend that such routine tasks soon diminish the highly educated officer's interest in law enforcement, which leads to greater job dissatisfaction, increasing turnover rates and higher hostility levels toward non–college-educated officers.

Critics of required higher education assert the skills effective officers need can be learned only on the street, not in a classroom. All controversy aside, the trend in today's law enforcement agencies appears to be supportive of high education standards for officers.

Residency Requirements   Over the years cities and municipalities have waived residency requirements to obtain better candidates. Though residency is still generally not required, some cities are again beginning to accept only candidates who reside within their boundaries.

 It is usually preferred and sometimes required that police officers live in the community they serve.

Sometimes compromises have been made whereby candidates are given one year to move into the community they serve. City and municipal politicians feel that by living in the community, a police officer becomes more closely identified with that community, more sensitive to its crime problems and more willing to participate in community activities.

Local residency is particularly important for departments instituting community policing. In addition politicians' self-interests dictate that their police officers live in the community so they can contribute their fair share of taxes. Some officers, however, may not be able to afford the cost of housing in the community they serve.

The Written Examination

Some departments use a civil service examination. Others use examinations designed specifically for their department. In either case the examinations do not usually test knowledge of police work or procedures but rather various abilities and aptitudes. Their primary function is to screen out those who lack the "basic material" to be a police officer.

Written examinations are usually in multiple-choice format and last two to three hours. They may test spelling, grammar and mathematical ability. They may also test reasoning ability, problem solving, reading comprehension, interpersonal communications skills or ability to process information.

Critics, however, claim written exams cannot measure common sense and penalize those who do not test well. Such tests may also inadvertently "weed out" candidates who possess other valuable skills that cannot be measured on paper. Another downside to written exams is the potential for adverse impacts against minority applicants and those for whom English is not their primary language.

Most written examinations are a straight pass/fail situation, serving as an entry into the next phase of the selection process. Some agencies, however, factor the score on this examination into their final selection decision. Many reference books and study guides are available to help candidates prepare for written law enforcement examinations. Those candidates who do well on the written test go on to physical fitness testing.

Physical Fitness Tests

Most police departments require physical fitness tests of applicants. Physical fitness tests determine a candidate's coordination and muscular strength and ascertain whether the candidate is in good physical condition. The type of test varies with police agencies throughout the country.

A candidate may be required to run a designated number of yards and while doing so hurdle a three-foot barrier, crawl under a 24-inch bar, climb over a four- or six-foot wall with both hands on top of the wall and sprint the remaining distance—all within a designated time monitored by a police officer with a stopwatch. Candidates may also be required to climb ropes or fire ladders and do chin-ups or push-ups. Other variations of the physical fitness test may be required, but usually only a minimum of strenuous activity is obligatory. Figure 12.2 illustrates the physical fitness course used at the Criminal Justice Institute of Broward Community College in Ft. Lauderdale, Florida.

 Physical fitness tests evaluate a candidate's coordination, speed and strength. The most common physical fitness tests are similar to military obstacle courses that must be completed in a designated time.

Physical fitness tests are necessary because they simulate what an officer may have to do on the street—jumping over a fence, climbing a wall or chasing someone through backyards or streets. Candidates who are considerably overweight rarely pass the physical fitness test. Research by Lonsway (2003, p.237) found a striking lack of agreement regarding which physical capabilities should be tested. A survey of 62 agencies indicated that the vast majority (89 percent) used some form of physical agility testing for entry-level selection, and agencies with a test had 31 percent fewer sworn women than agencies without such a test. Moore (2002, p.29) asserts: "Entry-level physical ability tests are often outdated, are not job-related and test for physical requirements not needed to perform the job of a modern law enforcement officer. These tests often put unnecessary emphasis on upper body strength and rely on methods of testing that eliminate large numbers of women who are, in fact, well qualified for the job."

Psychological Testing

Osofsky et al. (2001, p.38) explain: "Since the mid-1960s, psychological assessments have been relatively common as part of the police officer's selection process." Psychological tests are administered to determine if the person is emotionally suited for a career in law enforcement. Employers use psychological tests to learn about the applicant's present state of mind, what is important to that person and how that person is likely to respond to certain stimuli.

Psychological tests commonly used during officer selection include the Minnesota Multiphasic Personality Inventory–2 (MMPI–2), the California Psychological Inventory (CPI), the Myers-Briggs Type Indicator™, the Watson-Glaser Critical Thinking Appraisal and the Strong Interest Inventory.

The Interview

The interviewing board usually consists of three to five skilled interviewers knowledgeable in their fields. They may be staff officers from the agency doing the hiring or from other agencies, psychologists, sociologists or representatives of

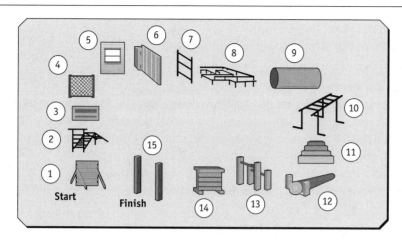

Figure 12.2 Physical Fitness Course

The course diagram shows numbered obstacles:

START

1) 6' Wall
2) LADDER CLIMB – Run across flat landing and down ramp
3) HURDLE – Use hands only!
4) CHAIN LINK FENCE CLIMB – Reach, lift and climb over fence
5) WINDOW CLIMB THROUGH
6) WOODEN GATE – Open fence gate door, go through and close door
7) HURDLE – Climb over
8) RUNNING MAZE – Enter at left. DO NOT touch siding
9) TUNNEL CRAWL – Crawl through. DO NOT dive!
10) HAND BAR WALK – Reach with hands, walk across
11) HIGH STEPPER – Lift feet high
12) LOG WALK – Slanted, walk across
13) HORIZONTAL HAND WALK – Use hands, push off ground and walk across bars
14) SHORT WALL – Jump up and over
15) POLE RUN – Run to your right, go $1^1/_2$ times around. DO NOT touch poles!

FINISH

SOURCE: Criminal Justice Institute, Broward Community College, Ft. Lauderdale, FL. Reprinted by permission.

a community service organization. The entire interviewing board may consist of members of a police or civil service commission. In smaller jurisdictions oral boards are sometimes replaced by an interview with the mayor, a member of the city council or the chief of police.

 Interviews are used to evaluate an applicant's appearance, alertness, communication ability, social adaptability, judgment, emotional stability, and interest in and suitability for the job.

Interviews, whether structured or unstructured, are designed to elicit answers revealing the candidates' personalities and suitability for police work, *not* to determine their technical knowledge in the police field. Candidates should be prepared to answer questions such as:

- Why do you want to be a police officer?
- What have you done to prepare for a career in law enforcement?
- What do you believe are the causes of crime?
- How do you feel about community policing?
- What is the last book you have read?

- What was your favorite subject in school?
- When did you last get drunk?
- Why did you select this department to apply to?

Interviews also test a candidate's ability to use good judgment in specific situations. For example:

- A person is standing on the corner making a speech regarding the overthrow of the government. He is drawing a crowd, and a certain amount of animosity is being shown toward the speaker, indicating future trouble. How would you handle this situation?
- You are working radar and you clock the mayor going 39 mph in a 30 mph zone. How would you handle this situation?

The interview usually lasts about 30 minutes. The same questions are posed to each candidate to allow comparison of answers. After the interview, each candidate's qualifications are evaluated and the candidate is given an overall rating, which is combined with the scores of the other examinations to yield a composite (total) score.

The Background Investigation

The applicant's background is a critical factor, and the background investigation serves two vital purposes: (1) it examines and verifies the past work and educational record of the candidate and (2) it determines if anything in the candidate's background might make him or her unsuitable for police work.

Fuss and Snowden (2004, p.60) stress: "A thorough background investigation not only ensures that the most qualified candidates are hired, but also can help a department avoid damaging legal actions and give an indication of an individual's competence, motivation and personal ethics. . . . A thorough background investigation can make the difference between putting a qualified individual on the streets to protect and serve society or an unqualified, tainted individual who can cause harm to himself, society and the hiring department."

The extensiveness of the background investigation is limited only by the number of candidates being investigated and time available. Normally all information given by the applicant on the personal history sheet must be verified. Birth and age records are verified through vital statistics, and driving records are verified through the driver's license bureau. Adverse driving records containing drunken driving, driving after suspension or revocation of license, or a consistent pattern of moving violations may cause disqualification.

Candidates are fingerprinted, and the prints are sent to the FBI to determine if the candidate has a criminal record. The candidate's criminal record is also checked at the local and state levels, usually through fingerprints, name and date of birth. Juvenile records are normally discounted unless a person has committed a heinous crime.

Ironically because of the transient nature of our population, a person wanted on a warrant in one part of the country has applied for a police officer's position in another part of the country. The criminal record check has sometimes resulted in their apprehension.

Military records are usually checked to verify service and eligibility under the veteran's preference acts of some states. The check also determines if the candidate was involved in any court-martials or disciplinary actions.

All personal and professional references listed on the history sheet are interviewed. Interviewing of references is sometimes criticized because candidates obviously will list only those who see them favorably; however these references may lead to others who know the candidates and have a different view of them. When candidates list out-of-town references, letters or questionnaires are usually mailed.

Previous employers are contacted to verify the applicant's work record. An inability to hold continuous employment may indicate trouble getting along with supervisors. A high absentee rate may indicate lack of interest or initiative or health problems.

The financial status of the candidate is also determined, usually through a credit records check. Those whose expenditures exceed their total incomes may be candidates for bankruptcy or bribery. Good credit indicates the person can live within his or her means and possesses self-control. The candidate may be required to submit a financial statement.

Educational records from high school, college and any other schools attended are usually checked through personal contact. The education record may indicate interests, achievements, accomplishments and social lifestyle while attending school. The scholastic record reflects not only intelligence but also study habits. Any degrees, certificates of achievement or awards are usually noted.

Polygraph examinations are growing in popularity as tools to verify information from background investigations, with the majority of police departments currently using this test. Although some states have banned use for preemployment purposes, where it is used to screen police candidates, it is necessary to determine why it is being given. Some departments use the polygraph extensively, especially if they have many transient applicants from other parts of the country. Some agencies use it to determine if the candidate has ever engaged in criminal activity and was ever apprehended. Some want to know if the candidate has any sexually deviant behaviors. Others use it to verify the information the candidate has given on the application and history sheet.

 The background investigation includes:
- Verification of all information on the application and history sheet.
- Check of driving record.
- Fingerprinting and a check of any criminal record.
- Check of military records.
- Interviews with personal references, acquaintances, past employers, neighbors and teachers.
- Check of financial status.
- Check of past performance at schools and previous jobs.

Testing or Assessment Centers

Some police departments use a testing or assessment center in the selection process, also called **situational testing.** Used by corporate America for over six decades, assessment centers were first accessed by law enforcement agencies during the mid-1980s to help with promotional decisions. Today such testing centers offer many benefits to agencies when selecting and promoting law enforcement personnel.

The Medical Examination

Medical requirements vary from jurisdiction to jurisdiction, but the purpose is the same. With the current emphasis on health care, more importance is placed on the medical examination. Citizens, concerned that police officers may retire early because of poor health, are demanding physically fit officer candidates. The medical standards usually include a variety of factors with some—vision, hearing and the cardiovascular-respiratory system—being more important than others.

Good eyesight is of great importance. Candidates who wear glasses that correct their vision to 20/20 can qualify in most departments. Likewise candidates who wear hearing aids that correct their hearing to meet the agency's requirements can qualify.

Because of job stress and the hypertension that often accompanies it, the cardiovascular system is thoroughly checked. The respiratory and cardiovascular systems play a critical role in fitness. To a great degree, endurance, the ability to continue exertion over a prolonged time, is directly related to the capacity of the cardiovascular-respiratory system to deliver oxygen to the muscles.

 Vision, hearing and the cardiovascular-respiratory system are of prime importance in the medical examination.

Other medical factors often tested are the ratio of total cholesterol to HDL cholesterol (which identifies cardiovascular risk factors), blood pressure, smoking status, drug use and blood sugar level for diabetes. A physician who feels a candidate has a functional or organic disorder may recommend disqualification.

The Law Enforcement Candidate Ride-Along

Sokolove and Field (2002, p.55) describe the law enforcement candidate ride-along as a supplemental selection tool: "The police officer candidate ride-along readily affords qualified applicants an opportunity to observe the agency up close. The ride-along should optimally compel the candidate to genuinely answer a paramount question: do I see myself in this work environment for the long term? It is incumbent upon law enforcement agencies to seek and select candidates looking for a career and not simply a job."

Sokolove and Field stress: "The police officer candidate ride-along should be viewed as a selection component designed to minimize unnecessary and time-wasting mismatches of employees and organizations. Conversely, such an approach to officer selection will more successfully identify those individuals whose personal agendas most closely assimilate and correlate with the organization's mission and goals."

The Human Resource Roundtable

Another innovative selection tool is the human resource roundtable described by Clark et al. (2001, p.29): "A roundtable is a group discussion of an applicant's employment packet before making the final hiring decision. The roundtable brings together data, insight and perspective from human resources, the department psychologist, appropriate command-level personnel and the WSP [Washington State Patrol] labor and risk manager (an attorney) as needed. The three goals of the roundtable are (1) to hire the best applicants by decentralizing the final hiring decision, (2) to reduce the agency's exposure to litigation and (3) to continually evaluate and update the hiring process."

The Final Result

After all required tests are completed, they are analyzed, and a composite score is given for each candidate. A list is made of eligible candidates, and they are called as openings occur. Some larger police departments keep their eligibility lists for one to two years, depending on civil service requirements or other requirements mandated by states or municipalities.

Federal Guidelines and Regulations

The basic rule of thumb is that all requirements must be clearly job related. A **bona fide occupational qualification (BFOQ)** is one that is reasonably necessary to perform the job. It may, on the surface, appear to be discrimination. For example in law enforcement, applicants may be required to have normal or correctable-to-normal hearing and vision because these attributes are required to perform the job.

Equal Employment Opportunity Act

In 1964 Congress enacted the Omnibus Civil Rights Law, of which Title VII concerned employment opportunities and prohibited discrimination based on sex, race, color, religion or national origin. The law also established the Equal Employment Opportunity Commission (EEOC) as its administrator. This law affected only private business, not state and local governments, and therefore had little impact on police agency practices.

However, in 1972 Congress passed the Equal Employment Opportunity Act, which modified Title VII to include state and local units of government. This law was passed because six years after the EEOC published guidelines for employment and promotion testing, few state or local central personnel selection agencies had taken positive steps to meet the guidelines.

 The 1972 Equal Employment Opportunity Act prohibits discrimination due to sex, race, color, religion or national origin in employment of any kind, public or private, local, state or federal.

The EEOC legislation restricts the type of information that can be gathered from job applicants and requires all questions posed to applicants to be relevant to the job for which the applicant is applying. The following information cannot be asked about on application forms or during interviews: race or color, religion, national origin, age, marital status or ages of children, or if the person has ever been arrested. Applicants may be asked if they have ever been convicted of a crime and, if so, when and where it took place. Questions about education and experience are largely unrestricted.

Affirmative Action

The Affirmative Action Amendment (signed by President Nixon in 1973) further strengthened the power of the EEOC. **Affirmative action** refers to special endeavors by employers (including law enforcement agencies) to recruit, hire, retain and promote minority group members and to eliminate past and present employment discrimination. According to Walker et al. (2004, p.129): "The most controversial aspect of employment discrimination is the policy of affirmative action. The Office of Federal Contract Compliance defines affirmative action as 'results-oriented actions [taken] to ensure equal employment opportunity [which may include] goals to correct under-utilization . . . [and] backpay, retroactive seniority, makeup goals and timetables.' "

Affirmative action is more than simply not discriminating during hiring—it is actively favoring women and minorities. Though the increases in the number of women and minorities in law enforcement agencies across the country are to be applauded, problems still exist. Sometimes these advancements are made at the expense of others—most notably white males. This is referred to as **reverse discrimination**—giving preferential treatment in hiring and promoting to women and minorities to the detriment of white males.

Scuro (2004, p.24) notes: "In numerous prior decisions, the United States Supreme Court has held that mandatory quotas established to meet an affirmative action plan's racially motivated goals are unlawful and thereby unconstitutional under federal law." In *Griggs v. Duke Power Company* (1971) the Court clearly ruled that racially based quotas violated federal law. In the 2002–2003 term the Supreme Court handed down two landmark decisions regarding affirmative action. In *Grutter v. Bollinger* (2003) the Supreme Court upheld the University of Michigan's law school admissions racially based affirmative action plan that permitted race to be one factor used in the admissions process. However, in *Gratz v. Bollinger* (2003) it declared the University of Michigan's undergraduate admissions program unlawful because it made race a "final and critically decisive factor and used a point system in which the race of an undergraduate applicant was factored into the final score upon which final admission was predicated" (Scuro, 2004 p.26).

This issue has separated whites from minorities, men from women and the advocates of affirmative action from those who believe in a strict "merit" principle for employment and advancement. The majority position has been summarized as a concern that for every deserving minority group member who is provided a job or promotion through preferential quotas, a deserving, and often more qualified, nonminority person is deprived of a job or promotion. A growing number of majority member workers are complaining bitterly about their own civil rights being abridged, and some are filing reverse discrimination suits in court. Such suits, however, are not always easily won. In fact, the courts themselves have been deeply divided over the constitutionality of the reverse discrimination that some believe is implicit in minority quotas and double standards.

Frequently those who might be beneficiaries of affirmative action do not welcome it, as noted by a veteran female sergeant who is Hispanic and one-quarter Navajo (Oglesby, 2002):

> When I joined the Los Angeles County Sheriff's Department in 1981, there was no significant demand for affirmative action; everyone was hired on merit and ability. Today, some 20 years later, those endorsing affirmative action are overlooking the fact that all citizens have the right to be protected and served by the best possible teachers, police officers, firefighters, doctors and other professionals. When we merely turn the tables on discrimination from one group

to another, we defy all logic and common sense. When I am told that I as a female Hispanic must be entitled to affirmative action, which is preferential treatment, I become deeply insulted for the following reasons:

- The assumption is that I am incompetent and inferior to white males, therefore rendering me incapable of succeeding on my own merit.
- That assumption is degrading and undermines my morale and incentive to compete. Without that incentive, I will be less capable of competing with others in the future as that preferential treatment can easily become an addictive crutch.
- My peers will not respect me because they will assume that I have accomplished everything through means of affirmative action.
- The public will have less respect for me for the same reasons.
- Therefore, if my peers and the public don't respect me, how can I respect myself? Or, the reverse, if I don't fully respect myself, why should anyone else respect me?
- As long as we have affirmative action, women and minorities will not get the respect they deserve.
- You don't eliminate discrimination by practicing discrimination.

Americans with Disabilities Act

Further complicating the selection and employment process is the Americans with Disabilities Act (ADA), which President Bush (senior) signed into law in July 1990. The purpose of this civil rights law is to guarantee equal opportunity to jobs for qualified individuals with disabilities.

 The Americans with Disabilities Act (ADA) of 1990 prohibits discrimination in employment based on a disability.

Conditions excluded from protection include current use of illegal drugs, compulsive gambling, kleptomania, pyromania, sexual behavior disorders and dysfunctions, pedophilia, voyeurism, exhibitionism and psychological disorders caused by current use of illegal drugs.

During the application process, the ADA prohibits employers from asking any questions or conducting any medical examinations that would identify applicants with disabilities or the nature and extent of such disabilities. Tests for use of illegal drugs are not considered medical examinations under ADA. However, as Scuro (2001, p.31) notes: "In the decade of the ADA's existence and practical application in this country, there are still no uniform standards to be applied when addressing the daily personnel issues that are a part of the routine operations of both a public sector law enforcement agency or private sector corporation."

Employers can ask preemployment questions about the applicants' ability to perform essential job-related tasks.

Probation and Training

According to Kaminsky (2001, p.32): "The avowed purpose of the probationary period is to provide some protection to an organization while it determines whether or not the new employee is all that the organization hoped they would be when hired." It is expected that during this period training would be comprehensive and on-going. "As we begin the 21st century," say Birzer and Tannehill (2001, p.233), "the need for more and improved police training is gathering increasing momentum." They stress:

> There is an obvious need for police officers to acquire knowledge of the latest legal decisions, technological advances, and tactical developments in the field, and to remain proficient in a number of job-related skills. There is also an urgent need for police officers who are skilled communicators and decision makers, who are capable of helping citizens identify and solve problems in their communities, and who possess effective mediation and conflict-resolution skills.

Unfortunately, many departments stress the physical aspects of policing and weapons skills without emphasizing that communication is usually an officer's most valuable weapon. Some states have mandated that recruits must be given from 240 to 400 hours of police training within one year of employment. One year is also the usual length of time officers are placed on probation.

 The probationary period is a trial period, usually one year, during which the officer is observed while obtaining training and applying this training on the streets.

Police officers may obtain their training in a state police academy, a city academy or a specialized rookie school. The basic training of police officers varies with each jurisdiction and its needs, but most officers will be trained in constitutional law, laws of arrest, search and seizure and in the various requests for service, such as accident investigation, crisis intervention and first aid.

While in training, recruits may be required to return to the department and spend a specified number of hours on street patrol. Some jurisdictions alternate their training periods every two weeks, allowing an officer to apply on the street what was learned in basic recruit school.

While on the street, the recruits ride with a field training officer or FTO, usually a sergeant, who monitors their movements and helps them apply principles learned in rookie school. While in school the officers are evaluated and tested by their instructors, who periodically send progress reports to the chief. After completing training they continue to ride with one or more training officers who evaluate their street performance. Following successful completion of the probationary period, they are full-fledged police officers. After probation some states license the person to be a police officer. Legislatures in many states have adopted standards for police officers that must be met to satisfy the state's training requirements for licensing.

States have also mandated a certain amount of in-service training to keep the license current. Many of these in-service training requirements revolve around the behavioral sciences to give police officers a better understanding of the entire criminal justice system. Guest speakers from the corrections system, the court system and on many occasions from minority groups present their philosophy and objectives to police officers.

Preparatory police academies have been proposed as an alternative approach to law enforcement recruitment and training. Other training opportunities include national scholarship programs similar to the military's Reserve Officer Training Corps (ROTC).

These cadets are receiving military-type drill instruction at a training site. Physical training is a central part of the six-month to one-year probationary period common in most police departments.

Failure to Train

The ground rules for failure to train were initially established by the Supreme Court in *City of Canton v. Harris* (1989). In this case the Court held that inadequacy of officer training could serve as the basis for Section 1983 liability only where the failure to train was the result of the "deliberate indifference to the rights" of the persons with whom the officer comes into contact. The Court's decision in this case, according to Spector (2001, p.75), left departments with "a lot of wiggle room and avenues to escape liability for failure to train."

However, the rather amorphous "deliberate indifference" standard has been replaced by the ruling in *Brown v. Bryan* (2000) in which the Supreme Court refused to consider the county's appeal concerning municipal liability for failure to train. As Risher (2001, p.10) explains: "The court held that a municipality may be liable for the inadequate training and misconduct of just one officer. . . . Any misstep by an officer that results in injury may lead to a failure-to-train claim."

Spector (p.73) notes: "Now, plaintiffs' attorneys will take the effort to plow through individual defendant officer's training records to find some deficiency related to their client's claimed injury, and if they want to spend a few bucks they'll hire some expert to identify these training deficiencies." He (p.77) notes that in *Brown*, the sheriff testified he did not have sufficient funds to conduct training. The county ended up paying $642,300 for the failure-to-train claim.

Retention

The process of recruiting, selecting and training new officers is expensive and time consuming. Therefore it is essential that agencies retain their officers. Among the factors to consider—in addition to the personal satisfaction of the job and good working conditions—are salary and benefits, opportunities for promotion and the ability to avoid stress and burnout.

Vest (2003, p.13) reports on the 205th session of the FBI National Academy on recruitment: "When asked to rank the top five items that new employees want, symposium participants responded with: (1) salary, (2) benefits—leave time, medical coverage and retirement, (3) job security, (4) career development—specialization and promotion and (5) job satisfaction—pride, excitement and community." Vest also reports: "Participants from larger agencies indicated that job security; personal growth opportunities; and pay, benefits, and retirement coverage represented the most important factors."

Yearwood and Freeman (p.46) studied retention techniques and their perceived effectiveness on a scale of 0 to 9. They found the most frequently used technique was annual pay increases irrespective of performance, 81.5 percent, rated 5.9 effective. Education/training at agency expense was used by 76.6 percent, rated 5.6 effective. Promotions were used by 69.4 percent, rated 4.5 effective. Performance-based annual pay increase was used by 66.1 percent, rated 5.6 effective. Formal awards and recognition were used by 64.5 percent, rated 4.2 effective. Favorable work shift was used by 60.5 percent, rated 5.2 effective.

Salary and Benefits

Salaries among police departments in the country have little uniformity. A variety of factors influence a police officer's salary, such as the community's ability to pay, the cost of living in the area and the prevailing wages of similar police departments in surrounding areas.

Normally position-classification plans are implemented under a personnel ordinance or department rule book. Steps on the salary scale are established in each position classification. New recruits start at the bottom of the salary scale and receive increment raises after six months and each succeeding year until they reach their maximum salary, usually after three to five years. They obtain more salary only if granted a cost-of-living raise; however a promotion to the next rank would bring them into a higher salary bracket. Sergeants, lieutenants, captains and chiefs all have minimum and maximum starting levels, with the top salary usually reached after three years in the position.

To compensate those who do not attain a rank during their police careers, many police departments have adopted longevity plans whereby nonranking officers receive a certain percentage more of their salaries after the 10th year, the 15th year and so on. This seniority system has been attacked, however, on the grounds that it discourages initiative and further education.

When salary schedules are formulated, such fringe benefits as hospitalization and dental plans, insurance, vacation, sick leave and holidays are all considered. Police officers' indirect benefits from their employers are estimated to be approximately 33 percent, comparable to what business and industry currently allow their employees. In addition to the more common benefits of paid holidays and vacations, personal and family sick leave, and medical and dental insurance, other benefits a department might provide include a uniform and clothing allowance, child care, life insurance, disability insurance, hospitalization insurance, workman's compensation, military leave, deferred compensation, college incentive pay, tuition reimbursement, a retirement fund, a pension plan and a credit union.

Policies vary regarding how to pay officers for overtime on the job, going to court while on duty, attending required training sessions while off duty and being called back to duty in an emergency. Some departments pay overtime; others give compensatory time off. Police departments may belong to unions that bargain for them. Usually all conditions of employment are clearly spelled out in their contracts.

Promotional Opportunities

Orrick (2002, p.103) suggests: "Studies have repeatedly found that employees are more concerned with opportunities for advanced training and career development programs than salary alone." Unfortunately, promotional opportunities, especially in smaller departments, are quite limited. Moore (2004b, p.114) notes that lack of promotional and advancement opportunities are much more likely reasons for female officers leaving a department than child-care issues.

Stress and Burnout

No discussion of retention would be complete without recognizing the highly stressful nature of this profession. Police officers deal with crisis daily, usually that of someone else. Sometimes, however, the demands of the roles and how they are expected to be performed create enough stress to put police officers themselves into a crisis situation.

 A police officer's job is highly stressful and may result in a personal crisis for the officer.

Dr. Hans Selye (1907–1982), known as the "father of the stress field," first defined **stress** as the nonspecific response of the body to any demand placed on it. He later said stress was simply the wear and tear caused by living.

Stress can be either positive or negative. In ancient China the symbol for stress had two written characters—one for opportunity and one for danger. In fact the excitement/stress of police work is one important reason people enter the profession. Unfortunately much of the stress experienced by police officers and, indeed, the general population, is negative.

Stress may also be acute or chronic. Acute stress is temporary and often positive. It keeps a person alert and focused. Chronic stress, in contrast, is continuous and can be debilitating. Everyone experiences stressors in their lives. Bennett and Hess (2004, p.405) observe: "Some common stress producers of daily living are changing relationships, a lifestyle inconsistent with values (too committed), money problems (credit card debt, poor investments), loss of self-esteem (falling behind professionally, accepting others' expectations), and fatigue or illness (poor diet, lack of sleep or lack of exercise)." Police officers may experience any of these in addition to stressors unique to the profession. Reese (2001, p.14) adds: "Police officers can and often do become *vicarious victims*—stressed, altered and in some cases destroyed by the crimes they investigate."

While shift work and pursuing armed suspects are relatively visible occupational hazards of policing, law enforcement is filled with many other "hidden stressors." One such insidious stressor is isolation—long hours spent alone on patrol, set apart from the rest of society by a uniform, and being held to a higher, almost nonhuman, standard than the general public. Adding to this sense of isolation is the daily interaction with the "criminal element" and routine exposure to the worst of the human condition—violence, death, pain, loss, poverty, drug addiction and lies, lies, lies. Over time, the effects of such stressors may spill over into officers' personal lives, leading them to distrust even their own family and friends.

Another hidden stressor is the unspoken, perhaps subconscious, double standard many citizens hold regarding the law, their personal freedoms and the responsibilities of the police. Examples of some of the mixed messages officers receive from the public include: "Stop those crazy drivers from speeding through my neighborhood. But you'd better not give me a ticket for rushing home." Or "Get tough on drunk drivers—they should have the book thrown at them. But I know I'm competent to drive after a night of bar-hopping with my friends." Or "Keep us safe. But don't invade our privacy."

If the stresses become great enough, officers may burn out. Being aware of and reducing stressors can prevent officer **burnout,** which Hawkins (2001, p.343) describes as "a syndrome of emotional exhaustion, depersonalization, and reduced personal accomplishment." According to Bennett and Hess (pp.418–419): "Burnout occurs when someone is exhausted or is listless because of overwork. Burnout results from long-term, unmediated stress. . . . Those most likely to experience burnout are those who are initially most committed. You cannot burn out if you have never been on fire."

Strategies for reducing stress and avoiding burnout include physical exercise, proper nutrition, adequate sleep, social outlets, relaxation techniques and time management. Many police departments are recognizing the hazards of stress for their officers and are taking steps to reduce or eliminate the causes over which they have control.

Another negative result of stress related to traumatic incidents is **post-traumatic stress disorder (PTSD).** Kates (2001, p.30) notes the distinction between post-traumatic stress and post-traumatic stress *disorder,* saying the difference lies in the symptoms:

> Post-traumatic stress may include some PTSD symptoms such as nightmares and flashbacks, but it also features symptoms like depression, eating disorders, heavy drinking and gambling, which are not part of PTSD's roster of reactions. Post-traumatic stress symptoms are generally short-lived, unlike PTSD's symptoms. . . .
>
> To be diagnosed with PTSD, candidates must meet two specific criteria . . . [1] a person has experienced or witnessed a traumatic event that involves actual or threatened death or serious injury . . . [and 2] the person has responded with intense fear, helplessness or despair. These reactions pave the way for PTSD to be set in motion. . . .
>
> You could sum up PTSD simply by saying that it consists of three clusters or groupings of symptoms. Those groupings are called reliving, avoidance and arousal [which he describes as difficulty concentrating and falling or staying asleep, overreacting to situations and being overly alert].

Kates (p.31) says that officers with PTSD experience "days and nights teeming with nightmares, cold sweats, tears and misery unimaginable to most."

Long-term stress is not only destructive but may be fatal in police work. It can cause serious physical problems such as heart problems, and it can even lead to suicide.

Stress can have adverse effects on police behavior which may, in turn, lead to citizen complaints being filed against an officer or the agency. The complaint review process may occur internally by police department personnel or may be overseen by a civilian review board, which is another stressor in and of itself.

Civilian Review Boards

 A **civilian review board** consists of citizens who meet to review complaints filed against the police department or against individual officers. The use and benefits of **civilian review** remain highly controversial.

According to Farrow and Pham (2003, p.22): "Citizen oversight of police practices has long been a controversial issue in law enforcement." They note: "On one side of the debate, there are those who assert that internal review and control is the only way to manage the problem of misconduct. Basically, they argue that the involvement of citizens without intimate knowledge of law enforcement procedures and legal limitations will only muddle the review process." They (p.24) also note: "Those on the other side argue that under democratic systems of checks and balances, no one should be left to judge him- or herself. The wide-ranging powers and discretion of law enforcement officers and their vital position as gatekeepers of the criminal justice system make it imperative that members of the public have a means of redress if officers abuse their powers and seek protection from scrutiny behind the so-called blue wall of silence."

Although civilian review boards have been used since the mid-1950s, administrators today still resist such "interference by outsiders." Many police chiefs say their jobs are tough enough without having civilian review boards constantly looking over their shoulders. Police leaders insist that only police officers can understand and judge the actions of other officers and that civilian oversight diminishes police morale and impedes officer performance. Finn (2001, p.viii) notes:

> There is no single model of citizen oversight. However, most procedures have features that fall into one of four types of oversight systems:
>
> 1. Type 1: *Citizens investigate allegations* of police misconduct and *recommend findings* to the chief or sheriff.
> 2. Type 2: Police officers investigate allegations and develop findings; *citizens review and recommend* that the chief or sheriff approve or reject the findings.
> 3. Type 3: Complainants may *appeal findings* established by the police or sheriff's department *to citizens,* who review them and then recommend their own findings to the chief or sheriff.
> 4. Type 4: An auditor *investigates the process* by which the police or sheriff's department accepts and investigates complaints and reports on the thoroughness and fairness of the process to the department and the public.

Benefits of citizen oversight include improved public relations and department image with the community and improved policies and procedures. Although community residents appear to prefer citizen review over internal police investigation, dissatisfaction remains high, and the heralded benefits remain disputed.

An alternative to civilian review boards, a civilian ombudsman, has been used successfully in Boise, Idaho. As Boatman (2001, p.219) explains, a community ombudsman provides a liaison between police and residents and makes policy recommendations to the police, mayor and city council. The result: "The presence of a community ombudsman has seen minor complaints against police officers nearly double, but serious complaints have been cut in half" (p.220). Boatman concludes: "For the review process to work, it can be neither window dressing nor adversarial. Both the independence of the ombudsman and the ultimate responsibility and authority of the chief must be preserved."

Sexual Harassment

Sexual harassment has become an issue of concern because of the rising number of women in law enforcement and the resistance to change by many officers from the "old school" in the traditionally male-dominated occupation. In addition the number of sexual harassment cases has been increasing, and the monetary awards have been sometimes shocking.

Sexual harassment is prohibited by Title VII of the 1964 Civil Rights Act, which states: "It is unlawful for any employer to discriminate against any individual with respect to his compensation, terms, conditions or privileges of employment, because of such individual's race, color, religion, sex, or national origin." Most state laws also prohibit sexual harassment.

The federal government defines **sexual harassment** as "unwelcome sexual advances, requests for sexual favors, and other verbal or physical conduct of a sexual nature" ("Preventing Sexual Harassment," n.d., p.1). Holtz (2003a, p.118) notes:

> There are two broad categories of sexual harassment: Quid pro quo sexual harassment and hostile work environment sexual harassment.
>
> Quid pro quo sexual harassment is where the submission to, or rejection of, unwelcome sexual conduct or sexual demands is made a condition of employment. This is where the employee is forced to grant sexual favors in order to obtain, maintain or improve employment status. . . .
>
> Hostile work environment sexual harassment, on the other hand, contains four elements. The conduct is (1) unwelcome, (2) sufficiently severe or pervasive to alter the conditions of the victim's employment and create an abusive working environment, (3) perceived by the victim as hostile or abusive and (4) creates an environment that a reasonable woman/man would find intimidating, hostile or abusive.

Holtz (2003b, p.126) stresses: "Law enforcement supervisors and administrators must be proactive in maintaining a work environment that is free from any form of prohibited harassment or discrimination. Their role is to ensure strict adherence to and compliance with the agency's sexual harassment policy." Boertien (2002, p.73) likewise stresses: "Supervisory and management personnel must shoulder the responsibility for ensuring a safe, comfortable work environment for all agency members. This responsibility can be met by modeling appropriate behavior, drafting unequivocal procedures, providing employees with adequate support and resources, and reacting quickly to complaints. To do anything less is unacceptable and may prove costly in lost productivity, high employee turnover and costly monetary judgments."

Pederson (2001, p.128) reports on a Florida study of 3,000 policewomen in which 69 percent claimed to have been sexually harassed on the job. Forty percent said it occurred daily. The most common offenses were jokes, comments, cartoons, calendars and verbal harassment. And, as expected, male officers initiated the vast majority of harassing behavior.

Many female officers are reluctant to report sexual harassment, well aware of the common perception among male officers that women are overly sensitive and prone to emotionalism. For females who have struggled to overcome this stereotype, filing a sexual harassment complaint means risking further alienation by their peers. Harrington, director of the National Center for Women and Policing, explains what happens to an officer who files a complaint: "Offensive remarks may be made at roll call. There may be severe retaliation. Other officers may refuse to speak to her or refuse to cover her when she calls for help" (Pederson, p.130).

Although extensive evidence exists that sexual harassment has permeated even the most professional police agencies, administrators remain reluctant to acknowledge its presence and often exhibit surprisingly cavalier attitudes toward the problem. Preventing sexual harassment from occurring is the best strategy for handling the issue, and, as Pederson (p.128) asserts: "Creating awareness of sexual harassment is the first step toward preventing it."

A twist in the problem of sexual harassment is same-sex sexual harassment which, according to the Equal Employment Opportunity Commission (EEOC), is also actionable. The EEOC Compliance Manual states that "the victim does not have to be of the opposite sex from the harasser. Since sexual harassment is a form of sex discrimination, the crucial inquiry is whether the harasser treats a member or members of one sex differently from members of the other sex." The Supreme Court ruling in *Oncale v. Sundowner Offshore Services, Inc.* (1997) expanded the definition of illegal same-sex harassment.

All officers, males and females alike, must protect their interests and help eradicate sexual harassment that threatens to undermine the effectiveness of policing. Another way in which officers seek to protect their interests is by establishing police labor unions and other local employee organizations.

Unions

According to Berger (2002, p.6): "Police labor unions have long played an active role in the law enforcement community, and there is no argument that police officers have derived numerous benefits from belonging to unions." A **union,** in the broadest context, is any group authorized to represent the members of the law enforcement agency in negotiating such matters as wages, fringe benefits and other conditions of employment. A **union shop** is an agency where people must belong to or join the union to be hired. Most police officers are currently members of local employee organizations and are not directly enrolled in a national labor union. Collins (2004, p.12) notes: "Employers have an obligation to bargain with the appropriate union before making changes in or affecting wages, hours or other terms and conditions of employment. The duty to bargain is continuous and does not end with the negotiation of an agreement. It exists through the period covered by the contract."

The Fraternal Order of Police (FOP) was founded in 1915 and is the world's oldest, largest and most influential sworn law enforcement officer's organization.

It has more than 310,000 members in more than 2,100 lodges. According to its Web site, it is the "voice of law enforcement professionals . . . committed to improving the working conditions of law enforcement." One of the FOP's priorities was passing a collective-bargaining bill. This "right-to-unionize bill" was opposed by the International Association of Chiefs of Police (IACP) and the National Sheriffs' Association (NSA). The Senate ultimately defeated the bill ("In Unions There Is Strength," 2003, p.6).

For many law enforcement agencies, unions are a positive force; for others, they create problems and dissension; and in yet others, they are nonexistent. One frequent objection to unions is the tactics commonly employed, including slow-downs, "sickouts" and strikes. Although it is usually illegal for most public employees to strike, strikes by law enforcement officers have occurred in San Francisco, Tucson and Oklahoma City. Some of the strikes lasted only a few days, but others lasted weeks. In some instances strikers lost their jobs, but in other instances they obtained raises.

Other objections raised against unions include the fear that the law enforcement administrators and public officials who unionized police employees could abuse their collective bargaining power and that specific aspects of administration, such as transfers and promotions, could become bound up in arbitration and grievance procedures. Many administrators see the union as interfering with their leadership and with the officers in the ranks. In addition police unions have resisted changes in law enforcement organizations and techniques that affect their membership. For example the unions have opposed attempts to shift from two-person to one-person patrol cars. Unions have also objected to efforts to hire civilians in clerical positions, and they have resisted affirmative action efforts, seeking to maintain the status quo rather than to increase recruitment of women and minorities.

 Line officers usually favor unionization as it gives them collective bargaining power with the administration. Administrators, on the other hand, disapprove of some union tactics and feel unionization limits their power and authority.

Unions are strongest in the northeast and on the west coast. The International Union of Police Associations (IUPA) began in 1978 as the only union exclusively designed for law enforcement personnel and, as of June 2001, there were 4,000 police unions in the United States with 225,000 sworn law enforcement members and 11,000 retired members.

One highly debated issue related to union membership is who should belong. What ranks should be included? Should managers and supervisors belong to the same union as patrol officers? Another topic of concern to unions and their members is the growing presence of private police forces.

Privatization of Criminal Justice

Privatization refers to the practice of having nonsworn personnel, often private security officers, perform tasks traditionally performed by police officers. Private security forces include guards, patrols, investigators, armed couriers, central alarm respondents and consultants. Private security agencies and their officers perform many of the same functions as police and other government law enforcement agencies and their officers: they control entrances and exits to facilities; promote safety and security inside government buildings, courthouses and airports; safeguard equipment, valuables and confidential material; prevent and report fires and other property damage; and patrol restricted areas. Businesses and educational, industrial and commercial organizations often hire private security guards to protect their premises and investments. In addition, police agencies commonly subcontract with private companies and labs for evidence testing, fingerprint and handwriting analysis, and applicant screening.

There are, however, important differences between private security officers and police officers. Police officers are salaried with public funds, responsible to a chief of police and, ultimately, accountable to the community's citizens. Technically they are on duty 24 hours a day and have full authority to uphold the law, including the authority to make arrests and to carry a concealed weapon. Still police officers cannot be everywhere. Therefore many businesses and organizations have elected to hire special protection.

Basically two different types of private security may be hired: private patrols and on-site security officers. As the name implies, private patrols operate both on and off the premises of their employers and may check several customers' properties periodically during a specified time period. On-site security officers, however, stay on the property to safeguard the premises at all times. Another distinction exists between security officers employed by large industrial firms and night guards employed by small firms. The former are usually carefully screened, well paid and trained to perform specific duties. In contrast night guards are often retired from a regular job (sometimes as police officers), need only temporary work or are simply supplementing a regular income by taking on a second job.

 Private security officers differ from police officers in that private security officers are salaried with private funds, are responsible to an employer and have limited authority extending to only the premises they are hired to guard. Security officers have no authority to carry concealed weapons and, unless deputized, have no authority to make arrests except as a citizen's arrest. Furthermore, their uniform and badge must not closely resemble that of a regular police officer.

Many benefits to law enforcement may be realized through partnering with private security. While usually complementing law enforcement efforts, private security officers can assist in responding to burglar alarms, investigating internal theft and economic crimes, protecting VIPs and executives, moving hazardous materials, and controlling crowds and traffic for public events. Private policing, or privatization, also has an advantage in that security officers are not bound by many constraints public police officers are, such as having to give the Miranda warning to suspects. Furthermore private-sector development of police stations, sheriffs' stations and jails is being advocated as an option for replacing outdated facilities.

Some police departments hire out full-time sworn officers to private enterprises for a fee. In other cases, police officers find part-time, supplemental employment on their own, sometimes against the preference or policy of their department.

Moonlighting

Moonlighting, working at a part-time job while fulfilling the obligations of a full-time position, has been a source of controversy in the police field for many years and falls within a gray area some departments prefer to avoid.

Moonlighting is controversial and is handled differently from one department to the next.

Most police departments restrict the type of work that can be done and the number of hours an officer can work while off duty. Some cities allow their police officers to work off duty in only police-related areas; others allow them to work in only non–police-related areas. While allowing police officers to work off duty has definite advantages, disadvantages also exist, and most cities and municipalities have developed policies that place limits on the officer's off-duty time. Policies on moonlighting address issues such as how to obtain permission for off-duty work, what types of off-duty jobs are not permitted and so on. Policies must also adhere to the Fair Labor Standards Act (FLSA) rules concerning moonlighting officers and the conditions attached to dual employment, joint employment, "special detail" work and "volunteer" work. Standards regarding secondary employment of police officers are among the 439 standards outlined by the Commission on Accreditation for Law Enforcement Agencies (CALEA) for agencies seeking accreditation.

Accreditation

The CALEA was formed in 1979 to develop a set of law enforcement standards and to establish and administer an **accreditation** process through which law enforcement agencies could demonstrate *voluntarily* that they meet professionally recognized criteria for excellence in management and service delivery. The commission is the combined effort of the International Association of Chiefs of Police (IACP), the National Organization of Black Law Enforcement Executives (NOBLE), the National Sheriffs' Association (NSA) and the Police Executive Research Forum (PERF). Members of these four organizations direct approximately 80 percent of the law enforcement community in the United States.

 The Commission on Accreditation for Law Enforcement Agencies (CALEA) was formed to develop professional standards and to administer a voluntary accreditation process, although controversy exists over the value of such accreditation.

The CALEA standards address nine major law enforcement subjects: (1) role, responsibilities and relationships with other agencies; (2) organization, management and administration; (3) personnel structure; (4) personnel process; (5) operations; (6) operational support; (7) traffic operations; (8) prisoner and court-related activities; and (9) auxiliary and technical services. The goals of these standards are to help law enforcement agencies (1) strengthen crime prevention and control capabilities, (2) formalize essential management procedures, (3) establish fair and nondiscriminatory personnel practices, (4) improve service delivery, (5) solidify interagency cooperation and coordination and (6) boost citizen and staff confidence in the agency ("The Standards," 2001).

CALEA's accreditation process consists of five phases: (1) the application, (2) self-assessment, (3) on-site assessment, (4) commission review and (5) maintaining compliance and re-accreditation.

Supporters of national accreditation contend it is one way to elevate law enforcement to a professional status and to assure that certain standards are met. As of March 2004, 552 law enforcement agencies have been accredited by CALEA. For agencies willing to meet the challenge, accreditation may provide the following benefits:

- A set of clear, written policies and procedures so every employee knows what's expected
- Assurance that department operations are consistent with current professional standards
- Greater accountability within the agency and higher morale
- Improved management/union relations
- Enhanced defense against citizen complaints and lawsuits, and reduced litigation costs
- Controlled liability insurance costs and discounts from insurance carriers
- Increased professionalism, an enhanced reputation for the department and greater community advocacy
- Increased support of government officials bolstered by their confidence in the agency's ability to operate efficiently and meet community needs
- Greater justification for resource and budget requests
- A proven management system of written directives, sound training, clearly defined lines of authority, and routine reports that support decision making and resource allocation
- A better managed agency

In fact, CALEA states: "Many agencies report a decline in legal actions against them, once they become accredited" ("Benefits of Accreditation," 2001). Concurring, Moore (2004a, p.114) states: "One of accreditation's main selling points remains the correspondent lowering of liability insurance expenses, a claim that's been validated many times over."

Despite these potential benefits, accreditation does have critics. A pool of randomly selected law enforcement agencies indicated five major arguments against accreditation: (1) too expensive, (2) too time-consuming, (3) dubious benefits, (4) hard to justify to community government and (5) department administration does not believe in it. Table 12.1 summarizes the results of a survey of law enforcement administrators on the perceived benefits of accreditation.

Table 12.1   Perceived Benefits of Accreditation

Statement	Agreed	Disagreed	Unsure
Accreditation is more a status symbol or public relations tool than it is a valuable process.	53%	21%	26%
Accreditation has an appreciable impact on how well an agency performs.	54%	31%	15%
Accreditation does establish accountability within the office.	60%	28%	12%
Accreditation establishes uniformity in service delivery.	44%	32%	24%
Accreditation promotes efficient and effective administration and deployment of personnel.	36%	32%	32%
Accreditation provides stronger defense against lawsuits.	44%	40%	16%
Accreditation improves employee morale.*	24%	32%	44%

*Most significant finding

SOURCE: Adapted from Arthur G. Sharp. "Accreditation: Fact or Fixture?" *Law and Order,* March 2000, p.93.

While criticism of the accreditation process is not new, and controversy has surrounded such standards from the start, much of the debate in recent years has centered on whether these standards facilitate or inhibit the implementation of community policing. CALEA presents a compelling argument in support of the facilitation of community policing through accreditation and how the two processes complement each other ("Community Policing," 2001):

> Implementing community policing requires the kind of dynamic and multifaceted process that accreditation encourages . . . a process that involves every component of the department and every facet of the community and local government . . . a process that fosters employee and citizen advice and counsel . . . and, a strategy designed to stimulate dialogue and feedback.
>
> Earning accredited status and implementing community policing can galvanize community support for a law enforcement agency. It can turn interagency cooperation into coordination and community apathy into collaboration. Community participation is an integral part of the self-assessment that marks the beginning of an agency's efforts toward accreditation.
>
> The commentary of standard 45.2.1 (Community Relations) further highlights the importance of community participation: "Law enforcement agencies should establish direct contacts with the community served. Without grassroots community support, successful enforcement of many laws may be difficult, if not impossible. Input from the community can also help ensure that agency policies accurately reflect the needs of the community."
>
> The accreditation self-assessment process provides many opportunities to institutionalize community policing. For example, preparing compliance documentation for . . . "Law Enforcement Role and Authority" . . . offers a chance for agencies to study and redefine their mission, statement of ethics and values, and vision of policing. This is also a logical time to take stock of the community's collective vision and opinions. . . . [Other parts] of the standards manual address organization, management, and administrative issues. While working on these standards, law enforcement agencies can consider such community policing precepts as decentralized authority and flattened organizational hierarchies. . . .
>
> Has the agency achieved diversity in the workplace? Do recruit and in-service training classes develop community policing skills such as effective communication with members of various ethnic and racial groups? Do the agency's performance evaluation criteria include community policing factors like community mobilization skills, group facilitation, problem-solving, and referral skills? . . . These questions deal with the standards [covering the subject of] "The Personnel Process." . . .
>
> Finally, not only do the accreditation standards help weave community policing into an agency's internal fabric, they also provide a way to integrate such objectives into external service-delivery. Key community policing objectives that can be applied when working on standards related to law enforcement operations, operations support, and communications are:
>
> - enhancing the role and authority of patrol officers;
> - improving analysis and information management; and
> - managing calls-for-service.

In the Community Policing Consortium's monograph, *Understanding Community Policing: A Framework for Action,* CALEA's four founders advise that: "Community policing cannot be established through a mere modification of existing policy; profound changes must occur on every level and in every area of a police agency from patrol officer to chief executive, and from training to technology. A commitment to community policing must guide every decision and every action of the department."

There is no reason why accreditation's strategic planning process cannot be used to facilitate community policing and meaningful change in a law enforcement agency. The preceding discussion clearly underscores this conclusion. But if further evidence is needed, consider the common bonds of community policing and accreditation:

- both require citizen and local government support;
- both encourage productive change in service-delivery strategies; and
- both require a leadership style that takes advantage of agency and community resources to institute value-driven rather than rule-driven management.

Accreditation requires law enforcement agencies to document their policies. Community policing requires agencies to engage the community in a process of evaluating what ought to be documented. Both ask participants to take a critical look at the status quo. According to Wilcox (2004, p.21): "[Accreditation] takes effort and money, but the benefits far outweigh the costs, monetary and otherwise." Others would disagree.

Another approach being used to ensure accountability is police **credentialing**, whereby individual police officers are evaluated by the National Law Enforcement Credentialing Board (NLECB). The NLECB was established by the Fraternal Order of Police and is supported by other law enforcement groups. A three-year study established national standards to evaluate officers, including disciplinary record, community service and post-academy education and training. Officers must submit evidence of meeting the standards and are then allowed, for a fee of $250, to take a three-hour test consisting of 200 multiple-choice items.

Acceptance of credentialing is not automatic. Critics point out that there has never been agreement on just what constitutes an "outstanding police officer." Nor is there agreement that this can be ascertained through a multiple-choice test. In addition, there is no limit on the number of times an officer can pay the fee and take the same test over. A further obstacle is that historically most state-level Peace Officers Standards and Training (POST) boards have been reluctant to recognize any training or certification other than their own. Whether credentialing will become nationally recognized remains to be seen.

Another approach to demonstrate competence in a given area is certification. According to Sanow (2004, p.4): "Certification is simply a proof of proper training from the manufacturer or a peer-recognized group. Importantly, certification is also a way to share liability . . . with the organization providing the certification." Officers might become certified in using various forms of less lethal weapons, radar, batons, and so on. Certification is an important tool for officers and agencies wishing to enhance their professionalism.

Police Professionalism

Throughout this text policing has been referred to as a profession; however whether law enforcement technically qualifies as a profession is controversial. Part of the problem is that definitions of professionalism vary. To some, *professional* means simply an important job or one who gets paid, as opposed to an *amateur*. Sociologists, however, have identified certain elements that qualify an occupation as a profession.

Sociological Elements of Professionalism

 The three key elements of professionalism are (1) specialized knowledge, (2) autonomy and (3) a service ideal.

Specialized Knowledge   The time when someone could walk into a police department, fill out an application and be hired is gone in most parts of the country. Many departments now require a two-year college degree, and some require a four-year degree. In addition to a college degree, many departments require that applicants complete skills training. As noted, most larger departments also have their own rookie schools or academies where new police officers learn what is expected in a particular agency. As technology advances and as criminals become more sophisticated, more knowledge and training is expected to be required.

Autonomy   Professional autonomy refers to the ability to control entrance into the profession, to define the content of the knowledge to be obtained and to be responsible for self-monitoring and disciplining. In addition the autonomy of a profession is usually authorized by the power of the state; for example physicians, dentists, lawyers and teachers are licensed by the state. These professions are, in effect, legalized monopolies.

Law enforcement does fit the criterion of professional autonomy in that requirements to be a police officer are usually set by the legislature. The growth in the number of Peace Officers Standards and Training (POST) boards throughout the country to oversee the profession attests to this fact.

A Service Ideal   The third element of a profession, a service ideal, requires that members of the profession follow a formal code of ethics and be committed to serving the community. In this area police officers qualify as professionals, provided the department stresses the public servant aspects of police work.

The Final Analysis—Does Law Enforcement Qualify?

However, despite this positive development, in most states, the minimum education requirement to enter law enforcement has gone unchanged for decades. Although a college degree requirement has been advocated since the 1967 President's Commission, no states currently meet this goal. Some states, such as Wisconsin and Minnesota, do require a two-year associate's degree to enter law enforcement, a step in the right direction.

SUMMARY

The future success (or failure) of our criminal justice system, especially our law enforcement system, depends in large part on the quality and effectiveness of our police officers. Therefore valid recruitment, screening, testing and selection procedures must be used to assure that only well-qualified candidates are hired. Qualities of a good police officer include reliability, leadership, judgment, persuasiveness, communication skills, initiative, integrity, honesty, ego control, intelligence, sensitivity and problem-solving ability. Individuals possessing such skills are sought through a careful selection procedure.

Agencies are also seeking to hire more minorities and women. A racially balanced and integrated police department fosters community relations and increases police effectiveness. Studies show that women perform as well as men in police work, are less apt to use excessive force, can help implement community-oriented policing and can improve an agency's response to violence against women. In addition, an increased female presence among officers can reduce problems of sex discrimination and harassment and foster policy changes that benefit all officers.

Police officer selection usually includes a formal application, a written examination, a physical fitness test, a psychological examination, an interview, a thorough background investigation and a medical examination. Most agencies require that a police officer candidate be a U.S. citizen, have or be eligible for a driver's license in the state and not have been convicted of a felony. Additional requirements may specify educational level and residency in the community served. Most police agencies require a minimum of a high school education or equivalency certificate, and some require a two- or four-year degree. Many police agencies are now requiring some college education for employment and/or promotion. Whether such education helps the officers perform better has not been documented. Regarding residency, it is always preferred and sometimes required that police officers live in the community they serve.

Because fitness is an important quality of law enforcement officers, physical fitness tests are used to evaluate a candidate's coordination, speed and strength. The most common physical fitness tests are similar to military obstacle courses that must be completed in a designated time. The candidate also undergoes an oral interview to evaluate appearance, alertness, communication ability, social adaptability, judgment, emotional stability, and interest in and suitability for the job. The background investigation includes verification of all information on the application and history sheet; a check of driving record; fingerprinting and a check of any criminal record; a check of military records; interviews with personal references, acquaintances, past employers, neighbors and teachers; a check of financial status; and a check of past performances at schools and previous jobs. Finally, a medical examination is conducted to assess the candidate's vision, hearing and cardiovascular-respiratory system.

In addition to local and state requirements for recruitment and selection of police officers, certain federal guidelines and regulations must be met. Most important are the 1972 Equal Employment Opportunity Act, which prohibits discrimination due to sex, race, color, religion or national origin in employment of any kind, public or private, local, state or federal; and the Americans with Disabilities Act (ADA), which prohibits discrimination in employment based on a disability.

Once candidates have passed all tests in the selection process, they usually enter a one-year probationary period during which they are observed while obtaining training and while applying this training on the streets.

All police officers are subjected to the hazards of police work, and all are expected to fulfill the responsibilities of the job. Nevertheless, a police officer's job is highly stressful and may result in a personal crisis for the officer. Stress can have adverse effects on police behavior that may, in turn, lead to citizen complaints being filed against an officer or agency.

To help assure ethical behavior—individually and departmentally—some communities have established civilian review boards. A civilian review board consists of citizens who meet to review complaints filed against the police department or against individual officers. The use and benefits of civilian review remain highly controversial. Whether police officers should be unionized remains another controversial issue. Line officers usually favor unionization as it gives them collective bargaining power with the administration. Administrators, on the other hand, disapprove of some union tactics and feel unionization limits their power and authority.

Controversy also surrounds the privatization of criminal justice responsibilities. Privatization refers to the practice of having nonsworn personnel, often private security officers, perform tasks traditionally performed by police officers. Private security officers differ from police officers in that private security officers are salaried with private funds, are responsible to an employer and have limited authority extending only to the premises they are hired to guard. Security officers have no authority to carry concealed weapons and, unless deputized, have no authority to make arrests except as a citizen's arrest. Furthermore, their uniform and badge must not closely resemble that of a regular police officer. Many agencies permit their officers to moonlight in private security and other fields. Moonlighting is controversial and is handled differently from one department to the next.

The issues of accreditation and police professionalism are additional topics of controversy. The Commission on Accreditation for Law Enforcement Agencies was formed to develop professional standards and to administer a voluntary accreditation process, although controversy exists over the value of such accreditation. Many question whether policing qualifies as a profession. The three key elements of professionalism are (1) specialized knowledge, (2) autonomy and (3) a service ideal.

DISCUSSION QUESTIONS

1. What is the most common reason for rejection during the selection process?

2. What employment opportunities in law enforcement are available locally? In your county? Your state?

3. What are some societal factors interfering with police work?

4. How important do you think it is for officers to live in the community in which they work?

5. How much education do police officers need?

6. Does private policing represent a threat to public policing?

7. Do you favor or oppose civilian review boards? State your reasons.

8. Is sexual harassment a serious problem for police departments?

9. Do you support or oppose accreditation of police departments? Why?

10. Do you consider law enforcement a profession? What about the entire criminal justice field?

INFOTRAC COLLEGE EDITION ASSIGNMENTS

- Use InfoTrac College Edition to help answer the Discussion Questions as appropriate.

- Use InfoTrac College Edition to search for *police civilian review boards* and note the variety of approaches used to investigate police action. After reviewing some of the information, what is your opinion of these boards? Are they useful or not? Be prepared to discuss your view with the class.

- Read and outline one of the following articles to share with the class:

  - "The Americans with Disabilities Act" by Thomas D. Colbridge

  - "Defining Disability under the Americans with Disabilities Act" by Thomas D. Colbridge

- "Prohibited Discrimination under the Americans with Disabilities Act" by Thomas D. Colbridge
- "Police Officer Candidate Assessment and Selection" by David A. Decicco
- "Citizen Complaints: What the Police Should Know" by Richard R. Johnson
- "Getting Along with Citizen Oversight" by Peter Finn
- "Closing the Recruitment Gap: A Symposium's Findings" by Gary Vest
- "Focus on Accreditation: A Small Police Department's Success" by William L. Wilcox
- "Recruitment Strategies: A Case Study in Police Recruitment" by Mark A. Spawn

 ### INTERNET ASSIGNMENTS

- Using the key words *police stress,* research the reasons law enforcement officers become stressed. Do any of them surprise you? What, if any, suggestions are given to prevent or reduce such stress? Be prepared to share your findings with the class.
- Go to the Web site of a law enforcement department and find starting salary and benefit figures for an officer *with* a college degree and one *without* a degree. Bring your data to class and calculate a mean (average) and median figure for the departments surveyed.

 ### BOOK-SPECIFIC WEB SITE

The book-specific Web site at http://info .wadsworth.com/0534552803 hosts a variety of resources for students and instructors. Included are extended activities from each chapter in which students write a policy, use critical thinking skills to make choices in response to a given scenario, use InfoTrac College Edition with direct links to articles for participation in topical discussion forums and analyze court cases using Web links for research. Many activities can be printed or emailed to instructors. Plus, cited cases with Web links, interactive key term FlashCards, PowerPoint presentations, chapter objectives, and an extensive collection of chapter-based Web links provide additional information and activities to include in the curriculum.

REFERENCES

Armstrong, David and Polk, O. Elmer. "College for Cops: The Fast Track to Success." *The Law Enforcement Trainer,* September/October 2002, pp.24–26.

"Benefits of Accreditation." *CALEA Online,* November 29, 2001. www.calea.org/newweb/accreditation.

Bennett, Wayne W. and Hess, Kären M. *Management and Supervision in Law Enforcement,* 4th ed. Belmont, CA: Wadsworth Publishing Company, 2004.

Berger, William B. "Votes of No Confidence." *The Police Chief,* June 2002, p.6.

Birzer, Michael L. and Tannehill, Ronald. "A More Effective Training Approach for Contemporary Policing." *Police Quarterly,* June 2001, pp.233–252.

Boatman, Robert. "Monitoring the Police: The Civilian Ombudsman as a Community Liaison." *Law and Order,* October 2001, pp.219–220.

Boertien, Robert. "Hostile Workplace." *Law and Order,* December 2002, pp.70–73.

Bowman, Theron. "Educate to Elevate." *Community Links,* 2002, pp.11–13.

Bratton, William J. "Recruitment Crisis Gains Momentum." *American Police Beat,* October 2001, pp.1, 32.

Butterfield, Fox. "City Police Work Losing Its Appeal and Its Veterans." *The New York Times,* July 30, 2001, pp.1, A12.

Clark, Daniel W.; Olson, Joseph W.; Porter, Lowell M.; and Leichner, Robert M. "The Human Resource Roundtable: A Recruitment and Risk Management Tool." *The Police Chief,* December 2001, pp.29–35.

Collins, John M. "Labor Relations: Promulgating a New Rule." *The Police Chief,* June 2004, p.12.

Conroy, Dennis and Placide, MaCherie. *Prevention of Racially Biased Policing: Accountability and Supervision: Technical Assistance Guide.* City of Saint Paul (Minnesota) Police Department, 2003.

Domash, Shelly Feuer. "Who Wants This Job?" *Police,* May 2002, pp.34–39.

Farrow, Joe and Pham, Trac. "Citizen Oversight of Law Enforcement: Challenge and Opportunity." *The Police Chief,* October 2003, pp.22–29.

Finn, Peter. *Citizen Review of Police: Approaches and Implementation.* Washington, DC: NIJ Issues and Practices, March 2001. (NCJ 184430)

Fuss, Timothy and Snowden, Lynne. "Importance of Background Investigations." *Law and Order,* March 2004, pp.58–63.

Garcia, Venessa. "'Difference' in the Police Department: Women, Policing, and 'Doing Gender.'" *Journal of Contemporary Criminal Justice,* August 2003, pp.330–344.

Hawkins, Homer C. "Police Officer Burnout: A Partial Replication of Maslach's Burnout Inventory." *Police Quarterly,* September 2001, pp.343–360.

Holtz, Larry. "What Is Sexual Harassment?" *Law Enforcement Technology,* March 2003a, p.118.

Holtz, Larry. "Harassment Policies." *Law Enforcement Technology,* April 2003b, p.126.

"In Unions There Is Strength." *Law Enforcement News,* April 30, 2003, p.6.

Jones, Robin. "Recruiting Women." *The Police Chief,* April 2004, pp.165–166.

Kaminsky, Glenn F. "Effective Utilization of the Probationary Period." *The Law Enforcement Trainer,* March/April 2001, pp.32–33.

Kanable, Rebecca. "Strategies for Recruiting the Nation's Finest." *Law Enforcement Technology,* February 2001, pp.64–68.

Kates, Allen R. "Post-Traumatic Stress Disorder: Hoax or Reality?" *The Associate*, January/February 2001, pp.29–31.

Lonsway, Kimberly A. "The Role of Women in Community Policing: Dismantling the Warrior Image." *Community Links*, September 2001, pp.16–17.

Lonsway, Kimberly A. "Tearing Down the Wall: Problems with Consistency, Validity and Adverse Impact of Physical Agility Testing in Police Selection." *Police Quarterly*, September 2003, pp.237–277.

Lonsway, Kimberly and Campbell, Deborah. "Retaining Women Officers." *Law and Order*, May 2002, pp.107–111.

Lonsway, Kimberly; Wood, Michelle; and Spillar, Katherine. "Officer Gender and Excessive Force." *Law and Order*, December 2002, pp.60–66.

Maglione, Roslyn. "Recruiting, Retaining and Promoting Women: The Success of the Charlotte-Mecklenburg Police Department's Women's Network." *The Police Chief*, March 2002, pp.19–24.

Moore, Carole. "Is Accreditation Right for Your Agency?" *Law Enforcement Technology*, February 2004a, p.114.

Moore, Carole. "Female Officers Benefit Departments." *Law Enforcement Technology*, April 2004b, p.114.

Moore, Margaret M. "How Effectively Does Your Police Agency Recruit and Retain Women?" *The Police Chief*, March 2002, p.29.

National Center for Women and Policing. *Equality Denied: The Status of Women in Policing, 2000*. Washington, DC: National Center for Women and Policing, 2001.

Nichols, Mark. "Bucking the Trend." *American Police Beat*, January/February 2001, pp.1, 44.

Oglesby, Denise Chavez. Statement regarding affirmative action written for this text and updated in 2002.

Olson, Robert K. "Recruiting the Officers of the Future." *Subject to Debate*, August 2001, pp.2, 5.

Orrick, W. Dwayne. "Calculating the Cost of Police Turnover." *The Police Chief*, October 2002, pp.100–103.

Osofsky, Howard J.; Fralle, Penelope; and Greenleaf, Wayne. "Developing a Partnership to Enhance Police Recruitment and Retention." *The Police Chief*, January 2001, pp.38–46.

Pederson, Dorothy. "Sexual Harassment: Is the Atmosphere Right for It in Your Precinct?" *Law Enforcement Technology*, October 2001, pp.128–134.

"Preventing Sexual Harassment." St. Paul, MN: Equal Opportunity Division, Department of Human Relations, no date.

Prussel, Deborah and Lonsway, Kimberly A. "Recruiting Women Police Officers." *Law and Order*, July 2001, pp.91–96.

Recruiting and Retaining Women: A Self-Assessment Guide for Law Enforcement. Los Angeles: National Center for Women and Policing, 2001. http://www.ncjrs.org, site of the National Criminal Justice Reference Service.

Reese, James T. "6 Keys to Stress-Free Living." *The Associate*, January/February 2001, pp.14–17.

Risher, Julie A. "Police Liability for Failure to Train." *The Police Chief*, July 2001, p.10.

Sanow, Ed. "Certified or Lose in Court." *Law and Order*, July 2004, p.4.

Scuro, Joseph E., Jr. "The Americans with Disabilities Act in the 21st Century." *Law and Order*, February 2001, pp.31–33.

Scuro, Joseph E., Jr. "Supreme Court Redefines Affirmative Action." *Law and Order*, February 2004, pp.24–26.

Sokolove, Bruce and Field, Mark W. "The Law Enforcement Candidate Ride-Along: A Supplemental Selection Tool." *The Police Chief*, January 2002, pp.55–59.

Spawn, Mark A. "Recruitment Strategies: A Case Study in Police Recruitment." *FBI Law Enforcement Bulletin*, March 2003, pp.18–20.

Spector, Elliot. "Emerging Legal Standards for Failure to Train." *Law and Order*, October 2001, pp.73–77.

"The Standards." *CALEA Online*. November 29, 2001. www.calea.org/newweb/accreditation.

Strandberg, Keith. "Conquering Recruiting Challenges: Finding the Best Candidates for the Job." *Law Enforcement Technology*, January 2004, pp.40–45.

Streit, Corinne. "Recruiting Minority Officers." *Law Enforcement Technology*, February 2001, pp.70–75.

Sullivan, John J. "Getting What You Pay For . . . A Call to the Budget-Cutting Administrator." *The Law Enforcement Trainer*, May/June 2003, pp.25–27.

Vest, Gary. "Closing the Recruitment Gap: A Symposium's Findings." *FBI Law Enforcement Bulletin*, November 2003, pp.13–17.

Walker, Samuel; Spohn, Cassia; and DeLone, Miriam. *The Color of Justice: Race, Ethnicity, and Crime in America*, 3rd ed. Belmont, CA: Wadsworth Publishing Company, 2004.

Wilcox, William L. "Focus on Accreditation: A Small Police Department's Success." *FBI Law Enforcement Bulletin*, February 2004, pp.18–21.

Yearwood, Douglas L. and Freeman, Stephanie. "Recruitment and Retention of Police Officers in North Carolina." *The Police Chief*, March 2004, pp.43–49.

Cases Cited

Brown v. Bryan, 219 F.3d 450 (5th Cir. 2000)
City of Canton v. Harris, 489 U.S. 378 (1989)
Davis v. City of Dallas (1978)
Gratz v. Bollinger, No. 02-516, decided June 23, 2003
Griggs v. Duke Power Company, 401 U.S. 424 (1971)
Grutter v. Bollinger, No. 02-241, decided June 23, 2003
Oncale v. Sundowner Offshore Services, Inc., 95 F.3d 56 (5th Cir. 1996), *cert. granted* 117 S.Ct. 2430 (1997)

LAW ENFORCEMENT AND THE CRIMINAL JUSTICE SYSTEM

Law enforcement is one of three major components of our country's criminal justice system, which has its roots in the U.S. Constitution. The colonists cherished the freedom from tyranny they had fought for and wanted to assure that when they set up their new government no single entity would have absolute power. They also, however, wanted to assure that law and order were a part of this new country. The importance of a system of checks and balance and of establishing entities that could ensure law and order are seen in the first three articles of the Constitution.

The U.S. Constitution laid the foundation for the criminal justice system by establishing:

- The legislative branch to make laws (Article 1).
- The executive branch to enforce the laws (Article 2).
- The judicial branch to judge when the law had been broken (Article 3).

The three branches of government serve as a system of checks and balances on each other, providing a lateral balance of power. In addition, because the states feared an all-powerful government, even with its system of checks and balances, the Tenth Amendment to the Constitution established the principle of federalism. Federalism allowed the criminal justice system to develop at both the state and federal levels and established a vertical balance of power.

The states, in turn, allowed local jurisdictions to establish their own law enforcement agencies. This *intentionally fragmented system* with both vertical and horizontal checks and balances assures that no one entity will become too powerful, but it also poses problems of coordination when joint efforts such as homeland security are needed. Indeed, coordination is sometimes lacking among the components of the criminal justice system.

The first three sections of this text explored the law enforcement component of the criminal justice system. This final section presents basic information about the other two components of the system with which law enforcement interacts: courts and corrections (Chapter 13).

Courts and Corrections: Law Enforcement's Partners in the Criminal Justice System

Justice is truth in action.

—Disraeli

Do You Know . . .

- How the police aid the criminal justice process?
- What the typical hierarchy is within the state court system? The federal court system?
- How juvenile court differs from adult court?
- What the adversary system requires?
- Who the key players in the judicial process are?
- What the dual role of the prosecutor is?
- What the critical criminal justice stages are?
- What purpose a preliminary hearing serves?
- What one alternative to trial is?
- How the defense attorney may attempt to discredit the testimony of a police officer?
- What the purposes of corrections are?
- What correctional alternatives are being used in the United States?
- How jail differs from prison?
- What two philosophies are evident in U.S. prisons?
- How parole differs from probation?
- How community policing and community justice are alike?

Can You Define?

adversary system	complaint	general deterrence	judicial waiver
appellate jurisdiction	cross-examination	hung jury	jurisdiction
arraignment	deterrence	incapacitation	no bill
boot camp	discovery process	incarceration	*nolo contendere*
community justice	diversion	intermediate sanctions	original jurisdiction

CAN YOU DEFINE? (CONTINUED)

parole

petition

plea bargaining

preliminary hearing

preponderance of the
   evidence

presumption of
   innocence

pro bono work

probation

reasonable doubt

recidivism

rehabilitation

restitution

restorative justice

retribution

R.P.R.d

shock incarceration

specific deterrence

standing mute

venue

voir dire

writ of certiorari

writ of habeas corpus

zeitgeist

Introduction

The criminal justice system is a complex amalgamation of three major components: law enforcement, courts and corrections. Each component acts independently and interdependently as the total system functions. The natural flow of the criminal justice system is from law enforcement to courts to corrections, as shown in Figure 13.1.

The criminal justice system is an important part of our society. According to a press release by the Bureau of Justice Statistics ("Nation Spends . . .," 2004), the United States spent a record $167 billion on police protection, judicial and legal services and corrections activities during 2001. The criminal justice system cost each person in the country $586: about $254 per person for police protection, just over $130 per person for judicial and legal services and approximately $200 per person for correctional services both in the community and in confinement facilities.

As of March 2001 the nation's federal, state and local justice system employed almost 2.3 million people—about 1.1 million working in law enforcement, just under a half million in the courts, prosecution and public defense services, and nearly three-quarters of a million in corrections. The March 2001 payroll at all levels of government totaled $8.1 billion.

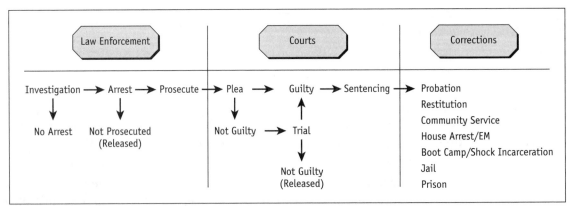

Note: This is an oversimplification to illustrate the key events in a person's "journey" through the criminal justice system.

Figure 13.1 Criminal Justice System Overview

Not only does the criminal justice system cost tax payers billions of dollars and employ millions of people, it deals with the lives of millions of people who break the law and their victims. Sometimes it deals with matters of life and death. Those who work within the system have awesome responsibilities that may be misunderstood by those outside the system.

This chapter begins with a brief discussion of the role of the police as gate-keepers to the criminal justice system. This is followed by an overview of the court systems in the United States, including state court systems, the federal court system, the Supreme Court and several specialized courts. Next the adversary system and its key players—the defendant, the prosecutor, the defense attorney and the judge—are introduced. This is followed by a description of the critical stages in the criminal justice system. Because not all cases result in a court trial, alternatives to such a trial are discussed next, including diversion and plea bargaining. This is followed by a description of the typical trial. The discussion of courts concludes with an explanation of sentencing alternatives and case review and appeal.

The second part of the chapter focuses on corrections, beginning with a discussion of the purposes of corrections and an examination of the correctional alternatives available, including probation, a host of intermediate sanctions and incarceration. Next parole and community-based reintegration programs are described, followed by a look at recidivism and the highly controversial issue of the death penalty versus life without parole. Next is a discussion of the role of the police in community corrections. The chapter concludes with an exploration of community justice and what the future criminal justice system might look like.

The Police as Gatekeepers to the Criminal Justice System

The police are the most visible element of the criminal justice system and play an integral role in its process. The criminal codes that guide police officers in enforcing laws are not a set of specific instructions. They are only rough maps of the territory in which police officers work. Regardless of how sketchy or complete the officers' education or experience, in reality they are interpreters of the law, holding enormous discretionary power, and may function as judge and jury at the start of every case. For example police officers who stop a person for speeding make a judicial decision when they give out a ticket. They might simply warn the next offender. By shooting and killing a fleeing felon who is likely to kill someone while trying to escape, the police officer delivers a capital penalty for a crime that may otherwise have netted probation or a prison term.

The police are the gatekeepers to the criminal justice system when they make an arrest. According to the FBI's Uniform Crime Reports, *Crime in the United States 2002* (2003, p.232), in 2002, law enforcement agencies nationwide made an estimated 13.7 million arrests for criminal infractions excluding traffic violations.

 Police officers aid the criminal justice process by (1) making arrests, (2) obtaining information and evidence, (3) writing reports, (4) identifying suspects and witnesses and (5) providing testimony in court.

Errors in any of these roles may seriously damage a case or even prevent a conviction. Police officers must become familiar with our courts, as well as each step of the criminal justice process, so they can intelligently bring about desired results.

An American Courtroom

Cole et al. (2004, p.251) describe the typical American courtroom:

> The typical American courtroom is not in the public minds' eye what it is in actuality. Most lower criminal courts in any city courtroom have little of the quiet dignity one expects to see when decisions concerning individual freedom and justice are made. The scene is usually one of noise and confusion as attorneys, police and prosecutors mill around conversing with one another and making bargains to keep the assembly line of the criminal justice process in operation. One might see a judge accepting guilty pleas and imposing sentences at a rapid pace, going through the litany of procedure in rote fashion. It is not surprising that visitors are shocked and that first offenders are confused by what they see.
>
> The courts, like the other parts of the justice system, function under conditions of mass production, congestion and limited resources. Even in the courts, the interests of the organization and of the principal actors often take precedence over the claims of justice.

Keep in mind this description of how the American judicial system often operates in reality while reading how it is intended to operate.

The Court System: An Overview

U.S. courts operate within a highly structured framework that may vary greatly from state to state. Many dualities exist within this framework, the most obvious being the dual system of state and federal courts.

Another duality within the courts is their **jurisdiction,** which refers not only to a geographic area but also to a court's authority to try a case or to hear an appeal, the duality being that of original versus appellate jurisdiction. A court with **original jurisdiction** has the authority to try cases, whereas a court with **appellate jurisdiction** has the authority to hear an appeal to set aside a conviction. In some cases, a court has both types of jurisdiction, for example the U.S. Supreme Court.

A court with authority to try cases is often called a *trial* court, and because such courts are often the first to record the proceedings, they are also referred to as *courts of record.* A court of last resort refers to the highest court to which a case may be appealed.

The State Court System

Durose and Langan (2003, p.1) report: "In 2000, state courts convicted an estimated 924,700 adults of a felony. . . . State courts accounted for 94 percent of the national total." Each state's constitution and statutory law establish its court's structure. Consequently great variety exists in the types of courts established, the names by which they are known and the number of levels in the hierarchy.

The hierarchy at the state level often goes up from courts of special or limited jurisdiction called justice of the peace (J.P.) courts, to trial courts or original and general jurisdiction courts (including probate court, municipal court, county court, circuit court, district court and superior court), to intermediate appellate courts, to the state supreme court.

Most cases originate in a municipal or county court, and it is in such courts that most law enforcement officers are called upon to testify. Although municipalities and counties are self-governed and have their own courts, they need to comply with state and federal laws. In some states cases may be appealed to an intermediate appellate court. In every state the state supreme court is the court of last resort at this level. Figure 13.2 illustrates the state court system. Cases may progress beyond this point, however, into the federal court system.

The Federal Court System

Durose and Langan (p.1) report that federal courts convicted 59,123 adults of a felony, only 6 percent of the national total.

 The federal court system is three tiered: district courts, appellate courts and the U.S. Supreme Court.

The three-tiered federal court system is illustrated in Figure 13.3. A state may be divided into federal districts (91 districts in 50 states), and several states may fall within a circuit (11 circuits plus a DC circuit).

The Supreme Court

The U.S. Supreme Court is presided over by nine justices appointed by the president of the United States, subject to Senate confirmation. The president also appoints a chief justice, who assigns the cases to the other justices. Most have been lawyers from the upper class and have been white, male, Protestant and graduates of prestigious universities. More than half were judges before their appointments.

The first black Supreme Court justice was Thurgood Marshall, appointed in 1967. Sandra D. O'Connor was the first woman Supreme Court justice, appointed in 1981. Table 13.1 displays the composition of the current Supreme Court.

The Constitution established tenure for "life on good behavior." Therefore, the only way to remove a justice is through impeachment unless voluntary retirement can be obtained. When the Supreme Court decides to hear a case, it grants a **writ of certiorari,** which is a request for a transcript of the proceedings of the case for review. When the Supreme Court rules on a case, the ruling becomes

The U.S. Supreme Court building, situated on Capitol Hill in Washington, DC, was constructed in 1935 and is undergoing modernization. The groundbreaking ceremony was held June 13, 2003, with completion expected in July 2008. Total cost of the project is estimated at $122 million.

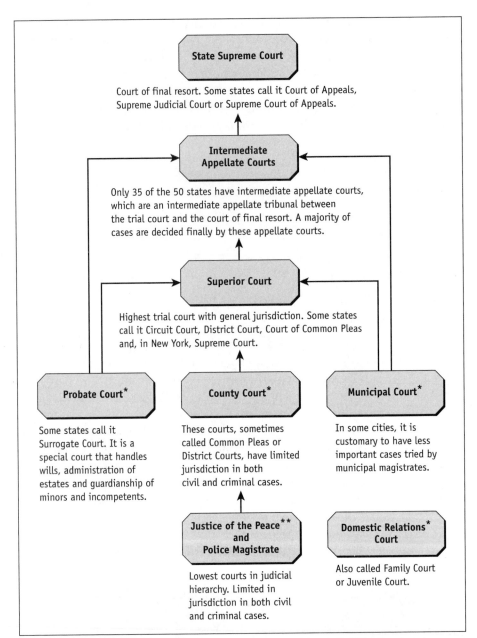

*Courts of special jurisdiction, such as probate, family or juvenile courts, and the so-called inferior courts, such as common pleas or municipal courts, may be separate courts or part of the trial court of general jurisdiction.
**Justices of the peace do not exist in all states. Where they do exist, their jurisdictions vary greatly from state to state.

Figure 13.2 State Judicial System

SOURCE: American Bar Association. *Law and the Courts.* Chicago: American Bar Association, 1974, p.20. Updated information provided by West Publishing Company.

J. J. Senna and L. J. Siegel. *Introduction to Criminal Justice,* 7th ed. St. Paul, MN: West Publishing Company, 1996, p.387. Reprinted by permission. All rights reserved.

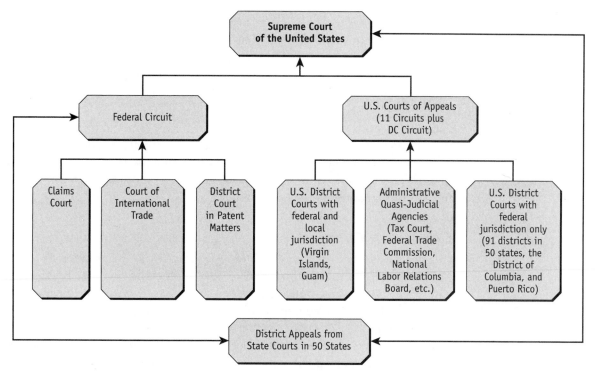

Figure 13.3 Federal Judicial System

SOURCE: American Bar Association. *Law and the Courts.* Chicago: American Bar Association, 1974, p.21. Updated information provided by the Federal Courts Improvement Act of 1982 and West Publishing Company.

J.J. Senna and L.J. Siegel. *Introduction to Criminal Justice,* 7th ed. St. Paul, MN: West Publishing Company, 1996, p.21. Reprinted by permission. All rights reserved.

Table 13.1 Supreme Court Justices in Order of Seniority

Name	Year of Birth	Home State	Year of Appointment	President	Senate Vote
William Rehnquist*	1924	Arizona	1971	Nixon	65–33
John Paul Stevens	1920	Illinois	1975	Ford	78–0
Sandra Day O'Connor	1930	Arizona	1981	Reagan	99–0
Antonin Scalia	1936	New York	1986	Reagan	98–0
Anthony Kennedy	1936	California	1988	Reagan	97–0
David Souter	1940	New Hampshire	1990	Bush	90–9
Clarence Thomas	1948	Georgia	1991	Bush	52–48
Ruth Bader Ginsburg	1933	New York	1993	Clinton	96–3
Stephen Breyer	1938	Massachusetts	1994	Clinton	87–9

*William Rehnquist was promoted from associate justice to chief justice in 1986.

SOURCE: David W. Neubauer. *America's Courts and the Criminal Justice System,* 6th ed. Belmont, CA: West/Wadsworth Publishing Company, 1999, p.457. Reprinted by permission.

precedent, commonly referred to as a landmark decision, which must be honored by all lower courts. The use of precedent in the legal system gives the Supreme Court power to influence and mold the everyday operating procedures of the police.

Specialized Courts

Specialized courts have developed to address specific criminal justice cases. It is hoped these alternatives to the traditional courtroom will dispense more equitable justice as applied to particular issues. Among the specialized courts are community courts, tribal courts, drug courts, gun courts, domestic violence courts, mental health courts and juvenile courts.

Community Courts

One recent alternative to the traditional courtroom is the community court. According to Clear and Cadora (2003, p.46): "Of the three main divisions of the criminal justice system—police, courts and corrections—the middle function, the courts, has the furthest conceptual distance to travel to become community oriented." Community courts are neighborhood based and seek to solve local problems. They bring together local resources and create problem-solving partnerships with community groups, government agencies and social service providers.

Feinblatt and Berman (2001, p.1) suggest: "Community courts are not effective when implemented as cookie-cutter models; to be effective, each must meet the needs of its neighborhood." They (p.2) outline six principles for community courts: "Bridging the gap between communities and courts, knitting together a fractured criminal justice system, helping offenders deal with problems that lead to crime, providing the courts with better information and building a courthouse that fosters these ambitions." They (p.4) note: "By definition, community courts embrace a variety of stakeholders, not only judges, police and prosecutors but tenant groups, victim organizations, businesses, schools and block associations as well."

Tribal Courts

A court system often overlooked is the tribal court, operated under the Department of the Interior. According to the National Tribal Justice Resource Center (2004):

> While each of the more than 560 federally recognized tribes in the U.S. possesses traditional methods of dispute resolution, formal court institutions are a relatively recent development in Indian Country. . . . It was not until 1934, with the passage of the Indian Reorganization Act, that tribes were encouraged by the federal government to enact their own laws and to establish their own justice systems. . . . Approximately 275 Indian nations and Alaska Native villages have established formal tribal court systems. There is widespread variety in the types of forums, and the law applied in each is distinctly unique to each tribe. Some tribal courts resemble Western-style judiciaries where written laws and rules of court procedure are applied. An increasing number of tribes are returning to their traditional means of resolving disputes through the use of peacemaking, elders' councils and sentencing circles.

The tribal court system includes trial and appellate courts, as well as specialized civil, criminal, family, healing and wellness, juvenile and drug courts. They hear cases pertaining to Native American law that affect both Native Americans and non-Native Americans living or operating a business within the jurisdiction of a Native American government.

Drug Courts

According to Harrison and Beck (2003, pp.10–11), drug offenders accounted for 20.4 percent of sentenced state inmates and 55 percent of sentenced federal inmates in 2001. To better handle the growing caseload of drug offenders, states have implemented drug courts. By providing drug treatment to offenders as soon as they enter the court system, instead of waiting until they have passed into the correctional component of criminal justice, drug courts have taken quite a different path from traditional court processes.

According to Harrell (2003, p.207): "The 14 years since the first drug court began operation in Miami have seen the number of drug courts grow exponentially, fueled by ardent practitioners and federal dollars." According to the OJP Drug Court Clearinghouse and Technical Assistance Project (2003), as of November 2003 there were 1,093 drug courts operating in all 50 states, the District of Columbia, Guam, Puerto Rico and 2 federal districts, plus another 414 drug court programs in the planning stages. Furthermore, data from the Tribal Court Clearinghouse indicates there were 30 fully operational tribal drug courts as of May 2003, with another 53 in the pilot or planning stages.

Drug courts are community-based courts designed to reflect community concerns and priorities, access community resources and seek community participation and support. Listwan et al. (2003, p.407), however, caution: "Drug courts are not a one-size-fits-all solution to the drug problem. Drug courts need to recognize that drug offenders have varying levels of needs and difficulties, which must be managed to reduce their criminal behavior."

Although the structure, scope and target populations of drug courts vary from one jurisdiction to another, the goals remain the same: to reduce recidivism and substance abuse and rehabilitate participants.

Gun Courts

Under the gun-court concept, one judge hears all gun cases from beginning to end. This judge makes all legal rulings, carries out all hearings and trials, and passes sentence on convicted offenders. A separate calendar is established for the gun cases. A successful gun court in Brooklyn, New York, led New York City Mayor Bloomberg to expand the program into Queens and the Bronx ("New York to Expand Gun Courts," 2003). Since the Brooklyn gun court began in April 2003, it tripled jail sentences from 14 percent to 44 percent, increased the median jail sentence from 90 days to one year and eliminated probation-only sentences for felony gun offenders. The gun court was also credited with reducing the number of shootings in the seven precincts it serves by 15 percent. According to Queens District Attorney Brown: "When criminals are afraid of carrying guns, the level of crime drops significantly. But unless those arrested are vigorously prosecuted and receive tough sentences when warranted, the law is meaningless."

Domestic Violence (DV) Courts

The first domestic violence court was established in Dade County, Florida, in 1992, and an estimated 300 such courts are in operation now. Ostrum (2003, p.105) suggests:

> The ideals of the specialized domestic violence court, with its focus on tailoring services to victims, enlisting community involvement and holding perpetrators accountable, are compelling. Specialized domestic violence courts tend to be based on principles and methods grounded in therapeutic jurisprudence. That is, these courts endeavor to move from the traditional adversarial process to a problem-solving orientation that places much more attention on the needs of the people involved, both victims and offenders, and in finding what is best for the community. In doing so, domestic violence courts seek to coordinate with medical, social services and treatment providers and establish special procedures and alternative sentencing options to promote effective outcomes.

Research by Gover et al. (2003, p.109) found: "Results indicate significantly lower rates of rearrests among defendants processed through the domestic violence court" (in Lexington County, South Carolina).

Mental Health Courts

Modeled after drug courts, mental health courts practice therapeutic jurisprudence, often altering the traditional dynamics of the courtroom. For example, in some courts prosecutors and defense lawyers come together to discuss their common goals for each defendant.

Denckla and Berman (2001, p.4) note: "Mentally ill individuals with a criminal record are often placed in a lose-lose situation. While incarcerated, their condition tends to worsen. And upon release, they are often unable to access available community treatment because of providers' reluctance to treat them. Many community mental health centers are unprepared or unwilling to treat people who have criminal records. The results are painfully clear; many defendants with mental illness churn through the criminal justice system again and again, going through a "revolving door" from street to court to cell and back again without ever receiving the support and services they need. It is fair to say that no one wins when this happens—not defendants, not police, not courts, not victims and not communities." Mental health courts seek to change this situation.

Law Enforcement News ("Mental Health Courts Are Catching on Like Crazy," 2002, p.7) reports: "Mental health courts have been springing up around the country since the first one was created in Broward County, Florida, in 1997." The article notes that the Justice Department will award up to $150,000 in grants over a two-year period to 20 pilot programs. Mental health courts are too new to have research support, but preliminary responses from those involved with such courts are positive.

Juvenile Courts

 Historically juvenile courts have been informal, private, nonadversary systems that stress rehabilitation rather than punishment of youths.

Juvenile courts try to secure care and guidance for each minor under the court's jurisdiction. Laws relating to juveniles try to preserve and strengthen family ties whenever possible, removing minors from parental custody only when the minor's welfare or safety or protection of the public cannot be adequately safeguarded without such removal. Juvenile court also has jurisdiction over neglected and dependent children and over those who encourage, cause or contribute to a child's delinquency.

Juvenile courts vary from state to state, but most begin with some sort of intake, which usually begins as a **petition**—a document alleging a juvenile is a delinquent, status offender or dependent and asking the court to assume jurisdiction of the child. It is the formal process for bringing a matter before the juvenile court. Often the petition originates with a law enforcement agency, but it can come from another source. The intake or initial screening is usually controlled and supervised by the juvenile court.

At the *adjudication hearing* (comparable to the preliminary hearing in the adult system) the youth is questioned about the alleged offense. If the evidence is insufficient, the petition may be dismissed. If enough evidence exists that the child is delinquent, a court date is set for the disposition hearing (comparable to the trial in the adult system).

At the *disposition hearing*, the judge has several alternatives. Based on the findings of the investigation, the judge may place the youth on probation or in a foster home, release the child to the parents, commit the child to an institution or make the child a ward of the court. Serious juvenile offenders may be committed to mental institutions, reformatories, prisons, and county and state schools for delinquents. Some cities, such as New York and Chicago, have set up youth courts that are adult courts using the philosophy of juvenile courts. These youth courts usually confine their hearings to misdemeanors. The usual sequence of events within the juvenile court is illustrated in Figure 13.4.

Waiver to Adult Court   When juveniles commit a series of serious crimes or a single particularly violent crime, juvenile courts can declare them to be under the jurisdiction of the adult (criminal) court. This **judicial waiver** allows juvenile court judges to transfer cases based on a juvenile's age, type of offense, prior record and dangerousness. Such juveniles are then charged and required to appear in adult criminal court. The age at which youths come under the jurisdiction of the criminal courts varies from state to state, ranging from age 16 to 19.

Juvenile Drug Courts   Like the adult court, the juvenile court also has a drug court component. According to Cooper (2001, p.1): "Juvenile drug courts are intensive treatment programs that provide specialized services for drug-involved youths and their families." Cooper (p.1) notes that since their inception in 1995, more than 140 juvenile drug courts have been established in the United States, and more than 125 are currently being planned. She (p.13) concludes: "Measured by indicators such as recidivism, drug use and educational achievement, juvenile drug courts appear to hold significant promise." Another approach to dealing with juveniles who enter into the juvenile justice system is the Teen Court Program.

Teen Court Programs   Teen Courts, also called Youth Courts and Peer Courts, are designed to address a variety of youthful problem behaviors, such as underage drinking, substance abuse, truancy and related offenses. The goal is to help

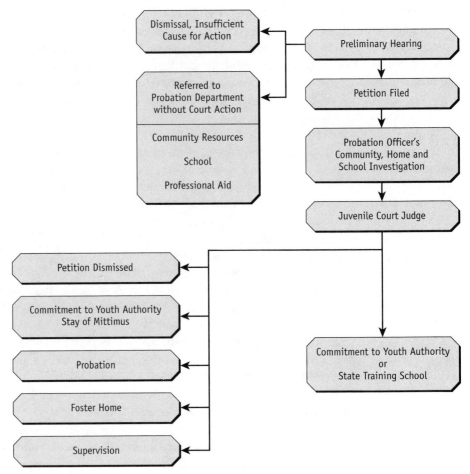

Figure 13.4 Juvenile Court Responsibility

SOURCE: Reprinted by permission of the International Association of Chiefs of Police.

youths to pursue a path leading to their becoming more responsible, productive citizens. Goodwin et al. (n.d., p.49) describe the Teen Court Program as a "community-based intervention/prevention program designed to provide an alternative response for the juvenile justice system for first-time, nonviolent, misdemeanor juvenile offenders, in which community youths determine the appropriate sanctions for the offender. The program will hold youthful offenders accountable and provide educational services to offenders and youth volunteers in an effort to promote long-term behavioral change that leads to enhanced public safety."

Having looked at the organizational structures of our various court systems, next turn your attention to a concept on which our entire criminal justice system rests: the adversary system.

The Adversary System

Our criminal justice system is based on an **adversary system**—the accuser versus the accused.

 Our adversary criminal justice system requires the accuser to prove beyond a reasonable doubt to a judge or jury that the accused is guilty of a specified crime.

Table 13.2 Evidentiary Standards of Proofs—Degrees of Certainty

Standard	Definition	Where Used
Absolute certainty	No possibility of error; 100 percent certainty	Not used in civil or criminal law
Beyond reasonable doubt; moral certainty	Conclusive and complete proof, without leaving any reasonable doubt as to the guilt of the defendant; allowing the defendant the benefit of any possibility of innocence	Criminal trial
Clear and convincing evidence	Prevailing and persuasive to the trier of fact	Civil commitments, insanity defense
Preponderance of evidence	Greater weight of evidence in terms of credibility; more convincing than an opposite point of view	Civil trial
Probable cause	U.S. constitutional standard for arrest and search warrants, requiring existence of facts sufficient to warrant that a crime has been committed	Arrest, preliminary hearing, motions
Sufficient evidence	Adequate evidence to reverse a trial court	Appellate review
Reasonable suspicion	Rational, reasonable belief that facts warrant investigation of a crime on less than probable cause	Police investigations
Less than probable cause	Mere suspicion; less than reasonable to conclude criminal activity exists	Prudent police investigation where safety of an officer or others is endangered

SOURCE: J. J. Senna and L. J. Siegel. *Introduction to Criminal Justice,* 9th ed. Belmont, CA: Wadsworth Publishing Company, 2002, p.391. Reprinted by permission. All rights reserved.

Presumption of innocence means that the accused is assumed innocent until proof to the contrary is clearly established. On the side of the accused are the defendant and the defense attorney. On the side of the accuser is the citizen (or victim), the prosecutor and the police officer. They bear the burden of proof.

An impartial judge or jury hears both sides of the controversy and then reaches a decision as to whether the accuser has proven the accused guilty beyond a **reasonable doubt,** explained as: "The state of mind of jurors when they do not feel a moral certainty about the truth of the charges and when the evidence does not exclude every other reasonable hypothesis except that the defendant is guilty as charged" (Neubauer, 2002, p.521). Reasonable doubt is a more stringent evidentiary standard than that required in a civil trial, where a mere **preponderance of the evidence** is standard. This standard simply means it is more likely than not, based on the bulk of the evidence, that the plaintiff's version of the case holds up. Table 13.2 illustrates the various evidentiary standards of proof or degrees of certainty required in varying circumstances.

Key Players in the Judicial Process

 Key players in the judicial process include the defendant, prosecutor, defense attorney, judge and jury.

The Defendant

Everyone, including a person suspected of committing a crime, has certain rights that must be protected at all stages of the criminal justice process. Defendants have all the rights set forth in the Bill of Rights. They may waive these rights, but if they do, the waiver should be in writing because proof of the waiver is up to the police officer or the prosecution. The police officer must be able to show that all rights have been respected and that all required procedures have been complied with.

The Fifth Amendment guarantees due process: notice of a hearing, full information regarding the charges made, the opportunity to present evidence before an impartial judge or jury and the right to refrain from self-incrimination. The Sixth Amendment establishes the requirements for criminal trials, including the right to a speedy public trial by an impartial jury and the right to have a lawyer. The Eighth Amendment forbids excessive bail and implies the right to such bail in most instances.

The criminal justice system is sometimes criticized when a defendant is found not guilty because of a technicality. Even though a person confesses to a hideous crime, if he or she was not first told of his or her rights and allowed to have a lawyer present during questioning, the confession is not legal. As noted by the Supreme Court in *Escobedo v. Illinois* (1964):

> No system of criminal justice can or should survive if it comes to depend for its continued effectiveness on the citizens' abdication through unawareness of their constitutional rights. No system worth preserving should have a fear that if an accused is permitted to consult with a lawyer, he will become aware of and exercise these rights. If the exercise of constitutional rights will thwart the effectiveness of a system of law enforcement, then there is something very wrong with that system.

Racial Minorities in Court   Walker et al. (2004, p.147) state: "Racial minorities are at a disadvantage in court both because of their race and because they are more likely than whites to be poor. This 'double jeopardy' makes it more difficult for minority defendants to obtain competent attorneys or secure release from jail prior to trial. This, in turn, hinders their defense and may increase the odds that they will be convicted and sentenced harshly." Walker et al. (p.145) also state: "Racial minorities, and particularly those suspected of crimes against whites, remain the victims of unequal justice." They (p.172) report: "There is evidence that defendant race/ethnicity continues to affect decisions regarding bail, charging and plea bargaining. Some evidence suggests that race has a direct and obvious effect on these pretrial decisions; other evidence suggests that the effect of race is indirect and subtle." However, their (pp.197–198) overall conclusion is somewhat more heartening:

> We conclude that contemporary court processing decisions are not characterized by *systematic* discrimination against racial minorities. . . .
>
> We are not suggesting that contemporary court processing decisions reflect *pure justice.* Researchers have demonstrated that court processing decisions in some jurisdictions reflect racial discrimination whereas decisions in other jurisdictions are racially neutral. Researchers have also shown that African Americans and Hispanics who commit certain types of crimes are treated more harshly than whites, and that being unemployed, having a prior criminal record or being detained prior to trial may have a more negative effect on court outcomes for people of color than for whites.
>
> These findings lead us to conclude that discrimination against African Americans and other racial minorities is not universal but is confined to certain types of cases, certain types of settings and certain types of defendants. We conclude that the court system of today is characterized by *contextual discrimination.*

The Prosecutor

A prosecutor is an official elected to exercise leadership in representing the government and, hence, the people in the criminal justice system. Prosecutors may be city, county, state, commonwealth or district attorneys or solicitors. They are usually elected to a two- or four-year term at the state level. At the federal level, they are appointed by the president.

Cole et al. (p.169) note: "Prosecutors are powerful because they are concerned with, and have some input in, many parts in the machine of criminal justice. . . . The prosecutor chooses the cases to be prosecuted, selects the charges that are to be brought into the courtroom, recommends the bail amount required for pretrial release, approves any negotiated agreements made with the defendant and urges judges to impose particular sentences."

As the legal representatives of the people and law enforcement, prosecutors are responsible to the people who elected them. They determine law enforcement priorities and are key in determining how much, how little and what types of crimes the public will tolerate. They serve the public interest and consider the public's need to feel secure, its sense of how justice should be carried out and the community's attitude toward certain crimes. Sometimes a case becomes so well publicized that the prosecutor is forced to "do something about it" or face defeat in the next election.

Prosecutors are also the legal advisors for police officers; they decide what cases should be prosecuted and how. They rely heavily on police officers' input in determining if a case should be brought to court. Often, however, misunderstanding and even ill will results when a prosecutor refuses a police officer's request for a complaint because of insufficient evidence or some violation of a criminal procedure, such as an illegal arrest. Plea bargaining may also cause ill will between a prosecutor and a police officer.

Because both police officers and prosecutors are striving for the same end—justice—they should be familiar with each other's problems. Police officers, for example, should understand what the prosecutor can and cannot do, which types of cases are worth prosecuting and the need for and advantages of plea bargaining in certain situations. Prosecutors, on the other hand, should be sensitive to the police officers' objections to legal technicalities and excessive paperwork and should include police officers in plea bargaining when possible or, at the least, inform them when such bargaining has occurred.

Prosecutors perform one other critical function in the criminal justice process. They are responsible for protecting the rights of all involved, including the suspect. In essence they have a dual responsibility. On the one hand, they are the leaders in the law enforcement community, the elected representatives of the public and the legal advisors to the police. On the other hand, they are expected to protect the rights of persons accused of crimes. In *Berger v. United States* (1935), Justice Sutherland defined the prosecutor's responsibility as being "the representative not of an ordinary party to a controversy, but of a sovereignty whose obligation to govern impartially is as compelling as its obligation to govern at all; and whose interest, therefore, in a criminal prosecution is not that it shall win a case, but that justice shall be done."

 Prosecutors have the dual function of leading the law enforcement community while at the same time protecting the rights of the accused.

Community Prosecution   Some prosecutors are also teaming up with citizens in the overall community justice movement. Swope (2001, p.11) has referred to community prosecution as the "missing link" and states: "The police are only the gatekeepers [to the justice system], and the law enforcement effort really has no teeth without the support of the prosecutor. . . . Community policing can never reach its full potential without the inclusion of the prosecutor as a full partner, joining the police and neighborhood residents."

This collaboration is also stressed by Boland (2001, p.38): "Because effective crime control is a joint effort, prosecutors need to ask other key actors, most importantly citizens and police, what they think they are getting from community prosecution. The best answers to these questions lie not in citywide random surveys, but in the police beats where the crime issue is defined in terms that are specific and concrete." According to Goldkamp et al. (2002, p.1): "Community prosecution initiatives put into practice the belief that crime problems are best prevented and solved when community members work with prosecutors and the police."

The Defense Attorney

The defense attorney represents the accused in court. Lawyers who represent the accused have the same duties and obligations whether privately retained, serving as a legal aid in the system or appointed by the court. They investigate the circumstances of the cases and explore facts relevant to their clients' guilt or innocence. They try to uncover evidence for their clients' defenses and organize the cases to present in court.

The majority of criminal cases are assigned to public defenders or to a few private lawyers who handle such cases. Public defenders are full- and part-time lawyers hired by the state or county government to represent people who cannot afford to hire a lawyer. Many lawyers donate time to represent the indigent, called *pro bono* work. Many others, however, are reluctant to do so.

Judges

Although most people think of trial judges when they hear the word *judge,* many different kinds of judges exist. In fact if a person comes to trial, he or she will already have encountered certain levels of the court system and judges acting within that system. The various types of judges and the functions they serve depend on the court to which they are appointed.

Judges have many important functions throughout the entire judicial process and can exercise great discretion by accepting or rejecting pleas, deciding in preliminary hearings if evidence is sufficient to justify prosecution or dismissing the charges; determining whether to grant bail, and if so, how much; deciding whether to grant delays; presiding over the trial; giving the jury instructions; and imposing the sentence if a defendant is found guilty. Judicial discretion, however, can also lead to a significant amount of sentencing disparity.

Having looked at the nature of the adversary system and most of the key players, now consider the critical steps normally involved in the criminal justice process.

Critical Stages in the Criminal Justice Process

The criminal justice process consists of the steps that occur between and including the filing of a complaint through the acquittal or sentencing of an offender. At various points along the way, a case may be dismissed, as illustrated in Figure 13.5.

 The criminal justice process consists of several critical stages: the complaint or charge, the warrant, arrest, booking, plea bargaining, preliminary hearing, grand jury hearing, the arraignment, the trial and sentencing.

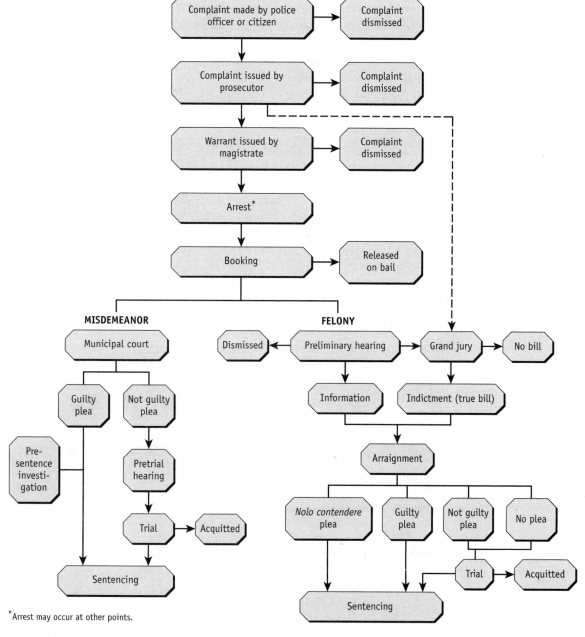

*Arrest may occur at other points.

Figure 13.5 The Criminal Justice Process from Complaint to Disposition

Usually the criminal justice process begins when a police officer or a citizen approaches the prosecutor to obtain a complaint. A **complaint,** also called the charge, is a legal document drawn up by a prosecutor that specifies the alleged crime and the supporting facts providing probable cause.

The police officer or citizen then presents the complaint to a judge and, in the judge's presence, swears to the accuracy of the content of the complaint and signs a statement to that effect. If the judge concurs with the charge, he or she grants an arrest warrant ordering the police to arrest the suspect.

The arrest may occur at several points throughout the criminal justice process. For example, it may have occurred without a complaint or warrant if the crime was committed in the presence of the arresting officer. The prosecutor also may choose to present the case to a grand jury for indictment before arresting a suspect.

After suspects are taken into custody, they are booked at the police station; that is, they are formally entered into the police records system. The suspect is photographed and fingerprinted. The prints are placed on file with the FBI in Washington, DC, and the suspect has a police arrest record.

Bail and Writ of Habeas Corpus

Usually one right of the accused is the right to be released from custody. Not only is this essential to the accused's immediate freedom, but it is in keeping with the premise that a person is innocent until proven guilty. After the formal booking process is completed, the suspect is usually entitled to be *released* on bail or on his or her *personal recognizance* (**R.P.R.d**) if the crime is a misdemeanor or released on a **writ of habeas corpus** or bond if the crime is a felony.

The judge decides how much bail is reasonable as a deposit to bring the defendant into court if released. Some defendants use a person or company that pays the bail for the defendant for an additional fee, typically a percentage of the amount of bail. Many argue that bail bonding discriminates against poor defendants and allows wealthy defendants to buy their way out of jail.

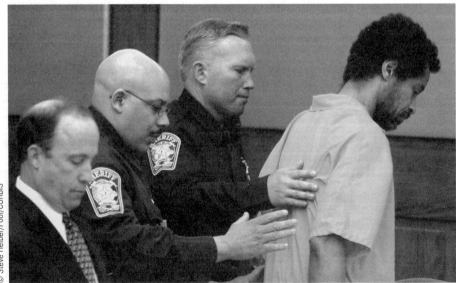

Convicted Beltway sniper Allen Muhammad is escorted out of court by two Prince William County (Virginia) sheriffs' deputies as his attorney stands by. Muhammad was convicted and sentenced to death.

Periodically a person in jail may be released on a **writ of habeas corpus**—a legal court order literally meaning "bring forth the body you have"—which commands that a person being held be brought forth immediately. This means of determining whether the jailing of the suspect is legal is used primarily when the justice process moves slowly and a prisoner is detained for an unreasonable time before the court appearance. Most states have guidelines as to how long a person may be jailed before being charged, released or making a court appearance. These guidelines range from 36 to 72 hours, taking into consideration Sundays and holidays.

Plea Bargaining

The client and defense lawyer may also try to plea bargain their case. **Plea bargaining** is legal negotiation between the prosecutor and the defense lawyer or the client to reach an agreement that avoids a court trial, conserving time and expense. According to Cole et al. (p.171): "For the overwhelming majority of cases, plea bargaining is the most important step in the criminal justice process. Very few cases go to trial; instead, a negotiated guilty plea developed through the interactions of prosecutors, defense lawyers and judges determines what will finally happen to most criminal defendants. It is generally accepted that up to 90 percent of felony defendants in the United States plead guilty."

Basically plea bargaining involves compromises and promises. From the prosecutor it might mean that if a series of charges had been filed, the defendant would be charged with only one; the other charges would be dismissed. It also might mean the prosecutor would reduce a charge if only one charge had been filed. A charge of burglary might be reduced to breaking and entering, which carries a lesser penalty.

A hazard of plea bargaining is that it makes police officers feel left out. Often officers will ask about a case only to find it has been disposed of in plea bargaining. As criminals are placed back into society, the police officers' problems in dealing with crime grow. If police officers are to deal with these problems, they should be consulted.

The Preliminary Hearing

In the **preliminary hearing**, the judge determines whether probable cause exists for believing that an offense has been committed and that the accused committed it. Most statutes and rules of criminal procedure require a preliminary hearing to be held within a "reasonable time."

 The preliminary hearing seeks to establish probable cause to prevent persons from being indiscriminately brought to trial.

The judge in a preliminary hearing is not bound by the rules of evidence that ordinarily control a trial. The prosecutor need only establish probable cause, not prove beyond a reasonable doubt that the crime was committed.

In reality the preliminary hearing is often a minitrial where the defense obtains as much information as possible to strengthen its case. Both prosecution and defense often use this stage of the criminal justice process for tactical purposes. In some instances overwhelming evidence may lead to a guilty plea or to a request for plea bargaining.

The **discovery process** requires that all pertinent facts on both sides be made available before the trial. Used properly the discovery process reduces questions of probable cause and other questions normally brought out in a preliminary hearing and encourages more final dispositions before trial, thereby saving court time. Available to both the prosecution and defense attorneys, it eliminates surprise as a legitimate trial tactic. The outcome of a preliminary hearing may be to (1) dismiss the charges, (2) present an information and bind the defendant over to a higher court or (3) send the case to a grand jury.

The Grand Jury

The U.S. Constitution requires an indictment by a federal grand jury before trial for most crimes against federal law. The consideration of a felony charge by a grand jury is not a trial. Only the prosecution's evidence is usually presented and considered. Contrary to the popular portrayal of grand juries on television and in movies, suspected offenders are usually not heard nor are their lawyers present to offer evidence on their behalf.

A grand jury meets in secret sessions and hears from witnesses to and victims of a crime. Like a preliminary hearing, it determines only whether enough evidence exists to accuse a person of a crime. In some states, by statute, a grand jury can hear evidence from suspects. However, the person being considered for indictment must sign a waiver of immunity and agree to answer all questions even though the testimony might be incriminating and may be used against them in a criminal trial. Their lawyers are not allowed to be present.

After the grand jury receives all testimony and evidence, it deliberates. If the majority of the grand jurors (or a specified number) agree that the person is guilty of a crime, they instruct the prosecutor to prepare an indictment specifying all the facts of the case. Grand juries may also issue what is called a **no bill,** meaning the jurors believe there is no criminal violation.

The Coroner's Jury

Coroners investigate violent deaths where suspicion of foul play exists. By law coroners may conduct autopsies as to the cause of death, and they may conduct inquests. The coroner's jury usually consists of six members. In some states the coroner's jury system has been abandoned and its functions performed by a professional medical examiner.

The Arraignment

When defendants are charged with a felony, they must personally appear at an **arraignment.** As in the preliminary hearing, they are entitled to counsel. The procedures of the arraignment vary by state, but generally defendants appear before the court, are read the complaint, information or indictment, and if they have not received a copy, they are given one. They then enter a plea.

Defendants have several alternatives when they appear for the formal arraignment. **Standing mute,** that is, refusing to answer, is entered by the judge as a not guilty plea. *Nolo contendere* means "no contest." By entering a plea of *nolo contendere,* defendants, in effect, throw themselves on the court's mercy. A *guilty plea* means the accused admits the charge or a lesser charge agreed to in plea bargaining. *Not guilty* means the accused denies the charge. Some states require defendants to automatically plead not guilty to such capital crimes as first-degree murder.

If defendants plead guilty or *nolo contendere,* a sentencing time is set. Usually a presentence investigation is ordered to determine if probation is warranted. If defendants make no plea or plead not guilty, they have the choice of a trial by a judge or by a jury. If defendants wish a jury trial, the case is assigned to the court docket and a date set. Before looking at the trial itself, next consider some alternatives to a trial.

Alternatives to a Trial—Diversion

 Before cases go to court, defense attorneys may explore the possibility of diverting the case from the criminal justice system by using a community agency.

For example in cases of mental incompetence, an attorney may seek to divert the case to a mental institution. **Diversion** is a discretionary decision that can occur at many points as the case progresses through the criminal justice process. For example a police officer diverts when he or she assumes custody of an intoxicated person and releases that person to the custody of family or a detoxification center. Likewise a prosecutor who delays prosecution while a defendant participates in psychiatric treatment diverts. In both cases a discretionary decision is made that there is a more appropriate way to deal with the defendant than to prosecute.

As might be expected, diversion has its opponents. Some feel this is "letting criminals off easy." However, major benefits can result, including saving court time; avoiding the stigma of conviction, particularly for first-time offenders; providing treatment for offenders whose criminal activity is the result of an addiction or disorder; allowing offenders to pay society back through community service or other work programs; and easing overcrowding in correctional facilities by leaving room for the truly violent and dangerous offenders.

The Trial

The trial is the climax in the criminal justice procedure. How well the police have investigated the case, compiled evidence and reported it, and dealt with the victim and witnesses are weighed in the courtroom. The trial also tests how well the prosecutor prepared the case.

The key figures in the trial are the judge, members of the jury, the defendant and defense attorney(s), the prosecuting attorney(s), police officer(s) and witnesses. The judge has charge of the trial and decides all matters with respect to the law. He or she also assures that all rules of trial procedure are followed.

The jury—people selected by law and sworn to examine the facts and determine the truth—decides all matters of fact. The trial begins with the jury selection. Before a jury can be assembled, the geographic location of the trial, called the **venue,** must be determined. A trial's venue is usually the same area in which the offense occurred. However, if a case has received such extensive publicity that picking an impartial jury from the local population is impossible, the trial may be moved to another part of the state, a process called a change of venue.

Jury Selection

Safeguards built into the jury selection process not only protect the defendant's rights but also assure the public that justice is done. Trial jurors are selected at random from voting or motor vehicle records or telephone directories by district or superior court judges or the commissioners of the county board. The defense attorney and then the prosecuting attorney question each person as to his or her qualifications to be a juror in this case. The judge may also question the prospective jurors. The random selection of potential jurors and the careful questioning of each, called *voir dire,* helps ensure selection of 6 or 12 fair and impartial jurors.

Some critics of the present jury system claim that our legal system has gotten too complex for the average person to render a fair decision. Many advocate replacing the present system with a three-judge tribunal.

Testimony

After the jury is selected and instructed by the judge, opening statements are presented. The prosecutor informs the jury of the state's case and how he or she intends to prove the charges against the defendant. The defense lawyer makes an opening statement in support of the accused or may waive this opening statement.

The prosecutor then presents evidence and the witness testimony, attempting to prove a crime has been committed and that the defendant did it. Through **cross-examination** the defense attorney tries to discredit prosecution witnesses, the evidence and the testimony of the police officers.

The Police Officer in Court   Almost all officers have a day in court. Because of overloaded court dockets, cases usually come up well after the officers' investigations; therefore officers must refer to their reports and their original notes to refresh their memories. A court appearance is an important part of any police officer's duty. All elements of the investigation are brought together at this point: the report, the statements of the witnesses, the evidence collected and possibly even a confession.

The prosecution needs to establish the elements of the crime by testimony of witnesses, physical evidence, documents, recordings or other admissible evidence. This information usually comes from police officers, their recollections, notes and reports. The prosecutor works with police officers in presenting the arguments for the prosecution.

According to Gil-Blanco (2001, p.74), police officers testify in approximately 90 percent of criminal cases brought to trial, and officers may be subpoenaed hundreds of times during their careers. In Gil-Blanco's survey of 78 San Jose police officers and sergeants, 52 percent said they had been subpoenaed in the range of 100 to 300 times; four officers reported being subpoenaed over 1,000 times (p.76). Thirty-eight percent reported having given "general" testimony 1 to 20 times, and 33 percent reported having given "general" testimony 100 to 300 times. In contrast, 70 percent reported having provided "expert" testimony 1 to 20 times; 4 percent reported having provided "expert" testimony 100 to 300 times.

Gil-Blanco (p.78) stresses: "The ability to present expert testimony persuasively is an essential skill every officer or investigator must have." In effect: "Whenever an officer gets on the stand, he or she is the subject of inquisition. Not only is that officer expected to know all the aspects of their case, they are also expected to know the law and to be above reproach. The officer is on 'stage' and expected to give vital and important information to their 'audience.' The testimony the officer gives is vital to a case and will not be available from other professional sources" (p.77). It is important for officers testifying in court to establish that they are experts by documenting their specialized training, experience and expertise (Kalk, 2001, p.39).

Attorney General John Ashcroft announced on December 11, 2001,
the first indictment of a key figure in the September 11, 2001,
attacks—six conspiracy charges against Zacarias Moussaoui, who
has been held as a material witness. Moussaoui, a French citizen of
Moroccan descent, faces the death penalty on four of the charges.
He will be tried in a federal court and not a military tribunal as
established by President George W. Bush. Moussaoui is shown in
this undated police photograph.

On the opposing side is the defense attorney, who uses several techniques to sway the jury away from the prosecution's argument. In a criminal case, the defense rarely expects to gain helpful information from police officers. The main intent is usually to discredit officers or their testimony.

 The defense attorney may try to confuse or discredit a police officer by (1) rapid-fire questioning, (2) establishing that the officer wants to see the defendant found guilty, (3) accusing the officer of making assumptions or (4) implying that the officer does not want anyone else to know what is in his or her notes.

An example of a defense team able to discredit a police officer was seen in the O. J. Simpson trial when defense attorneys were able to call into serious question the testimony given by former Los Angeles Police Department Detective Mark Fuhrman, in fact causing him to assert his Fifth Amendment right against self-incrimination.

Closing Statements and Jury Deliberation

After all testimony has been given, the jury hears the closing statements—a contest in persuasion first by the prosecution, stating that the jury should render a guilty verdict, then by the defense attorney, concluding that the client is surely innocent or at least not proven guilty beyond a reasonable doubt.

After the closing statements, the judge reads the instructions to the jury. This includes an explanation of the crime, what elements constitute the crime, alternate charges and the concepts of presumption of innocence and reasonable doubt. The jurors then retire behind closed doors to deliberate their findings.

© Reuters NewMedia Inc./CORBIS

They can return one of three findings: guilty, not guilty or no verdict. No verdict simply means that no agreement can be reached; this is also sometimes known as a **hung jury.**

After the jury has come to a decision, the judge is notified and the jury returns to the courtroom. With everyone present the jury foreman announces the verdict. Jurors may then be polled as to how each voted and asked if the verdict read by the foreman is the verdict of the juror. If the finding is guilty, the defendant may either be sentenced immediately or may be given a sentencing date. If found not guilty, he or she is set free. If a hung jury results, the defendant may be retried at the prosecutor's discretion.

Sentencing

Sentences for people convicted of crimes vary considerably from lenient to extremely severe penalties, from probation to many years in prison or even death. In many jurisdictions the court has the authority to set, within limits established by state statute, both maximum and minimum sentences. Judges have a host of intermediate choices available, as shown in Figure 13.6.

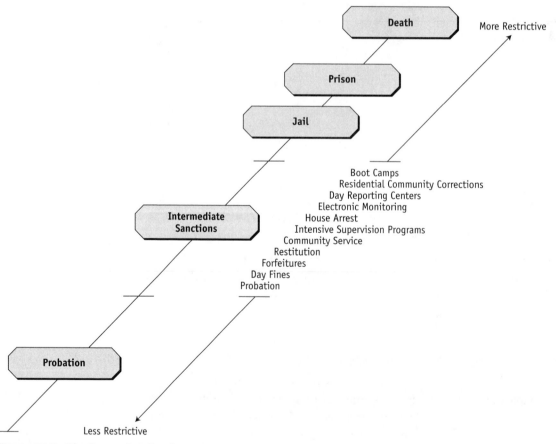

Figure 13.6 The Sentencing Continuum

SOURCE: Norman A. Carlson, Kären M. Hess and Christine M. H. Orthmann. *Corrections in the 21st Century: A Practical Approach.* Belmont, CA: West/Wadsworth Publishing Company, 1999, p.101. Reprinted by permission.

Three-Strikes Laws, Mandatory Minimums and Truth-in-Sentencing

In the effort to crack down on crime and get tough on criminals, sentences for repeat offenders and those convicted of certain crimes have become tougher. One popular sentencing reform has been "three-strikes" laws, first enacted in California, which require judges to impose life sentences on offenders who commit their third felony. Yet another get-tough-on-crime reform is the mandatory minimum sentences for certain offenses, most notably drug and weapons offenses. Truth-in-sentencing laws aim to restrict or stop early release practices and keep offenders incarcerated for the duration of their sentences.

Such legislation, however, is being criticized for its inability to achieve the desired results and its significant contribution to prison overcrowding. Kovandzic et al. (2004, p.463) found: "In cities with three-strike laws, homicide rates increased on average 13 to 14 percent over the short term and 16 to 24 percent over the long term, compared to cities without the laws." They conclude: "Despite their public support and political popularity, policy makers should seriously consider repealing three-strike laws. They are simply not the panacea for the nation's violent crime and may actually exacerbate the most violent crime—homicide."

Ehlers et al. (2004) report on a 10-year study of California's three-strikes law, noting:

- The California prison population experienced a 22.6 percent increase.
- The three-strike population grew from 254 in 1994 to 7,234 in September 2003, a 2,709 percent increase.
- The second-strike population experienced a 747 percent increase.
- Fifty-seven percent of three-strikers were in prison for a nonviolent offense.

Mandatory minimums have also been blamed for filling up the nation's prisons with nonviolent offenders more in need of treatment than incarceration. Such sentencing schemes, however, are falling out of favor with many judges.

When combined with mandatory minimums, truth-in-sentencing laws nearly guarantee our country's correctional facilities will remain at or above capacity. Critics contend that by requiring a drug offender sentenced to 10 years to serve the entire 10-year sentence behind bars with no chance of parole, there is little incentive for inmates to reform, partake in treatment programs or even display "good behavior" as no hope exists that such efforts may lead to early release. Furthermore, such sentencing practices keep offenders isolated from society longer than may be necessary and, thus, might impede their reintegration into the community following their release.

Prison and Jail Inmates at Midyear 2003 (2004) notes: "The nation's prison population rose by more than 2.9 percent between midyear 2002 and midyear 2003, the largest increase in four years. And the local jail population increased by 3.9 percent during the same period. . . . Prisons are no longer a response to increasing crime, and crime does not respond to increasing prisons. The prison system just grows like a weed in the yard. Unless states take affirmative steps to reduce the number of people they incarcerate, incarceration rates will continue to grow."

Case Review and Appeal

To assure that justice is served, the court system provides for a judicial review of cases and for a person convicted to appeal the conviction in most instances. Once the sentence has been passed, the corrections component of the justice system—the final stage in the administration of U.S. criminal justice—takes over.

The Corrections System: An Overview

Corrections is that portion of the criminal justice system that carries out the court's orders. It deals with both juvenile and adult offenders and consists of probation and parole systems, as well as jails, prisons and community-based programs to rehabilitate offenders. Glaze (2003, p.1) reports: "The total federal, state and local adult correctional population—incarcerated or in the community—grew by 150,700 during 2002 to reach a new high of more than 6.7 million. About 3.1 percent of the U.S. adult population, or 1 in every 32 adults, were incarcerated or on probation or parole at year-end 2002."

Purposes of Corrections

Throughout history, society has dealt with lawbreakers in many ways and has emphasized different goals and methods to accomplish those goals. The pendulum has swung from seeking pure revenge to viewing criminals as being ill and in need of treatment. It has swung from very public punishment, such as floggings and hangings, to very private punishment, such as solitary confinement. As the pendulum swings, the primary purposes to be served by corrections also shift. No matter where emphasis is placed, however, corrections generally serves four basic, often overlapping, purposes.

 The primary purposes of corrections are retribution, deterrence, incapacitation and rehabilitation.

This simple statement belies the complexity of the issues. What purpose or purposes corrections should serve has been and continues to be the subject of heated debate.

Retribution is punishment for the sake of punishment. Retribution is also referred to as revenge, "just deserts" or "an eye for an eye." It assumes that offenders are responsible for their actions, that they chose to break the law and deserve to be punished. Recently retribution has come to include restitution.

Deterrence sees corrections as a way to prevent future criminal actions, a more functional, proactive view. Deterrence aimed at offenders is called **specific deterrence.** It tries to make the consequences of committing crime so severe that when offenders return to society, they will not commit crime. Deterrence that serves as an example to society of the consequences of crime is called **general deterrence.**

Incapacitation refers to making it impossible for offenders to commit further offenses. Incapacitation can take many forms. One of the earliest forms was banishment. Currently, the most common method of incapacitation is incarceration. While imprisoned a criminal is no longer a threat to society. The most extreme form of incapacitation is capital punishment.

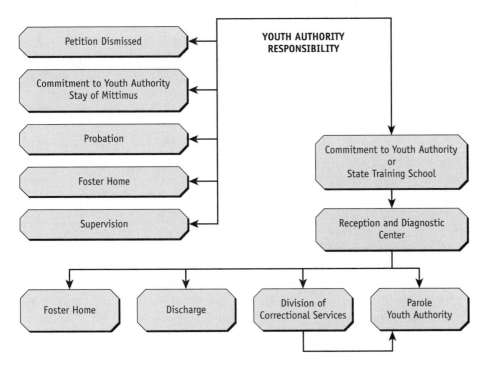

Figure 13.7   Youth Authority Responsibility

SOURCE: Reprinted by permission of the International Association of Chiefs of Police.

Rehabilitation sees the purpose of corrections to be clear from its name—to *correct* deviant behavior. Rehabilitation is proactive in that it focuses on the future needs of offenders, as well as the needs of the community to which the offenders may return. The problem of **recidivism,** or offenders returning to crime, raises questions about whether corrections can effectively rehabilitate offenders. Closely related to this purpose is the goal of reintegrating offenders into society as productive, law-abiding citizens.

Purposes of Juvenile Corrections

While these four correctional purposes also exist within the juvenile justice system, the primary focus of juvenile corrections has traditionally been, and continues to be, rehabilitation. In Figure 13.7 the various correctional avenues for juvenile offenders are shown, thus providing a sense of the emphasis placed on correcting deviant behavior in youths.

As noted, the courts have several sentencing alternatives for those convicted of crimes.

 Correctional alternatives include probation, intermediate sanctions, incarceration and, in some states, the death penalty. These same options exist for juvenile offenders, although probation is by far the most frequent disposition in juvenile delinquency cases.

Probation

A person found guilty of a crime may be placed on probation, the least restrictive and most common alternative to a jail or prison sentence. The American Correctional Association (ACA) defines **probation** as "a court-ordered disposition alternative through which an adjudicated offender is placed under the control, supervision, and care of a probation field staff member in lieu of imprisonment, so long as the probationer meets certain standards of conduct." A major benefit of probation is that it allows offenders to remain in the community, able to maintain important family ties and fulfill vital work, family and community obligations.

Who Gets Probation?

The court considers the presentence investigation (PSI) report and state statutes in determining if an offender should be put on probation, but some statutes involving mandatory sentences preclude the option. Probation is most often used with first-time offenders, property offenders, low-risk offenders and nonviolent offenders, such as those convicted of white-collar crimes. Probation operates on a "second-chance" philosophy. Consequently if a person is convicted a second time for a crime, that person is very unlikely to receive probation.

Probation is also the most widely used correctional alternative for juveniles, and over half of all adjudicated youths receive this sentence. The main goal of probation is rehabilitation with secondary goals of (1) protecting the community, (2) making juvenile offenders accountable and (3) providing youthful offenders with skills needed to live productively and responsibly in the community.

According to Glaze (p.1) in 2002, 3,995,165 individuals were on probation, an increase of 63,434 probationers or a 1.6 percent increase since 2001. Fifty percent of all probationers had been convicted of a felony, 49 percent of a misdemeanor and 1 percent of other infractions.

Conditions of Probation

Conditions of probation vary depending on the nature of the offense and the court's goals. The general purpose of probation is to help offenders maintain law-abiding behavior. Some courts are more treatment oriented in assigning conditions, whereas other courts are more punitive. One universal condition for all probationers is to obey the law. Other conditions may include adherence to a program of supervision, maintaining steady employment or refraining from engaging in a specific employment or occupation, completing prescribed educational or vocational training, meeting family responsibilities, staying away from certain types of people or places, performing community service and making restitution.

Partnerships between Law Enforcement and Probation Services

A constant theme throughout this text has been the importance of partnerships between entities within the criminal justice field, as well as partnerships between such agencies and the communities and individuals they serve. This vital relationship also extends to law enforcement and probation services. One way police and probation professionals build rapport and understanding is to participate in ride-along programs with each other.

The Growing Use of Probation

The first state to implement a formal probation program was Massachusetts in 1878. By 1927 juvenile probation programs were operating in every state, but it was not until 1957 that every state was providing similar services for adult offenders.

Probation is the fastest-growing sentencing alternative in the United States. The increased use of this disposition has led to an overload on the probation system and has fueled the increasing demand for an effective network of diversionary community-based programs known as intermediate sanctions. Often standard probation is combined with forms of intermediate punishment to increase the level of punishment and restriction imposed on the offender.

Intermediate Sanctions/Community Corrections

Intermediate sanctions, also called *community corrections,* exist along a continuum of increasing control and are tougher than traditional probation but less restrictive and costly than imprisonment (recall Figure 13.6). As Cole et al. (p.310) note: "Since the early nineteenth century, supervision in the community has been recognized as an appropriate punishment for some offenders." Community corrections includes any activities in the community aimed at helping offenders become law-abiding citizens and requires a complicated interplay among judicial and correctional personnel from related public and private agencies, citizen volunteers and civic groups. Probation, as just discussed, is the oldest community-based correctional program and provides a foundation on which to build a wide range of community-based services. The use of control and surveillance is basic to a sound community corrections system.

Day fines are based on an offender's daily income and differ from straight fines in that the judge considers not only the nature of the crime but also the offender's ability to pay. Day fines, while not particularly severe, do appear to provide effective punishment and deterrence while allowing the offender to remain in the community, able to tend to family needs.

Forfeiture, like day fines, imposes a financial penalty on offenders. However while fines are currency-based penalties, forfeiture involves seizing an offender's illegally used or acquired property or assets. Forfeiture is usually an add-on punishment used in conjunction with another sentence.

Restitution has become an increasingly common criminal sanction, often imposed as a condition of probation, whereby an offender reimburses a victim, most often with money though occasionally with services. The three goals of **restitution** are to (1) punish and rehabilitate offenders, (2) deter future crimes and (3) provide compensation to victims.

Community service, like restitution, is usually imposed not as a sole penalty but as a condition of probation. Community service often requires the offender to perform unpaid labor to pay a debt to society, with assignments ranging from cleaning litter along roadsides, to janitorial work in churches or schools, to building parks and playgrounds, repairing public housing and serving as a volunteer in a hospital or rehab center.

Intensive supervision programs (ISPs), also called *intensive supervised probation,* involve more supervision and greater restrictions than standard probation. They emphasize offender control and surveillance rather than treatment and rehabilitation. Although no single specific model exists for ISPs, common elements found in the various programs across the country include frequent personal contacts between the probation officer and the offender; strict enforcement of conditions, such as curfews and random drug and alcohol testing; fulfillment of restitution and community service obligations; mandatory employment; participation in treatment programs or educational classes; routine checks of local and state arrest records; and house arrest and electronic monitoring. Interestingly, several studies have found that the increased supervision and surveillance involved in ISPs leads to increased levels of probation violations (Giblin, 2002, p.116). This suggests the more one looks for something, the more likely it is one will find it.

House arrest, also known as *home confinement* or *home detention,* requires offenders to remain in their homes during specified times and to adhere to a strict curfew. Probation officers may monitor those under house arrest by random calls and home visits, or they may rely on technology to help keep track of offenders through electronic monitoring (EM). Such monitoring systems typically use radio frequency "tethers" consisting of a tamper-proof, water-resistant transmitter worn on the offender's ankle and a receiver placed in the offender's home. The transmitter communicates with the receiver, which has a preset range in which the offender must stay during the times they are to be at home, and sends an alarm to the supervising officer when the offender steps "out of bounds."

Day reporting centers (DRCs) are nonresidential facilities where offenders must appear daily. First used in the United States during the 1970s for juvenile offenders and deinstitutionalized mentally ill persons, day reporting centers today serve as an alternative to sending both juvenile and adult offenders to jail or prison. While the emphasis at day reporting centers is on helping offenders find jobs, a variety of counseling and treatment programs are often also available.

For those offenders for whom live-in sanctions are more appropriate, residential community corrections are available—an alternative just a step away from incarceration. These residences provide a semisecure correctional environment within the community while addressing the dual objectives of community protection and offender reintegration. Such centers may take many forms, including halfway houses, prerelease centers, transition centers, work furlough and community work centers, community treatment centers and restitution centers. Offenders may live either part-time or full-time at these facilities, depending on the conditions set forth by the court.

Intermediate Sanctions for Juveniles

Community corrections programs for juvenile offenders include shelters; ranches, forestry camps and farms; group homes; and halfway houses. Juveniles requiring greater supervision and more security may be placed in correctional facilities such as detention centers, training schools and boot camps.

Boot Camps

For some offenders community corrections are not the answer. One alternative is **boot camp,** also known as **shock incarceration.** If a judge rules shock incarceration the appropriate sentence, the offender has a choice: consent to the placement and serve a relatively shorter sentence (typically 90 to 180 days), or refuse and be placed in prison to serve a longer sentence.

The dual goals of boot camps are to rehabilitate offenders and reduce prison overcrowding. Structured after the military boot camp, strict discipline and physical labor are elements of many shock incarceration programs. Education and behavior modification are also common elements of shock incarceration programs.

Sumter County Correctional Institution "Boot Camp" in Bushnell, Florida. Here juvenile offenders experience militaristic training and discipline.

According to MacKenzie et al. (2001, p.1): "Despite their growing popularity, correctional boot camps are controversial. The controversy primarily is over whether the camps are an appropriate way to manage and treat juvenile delinquents and what impact the camps have on the adjustment and behavior of juveniles while they are confined and after they are released." MacKenzie et al. (p.1) compared 27 boot camps to 22 more traditional facilities and found: "Juveniles in boot camps more frequently reported positive responses to their institutional environment. Boot camp juveniles said they were better prepared for release, were given more therapeutic programming, had more structure and control, and were more active than comparison facility youths." In assessing these results, it should be kept in mind that most boot camps are selective about who they accept, limiting admission to first-time, nonviolent offenders who have no psychological problems and are not suicide risks.

Incarceration

Many types of correctional facilities exist for the **incarceration** (confining) of offenders. The primary goal of these correctional institutions is to protect society. Secondary goals may be to deter, rehabilitate and reintegrate offenders into society. While corrections tries to rehabilitate offenders, conditions cannot be such that the prison is a pleasant place to be. Inmates should dread a return. Unfortunately, however, too often our correctional institutions do not rehabilitate but actually contribute to and reward criminal behavior.

The type of correctional institution in which an offender is incarcerated usually depends on the type of crime committed and the offender's past record. Incarceration options include local and county jails and state and federal prisons.

Jails

Jails are an important part of the U.S. criminal justice system and go by a variety of names, including houses of detention and houses of corrections, but their definitions are generally the same. A jail is a place of confinement, typically administered by local law enforcement, although occasionally by a regional or state law enforcement agency.

Jails serve the dual function of (1) detaining individuals waiting to appear before the court, either for trial (preconviction) or for sentencing (postconviction), and (2) holding those sentenced to a year or less of incarceration. Although jails vary considerably in their management and operational philosophies, the basic responsibilities of jail personnel remain constant, including the intake and classification of inmates, orientation of new residents, transportation of inmates between the jail and court and the release of inmates.

Jails differ from lockups in that lockups, commonly located in city halls or police stations, are temporary holding facilities, authorized to hold individuals for a maximum of 48 hours. Jails differ from prisons in that prisons are state or federally administered and hold only those convicted of a crime and sentenced, not those awaiting trial or sentencing.

Jail differs from prison in that its inmates are there for shorter terms, usually for less serious crimes.

At year-end 2002, 665,475 individuals were in jail, an increase of 5.4 percent since 2001 (Glaze, p.1). The turnover rate of the jail population is relatively high, with offenders being booked and release and coming and going much more often than inmates in prison. O'Toole (2001) notes: "It takes two years for the nation's prison population to turn over once, while the jail population turns over 20 to 25 times each [year]. . . . The reality of jail population dynamics is that the vast majority of inmates are released within a few days, and those who are not released early tend to remain in custody throughout the adjudication process."

The numbers of juveniles and female adults in the jail population have been increasing faster than the number of male adults, yet the vast majority of jail inmates, nearly 90 percent, remain male adults. The rate of jail incarceration for blacks is five times higher than the rate for whites. A significant proportion of those in jail have not yet been convicted of a crime. Issues of concern vary slightly between state and federal jail facilities, including overcrowding, assaults, inmate suicide and inmate rights.

The other major type of correctional institution in the United States, where the inmates *have* been convicted of a crime, is the prison.

Prisons

Prisons are often what come to people's minds when they think of *corrections*. A prison is administered by a warden or superintendent and holds convicted offenders sentenced to more than one year of incarceration. Just as the United States has both a state and federal court system, it also has a state and federal prison system. Since 1930 the Federal Bureau of Prisons (BOP), an agency within the Department of Justice, has been the authority charged with running our nation's federal facilities, which house those convicted of federal offenses.

Because of overcrowding, newer institutions are being built with four tiers to accommodate more inmates. To many people this looks like warehousing prisoners.

The word *prison* usually conveys a mental picture of rows of cage-like cells several levels high, crowded mess halls and a "yard" where prisoners engage in physical activities, organized and not so organized, all patrolled by tight-lipped, heavily armed guards. While perhaps once accurate, this dramatic image no longer typifies modern prisons.

 Prisons may be punitive or treatment oriented. Punitive-oriented prisons are more formal and rigid, with an emphasis on obedience. Obedience is sought through negative incentives. Treatment-oriented prisons are more informal and flexible, with positive incentives for good behavior.

According to Austin and Irwin (2001, p.1): "The United States has been engaged in an unprecedented imprisonment binge. Between 1980 and 1998, the prison population ballooned from 329,821 to 1,302,019—a rise of 295 percent." By year-end 2000, the number of inmates in state and federal prison was 1,312,354, or 478 out of every 100,000 U.S. residents, which is markedly higher than the 1990 incarceration rate of 292 sentenced prisoners per every 100,000 residents (Beck and Harrison, 2001, pp.2, 4). At year-end 2002, 1,367,856 individuals were in prison, an increase of 2.8 percent from 2001 (Glaze, p.1).

Race and gender differences are noted among the prisoner population. Beck and Harrison (p.11) report: "At year-end 2000 black inmates represented an estimated 46% of all inmates with sentences of more than 1 year, while white inmates accounted for 36% and Hispanic inmates, 16%." In addition, they found nearly 1 out of every 10 black males age 25 to 29 were in prison in 2000 (p.11).

Women comprise a relatively small percentage of prisoners—6.6 percent (91,612) at year-end 2000 (Beck and Harrison, p.5). However, the number of women in prison has more than doubled since 1990. Austin et al. (2001, p.15) observe: "Between 1980 and 1999, the total number of incarcerated males increased 303 percent whereas that number increased 576 percent for females." The two most significant sources of growth for the female inmate population from 1990 to 2000 were a 28 percent increase in the number of violent women offenders and a 35 percent increase in female drug offenders (Beck and Harrison, p.12).

As with jails, our nation's prisons face several critical issues, including:

- Overcrowding—at year-end 2000, 22 states and the federal prison system were operating at 100 percent or more of their highest capacity (Beck and Harrison, p.9).
- Prison gangs—virtually every correctional system in the nation has had some experience with prison gangs.
- Criminalizing environment—socialization that occurs in prison may draw offenders away from a community's values and norms and strengthen their criminal tendencies. This phenomenon, which Clemmer (1971) identified as *prisonization,* leads prisoners to identify with and learn to coexist with other criminals and lose touch with any conventional values they may have had on the outside.
- Privatization—the provision of correctional services by organizations outside the governmental framework, either nonprofit or for profit, remains highly controversial. While proponents contend privatization will streamline and reduce the costs of corrections to the community, critics argue private prisons, motivated by the "bottom line," will cut corners, from cheaper, inferior construction materials to hiring inexperienced personnel, making decisions that enhance profits at the expense of security, quality of service and the rights and well-being of inmates. However, as Austin and Coventry (2001, p.38) report: "No data [exists] to support the contention that privately operated facilities offer cost savings over publicly managed facilities. Similarly, no definitive research evidence would lead to the conclusion that inmate services and the quality of confinement are significantly improved [or diminished] in privately operated facilities."

Regardless of whether an offender is housed in a public or private correctional facility, the reality for most inmates is that one day they will be released.

Parole

Parole is the conditional release from prison before the expiration of the sentence and the period of supervision in the community following this release. It is the most frequent type of release from a correctional facility. At year-end 2002, 753,141 adults were under parole supervision, an increase of 2.9 percent from 2001 (Glaze, p.1).

 Parole differs from probation in that a person who is paroled has spent some time serving a prison sentence. It is similar to probation in that both require supervision of the offender and set up certain conditions the offender must meet.

Administratively, parole, like law enforcement, is part of the executive branch of government; probation is under the courts and part of the judicial branch of government.

Factors influencing whether a person serving a sentence is eligible for or, indeed, is granted parole include the type of offense committed, the offender's prior record, state statutes, the inmate's behavior while incarcerated, participation in programs, whether the inmate has a plan for life on the outside and if the inmate poses any public risk. In some jurisdictions parole is prohibited by statute for certain crimes. In other jurisdictions, however, people sentenced to prison are immediately eligible for parole. The type of parole release or reentry program granted depends on the inmate's individual needs and the variety of programs offered in a particular area. Common release programs include furloughs, work release, educational release and halfway houses.

Conditions of parole typically include regular meetings between the parolee and the parole officer, a requirement to acquire and hold a job, a promise to act lawfully, a restriction on leaving the county or state without permission, a prohibition on purchasing or using a firearm and submission to random or routine drug testing. Violation of the conditions of parole typically send the offender back to prison.

Parole has had many advocates and critics over the years. Proponents assert parole plays an important role in relieving the pressures of our overcrowded prisons, while opponents claim parole lets offenders off by shortening their stay behind bars and exposes the public to criminals who have not yet paid their debt or who still pose a threat to society. Clearly the parole process is not perfect, and many states have chosen to abolish it. However many states still rely on parole to return inmates to society. Once an inmate is released, it is the parole officer's task to supervise the parolee. For those offenders who are paroled, it is often a condition of their parole that they participate in some program to integrate them back into society.

Travis and Petersilia (2004, p.429) contend that a two-part jurisprudential logic be applied to parole: "Namely that (a) completion of a prison sentence represents payment of a debt to society, and (b) every substantial period of incarceration should be followed by a period of managed reentry."

Community-Based Reintegration Programs

Community-based institutional programs aimed at reintegration of the offender into society include halfway houses and restitution centers.

Halfway Houses

As the name implies, halfway houses are community-based institutions for people who are halfway into prison, that is, on probation, or halfway out of prison, that is, on or nearing parole. Halfway houses serving those nearing parole or actually discharged from prison are sometimes called "prerelease centers." Halfway houses typically provide offenders with a place to live, sleep and eat. Counselors help offenders return to society, sometimes helping them find suitable jobs or providing transportation to jobs.

Restitution Centers

A new variation of the halfway house is the restitution center. A restitution center differs from a halfway house in that at the restitution center offenders work to partially repay their victims. Like the halfway house, restitution centers offer an alternative to prison, either for those who are halfway into or halfway out of prison.

Other Reintegration Methods

Several other approaches to reintegrating offenders into society have been used, with varying degrees of success. Three common reintegration methods are furloughs, work release and study release. In all cases the possibility of escape from the directives of the criminal justice system must be considered.

Furloughs are short, temporary leaves from a prison or jail, supervised or unsupervised, although generally the latter. They are often used as positive motivators for good behavior. They may be granted for family emergencies, for a weekend with a spouse or for job interviewing. Work and study release are also positive motivators for good behavior that also help reintegrate offenders into society. Often such programs are conducted through halfway houses or through local jails.

The conditions of furloughs, work release and study release programs are usually very explicit and rigid. For example a strict curfew may be established; going into a bar may be prohibited; and associating with known criminals may be forbidden. People on work programs usually have their pay closely controlled. They may be required to pay a portion of their room and board, and, if married, to send part of their earnings to their dependents.

Recidivism

The problem of released criminals returning to crime is of great concern. According to Glaze (p.6): "Of those parolees discharged in 2002, 41 percent had been returned to incarceration either because of a rule violation or new offense. Another 9 percent had absconded." This pattern of crime to prison to parole to crime and back to prison ad infinitum describes what has become known as the "revolving door of criminal justice," a loop involving all three components of the justice system.

Nowhere is the issue of recidivism of greater concern than when considering how to handle offenders who have committed heinous and violent crimes. Because the general population and the courts agree such offenders should not be returned to society, the question then becomes a matter of life versus death: should we keep these offenders locked up forever (life) or execute them (death)?

The Death Penalty versus Life without Parole

Thirteen states executed 71 prisoners during 2002. The number executed was five times greater than in 2001. Those executed during 2002 had been under sentence of death an average of 10 years and 7 months, 15 months less than that for inmates executed in 2001. At year-end 2003, 3,374 prisoners were under sentence of death.

Many brutal methods have been used throughout history to execute condemned criminals, including being buried alive, thrown to wild animals, boiled in oil, stoned, pressed to death, stretched on a rack, disemboweled and beheaded. Capital punishment in the United States "evolved" as society searched for more humane ways of killing its condemned—from hangings in the early years, to the first electrocution in 1890, the invention of the gas chamber in 1923, the use of a firing squad and finally the adoption of lethal injections in 1977. Today, lethal injection is the predominant method of execution in the United States, used in 37 states. Nine states authorize electrocution; four states, lethal gas; three states, hanging; and three states, firing squad. The three most common methods of execution in the United States—electrocution, asphyxiation and lethal injection—are not used in any other developed country.

As correctional philosophies and practices fluctuate, and the pendulum swings from punishment to rehabilitation and back, so too do attitudes concerning capital punishment. Gallup polls conducted between 1936 and 2001 show support for the death penalty reached its lowest point in 1966 (42 percent favored it) and peaked in 1994, with 80 percent favoring capital punishment for someone convicted of murder ("Death Penalty," 2002). The Gallup Poll, taken October 11–14, 2001, showed 68 percent of adults polled were in favor of the death penalty.

Supporters of capital punishment see it as both a deterrent and as a form of retribution. They also assert that imprisoning for life those convicted of capital crimes will only further burden an already overcrowded prison system.

Those who argue against the death penalty contend it is morally reprehensible and self-defeating, sending the message "it's okay to punish an act of killing with an act of killing" or "it's okay to extinguish those who have done wrong." Some opponents assert that such state-sanctioned killings cheapen the value of human life and dull society to issues concerning intentional death. Others criticize the disparity shown by the court when deciding who should receive capital punishment. Indeed several studies have shown that the financial status of the offender and the location of the offense are factors in determining who receives a death sentence. Another disparity concerning the death penalty centers on the gender of the offender—women are conspicuously absent on death row.

Race of the offender, however, has been found not to be a factor in capital punishment cases. Citing a study of nearly 1,000 potential death penalty cases in U.S. Attorneys' offices across the country, Attorney General John Ashcroft concluded: "There is no evidence of racial bias in the administration of the federal death penalty. Our analysis has confirmed that black and Hispanic defendants were less likely at each stage of the department's review process to be subjected to the death penalty than white defendants" ("Expanded Study . . .," 2001, p.4).

Many opponents to capital punishment suggest life without parole (LWOP) as a suitable alternative, bolstering their argument by citing the potential good the inmate might do if allowed to live, including providing restitution to the victim's family and participating in the rehabilitation of other inmates (on and off death row). In fact, many death row inmates consider LWOP a worse alternative than execution, saying they would rather be put to death than rot behind bars for the rest of their lives, which may last decades.

Given the relatively young age at which many murderers commit their crimes and the likelihood these prisoners will spend many years behind bars if given LWOP, concern over the cost to warehouse these criminals has become another issue of the debate. Capital punishment proponents estimate that at $10,000 to $20,000 a year, a 20-year-old who lives 60 years in prison would cost society more than $1 million. However, dollar estimates for executions that include the full cost of appeals are also often in the millions.

Mental Competence and the Death Penalty   The Supreme Court has ruled that capital offenders are not necessarily or automatically exempt from receiving a death sentence simply because they are mentally retarded, although more than a dozen states and the federal government expressly prohibit such executions. Amnesty International USA ("Death Penalty Facts," 2001) reports that since 1976 and as of September 8, 2001, the United States has executed 35 mentally retarded offenders.

While *retardation* does not exclude the possibility of capital punishment as a sentence, a diagnosis of *mental illness* often does eliminate the death penalty as a sentencing option for capital offenders. The National Mental Health Association (2001) notes that over the past 30 years, the number of people with mental illness and other mental disabilities on death row has steadily increased, and it estimates 5 to 10 percent of death row inmates have a serious mental illness.

Many courts have upheld the forcible medication of criminal defendants to restore their competency to stand trial, as long as the state does not *over*medicate the defendant in its attempts to restore competency. Other courts have held that medicating an objecting person, with the ultimate goal of executing that offender once competent, constitutes cruel and unusual punishment. Another issue of grave concern regarding capital punishment is the execution of innocent people.

Innocence, Wrongful Conviction and the Death Penalty   Debate has also erupted over the possibility of innocent people being executed. According to Amnesty International USA (2001), 350 people have been wrongfully convicted of capital or potentially capital crimes in the United States since 1990, 23 of whom were executed. From 1973 to 2001, 98 people were released from death row after evidence of their wrongful conviction surfaced. In January 2001, the case against Peter Limone was dropped by the state of Massachusetts after the main witness admitted fabricating much of his testimony. Limone had spent 33 years on death row. Another article, "10 Death Row Inmates Exonerated . . .," (2004, p.5), reports: "Ten persons were exonerated from death row in 2003, tying the record for the most 'exonerees' in a single year. A total of 112 death row inmates have been exonerated since the 1970s."

Many argue that the potential for even one mistake should be reason enough to abolish capital punishment. Others, however, assert that to abolish the death penalty out of fear of error is to second-guess the integrity of the system or to undermine the very credibility of our criminal justice system. The controversy regarding capital punishment and life without parole is likely to continue. There is little doubt, however, that capital punishment is the ultimate form of retribution. Many argue restorative justice might seem to be a better approach.

The Restorative Justice Model

Historically justice in this country has focused on offenders and the state punishing them (retribution). Victims and the community have traditionally been ignored. In keeping with the trend of expanding community involvement in criminal justice, restorative justice is becoming an increasingly popular alternative to retributive justice. **Restorative justice** seeks to use a balanced approach involving offenders, victims, local communities and government to alleviate crime and violence and obtain peaceful communities.

More and more, crime is being viewed and redefined as a violation against another person, not simply a harm against the state. Bazemore and Umbreit (2001, p.1) report: "Reconciling the needs of victims and offenders with the needs of the community is the underlying goal of restorative justice. Unlike retributive justice, which is primarily concerned with punishing crime, restorative justice focuses on repairing the injury that crime inflicts." Table 13.3 lists the various facets of restorative justice and how it involves crime victims, offenders, citizens, families and community groups.

Smith (2001, p.1) links restorative justice and public safety as important components of community corrections: "Public safety and restorative justice are big

Table 13.3   The Restorative Justice Response to Crime

Crime Victims

- Receive support, assistance, compensation, information and services.
- Receive restitution and other reparation from the offender.
- Are involved and encouraged to provide input at all points in the system and direct input into how the offender will repair the harm done.
- Have the opportunity to face the offender and tell their story to the offender and others if they so desire.
- Feel satisfied with the justice process.
- Provide guidance and consultation to professionals on planning and advisory groups.

Offenders

- Pay restitution to their victims.
- Provide meaningful service to repay the debt to their communities.
- Face the personal harm caused by their crimes by participating in victim-offender mediation if the victim is willing or through other victim awareness processes.
- Complete work experience and active and productive tasks that increase skills and improve the community.
- Improve decision-making skills and have opportunities to help others.
- Are monitored by community adults as well as juvenile justice providers and are supervised to the greatest extent possible in the community (if young offenders).

Citizens, Families and Community Groups

- Are involved to the greatest extent possible in offender accountability and rehabilitation and community safety initiatives.
- Work with offenders on local community service projects.
- Provide support to victims. Provide support to offenders as mentors, employers and advocates.
- Provide work for offenders to pay restitution to victims and for service opportunities that provide skills and also allow offenders to make meaningful contributions to the quality of community life.
- Play an advisory role to courts and corrections and an active role in disposition through one or more neighborhood sanctioning processes.
- Assist families in helping young offenders repair the harm and in increasing competencies (if community groups).

SOURCE: G. Bazemore. "What's New About the Balanced Approach?" *Juvenile and Family Court Journal*, vol. 48, no. 1, 1997, pp.1–23. Reprinted by permission of the author.

ideas now making claims on the future of community corrections." He (p.2) explains that traditionally public safety has been equated with more arrests, more prisoners, longer sentences and lower recidivism, but that these are "poor proxies" for public safety. Instead: "As an objective for community corrections, public safety is best conceived as the condition of a place, at times when people in that place are justified in feeling free of threat to their persons and property." In effect: "This view of public safety directly challenges offender-focused probation and parole case management. It emphasizes instead the need for unofficial, naturally occurring guardians of people and places. Guardians may include spouses, family members, friends, neighbors, employers and businesspeople. When such guardians are in place, public safety exists. In their absence, public safety is in jeopardy."

Smith (p.3) notes the conceptual overlap between public safety and restorative justice: "Both public safety and restorative justice incorporate each other's essential features. The triangular 'web of interdependency' (victims, offenders, community) on which restorative processes rely has much in common with the networks of naturally occurring guardians on which public safety depends."

Community Corrections and the Role of Police

Traditionally correctional institutions were isolated from other human service agencies and were required merely to hold prisoners and to provide some form of nominal supervision for those on probation and parole. More recently, however, corrections is expected to take a more positive approach, seeking rehabilitation whenever possible. These revised expectations make it necessary to link corrections to the community in every phase of operation.

A community approach to corrections has three significant advantages: humanitarian, restorative and managerial. The humanitarian aspect is obvious because no one should be subjected to custodial control unnecessarily. Second, restorative measures should help offenders achieve positions in the community in which they do not violate the law. Third, the managerial goal of cost effectiveness can often be achieved because any shift from custodial control saves money.

Community correctional programs cannot succeed without the understanding and cooperation of the police because those within these programs *will* come in contact with the police, and the nature of that contact will directly affect the offender's adjustment. The police can make affirmative contributions to community-based corrections programs. They know the resources available and the pitfalls to be avoided. In essence the police are an integral part of any successful corrections program, from using good judgment in making arrests to helping those on parole or probation to reenter the community.

Community Justice

Just as the community policing philosophy is gaining the acceptance of police departments, courts and corrections across the country, community justice is also finding its advocates, building upon the restorative justice model. And like community policing, "**community justice** is about creating new relationships both within the justice system and with stakeholders in the community such as residents, merchants, churches and schools, and testing new and aggressive approaches to public safety rather than merely responding to crime" (Feinblatt and Berman, p.1). Also, like community policing, community justice has at its core partnerships and problem solving, as evidenced by the six central goals of:

- Restoring the community.
- Bridging the gap between communities and courts.
- Knitting together a fractured criminal justice system.
- Helping offenders deal with problems that lead to crime.
- Providing the courts with better information.
- Building a courthouse that fosters these ambitions (Feinblatt and Berman, p.2).

Community justice initiatives often start because citizens are dissatisfied with the criminal justice system, viewing it as slow, formal and unable to cope with matters, especially low-level offenses, that need rapid and informal attention: "If community justice is to be created, two things must happen: The criminal justice system's relation to the community must be realigned, and community members must work to create civility" (*Community Justice in Rural America,* 2001 . . ., pp.9–12). As explained by Clear and Cadora (pp.1–2):

> Community justice is an emerging, innovative idea about the way criminal justice operations ought to be carried out in places where public safety is a significant problem and criminal justice is a significant fact of life. We call these locations high-impact areas because they are places where both crime and criminal justice responses to crime exist in concentrated levels. . . .
>
> Two assumptions are inherent within the idea of community justice. First, it is assumed that within existing jurisdictions, such as states or large cities, there are critically important differences from one community to another, and these differences suggest that criminal justice strategies need to be tailored to fit those differences. . . . The second assumption is that formal systems of social control, such as the criminal justice system, are not the main mechanisms of public safety. Rather, informal social controls—families, neighbors, social organizations, and friendship relations—form the most important foundation for public safety. . . .
>
> Thus, community justice can be thought of as a broad strategy that includes the following priorities:
>
> 1. Community justice selects high-impact locations—places where there is a concentration of crime and criminal justice activity—for special strategies to improve the quality of community life, especially by promoting public safety.
> 2. Community justice approaches its tasks in these areas by working to strengthen the capacity of informal systems of social control: families, neighborhood groups, friends and social supports. This means that instead of adopting the usual *reactive* strategy of merely responding to criminal cases as they occur, community justice undertakes a *proactive* strategy designed to work in partnership with these informal social control sources to strengthen the foundation for public safety.
> 3. In order to strengthen community capacity, community justice initiatives develop partnerships with residents, businesses and other social services to coordinate the way public safety problems are addressed.
>
> Community justice, therefore, is both a strategy and a philosophy.

 Community policing and community justice share several commonalities:
- Each can be considered both a strategy and a philosophy.
- Both are proactive rather than reactive.
- Both seek to form partnerships to solve community problems.

Clear and Cadora (p.104) note: "There are three essential components of community justice: place, adding value and public safety. . . . Community justice cannot occur without [these] three components. . . . It is the fact of place that makes the approach one of 'community.' It is the commitment to adding value that enables the community approach to do justice. Finally, the ultimate aim of all community justice is a better experience of public safety." They (pp.118–119) conclude: "There is no question that community justice is no longer an emerging idea but a prominent new conceptualization of the way criminal justice ought to be delivered. Community justice has developed deep roots in police practice, informs most of the current innovation in courts, and has become an important new force in correctional practice."

A Look to the Future

So what does the future hold for law enforcement and the criminal justice system? Roth (2005, p.351) contends: "The criminal justice system is changing more quickly than ever before. What was once a slow evolution based on experimentation and innovation has turned into a dynamic and proactive attempt to contain and suppress criminal behavior that was almost unthinkable in years past."

Youngs (2003, p.97) reports on the joint effort of the Society of Police Futurists International and the FBI-sponsored Futuristics and Law Enforcement: The Millennium Conference. They identified five areas of concern that must be addressed: (1) the future of technology and its effect on law enforcement, (2) the future of leadership and management in policing agencies, (3) future crime/future law, (4) the future of policing practices and philosophies and (5) the changing face of American demographics and American policing. Youngs (pp.98–101) suggests:

> Agencies must have proactive planning programs to monitor trends, discuss and develop new strategies, and facilitate and respond to emerging trends. Law enforcement must form a variety of partnerships with both public and private entities due to lack of knowledge and resources with which to combat cyber crime and manage diversity. . . . Management styles will change emphasizing leadership ability and interpersonal relationship building. . . . Citizen involvement will increase and be paramount. . . . Citizens will be able to log on and track crime in their neighborhoods and vote on issues affecting them. . . . Terrorism will take many forms, such as attacks against the infrastructure through computer networks, weapons of mass destruction, genomic or genetic terrorism attacking food production and preparation, and traditional random violent attacks. . . . Citizens are likely to trade some civil liberties for protection against terrorism and cyber-crime. . . . It could be that by 2050 society will have a new generation that deals with the process of change in a way that allows rapid growth without the chaos each technological development now brings.

Youngs (p.98) provides a timeline prediction of trends that those responsible for planning for the future might want to consider (see Figure 13.8).

During the closing plenary session at the National Criminal Justice Association's National Forum 2003, panelists were asked to look to the year 2010 and communicate their visions for the future of criminal justice, including the issues that criminal justice decision makers might be facing at that time.

> Overall, panelists saw improved access to technology for the public safety community, with movement away from 'cookie cutter' approaches in policing toward more intelligence-driven policing. At the same time, law enforcement will deal more with the globalization of crime, and it will be even more important then, than now, for jurisdictional boundaries to be broken and regional governance models to be developed. In 2010 criminal justice will have overcome the interoperability obstacle; improved national information

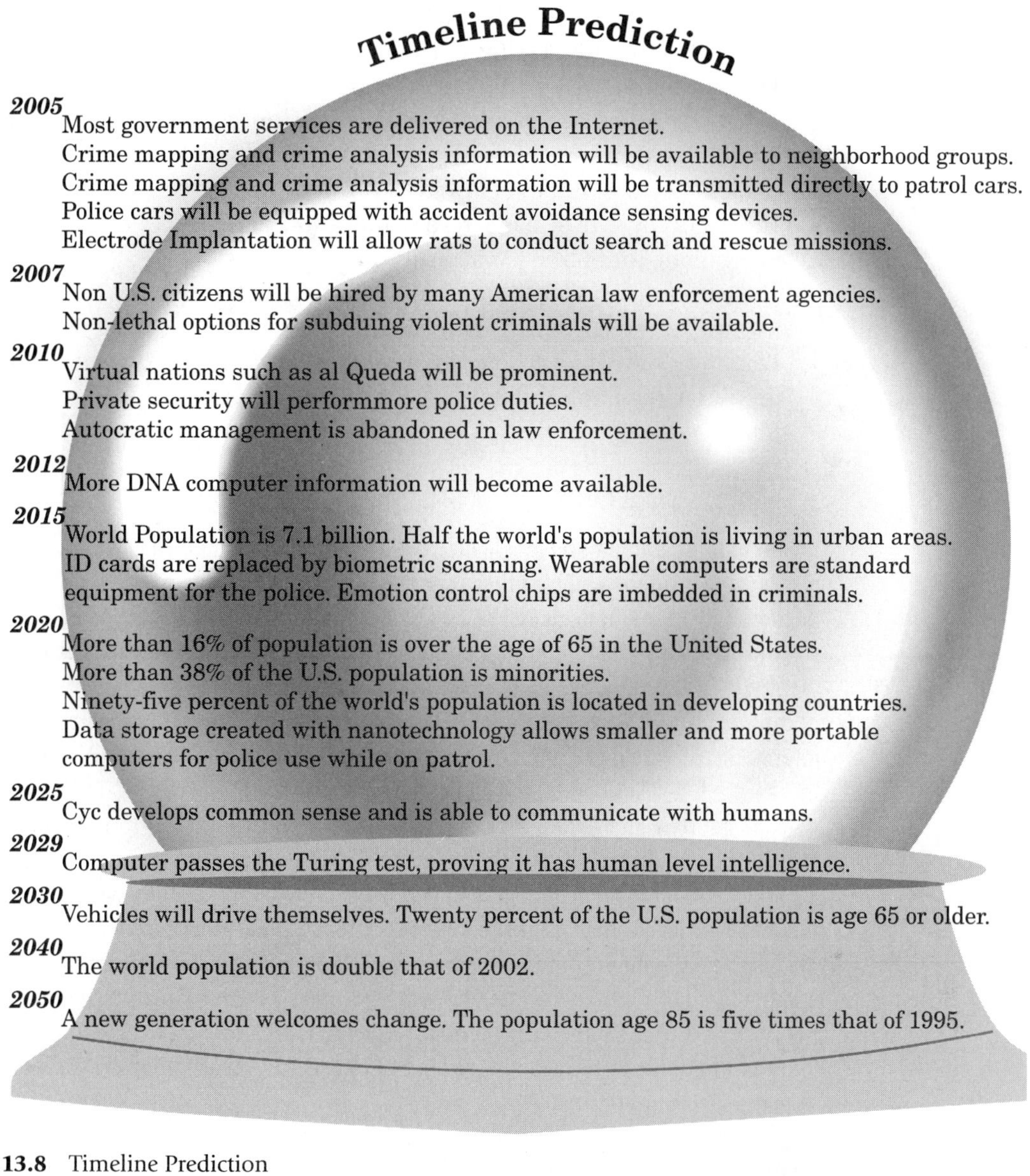

Timeline Prediction

2005
Most government services are delivered on the Internet.
Crime mapping and crime analysis information will be available to neighborhood groups.
Crime mapping and crime analysis information will be transmitted directly to patrol cars.
Police cars will be equipped with accident avoidance sensing devices.
Electrode Implantation will allow rats to conduct search and rescue missions.

2007
Non U.S. citizens will be hired by many American law enforcement agencies.
Non-lethal options for subduing violent criminals will be available.

2010
Virtual nations such as al Queda will be prominent.
Private security will performmore police duties.
Autocratic management is abandoned in law enforcement.

2012
More DNA computer information will become available.

2015
World Population is 7.1 billion. Half the world's population is living in urban areas.
ID cards are replaced by biometric scanning. Wearable computers are standard
equipment for the police. Emotion control chips are imbedded in criminals.

2020
More than 16% of population is over the age of 65 in the United States.
More than 38% of the U.S. population is minorities.
Ninety-five percent of the world's population is located in developing countries.
Data storage created with nanotechnology allows smaller and more portable
computers for police use while on patrol.

2025
Cyc develops common sense and is able to communicate with humans.

2029
Computer passes the Turing test, proving it has human level intelligence.

2030
Vehicles will drive themselves. Twenty percent of the U.S. population is age 65 or older.

2040
The world population is double that of 2002.

2050
A new generation welcomes change. The population age 85 is five times that of 1995.

Figure 13.8   Timeline Prediction

SOURCE: Alan C. Youngs. "Law Enforcement in 2003 and Beyond." *Law and Order*, April 2003, p.98. Reprinted by permission.

sharing and data analysis; and learned to 'do more with less' through the leveraging of resources, use of technology (to solve/forecast crime and track/monitor/identify offenders), and increased private sector partnerships to help protect the public ("National Forum's Final Plenary Session: 'Fast Forward—What Can We Expect?'" 2003).

Philip Ramer, director of intelligence for the Florida Department of Law Enforcement, expressed optimism that the public sector will catch up with the private sector technologically—there will be greater intelligence sharing and information analysis, and regional governance models will emerge, especially as this relates to communications interoperability.

Paul Wormeli, vice president of PEC Solutions, noted that seven years is not long enough to see any significant changes in the criminal justice system. He contended that the **zeitgeist**—the general intellectual, moral or cultural "spirit" of the times—will not change until we are ready, but we must first have the will, opportunity and means. Wormeli outlined three drivers of change on the criminal justice system as it moves toward 2010:

- The economy, which has forced reallocation of resources and caused declining revenue for public service.
- The war on terrorism, which is now driving much of the workload in criminal justice and has further reduced resources.
- Technology, which has helped lower costs while providing greater capabilities for protecting public safety.

 SUMMARY

Police officers aid the criminal justice process by (1) making arrests, (2) obtaining information and evidence, (3) writing reports, (4) identifying suspects and witnesses and (5) providing testimony in court. They routinely interact with both the courts and corrections.

Our judicial system operates at both the state and federal levels. The hierarchy at the state level often goes up from courts of special or limited jurisdiction called justice of the peace (J.P.) courts, to trial courts or original and general jurisdiction courts, to intermediate appellate courts, to the state supreme court. The federal court system is three tiered: district courts, appellate courts and the U.S. Supreme Court. A specialized type of court is the juvenile court, historically informal, private and nonadversarial, stressing rehabilitation rather than punishment of youths.

Our criminal justice system is based on the adversary system, which requires that the accuser prove beyond a reasonable doubt to a judge or jury that the accused is guilty of a specified crime. The criminal justice process consists of several critical stages: the complaint or charge, the warrant, arrest, booking, plea bargaining, preliminary hearing, grand jury hearing, the arraignment, the trial and sentencing. The preliminary hearing seeks to establish probable cause to prevent people from being indiscriminately brought to trial.

Not all cases go to court. Alternatives to a trial include diversion. Police officers' testimony at the trial is of great importance. They should be aware of tactics often used by defense attorneys to confuse or discredit a police officer who is testifying: (1) rapid-fire questioning, (2) establishing that the officer wants to see the defendant found guilty, (3) accusing the officer of making assumptions or (4) implying that the officer does not want anyone else to know what is in his or her notes.

Once a case has passed through the court system and a disposition is reached, the case then moves into the corrections phase of the justice system. Corrections is that portion of the criminal justice system that carries out the court's orders. The primary purposes of corrections are retribution, deterrence, incapacitation and rehabilitation. Correctional alternatives available to the courts include probation, intermediate sanctions, incarceration and, in some states, the death penalty. These same options exist for juvenile offenders, although probation is by far the most frequent disposition in juvenile delinquency cases.

Many offenders, especially repeat offenders, are sentenced to correctional institutions, jails or prisons. Jail differs from prison in that its inmates are there for shorter terms, usually for less serious crimes. Prisons may be punitive oriented or treatment oriented. Punitive-oriented prisons are more formal and rigid, with an emphasis on obedience. Obedience is sought through negative incentives. In contrast, treatment-oriented prisons are more informal and flexible, with positive incentives for good behavior.

Most people sentenced to jail or prison become eligible for parole. Parole differs from probation in that a person who is paroled has spent some time serving a prison sentence. It is similar to probation in that both require supervision of the offender and set up certain conditions that must be met by the offender. Parole and probation often involve community-based institutional programs aimed at reintegrating offenders into society, including halfway houses, restitution centers, furloughs, and work release and study release programs.

Just as community policing has had a major impact on contemporary law enforcement, similar approaches in the courts and corrections have resulted in a move toward community justice. Community policing and community justice share several commonalities. Each can be considered both a strategy and a philosophy. Both are proactive rather than reactive. Both seek to form partnerships to solve community problems.

DISCUSSION QUESTIONS

1. Is the jury system really fair?
2. Should the police be consulted when plea bargaining is used?
3. Is our system truly an adversary system when the prosecutor also has to protect the accused's rights?
4. Do you feel diversion is an acceptable alternative in some instances? If so, when? If not, why?
5. What are your views on capital punishment? A sentence of life without parole? Which do you feel would be the harsher sentence?
6. Why do you think the United States has the highest incarceration rate and number of people behind bars?
7. Explain the relationships among community policing, community justice and restorative justice.
8. Does your community use any forms of community policing, community prosecution, community courts or community corrections? If so, what?
9. What do you perceive to be the greatest challenges facing law enforcement and the criminal justice system in the future?
10. Should law enforcement have more input into the other two components of the criminal justice system? If so, how?

 ### INFOTRAC COLLEGE EDITION ASSIGNMENTS

- Use InfoTrac College Edition to answer the Discussion Questions as appropriate.
- Use InfoTrac College Edition to research *restorative justice.* Find and outline at least two articles on the subject. **OR**

- Use InfoTrac College Edition to research *capital punishment.* Outline one article in favor of and one article opposed to this form of "corrections." With either option, be prepared to share your findings with the class. **OR**
- Read and outline "Forging a Police-Probation Alliance" by Brian McKay and Barry Paris.

 ### INTERNET ASSIGNMENT

- Research *community justice* on the Web at http://www.communityjustice.org. Outline at least two references. Be prepared to share your outline with the class.

 ### BOOK-SPECIFIC WEB SITE

The book-specific Web site at http://info .wadsworth.com/0534552803 hosts a variety of resources for students and instructors. Included are extended activities from each chapter in which students write a policy, use critical thinking skills to make choices in response to a given scenario, use InfoTrac College Edition with direct links to articles for participation in topical discussion forums and analyze court cases using Web links for research. Many activities can be printed or emailed to instructors. Plus, cited cases with Web links, interactive key term FlashCards, PowerPoint presentations, chapter objectives, and an extensive collection of chapter-based Web links provide additional information and activities to include in the curriculum.

REFERENCES

Amnesty International USA. "Death Penalty Facts." 2001. http://www.amnesty-usa.org/abolish/reports. html.

Austin, James and Coventry, Garry. *Emerging Issues on Privatized Prisons.* Washington, DC: Bureau of Justice Assistance and the National Council on Crime and Delinquency, February 2001. (NCJ 181249)

Austin, James and Irwin, John. *It's about Time: America's Imprisonment Binge,* 3rd ed. Belmont, CA: Wadsworth Thomson Learning, 2001.

Austin, James; Bruce, Marino A.; Carroll, Leo; McCall, Patricia L.; and Richards, Stephen C. "The Use of Incarceration in the United States." *The Criminologist,* May/June 2001, pp.14–16.

Bazemore, Gordon and Umbreit, Mark. *A Comparison of Four Restorative Conferencing Models.* Washington, DC: OJJDP Juvenile Justice Bulletin, February 2001.

Beck, Allen J. and Harrison, Paige M. *Prisoners in 2000.* Washington, DC: Bureau of Justice Statistics Bulletin, August 2001. (NCJ 188207)

Boland, Barbara. *Community Prosecution in Washington, DC.* Washington, DC: National Institute of Justice Research Report, April 2001.

Clear, Todd R. and Cadora, Eric. *Community Justice.* Belmont, CA: Wadsworth Publishing Company, 2003.

Clemmer, Donald. "The Process of Prisonization." In *The Criminal in Confinement,* edited by Leon Radzinowicz and Marvin Wolfgang. New York: Basic Books, 1971, pp.92–93.

Cole, George F.; Gertz, Marc G.; and Bunger, Amy. *The Criminal Justice System: Politics and Policies,* 9th ed. Belmont, CA: Wadsworth Publishing Company, 2004.

Community Justice in Rural America: Four Examples and Four Futures. Washington, DC: Bureau of Justice Assistance Monograph, February 2001. (NCJ 182437)

Cooper, Caroline S. *Juvenile Drug Court Programs.* Washington, DC: Juvenile Accountability Incentive Block Grants Program Bulletin, May 2001.

Crime in the United States 2002. Washington, DC: Federal Bureau of Investigation, 2003.

"Death Penalty." Gallup Organization, 2002. http://www. gallup.com/poll/topics/death_pen.asp.

Denckla, Derek and Berman, Greg. *Rethinking the Revolving Door: A Look at Mental Illness in the Courts.* New York: Center for Court Innovation, 2001. http://www .courtinnovation.org/pdf/mental_health.pdf.

Durose, Matthew R. and Langan, Patrick A. *Felony Sentences in State Courts, 2000.* Washington, DC: Bureau of Justice Statistics Bulletin, June 2003. (NCJ 198821)

Ehlers, Scott; Schiraldi, Vincent; and Ziedenberg, Jason. *Still Striking Out: 10 Years of California's Three Strikes.* Washington, DC: Justice Policy Institute, July 1, 2004. www.justicepolicy.org

"Expanded Study Shows No Bias in Death Penalty, Ashcroft Says." *Criminal Justice Newsletter,* June 18, 2001, pp.4–5.

Feinblatt, John and Berman, Greg. *Responding to the Community: Principles for Planning and Creating a Community Court.* Washington, DC: Bureau of Justice Assistance Bulletin, February 2001. (NCJ 185986)

Giblin, Matthew J. "Using Police Officers to Enhance the Supervision of Juvenile Probationers: An Evaluation of the Anchorage CAN Program." *Crime and Delinquency,* January 2002, pp.116–137.

Gil-Blanco, Jorge. "Courtroom Coliseum." *Police,* October 2001, pp.74–78.

Glaze, Lauren E. *Probation and Parole in the United States, 2002.* Washington, DC: Bureau of Justice Statistics Bulletin, August 2003. (NCJ 201135)

Goldkamp, John S.; Irons-Guynn, Cheryl; and Weiland, Doris. *Community Prosecution Strategies: Measuring Impact.* Washington, DC: Bureau of Justice Assistance Bulletin, November 2002.

Goodwin, Tracy with Steinhart, David J. and Fulton, Betsy A. *Peer Justice and Youth Empowerment: An Implementation Guide for Teen Court Programs.* U.S. Department of Transportation, National Highway Traffic Safety Administration; American Probation and Parole Association; and the U.S. Department of Justice, Office of Juvenile Justice and Delinquency Prevention, no date.

Gover, Angela R.; MacDonald, John M.; and Alpert, Geoffrey P. "Combating Domestic Violence: Findings from an Evaluation of a Local Domestic Violence Court." *Criminology and Public Policy,* November 2003, pp.109–132.

Harrell, Adele. "Judging Drug Courts: Balancing the Evidence." *Criminology and Public Policy,* vol. 2, no. 2, 2003, pp.207–212.

Harrison, Paige M. and Beck, Allen J. *Prisoners in 2002.* Washington, DC: Bureau of Justice Statistics Bulletin, July 2003. (NCJ 200248)

Kalk, Dan. "Checkpoints, Pursuits and Court Dates." *Police,* March 2001, pp.39–41.

Kovandzic, Tomislav; Sloan, John J.; and Vieraitis, Lynne. "Unintended Consequences of Politically Popular Sentencing Policies: The Homicide Promoting Effects of 'Three Strikes' in U.S. Cities (1980–1999)." in *The Criminal Justice System: Politics and Policies,* 9th ed., edited by George F. Cole, Marc G. Gertz and Amy Bunger. Belmont, CA: Wadsworth Publishing Company, 2004, pp.456–469.

Listwan, Shelley Johnson; Sundt, Jody L.; Holsinger, Alexander M.; and Latessa, Edward J. "The Effect of Drug Court Programming on Recidivism: The Cincinnati Experience." *Crime and Delinquency,* July 2003, pp.389–411.

MacKenzie, Doris Layton; Gover, Angela R.; Armstrong, Gaylene Styve; and Mitchell, Ojmarrh. *A National Study Comparing the Environments of Boot Camps with Traditional Facilities for Juvenile Offenders.* Washington, DC: National Institute of Justice Research in Brief, August 2001.

"Mental Health Courts Are Catching on Like Crazy." *Law Enforcement News*, October 15, 2002, p.7.

"Nation Spends $167 Billion on Criminal and Civil Justice Services." Washington, DC: Bureau of Justice Statistics Press Release, May 2, 2004.

"National Forum's Final Plenary Session: 'Fast Forward— What Can We Expect?' "*National Criminal Justice Association Justice Bulletin*, August 2003, pp.1, 12–13.

National Mental Health Association. *Death Penalty and People with Mental Illness*. Policy Position: P-44. 2001. http://www.mhami.org/policy44.html.

National Tribal Justice Resource Center. A Project of the National American Indian Court Judges Association, 2004. http://www.tribalresourcecenter.org.

Neubauer, David W. *America's Courts and the Criminal Justice System*, 7th ed. Belmont, CA: Wadsworth Publishing Company, 2002.

"New York to Expand Gun Courts." *Newsday*, December 18, 2003.

"Number of Death Row Inmates Declined for Third Straight Year." *NCJA Justice Bulletin*, 2004, p.18.

OJP Drug Court Clearinghouse and Technical Assistance Project. *Summary of Drug Court Activity by State and County*. Washington, DC: American University, November 7, 2003. http://www.american.edu/academic.depts/spa/justice/publications/drgchart2k.pdf.

Ostrom, Brian J. "Domestic Violence Courts." *Criminology & Public Policy*, November 2003, pp.105–108.

O'Toole, Michael. "Jails and Prisons: The Numbers Say They Are More Different Than Generally Assumed." *American Jails*, 2001. http://www.corrections.com/aja/mags/magazine.html.

Prison and Jail Inmates at Midyear 2003. Washington, DC: Bureau of Justice Statistics Bulletin, May 2004. (NCJ 203 947)

Roth, Mitchel P. *Crime and Punishment: A History of the Criminal Justice System*. Belmont, CA: Wadsworth Publishing Company, 2005.

Smith, Michael E. *What Future for "Public Safety" and "Restorative Justice" in Community Corrections? Sentencing and Corrections Issues for the 21st Century*. Research in Brief. Papers from the Executive Sessions on Sentencing and Corrections, No. 11, June 2001.

Swope, Ross E. "Community Prosecution: The Real Deal." *Law Enforcement News*, January 15/31, 2001, pp.11, 14.

"10 Death Row Inmates Exonerated in 2003, Tying a Record, DPIC [Death Penalty Information Center] Says." *Criminal Justice Newsletter*, January 2, 2004, p.5.

Travis, Jeremy and Petersilia, Joan. "Reentry Reconsidered: A New Look at an Old Question." In *The Criminal Justice System: Politics and Policies*, 9th ed., edited by George F. Cole, Marc G. Gertz and Amy Bunger. Belmont, CA: Wadsworth Publishing Company, 2004, pp.415–434.

Walker, Samuel; Spohn, Cassia; and DeLone, Miriam. *The Color of Justice: Race, Ethnicity and Crime in America*, 3rd ed. Belmont, CA: Wadsworth Publishing Company, 2004.

Youngs, Alan C. "Law Enforcement in 2003 and Beyond." *Law and Order*, April 2003, pp.96–101.

CASES CITED

Berger v. United States, 295 U.S. 78 (1935)

Escobedo v. Illinois, 378 U.S. 478 (1964)

Glossary

The number following the definition refers to the chapter(s) in which the term is defined.

accreditation—Being approved by an official review board as meeting specific standards. (12)

actus reus—A guilty, measurable act, including planning and conspiring. (2)

administrative services—Those services such as recruiting, training, planning and research, records, communications, crime laboratories and facilities, including the police headquarters and jail. (4)

administrative warrant—Official permission to investigate the cause of a fire after the fire has been extinguished. (8)

adversary system—The criminal justice system used in the United States that puts the accuser versus the accused. The accuser must prove that the one accused is guilty. (13)

affidavit—A statement reduced to writing, sworn to before a judge or notary having authority to administer an oath. (8)

affirmative action—Results-oriented actions taken to ensure equal employment opportunity, may include goals to correct underutilization and backpay, retroactive seniority, makeup goals and timetables. (12)

aggravated assault—An unlawful attack upon a person for the purpose of inflicting severe bodily injury or death. (3)

aggravated rape—Having sexual intercourse through use of force, threats or immediate use of force, or taking advantage of an unconscious or helpless person or a person incapable of consent because of mental illness or a defect reasonably known to the attacker. (3)

aggressive patrol—Designed to handle problems and situations requiring coordinated efforts. Also called *specialized patrol* or *directed patrol*. (6)

American creed—The belief in individual freedom. (2)

American Dream—Belief that anyone who works hard and is willing to sacrifice for a while can be successful. (5)

amphetamines—Stimulants taken orally as tablets or capsules or intravenously to reduce appetite and/or to relieve mental depression. (9)

appellate jurisdiction—A higher court with the power to hear and decide an appeal to the decision of an original court without holding a trial. (13)

arraignment—A court procedure whereby the accused is read the charges against him or her and is then asked how he or she pleads. (13)

arrest—To deprive a person of liberty by legal authority. Usually applied to the seizure of a person to answer before a judge for a suspected or alleged crime. (8)

arson—Intentionally damaging or destroying, or attempting to damage or destroy, by means of fire or explosion the property of another without the consent of the owner or one's own property, with or without the intent to defraud. (3)

assault—An unlawful attack by one person upon another for the purpose of inflicting bodily harm. (3)

asset forfeiture—Allows seizure of assets and property used in connection with a crime. (2)

asymmetric warfare—Conflict in which a much weaker opponent takes on a stronger opponent by refusing to confront the stronger opponent head on. (10)

authority—The right to direct and command. (2)

bail—Payment by an accused of an amount of money, specified by the court based on the nature of the offense, to ensure the presence of the accused at trial. (2, 12)

balancing—Occurs when officers unfairly stop unoffending motorists to make the numbers come out right; for example if an officer stops a black motorist, he or she must stop X number of white motorists to make the numbers come out right. (11)

ballistics—A science dealing with the motion and impact of projectiles such as bullets and bombs. (7)

barbiturates—Depressants usually taken orally as small tablets or capsules to induce sleep and/or to relieve tension. (9)

battery—Physical assault. (3)

bias crime—Unlawful action designed to frighten or harm an individual because of his or her race, religion, ethnicity or sexual orientation. Also called *hate crime*. (3)

Bill of Rights—The first 10 amendments to the U.S. Constitution. (2)

bioterrorism—Involves such biological weapons of mass destruction (WMDs) as anthrax, botulism and smallpox to cause fear in a population. (10)

Bloods—Well-known African American gang. Rivals of the Crips. (9)

bona fide occupational qualification (BFOQ)—Skill or knowledge that is reasonably necessary to perform a job and, consequently, may be a requirement for employment. (12)

boot camp—Patterned after the traditional military boot camps for new recruits, a system of incarceration for youths that stresses strict and even cruel discipline, hard work and authoritarian decision making and control by a drill sergeant. Also called *shock incarceration*. (13)

Bow Street Runners—The first English detective unit; established in London by Henry Fielding in 1750. (1)

broken-window phenomenon/theory—Maintains that if a neighborhood is allowed to run down, it will give the impression that no one cares and crime will flourish. (5, 9)

burglary—An unlawful entry into a building to commit a theft or felony. (3)

burnout—A psychological state that occurs when someone is made exhausted and listless and rendered unserviceable or ineffectual through overwork, stress or intemperance. (12)

career criminal—An offender arrested five or more times as a juvenile. Also called a *chronic criminal.* (3)

carjacking—Stealing a car from the driver by force. (3)

case law—A collection of summaries of how statutes have been applied by judges in various situations; the precedents that have been established by the courts. (2)

chain of evidence—Documenting who has had possession of evidence from the time it was discovered and taken into custody until the present time. (7)

choloization—Asserting with pride a Chicano identity and denying being Americanized. (9)

chronic criminal—An offender arrested five or more times as a juvenile. Also called a *career criminal.* (3)

civil injunction—A lawsuit that, if granted by the court, requires or limits certain actions by the defendants and serves, in essence, as a protective order from the city. (9)

civil law—All restrictions placed upon individuals that are noncriminal in nature; seeks restitution rather than punishment. (2)

civil liberties—An individual's immunity from governmental oppression. (2)

civil rights—Claims that the citizen has to the affirmative assistance of government. (2)

civilian review—A process by which citizens' complaints about police behavior are reviewed by individuals who are not sworn police officers. (12)

civilian review board—Consists of citizens who meet to review complaints filed against the police department or against individual officers. (12)

classical theory—Theory developed by eighteenth-century Italian criminologist Cesare Beccaria that sees people as free agents with free will. People commit crimes because they want to. (3)

code of silence—A pact among officers that they will not make known any misconduct of fellow officers. (2)

cold crimes—Crimes discovered after the perpetrator has left the scene. (6)

common law—In England, the customary law set by judges as disputes arose; the law in force prior to and independent of legislation. (2)

community era—(1980–present) the third era of policing. Characterized by authority coming from community support, law and professionalism; broad provision of services, including crime control; decentralized organization with more authority given to patrol officers; an intimate relationship with the community; and use of foot patrol and a problem-solving approach. (1)

community justice—Creates new relationships both within the justice system and with stakeholders in the community; has at its core partnerships and problem solving. (13)

community policing—A philosophy that emphasizes a problem-solving partnership between the police and the citizens in working toward a healthy, crime-free environment. Also called *neighborhood policing.* (4)

complainant—A person who makes a charge against another person. (7)

complaint—A legal document drawn up by a prosecutor that specifies an alleged crime and the supporting facts providing probable cause. (13)

conflict theory—Contends that certain behaviors are criminalized to keep the dominant class in power. (2)

consensus theory—Holds that individuals within a society agree on basic values, on what is inherently right and wrong. (2)

consent—To agree; to give permission; voluntary oral or written permission to search a person's premises or property. (8)

constable—An elected official of a hundred, responsible for leading the citizens in pursuit of any lawbreakers. The first English police officer and, as such, in charge of the weapons and horses of the entire community. (1)

constitution—A system of fundamental laws and principles that prescribes the nature, functions and limits of a government or other body. The basic instrument of government and the supreme law of the United States; the written instrument defining the power, limitations and functions of the U.S. government and that of each state. (2)

constitutional law—Statutes based on the federal or state constitutions. (2)

contagion effect—Media coverage of terrorism inspires more terrorism. (10)

contamination—Something foreign is introduced into or evidence is removed from a crime scene. (7)

contraband—Any article forbidden by law to be imported or exported; any article of which possession is prohibited by law and constitutes a crime. (8)

corporate gangs—Gangs that have strong leaders and focus on illegal money-making ventures, often drug trafficking. (9)

corpus delicti—The body of the crime, the elements making up a specific crime. (2)

corruption—The misuse of authority by an officer for personal gain. Includes accepting gratuities and bribes as well as committing theft or burglary. (11)

CPTED—Crime prevention through environmental design. Focuses on "defensible space," using access control, lighting and surveillance as key strategies in preventing crime. (5)

crack—A form of cocaine available at greatly reduced cost. (9)

credentialing—Process whereby individual police officers are approved by a board as meeting certain standards. (12)

crime—An action harmful to another person and/or to society and made punishable by law. (2)

crime control—The basic purpose of criminal justice is to keep crime controlled. (2)

criminal intent—A resolve, design or mutual determination to commit a crime, with full knowledge of the consequences and exercise of free will. (2)

criminal law—The body of law that defines crimes and assigns punishments for them. (2)

criminalistics—A branch of forensic science that deals with physical evidence related to a crime, including fingerprints, firearms, tool marks, blood, hair, documents and other types of physical evidence. (7)

Crips—Gang with the reputation of being the toughest African American gang in Los Angeles; rivals of the Bloods. (9)

cross-examination—Questioning of an opposing witness in a trial or hearing. (13)

curtilage—That portion of property associated with the common use of land—for example, buildings, sheds and fenced-in areas. (8)

custodial interrogation—Questioning a person who is not free to leave. (2)

custody—State of being kept or guarded, or being detained. (8)

cyanoacrylate—Super glue; used in fingerprinting. (7)

cybercops—Investigators of computer crimes. (3)

cybercrime—Computer crime. (3)

cyberterrorism—Terrorism that initiates or threatens to initiate the exploitation of or attack on computerized information systems. (10)

dark figure of crime—The actual, unknown number of crimes being committed. (3)

de facto arrest—Occurs when officers who lack probable cause to arrest take a suspect in for questioning; officers' actions have the appearance of an arrest—that is, the suspect is not free to leave. (8)

de facto segregation—Actual separation, often geographically into ghettos. (5)

deadly force—Any force intended to cause death or serious physical injury. (11)

deinstitutionalization—Releasing into society those who have been under the care of the state. Frequently refers to the massive release of mentally ill individuals into society in the 1960s and 1970s, many of whom became homeless. (5)

delinquency—Actions or conduct by a juvenile in violation of criminal law or constituting a status offense. An error or failure by a child or adolescent to conform to society's expectations of social order, either where the child resides or visits. (3)

delinquent—A child judged to have violated a federal, state or local law; a minor who has done an illegal act or who has been proven in court to misbehave seriously. A child may be found delinquent for a variety of behaviors not criminal for adults (status offenses). (3)

deliriants—Volatile chemicals that can be sniffed or inhaled to produce a "high" similar to that produced by alcohol. (9)

demographers—Individuals who study the characteristics of human populations. (5)

determinism—Maintains that human behavior is the product of a multitude of environmental and cultural influences. (3)

deterrence—Sees corrections as a way to prevent future criminal actions. Tries to show offenders that the price of committing crimes is too great. (13)

differential response strategies—Suiting the response to the call. (6)

diffusion of benefits—Crackdowns can reduce crime and disorder outside the target area or reduce offenses not targeted in the crackdowns. (6)

direct victims—Those who are initially harmed by injury, death or loss of property as a result of crimes committed. Also called *primary victims.* (3)

directed patrol—Uses crime statistics to plan shift and beat staffing, providing more coverage during times of peak criminal activity and in high-crime areas. Designed to handle problems and situations requiring coordinated efforts. Also called *specialized patrol* or *aggressive patrol.* (6)

discovery crimes—Illegal acts brought to the attention of the victim and law enforcement after the act has been committed—a burglary, for example. (7)

discovery process—A system that requires all pertinent facts be made available to the prosecutor and the defense attorney before the trial. (13)

discretion—The freedom of an agency or individual officer to make choices as to whether to act; freedom to act or judge on one's own. (4)

discrimination—Showing a preference or prejudice in treating individuals or groups. (11)

disparity—A simple difference, not necessarily caused by any kind of bias. (11)

diversion—Bypassing the criminal justice system by assigning an offender to a social agency or other institution rather than trying him or her in court. (13)

DNA profiling—Uses the material from which chromosomes are made to positively identify individuals. No two individuals except identical twins have the same DNA structure. (7)

double jeopardy—Unconstitutionally being tried for the same crime more than once. (2)

drug gangs—Smaller than other gangs; more cohesive; focused on the drug business; strong, centralized leadership with market-defined roles. (9)

drug-defined offenses—Illegal acts involving drugs, that is, the crime occurs as a part of the drug business or culture, for example marijuana cultivation or cocaine distribution. Also called *systemic* offenses. (9)

drug-related offenses—Illegal acts in which the effect of a drug is a contributor, such as when a drug user commits crime because of drug-induced changes in physiological functions, cognitive ability and mood, or in which the need for the drug is a factor, as when a drug user commits crime to obtain money to buy drugs. (9)

dual motive stop—When the officer has an ulterior motive for the stop. Also called a *pretext stop.* (8)

due process of law—Not explicitly defined, but embodies the fundamental ideas of American justice expressed in the Fifth and Fourteenth Amendments. (2)

ecclesiastical law—Law of the church. (2)

eco-terrorism—Terrorism aimed at inflicting economic damage on those who profit from the destruction of the natural environment. (10)

8% problem—A group of repeat offenders dramatically different from those who are arrested only once and who account for a disproportionate amount of youth crime. (3)

elements of the crime—The distinctive acts making up a specific crime. The elements make up the *corpus delicti* of the crime. (2)

embezzle—A person steals or uses for him- or herself money or property entrusted to him or her. (3)

emergency situations—Circumstances where a police officer must act without a magistrate's approval (without a warrant). (8)

E911 (enhanced 911)—Requires wireless carriers to identify the location of the caller to within 125 meters at least two-thirds of the time. (4)

entrapment—Occurs when an officer induces someone to commit a crime for the purpose of prosecuting that person. (8)

environmental anomalies—Unusual activities that warrant further investigation. (6)

equal protection—Requires that a state cannot make unreasonable, arbitrary distinctions between different persons as to their rights and privileges. (2)

equity—A concept that requires that the "spirit of the law" take precedence over the "letter of the law." (2)

ethics—Involves moral behavior, doing what is considered right and just. The rules or standards governing the conduct of a profession. (11)

evidence—All the means by which any alleged matter or act is either established or disproved. (7)

excessive force—Force beyond that which is reasonably necessary to accomplish a legitimate law enforcement purpose. (11)

Exclusionary Rule—A U.S. Supreme Court ruling that any evidence seized in violation of the Fourth Amendment will not be admissible in a federal or state trial. (2)

exculpatory evidence—Evidence favorable to the accused. (11)

exigent circumstances—The same as *emergency situations.* (8)

extenuating circumstances—Requiring immediate action; emergency situations. (8)

federalism—A principle reserving for the states the powers not granted to the federal government or withheld from the states. (2)

felony—A major crime—for example, murder, rape, arson; the penalty is usually death or imprisonment for more than one year in a state prison or penitentiary. (2)

fence—A professional receiver and seller of stolen property. (3)

field detention—Holding suspects with less than probable cause. (8)

field identification—At-the-scene identification, made within a reasonable time after a crime has been committed. (7)

field inquiry—Briefly detaining or stopping persons to determine who they are and/or what they are up to. (8)

field services—The operations or line divisions of a law enforcement agency, such as patrol, traffic control, investigation and community services. (4)

fighting words—Utterances likely to cause violence. (2)

first-degree murder—Willful, deliberate and premeditated (planned) taking of another person's life. (3)

follow-up investigation—Investigation after the preliminary investigation. (7)

force—Action taken to compel an individual to comply with an officer's request. (11)

forced entry—An announced or unannounced entry into a dwelling or a building by force for the purpose of executing a search or arrest warrant to avoid the needless destruction of property, to prevent violent and deadly force against the officer and to prevent the escape of a suspect. (8)

forensic science—The study of evidence. (7)

Frankpledge system—Norman modification of the tithing system requiring loyalty to the king's law and mutual local responsibility in maintaining the peace. (1)

frisk—A patting down or minimal search of a person to determine the presence of a dangerous weapon. (8)

gang—A group of people who form an allegiance for a common purpose and engage in unlawful or criminal activity. (9)

general deterrence—Deterrence to serve as an example to others of the consequences of crime. (13)

ghetto—Area of a city inhabited by people of an ethnic or racial group who live in poverty and apparent social disorganization often resulting from involuntary segregation. (5)

ghetto syndrome—A vicious cycle of poverty and welfare dependency in which an individual's inability to go to college or prepare for well-paying jobs leads to lack of motivation, which leads to unemployment, poverty and welfare dependency, perpetuating the cycle. (5)

ghosting—Falsifying patrol logs to make the numbers come out right in response to alleged racial profiling practices. (11)

graffiti—Writing or drawing on buildings and walls. A common form of communication used by gang members to mark their territory. Sometimes called the newspaper of the street. (9)

grand jury—A group of citizens, usually 23, convened to hear testimony in secret and to issue formal criminal accusations (indictments) based upon probable cause if justified. (2)

grand larceny—Theft of property valued above a certain amount, in contrast to petty larceny, a less serious offense. (3)

gratuities—Tokens of appreciation. (11)

hallucinogens—Drugs that produce distortion, intensify sensory perception and lessen the ability to discriminate between fact and fantasy; physical characteristics allow them to be disguised as tablets, capsules, liquids or powders. (9)

hate crime—Unlawful act designed to frighten or harm an individual because of his or her race, religion, ethnicity or sexual orientation. Also called *bias crime*. (3)

hearsay—See *hearsay evidence*. (2)

hearsay evidence—Secondhand evidence. Facts not in the personal knowledge of a witness, but a repetition of what others said. (2)

hedonistic/social gangs—Only moderate drug use and offending, involved mainly in using drugs and having a good time; little involvement in crime, especially violent crime. (9)

homicide—The willful killing of a human by another human. Also called *murder*. (3)

homophobia—A fear of gays and lesbians. (11)

hot spots—Specific locations with high crime rates. (5, 6)

Hue and Cry—A shout by a citizen who witnessed a crime, enlisting the aid of others in the area to chase and catch the offender. May be the origin of the general alarm and the citizen's arrest. (1)

hundreds—Groups of 10 tithings. (1)

hung jury—A jury that cannot reach a decision. The result is a "no verdict" decision that can result in a retrial. (13)

identity theft—One of the country's fastest-growing crimes involving misappropriation of names, Social Security numbers, credit card numbers or other pieces of personal information for fraudulent purposes. (3)

image—How one is viewed; the concept of someone or something held by the public. Police image results from the media's portrayal of police and from everyday contacts between individual police officers and citizens. (4)

immediate control—Within a person's immediate reach. Also called *wingspan*. (8)

implied consent laws—State that any person driving a motor vehicle is deemed to have consented to a chemical test of the alcohol content of his or her blood if arrested while intoxicated. Refusal to take such a test can be introduced in court as evidence. (6)

incapacitation—Making it impossible for offenders to commit further offenses. (13)

incarceration—Being confined in jail or prison. (13)

incident—An isolated event that requires a police response. (5)

incident-driven policing—Where calls for service drive the department. A reactive approach with emphasis on rapidity of response. (6)

incivilities—Visible signs of people not caring about their community, for example, broken windows, unmowed lawns, piles of accumulated trash, litter, graffiti, abandoned buildings, rowdiness, drunkenness, fighting and prostitution. (5)

incorporation doctrine—Holds that only those provisions of the Bill of Rights that are fundamental to the American legal process are made applicable to the states through the due process clause. Also called *selective incorporation*. (2)

Index Crimes—Categories of crime used in the Uniform Crime Report: Part I or Part II depending on the seriousness of the crime. (3)

indicted—Formally charged with a specific crime by a grand jury, based on probable cause. (2)

indigent—Destitute, poverty-stricken, with no visible means of support. (2)

indirect victims—Family members and friends of victims who also feel pain and suffering along with the victim. Also called *secondary victims*. (3)

inevitable discovery doctrine—Holds that illegally obtained evidence may be admitted at trial if the prosecution can prove that the evidence would have been discovered sooner or later (inevitably). (8)

infamous crime—An especially heinous crime. (2)

informant—Person who furnishes information concerning accusations against another person or persons. (7)

inspection warrant—See *administrative warrant*. (8)

instrumental gangs—Gangs formed for the express purpose of criminal activity. They pose a greater threat than cultural gangs because they typically have a higher degree of organization. (9)

instruments of a crime—The means by which a crime is committed or the suspects and/or victims transported, for example, gun, knife, burglary tools, car, truck. (8)

integrated patrol—An operational philosophy that combines community-based policing with aggressive enforcement and provides a balanced, comprehensive approach to addressing crime problems throughout an entire jurisdiction rather than merely in targeted areas within a community. (5)

integrity—A series of concepts and beliefs that provide structure to an agency's operation and officers' professional and personal ethics, including, but not limited to, honesty, honor, morality, allegiance, principled behavior and dedication to mission. (11)

intent—See *criminal intent*. (2)

interdiction—Cutting off or destroying a line of communication—in the case of drug control, halting the flow of drugs into the United States. (9)

intermediate sanctions—Sanctions that are tougher than traditional probation but less stringent, and less expensive, than imprisonment. (13)

interoperability—The capacity of various telecommunications and computing devices to "talk" to each other. (4, 10)

interrogate—To question a suspect. (7)

interview—To question a witness or person with information relating to an incident. (7)

involvement crimes—Illegal acts discovered while being committed. (7)

jihad—A holy war. (10)

judicial waiver—The juvenile court waives jurisdiction and transfers a case to criminal court. Also known as *binding over*, *transferring* or *certifying* juvenile cases to criminal courts. (13)

jurisdiction—The geographic area within which a court (or public official) has the right and power to operate. Also refers to individuals and subjects over which a court has the right and power to make binding decisions. (13)

justifiable homicide—Includes killing in self-defense or in the defense of another person if the victim's actions and capability present imminent danger of serious injury or death. (3)

larceny/theft—The unlawful taking and removing of the property of another with the intent of permanently depriving the legal holder of the property. (3)

latent fingerprints—Prints made by sweat or grease that oozes out of the pores from little wells under the ridges at the ends of the fingers. (7)

law—A body of rules for human conduct that are enforced by imposing penalties for their violation. (1)

Leges Henrici—A document that made law enforcement a public matter and separated offenses into felonies and misdemeanors. (1)

less-lethal force—Force that has less potential for causing death or serious injury than traditional tactics. (11)

lex talionis—An eye for an eye. (1)

liability—A legal obligation incurred for an injury suffered/complained that results from failure to conduct a specific task/activity within a given standard. (11)

litigaphobia—Fear of a lawsuit. (2, 11)

magistrate—A judge. (8)

Magna Carta—A decisive document in the development of constitutional government in England that checked royal power and placed the king under the law (1215). (1)

mala in se—"Bad in itself," a crime so offensive, such as murder or rape, that it is obviously criminal. (2)

mala prohibita—"Bad because it is forbidden," a crime that violates a specific regulatory statute and would not usually be considered a crime if no law prohibited it, for example, certain traffic violations. (2)

malice—Hatred or ill will, disregard for the lives of others. (3)

manslaughter—Accidentally causing the death of another person. No malice or intent is involved. (3)

medical model—In corrections, assumes criminals are victims of society and need to be "cured." (5, 13)

mens rea—Guilty intent. Literally, a guilty mind. (2)

methamphetamine—A powerful stimulant emerging as a major problem for law enforcement because of its tendency to invoke violence in the user. (9)

misdemeanor—A minor offense—for example, breaking a municipal ordinance, speeding; the penalty is typically a fine or a short imprisonment, usually less than one year, in a local jail or workhouse. (2)

mobility—Movable; not firm, stationary or fixed—for example, an automobile that is capable of being moved quickly with relative ease. (8)

modus operandi (M.O.)—A method of criminal attack specific to an individual offender. (7)

monikers—Street names of gang members. (9)

moonlighting—Working at a second, part-time job while fulfilling the obligations of a full-time position. (12)

moral law—Laws made by society and enforced solely by social pressure. (2)

motive—Reason for doing something. (2)

motor vehicle theft—The unlawful taking or stealing of a motor vehicle without the authority or permission of the owner. Includes automobiles, trucks, buses, motorcycles, motorized boats and aircraft. (3)

mules—Individuals who smuggle cocaine for professional drug dealers. Often tourists or students. (9)

multiple hurdle procedure—The numerous tests that applicants for police positions must pass. (12)

murder—See *homicide.* (3)

narcotics—Drugs that produce sleep and lethargy or relieve pain; usually opiates. (9)

negligence—Failure to exercise a reasonable amount of care in a situation that causes harm to someone or something. (2)

negligent homicide—An accidental death that results from the reckless operation of a motor vehicle, boat, plane or firearm. (3)

nightcap warrants—Nighttime search or arrest warrants. (8)

nighttime search warrants—Search warrants issued by a magistrate that authorize a police officer to execute the warrant during the night. (8)

no bill—Issued by a grand jury if it decides that no crime has been committed. (13)

no-knock search warrant—Authorization by a magistrate upon the issuance of a search warrant to enter a premise by force without notification to avoid the chance that evidence may be destroyed if the officers' presence was announced. (8)

nolo contendere—"I will not contest it." A defendant's plea of "no contest" in a criminal case. It means he or she does not directly admit guilt, but submits to sentencing or other punishment. (13)

nystagmus—An uncontrolled bouncing or jerking of the eyeball of an intoxicated person when he or she looks to the extreme right or left, and up or down. (9)

one-pot approach—Equating poor and abused children with delinquent and criminal children and provided that they be treated in essentially the same way. (1)

open fields doctrine—Holds that land beyond what is normally associated with use of that land, that is, undeveloped land, can be searched without a warrant. (8)

ordinances—Local laws or regulations. (2)

ordinary care—Such degree of care, skills and diligence as a person of ordinary prudence would employ under similar circumstances. (8)

ordinary law—Statutes passed at the federal or state level that are not based on the Constitution. (2)

organized crime—Conspiratorial crime involving a hierarchy of persons who coordinate, plan and execute illegal acts using enforcement and corruptive tactics. (3)

organized gangs—Heavy involvement in all kinds of crime, heavy use and sale of drugs; may resemble corporations, with separate divisions handling sales, marketing, discipline and so on; discipline is strict, and promotion is based on merit. Also called *corporate gangs.* (9)

original jurisdiction—A court's power to take a case, try it and decide it. In contrast to an appellate court that hears appeals to the decisions of the original court. (13)

paradigm shift—A change in the thinking and attitudes toward a concept or model. (5)

parens patriae—The right of the government to take care of minors and others who cannot legally take care of themselves. (1)

parish—The area in which people lived who worshipped in a particular parish church. (1)

parish constable system—An early system of law enforcement used primarily in rural areas of the United States. (1)

parole—A release from prison before a sentence is finished. Continued release depends on good behavior and reporting to a parole officer. The most frequent type of release from a correctional institution. (13)

participatory leadership—Each individual has a voice in decisions, but top management retains the ultimate decision-making authority. (5)

party gangs—Commonly called "party crews"; relatively high use and sale of drugs, but only one major form of delinquency—vandalism; compete over who throws the biggest party, with alcohol, marijuana, nitrous oxide, sex and music critical party elements. (9)

pat down—An exploratory search of an individual's clothing. The "search" phase of a stop and frisk. (8)

petition—A written request for some action; a form of communication with the government; guaranteed by the First Amendment. (2) In the juvenile justice system, a document alleging a juvenile is a delinquent, status offender or dependent and asking the court to assume jurisdiction of the child. (13)

petty larceny—Theft of property valued below a certain amount, in contrast to grand larceny, the more serious offense. (3)

phantom wireless 911 calls—Occur when a cell phone is preprogrammed to call 911 if a 9 or 1 key is pressed, if the redial is pressed after a 911 call has been placed or when an older cell phone's batteries are low. (4)

phishing—A form of Internet fraud. (3)

pilfer—A person steals or uses money or property entrusted to him or her. (3)

plain feel/touch doctrine—Related to the plain view doctrine. An officer who feels/touches something suspicious during the course of lawful activity can investigate further. (8)

plain view—Evidence that is not concealed and is seen by an officer engaged in a lawful activity; what is observed in plain view is not construed within the meaning of the Fourth Amendment as a search. (8)

plea bargaining—A compromise between the defense and prosecuting attorneys that prearranges the plea and the sentence, conserving time, effort and court expenses. (13)

police authority—The right to direct and command. (4)

police power—The power of the federal, state or municipal governments to pass laws regulating private interests, to protect the health and safety of the people, to prevent fraud and oppression and to promote public convenience, prosperity and welfare. (2)

political era—(1840–1930) the first era of policing. Characterized by authority coming from politicians and the law, a broad social service function, decentralized organization, an intimate relationship with the community and extensive use of foot patrol. (1)

positivist theory—Theory developed at the turn of the century by Italian criminologist Cesare Lombroso that sees criminals as "victims of society" and of their own biological, sociological, cultural and physical environments. (3)

post-traumatic stress disorder (PTSD)—A psychological illness that happens after a highly stressful event or series of events, commonly associated with shooting incidents. (12)

power—The force by which others can be made to obey. (2)

precedent—What has come before. (2)

predatory gangs—Heavily involved in serious crimes (robberies, muggings) and the abuse of addictive drugs such as crack cocaine; may engage in selling drugs, but not in an organized fashion. (9)

preliminary hearing—That stage in the judicial system seeking to establish probable cause for believing that an offense has been committed and that the accused committed it thus preventing persons from being indiscriminately brought to trial. (13)

preliminary investigation—Actions performed immediately upon receiving a call to respond to the scene of a crime. Usually conducted by patrol officers. (7)

premeditated—Planned ahead of time, as in premeditated murder. (3)

preponderance of the evidence—The greater weight of the evidence. One side is more credible than the other. Standard of proof used in civil trials. (13)

presumption of innocence—The accused is assumed innocent until proof to the contrary is clearly established. (13)

pretext stop—When an officer stops a vehicle for ulterior motives. Also called a *dual motive stop*. (6, 8)

primary victims—Individuals directly affected by an incident, such as the person who is robbed, burglarized or raped. (3)

privatization—Civilians performing duties normally performed by sworn personnel who may be volunteers, paid civilians or private security personnel. (12)

pro bono **work**—Work done for free. Lawyers volunteer their time to be public defenders. (13)

proactive—Seeking to find the causes of crime and to rectify those problems, thereby deterring or even preventing crime. Acting before the fact rather than reacting to something that has already occurred. (1)

probable cause—Reasonable grounds for presuming guilt; facts that lead a person of ordinary care and prudence to believe and conscientiously entertain an honest and strong suspicion that a person is guilty of a crime. (8)

probation—The conditional suspension of a sentence of a person convicted of a crime but not yet imprisoned for that crime. The defendant is placed under the supervision of a probation officer for a set period of time and must meet specific conditions. (13)

problem-oriented policing—A departmental-wide strategy aimed at solving persistent community problems. Police identify, analyze and respond to the underlying circumstances that create incidents. (5)

procedural criminal law—Laws specifying how law enforcement officers are to carry out their responsibilities. (2)

procedural due process—Deals with notices, hearings and gathering evidence in criminal matters. (2)

professional model—The style of policing used during the reform era, based on the philosophies of August Vollmer and O. W. Wilson. (1)

protective sweep—A quick and limited search of premises, incident to an arrest and conducted to protect police officers and/or others. (8)

public offenses—Any crime. Includes felonies and misdemeanors. (8)

public safety exception—Allows police officers to question suspects without first giving the Miranda warning if the information sought sufficiently affects the officers' or the public's safety. (8)

pure speech—Words without any accompanying action. (2)

pursuit—An active attempt by a law enforcement officer on duty in a patrol car to apprehend one or more occupants of a moving motor vehicle, providing the driver of such vehicle is aware of the attempt and is resisting apprehension by maintaining or increasing his speed or by ignoring the law enforcement officer's attempt to stop him. (11)

racial profiling—Any police-initiated action that relies on the race, ethnicity or national origin rather than the behavior of an individual that leads the police to believe a particular individual is engaged in criminal activity. (6, 11)

random patrol—Having no set pattern; by chance; haphazard. (6)

rape—Carnal knowledge of a woman or man through the use of force or the threat of force. Also called *sexual assault*. (3)

rattle watch—A group of citizens patrolling at night and armed with rattles to call for help. Used in New Amsterdam in the 1650s. (1)

reactive—Responding to crimes after they have been committed. (1)

reasonable—Sensible; just; well-balanced; good, sound judgment; that which would be attributed to a prudent person. (8)

reasonable doubt—That state of a case in which, after comparing and considering all the evidence, the jurors cannot say they feel an abiding conviction of the truth of the charge. Moral uncertainty of the truth of the charges. (13)

reasonable force—Force no greater than that needed to achieve the desired end. (11)

recidivism—Repeated or habitual offending. (13)

recidivist—One who habitually or repeatedly breaks the law. (3)

reeve—The top official of a hundred. (1)

reform era—(1930–1980) the second era of policing. Characterized by authority coming from the law and professionalism; crime control as the primary function of law enforcement; a centralized, efficient organization; professional remoteness from the community; and an emphasis on preventive motorized patrol and rapid response to crime. (1)

regulators—Respectable settlers of average or affluent means who joined others as vigilantes to attack and break up outlaw gangs and restore order in the 1760s. (1)

rehabilitation—Correcting deviant behavior. (13)

residual deterrence effect—The positive effects of crackdowns that continue after a crackdown ends. (6)

restitution—Compensating or making up for loss, damage or injury. Requiring an offender to repay the victim or the community in money or services. (13)

restorative justice—Seeks to use a balanced approach involving offenders, victims, local communities and government to alleviate crime and violence and obtain peaceful communities. (13)

retribution—Punishment for the sake of punishment; revenge. (13)

reverse discrimination—Giving preferential treatment in hiring and promoting to women and minorities to the detriment of white males. (12)

reverse 911 (R911)—As the name implies, allows agencies to alert the public in emergencies. (4)

riflings—Spiral grooves cut into a gun barrel during its manufacture. (7)

riot act—An order permitting the magistrate to call in the military to quell a riot. (1)

risk factors—Elements related to how and where people live that affect the likelihood of their victimization. (3)

ritual—A system of rites; a ceremonial act. (3)

ritualistic crime—An unlawful act committed during a ceremony related to a belief system. It is the crime, not the belief system, that must be investigated. (3)

road rage—An angry, frequently violent response to an aggressive-driving incident. Not the same as aggressive driving. (6)

robbery—Stealing anything of value from the care, custody or control of a person in his or her presence, by force or by the threat of force. (3)

roll call—The briefing of officers before their tour of duty to update them on criminal activity and calls for service. (4)

R.P.R.d—Release on personal recognizance. (13)

SARA model—Four strategies used in problem-oriented policing: scan, analyze, respond, assess. (5)

saturation patrol—Involves an increased enforcement effort targeting a specific geographic area to identify and arrest impaired drivers. (6)

scavenger gangs—Gangs that have few goals and primarily provide an outlet for impulsive behavior and meet the need to belong. (9)

scienter—A degree of knowledge that makes an individual legally responsible for the consequences of his or her acts. (2)

scofflaws—People who habitually violate the law. (6)

search—Examination of a person or property for the purpose of discovering evidence to prove guilt in relation to a crime. (8)

search warrant—A judicial order directing a peace officer to search for specific property, seize it and return it to the court; it may be a written order or an order given over the telephone. (8)

secondary victims—Family members and friends of victims who also feel pain and suffering along with the victim. Also called *indirect victims*. (3)

second-degree murder—The unpremeditated but intentional killing of another person. (3)

seizure—A forcible detention or taking of a person or property in an arrest. (8)

selective enforcement—Targets specific crashes and/or high-crash areas. (6)

selective incorporation—Holds that only those provisions of the Bill of Rights that are fundamental to the American legal process are made applicable to the states through the due process clause. Also called the *incorporation doctrine*. (2)

self-incrimination—An individual is required to provide answers to questions that might convict him or her of a crime. (2)

serious delinquent gangs—Heavy involvement in both serious and minor crimes, but much lower involvement in drug use and drug sales than party gangs. (9)

sexual assault—See *rape*. (3)

sexual harassment—Has two conditions: (1) it must occur in the workplace or an extension of the workplace (department sanctioned) and (2) it must be of a sexual nature that does not include romance or that is not of a mutually friendly nature. The harassment must be unwelcome, unsolicited and deliberate. (12)

sheriff—The principal law enforcement officer of a county. (1)

shire-reeve—The top official of a shire (county). The forerunner of our county sheriff. (1)

shires—Counties in England. (1)

shock incarceration—Patterned after the traditional military boot camps for new recruits, a system of incarceration for youths that stresses strict and even cruel discipline, hard work and authoritarian decision making and control by a drill sergeant. Also called *boot camp*. (13)

simple assault—An unlawful attack by one person on another, but without the intention of causing serious, permanent injury. (3)

simple rape—Misleading a victim into having sexual intercourse. (3)

sinsemilla—Marijuana grown indoors in the United States. (9)

situational testing—Job-related simulation exercises to assess a candidate's qualifications for a law enforcement position. (12)

slave patrols—Special enforcement officers during the mid-1790s who were allowed to enter any plantation and break into slaves' dwellings, search slaves' persons and possessions at will and beat and even kill any slaves found violating the slave code. (1)

sleeper cell—A group of terrorists who blend into a community. (10)

social capital—The bond among family members and their immediate, informal groups as well as the networks tying individuals to broader community institutions such as schools, civic organizations, churches and to various levels of government, including the police. (5)

social gangs—Only moderate drug use and offending, involved mainly in using drugs and having a good time;

little involvement in crime, especially violent crime. Also called *hedonistic gangs*. (9)

social law—Law made by society and enforced solely by social pressure. (2)

solvability factors—Factors affecting the probability of successfully concluding a case. (7)

specific deterrence—Deterrence aimed at offenders. Attempts to make the consequences of committing crime so severe that when offenders return to society, they will not commit crime. (13)

speech plus—Words accompanied by some sort of action, such as burning a flag. (2)

spoils system—A political system whereby "friends" of politicians were rewarded with key positions in the police department. (1)

standing mute—Refusing to answer as to guilt or innocence at an arraignment. Entered as a "not guilty" plea. (13)

status offenses—Crimes restricted to persons under the legal age—for example, smoking, drinking, breaking curfew, absenting from home, truancy, incorrigibility. (3)

statutory law—Law passed by a legislature. (2)

statutory rape—Rape without force, but still against the law, as in having intercourse with an minor. (3)

stereotype—Oversimplified conception, opinion or belief, often associated with specific racial or ethnic groups; seeing all members of a group as the same with no individuality. (5)

stop—Briefly detaining someone who is acting suspiciously. A stop is *not* an arrest. (8)

stop and frisk—A protective search for weapons that could be used to assault police officers and others—for example, knives, guns and clubs. (8)

stress—Physical, chemical or emotional factors that cause bodily or mental tension; mentally or emotionally disruptive or disquieting influence; distress. (12)

strict liability—Intent is not required; the defendant is liable regardless of his or her state of mind when the act was committed. (2)

subculture—Any group demonstrating specific patterns of behavior that distinguish it from others within a society. Policing has been referred to as "The Blue Brotherhood." (4)

subpoena—A written legal document ordering the person named in the document to appear in court to give testimony. (2)

substantive criminal law—Statutes specifying crimes and their punishments. (2)

substantive due process—Protects individuals against unreasonable, arbitrary or capricious laws and limits arbitrary government actions. (2)

suppressible crimes—Crimes that commonly occur in locations and under circumstances that provide police officers a reasonable opportunity to deter or apprehend offenders. Includes robbery, burglary, car theft, assault and sex crimes. (7)

symbolic speech—Tangible forms of expressions such as wearing buttons or clothing with political slogans or displaying a sign or flag. Protected by the First Amendment. (2)

target hardening—Making it more difficult for crime to occur. For example, using access control, lighting and surveillance. (5)

territorial gangs—Gangs that establish their turf and defend it. (9)

terrorism—The use of force or violence against persons or property in violation of the criminal laws of the United States for purposes of intimidation, coercion or ransom. (10)

theft—Stealing of any kind. (3)

threshold inquiry—Same as a *stop*, that is, briefly detaining an individual who is acting suspiciously. (8)

tithing—In Anglo-Saxon England, a unit of civil administration consisting of 10 families; established the principle of collective responsibility for maintaining law and order. (1)

tithing system—Established the principle of collective responsibility for maintaining local law and order by organizing families into groups of 10 families known as a *tithing*. (1)

tort—A civil wrong for which the court seeks a remedy in the form of damages to be paid. (2)

totality of circumstances—Taking into account all factors involved in a given situation. (7, 8)

traditional gangs—Gangs that can trace their heritage back several generations and have a strong system of tradition. (9)

turf—The geographic territory claimed by a gang. (9)

typologies—Systematic classifications, as in styles of policing. (4)

undercover—Long-term, ongoing investigations into criminal activity in which officers do not wear uniforms or drive marked cars and may use assumed names and fictitious identities. (7)

union—Any group authorized to represent the members of the law enforcement agency in negotiating such matters as wages, fringe benefits and other conditions of employment. (12)

union shop—An agency where people must belong to or join the union to be hired. (12)

venue—The local area where a case may be tried. It is usually required that the trial for an offense be held in the same area in which the offense occurred. (13)

victim impact statement (VIS)—A written or spoken statement detailing the medical, financial and emotional injuries resulting from a crime. The information is usually provided to a probation officer who writes a summary to be included in the defendant's presenting packet. (3)

victim statement of opinion (VSO)—A spoken or written statement to the judge in which victims tell the court their opinions on what sentence the defendant should receive. More subjective than the victim impact statement. (3)

vigilante—A person who takes the law into his or her own hands, usually in the absence of effective policing. (1)

voir dire—The random selection of potential jurors and the careful questioning of each. (13)

waiver—The intentional giving up of a right. (8)

wannabes—Youths who dress and act like gang members and hang out on the fringes of the gang, hoping to be invited in some day. (9)

warrant—A written order issued by an officer of the court, usually a judge, directing a person in authority to arrest the person named, charge that person with the named offense and bring him or her before the issuing person or court of jurisdiction. (2)

Watch and Ward—A system of law enforcement that was used to protect citizens 24 hours a day; the day shift was called the "ward" and the night shift the "watch." (1)

white-collar crime—Occupational or business-related crime. Also called *economic crime.* (3)

wingspan—The area within a person's reach. Also known as *immediate control.* (8)

witness—Can be a complainant, an accuser, a victim or an observer of an incident. (7)

writ of certiorari—A request for a transcript of the proceedings of a case for review. Granted when the Supreme Court decides to hear a case. (13)

writ of habeas corpus—A legal court order literally meaning "bring forth the body you have," which commands that a person being held be brought forth immediately. (13)

xenophobia—Fear or hatred of strangers or foreigners. (3)

zeitgeist—The general intellectual, moral and cultural "spirit" of the times. (13)

zones of privacy—Areas safe from governmental intrusion. (2)

Author Index

Subject Index

Photo Credits

This page constitutes an extension of the copyright page. We have made every effort to trace the ownership of all copyrighted material and to secure permission from copyright holders. In the event of any question arising as to the use of any material, we will be pleased to make the necessary corrections in future printings. Thanks are due to the following authors, publishers, and agents for permission to use the material indicated.

Chapter 1. 11: © AP / Wide World Photos 17: © Brown Brothers 35: Courtesy of the Stephan H. Hart Library, Colorado Historical Society

Chapter 2. 46: © Aaron Haupt/Photo Researchers, Inc. 57: John Blanding © Reuters/CORBIS 63: © Bettmann/CORBIS

Chapter 3. 83: © Al Golub/Pool/Reuters/CORBIS 89: © Mark Richards/PhotoEdit 109: © AP/Wide World Photos

Chapter 4. 116: © AP/Wide World Photos 128: © Richard Bermack 137: © CBS/Landov

Chapter 5. 148: © Tom Carter/PhotoEdit 157: © James L. Shaffer 166: © Mark Richards/PhotoEdit

Chapter 6. 188: Copyright © 2002 Oxnard Police Department 194: © AP/Wide World Photos 196: © Shelley Boyd/PhotoEdit

Chapter 7. 226: Carla M. Cataldi © AP/Wide World Photos 236: © AP/Wide World Photos 238: © Joel Gordon 2001

Chapter 8. 251: Jeff Klein © AP/Wide World Photos 268: © Mark Reinstein/Index Stock Imagery 271: © Michael Newman/PhotoEdit—All rights reserved.

Chapter 9. 297: © Mark Richards/PhotoEdit 319: © AP/Wide World Photos 327: © Joel Gordon

Chapter 10. 349: bottom left, Jerry Torrens © AP Photo/Wide World Photos 349: bottom right, © Cleve Bryant/PhotoEdit 360: © AP/Wide World Photos

Chapter 11. 368: Richard Sheinwald © AP/Wide World Photos 380: © Stephen Ferry/Getty Images

Chapter 12. 423: © Michael Newman/PhotoEdit

Chapter 13. 447: Getty Images/PhotoDisc 460: © Steve Helber/Pool/CORBIS 465: © Reuters NewMedia Inc./CORBIS 473: © UPI/Bettmann Newsphotos/CORBIS 475: © Laimute E. Druskis/Stock Boston